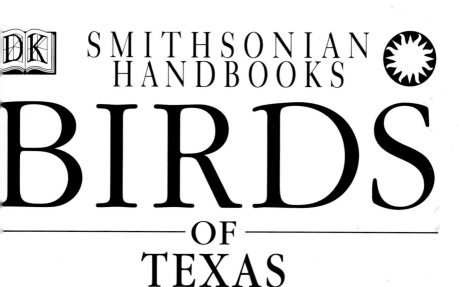

SMITHSONIAN
HANDBOOKS
BIRDS
—OF—
TEXAS

SMITHSONIAN HANDBOOKS

BIRDS
— OF —
TEXAS

Fred J. Alsop III

LONDON, NEW YORK, MUNICH,
MELBOURNE AND DELHI

Editor-in-Chief Russell Greenberg, PhD
Director of the Migratory Bird Center at the National Zoological Park

Senior Editor Jill Hamilton
Art Editors Gus Yoo, Megan Clayton
Editorial Director Chuck Wills
Creative Director Tina Vaughan
Publisher Sean Moore
Production Manager Chris Avgherinos
DTP Designer Russell Shaw
Picture Research Martin Copeland, Mark Dennis

Produced by Southern Lights Custom Publishing
Editorial Director Shelley DeLuca
Production Director Lee Howard
Graphic Design Miles Parsons, Tim Kolankiewicz, Scott Fuller
President Ellen Sullivan

First American Edition, 2002
4 6 8 10 9 7 5 3

Published in the United States by
DK Publishing, Inc.
375 Hudson Street
New York, New York 10014

DK Publishing, Inc. offers special discounts for bulk purchases for sales promotions
or premiums. Specific, large-quantity needs can be met with special editions, including
personalized covers,excerpts of existing guides, and corporate imprints. For more
information, contact Special Markets Department, DK Publishing, Inc.,
375 Hudson Street, New York, New York 10014; Fax: 212-689-5254.

A Cataloging-in-Publication record is available from the Library of Congress.

0-7894-8388-2

Printed and bound by South China Printing Company in China.
Color reproduction by Colourscan, Singapore.

See our complete product line at
www.dk.com

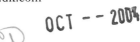

OCT – – 2004

LONELY BRANC

CONTENTS

INTRODUCTION

Birdwatching, or birding as it is now commonly called, is practiced by more than 60 million North Americans – making it the single largest hobby on the continent. North America is an exciting place to go birding because it contains birds representing more than 920 species that are permanent or summer residents, visit regularly, or stray occasionally to the continent.

AVIAN DIVERSITY
Having attained the power of flight more than 150 million years ago, birds might be expected to be uniformly distributed in every corner of the Earth. But they are not. They are bound to the earth by the habitats to which they have adapted, and they are limited by geographical barriers as well as the history of their lineage.

Different species are often associated with major plant communities, or biomes, that provide them with critical habitat requirements for part or all of their annual cycle. Polar regions of permanent ice and snow are home to

The SPOTTED OWL inhabits old-growth forests and wooded canyons.

Ivory Gulls; the arctic tundra to Snowy Owls, ptarmigans, jaegers, Gyrfalcons, and countless shorebirds in summer. The great block of northern coniferous forests provide seeds for crossbills, grosbeaks, finches, and nuthatches; in summer, insects for flycatchers, vireos, and warblers abound. Deciduous forests, southern pine forests, grasslands, and deserts all hold particular species of birds different from those in other biomes. Other species, such as herons, are adapted for freshwater ponds, lakes, rivers, and streams; still others for marshes and seashores as well as the open ocean.

The GREAT BLUE HERON has adapted to freshwater habitats.

BIRDWATCHING IN NORTH AMERICA

The incredible diversity of North America's avian population is evidenced by the more than 920 species of birds that are now accepted as having occurred in North America. These species can be found in a wide variety of habitats, from spectacular mountain ranges, vast grasslands, hot and cold deserts, chaparral, deciduous and coniferous forests, swamps and pine forests, tundra, glaciers, and ice fields. Inhabiting this vast area are billions of individual birds.

The VERMILION FLYCATCHER thrives in arid and semiarid habitats.

Many birdwatchers practice their hobby close to their own backyards. They learn to recognize the species they see most often and occasionally identify a "new" species for the yard, perhaps even photograph the birds they see. Some are so passionate that they travel North America identifying as many species as they can, often covering many miles on short notice to observe a newly discovered vagrant.

Not even the most ardent birder has seen all of the species recorded on the North American continent. But that is part of the fun and challenge of birding. It holds something for every level of interest, and the amateur birder stands as much chance as the professional of making a discovery that sheds important light on the field of ornithology.

MALLARDS are found almost anywhere there is shallow freshwater, including the mountains of the Southwest.

HOW THIS BOOK WORKS

Until now, no tool for identifying birds has also provided access to information on behavior, nesting, flight patterns, and similar birds in a compact and user-friendly format. Written for the novice as well as the experienced birder, this book showcases in individual page profiles each of the 503 species of birds

The CANADA GOOSE can be found almost anywhere in North America at some point during the year.

documented as occurring in the state of Texas. The species are in taxonomic order and include all those known to breed in Texas and adjacent islands and seas within two hundred miles of the coast, as well as all species documented as regular visitors by the American Ornithologists' Union (AOU) and the American Birding Association (ABA). Species recorded as casual, vagrant, or accidental visitors are listed separately beginning on page 543. Only those species listed on the current AOU *Check-list of North American Birds* (7th edition, 1998 and its 42nd Supplement, 2000)' and the ABA 1998–99 ABA *Check-list Report, Birding* 31: 518–524 are included. Other species that have been seen but not yet accepted by the AOU or ABA are not included. Excluded also are a host of introduced exotic species that are not yet recognized by either the AOU or the ABA as having viable breeding populations.

FINDING YOUR BIRD

To find a bird, scan the pages of the book, or look up its scientific or common name in the index. The species are in taxonomic order, beginning with the non-passerines such as grebes, ducks, hawks, owls, doves, hummingbirds, and woodpeckers. They are followed by the passerines, the perching or songbirds, which are introduced on page 299. The species profiles will help you identify a bird as well as learn about its natural history.

LEAST GREBE (non-passerine)
Birds that do not perch and sing are in the first part of this book.

TOWNSEND'S WARBLER (passerine)
Birds that do perch and sing are in the second part of this book.

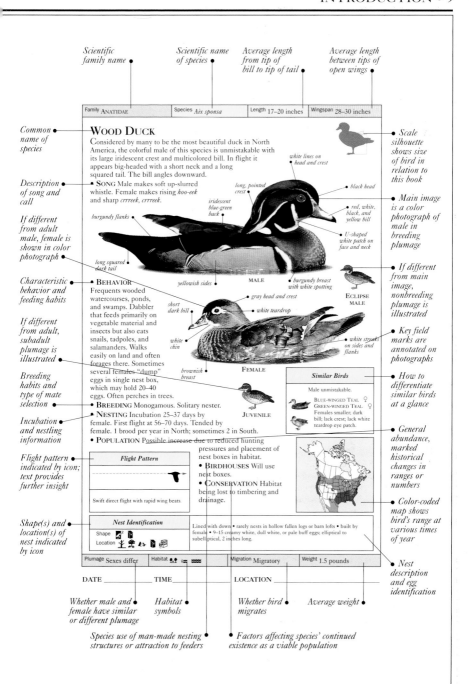

Scientific family name

Scientific name of species

Average length from tip of bill to tip of tail

Average length between tips of open wings

Common name of species

Description of song and call

If different from adult male, female is shown in color photograph

Characteristic behavior and feeding habits

If different from adult, subadult plumage is illustrated

Breeding habits and type of mate selection

Incubation and nestling information

Flight pattern indicated by icon; text provides further insight

Shape(s) and location(s) of nest indicated by icon

Whether male and female have similar or different plumage

Habitat symbols

Species use of man-made nesting structures or attraction to feeders

Whether bird migrates

Average weight

Factors affecting species' continued existence as a viable population

Scale silhouette shows size of bird in relation to this book

Main image is a color photograph of male in breeding plumage

If different from main image, nonbreeding plumage is illustrated

Key field marks are annotated on photographs

How to differentiate similar birds at a glance

General abundance, marked historical changes in ranges or numbers

Color-coded map shows bird's range at various times of year

Nest description and egg identification

Family ANATIDAE **Species** Aix sponsa **Length** 17–20 inches **Wingspan** 28–30 inches

WOOD DUCK

Considered by many to be the most beautiful duck in North America, the colorful male of this species is unmistakable with its large iridescent crest and multicolored bill. In flight it appears big-headed with a short neck and a long squared tail. The bill angles downward.

• SONG Male makes soft up-slurred whistle. Female makes rising *hoo-eek* and sharp *crrreek, crrreek.*

• BEHAVIOR Frequents wooded watercourses, ponds, and swamps. Dabbler that feeds primarily on vegetable material and insects but also eats snails, tadpoles, and salamanders. Walks easily on land and often forages there. Sometimes several females "dump" eggs in single nest box, which may hold 20–40 eggs. Often perches in trees.

• BREEDING Monogamous. Solitary nester.

• NESTING Incubation 25–37 days by female. First flight at 56–70 days. Tended by female. 1 brood per year in North; sometimes 2 in South.

• POPULATION Possible increase due to reduced hunting pressures and placement of nest boxes in habitat.

• BIRDHOUSES Will use nest boxes.

• CONSERVATION Habitat being lost to timbering and drainage.

white lines on head and crest

long, pointed crest

black head

red, white, black, and yellow bill

iridescent blue-green back

U-shaped white patch on face and neck

burgundy flanks

long squared dark tail

yellowish sides

MALE

short dark bill

white chin

brownish breast

FEMALE

burgundy breast with white spotting

ECLIPSE MALE

gray head and crest

white teardrop

white streaks on sides and flanks

JUVENILE

Similar Birds

Male unmistakable.

BLUE-WINGED TEAL ♀
GREEN-WINGED TEAL ♀
Females smaller; dark bill; lack crest; lack white teardrop eye patch.

Flight Pattern

Swift direct flight with rapid wing beats.

Nest Identification

Shape
Location

Lined with down • rarely nests in hollow fallen logs or barn lofts • built by female • 9–15 creamy white, dull white, or pale buff eggs; elliptical to subelliptical, 2 inches long.

Plumage Sexes differ **Habitat** **Migration** Migratory **Weight** 1.5 pounds

DATE _____ TIME _____ LOCATION _____

GUIDE TO VISUAL REFERENCES

PHOTOGRAPHS

Because users of this guide will be viewing these birds in backyards, woodlands, and other natural environments, realistic photographs are used as visual reference. Some rare and seldom-photographed species are illustrated. Unless otherwise noted, the primary image shows the male bird in breeding plumage. If the adult female has significantly different plumage from the male a second image depicts the female in breeding plumage. If field marks are not visible in a photograph they are described in the accompanying text.

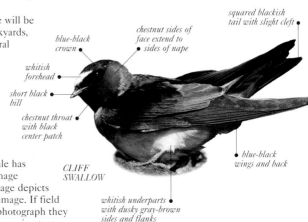

squared blackish tail with slight cleft

chestnut sides of face extend to sides of nape

blue-black crown

whitish forehead

short black bill

chestnut throat with black center patch

blue-black wings and back

CLIFF SWALLOW

whitish underparts with dusky gray-brown sides and flanks

ILLUSTRATIONS

Many birds also have other plumages, including the winter plumage, which are depicted in illustrations. The plumage of the immature if different from both adults also is illustrated. Some species have different color morphs, which are also illustrated.

LIGHT MORPH JUVENILE   WINTER PLUMAGE   WHITE MORPH

SIMILAR BIRDS

In many cases it can be difficult to distinguish between certain species in the field. Therefore, the accounts feature pictures of similar birds with accompanying text that identifies the distinct features and behavior that clearly set them apart. Male and female symbols indicate the sex of the bird that could be mistaken for the species being profiled.

Similar Birds

CAVE SWALLOW
Pale cinnamon-buff throat; cinnamon forehead; richer cinnamon-rust rump.

DISTRIBUTION MAP

Each species profile has a map showing where the bird is likely to be seen either all year long (permanent resident), in the breeding season (summer resident), or in the winter (winter resident). The maps depict only those parts of each species' range within North America and up to approximately 100 miles offshore north of central Mexico to the northern borders of Canada.

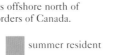 permanent resident   summer resident   winter resident

SCALE SILHOUETTES
These show the silhouette of the bird overlaid proportionally on a copy of this book.

NEST IDENTIFICATION
The Nest Identification box provides icons describing nest shape and location.

Flight Pattern

Swift graceful flight alternating several deep, rapid wing beats with long elliptical glides with sharp sweeping upturns at the end. Soars on thermals and updrafts.

FLIGHT PATTERN
Each bird's flight pattern is shown in its species profile by an icon. For more information on flight patterns, see page 20.

Nest Identification	Pellets of clay or mud, with lining of grasses, down, and feathers • usually under eaves of buildings or under dams or bridges; sometimes on ridges of canyons; rarely on trunk of conifer tree under overhanging branch • built by both sexes • 3–6 white, cream, or pinkish eggs, marked with browns; oval to long oval, 0.8 x 0.5 inches.
Shape ⬤	
Location 🏚 〰 🐿 🏠	

Shape					
Burrow Excavated	Burrow Preformed	Crevice	Deep Cup	Floating	Man-made
None	Open Cup	Pendant	Platform	Saucer	Scrape
Shallow	Sphere	Tree Cavity Primary	Tree Cavity Secondary		

Location							
Bank	Building	Bridge	Cave	Chimney	Cliff	Conifer
Decidous	Floating	Grass	Gravel Roof	Hollow Log	Man-made	Pebbles
Reed/Cattails	Shrub	Snag	Bare Soil	Stump		

Habitat 🐦 🪨 〰

HABITAT
At the bottom of each species account is a set of icons representing all the habitat types in the order in which the bird is found, from the most to the least likely.

🌳 forest: coniferous, broadleaf, temperate, or tropical

🌲🌳 open forest; more space between the trees, tundra forest, semiopen areas

🌳 forest edge, oak and riparian

🌾 grassland with scattered trees (includes farmland, citrus groves, orchards)

🌿 bushes, shrubs, thickets and undergrowth; tropical lowland

🌵 areas of scrub vegetation, frequently with thorns

___ open landscapes: grassland, tundra, savanna, coastal ponds/sloughs – salt, brackish or freshwater, coastal marshes, coastal wetlands, salt marshes, prairie potholes

⚊ ⚊ semidesert

🌱 desert

〰 lakes, rivers and vicinity, sandspits, mudflats, ponds

〰 upland streams and vicinity

〰 open sea, low flat islands

〰 rocky or sandy seashore, bay islands, coastal islands, shallow coastal habitats, coastal bays, coastal mangroves, tidal flats, sand spits, mudflats

〰 freshwater marshes, swamps

🪨 rocky places or cliffs (both on the coast and inland)

▲ mountains, wooded canyons

ANATOMY OF BIRDS

Birds are the most diverse terrestrial vertebrates with more than 9,800 extant species. Mammals are the only other homeothermic group with whom they share the planet. Yet, although mammal species number less than half that of birds, the mammals are much more varied in body shape and size. Mammals vary in form from primates to giraffes to armadillos, with specialists in running, hopping, flying, swimming, burrowing, digging, and climbing. Birds, however, all look like birds – with the same basic architecture, a body shape dictated by the demands of flight.

FEATHERS

Birds have three basic types of feathers: down, contour, and flight (wing and tail) feathers. Down feathers are next to the bird's skin for insulation. The contour is the most commonly recognized feather and the one that covers most of the bird's body. Typical contour feathers consist of a central shaft or quill and the flattened portion or vane. Contour feathers that extend beyond the wings and tail are the flight feathers.

DOWN   **CONTOUR**   **FLIGHT**
(**WING AND TAIL**)

BONES

In most species both the wings and the legs must be strong enough to transport the full weight of the bird, yet light enough to fly. Some bones have been fused and some bear internal struts. Ribs are overlapped for strength; others are hollowed, thinned, and reduced in numbers for lightness. In flying birds, and those flightless birds like penguins that use flipperlike forelimbs to "fly" under-water, the sternum, or breastbone, bears a thin knifelike keel to which the large flight muscles of the breast, the pectoral muscles, are attached.

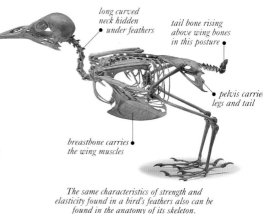

*long curved
neck hidden
• under feathers*

*tail bone rising
above wing bones
in this posture •*

*• pelvis carries
legs and tail*

*breastbone carries •
the wing muscles*

*The same characteristics of strength and
elasticity found in a bird's feathers also can be
found in the anatomy of its skeleton.*

BILLS

Birds' bills are composed of a horny sheath overlying a bony core. The entire lightweight structure has evolved in countless ways to the specialized needs of its owner, from seed-cracking to nectar probing and from fish-catching to fruit-picking. Birds also use their bills to build nests, preen, and court. Bills may change in size and/or color in breeding season.

The ROSEATE SPOONBILL uses its spoon-shaped bill to scoop food from water.

The EVENING GROSBEAK uses its conical bill to crunch seeds.

The BUFF-BELLIED HUMMINGBIRD uses its long needlelike bill to probe into flowers for nectar.

The RED CROSSBILL's bill features mandibles crossed at the tips that are ideal for digging the seeds out of pinecones.

LEGS AND FEET

The legs of birds are thin, strong, and springy, and in most species lack feathers on their distal parts where they are instead covered with scales. Muscles, which are concentrated on the portion of the leg nearest the body, control the extremities with a series of tendons. Toes generally number four with three forward and one opposable toe pointed backward, but some North American birds have only three. Toes are covered by scales and have claws at their tips which in birds of prey are enlarged into strong talons.

The AMERICAN ROBIN has a typical bird's foot: four toes with three forward and one back.

Some, like the HAIRY WOODPECKER, have two toes forward and two back.

The MALLARD has three webbed toes and one vestigial toe in back.

The DOUBLE-CRESTED CORMORANT has four webbed toes.

The BALD EAGLE has claws enlarged and elongated into talons.

WINGS AND TAILS

The shapes of wings and tails are an adaptation to where and how a bird flies. Look carefully at flight silhouettes: forest raptors (a) have rounded wings for living in dense vegetation; swallows (b) have narrow tapering wings. The tapering wings and narrow tail of a falcon (c) contrast with the broad splayed wings and broad tail of an eagle (d), which allow an eagle to soar. Terns (e) have long elegant wings; albatross wings (f) are very long, with an extended inner section for flying over water like a sailplane.

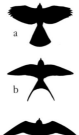
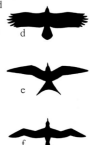

TOPOGRAPHY OF A BIRD

As you consult the species profiles in this book you will encounter a number of ornithological terms that describe the "landscape," or groups of feathers, of a bird's body. Learning these terms will help you use your field guide and, when you look at living birds, prompt you to see more detail with each sighting.

TIPS FOR THE FIELD

1. Start by looking at the bird's head. Note its bill and the markings on its face.
2. Get a feel for the bird's overall shape and size and note body markings.
3. Note shapes and markings of tail and wings.
4. Watch it fly and note markings visible in flight.

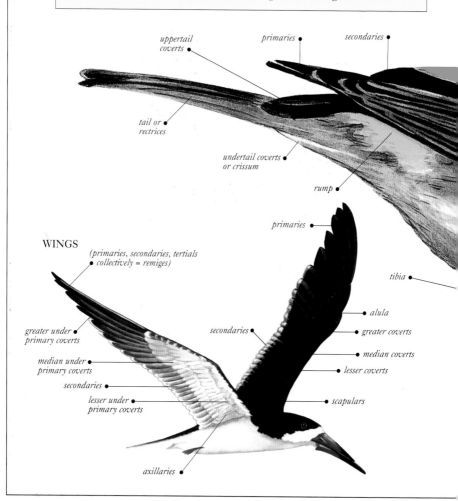

uppertail coverts

primaries

secondaries

tail or rectrices

undertail coverts or crissum

rump

primaries

WINGS

(primaries, secondaries, tertials collectively = remiges)

tibia

alula

greater coverts

greater under primary coverts

secondaries

median under primary coverts

secondaries

lesser under primary coverts

median coverts

lesser coverts

scapulars

axillaries

HEAD

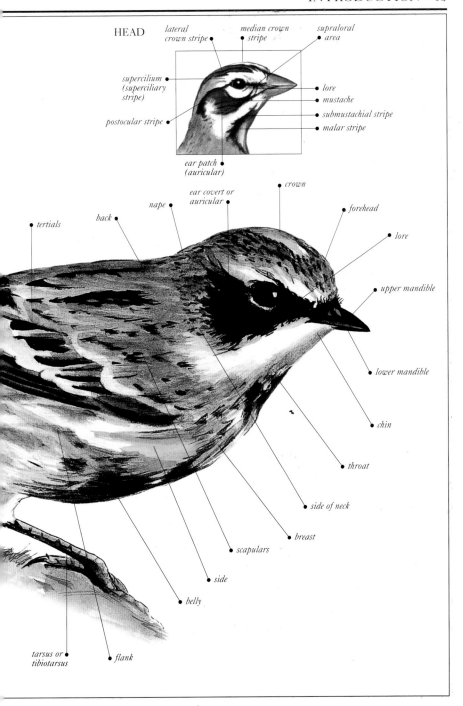

lateral crown stripe

median crown stripe

supraloral area

supercilium (superciliary stripe)

lore

mustache

postocular stripe

submustachial stripe

malar stripe

ear patch (auricular)

crown

ear covert or auricular

nape

forehead

back

lore

tertials

upper mandible

lower mandible

chin

throat

side of neck

breast

scapulars

side

belly

tarsus or tibiotarsus

flank

VARIATIONS WITHIN SPECIES

Birds are the most colorful of all terrestrial vertebrates. Their coloration varies widely not only from species to species but within species. Often plumage colors differ between the sexes, between adults and their young, and from season to season. All of these different color patterns increase the challenge of identification for the birder.

MALE/FEMALE VARIATIONS

Within a species, adult males often differ in color and pattern of plumage, and sometimes in size, from adult females.

PAINTED BUNTINGS have three distinct plumages.

MALE   FEMALE   JUVENILE

JUVENILE PLUMAGE VARIATIONS

On an individual bird, color changes occur when feathers molt, or drop from their follicles to be replaced by new feathers. In its life span a bird will molt many times. After its first molt, when it loses its natal down, the bird will attain its *juvenile plumage*. This will be its first plumage with contour and flight feathers. This plumage often does not resemble that of either adult and is worn briefly for a few weeks or months. For the purposes of this book the term "juvenile" is used to refer to subadult plumaged birds that may, or may not, be sexually mature.

MALE   FEMALE   JUVENILE

Male and female NORTHERN CARDINALS have different plumages, while juveniles resemble females.

OTHER SUBADULT PLUMAGES

Although in many species, such as the bunting and cardinal, the juvenile attains adult plumage after its first year, there are species in which it takes the juvenile longer to do this. It may take juveniles of some species two years or more. These individuals may experience what are known as first, second, or even third winter or summer plumages before attaining the plumage of adult birds. The Ring-billed Gull is one such example.

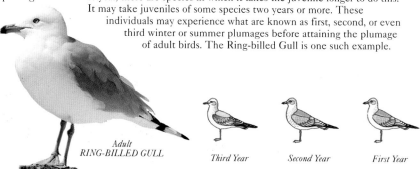

Adult
RING-BILLED GULL

Third Year   *Second Year*   *First Year*

SEASONAL VARIATIONS IN ADULT BIRDS

Most adult birds have two molts a year with a complete molt of all feathers after the breeding season and a partial molt in late winter/early spring in which only the head and body feathers are replaced.

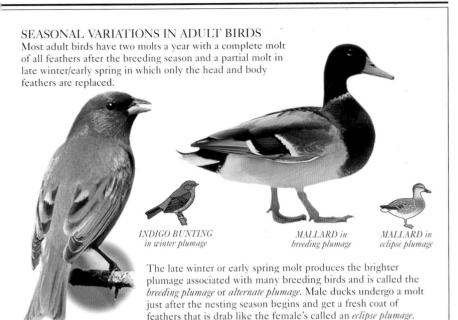

INDIGO BUNTING in winter plumage

MALLARD in breeding plumage

MALLARD in eclipse plumage

INDIGO BUNTING in breeding plumage

The late winter or early spring molt produces the brighter plumage associated with many breeding birds and is called the *breeding plumage* or *alternate plumage*. Male ducks undergo a molt just after the nesting season begins and get a fresh coat of feathers that is drab like the female's called an *eclipse plumage*. Fall molts produce a plumage called *winter plumage*, *fall plumage*, or *basic plumage*.

OTHER VARIATIONS

Some genetic variations in color and pattern can be seen among populations representing different geographical races of a species. These races are also referred to as subspecies.

SLATE-COLORED JUNCO *OREGON JUNCO* *PINK-SIDED JUNCO* *WHITE-WINGED JUNCO* *GRAY-HEADED JUNCO*

The DARK-EYED JUNCO has five adult plumage variations associated with different geographical regions.

Hybrids between species may produce birds that share some characteristics of each parent but still have a very different appearance.

Some species have two or more color phases or morphs.

LAWRENCE'S WARBLER *BREWSTER'S WARBLER*

Results from crosses between Golden-winged Warblers and Blue-winged Warblers and their offspring.

The EASTERN SCREECH-OWL has red, gray, and brown morphs.

HOW TO IDENTIFY BIRDS

Birds that come to backyard feeders often stay long enough for you to study them in detail, but not all birds are so cooperative and often a fleeting glimpse is all you get. Learn to get the best look you can under the conditions and to see the entire bird well. First impressions of a bird, especially a new species for you, will give you clues for comparing it with birds you already know. What you are looking for are field marks, those physical clues that include size, shape, color patterns, and behavior, and also the habitat the bird is in and the sounds it may make.

Learn to routinely and quickly look at the details of the head; markings on the body, wings, and tail; and the shapes of the bird's parts.

HEAD
Is the crown:

striped   streaked   capped   crested

Look for other markings on the face such as:

superciliary stripes   eye lines   eye rings   spectacles

mustache marks   malar marks   ear patches   a mask through the eye

BODY PLUMAGE
Are the underparts:

plain and unmarked   streaked   spotted

TAIL
Is the tail:

forked   rounded   fan-shaped   wedge-shaped   pointed

notched   square   short   long

MARKINGS
Does it have distinctive wing or tail markings such as:

bars   bands   spots   contrasting colors

BILL
Is the bill:

cone-shaped   needlelike   hooked   decurved   spatulate   long or short

SONG
Many expert birders rely on their ears as much as their eyes to identify birds. Any of the many cassette tapes, CDs, or videos can help you learn the songs, calls, and other sounds birds make.

BEHAVIOR
The behavior of the bird will also provide clues to its identity. Does it bob, wag, or pump its tail either up and down or back and forth? Note its flight pattern. Does it back down a tree or go headfirst? For more information on Behavior, see page 24.

IDENTIFYING BIRDS IN FLIGHT

How a bird flies – the speed of the wing stroke as well as the pattern – can often help you recognize a species.

Direct – steady flight with regular wing beats, along a constant line; typical of most species, including waterfowl, herons, doves, crows, shorebirds, and many songbirds.

Dynamic soaring – glides over water "downhill" with the wind to its back and when close to the surface quickly turns 180 degrees back into the wind. There the bird is lifted back up to near the original height upon which it turns back and soars "downhill" again. Characteristic of many pelagic species, including albatrosses, shearwaters, and petrels.

Flap and glide – alternates a burst of several wing beats with a short or long level glide. Many birds of prey, both hawks and owls, use this flight pattern as do Black Vultures, ibis, and pelicans.

Flightless – many species living in environments free of predators have given up the energy-demanding activity of flight. The only flightless North American species, the Great Auk, was hunted to extinction in 1844.

Glide – wings are held fully or partially extended as the bird loses altitude. Many birds glide down to a landing, or from perch to perch. Hawks may glide from the top of one thermal to the bottom of the next in migration.

Hawking – flying up from the ground or down from an aerial perch to seize a flying insect and looping back down to the same or nearby perch. Characteristic of flycatchers and other small, active insect-eating birds such as warblers, the Cedar Waxwing, and several species of woodpeckers.

Hovering – rapid wingbeats while the bird remains suspended in one spot over the ground or water. Typical of hummingbirds, kingfishers, American Kestrel, Osprey, Rough-legged Hawk and many small birds that hover briefly to glean food from vegetation.

Mothlike – an erratic, sometimes bouncy, slow flight seen in nightjars, a few storm-petrels, and in the display flights of some small birds.

Skims – the flight pattern of the Black Skimmer in which the bird flies a steady course with its lower mandible cleaving the surface of still water as it feeds.

Static soaring – requires about a twentieth of the energy of flapping flight. Birds soar on rising heated columns of air, thermals, or on deflected currents and updrafts. Large hawks, eagles, vultures, storks, White Pelicans, and gulls soar this way.

Straight line formation – an energy-saving style of flight used by some larger birds such as cormorants, pelicans, ibis, some waterfowl, and others. Birds may fly one behind the other, or abreast as do some scoters and eiders.

Undulating – some small birds conserve energy by rising on one or more wing beats and then folding the wings to the body and swooping down to the next wing beat. Characteristic of woodpeckers, finches, and chickadees.

V formation – an energy-saving flight style used by some larger birds, including ducks, geese, cranes, and cormorants.

Zigzag – a pattern used by birds flushed from the ground as a way to elude predators. The Common Snipe and several species of quail are good examples.

BIRD SILHOUETTES

The first step in identifying a bird is to narrow down the possibilities to one or two families. Most species in a family share a unique combination of physical traits, such as the size and shape of the bill, that gives the family a distinctive silhouette. Some larger families are broken into subfamilies. For example, buteos and accipiters, both hawks in the family Accipitridae, have very different flight silhouettes. Identification becomes easier once you have learned the characteristic shape of each family and subfamily. The silhouettes shown here will help you place birds into their family groupings.

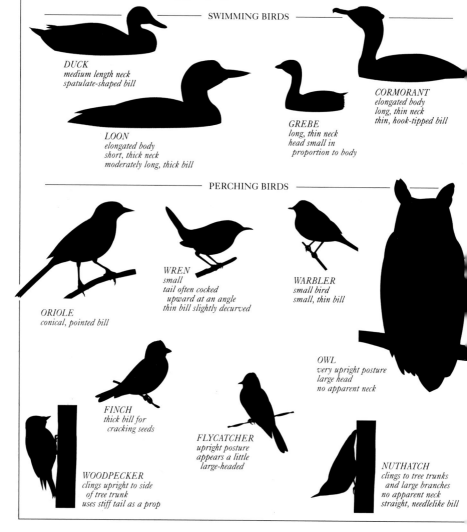

SWIMMING BIRDS

DUCK
medium length neck
spatulate-shaped bill

LOON
elongated body
short, thick neck
moderately long, thick bill

GREBE
long, thin neck
head small in
proportion to body

CORMORANT
elongated body
long, thin neck
thin, hook-tipped bill

PERCHING BIRDS

ORIOLE
conical, pointed bill

WREN
small
tail often cocked
upward at an angle
thin bill slightly decurved

WARBLER
small bird
small, thin bill

OWL
very upright posture
large head
no apparent neck

FINCH
thick bill for
cracking seeds

FLYCATCHER
upright posture
appears a little
large-headed

WOODPECKER
clings upright to side
of tree trunk
uses stiff tail as a prop

NUTHATCH
clings to tree trunks
and large branches
no apparent neck
straight, needlelike bill

STANDING BIRDS

THRASHER
thrushlike but with
  longer tail
  medium length bill

PEEP
thin bill
dumpy body
moderately long legs

THRUSH
thin bill
plump body
relatively long legs

HERON
long neck and legs
daggerlike bill

CORVID
short neck
strong bill
heavy body

FLYING BIRDS

GOOSE
heavy body
small head
long, outstretched neck

ACCIPITER
broad wings
long, relatively
  narrow tail

BUTEO
broad wings and tail
individual primary
  feathers visible on wing

SWIFT
long, very thin,
  swept-back wings
  almost no visible tail

SWALLOW
long, pointed,
  swept-back wings

GULL
long, angular wings
spread tail
moderate bill

FALCON
narrow tail
relatively
  narrow,
  pointed wings

VULTURE
large bird
small head
long, broad-based wings
  with visible primaries

BEHAVIOR

A large portion of the bird behavior we admire is instinctive and associated with particular species and families. So as you look for field marks, notice the bird's body language. It will give you many clues to its identity.

TAIL MOVEMENT

Some birds flip their tails as they move or perch. The tail may be cocked at an angle over the back, fanned open or closed, wagged, bobbed, or pumped up or down. Some birds constantly bob their bodies up and down as they walk or stand; others bob or jerk occasionally, while others sway back and forth as they walk.

BODY MOVEMENT

Some birds hop like a sparrow. Some run or walk. They may climb trees straight up, hitch up or back down them, walk headfirst down them, or cling upside down. Many birds wade like herons and egrets, or swim like ducks and geese. Some aquatic species feed by dabbling or tipping up their bodies with their heads and necks beneath the surface. Others dive completely below the surface.

BEWICK'S WREN holds its tail high above its back as it hops, often flicking it from side to side.

The PAINTED REDSTART spreads its tail, flashing the white outer tail feathers.

The BLUE-WINGED TEAL dabbles for food.

The TRICOLORED HERON wades.

FORAGING

Notice whether the bird forages on the ground, in the treetops, or at the mid-story level. Shorebirds may stay on the dry sand or away from the water's edge on a mudflat, or they may wade in the shallows, while some species may wade up to their bellies. Some shorebirds pick at their food while others drill and probe rapidly in the mud.

A juvenile WHITE IBIS probes with its bill for food in shallow water.

These MOURNING DOVES are foraging on the ground.

DISPLAY BEHAVIORS

Many species exhibit distinctive display behaviors during breeding season. They may dance like Prairie-Chickens, cranes, or Western Grebes; "skylark" like sparrows or buntings; or put on the aerial shows of woodcock and snipe. Many species, especially ground-nesters, will try to lead intruders away from the nest with distraction displays including the broken-wing or crippled-bird act.

The GREAT EGRET flashes its long white plumes in courtship display.

ABUNDANCE AND DISTRIBUTION

What does it mean when someone says a bird is "common" or that a species is "abundant" or "rare?" To appreciate a bird species' presence (or lack of it) in a given region you need to consider the factors of habitat, geographical range, and season of the year. Keep in mind that the distribution and abundance of birds, among the most mobile of the earth's creatures, are not static and the boundaries of populations often change. Birds are easily impacted by changes in climate and habitat brought about by natural or human causes, with seasonal migrations being the most obvious result. Thus knowing the seasonal occurrence of a bird is important in confirming its identification. The range maps in this guide are color-coded to provide you with this information. You can get even more specific information from local checklists, local bird books, websites, and local birders.

• _Abundant_ means a species is so conspicuous that birders usually observe more than 25 individuals daily in proper habitat and season.

Common means • birders are likely to see 5–25 individuals daily in proper habitat and season.

BLACK-CAPPED CHICKADEE

EUROPEAN STARLING

Uncommon species • can be widespread but may not be observed by birders searching for it in proper habitat and season.

Fairly common means a species is common enough that birders should observe at least one individual daily in proper habitat and season. •

YELLOW-THROATED VIREO

LONG-EARED OWL

Casual means a bird that wanders into North America at infrequent intervals and is not observed annually, but exhibits a pattern of occurrence over several decades. •

Rare can mean either that the species is widely distributed outside North America but exists in low numbers here, or that the entire population • is small and local.

WHITE-THROATED ROBIN

ANTILLEAN NIGHTHAWK

Irruptive means the species is erratic in its movements – present and even numerous in a region in one year and absent the next.

SNOWY OWL

Vagrant is a migrant that has strayed off its usual route.

WHITE-EYED VIREO

RING-NECKED PHEASANT

Introduced means a non-native species deliberately released in a legal effort to establish a population.

Exotic means a non-native species illegally released or escaped, such as the many parrot species in south Florida, or a non-native species that has arrived in the region on its own like the Cattle Egret, or with passive human assistance (such as hitching a transoceanic ride on a ship).

Permanent residents live in the same geographic region all year.

NORTHERN CARDINAL

CATTLE EGRET

Summer residents breed and raise their young in one region and leave to winter in another region, usually to the south.

CEDAR WAXWING

SHY ALBATROSS

Accidentals are species that have occurred fewer than ten times in a region.

Transients pass through a region only once or twice a year during their spring and/or fall migrations.

AMERICAN TREE SPARROW

Winter residents arrive in a region only during the winter months after their breeding season, and usually breed to the north of it.

SEMIPALMATED SANDPIPER

WATCHING BIRDS IN THE BACKYARD

If you provide suitable food, shelter, and water, birds will come to your backyard. If you offer a variety of these necessities you will attract a greater diversity of birds. Place your feeders, nesting boxes, and birdbaths where the birds will feel safe from people and animals and where you can see the birds as you go about your daily routine.

FOOD AND FEEDERS

Many people enjoy feeding birds year-round. Basic types of feeders include platform feeders, hopper feeders, tube feeders, ball feeders, window feeders, fruit feeders, nectar feeders, and suet feeders. Standard foods include black (oil) sunflower seed (the best single seed), striped sunflower seed, hulled sunflower (chips/hearts) seed, niger (called "thistle") seed, safflower seed, white proso millet seed, red millet seed, milo seed, corn (whole kernel, shelled, and cracked), peanuts, peanut butter, suet and suet mixes, fruits, and nectar.

HOUSE FINCHES and a NORTHERN CARDINAL find food and shelter.

AMERICAN GOLDFINCHES at a tube feeder

A female RED-BELLIED WOODPECKER finds suet in a wire cage feeder.

WATER

Birds need water as much as they need food. If you include even one dependable source of water in your yard you will attract a great variety of birds to drink, bathe, and cool off. If there is running water or dripping water element even more species will come. There are many styles of water containers to choose from but the only requirement is: Maintain a stable supply of clean water in a shallow container no deeper than three inches.

NORTHERN CARDINAL at a traditional birdbath

"Hotel" for PURPLE MARTINS

Two types of nest boxes you can make yourself

SHELTER AND NEST BOXES

Planting trees, shrubs, and other vegetation not only provides food for birds but shelter and nesting places. Many species will use nest boxes. Others will use nesting shelves or ledges, and larger species will use raised nesting platforms. Nesting boxes can be made of wood, aluminum, or plastic; natural gourds are often used for martins and swallows.

Urban nest for MOURNING DOVES

WATCHING BIRDS IN THE FIELD

Very little gear is needed to watch birds, other than your own curiosity. Two indispensable items are a good pair of binoculars and a good field guide. Birding with experienced birders who know the area is also valuable in getting you off to a good start. It is a good idea to keep a small notebook handy. Later you may want to add a camera and telephoto lens; a spotting scope with tripod becomes a good investment for the more serious birder.

A long-lens camera and binoculars allow birders to photograph and see birds that might otherwise be missed.

BINOCULARS
Look for magnifying ranges of
7x to 10x power.

BINOCULARS

Look for magnifying ranges from 7x to 10x power. The outside diameter of the lenses that are farthest from your eyes (the objective lenses) should range from 35mm to 50mm. The power of magnification and the diameter of the objective lenses (the latter helps determine light-gathering ability) are combined and stamped on the binoculars as two numbers such as: 7 x 35, 7 x 50, or 8 x 42. Small compact binoculars such as 8 x 23 are lightweight and tempting to carry in the field, but the small size of the objective lenses limits the amount of light they can gather, making birdwatching under low light difficult.

BASIC PHOTOGRAPHY EQUIPMENT

The best camera body for bird photography is a 35mm single lens reflex (SLR). This camera allows you to view the subject directly through the lens. Many birds move quickly so your camera should have a fast shutter speed of at least 1/500 sec or higher, and the films you use with natural light should have high exposure speeds in the range of 200–400 ISO (ASA). A telephoto lens will allow you to photograph a larger image; you will need one in the 300mm to 500mm range. A sturdy tripod is required for sharp exposures. Use blinds to conceal yourself from the bird and let you get much closer. Automobiles will work as long as you stay inside.

TRIPOD
*To improve the sharpness
of your exposures*

CAMERA
35mm single lens reflex (SLR)

TELEPHOTO LENS
*Look for a lens in the 300mm to
500mm range.*

A temporary moveable blind in the form of a simple tent can conceal birders enough to put wary birds at ease.

HOW TO BE A BETTER BIRDER

There are many ways to improve your birding skills and increase your enjoyment of birdwatching.

STUDY AT HOME
Time spent at home studying your field guide will make a big difference. Find local checklists of birds, or state and regional bird books, that provide even more specific information about the birds in your area. Listen to recordings of bird songs and calls.

Patience is one of a birder's most important skills.

IMPROVE YOUR FIELD SKILLS
Birds have keen color eyesight and hearing. They are frightened by sudden movements, loud noises, and bright clothing that does not "blend" with the background. Experienced birders move deliberately, stalking quietly. They converse in low tones and stand patiently.

Birds are curious and attracted to sounds. When you make "pishing" noises (forcing air out through clenched teeth as if saying "pish, pish, pish"), or "squeaking" (making a high-pitched squeak by sucking air through closely pursed lips, a sound that can be amplified by "kissing" the back of your hand) many birds' curiosity will be piqued and they will come closer. Often they produce alarm notes or assembly calls, causing even more birds to come out where you can see them.

KEEP A RECORD
Keeping good records of the birds you see will help you learn when seasonal species are present and how abundant they may be. There is still much science does not know about birds, particularly about behavior and abundance in some habitats, and the amateur birder can make valuable contributions.

PRACTICE BIRDING ETHICS

Birding is not without its responsibility to the welfare of the bird. The American Birding Association has compiled a Code of Ethics for its members. (Copies can be obtained by writing to the ABA at the address below.) Their basic message is that birders' actions should not endanger the welfare of birds or other wildlife; they should not harm the natural environment; and birders must always respect the rights of others, especially their rights to privacy and private property rights.

A female feeds baby BLUEBIRDS.

The welfare of fledgling SCREECH-OWLS like these depends on birders who practice good ethics.

BIRD PROTECTION IN BREEDING SEASON

Remember that birds are sensitive to disturbance. Nothing should be done that will frighten them or alter the surroundings of their nest. Once frightened, they may abandon the nest, and this could set their breeding back a whole year.

RUBY-THROATED HUMMINGBIRD feeds her young

JOIN A CLUB

Every state and province has established bird clubs. Many local clubs are associated with state, provincial, or regional ornithological societies that network activities, have regular meetings, and publish newsletters. You can locate your nearest bird clubs on the internet, or though the Conservation Directory of the National Wildlife Federation, your state conservation or wildlife department, local library, or newspaper.

Birding organizations exist on the national and international level as well. Some national organizations and their publications are:
• American Birding Association, PO Box 6599, Colorado Springs, CO 80934; *Birding.*
• American Ornithologists' Union, *The Auk;* Association of Field Ornithologists, *Journal of Field Ornithology;* Cooper Ornithological Society, *The Condor;* Wilson Ornithological Society, *Wilson Bulletin.* All can be contacted c/o Ornithological Societies of North America, 810 E. 10th Street, Lawrence, KS 66044.
• Laboratory of Ornithology at Cornell University, 159 Sapsucker Woods Road, Ithaca, NY 14850; *Living Bird* quarterly.
• National Audubon Society, 700 Broadway, New York, NY 10003; *Audubon.*

CONSERVATION

We are lucky that here in North America we have lost relatively few bird species to extinction. Laws to protect some species were passed as early as the late 1700s, but even then some came too late or were not enforced. Today, all species of birds native to North America are protected by state, provincial, and federal laws and cannot be collected or held in captivity without a legal permit (introduced, non-native species are not so protected). Some species, considered game species, are managed and can be legally harvested during hunting seasons.

Still, many species of North American birds are in decline. Several species require management because their populations have become dangerously low. These species are given additional protection and listed by state, provincial, or federal authorities as "threatened" or "endangered." The bird conservation effort across America is joined by organizations such as the National Audubon Society, the American Bird Conservancy, and Partners in Flight.

The WOOD STORK is declining due to habitat destruction and the disruption of water flow through southern Florida.

Some populations of LEAST TERN are endangered due to human disturbance of nesting areas.

The latter group is an Americas-wide coalition of more than 160 organizations and government agencies. Many of our continent's birds have not fared well at the hands of man. They have been persecuted as pests, victimized by wanton shooting, deprived of habitat, subjected to poisons, forced into competition by

The SPECTACLED EIDER has seen major decline in recent years due to the introduction of firearms into its limited nesting range.

introduced species, and preyed upon by brood parasites. Many of the species that nest in North America, particularly songbirds and shorebirds, are neotropical migrants wintering in other countries where they are exposed to similar stresses, often with less protection.

Birds and other wildlife need our help now more than ever before. Conservation requires the support of every citizen to prevent the continued loss of our natural heritage.

The CALIFORNIA CONDOR is now nearly extinct in the wild due to hunting and lead poisoning.

LAUGHING GULLS and BROWN PELICANS live side by side with America's offshore oil industry.

EXTINCTION

The North American continent north of Mexico hosts more than 700 species of native nesting birds. Direct persecution and indirect population stresses caused by loss of required habitat – both factors generated by humans – have resulted in a small percentage that are now either extinct or on the very brink of extinction. Likewise, many other species are declining and some are in serious trouble. The first to go was the Great Auk, the only flightless species on the continent, after centuries of unregulated exploitation. Many of these species were abundant, and some, like the Passenger Pigeon, were among the most numerous species in North America. Often sheer numbers made them easy to kill in quantity and their marketing profitable. Improvements in firearms and transportation, plus the conversion of the vast eastern forests into farmland, hastened the decline of these species.

Today we are more enlightened. We have enacted laws and extended efforts to save species. There are preservation success stories with species like Peregrine Falcons, Bald Eagles, Brown Pelicans, Ospreys, Whooping Cranes, and Trumpeter Swans. But, there is still much to do as human populations continue to alter critical habitats.

The Eskimo Curlew, Ivory-billed Woodpecker, and Bachman's Warbler are considered probably extinct. The two species on the following page, the Passenger Pigeon and Carolina Parakeet, are now classified as extinct.

Family SCOLOPACIDAE	Species *Numenius borealis*	Length 14 inches	Wingspan 23–27 inches

ESKIMO CURLEW

Once among the most numerous shorebirds in North America, this bird was rare by the 20th century due to unrestricted shooting during fall migration on the North Atlantic Coast, on the wintering grounds in Argentina, and in spring migration in Texas and on the Great Plains. Gregarious by nature, large flocks attracted market and sport hunters, who killed them by the wagonload and shipped them to eastern cities. Most records in the 20th century were in spring on the Texas coast; the last specimen was recorded in Barbados in 1963, and the last sight records were in 1982 in Canada.

• **SONG** Soft tremulous twittering whistles in flight. Calls thin high-pitched squeaks and whistles.

• **BEHAVIOR** Gregarious in migration and on wintering grounds; often in large flocks. Approachable; habit of returning to site after shots fired into flock made it vulnerable to hunters. Nested on Arctic tundra; wintered in open areas, prairies, and agricultural fields.

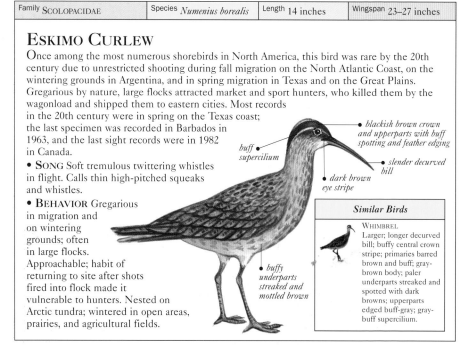

buff supercilium

blackish brown crown and upperparts with buff spotting and feather edging

slender decurved bill

dark brown eye stripe

buffy underparts streaked and mottled brown

Similar Birds

WHIMBREL
Larger; longer decurved bill; buffy central crown stripe; primaries barred brown and buff; gray-brown body; paler underparts streaked and spotted with dark browns; upperparts edged buff-gray; gray-buff supercilium.

Family PICIDAE	Species *Campephilus principalis*	Length 19.5 inches	Wingspan 30–32 inches

IVORY-BILLED WOODPECKER

black forecrest

red crest

white streak from eye to back of wing

ivory-white bill

white patch on folded wing

black overall

The largest woodpecker north of Mexico depended on large tracts of primeval bottomland and swamp forests to sustain its feeding habits. The head and bill were used by Native Americans for trade items and early settlers valued them for good luck, but it was the felling of the large southern forests and the loss of its food supply that doomed this woodpecker. Once it became rare, people hunted the remaining birds for museum and private collections. An estimated twenty-two birds existed in the US in 1938; the last records were in the 1940s. Unverified sightings are still being reported from the South, and a Cuban subspecies was confirmed to be alive in the late 1980s.

• **SONG** Nasal clarinet-like *yank, yank, yank*, often in a series like a large White-breasted Nuthatch.

• **BEHAVIOR** In pairs, mated for life, or in small family groups just after nesting season. Fed on wood-boring insects under bark of dead or dying trees, some fruits and berries. Ranged from Ohio River Valley to east Texas, Gulf Coast, and also to the state of Florida.

Similar Birds

PILEATED WOODPECKER
Smaller • male has red crest and mustache mark; black mask extends from lores to nape; white supercilium begins behind eye; white chin; white line extends from base of bill to sides of breast • female has black forehead and mustache.

Family PARULIDAE	Species *Vermivora bachmanii*	Length 4.25–4.75 inches	Wingspan 6.75–7.5 inches

BACHMAN'S WARBLER

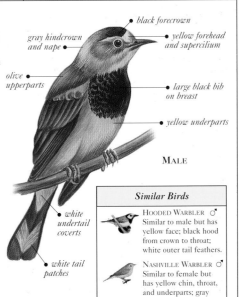

gray hindcrown and nape

black forecrown

yellow forehead and supercilium

olive upperparts

large black bib on breast

yellow underparts

MALE

white undertail coverts

white tail patches

Possibly never very numerous, this songbird lived in bottomland forests and swamps and their canebrakes along the coastal plain from southern Kentucky and Missouri to South Carolina. It was found in the Gulf coastal states in migration on its way to and from wintering grounds in Cuba and in some locations along the Suwannee River in Florida. The clearing of these forests for timber and agricultural drainage hastened the decline. The last certain US record was near Charleston, South Carolina, in 1962; and the last individual seen was a wintering female in Cuba in 1981.

• **SONG** Buzzy trill of 6–8 notes on a single pitch; similar to Worm-eating Warbler or Chipping Sparrow but higher pitched. Persistent singer on breeding grounds.

• **BEHAVIOR** Solitary or in pairs. Foraged at middle to high level in trees. Nested in thickets within 3 feet of ground in briers, canebrakes, or bushy tangles. Gleaned insects from foliage and branches.

Similar Birds

HOODED WARBLER ♂
Similar to male but has yellow face; black hood from crown to throat; white outer tail feathers.

NASHVILLE WARBLER ♂
Similar to female but has yellow chin, throat, and underparts; gray head, crown, and nape.

Family COLUMBIDAE	Species *Ectopistes migratorius*	Length 16 inches	Wingspan 24–25.5 inches

PASSENGER PIGEON

The most abundant bird in North America at the time of European settlement may have made up a quarter of its bird population. The Passenger Pigeon and the eastern deciduous forest upon which it depended were destroyed simultaneously. John James Audubon described migrating flocks that stretched for miles in the sky and took three days to pass over, and which he estimated to contain over a billion birds. As the forest was reduced to farmland, the birds were hunted throughout the year. The last known wild specimen was shot in 1898; and the last surviving bird, Martha, a captive reared individual, died at age 29 in the Cincinnati Zoo in 1914.

• **SONG** Loud grating croaking, chattering, or clucking notes. Not dovelike.

• **BEHAVIOR** Highly gregarious; lived, foraged, wandered, and nested in large groups. Fed on tree seeds, fruits, berries, buds, and invertebrates. Nomadic; went where food was plentiful. Nested from Missouri, Kentucky, and Virginia northward into southern Canada and west to Kansas. Wintered south to Gulf Coast.

MALE

blue-gray head and upperparts

tawny breast

blue-gray upperparts

brownish gray breast

sandy-gray underparts

sandy gray underparts

FEMALE

Similar Birds

MOURNING DOVE Smaller; pinkish fawn head and underparts; brownish gray upperparts; white-tipped outer tail feathers; black spots on upper inner wing; black spot on lower cheek.

Family PSITTACIDAE	Species *Conuropsis carolinensis*	Length 16 inches	Wingspan 24–26 inches

CAROLINA PARAKEET

Once abundant in the East from eastern Nebraska to New York and south to the Gulf Coast, this beautiful parakeet was hunted for its feathers, the pet trade, for sport, and as a pest of orchards, cornfields, and gardens. Flocks had such strong bonds that when some of their numbers were killed the remainder of the flock returned to their bodies repeatedly until all were shot. By the late 1870s it existed only in remote Florida swamps; the last known birds were shot in the early 1900s, and the last reported individual of the only endemic US parrot died in the Cincinnati Zoo in the year 1914.

• **SONG** Loud quarrelsome screams given in flight.

• **BEHAVIOR** Social. Gregarious, occurring in flocks except in breeding season when pairs nested in dense colonies. Mated for life. Roosted communally in hollow trees. Fed in bottomland forests, riverbanks, and cypress swamps on tree seeds, thistle, cocklebur, grass seeds, fruits, and berries.

yellow head with orange cheeks, forehead, and crown

large hooked pinkish cream bill

green body, wings, and tail

pointed tail, yellow below

Similar Birds

No similar native species.

SPECIES PROFILES

The following section (pp. 40–542) contains a full-page profile for each of the 503 bird species known to occur regularly in the state of Texas and its adjacent islands and seas within 200 miles of the coast. The profiled species represent 71 families in 21 orders. They are arranged in taxonomic order, according to the American Ornithologists' Union Check-list of North American Birds (7th Edition, 1998, and its 42nd Supplement, 2000). Additional species that occur less regularly within this region may be found in a separate section at the back of this book, beginning on page 543.

Family GAVIIDAE	Species *Gavia stellata*	Length 24–27 inches	Wingspan 42–45 inches

RED-THROATED LOON

This is the smallest loon and the only one without profuse white spotting on its upperparts in the breeding plumage. When the bird is on the water, its slender bill appears upturned and is often held pointed upward by the swimming bird. In juvenile and winter plumage both sexes have a gray crown and hindneck, dark gray back with many small white spots, pale upturned bill, and a white face, sides, foreneck, and underparts.

gray head and neck

dark slender upturned bill

medium gray back with small, indistinct spots

thin black stripes on hindneck

dull red patch on foreneck

- **SONG** Usually silent. On breeding ground, prolonged wails and gooselike *kwuk-kwuk-kwuk*.
- **BEHAVIOR** Flies with neck drooping. Only loon to leap directly into flight from water or land. Feeds primarily on fish, which it catches in dives down to 90 feet. Solitary except on wintering grounds and in migration, when hundreds may congregate in bays along the coast.
- **BREEDING** Usually a solitary nester. Sometimes forms loose colonies.
- **NESTING** Incubation 24–29 days by both sexes. Precocial young leave nest and take to water about 1 day after hatching, then fly at about 49–60 days. 1 brood per year.
- **POPULATION** Common to fairly common on breeding grounds; fairly common on coast in winter; casual to very uncommon inland in winter. Populations stable.
- **CONSERVATION** Vulnerable to loss of habitat due to development in high Arctic and to pollution, particularly oil spills, in wintering areas. Many drown in gill nets.

WINTER PLUMAGE

Similar Birds

ARCTIC LOON
PACIFIC LOON
Breeding adults have dark throat; dark flanks; large white spots on back • in winter plumage, lack white spots on back; bill not upturned; dark gray of crown and hind neck contrast sharply with white face and foreneck. • Arctic Loon in the West only.

Flight Pattern	
Direct flight with swift rapid wing beats.	

Nest Identification	
Shape 🪹 Location ▬ ✸✸✸	Moist depression or heap of damp vegetation mixed with mud • male sometimes constructs copulation platform away from nest • 1–3 olive-green to dark brown eggs, sometimes with blackish brown spots.

Plumage Sexes similar	Habitat 〰️ 〰️	Migration Migratory	Weight 3.4 pounds

DATE _____ TIME_____ LOCATION _____

Family GAVIIDAE	Species *Gavia immer*	Length 28–36 inches	Wingspan 50–58 inches

COMMON LOON

Frequenting quiet lakes and usually sleeping on the water, this large bird rarely comes on land except to nest. It must run at least 20 yards across water to gain enough momentum to fly. Loons require such pristine conditions to nest that their presence as a nesting bird is a good indicator of the wilderness condition of a lake and the frequency of human activity on it. Winter adults have gray or brown upperparts; an irregular or broken pattern on the head to the base of the eye and the sides of the neck; white underparts, chin, and foreneck; a blue-gray bill; and a white eye ring.

glossy black head with greenish sheen

red-brown eyes

stout, straight black bill

checkered black-and-white back

glossy black throat

broken white neck collar

white breast and belly

WINTER PLUMAGE

- **SONG** Usually silent away from breeding areas. Different calls on breeding grounds: tremolo or "loon's laughter"; yodel, sounding like *yodel-ha-oo-oo*; wail; and talking *kwuk*.
- **BEHAVIOR** Rides low on water. Dives to 200 feet to catch fish. Eats freshwater and saltwater fish, crustaceans, amphipods, snails, leeches, frogs, salamanders, and aquatic insects. Eats larger prey on surface and smaller prey underwater. Can stay underwater up to 60 seconds. Loons migrate alone or in small groups.
- **BREEDING** Monogamous. Solitary nester on islands, always within a few feet of water. May use same nest year after year.
- **NESTING** Incubation 26–31 days by both sexes, mostly by female. Precocial young leave nest soon after hatching; fed and raised by both sexes. First flight at 70–80 days. 1 brood per year.
- **POPULATION** Fairly common. Decrease in some breeding areas in southern parts of range.
- **CONSERVATION** Prone to environmental loss due to human disturbance and reduced food supply resulting from acid rain. Some abandon nests due to human activity. Some breeding grounds protected by volunteers.

Similar Birds

YELLOW-BILLED LOON Pale yellow bill in all plumages, with dusky base in winter; bill is larger and culmen is less curved • in winter has paler head and neck and brown patch over ear.

Flight Pattern

Rapid direct flight with strong wing beats. Head, neck, and legs extended and drooping slightly below midline of body give hunchbacked appearance.

Nest Identification	
Shape ～ Location ▬ ⌂	Bed of stems, grasses, and twigs • floating in bog; or on ground, hidden in crevices or muskrat houses • built by both sexes • 1–3 olive-green to dark brown eggs usually scattered with dark brown spots; subelliptical to oval, 3.5 x 2.2 inches.

Plumage Sexes similar	Habitat ～ ～	Migration Migratory	Weight 9.1 pounds

DATE _____ TIME_____ LOCATION _____

Family PODICIPEDIDAE	Species *Tachybaptus dominicus*	Length 9–10 inches	Wingspan 20 inches

LEAST GREBE

As its name suggests, this is the smallest of the North American grebes. It also has the most restricted range, barely crossing the southern border from Mexico. It may hide among tall vegetation in shallow, warm ponds, sloughs, and ditches in which it forages and nests. Apart from its size, it can be distinguished from other grebes by its golden eyes and short dark bill. In winter the sides of the head are brown rather than gray, the back and bill are lighter in color, and there is less black on the back of the head and neck.

golden eyes •

short • neck

• purplish face and neck

• small slender bill

WINTER PLUMAGE

• **SONG** Bold, resonating trumpetlike note.
• **BEHAVIOR** Feeds primarily on aquatic insects. Like all other grebes, eats its own feathers, which may form a ball in the stomach. The purpose of this unusual behavior is unknown, but it may protect the gastrointestinal track from the sharp bones of the fish they ingest.
• **BREEDING** Monogamous. Occasionally forms loose colonies.
• **NESTING** Incubation 21 days by both sexes. Young stay in nest 2 weeks. Carried by parents for 3–4 days. Fed by both sexes. 2–3 broods per year, with more in the Tropics.
• **POPULATION** Common.
• **CONSERVATION** Readiness to use newly created bodies of water may be employed as a means of increasing populations.

Similar Birds

PIED-BILLED GREBE
Larger; thicker, light-colored bill; eye ring and dark (not golden) eye.

Flight Pattern
– – – – – – – – – – – ➤
Direct flight with rapid wing beats.

Nest Identification	
Shape ⌒ Location ⋰	Platform of decaying vegetation • either floating or anchored by aquatic plants in middle of secluded pond • built by both sexes • 2–7 whitish to very pale blue-green eggs that become nest stained; long pyriform, 1.3 inches long.

Plumage Sexes similar	Habitat ≈≈ ⌇ ⌁	Migration Nonmigratory	Weight 4.5 ounces

DATE _____ TIME_____ LOCATION _____

Family PODICIPEDIDAE	Species *Podilymbus podiceps*	Length 12–15 inches	Wingspan 22.5 inches

PIED-BILLED GREBE

The most widespread and best-known grebe in North America sometimes hides from intruders by sinking until only its head shows above water or by diving like other members of the group. This stocky grebe has a large head and short thick bill that gives it a chickenlike profile, easily distinguishing it from other grebes, even at a distance. The bill is light-colored and has a black ring around it during the breeding season but lacks the ring in winter.

large head

dark eye

eye ring

brownish gray body

short neck

dark ring on short thick bill

WINTER PLUMAGE

- **SONG** Loud, cuckoolike call, *cuck, cuck, cuck, cow-cow-cow, cow-ah-cow-ah.*
- **BEHAVIOR** Forages by diving from the surface and swimming underwater, propelled by its feet. Feeds some on vegetation, but about half of the diet is made up of aquatic insects with the remainder split almost equally between small fish and crustaceans.
- **BREEDING** Monogamous. Solitary nester.
- **NESTING** Incubation 23–27 days by both sexes, but female does more. Young move from nest to adult's back less than an hour after hatching. Nest use stops in 24–42 days. First flight at 35–37 days. Young fed by both sexes. 1–2 broods per year.
- **POPULATION** Very common in range.
- **CONSERVATION** May be declining due to habitat loss.

Similar Birds

LEAST GREBE Smaller with golden (not dark) eye; slender, dark bill; much more restricted North American range.

Flight Pattern

Direct flight with rapid wing beats.

Nest Identification

Shape ⌒⌒   Location ⋔⋔

Platform of decaying vegetation • inconspicuously anchored to vegetation in open water among reeds or rushes • built by both sexes • 2–10 pale bluish white or nest-stained eggs; elliptical to subelliptical, 1.7 inches long.

Plumage Sexes similar	Habitat 〜〜 〜	Migration Some migrate	Weight 15.6 ounces

DATE _____ TIME_____ LOCATION _____

Family PODICIPEDIDAE	Species *Podiceps auritus*	Length 12–15 inches	Wingspan 24 inches

HORNED GREBE

The "horns" for which this bird is named are actually tufts of golden feathers above and behind the eyes, which are present only during the bird's breeding season. In summer the reddish neck of the Horned Grebe distinguishes it from the Eared Grebe, which shares much of the breeding range. The Horned Grebe's life is tied to water, breeding in freshwater habitats and often spending the winter both in freshwater and in saltwater.

• **SONG** This grebe gives an abrasive *keark, keark* or *yark, yark*. It also makes a repeated prattling sound followed by shrill screams.

golden "horns"

black head

reddish neck

dark straight bill

short tail

• **BEHAVIOR** The Horned Grebe eats as its primary diet mostly fish and some crustaceans as well as aquatic insects. Tamer than other grebes, it often allows a close approach by humans. Its nests are often built so that they are concealed poorly or not at all.

WINTER PLUMAGE

• **BREEDING** Monogamous. Most often a solitary nester; sometimes in loose colonies of 4–6 pairs.

• **NESTING** Incubation 22–25 days by both sexes. Precocial young fed by both sexes. First flight at 45–60 days. 1 brood per year, sometimes 2.

• **POPULATION** Common.

• **CONSERVATION** Declining apparently due to oil spills and habitat loss.

Similar Birds

EARED GREBE
More triangular head; has black neck in summer • dusky neck and black cheeks in winter.

WESTERN GREBE CLARK'S GREBE
Black above and white below; much larger; much longer necks and bills.

Flight Pattern

Direct flight with rapid wing beats.

Nest Identification

Shape Location

Floating heap of wet plant material, including underwater plants, rotting vegetation, rubbish, and mud • often anchored to vegetation • 3–7 whitish to very pale green eggs, usually nest-stained; 1.7 inches long.

Plumage Sexes similar	Habitat	Migration Migratory	Weight 1 pound

DATE _____ TIME_____ LOCATION _____

Family PODICIPEDIDAE	Species *Podiceps grisegena*	Length 17–21 inches	Wingspan 30–32 inches

RED-NECKED GREBE

Slightly smaller than the Western and Clark's Grebes, this bird's neck is much thicker in appearance. In flight it is the only grebe that shows white leading and trailing edges on the inner wing. Although it requires large bodies of freshwater for breeding, most of the population spends the winter months on saltwater.

- **SONG** On breeding ground, utters drawling cries and *crick-crick*; during courtship both sexes make loonlike calls of *ah-ooo, ah-ooo, ah-ooo, ah-ah-ah-ah-ah.*
- **BEHAVIOR** Feeds primarily on small fish and crustaceans that it gathers in dives to 25–30 feet.

blackish cap

long, thick yellow bill with dark tip

whitish cheeks

reddish foreneck and breast

blackish upperparts

dark gray sides

JUVENILE   WINTER PLUMAGE

One of the shyest grebes around the nest, it often slips away in the presence of intruders.

- **BREEDING** Monogamous. Usually a solitary nester but sometimes breeds in small colonies.
- **NESTING** Incubation 20–23 days by both sexes. Young fed by both sexes. First flight at 49–70 days. 1 brood per year.
- **POPULATION** Fairly common in suitable habitat in breeding range and along both North Atlantic and North Pacific coasts in winter. Casual to rare inland from US states bordering Canada south to the Gulf Coast in winter.
- **CONSERVATION** Declining overall due to pesticides, oil spills in marine environments, and habitat loss. Recent declines due to egg inviability, shell thinning from pesticides and PCBs, and increased egg predation by raccoons.

Similar Birds

WESTERN GREBE
CLARK'S GREBE
Similar in size; long necks always white below; pale to whitish sides; red eyes, not dark as in Red-necked Grebe.

Flight Pattern	
Direct flight with rapid wing beats.	

Nest Identification	
Shape Location	Plant material, fresh and decaying reeds • floating or anchored in shallow water • built by both sexes • 2–6 bluish white or very pale buff eggs that become nest-stained brown, 2.1 inches long.

Plumage Sexes similar	Habitat	Migration Migratory	Weight 2.3 pounds

DATE _____ TIME_____ LOCATION _____

Family PODICIPEDIDAE	Species *Podiceps nigricollis*	Length 12–13 inches	Wingspan 22.5 inches

EARED GREBE

The "ear" for which this bird is named is a wide golden tuft of feathers behind the eyes, present only in breeding plumage. It has a more triangular-shaped head than other grebes and is the only one that has a black neck during breeding season. The neck remains dusky gray in winter – a good field mark. The slender, dark bill appears slightly upturned.

triangular-shaped head

golden "ears"

black neck

slender, dark upturned bill

WINTER PLUMAGE

- **SONG** Utters soft *poo-eee-chk* in courtship. Also has grating shrieks.
- **BEHAVIOR** Pairs and family groups during the nesting season but often nests in dense colonies of up to several hundred pairs. Breeding pairs have several mutual displays, including an upright "penguin dance" side-by-side on the water. Forages by diving and swimming underwater for aquatic insects, which make up most of its summer diet. Many winter in marine environments, where shrimplike crustaceans become their principal food. A gregarious bird that often gathers in large flocks in winter. Tends to ride higher on the water than the somewhat similar Horned Grebe.
- **BREEDING** Monogamous. Colonial.
- **NESTING** Incubation 20–22 days by both sexes. Precocial young leave nest after last egg hatches. Fed by both sexes. Become independent 21 days after hatching. 1 brood per year, sometimes 2.
- **POPULATION** Common. Becoming increasingly more common in the East in winter. Numbers concentrated on lakes in Great Basin during migration.

Similar Birds

HORNED GREBE
Reddish neck in summer • white in winter plumage; white cheeks (not blackish like Eared Grebe) in winter • gold feathers in breeding plumage are restricted to "horns" above and behind the eye, not over the ears.

Flight Pattern

Direct flight with rapid wing beats.

Nest Identification

Shape ⌒⌒   Location ⅃⅃⅃

Made from fresh and decayed vegetation • floating but anchored by standing vegetation • built by both sexes • 1–9 whitish or bluish white eggs that become nest-stained brown, 1.7 inches long.

Plumage Sexes similar	Habitat 🌿 〰️	Migration Migratory	Weight 10.3 ounces

DATE _____ TIME_____ LOCATION _____

| Family PODICIPEDIDAE | Species *Aechmophorus occidentalis* | Length 22–29 inches | Wingspan 31–40 inches |

WESTERN GREBE

Identical in shape and size to Clark's Grebe, the Western Grebe shares much of the same range. It has a long swanlike neck and a slender, greenish yellow bill. Like all other grebes, it has feet modified for swimming, and the toes are lobed, not webbed as in waterfowl. Fish make up most of its diet.

- **SONG** Bold *crick-kreek*. Grating, whistled *c-r-r-ee-er-r-r-ee*.
- **BEHAVIOR** Both Western and Clark's Grebes have a structure in the neck that allows rapid,

black of cap extends below eye

long, slender neck

dark back

long, slender, greenish yellow bill

grayish sides

spearlike thrusting of the bill. Like all other grebes, it practices the peculiar behavior of carrying newly hatched young snuggled in the feathers of its back as it swims, and even as it dives if disturbed by an intruder.

- **BREEDING** Monogamous. Colonial.
- **NESTING** Incubation 23–24 days by both sexes. Precocial young climb onto parents' backs within minutes of birth and leave nest soon after. Young fed by both sexes. First flight at 63–70 days. 1 brood per year.
- **POPULATION** Fairly common to common. Casual in East during fall migration and winter.

WINTER PLUMAGE

Similar Birds

CLARK'S GREBE
Almost identical in all plumages but paler with white face extending above eye; orange (not yellow-green) bill
- more similar head pattern in winter, when Western may have whiter lore and Clark's may have darker lore.

HORNED GREBE
In winter, plumage also black and white but much smaller; shorter neck; short, dark bill.

- **CONSERVATION** From 1890s to 1906, thousands shot for feathers to make hats, coats, and capes. Oil spills and gill nets currently major causes of mortality. Vulnerable also to loss of habitat.

Flight Pattern
Direct flight with rapid wing beats.

Nest Identification	
Shape ♧ Location ⚮	Made of plant material • floating or anchored to standing vegetation in shallow water • built by both sexes • 1–7 pale bluish white eggs that become nest-stained brown; subelliptical to long elliptical, some tending toward oval, 2.3 inches long.

| Plumage Sexes similar | Habitat ⚟ ≈≈ ⚞ | Migration Some migrate | Weight 3.3 pounds |

DATE _____ TIME_____ LOCATION _____

Family PODICIPEDIDAE	Species *Aechmophorus clarkii*	Length 26 inches	Wingspan 30–40 inches

CLARK'S GREBE

Until recently this bird was considered a pale morph of the Western Grebe, which it closely resembles in size, shape, behavior, habitat selection, and range. It differs in bill color and by having a white face above and below the eyes, topped by a black cap. The range is not well known.

• **SONG** Ascending *kree-eek*.

• **BEHAVIOR** Gregarious; often colonial during the breeding season; wintering mostly in large numbers along the Pacific Coast in salt water. Has structure in neck that allows rapid, spearlike thrusting of bill. Like other grebes, legs set far back under the body make walking on land slow and laborious but swimming

• *white face above and below eyes*

• *very short tail*   • *pale sides and flanks*

WINTER PLUMAGE

and diving easy. Courtship behavior much like Western Grebe, with water "dances" including pairs running across the surface with bodies vertical and necks thrust forward.

• **BREEDING** Monogamous. Colonial.

• **NESTING** Incubation 23–24 days by both sexes. Precocial young climb onto parents' backs within minutes of birth. First flight at 63–77 days. Young fed by both sexes. 1 brood per year.

• **POPULATION** Common to fairly common in number; accidental in the East.

Similar Birds

WESTERN GREBE
Only other large, black-and-white grebe with a long neck; yellow-green bill instead of orange; black of cap extends down through eye.

• **CONSERVATION** Plume hunters once devastated populations. Oil spills and accidental drowing in gill nets are current major causes of mortality; also vulnerable to loss of habitat.

Flight Pattern
Direct flight with rapid wing beats.

Nest Identification	
Shape ⌒⌒ Location ⅃⅃⅃	Made of floating detritus • in shallow water • built by both sexes • 1–6 bluish white eggs that become nest-stained brown, 2.3 inches long.

Plumage Sexes similar	Habitat 〜 ≈≈ ≋	Migration Some migrate	Weight 3.3 pounds

DATE _____ TIME_____ LOCATION _____

Family PROCELLARIIDAE	Species *Calonectris diomedea*	Length 18–21 inches	Wingspan 44 inches

CORY'S SHEARWATER

The largest shearwater found along the Atlantic Coast skims the surface of the ocean with slow wing beats and a buoyant flight similar to that of the albatross. When this bird is seen flying straight ahead, its wings show a distinctive downward bow from wrist to wing tip. The large pale bill as well as the way the brown upperparts blend gradually with the white underparts without producing a capped appearance is distinctive. Cory's is the only Atlantic shearwater that occasionally soars.

brownish gray upperparts

narrow pale tips of uppertail coverts contrast with dark tail

large pinkish yellow bill with dusky tip

white underparts

dusky trailing edge on underwing

dusky primaries

- **SONG** Generally silent except on breeding grounds.
- **BEHAVIOR** Gregarious, often forming flocks that number in the hundreds or thousands. Frequently follows predatory fish to feed on the bait fish they drive to the water's surface. Feeds at night on crustaceans and large squid it takes from the surface. Has a keen sense of smell.
- **BREEDING** Monogamous. Colonial.
- **NESTING** Incubation 52–55 days by both sexes. Semialtricial young stay in nest about 90 days, although parents abandon young while still in nest. Young are fed by both sexes at night.
- **POPULATION** Numerous, but showing some decline.

Similar Birds

GREATER SHEARWATER Dark bill; distinct dark cap with white collar across nape; clear white rump band; smudge of dusky color on belly; clear contrast between dark upperparts and white underparts.

Flight Pattern

Soars if wind is up, looping and circling on fixed wings. Or, deep wing beats with wings bowed downward in long low glide.

Nest Identification

Shape 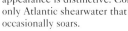 Location

Both sexes work together to either dig a new burrow or clean out a previously used burrow • sometimes under a rock • no material added • 1 white egg; blunt oval or subelliptical, 2.8 inches long.

Plumage Sexes similar	Habitat	Migration Migratory	Weight 1.2 pounds

DATE _____ TIME_____ LOCATION _____

Family PROCELLARIIDAE	Species *Puffinus griseus*	Length 18–20 inches	Wingspan 37–43 inches

SOOTY SHEARWATER

A common summer visitor off both the Atlantic and Pacific Coasts, this stocky short-necked sooty brown bird is probably the best-known shearwater in North American waters. It normally feeds well offshore, but during strong onshore winds hundreds of birds may be seen by observers from the shoreline. Look for the long slender dark wings with silvery gray underwing coverts. Some birds may have a white underwing lining. Legs and feet are blackish.

silvery gray underwing coverts

long slender dark wings

long dark bill

dark sooty brown plumage, darkest on tail and primaries

• **SONG** The Sooty Shearwater is silent except for noisy squeals when squabbling for food. Also makes inhaled and exhaled *koo-wah-koo-wah-koo-wah* when on breeding grounds.

• **BEHAVIOR** This bird often gathers in large flocks. Does not follow ships like some other seabirds, but is attracted to fishing trawlers. Flies with long glides on long narrow slightly swept-back wings. Sometimes makes short dives for fish, squid, and crustaceans. May plunge to dive on open wings from several feet above water.

• **BREEDING** Colonial. The Sooty Shearwater nests on various isolated islands in the southern oceans.

• **NESTING** Incubation 52–56 days by both sexes. Semialtricial young remain in nest for about 97 days. Adults usually leave at night. Young fed by both sexes at night.

• **POPULATION** The Sooty Shearwater is an abundant bird, with a total population of more than 10 million.

Similar Birds

SHORT-TAILED SHEARWATER
Shorter bill; less contrasting grayer underwing linings often restricted to a panel on the median secondary coverts and extending slightly onto the inner median primary coverts; underwings may be dark overall, lacking pale panels • only in the West.

Flight Pattern

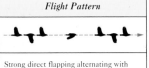

Strong direct flapping alternating with long glides.

Nest Identification

Shape   Location

Made of leaves and grass • up to 10 feet long • built by both sexes • 1 white egg; elliptical, 1.9 x 3 inches.

Plumage Sexes similar	Habitat	Migration Migratory	Weight 1.8 pounds

DATE _____ TIME_____ LOCATION _____

Family PROCELLARIIDAE	Species *Puffinus lherminieri*	Length 12 inches	Wingspan 27 inches

AUDUBON'S SHEARWATER

The smallest shearwater regularly seen off the Atlantic beats its wings more rapidly than any other Atlantic shearwater. This stocky bird with broad wings has dark brown upperparts, matching its tail, which is long for a shearwater. Pinkish legs and feet, dark undertail coverts, and dark tail are visible from below.
• **SONG** Generally this shearwater is silent. However, it has been heard to emit a variety of sounds including squeals, grunts, and cooing produced on its breeding grounds and during confrontations with other birds.

dark upperparts

dark tail and undertail coverts ·

hooked dark bill

white underparts

• **BEHAVIOR** Away from its breeding areas, Audubon's Shearwater is often seen in flocks that may number up to hundreds of birds. As a rule, this shearwater does not usually follow ships. It tends to spend most of its time on the water, where it may dive for its primary diet of marine organisms and animals, especially fish and squid.
• **BREEDING** This shearwater nests in colonies on small isolated islands, usually in rock crevices or under clumps of dense vegetation.
• **NESTING** Incubation 51 days by both sexes. Semialtricial young stay in nest 71–73 days. Fed by both sexes at night. 1 brood per year.

Similar Birds

LITTLE SHEARWATER More white in face and under wings; white undertail coverts; grayish legs and feet; different flutter-and-glide flight.

MANX SHEARWATER Larger; different flight pattern with more soaring and less flapping.

• **POPULATION** Declining.
• **CONSERVATION** Protected in only part of its breeding range. Caribbean populations disturbed by humans; adults and young taken from nest burrows for food.

Flight Pattern
Flap and glide flight with rapid wing beats.

Nest Identification	
Shape  Location 	No lining • on ground or in rock crevice • built by both sexes • 1 white egg, 2 inches long.

Plumage Sexes similar	Habitat 〰〰	Migration Migratory	Weight 5.9 ounces

DATE _____ TIME_____ LOCATION _____

Family HYDROBATIDAE	Species *Oceanites oceanicus*	Length 6–7.5 inches	Wingspan 16–17 inches

WILSON'S STORM-PETREL

This is the storm-petrel that is most commonly seen off the Atlantic Coast, and it may be one of the most abundant birds in the world. It is the smallest storm-petrel seen off the Atlantic Coast. Few pelagic birds are easily identified from a rocking boat at sea, but this species can be identified by its short squared tail and feet extending beyond the tip of the

dark sooty brown plumage

dark bill

paler bar on upper surface of inner wings

yellowish green webbing between toes

squared to slightly rounded tail

broad U-shaped white band on rump extends to undertail coverts

dark legs

tail, its rather short rounded wings, and its large U-shaped white rump patch. These birds often come very close to boats, crisscrossing the wake of the boat and providing excellent views and easier confirmation of their identity.

• **SONG** Usually silent at sea, but makes noisy chattering sounds around nesting colonies.

• **BEHAVIOR** Generally flies close to water surface with purposeful shallow wing beats similar to those of a swallow or small tern. Frequently patters feet on water while holding wings above the body as it feeds on small marine organisms, often "dancing" on the surface and almost hovering in one place as the winds lift it kitelike a few inches off the surface of the water. Frequently follows ships and chum lines (slicks of fish oils); attends fishing boats and whales as it forages.

Similar Birds

LEACH'S STORM-PETREL Larger; longer forked tail without feet protruding beyond tip; mothlike flight pattern.

BAND-RUMPED STORM-PETREL Larger; longer tail; flight pattern is with shallow wing beats followed by stiff-winged glides similar to those of a shearwater.

• **BREEDING** Colonial.

• **NESTING** Incubation 40–50 days by both sexes. Semialtricial young fed by both sexes. Young leave nest at 46–97 days.

• **POPULATION** Large and apparently stable.

Flight Pattern

Direct flight with steady shallow wing beats.

Nest Identification

Shape ⬛ Location ▬

No built nest • hides egg in hole or crevice • 1 white egg, usually with reddish brown spots on larger end.

Plumage Sexes similar	Habitat 〜〜 ⌂	Migration Migratory	Weight 1.1 ounces

DATE _____ TIME_____ LOCATION _____

Family SULIDAE	Species *Sula dactylatra*	Length 26–34 inches	Wingspan 60–62 inches

MASKED BOOBY

Sometimes called the Blue-faced Booby, this species can be seen far from shore perched atop the backs of sea turtles or napping with its head concealed in its back feathers. One of the largest of the booby family and an adept diver, it can plunge vertically from 40 feet in the air to 6–10 feet underwater.

- **SONG** Male makes high-pitched whistle; female makes louder, lower honk or trumpet. Rarely vocal except on breeding grounds or while feeding.
- **BEHAVIOR** Eats flying fishes and small squid by plunge diving. Usually found far from land because it prefers deep water where its prey

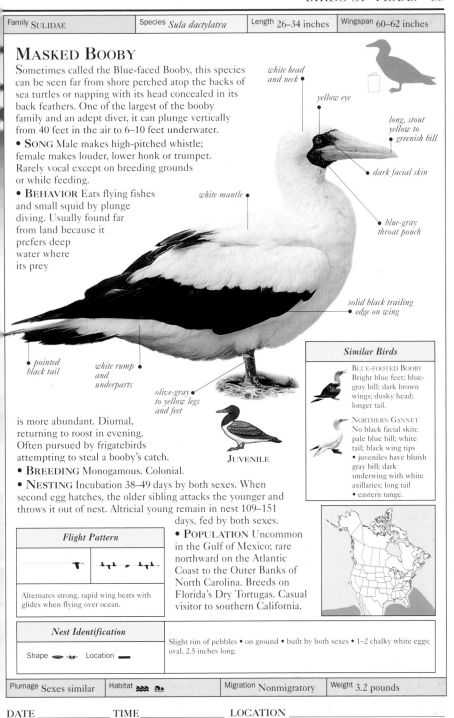

white head and neck

yellow eye

long, stout yellow to greenish bill

dark facial skin

white mantle

blue-gray throat pouch

solid black trailing edge on wing

pointed black tail

white rump and underparts

olive-gray to yellow legs and feet

JUVENILE

Similar Birds

BLUE-FOOTED BOOBY Bright blue feet; blue-gray bill; dark brown wings; dusky head; longer tail.

NORTHERN GANNET No black facial skin; pale blue bill; white tail; black wing tips • juveniles have bluish gray bill; dark underwing with white axillaries; long tail • eastern range.

is more abundant. Diurnal, returning to roost in evening. Often pursued by frigatebirds attempting to steal a booby's catch.
- **BREEDING** Monogamous. Colonial.
- **NESTING** Incubation 38–49 days by both sexes. When second egg hatches, the older sibling attacks the younger and throws it out of nest. Altricial young remain in nest 109–151 days, fed by both sexes.
- **POPULATION** Uncommon in the Gulf of Mexico; rare northward on the Atlantic Coast to the Outer Banks of North Carolina. Breeds on Florida's Dry Tortugas. Casual visitor to southern California.

Flight Pattern

Alternates strong, rapid wing beats with glides when flying over ocean.

Nest Identification

Shape ⌒ 🌿   Location ▬

Slight rim of pebbles • on ground • built by both sexes • 1–2 chalky white eggs; oval, 2.5 inches long.

Plumage Sexes similar	Habitat 〰〰 ⌒	Migration Nonmigratory	Weight 3.2 pounds

DATE _____ TIME_____ LOCATION _____

Family SULIDAE	Species *Sula leucogaster*	Length 26–29 inches	Wingspan 52–59 inches

BROWN BOOBY

Because of its habit of landing aboard ships and not trying to escape, sailors nicknamed this bird "booby," meaning "dunce" in Spanish. The Brown Booby is one of the most common boobies and prefers to feed and travel in large flocks. The female can be distinguished from the male by its yellow (rather than blue) orbital ring and yellow bill. Males of the subspecies *brewsteri*, rarely observed in North America, have white foreheads and whitish tan heads and necks. Juveniles have gray facial skin and underparts, and underwings washed with dusky brown.

• blue orbital ring

• bluish gray bill

• dark brown overall

JUVENILE

• sharp demarcation between brown neck and white underparts

• blackish brown upperwing

• **SONG** Usually silent at sea. On breeding grounds, a harsh honking. Also gives harsh brays and a hoarse hissing whistle.
• **BEHAVIOR** Gregarious. Marine and pelagic but often seen from shore. Eats parrot fishes, mullets, flatfishes, and halfbeaks. Feeds inshore more often than other boobies by making shallow plunging dives from 30–50 feet above the water. Prefers to perch rather than sit on the water and comes ashore at night to roost in trees, shrubs, wharfs, buildings, etc. Attracted to ships and will perch in their rigging.
• **BREEDING** Monogamous. Colonial.
• **NESTING** Incubation 40–47 days by both sexes. Altricial young stay in or near nest; fed by both sexes. First flight at 84–119 days. 1 brood per year.
• **POPULATION** Casual to rare in South Florida and Florida Keys, Gulf Coast, and Gulf of California. Accidental elsewhere. Wide range of nesting sites has kept population stable.
• **CONSERVATION** Vulnerable to breeding colony disturbances as well as introduced predators.

dark brown wedge-shaped tail

yellowish feet and legs

Similar Birds

RED-FOOTED BOOBY
Brown morph and juvenile similar • brown overall; brown underwing; gray to pinkish bill, legs, and feet.

BLUE-FOOTED BOOBY
Juvenile similar • white patch at base of neck; white rump.

MASKED BOOBY
Juvenile similar • brown coloring extends only to throat; has complete white collar.

NORTHERN GANNET
Juvenile similar • larger; dark gray upperparts with light spots and spangling; grayish underparts • eastern range.

Flight Pattern

Strong, moderately rapid wing beats interrupted by sailing glide; also powerful, deep wing beats.

Nest Identification

Shape ⚬ Location 🪹

Grass, twigs, and debris • on ground • 1-3 whitish to pale blue-green eggs with chalky coating, often nest stained; ovate to elliptical ovate, 2.4 x 1.6 inches.

Plumage Sexes differ	Habitat 〰 〰	Migration Nonmigratory	Weight 2.4 pounds

DATE _____ TIME_____ LOCATION _____

| Family SULIDAE | Species *Morus bassanus* | Length 35–40 inches | Wingspan 65–71 inches |

NORTHERN GANNET

Like a large white flying cross pointed at all ends – long pointed black-tipped wings, long pointed white tail, and long bill often pointed downward toward the water – this is the largest indigenous seabird of the North Atlantic. Gannets feed and travel in small flocks, but nest in huge dense colonies of five thousand or more birds. They stay at sea the first three years of life, then head for land only to breed. Juveniles have dark gray upperparts and heavily spotted, paler gray underparts, then become pied black, white, and gray as they progress into adult plumage. Males are larger than females.

creamy yellow to golden orange wash on head

long pale blue bill

black bare skin at base of bill

white overall

JUVENILE

• **SONG** Silent at sea except when feeding. Clamorous honking and various low groans and clucks around nest.

• **BEHAVIOR** Gregarious. Dives underwater, as deep as 50 feet, plunging like an arrow from up to 100 feet high. Grabs fish and squid with bill. Roosts on water after feeding; sleeps in large rafts. Returns to nesting site annually; sites used for hundreds of years. Ranges primarily over continental shelf. Rarely pelagic over truly deep waters.

long black-tipped wings

long pointed white tail

dark gray legs and webbed feet

• **BREEDING** Monogamous; mates for life. Colonial. Mated pairs perform complex "dance" at nest, similar to that of albatross, in which they face each other, wings slightly raised and opened, tail raised and spread. This is followed by a repeated series of bows, bills raised and waved in air, more bows, and feigned caressing of each other's breast.

• **NESTING** Incubation 42–44 days, by both sexes; male does more. Young stay in nest 95–107 days. Both parents feed by regurgitation. 1 brood per year.

Similar Birds

MASKED BOOBY
Yellow bill; black facial skin; black tail; solid black edging (all flight feathers) on wings.

RED-FOOTED BOOBY
White morph • smaller; white or black tail; all flight feathers and primary coverts are black; coral-red feet.

• **POPULATION** Common. Often seen from shore in migration and winter. Rare to casual on Great Lakes in fall.

• **CONSERVATION** Vulnerable to oil spills, human disturbance at nesting colonies.

Flight Pattern	

Alternates rapid wing beats with short glides at frequent intervals. Soars to great heights. Glides low in strong winds.

Nest Identification	
Shape ⌒ ⟶ Location ▓	Pile of seaweed and refuse • on ridges of cliff • 1 chalky light blue egg becoming nest stained; ovate to elliptical ovate; 3.0 x 1.8 inches.

| Plumage Sexes similar | Habitat ≈≈ ≋ ≈ | Migration Migratory | Weight 6.5 pounds |

DATE _____ TIME_____ LOCATION _____

Family PELECANIDAE	Species *Pelecanus erythrorhynchos*	Length 60–63 inches	Wingspan 96–110 inches

AMERICAN WHITE PELICAN

One of the most distinctive birds in North America, this huge pelican, with its immense bill and vast wingspan, is one of the largest waterbirds. Making their summer home near inland lakes, breeding birds shed the upper mandible plate after the eggs are laid and show a dull grayish crown and nape. In flight the head is drawn back on the shoulders with the bill resting on the breast, and the black primaries and outer secondaries contrast sharply with the white plumage. Young have a dull grayish bill and a brownish wash on the head, neck, and upper wing coverts.

• *pale yellow crest*

black wing tips and outer trailing edge of wing •

graduated plates on upper mandible •

• *oversized orange-salmon bill*

short orange-red legs and feet •

• **SONG** Mostly silent. On nesting grounds guttural croaks.

WINTER PLUMAGE

• **BEHAVIOR** Entire flock may work communally to catch fish by "herding" them into shallow water or an enclosed area, then scooping the fish out of the water with pouches that can hold up to 3 gallons of water. Eats fish of little or no commercial value.

• **BREEDING** Monogamous. Colonial.

• **NESTING** Incubation 29–36 days by both sexes. Young stay in nest 17–28 days; fed by both sexes. Gather in groups called pods after fledging and continue to be fed by adults. First flight at 9–10 weeks. 1 brood per year.

• **POPULATION** Fairly common to common. Breeds in western lakes; winters in southwest and Gulf Coast states. Casual wanderer in migration.

Similar Birds	
	WOOD STORK Black trailing edge to wing (all flight feathers); black tail; dark head and bill; long legs trail beyond tail in flight.
	BROWN PELICAN Gray-brown upperparts; dark wings; darker bill; plunge dives for fish while flying.

• **CONSERVATION** Some decrease due to habitat loss and pesticide poisoning; however, has increased since 1970s. Despite legal protection most deaths due to shooting.

Flight Pattern

Strong slow deep wing beats. Soars high on thermals. Flies in straight line or V formation.

Nest Identification

Shape — Location ▬

Made of built-up dirt and rubbish • on flat ground • 1–2 dull or chalky white eggs; ovate to elongate-ovate with some nearly elliptical–oval, 3.5 x 2.2 inches.

Plumage Sexes similar	Habitat 〰 ✓ 〰	Migration Migratory	Weight 15.4 pounds

DATE _____ TIME_____ LOCATION _____

Family PELECANIDAE	Species *Pelecanus occidentalis*	Length 48–50 inches	Wingspan 78–84 inches

BROWN PELICAN

Louisiana's state bird is the smallest of the world's pelicans. Strictly a marine bird, it almost faced extinction because of pesticides and hydrocarbons that led to the thinning of its eggshells and reproductive failure in many colonies in the 1960s and 1970s. The population is now recovering, although it is still listed as threatened. It is rarely seen inland except around the Salton Sea. The color of its gular pouch varies from red in the West to blackish in the East. Young birds are brownish with a whitish belly.

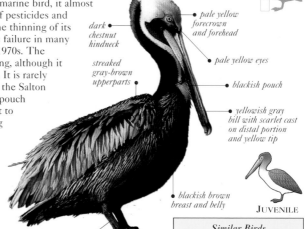

white head and neck

pale yellow forecrown and forehead

dark chestnut hindneck

streaked gray-brown upperparts

pale yellow eyes

blackish pouch

yellowish gray bill with scarlet cast on distal portion and yellow tip

blackish brown breast and belly

JUVENILE

- **SONG** Adults are silent except for occasional low croaking. Young make snakelike hiss.
- **BEHAVIOR** Coastal and pelagic. Eats fish taken near the surface by plunge-diving from air and scooping up prey with pouch. Sometimes attended by gulls that attempt to steal the catch before it can be swallowed. Gregarious. Often flies in long lines close to the water, with each bird closely following the flight path of the one ahead and all flapping and gliding in unison.

black legs and webbed feet

- **BREEDING** Monogamous. Colonial.
- **NESTING** Incubation 28–30 days by both sexes. Young begin to walk out of nest at 35 days if nest site is on ground, but do not leave nest until 63–80 days, when able to fly, if nest is elevated in shrub or tree. Tended and fed by both sexes. 1 brood per year.
- **POPULATION** Fairly common to common on Pacific Coast from central California southward, on the Atlantic Coast from Maryland southward around the tip of Florida, and westward along the entire Gulf Coast. Wanders north along coast in spring and summer. Rare inland, but common in Salton Sea.
- **CONSERVATION** Listed as threatened. Declined in mid-1900s due to pesticides; currently recovering in number.

Similar Birds

AMERICAN WHITE PELICAN
Black wing tips and outer secondaries; white body; huge salmon bill; orange-red legs and feet; does not plunge dive for food.

NORTHERN GANNET
Juvenile has dark gray upperparts with pale speckling; paler underparts; pointed, straight pale bill; pointed tail with white U patch at base; long dark-tipped wings
• Atlantic and Gulf Coast range.

Flight Pattern
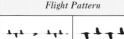
Graceful, powerful flight with deliberate wing beats alternating with short glides. Flies in straight line formation.

Nest Identification	
Shape ⌣ ⌣ Location ▬ ♣ ♣	Sticks, reeds, and grass • in vegetation 6–20 feet high or on ground built up 4–10 inches • built by female with materials gathered by male • 2–4 white eggs often nest-stained; long oval, 2.8 x 1.8 inches.

Plumage Sexes similar	Habitat ⟿ ≈	Migration Migratory	Weight 8.2 pounds

DATE _____ TIME_____ LOCATION _____

Family PHALACROCORACIDAE	Species *Phalacrocorax brasilianus*	Length 23–29 inches	Wingspan 40 inches

NEOTROPIC CORMORANT

Primarily found along the Mexican border, Neotropic Cormorants can be spotted perched on fence posts or in trees. This small slender cormorant with a long tail frequently holds its neck in an S-shape. The throat pouch is yellow-brown and has a white edge when the bird is breeding. It inhabits freshwater, brackish water, or saltwater. Juveniles are brownish in color.

- **SONG** Low guttural piglike grunts.
- **BEHAVIOR** With eyes adapted for underwater as well as aerial vision, all cormorants swim well and dive for fish from the surface. Occasionally hunts cooperatively, beating the water with its wings to confuse fish. Also eats amphibians and crustaceans. Often perches upon leaving water and holds wings and tail open in "spread eagle" fashion to dry them. Unlike other North American cormorants, often perches on wires.
- **BREEDING** Monogamous. Colonial.
- **NESTING** Incubation 25–30 days by both sexes. Altricial young fed by both sexes; swim and dive at 8 weeks, feed until 11 weeks, and become independent at 12 weeks. 1 brood per year.

long hooked bill

pointed posterior edge of brownish yellow throat skin reaches behind eye

brownish upperparts scaled black

pointed feathers on back and scapulars

white tufts on the sides of the head in breeding plumage

long slender body

JUVENILE

Similar Birds

DOUBLE-CRESTED CORMORANT Larger; heavier looking; shorter tail; rounded tips on scapular and back feathers; yellow-orange throat pouch; green sheen on head, neck, and underparts.

BRANDT'S CORMORANT Bluish facial and throat skin • West Coast range.

- **POPULATION** Widespread in Mexico; rare to casual in states along Mexican border from southern California to New Mexico; fairly common in southern Texas. Increasing and spreading north inland.

Flight Pattern
Typically flies fairly low over water with strong rapid wing beats.

Nest Identification	
Shape Location	Made of sticks with depression at center • lined with twigs and grass • built by both sexes • 2–6 (usually 4) chalky bluish eggs, soon becoming nest-stained; oval to long subelliptical.

Plumage Sexes similar	Habitat	Migration Nonmigratory	Weight 2.8 pounds

DATE _____ TIME_____ LOCATION _____

Family PHALACROCORACIDAE	Species *Phalacrocorax auritus*	Length 32 inches	Wingspan 52 inches

DOUBLE-CRESTED CORMORANT

The most widespread cormorant in North America appears blackish overall from a distance, but may appear to have a green sheen in certain lighting. During breeding season it shows two small tufts of feathers; they are black in eastern birds, but larger and mostly white in western birds. Its wings are not completely waterproof, so upon leaving the water the bird often perches on exposed objects with its wings held out to catch the sun's rays and dry its feathers. This cormorant swims low in the water with its bill tilted slightly upward. In flight it has a distinct crook in its neck. Immature birds are brown with white face, foreneck, and breast.

bright orange-yellow facial skin

long pale hooked bill

bright orange-yellow gular skin

brown upperparts with black scaling

green sheen on neck, head, and underparts

blackish overall

JUVENILE

- **SONG** Deep guttural grunt.
- **BEHAVIOR** Gregarious. Dives for fish, crustaceans, and amphibians from surface. Excellent diver, using feet for propulsion. Able to stay at 5–25 feet below surface for 30–70 seconds.

black legs and feet

- **BREEDING** Monogamous. Colonial.
- **NESTING** Incubation 28–30 days by both sexes. Altricial young may leave nest at 21–28 days but may return to be fed by both sexes. First flight at 35–42 days. Independent at 63–70 days. 1 brood per year.
- **POPULATION** Common. Fluctuates because of persecution at nesting colonies, although increasing and expanding range, particularly in interior, in last 2 decades of the 20th century.
- **CONSERVATION** Often killed by fishermen who believe birds compete with them. Many populations hit hard, especially on California coast, in 1960s and 1970s by DDT, causing reproductive failures.

Similar Birds

NEOTROPIC CORMORANT Smaller; longer tail; posterior edge of gular skin often pointed with whitish border.

BRANDT'S CORMORANT Dark face; blue throat patch with buff border; shorter tail; flies with head and neck held straight • strictly coastal and pelagic western range.

GREAT CORMORANT Larger throat pouch bordered by white feathers; white cheeks and flank patches (breeding) • East Coast range.

Flight Pattern
Strong powerful direct flight. Sometimes soars briefly on thermals. Groups fly in straight line or V formation.

Nest Identification	
Shape ⌒⌒ Location 🌲🏠🪨 ▬	In trees made of sticks and debris and lined with leafy twigs and grass • on rocks often made of seaweed and trash gathered at water's edge • near water • built by female • 2 nest-stained bluish white eggs; long subelliptical, 2.4 x 1.5 inches.

Plumage Sexes similar	Habitat 〰️ 🦆 🐟	Migration Migratory	Weight 4.0 pounds

DATE _____ TIME_____ LOCATION _____

Family ANHINGIDAE	Species *Anhinga anhinga*	Length 35 inches	Wingspan 45–48 inches

ANHINGA

Although clumsy on perches and slow on the ground, the Anhinga is a graceful flier capable of soaring to great heights. It is also called the snakebird because of its long thin neck and small narrow head, which appears serpentine when this bird swims with its body submerged to the neck. Water turkey, its other common name, comes from the long buff-tipped tail.

ruby-red to scarlet eyes

silver-white streaks and spots on upper back and forewings

long pointed yellowish brown bill

long thin neck

black plumage with green gloss

MALE

- **SONG** Mostly silent. Low grunt similar to that of the cormorant. When quarreling makes distinct rapid clicking sound, *guk-guk-guk-guk-guk*.
- **BEHAVIOR** Swims underwater and uses sharply pointed bill to spear fish. Eats small to

long fanlike tail with buff terminal band

FEMALE

pale buff neck and head

pale buff breast

blackish brown body

medium freshwater fish, frogs, water snakes, and leeches. Also known to take goldfish from outdoor ponds. Spends much time perched after swimming with wings and tail spread out to dry.
- **BREEDING** Monogamous. Usually colonial, often with egrets and herons. Bare facial skin and eye of male become blue-green and lacy black-and-white plumes appear on head and neck in breeding condition.
- **NESTING** Incubation 25–29 days by both sexes. Fed by both sexes. Altricial young will jump out of nest after 14 days if disturbed. 1 brood per year.
- **POPULATION** Fairly common to common in breeding range. Casual wanderer north of breeding range.
- **CONSERVATION** In the past often killed by fishermen fearing competition from the fishing abilities of this bird.

Similar Birds

NEOTROPIC CORMORANT
Brownish yellow facial and throat skin; blackish overall with green sheen; browner upperparts scaled with black; shorter thicker neck; hooked bill; swims on water's surface between dives.

DOUBLE-CRESTED CORMORANT
Larger; heavier; shorter thicker neck; shorter tail; yellow-orange throat pouch; hooked bill; swims on water's surface between dives.

Flight Pattern

Strong graceful direct flight. Often soars like a raptor.

Nest Identification

Shape ♙♙   Location 🌳🌳

Sticks • often lined with grass and leaves • built by female; male sometimes gathers materials • sometimes uses nest of Snowy Egret and Little Blue Heron • 2–5 white to pale blue eggs that become nest-stained; 2.1 inches long.

Plumage Sexes differ	Habitat 〰 〰 〰	Migration Most do not migrate	Weight 2.7 pounds

DATE _____ TIME_____ LOCATION _____

Family FREGATIDAE	Species *Fregata magnificens*	Length 37–41 inches	Wingspan 82–94 inches

MAGNIFICENT FRIGATEBIRD

The male has a most striking courtship display when he inflates his throat sac into a huge brilliant red balloon. In flight it looks almost sinister with its black plumage, long thin crooked wings, and deeply forked tail often folded into a point. Juveniles are black without gloss and have a white head, neck, sides, breast, and belly. Even when not nesting, flocks of these birds often gather at their permanent roosts in treetops, or on high cliffs.

• **SONG** Clacks bill; nasal *kack* or *ka-ack*; soft chippering at nesting grounds. Silent at sea.

• **BEHAVIOR** Soars over sea to find food. Dives for prey and catches it in bill from surface. Eats fish, crustaceans, and jellyfish. Attacks other large seabirds in flight until they drop or disgorge their catch, which the frigatebird then catches in midair. Roosts communally and is gregarious.

• **BREEDING** Monogamous. Colonial.

• **NESTING** Incubation 40–50 days by both sexes. Fed by both sexes. First flight at 20–24 weeks. Young never left unguarded because other birds in colony may eat eggs and hatchlings. Most females do not breed every year.

• **POPULATION** Total difficult to monitor. Rare to casual on Salton Sea and along California coast to Washington. Breeds on Dry Tortugas off Florida Keys. Fairly common to casual along Gulf of Mexico, Florida coasts, and north to North Carolina. Rare straggler north to Maritimes and inland, especially after storms.

• **CONSERVATION** Frigatebirds are legally protected, but they are still killed in the nest by local people, who hunt at night with flashlights and clubs. Some years no young survive.

straight hooked gray bill

entirely black with purple gloss on back and head

bright red pouch usually shows as red patch on throat when not distended

MALE

JUVENILE

straight hooked gray bill

black without gloss

white breast and sides

FEMALE

long, narrow pointed wings

long deeply forked tail

Similar Birds

GREAT FRIGATEBIRD
♂ Male has pale brownish alar bar; scalloped pale grayish axillars; green gloss on head and back • female has gray-white throat, breast, and upper belly; red orbital ring; broader black belly patch • juvenile has white head, neck, and breast; neck and head tinged with rust-brown.

Flight Pattern
Very high effortless soaring flight. Extremely graceful and buoyant in the air.

Nest Identification	
Shape Location 🌳🌿	Sticks, twigs, grass, and reeds • in mangroves, trees, or bushes, 2–20 feet above ground • built by female with materials gathered by male, which often steals from neighbors' nests • 1 white egg; rarely 2.

Plumage Sexes differ	Habitat 〰	Migration Nonmigratory	Weight 2.8 pounds

DATE _____ TIME _____ LOCATION _____

Family ARDEIDAE	Species *Botaurus lentiginosus*	Length 23 inches	Wingspan 42–50 inches

AMERICAN BITTERN

When it senses danger, the American Bittern hides by standing motionless with its bill pointed upward and its body tightly contracted. Thus it can be mistaken for a wooden stake in the marshes, saltwater and freshwater bogs, and wetland ponds it inhabits. The dark and light vertical streaks blend with shadows and highlights cast by surrounding vegetation, so the bird often goes unnoticed even from a few feet away. In flight the somewhat pointed dark outer wings contrast sharply with the inner wings and body.

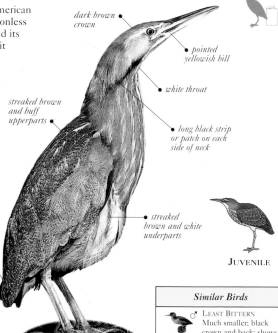

dark brown crown

pointed yellowish bill

white throat

streaked brown and buff upperparts

long black strip or patch on each side of neck

streaked brown and white underparts

JUVENILE

- **SONG** *Oonk-a-lunk* or *punk-er-lunk*, often heard at dusk; it is one of the strangest sounds produced by any bird; sounds like someone driving a stake into the mud with a wooden mallet.

pointed wings with contrasting dark tips

- **BEHAVIOR** Stands motionless, often hidden by marsh vegetation, on ground or in water to search for prey. Eats frogs, small eels, small fish, small snakes, salamanders, crayfish, small rodents, and water bugs.
- **BREEDING** May be polygamous. Solitary nester.
- **NESTING** Incubation 24–29 days by female. Young stay in nest 14 days. Fed by both parents. 1 brood per year.

Similar Birds

♂ **LEAST BITTERN** Much smaller; black crown and back; shows buff wing patches in ♀ flight.

YELLOW-CROWNED NIGHT-HERON
BLACK-CROWNED NIGHT-HERON
Juveniles have more heavily spotted upperparts; lack black mustache lines on face.

- **POPULATION** Fairly common. Declining in the South from marshland drainage.
- **CONSERVATION** Protected by law. Wetland conservation is critical for this species.

Flight Pattern
Strong direct flight with deep rapid wing beats.

Nest Identification	
Shape  Location	Grasses, reeds, and cattails • lined with fine grasses • on dense marsh ground, dry ground above water, or mud in tall vegetation • built by female • 2–7 pale brown to olive-buff eggs, 1.9 inches long.

Plumage Sexes similar	Habitat	Migration Migratory	Weight 1.6 pounds

DATE _____ TIME_____ LOCATION _____

Family ARDEIDAE	Species *Ixobrychus exilis*	Length 11–14 inches	Wingspan 16–18 inches

LEAST BITTERN

This shy bird of the marshes is the smallest heron in North America. Because of the thick vegetation it frequents and its retiring nature, it often goes unnoticed and is probably more common than reported. Its small size and buff inner wing patches seen in flight quickly separate it from all other species. Adult females have a dark brown crown, back, and tail; juveniles are similar but more heavily streaked.

black crown

buff head, neck, and sides

black back and tail

MALE

pinkish yellow bill

white chin

white underparts streaked with buff

dark brown crown

dull yellow legs

FEMALE

• **SONG** Call is series of harsh *kek* notes. Song is softer *ku* notes, somewhat dovelike.
• **BEHAVIOR** Shy secretive denizen of the marsh. Seldom seen or heard. When approached closely often freezes in place with neck stretched upward, bill pointed skyward, and body compressed. May sway back and forth with rhythm of surrounding vegetation to help blend into background. When flushed, flies weakly yet migrates long distances.
• **BREEDING** Monogamous. Solitary to loose colonies.
• **NESTING** Incubation 17–20 days by both sexes. Semialtricial young remain in nest 25 days. Fed by both sexes. Has 1–2 broods per year.

Similar Birds

GREEN HERON Larger; lacks buff coloration and wing patches in flight.

• **POPULATION** Thought to be declining because of habitat loss, although still abundant in parts of North America.
• **CONSERVATION** Neotropical migrant. Conservation of wetlands key to population success.

Flight Pattern

Weak direct flight with slow labored wing beats.

Nest Identification

Shape ___ Location 🌾🌳

Platform • bent marsh vegetation with sticks and grass on top • well concealed in marsh growth, near or over water, on ground, or in low shrub • built by both sexes • 2–7 pale green or blue eggs; elliptical, 1.2 inches long.

Plumage Sexes differ	Habitat 〰	Migration Migratory	Weight 3.0 ounces

DATE _____ TIME_____ LOCATION _____

Family ARDEIDAE	Species *Ardea herodias*	Length 46–52 inches	Wingspan 77–82 inches

GREAT BLUE HERON

Often called "crane" or "blue crane" by locals, the Great Blue Heron is the largest, most widespread, and best-known heron in North America. Its size, long yellowish bill, and mostly bluish gray body readily distinguish it. In the breeding season several long black occipital plumes adorn the back of the crown. In south Florida a paler white-headed form was formerly considered a separate species called Ward's or Wurdemann's Heron. An all-white morph with yellowish legs found in southern Florida is called the Great White Heron and formerly was also considered a separate species.

bold black line on both sides of crown

long, stout yellowish bill

white face

black-and-white streaks on midline of foreneck

blue-gray body

chestnut "pants"

WURDEMANN'S HERON

short tail

blackish yellow legs

JUVENILE

- **SONG** Mostly silent except at colonies, where it makes series of squawks and low croaks.
- **BEHAVIOR** In flight the long neck is folded back into a compact S-shape typical of other herons and egrets, and the long legs trail far out behind the short dark tail. Feeds by standing still in water for long periods and grabbing fish and other animals that come within range of a lightning thrust of its daggerlike bill, or by walking slowly along waterways or through marshy vegetation or grassy fields.
- **BREEDING** Monogamous. Colonial.
- **NESTING** Incubation 25–30 days by both sexes. Semialtricial young remain in nest 65–90 days. Fed by both sexes. 1 brood per year in the North, 2 per year in the South.

Similar Birds

SANDHILL CRANE
Bald red crown; bustlelike tail coverts; flies with neck extended.

- **POPULATION** Stable, common, and widespread.
- **CONSERVATION** This species and other "long-legged waders" have benefited from state and federal protection, particularly of breeding colonies.

Flight Pattern

Direct flight with slow steady wing beats.

Nest Identification	
Shape	Sticks • lined with twigs and leaves • usually in trees 20–60 feet above ground or water; sometimes in low shrubs; rarely on ground, rock ledges, or coastal cliff • built by female from materials gathered by male • 2–7 pale blue or light bluish green eggs; oval to long oval, long elliptical, or subelliptical; 2.5 inches long.
Location	

Plumage Sexes similar	Habitat	Migration Northern birds migrate	Weight 5.7 pounds

DATE _____ TIME_____ LOCATION _____

Family ARDEIDAE	Species *Ardea alba*	Length 37–41 inches	Wingspan 55 inches

GREAT EGRET

The largest white egret found over most of its range can be distinguished from other white egrets and juvenile herons by its size, yellow bill, black legs and feet. This tall, slender-necked bird develops long trains of lacy plumes on its back that extend beyond the tail when breeding, and its yellow bill appears more orange in color.

- **SONG** Bold throaty croaking or repeated *cuk, cuk.*
- **BEHAVIOR** Prefers to feed in open areas from salt marshes to freshwater habitats.

black feet and legs

yellow bill

white plumage

Diurnal in its activities, it flies singly or in groups to communal roosts in trees for the night. Feeds on wide variety of small aquatic animals and animals found in wetland environs, from fish to frogs, snakes, crayfish, and large insects.

- **BREEDING** Monogamous. Colonial, usually with other species of herons, egrets, ibis, and other similar species.
- **NESTING** Incubation 23–26 days by both sexes. Young stay in nest 21 days. Fed by both sexes. 1 brood per year.
- **POPULATION** Decimated by plume hunters in late 1800s. Protected since early 20th century. In recent decades breeding range has expanded northward.
- **CONSERVATION** With full protection in North America, species is increasing. Still, factors such as polluted waters, coastal development, and draining of wetlands negatively impact egrets.

Similar Birds

GREAT BLUE HERON
Wurdemann's Heron (morph) is larger with yellowish legs and feet.

SNOWY EGRET
Smaller; dark bill.

REDDISH EGRET
White morph smaller with dark bill.

LITTLE BLUE HERON
Juvenile smaller with dark bill.

CATTLE EGRET
Much smaller; yellow legs and feet.

Flight Pattern
Buoyant direct flight with deep steady wing beats.

Nest Identification	
Shape Location	Made of sticks • unlined or lined with fine material • in tree or shrub, usually 10–40 feet above ground • built by both sexes • 1–6 pale blue-green or light blue eggs, 2.2 inches long.

Plumage Sexes similar	Habitat	Migration Some migrate	Weight 2.0 pounds

DATE _____ **TIME** _____ **LOCATION** _____

Family ARDEIDAE	Species *Egretta thula*	Length 22–27 inches	Wingspan 38–45 inches

SNOWY EGRET

This is perhaps the most beautiful of all North American egrets and herons in its nuptial plumage, and the daintiest with or without it. This energetic medium-sized white egret has black legs and bright yellow "slippers." Slaughtered by the thousands for its soft, lacy breeding finery, it was the most persecuted of all egrets by plume hunters in the late 19th and early 20th centuries.

yellow eyes

long, slender black bill

yellow lores

white plumage

• **SONG** Generally silent. Vocalizations are harsh squawks.

• **BEHAVIOR** Most active heron when feeding. Rushes after prey in manner of Reddish Egret. Often sticks one foot forward in water and rapidly vibrates it to startle prey. Crustaceans, insects, and fish are important components of diet.

• **BREEDING** Monogamous. Colonial, often nests in mixed colonies with other herons and egrets.

• **NESTING** Incubation 20–24 days by both sexes. Semialtricial young stay in nest 30 days. Fed by both sexes. 1 brood per year.

• **POPULATION** Increasing. Range expanding northward.

bright yellow feet

black legs

WINTER PLUMAGE

Similar Birds

CATTLE EGRET Stockier; shorter neck; yellow bill and legs.

GREAT EGRET Much larger; yellow bill; black feet.

LITTLE BLUE HERON Juvenile has greenish legs; gray bill with black tip.

• **CONSERVATION** Seemingly thriving today, but almost extirpated in the early 20th century by demand for its "cross aigrettes" for ladies' fashions.

Flight Pattern

Buoyant direct flight with steady fast wing beats.

Nest Identification

Shape   Location

Sticks • lined with fine twigs and rushes • in short tree or shrub, 5–10 feet high • sometimes on ground • built by both sexes • 2–6 pale blue-green eggs, 1.7 inches long.

Plumage Sexes similar	Habitat	Migration Migratory	Weight 13.1 ounces

DATE _____ TIME_____ LOCATION _____

Family ARDEIDAE	Species *Egretta caerulea*	Length 24–29 inches	Wingspan 40–41 inches

LITTLE BLUE HERON

Adults appear entirely dark at a distance, but at closer range they are slate-colored with a purplish maroon head and neck. This is the only dark heron species in North America in which the juvenile is white. The juvenile begins molting into adult plumage in its first spring and gradually acquires more blue-gray feathers, achieving a calico appearance in the transition from white to slate gray.

purplish maroon neck and head

gray bill with black tip

gray body

greenish gray legs

JUVENILE

- **SONG** Breeding male makes *eh-oo-ah-eh-eh*. Both sexes make loud nasal *skea* or *scaah* and low clucking notes.
- **BEHAVIOR** Prefers fresh water but can be found in brackish water and salt marshes. A stealthy stalker, it moves slowly as it wades in shallow water or along water's edge for prey. Feeds on a variety of small vertebrates, crustaceans, and large insects. Roosts in trees and shrubs at night.
- **BREEDING** Monogamous. Colonial; often nests in heronries with other species.
- **NESTING** Incubation 20–24 days by both sexes. Semialtricial young stay in nest 42–49 days. Fed by both sexes. Has 1 brood per year.
- **POPULATION** Increasing and expanding.
- **CONSERVATION** Responding to protection of nesting colonies.

Similar Birds

REDDISH EGRET Dark morph similar to adult; rufous head and neck; pink bill with black tip • white morph similar to juvenile.

TRICOLORED HERON White underparts.

Flight Pattern

Direct flight with steady quick wing beats.

Nest Identification

Shape   Location

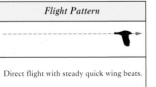

Sticks and twigs • unlined or lined with finer material • usually in tree or shrub, 3–15 feet high • occasionally on ground • built by both sexes • 1–6 pale blue-green eggs; elliptical to subelliptical, 1.7 inches long.

Plumage Sexes similar	Habitat	Migration Migratory	Weight 12.9 ounces

DATE _____ TIME_____ LOCATION _____

| Family ARDEIDAE | Species *Egretta tricolor* | Length 24–26 inches | Wingspan 36 inches |

TRICOLORED HERON

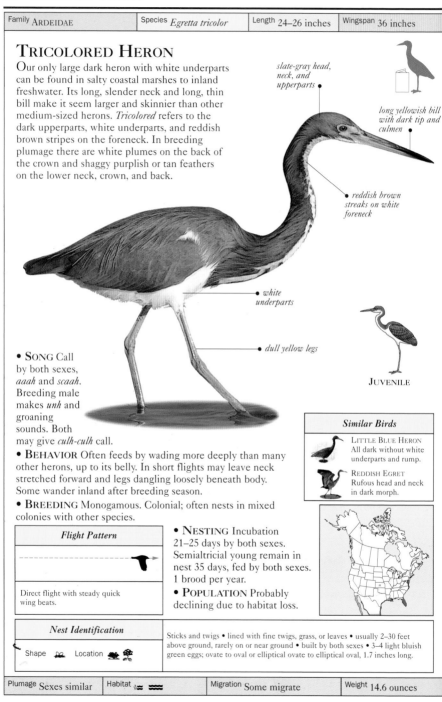

Our only large dark heron with white underparts can be found in salty coastal marshes to inland freshwater. Its long, slender neck and long, thin bill make it seem larger and skinnier than other medium-sized herons. *Tricolored* refers to the dark upperparts, white underparts, and reddish brown stripes on the foreneck. In breeding plumage there are white plumes on the back of the crown and shaggy purplish or tan feathers on the lower neck, crown, and back.

slate-gray head, neck, and upperparts

long yellowish bill with dark tip and culmen

reddish brown streaks on white foreneck

white underparts

dull yellow legs

JUVENILE

• **SONG** Call by both sexes, *aaah* and *scaah*. Breeding male makes *unh* and groaning sounds. Both may give *culh-culh* call.

• **BEHAVIOR** Often feeds by wading more deeply than many other herons, up to its belly. In short flights may leave neck stretched forward and legs dangling loosely beneath body. Some wander inland after breeding season.

• **BREEDING** Monogamous. Colonial; often nests in mixed colonies with other species.

Similar Birds

LITTLE BLUE HERON
All dark without white underparts and rump.

REDDISH EGRET
Rufous head and neck in dark morph.

Flight Pattern
Direct flight with steady quick wing beats.

• **NESTING** Incubation 21–25 days by both sexes. Semialtricial young remain in nest 35 days, fed by both sexes. 1 brood per year.

• **POPULATION** Probably declining due to habitat loss.

Nest Identification	
Shape 〰 Location 🌳🌿	Sticks and twigs • lined with fine twigs, grass, or leaves • usually 2–30 feet above ground, rarely on or near ground • built by both sexes • 3–4 light bluish green eggs; ovate to oval or elliptical ovate to elliptical oval, 1.7 inches long.

| Plumage Sexes similar | Habitat 〰 〰 | Migration Some migrate | Weight 14.6 ounces |

DATE _____ TIME_____ LOCATION _____

Family ARDEIDAE	Species *Egretta rufescens*	Length 27–32 inches	Wingspan 46 inches

REDDISH EGRET

This coastal inhabitant is an uncommon to rare egret with two distinct color morphs, white and dark. The dark morph is more common.

- **SONG** Generally silent. On nesting grounds, low croaks and soft clucking notes.
- **BEHAVIOR** A bird of coastal salt pans and shallow tidal flats that can often be identified at some distance by its unusual feeding behavior. Often dashes after prey, running and lurching in first one direction and then another with wings jutting in and out or held skyward in canopy fashion. Sometimes feeds by stirring bottom mud with a foot and striking escaping prey.
- **BREEDING** Monogamous. Colonial.
- **NESTING** Incubation 25–26 days by both sexes. Semialtricial young stay in nest 42–49 days, fed by both sexes. 1 brood per year.

rufous head and neck

pink bill with black tip

DARK MORPH

gray body

dark blue legs and feet

JUVENILE

head and neck appear shaggy

white body

WHITE MORPH

dark blue legs and feet

pink bill with black tip

Similar Birds

LITTLE BLUE HERON Smaller; darker; lacks rufous head; neck and bill dark gray with black tip; greenish gray legs.

GREAT EGRET Larger; yellow bill; black legs and feet.

Flight Pattern

Direct flight with buoyant steady wing beats.

- **POPULATION** Rare to uncommon. Nearly killed off by plume hunters in late 1800s. Numbers have been increasing gradually with complete protection. Current total US population about 2,000 pairs.

Nest Identification

Shape   Location

Platform of sticks and grasses with little or no lining • on ground in Texas; 3–15 feet high in tree in Florida • built by both sexes • 2–7 pale blue-green eggs, 2 inches long.

Plumage Sexes similar	Habitat	Migration Most do not migrate	Weight 15.9 ounces*

DATE _____ TIME_____ LOCATION _____

Family ARDEIDAE	Species *Bubulcus ibis*	Length 19–21 inches	Wingspan 36–38 inches

CATTLE EGRET

This is the only small white egret with the combination of a yellow bill and yellow legs and feet. Breeding adults have patches of buff-orange on crown, nape, lower foreneck, and back. Nonbreeding adults and immature birds lack the buff-orange patches and have yellow bill, legs, and feet. A big-headed, thick-necked, short-legged egret of the Old World (originally found in Spain, Portugal, and Africa), it introduced itself to South America in the 1880s and to Florida by the early 1940s. From there it moved over most of the US and into southern Canada.

- **SONG** Various croaking sounds at breeding colonies; otherwise silent.

- *buff-orange patches on crown, nape, and back*
- *yellowish orange bill*
- *short thick neck*
- *buff-orange patches on lower foreneck*
- *white plumage*
- *yellowish orange feet*
- *short yellowish orange legs*

JUVENILE

- **BEHAVIOR** Associates with cattle, horses, or other livestock in moist or dry pastures, where it feeds primarily on large insects disturbed by feeding livestock. Several birds may accompany a single cow, often riding on its back. Also follows tractors plowing fields to feed on the exposed insects and grubs. Largely diurnal, flying at dusk to communal roosts with other egrets, herons, and ibis to spend the night perched in trees or shrubs. They often form the nucleus of nesting colonies of other species of heron and egrets, and their presence may encourage the nesting of these birds in the heronries.

- **BREEDING** Monogamous. Colonial; often found in mixed breeding colonies with other species.

- **NESTING** Incubation 21–26 days by both sexes. Semialtricial young remain in nest about 45 days. Fed by both sexes. 1 brood per year.

- **POPULATION** North American population increasing.

- **CONSERVATION** Nesting colonies protected.

Similar Birds

SNOWY EGRET
Longer, more slender neck; black bill and legs.

LITTLE BLUE HERON
Juvenile is larger with longer, more slender neck; greenish gray legs and feet; black-tipped grayish bill.

GREAT EGRET
Larger; black legs and feet.

Flight Pattern
Direct flight with steady, rather rapid wing beats.

Nest Identification	
Shape Location	Sticks and reeds • lined with leafy green twigs • in tree or shrub • built by female from materials gathered by male • 1–9 pale blue or light bluish green eggs; subelliptical or elliptical, 1.9 inches long.

Plumage Sexes similar	Habitat	Migration Migratory	Weight 11.9 ounces

DATE _____ TIME_____ LOCATION _____

Family ARDEIDAE	Species *Butorides virescens*	Length 18–22 inches	Wingspan 26 inches

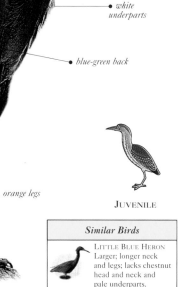

GREEN HERON

Looking similar to a crow while flying, the Green Heron has a thicker neck and more bowed wing beats. It is a widely distributed heron found in almost every wetland in summer. Perhaps more blue than green on the back, this heron has a dark cap ending in a shaggy crest on the occiput, with a chestnut head and neck. Its legs appear more yellowish in nonbreeding season. Juvenile plumage has more brown on the upperparts, heavily streaked underparts, a white chin, and dull yellow legs.

- **SONG** Bold abrasive *kyowk* or *skeow*; sometimes soft *kuck, kuck* notes.
- **BEHAVIOR** Diurnal species that retires to ground or close to it for the night. Often walks slowly when hunting or stands and waits motionless in water or on an overhanging perch for prey to come close enough for a quick strike. When disturbed, often nervously flicks its short tail and elevates shaggy crest. Has been seen placing food or bait in the water deliberately to attract fish. Often perches in trees and shrubs.
- **BREEDING** Monogamous. Usually solitary pairs; occasionally forms small colonies. Sometimes nests rather distant from water.

dark cap

thin brownish yellow bill

chestnut head and most of neck

white underparts

blue-green back

orange legs

JUVENILE

- **NESTING** Incubation 19–25 days by both sexes. Young remain in nest for 16–17 days, fed by both sexes. 1 or 2 broods per year.
- **POPULATION** Common and stable.

Similar Birds

LITTLE BLUE HERON
Larger; longer neck and legs; lacks chestnut head and neck and pale underparts.

Flight Pattern

Direct flight with slow steady arched wing beats.

Nest Identification

Shape ⌣ Location 🌳 🌲 🌿 〽️

Sticks and twigs • in tree or shrub, 5–30 feet off ground • built by both sexes • 2–7 pale green or blue-green eggs; elliptical to subelliptical, 1.5 inches long.

Plumage Sexes similar	Habitat 〰️ 〰️ 〰️	Migration Some migrate	Weight 7.5 ounces

DATE _____ TIME _____ LOCATION _____

Family ARDEIDAE	Species *Nycticorax nycticorax*	Length 25–28 inches	Wingspan 44–45 inches

BLACK-CROWNED NIGHT-HERON

The scientific name of this bird means "Night Raven," and it refers to the nature of the bird, as does the common name of Night-Heron. A stocky bird with short legs and a thick, short neck, it prowls freshwater pools, marshes, and streams and coastal estuaries across much of North America. In flight the toes often protrude beyond the short tail. Juvenile plumage shows brown above with white spots and streaking, buff-brown below with dark brown spots and streaking. Juveniles have a yellowish bill with a dark tip and greenish yellow legs and feet.

black cap and nape

dark bill

red eyes

white face and underparts

black back

breeding adults have 2–3 long white plumes on back crown

gray sides of neck, wings, and tail

yellow legs and feet

JUVENILE

- **SONG** Low, harsh *woe* and guttural *quock* or *quaik*.
- **BEHAVIOR** Primarily nocturnal. Roosts in trees by day and actively feeds at night. Some feed during daylight hours. Omnivorous, feeding on whatever is most handy. Diet ranges from fish to mollusks, small rodents, frogs, snakes, crustaceans, plant material, eggs, and young birds. Often stands very still in water for long periods of time, expertly grabbing fish that swim too close.
- **BREEDING** Monogamous. Colonial.
- **NESTING** Incubation 21–26 days by both sexes. Young stay in nest 28 days. Fed by both sexes. First flight at 42 days. After 49 days, may follow parents to foraging areas to beg and be fed. 1 brood per year.

Similar Birds

AMERICAN BITTERN
Similar to juvenile
- thinner long yellowish bill; dark mustache stripes; lacks white spotting above.

YELLOW-CROWNED NIGHT-HERON
Similar to juvenile
- more gray-brown with smaller white spots; thick dark bill; thinner neck; longer legs.

- **POPULATION** Overall stable or increasing.
- **CONSERVATION** Benefited from general protection by state, federal, and conservation agencies. Loss of wetland habitat affects food supply and reproduction.

Flight Pattern
Direct flight with slow steady wing beats.

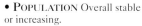

Nest Identification	Sticks, twigs, and reeds • lined with finer material • on or above ground as high as 150 feet • built by female with materials gathered by male • 1–7 pale green or light bluish eggs; oval, 2 inches long.
Shape	
Location	

Plumage Sexes similar	Habitat	Migration Migratory	Weight 1.9 pounds

DATE _____ TIME_____ LOCATION _____

Family ARDEIDAE	Species *Nyctanassa violacea*	Length 22–28 inches	Wingspan 42–44 inches

YELLOW-CROWNED NIGHT-HERON

At home in coastal mangroves, inland swamps, and riparian woodlands, this short-necked, stocky heron has a gray body and a large black head boldly marked with a white cheek patch and white crown with yellowish tints on the forehead. During breeding season adult males and females have long white occipital plumes on the back of the head. The long yellow legs protrude well beyond the short tail in flight.

long white occipital plumes

thick dark bill

large black head with yellowish white crown and white cheek patches

slender neck

JUVENILE

long yellow legs

• **SONG** Short *woe* or *wok*. Its *quak* is higher and less harsh than that given by the Black-crowned Night-Heron.

• **BEHAVIOR** While mostly nocturnal, it is often active during the day. Exhibits strong preference for crustaceans, although it eats a variety of other aquatic organisms from fish to shellfish.

• **BREEDING** Monogamous. Solitary nester or forms small loose colonies. Also joins large nesting colonies with other herons and egrets, often chooses nesting site located on periphery of the colony.

Similar Birds

BLACK-CROWNED NIGHT-HERON
Black back; white head with black cap; short yellowish legs
• juvenile has brown crown; brown upperparts with large white spots and streaks; whitish-tan underparts with brown streaking; short yellow-green legs and feet; yellowish bill with black tip.

• **NESTING** Incubation 21–25 days by both sexes. Semialtricial young remain in nest 25 days, fed by both sexes. Probably 1 brood per year.

• **POPULATION** Stable.

Flight Pattern
Direct flight with steady deep wing beats.

Nest Identification	
Shape 🐾 Location 🌿🌳	Sticks • lined with twigs or sometimes leaves • either on ground or in tree 30–40 feet high • built by both sexes • 2–8 pale blue-green eggs; oval to long oval, 2 inches long.

Plumage Sexes similar	Habitat 🌾 🌿 〰️ 〰️	Migration Migratory	Weight 1.6 pounds

DATE _____ TIME_____ LOCATION _____

Family THRESKIORNITHIDAE	Species *Eudocimus albus*	Length 21–27 inches	Wingspan 38 inches

WHITE IBIS

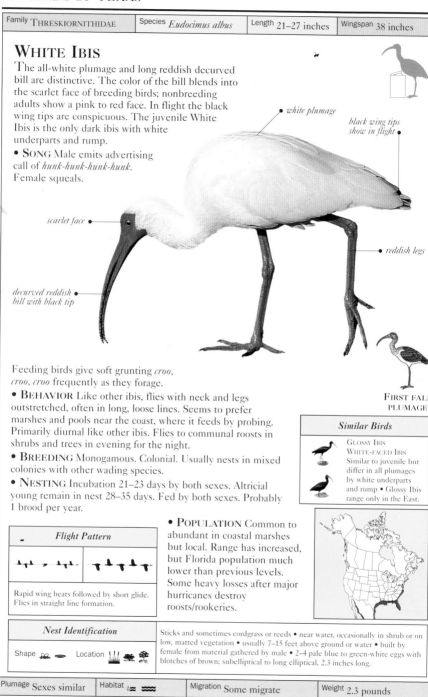

The all-white plumage and long reddish decurved bill are distinctive. The color of the bill blends into the scarlet face of breeding birds; nonbreeding adults show a pink to red face. In flight the black wing tips are conspicuous. The juvenile White Ibis is the only dark ibis with white underparts and rump.

• **SONG** Male emits advertising call of *hunk-hunk-hunk-hunk.* Female squeals.

white plumage

black wing tips show in flight

scarlet face

reddish legs

decurved reddish bill with black tip

Feeding birds give soft grunting *croo, croo, croo* frequently as they forage.

• **BEHAVIOR** Like other ibis, flies with neck and legs outstretched, often in long, loose lines. Seems to prefer marshes and pools near the coast, where it feeds by probing. Primarily diurnal like other ibis. Flies to communal roosts in shrubs and trees in evening for the night.

• **BREEDING** Monogamous. Colonial. Usually nests in mixed colonies with other wading species.

• **NESTING** Incubation 21–23 days by both sexes. Altricial young remain in nest 28–35 days. Fed by both sexes. Probably 1 brood per year.

FIRST FALL PLUMAGE

Similar Birds

GLOSSY IBIS WHITE-FACED IBIS Similar to juvenile but differ in all plumages by white underparts and rump • Glossy Ibis range only in the East.

• **POPULATION** Common to abundant in coastal marshes but local. Range has increased, but Florida population much lower than previous levels. Some heavy losses after major hurricanes destroy roosts/rookeries.

Flight Pattern
Rapid wing beats followed by short glide. Flies in straight line formation.

Nest Identification	
Shape	Location	Sticks and sometimes cordgrass or reeds • near water, occasionally in shrub or on low, matted vegetation • usually 7–15 feet above ground or water • built by female from material gathered by male • 2–4 pale blue to green-white eggs with blotches of brown; subelliptical to long elliptical, 2.3 inches long.

Plumage Sexes similar	Habitat	Migration Some migrate	Weight 2.3 pounds

DATE _____ TIME_____ LOCATION _____

Family THRESKIORNITHIDAE	Species *Plegadis falcinellus*	Length 19–26 inches	Wingspan 36–38 inches

GLOSSY IBIS

From a distance this large bird with a dark decurved bill appears dark overall in the freshwater or saltwater marshes it frequents, but closer observation reveals deep chestnut plumage glossed with metallic greens and purples. The species occurs widely in the Old World and evidence suggests that perhaps it introduced itself to North America in the 1800s. Its North American range may be limited due to its recent arrival on the continent, as well as competition with the already established White Ibis. Breeding plumaged birds show intense green patches in their wings, greenish legs with red joints, pale blue around the face and blue-gray facial skin in the loral region.

dark iris

metallic green and purple gloss on back, wings, head, and neck

dark gray lores bordered with pale blue

brownish black decurved bill

chestnut plumage

- **SONG** Guttural, grating croak, *ka-onk*.
- **BEHAVIOR** Gregarious. Flies in lines or groups, with individuals often changing position in the flock. In flight the head, neck, and legs are extended. Highly prone to wandering, thus turns up at great distances from breeding range, especially in spring. Uses long bill to probe for food, particularly crayfish and crabs in their holes. Also readily eats water snakes. Often feeds with other large wading birds, including the White Ibis. Flies to roost late in the day and frequently is seen roosting with other species of ibis, herons, and egrets.
- **BREEDING** Monogamous. Colonial; often nests in mixed colonies with other ibis, herons, and egrets.

Similar Birds

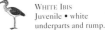

WHITE-FACED IBIS Reddish legs and lores bordered with white; white line around lore encircles eye; red iris.

WHITE IBIS Juvenile • white underparts and rump.

- **NESTING** Incubation about 21 days, mostly by female. Semialtricial young remain in nest for about 28 days, fed by both sexes. 1 brood per year.
- **POPULATION** Common but local. Greatly increased and expanded during 20th century.

Flight Pattern
Several shallow rapid wing beats followed by a short glide. Flies in straight line formation.

Nest Identification	
Shape Location	Platform of sticks and marsh plants with depression in center • occasionally lined with leaves • in shrubs or low trees; on the ground on islands • built by both sexes • 1–5 pale blue or green eggs, 2 inches long.

Plumage Sexes similar	Habitat	Migration Migratory	Weight Undetermined

DATE _____ TIME_____ LOCATION _____

Family THRESKIORNITHIDAE	Species *Plegadis chihi*	Length 20–26 inches	Wingspan 36–38 inches

WHITE-FACED IBIS

This bird is almost identical to the Glossy Ibis in all plumages; winter-plumaged birds and juveniles must be inspected closely to distinguish between the two species. The best field marks are leg and lore color (pinkish in winter and juvenile birds, red in breeding birds). In breeding plumage white feathers border the lores and extend behind the eye and under the chin. In summer and winter, adult White-faced Ibis has a red iris.

pink to red lores

dark chestnut and brownish olive plumage

white "face" ring of feathers outlines chin, lores, and eyes

decurved bill

bronze and green metallic glosses

reddish legs

• **SONG** Feeding call is a multisyllable *oink*. Also gives low-pitched *graa, graa, graa.*
• **BEHAVIOR** Gregarious. Flies in straight line formations. Feeds by probing with long bill, eating crayfish and other invertebrates, as well as frogs and fish. Usually frequents freshwater marshes, but coastal birds forage in salt marshes and include crabs in diet.
• **BREEDING** Monogamous. Colonial; often nests in mixed colonies with other ibis, herons, and egrets.
• **NESTING** Incubation 17–26 days by both sexes. Young stay in nest about 28 days. Fed by both sexes. 1 brood per year.
• **POPULATION** Uncommon to fairly common, but local. Local numbers fluctuate, but total North American population has increased since the 1970s. Range also has expanded eastward.
• **CONSERVATION** Serious concern in early 1970s, when reproduction failed in many colonies due to eggshell thinning from pesticides present in food chain.

Similar Birds

GLOSSY IBIS
Blue-gray lores; dark legs; dark eye.

Flight Pattern

Several shallow rapid wing beats followed by short glide. Flies in straight line formation.

Nest Identification

Shape   Location

Bulrushes or other plant stems with depression in center • usually in thick marsh growth or short trees • built by both sexes • 2–5 pale blue-green to dark turquoise eggs; mostly elliptically ovate, some almost round; 2 inches long.

Plumage Sexes similar	Habitat	Migration Most migrate	Weight 1.6 pounds

DATE _____ TIME_____ LOCATION _____

Family THRESKIORNITHIDAE	Species *Ajaia ajaja*	Length 30–40 inches	Wingspan 50–53 inches

ROSEATE SPOONBILL

The only spoonbill native to North America, this is also the only large pink wading bird normally found on our southern coasts. Adults and juveniles alike are unmistakable with large spatulate bills. In flight the adult bird looks almost entirely pink and flies with its neck and legs extended. During breeding season the head sometimes becomes a copper-buff color. Juveniles are pale whitish overall.

- **SONG** Soft quacking sounds when disturbed.
- **BEHAVIOR** Feeds while wading in shallow water by rhythmically sweeping its spoonbill back and forth. Sensitive nerve endings snap bill shut

bare greenish head

gray-green spatulate bill

white back

white neck and breast

red coverts form red bar on folded wing

pink wings, rump, and underparts

pinkish red legs and feet

on any prey encountered. Often quite tame. Individuals and flocks frequently found in company of other wading birds.

- **BREEDING** Monogamous. Colonial; often nests in mixed colonies with other wading birds.
- **NESTING** Incubation 22–24 days by both sexes. Young stay in nest 35–42 days. Fed by both sexes. Capable of strong flight in 49–56 days. 1 brood per year.
- **POPULATION** Fairly common but local. Virtually eliminated from US in 1860s as water colonies were destroyed. Recolonization began in Texas and Florida in early 20th century. Still vulnerable to degradation of feeding and nesting habitats.
- **CONSERVATION** Drainage for development and mosquito control threatens foraging habitat.

Similar Birds
 **GREATER FLAMINGO** Much larger in size; entirely pink; longer legs and neck.
SCARLET IBIS Much deeper red; slender decurved bill.

Flight Pattern
Steady flapping wing beats with short glides in between.

Nest Identification	Platform with deep hollow in center • made of sticks • lined with twigs and leaves • in mangroves, trees, and shrubs • usually 5–15 feet above ground or water • built by female with material from male • 1–5 white eggs, spotted with brown and occasionally wreathed, 2.6 inches long.
Shape 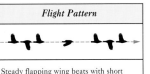 Location	

Plumage Sexes similar	Habitat	Migration Some migrate	Weight Undetermined

DATE _____ TIME_____ LOCATION _____

Family CICONIIDAE	Species *Mycteria americana*	Length 35–45 inches	Wingspan 65 inches

WOOD STORK

Numbers of the only stork that breeds in North America are much reduced from their former levels. This large bird of southern wetlands and swamps appears all white on the ground, except for its bare grayish "flinthead" and upper neck, blackish gray legs with pink feet, and black tail. In flight the trailing edge of the wings is black. Storks fly with legs and neck extended. Some wander northward after the breeding season in late summer and are irregularly recorded north to California, Tennessee, and Massachusetts; casually as far north as southern Canada. Many retreat to Florida in winter.

- **SONG** Usually silent. Adults clatter and snap bills during courtship and copulation. Adults also infrequently produce airy, low, rasping fizz or hiss reminiscent of Turkey Vulture.
- **BEHAVIOR** Walks or wades in shallow water up to its belly with head down when feeding. Reproductive cycles triggered by drying up of waterholes that concentrate fish in sufficient numbers for efficient feeding of young.
- **BREEDING** Monogamous. Colonial.
- **NESTING** Incubation 27–32 days by both sexes. Young stay in nest 55–60 days. Fed by both sexes. 1 brood per year likely.
- **POPULATION** Fairly common. Destruction of habitat and disruption of water flow through south Florida major causes of decline. Recently shifted range to South Carolina.
- **CONSERVATION** Endangered in US due to loss of breeding habitat.

• *bare gray head and upper neck*

• *thick gray-brown decurved bill*

• *white body*

JUVENILE

Similar Birds

GREAT EGRET
Slender white neck; feathered head; yellow beak.

AMERICAN WHITE PELICAN
Short legs do not trail behind white tail; much longer orange beak; shorter neck.

WHITE IBIS
Smaller; entirely white except for red legs, feet, face, and decurved bill with black tip • in flight, body appears white with black wing tips; red features may look dark • flight pattern differs, with several rapid wing beats alternating with a glide.

• *blackish gray legs*

Flight Pattern

Alternates between strong flapping flight and gliding. Masterful at soaring, riding high on thermals.

Nest Identification

Shape   Location

Large sticks • lined sparsely with fine materials and green leaves • 50–80 feet above ground in large cypress trees standing in water • built by both sexes • 2–5 whitish eggs, elliptical to subelliptical, 2.7 inches long.

Plumage Sexes similar	Habitat	Migration Nonmigratory	Weight 6.0 pounds

DATE _____ TIME_____ LOCATION _____

Family CATHARTIDAE	Species *Coragyps atratus*	Length 23–27 inches	Wingspan 54–60 inches

BLACK VULTURE

Alternating between several quick flaps and a short sail on flat wings, this bird seems to labor on the wing more than the Turkey Vulture that it superficially resembles. In flight the wings are wide, with the six outermost primaries showing white bases beneath. The tail of this vulture is short and squared, barely extending beyond the wing, and the feet often protrude beyond it.

wrinkled grayish black skin on head and neck

sooty black plumage

whitish bill

short neck

white outer primaries

long gray-white legs and gray-white feet

• **SONG** Usually silent, but when competing for food it makes grumbling, barking, and hissing noises.
• **BEHAVIOR** Solitary or found in small to large groups. Often roosts communally. Diet consists primarily of carrion. Aggressive in nature for a vulture, it often dominates carrion when other species are present. Sometimes attacks and kills prey. It spreads its wings when on the roost, especially in the morning, to catch the ultraviolet rays of the sun.
• **BREEDING** Monogamous. Colonial.
• **NESTING** Incubation 37–48 days by both sexes. Semialtricial young remain in nest 80–94 days, and are fed by both sexes. 1 brood per year.
• **POPULATION** Fairly common to common. Decline in the Southeast has been due to the loss of safe nesting habitat. Overall, there has been a slight increase in the Northeast as range has expanded.

Similar Birds

TURKEY VULTURE
Bare red head (black on juvenile); long rectangular tail; 2-toned wings from below (black in front, silver-gray trailing edge); holds wings in dihedral when soaring.

Flight Pattern
Several quick deep wing beats followed by a glide; soars on thermals.

Nest Identification	
Shape ⚬ ◲ ▯ Location 🌿 🪨 🏚 🐾 — ⛰	No nest • lives in dark recesses or under cover in caves, hollow logs, stumps, tree trunks, or abandoned buildings • 2 light grayish green or bluish white eggs, usually marked with brown or lavender; elliptical ovate or elongate ovate, 3 inches long.

Plumage Sexes similar	Habitat ___	Migration Some migrate	Weight 4.8 pounds

DATE _____ TIME_____ LOCATION _____

Family CATHARTIDAE	Species *Cathartes aura*	Length 26–32 inches	Wingspan 68–72 inches

TURKEY VULTURE

Commonly known as a "buzzard," this bird ranges throughout the United States and into southern Canada and south to South America. It gets its name from the red skin on its head and dark body feathers that resemble a turkey. This carrion feeder is perhaps most often seen in flight, when its two-tone wings, black in front and silver-gray flight feathers behind, are most visible. Soaring birds hold their wings above their backs in a shallow V called a dihedral and rock from side to side as if unsteady in the air.

gray flight feathers

brown-edged dark upperwing coverts and upperparts

bare-skinned red head and dull red neck

semicircle of whitish to greenish warts below and in front of eyes

slightly hooked white bill

long slim tail

pale pinkish white legs

- **SONG** Usually silent. Makes hisses, grunts, or growls around food.
- **BEHAVIOR** Circles just above treetops and up to 200 feet high, searching for prey by smell and sight. Birds gather quickly after an animal dies. Feeds primarily on fresh or rotten carrion. Also eats roadkill (many become victims to autos themselves); stillborn livestock and afterbirth; and dead young of egrets, herons, ibis, and similar species, at heronries. Has been known to eat vegetables and even pumpkins if shortage of food. Master at soaring. Often roosts communally at night.
- **BREEDING** Monogamous.
- **NESTING** Incubation 38–41 days by both sexes. Semialtricial young stay in nest 66–88 days; both sexes feed by regurgitating. 1 brood per year.
- **POPULATION** Common. Very slight overall increase.
- **CONSERVATION** Remarkably resistant to most diseases, especially those likely to be present in carrion.

JUVENILE

Similar Birds

BLACK VULTURE
Very black, including head and stubby tail; longer whiter legs often protrude beyond tail in flight; white primaries under wing tip; flaps and glides more.

GOLDEN EAGLE
Much larger; looks heavier; shorter fan-shaped tail; larger feathered head; large strongly hooked yellow beak; flies with wings held in flat plane.

ZONE-TAILED HAWK
Black; feathered head; bold white tail bands; barred black flight feathers; yellow cere, legs, and feet.

Flight Pattern
Circles with wings in shallow V and rocks unsteadily; moderately slow steady wing beats when not soaring.

Nest Identification	
Shape ♣ Location	Bare floors of caves, rock outcroppings, hollow trees, empty buildings, and rocks on cliffs • 1–3 white or cream eggs, often splashed with brown; subelliptical, long oval, or elliptical, 2.8 inches long.

Plumage Sexes similar	Habitat	Migration Migratory	Weight 3.2 pounds

DATE _____ TIME _____ LOCATION _____

Family ANATIDAE	Species *Dendrocygna autumnalis*	Length 19–22 inches	Wingspan 34–36 inches

BLACK-BELLIED WHISTLING-DUCK

This gooselike duck with long legs and neck is much more common in the American tropics. In flight its long white wing patch contrasts sharply with the black flight feathers, and the reddish feet protrude beyond the black tail. It is the only North American duck with an entirely red spatulate bill. Juveniles are paler above and below, lacking the black belly and having bars of black mottling on their sides, flanks, and lower bellies; bills are gray.

- **SONG** High-pitched 4-note whistle, *pe-che-che-ne* or *wha-chew-whe-whe-whew*, often is given in flight.
- **BEHAVIOR** Often in small groups. Flocks on shallow water; perches in trees. Feeds primarily at night. Frequently retreats to woodlands when disturbed; easily maneuvers between trees. Primary diet aquatic vegetation, cultivated grains, and seeds.
- **BREEDING** Monogamous.
- **NESTING** Incubation 25–30 days by both sexes, but primarily by male. Young precocial; leave nest 18–24 hours after hatching. Tended by both sexes for at least 144 days. Possibly 2 broods per year. "Dump" nests produced by more than one female laying eggs in a single nest are common, which results in documented nests containing more than 100 eggs.
- **POPULATION** Uncommon to casual. Local.
- **BIRDHOUSES** Will nest in tree boxes.

white eye ring

grayish white face and foreneck

red bill

long neck

bright chestnut back

chestnut breast and neck

white wing patch

long pinkish red legs

black belly, rump, and tail

JUVENILE

Similar Birds

FULVOUS WHISTLING-DUCK Gray-blue bill, legs, and feet; paler brown plumage; lacks black belly.

Flight Pattern
Direct flight with strong rapid wing beats.

Nest Identification	
Shape  Location	8–30 feet above ground in elms, willows, and other trees • also on ground among rushes, weeds, or grasses near water's edge • built by female • 12–16 white or creamy white eggs, 2 inches long.

Plumage Sexes similar	Habitat	Migration Migratory	Weight 1.8 pounds

DATE _____ TIME_____ LOCATION _____

Family ANATIDAE	Species *Dendrocygna bicolor*	Length 18–21 inches	Wingspan 36 inches

FULVOUS WHISTLING-DUCK

In its upright stance with its long legs and neck, this duck is somewhat gooselike in appearance. One of the most widely distributed waterfowl in the world, this rich fulvous brown duck resembles no other North American duck on land or water. It flies with a noticeable droop in its long neck and with legs and feet extended beyond the tail. Its white rump patch contrasts against the black tail.

tawny-fulvous head and neck

dark cap and line extending down midline of hindneck

brownish black back with feathers edged tawny-brown

gray-blue bill

black tail

white rump

white slashes on sides

tawny-fulvous underparts

- **SONG** High squeaking 2-syllable whistle, *pe-chee*, usually is given while bird is in flight.
- **BEHAVIOR** Feeds at night. Walks on land. Eats grass and weed seeds. Forages in fields for waste grain; seems to be particularly fond of rice. Roosts by day in dense vegetation. Often found in large flocks.
- **BREEDING** Monogamous.
- **NESTING** Incubation 24–26 days by both sexes. Young stay in nest 55–63 days. Young tended by both sexes but find own food. 1 brood per year.

Similar Birds

BLACK-BELLIED WHISTLING-DUCK
Bold white wing stripe in flight; black belly; red bill, legs, and feet.

- **POPULATION** Uncommon to fairly common locally. Decline in Southwest; increase in Southeast.
- **CONSERVATION** Considered a "pest" species by some rice farmers in the South.

Flight Pattern

Direct heronlike flight with slow deep wing beats.

Nest Identification

Shape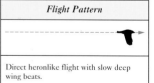

Location

Woven grass, sedges, and cattails • no down added • on ground next to water or in dense marsh just above water in bulrushes or dense beds of cattails • rarely in tree cavity • built by female • 12–14 white or buff-white eggs; bluntly ovate, short ovate, or oval; 2.1 inches in diameter.

Plumage Sexes similar	Habitat 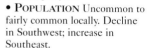	Migration Migratory	Weight 1.6 pounds

DATE _____ **TIME** _____ **LOCATION** _____

Family ANATIDAE	Species *Anser albifrons*	Length 26–34 inches	Wingspan 53–62 inches

GREATER WHITE-FRONTED GOOSE

This is the only North American goose with the combination of a white face at the base of the bill, dark barring on the belly, and orange-yellow legs and feet. In flight the blue-gray wing coverts contrast with the brown body and U-shaped rump patch, and the "specklebelly" is easily seen. Huge numbers winter on the eastern Great Plains. Individuals or small flocks, often mixed in with other species of geese, may show up

dark brownish gray head, neck, and upperparts

white on front of head and around base of bill extends to forehead

pink bill with white tip

brownish gray underparts with heavy dark mottling and barring

black tail

white undertail coverts

orange-yellow legs and feet

anywhere in eastern Canada or the northeastern US outside their normal range.
- **SONG** High-pitched laughing *kah-lah-aluek* and loud *wah-wah-wah*.
- **BEHAVIOR** Dabbles and walks well on land. Feeds on grasses, grain, aquatic plants, and insects. Favors freshwater pools, lakes, and marshes. In winter found in grasslands and agricultural fields. Flies high in V formations with clamorous "talking" among individuals in flock.
- **BREEDING** Monogamous.

Similar Birds

SNOW GOOSE
Juvenile dark morph has dark legs and bill; lacks white on face; lacks dark barring on underparts.

EMPEROR GOOSE
Juvenile has dark bill; lacks dark barring on belly • western range.

BEAN GOOSE
Black bill with yellow band near tip; gray-brown overall; darker brown on upperparts; orange feet and legs; whitish center to belly • western range.

- **NESTING** Incubation 22–28 days by female. Young precocial; first flight at 38–49 days. Tended by both sexes. 1 brood per year.
- **POPULATION** Common to fairly common. Midcontinent numbers increasing.

Flight Pattern

Steady direct flight with rapid wing beats. Flies in V formation.

Nest Identification

Shape ⚬ ⚬ Location ▬ ▬▬

Plant material and down • on ground near water in open, wet tundra • built by female • 3–6 buff, cream, pinkish white, or nest-stained eggs; elliptical to ovoid, 3.1 inches long.

Plumage Sexes similar	Habitat	Migration Migratory	Weight 6.0 pounds

DATE _____ TIME_____ LOCATION _____

Family ANATIDAE	Species *Chen caerulescens*	Length 25–31 inches	Wingspan 53–60 inches

SNOW GOOSE

This species comprises two color morphs that, until the last quarter of the 20th century, were considered separate species: Snow Goose for the white morph and Blue Goose for the dark or blue morph. The plumage of the white morph is entirely white in adults except for black primary feathers. Blue morph adults have a white head and neck with a dusky gray-brown body and white tail coverts.

- **SONG** Shrill falsetto notes and occasional softened honking. High-pitched nasal barking continuously in chorus in flight.
- **BEHAVIOR** Flies in bunched flocks or in broad U formations. Dabbler that walks easily on land. Grazes on tender shoots, waste grain, and other vegetable matter. Color morphs tend to segregate on breeding grounds, but mixed partners sometimes do pair and nest.
- **BREEDING** Monogamous. Colonial; densities of up to 1,200 pairs per square mile.
- **NESTING** Incubation 23–25 days by female. Precocial young leave nest soon after hatching, tended by both parents. First flight at 38–49 days. 1 brood per year.
- **POPULATION** Very common to abundant. Increasing overall, with blue morph increasing and white morph decreasing, because of selection by predators on breeding grounds and hunters on wintering grounds.
- **CONSERVATION** Some management in certain areas of breeding range to prevent overpopulation and destruction of habitat by increased populations.

black primaries

DARK MORPH
ADULT

pink bill   white body

black "grinning patch" on cutting edges of mandibles

WHITE MORPH
ADULT

WHITE MORPH
JUVENILE

DARK MORPH
JUVENILE

Similar Birds

ROSS'S GOOSE
Smaller; short, stubby bill; rounder head; lacks grinning patch.

EMPEROR GOOSE
Similar to dark morph • black throat and foreneck; bright orange-yellow legs and feet • western range.

Flight Pattern

Strong direct flight with moderate wing beats.

Nest Identification

Shape ⌣ ⬭   Location ▬ ⁂

Built by female • filled with mosses • lined with grasses and down • 3–5 white or nest-stained eggs, 3.2 inches long.

Plumage Sexes similar	Habitat	Migration Migratory	Weight Undetermined

DATE _____ TIME _____ LOCATION _____

Family ANATIDAE	Species *Chen rossii*	Length 21–26 inches	Wingspan 47–54 inches

ROSS'S GOOSE

Often seen with the Snow Goose, North America's smallest goose is said to have a gentle expression. Like the Snow Goose, Ross's Goose has both a white morph and a very uncommon blue morph. It can be distinguished from the Snow Goose from a distance by its smaller size and shorter neck and at closer range by its stubby triangular bill, which lacks the "grinning patch." In flight it has faster wing beats than the Snow Goose.

round head

short neck

stubby, triangular, deep pinkish red bill with warty bluish base

black wing tips

snow-white body

WHITE MORPH

BLUE MORPH

- **SONG** Low throaty *kug* or weak *kek*, *kek* or *ke-gak*, *ke-gak*. Similar to call of smaller races of Canada Goose.
- **BEHAVIOR** Eats fresh grasses and grains. Often can be seen feeding with Snow Geese.
- **BREEDING** Monogamous. Colonial.
- **NESTING** Incubation 21–24 days by female. Precocial young are tended by both sexes. First flight at 40–45 days. Has 1 brood per year.
- **POPULATION** Rare to uncommon in migration and outside its wintering grounds in California, New Mexico, and the states along lower Mississippi River. Fairly common on breeding grounds.
- **CONSERVATION** Numbers were decimated by market hunting, especially in California, until it was regulated early in the 20th century. Populations increased in the last half of the 20th century.

Similar Birds

SNOW GOOSE
Longer neck and bill; has "grinning patch" on cutting edge of bill; flatter head; rusty stains often visible on face in summer; slower wing beats.

Flight Pattern
Rapid direct flight with strong wing beats. Flies in V formation.

Nest Identification	
Shape · Location	Soft grasses, moss, and twigs • lined with small amount of down • built by female • 4–5 white eggs; subelliptical, 2.9 x 1.9 inches.

Plumage Sexes similar	Habitat	Migration Migratory	Weight 3.7 pounds

DATE _____ TIME _____ LOCATION _____

| Family ANATIDAE | Species *Branta canadensis* | Length 25–45 inches | Wingspan 75 inches |

CANADA GOOSE

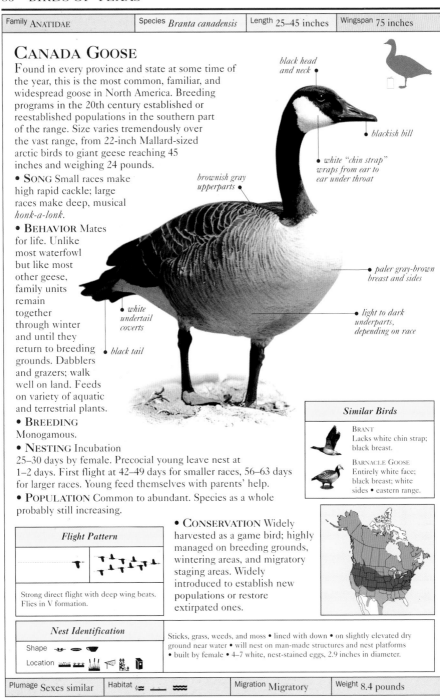

Found in every province and state at some time of the year, this is the most common, familiar, and widespread goose in North America. Breeding programs in the 20th century established or reestablished populations in the southern part of the range. Size varies tremendously over the vast range, from 22-inch Mallard-sized arctic birds to giant geese reaching 45 inches and weighing 24 pounds.

black head and neck

blackish bill

white "chin strap" wraps from ear to ear under throat

brownish gray upperparts

- **SONG** Small races make high rapid cackle; large races make deep, musical *honk-a-lonk*.

paler gray-brown breast and sides

- **BEHAVIOR** Mates for life. Unlike most waterfowl but like most other geese, family units remain together through winter and until they return to breeding grounds. Dabblers and grazers; walk well on land. Feeds on variety of aquatic and terrestrial plants.

white undertail coverts

black tail

light to dark underparts, depending on race

- **BREEDING** Monogamous.
- **NESTING** Incubation 25–30 days by female. Precocial young leave nest at 1–2 days. First flight at 42–49 days for smaller races, 56–63 days for larger races. Young feed themselves with parents' help.
- **POPULATION** Common to abundant. Species as a whole probably still increasing.

Similar Birds

BRANT
Lacks white chin strap; black breast.

BARNACLE GOOSE
Entirely white face; black breast; white sides • eastern range.

- **CONSERVATION** Widely harvested as a game bird; highly managed on breeding grounds, wintering areas, and migratory staging areas. Widely introduced to establish new populations or restore extirpated ones.

Flight Pattern
Strong direct flight with deep wing beats. Flies in V formation.

Nest Identification	
Shape	Sticks, grass, weeds, and moss • lined with down • on slightly elevated dry ground near water • will nest on man-made structures and nest platforms • built by female • 4–7 white, nest-stained eggs, 2.9 inches in diameter.
Location	

| Plumage Sexes similar | Habitat | Migration Migratory | Weight 8.4 pounds |

DATE _____ TIME_____ LOCATION _____

Family ANATIDAE	Species *Branta bernicla*	Length 22–26 inches	Wingspan 43–48 inches

BRANT

A tundra species most often seen wintering along sea coasts, this small short-necked goose is not much larger than a Mallard. The two races in North America differ in appearance. Both have dark brown backs, but whereas the western bird has a dark belly, the eastern form has a paler one and its white patches do not meet at the front of the neck. In both plumages the white rump is conspicuous in flight.

- **SONG** Call is throaty drawled *c-r-r-onk, crr-ronk.*
- **BEHAVIOR** Often flies low in ragged bunches with position of birds changing often and without appearance of a leader. Incubating birds sit tightly on nest and lie low with neck and head stretched flat, blending with surrounding tundra. Relatively tame. Feeds primarily on vegetable matter.
- **BREEDING** Monogamous. Mates for life. Forms loose colonies.
- **NESTING** Incubation 22–26 days by female. First flight at 40–50 days. Tended by both sexes.
- **POPULATION** Common and local. May be declining.
- **CONSERVATION** A die-off of eelgrass, a major source of food for the Brant, on the Atlantic Coast in the 1930s had serious impact on population. No long-term damage reported, because the Brant switched to another food source. Eelgrass made a partial recovery.

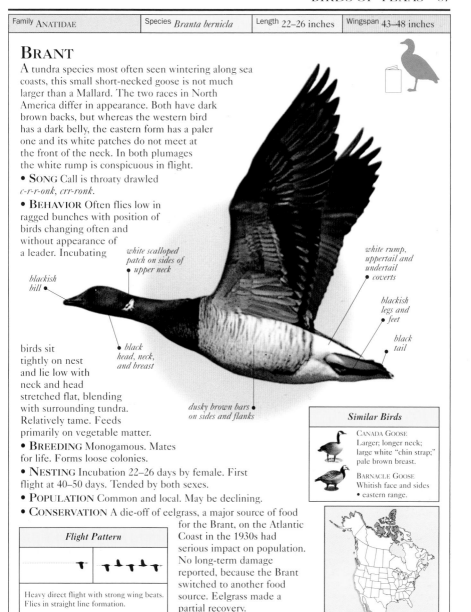

white scalloped patch on sides of upper neck

blackish bill

black head, neck, and breast

dusky brown bars on sides and flanks

white rump, uppertail and undertail coverts

blackish legs and feet

black tail

Similar Birds

CANADA GOOSE
Larger; longer neck; large white "chin strap;" pale brown breast.

BARNACLE GOOSE
Whitish face and sides • eastern range.

Flight Pattern
Heavy direct flight with strong wing beats. Flies in straight line formation.

Nest Identification	
Shape ⌣ ⌣ Location ▬ ▬ ✸✸	Shallow bowl of grass and other materials • heavily lined with down • on small island in tundra pond, usually 1–5 miles from coast • built by female • 1–7 creamy white or buff eggs; subelliptical to elliptical, 2.9 inches in diameter.

Plumage Sexes similar	Habitat ⌇⌇ ≈≈ ▬	Migration Migratory	Weight 3.0 pounds

DATE _____ TIME_____ LOCATION _____

Family ANATIDAE	Species *Cygnus columbianus*	Length 47–58 inches	Wingspan 6–7 feet

TUNDRA SWAN

The most common and widespread swan in North America, this species breeds on arctic tundra and winters principally on the Atlantic and Pacific Coasts. Wintering concentrations on some coastal bays and lakes are spectacular in scope and activity. Swans are often associated with water; they are exceptionally fast swimmers. When flying they are large spectacular birds with long triangular wings, snow white to the tips of all flight feathers. The thin outstreached neck appears like a line more than half the length of the body, with a black point at the end.

• **SONG** Clamoring notes or yodeling; soft musical laughter, *wow-HOW-ow*, heavily accented on second syllable; repeated *who-who's*.

• **BEHAVIOR** Dabbler; plunges long neck and head beneath water to pick aquatic

yellow to orange spot in front of eye (most birds)

black bill with slightly concave profile to rounded head

black lores pointed to just in front of eye make straight line across forehead

entirely white body

JUVENILE

vegetation and dig up roots of submerged plants. Like other swans, runs across water beating its wings to achieve takeoff. Once in flight flies with neck and head thrust straight forward and feet protruding beneath tail.

• **BREEDING** The Tundra Swan is monogamous. It finds a mate and pairs for life. It is also known to be a solitary nester that is widespread over the tundra.

• **NESTING** Incubation 31–40 days, mostly by female. Precocial young tended by both sexes. First flight at 60–70 days. 1 brood per year.

• **POPULATION** Common on breeding range. Common to rare on wintering range. Increasing.

Similar Birds

TRUMPETER SWAN
Larger; bill slopes into flat forehead; no yellow spot in front of eye; black lores taper to point touching eye and form a V across forehead; pink "smile line."

Flight Pattern

Strong direct flight with steady wing beats. Flies in straight line or V formation.

Nest Identification

Shape ⌣⌣ ⌣   Location ▬▬ ✱✱✱

Low mound of plant material such as mosses, dried grasses, and sedges • near lake or other open water on ridge or island • built by both sexes, but male does more • 4–5 creamy white or nest-stained eggs; elliptically ovate, 4.2 inches long.

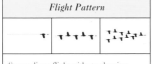

Plumage Sexes similar	Habitat ▬▬ ⬚≈ ≈≈	Migration Migratory	Weight 15.7 pounds

Family ANATIDAE	Species *Cairina moschata*	Length 25–35 inches	Wingspan 54–60 inches

MUSCOVY DUCK

Widely domesticated and gooselike, Muscovy Ducks appear heavy and laboring when flying, with the body low and head held high. White upper and lower wing coverts are conspicuous in flight. Males are much larger than females and have bare facial skin, a black to reddish knob at the base of the bill, a crested head, and black legs and feet. Females are smaller and duller in color.

crested head •

black upperparts with metallic green gloss •

bare black to • *red face*

knob at base • *of bill*

• *black bill banded with bluish white*

dusky black • *underparts*

white patch in • *folded wing*

DOMESTIC
WHITE FORM

Domesticated birds vary in their mix of dark and light plumage and often have larger red wart patches on the face.

• **SONG** Usually silent. Male hisses; female may give rare guttural croak or quack.

• **BEHAVIOR** Inhabits forested watercourses where it roosts in trees at night and nests in natural cavities. Feeds primarily on vegetable matter, particularly seeds, which it forages for in pools, rivers, bottomland, hardwoods, and grain fields. Generally solitary or in pairs; infrequently in small groups.

• **BREEDING** Polygamous. Males do not form pair bonds with females and aggressively drive other males away.

• **NESTING** Breeding biology poorly known; incubation estimated at 35 days.

• **POPULATION** Uncommon and local. Wild birds restricted to the lower Rio Grande Valley.

• **CONSERVATION** Nest box program has been successful in northern Mexico.

Similar Birds

NEOTROPIC
CORMORANT
More slender body; longer, thinner neck and tail; lacks white patches on wing.

Flight Pattern

- - - - - - - - - - - - ➤

Strong direct gooselike flight.

Nest Identification

Shape 〰² ▯   Location 🌸 ▯

Nest boxes lined with little or no down • in cavities in trees, 9–60 feet above the ground • 8–10 white eggs with greenish sheen.

Plumage Sexes differ	Habitat 🌳	Migration Nonmigratory	Weight 6.4 pounds

DATE _____ TIME_____ LOCATION _____

Family ANATIDAE	Species *Aix sponsa*	Length 17–20 inches	Wingspan 28–30 inches

WOOD DUCK

Considered by many to be the most beautiful duck in North America, the colorful male of this species is unmistakable with its large iridescent crest and multicolored bill. In flight it appears big-headed with a short neck and a long squared tail. The bill angles downward.

• **SONG** Male makes soft up-slurred whistle. Female makes rising *hoo-eek* and sharp *crrreek, crrreek.*

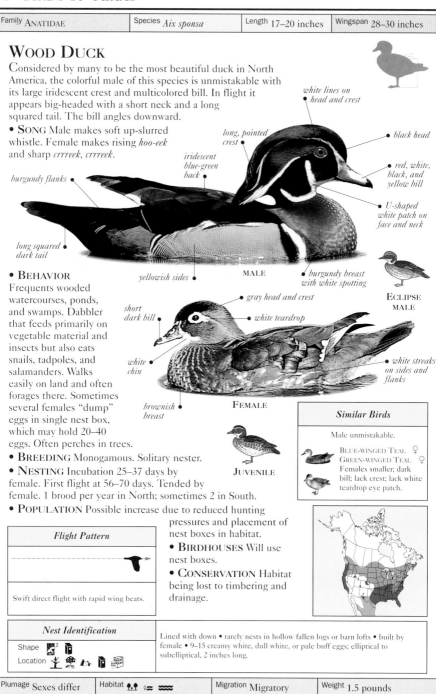

white lines on head and crest

long, pointed crest

iridescent blue-green back

black head

red, white, black, and yellow bill

U-shaped white patch on face and neck

burgundy flanks

long squared dark tail

yellowish sides

MALE

burgundy breast with white spotting

ECLIPSE MALE

gray head and crest

short dark bill

white teardrop

white chin

white streaks on sides and flanks

brownish breast

FEMALE

JUVENILE

• **BEHAVIOR** Frequents wooded watercourses, ponds, and swamps. Dabbler that feeds primarily on vegetable material and insects but also eats snails, tadpoles, and salamanders. Walks easily on land and often forages there. Sometimes several females "dump" eggs in single nest box, which may hold 20–40 eggs. Often perches in trees.

• **BREEDING** Monogamous. Solitary nester.

• **NESTING** Incubation 25–37 days by female. First flight at 56–70 days. Tended by female. 1 brood per year in North; sometimes 2 in South.

• **POPULATION** Possible increase due to reduced hunting pressures and placement of nest boxes in habitat.

• **BIRDHOUSES** Will use nest boxes.

• **CONSERVATION** Habitat being lost to timbering and drainage.

Similar Birds

Male unmistakable.

BLUE-WINGED TEAL ♀
GREEN-WINGED TEAL ♀
Females smaller; dark bill; lack crest; lack white teardrop eye patch.

Flight Pattern

Swift direct flight with rapid wing beats.

Nest Identification

Shape

Location

Lined with down • rarely nests in hollow fallen logs or barn lofts • built by female • 9–15 creamy white, dull white, or pale buff eggs; elliptical to subelliptical, 2 inches long.

Plumage Sexes differ	Habitat	Migration Migratory	Weight 1.5 pounds

DATE _____ TIME_____ LOCATION _____

Family ANATIDAE	Species *Anas strepera*	Length 18–23 inches	Wingspan 31–36 inches

GADWALL

The male Gadwall is the grayest dabbling duck. Its gray body contrasts with the black rear and blends into the brown back, neck, and head. In flight both sexes show a white speculum. On water or land the white secondaries often appear as a narrow white patch in the folded wing. The male has yellowish legs and feet.

brown head and neck

dark bill

• SONG Female makes series of loud quacks that fall in pitch, *kaaak, kaaak-kak-kak-kak.* Male makes single low quack and shrill whistling sound.

brownish back

MALE

black tail coverts

gray body

gray upper mandible with orange sides

mottled brown back and sides

FEMALE

ECLIPSE MALE

• BEHAVIOR Dabbler. Feeds in shallows primarily on plant material. Often forages in grain fields and into wood lots for acorns. Walks well on land compared to most ducks. Flies in small flocks. Usually shy and wary; sociable and gregarious. Often feeds by dabbling with head underwater instead of tipping up like many other puddle ducks.
• BREEDING Monogamous. Solitary nester.
• NESTING Incubation 24–27 days by female. Young precocial; first flight at about 48–56 days. Tended by female. 1 brood per year.
• POPULATION Uncommon. Increasing due to expansion of nesting habitat because of unusually wet conditions in breeding range in late 1990s.

Similar Birds

MALLARD ♀
Blue speculum bordered with white; orange legs and feet.

Flight Pattern

Fast direct flight with rapid wing beats.

Nest Identification

Shape — — Location

Grasses and weeds • lined with down • near water or dry land, surrounded by dense weeds or grass • built by female • 7–15 white to dull cream eggs.

Plumage Sexes differ	Habitat	Migration Migratory	Weight 2.2 pounds

DATE _____ TIME_____ LOCATION _____

Family ANATIDAE	Species *Anas penelope*	Length 18–20 inches	Wingspan 30–32 inches

EURASIAN WIGEON

Although the Eurasian Wigeon is not known to nest on this continent, this dabbling duck has been a rare but regular visitor in winter on both coasts in North America for the last forty to fifty years. The adult female has a cinnamon-buff head in contrast to the male's reddish head. The female also has two morphs: rufous and gray. In flight it is best distinguished from the American Wigeon by its dusky axillars and underwing linings.

buff crown

reddish head

gray overall

creamy forehead cap

blue-gray bill

brownish rose breast

white patch on forewings

MALE

cinnamon-buff head

ECLIPSE MALE

• **SONG** Male makes wild musical whistle, *whee-oo*, and short cheeping note. Female makes hoarse croak and sharp quack when alarmed.
• **BEHAVIOR** Highly gregarious after breeding season, often forming large flocks on the Eurasian wintering grounds. Dabbles in mud or tips up in shallow water to eat favorite foods: pond weeds, eelgrass, and other aquatic plants. Eats seeds but prefers leaves, stems, and buds. Also eats snails, beetles, and crickets. Walks well on land and often forages in fields and wooded lots some distance from water.
• **BREEDING** Monogamous. Semicolonial.
• **NESTING** Incubation 24–25 days by female. Precocial young leave nest shortly after hatching and find own food but still tended by female. First flight at 60–70 days.
• **POPULATION** Rare to uncommon visitor on both coasts but more common on the West Coast. Rare inland.

white belly

FEMALE

Similar Birds

♂ AMERICAN WIGEON Larger • male has gray head with wide green postocular patch; bright white crown; wine sides; white underwing linings show in flight • female generally grayer with white underwing linings.

Flight Pattern
- - - - - - - - - - - - ➤
Swift direct flight with rapid wing beats.

Nest Identification	
Shape ⌒ ⬭ Location 🌱 ❀ 🌿	Lined with grass and large amount of down • built in depression on ground, well hidden in tall grass • 7–9 whitish to pale buff or cream-white eggs • eggs identical to those of American Wigeon.

Plumage Sexes differ	Habitat 〜 〜 〜 �−	Migration Migratory	Weight 1.8 pounds

DATE _____ TIME_____ LOCATION _____

Family ANATIDAE	Species *Anas americana*	Length 18–23 inches	Wingspan 30–35 inches

AMERICAN WIGEON

This species is identified in flight by the bold white patches on its forewings, which are gray on females, and the white underwing linings. The male has a conspicuous white forehead and crown, leading hunters to nickname it "baldpate." Both males and females are more rusty brown on their breast and sides than other dabbling ducks. Legs and feet are gray. In flight females show a white belly and undertail coverts and a green speculum.

gray head with wide green postocular stripe

white forehead and crown

• SONG Throaty whistle, *whew, whew, whew*. Female makes weak guttural quack.

black tail and undertail coverts

MALE

black-tipped blue-gray bill

white of underparts extends onto flanks

• BEHAVIOR Dabbler. Flies in tight flocks that may twist and turn like those of teals. Eats plant material. Will graze on shore and in fields. Often feeds in shallow water with other duck species. Wary; takes flight quickly when it is disturbed.

gray bill with black tip

gray head and neck

brown back with rusty shoulders

reddish brown breast and sides

ECLIPSE MALE

rufous-brown breast, sides, and flanks

FEMALE

Similar Birds

♂ EURASIAN WIGEON
Rufous-brown head; creamy buff forehead and crown; gray sides and back • female shows dusky underwing linings in flight; gray-morph has brownish gray head, throat, and breast; rufous morph has rufous head, neck, throat, and breast.

• BREEDING Monogamous. Solitary. Nests on dry land, sometimes far from water; often on small islands.

• NESTING Incubation 22–25 days by female. Precocial young stay in nest 45–63 days. Fed by female. 1 brood per year.

• POPULATION Common and apparently stable. Breeding range expanding eastward in Canada and northeastern US. Increase has been due to wet conditions as well as increase in nesting sites.

• CONSERVATION No issues at present; carefully monitored and managed.

Flight Pattern
— — — — — — →
Swift direct flight with strong wing beats.

Nest Identification	
Shape Location	Grasses and weeds lined with down • on dry land, sometimes on island • built by female • 6–12 white to creamy white eggs; elliptical, 2.1 inches in diameter.

Plumage Sexes differ	Habitat	Migration Migratory	Weight 1.7 pounds

DATE _____ TIME_____ LOCATION _____

Family ANATIDAE	Species *Anas rubripes*	Length 19–24 inches	Wingspan 33–36 inches

AMERICAN BLACK DUCK

The darkest dabbling duck on the water looks almost black at a distance, with a paler head and foreneck. In flight the white wing linings contrast boldly with the dark body and wings. The purplish blue speculum is bordered with black, and the posterior border often has a narrow white edge. It is as large as a Mallard. Into the 1940s this was the most abundant duck in eastern and central North America and was the most heavily hunted without noticable decline in numbers. Today it seems to be losing steadily to years of heavy hunting preasure and increasing displacement by Mallards.

greenish bill with black flecking

FEMALE

yellow bill

brownish black body • pale brownish gray head and foreneck

MALE

brownish black body

- **SONG** Typical female gives loud duck quack; male makes lower croak.
- **BEHAVIOR** Dabbler. Very alert and wary; one of the quickest ducks into the air when disturbed, thrusting upward energetically off water or land. Feeds in shallow water, taking mostly plant materials in winter and a variety of aquatic insects in summer.
- **BREEDING** Monogamous. Solitary nester. Sometimes hybridizes with Mallard.
- **NESTING** Incubation 23–33 days by female. Precocial young stay in nest 58–63 days. Fed by female. 1 brood per year.
- **POPULATION** Fairly common.
- **CONSERVATION** Management warranted due to decline in numbers, which may be caused by changes to its habitat and deforestation. Both of these circumstances seem to favor Mallards, which tend to replace Black Ducks where the two species coexist.

Similar Birds

MALLARD ♀
Female lacks contrast between head and body; paler brown; yellow-orange bill with blackish mottling; bright orange feet; metallic blue speculum bordered with a white front and back; white tail.

Flight Pattern

Swift direct flight with strong wing beats.

Nest Identification

Shape

Location

Shallow depression with plant material added • lined with down • on ground among clumps of dense vegetation • sometimes in raised situation, as on top of stump • built by female • 6–12 creamy white to greenish buff eggs.

Plumage Sexes differ	Habitat	Migration Migratory	Weight 3.1 pounds

DATE _____ TIME _____ LOCATION _____

Family ANATIDAE	Species *Anas platyrhynchos*	Length 23 inches	Wingspan 30–40 inches

MALLARD

One of the best-known waterfowl in the world, the Mallard can be found almost anywhere shallow freshwater occurs. Some even reside in salt marshes and bays. The male is larger than the female. Many domesticated forms are entirely white with an orange bill, legs, and feet.

• **SONG** Female makes loud *quack-quack-quack, quack, quack-quack,* descending in scale. Male sounds double note and low reedy *kwek-kwek-kwek.*

• **BEHAVIOR** Generally found in shallow freshwater, where it dabbles primarily for plant food, also taking insects, mollusks, and crustaceans. Sometimes dives underwater. Walks well and often forages on shore in fields and woodlots. Leaps directly into flight from water. Frequently hybridizes.

• **BREEDING** Monogamous. Solitary nester.

• **NESTING** Incubation 26–30 days by female. Precocial young leave nest soon after hatching. 1 brood per year.

• **POPULATION** Common to abundant.

• **FEEDERS** Corn or grains. In city parks some are tame enough to be hand-fed by humans.

• **CONSERVATION** One of the ducks harvested in greatest numbers by waterfowl hunters. Prone to lead poisoning from ingesting spent lead shot with food from bottom ooze.

yellow bill

shiny green head

gray-brown back

metallic blue-violet speculum with white borders

white collar

2 curled-up black tail feathers

purple-chestnut breast

white sides and underparts

white tail

orange feet and legs

MALE

orange and brown mottled bill

metallic blue-violet speculum with white borders

ECLIPSE MALE

white tail

orange feet and legs

FEMALE

Similar Birds

Female resembles many other female ducks, but blue speculum bordered white is unique.

NORTHERN SHOVELER ♂
Long dark bill; white breast; chestnut sides.

COMMON MERGANSER ♂
Narrow red bill; puffy or crested head.

RED-BREASTED MERGANSER ♂
Narrow red bill; puffy or crested head.

Flight Pattern

Swift direct flight with strong wing beats.

Nest Identification

Shape

Location

Shallow pool of plant material gathered at the site, lined with down • may be more than 1 mile from water, usually on ground among concealing vegetation • built by female • 5–14 greenish buff or grayish buff eggs, 2.3 inches long.

Plumage Sexes differ	Habitat	Migration Migratory	Weight 2.4 pounds

DATE _____ TIME_____ LOCATION _____

Family ANATIDAE	Species *Anas fulvigula*	Length 21 inches	Wingspan 30–33 inches

MOTTLED DUCK

A large resident duck of southern marshes and coastal prairies, this bird is paler than the American Black Duck but also shows white wing linings in flight that contrast with its darker body. In flight it shows a metallic greenish purple speculum that is bordered on both sides by a black bar, and the trailing bar is also bordered with a narrow white line. Although the current population is stable, it is not as large as it was in the beginning of the 20th century as the toll from civilization's expanding development and agriculture's draining of southern marshlands has outweighed the toll from hunting.

fine dark streaking on back of head and sides of neck

brown body with buff mottling

yellow-orange bill without mottling

• **SONG** Male makes a low, raspy *kreeeb, kreeeb, kreeeb.* Female's quack similar to that of a female Mallard.

• **BEHAVIOR** Usually in pairs or small groups. Pairs persist for most of the year except during the postbreeding season molt. A somewhat tame dabbling duck that eats more animal food than the closely related Mallard. Feeds primarily on mollusks, crustaceans, and insects, but also eats vegetable matter. Courtship and pair formation for this species take place on the wintering grounds while Mallards, American Black Ducks, and other duck species are still present.

• **BREEDING** Monogamous. Solitary nester.

• **NESTING** Incubation 24–28 days by female. First flight at about 60–70 days. Fed by female. 1 brood per year.

• **POPULATION** Common. Stable. Introduced on South Carolina coast.

• **CONSERVATION** Heavily hunted in season.

Similar Birds

AMERICAN BLACK DUCK Much darker blackish brown with streaked cheeks and throat.

MALLARD ♀ Female has orange and brown bill with dark mottling; white borders on both sides of blue-purple speculum.

Flight Pattern

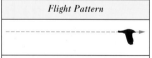

Direct flight with strong rapid wing beats.

Nest Identification	Shallow bowl of grasses and reeds • lined with down and breast feathers • in dense growth in marsh, usually within 600 feet of water, supported in dense clumps of grass • may be several inches above ground • built by female • 8–12 creamy white to greenish white eggs; elliptical, 2.2 inches long.
Shape	
Location	

Plumage Sexes similar	Habitat	Migration Nonmigratory	Weight 2.3 pounds

Family ANATIDAE	Species *Anas discors*	Length 14–16 inches	Wingspan 23–31 inches

BLUE-WINGED TEAL

One of the smallest ducks in North America travels great distances between breeding and wintering grounds, as much as 7,000 miles. Both sexes have a large pale blue patch on the forewings and a long metallic green speculum that is visible when wings are spread. Males in breeding colors have a gray-violet head bordered by a bold white facial crescent.

gray-violet head

short dark bill

white crescent on face

MALE

- **SONG** In flight, the male often makes a high sibilant *tseel*. The female makes *wak* quacking sound.

tawny brown body with dark spotting

- **BEHAVIOR** Very fast taking off from the water, this bird flies quickly and rapidly, often twisting and turning in small compact flocks. Plants make up the bulk of its diet. Often forages in shallow waters. One of the earliest ducks to migrate southward to wintering areas. More than 90 percent of population winters south of US border. Tame, often allowing close approach.

white flank patch

yellowish legs and feet

pale grayish brown head

brown body with dark chevron-shaped spots

FEMALE

- **BREEDING** Monogamous. Solitary nester.
- **NESTING** Incubation 22–27 days by female. First flight at 35–49 days. Tended by female. 1 brood per year.
- **POPULATION** Fairly common in the East; uncommon in the West. Apparently stable.
- **CONSERVATION** Most Blue-Winged Teals winter south of US borders, so Latin American cooperation is needed to further conservation efforts.

Similar Birds

NORTHERN SHOVELER ♀
Much larger; spatulate bill.

GREEN-WINGED TEAL ♀
Larger bill; lacks white undertail coverts and blue forewing patch in flight.

CINNAMON TEAL ♀
Longer bill; richer brown; less distinct eye line.

Flight Pattern

Fast direct flight with steady wing beats.

Nest Identification

Shape — Location —

Shallow depression with some grass or weeds added • lined with down • on ground in prairie, hayfield, or coastal meadow • built by female • 6–15 white, olive-white, dull white, or tinged olive eggs; ovate to elliptical ovate, 1.8 inches in diameter.

Plumage Sexes differ	Habitat	Migration Migratory	Weight 14.4 ounces

DATE _____ TIME_____ LOCATION _____

Family ANATIDAE	Species *Anas cyanoptera*	Length 14–17 inches	Wingspan 24–30 inches

CINNAMON TEAL

The male, with its rich cinnamon hues, is one of the most recognizable ducks in western North America. The female's warm earth tones blend well with the cattails and reeds that surround its home. The Cinnamon Teal and the Ruddy Duck are the only waterfowl to breed in both North and South America. In flight the upper forewing features a large pale powder-blue patch and the speculum is metallic green with a white border. Juveniles and eclipse males resemble females.

cinnamon head and neck

long spatulate blue-black bill

cinnamon underparts

MALE

- **SONG** Male has low-pitched prattling *chuk-chuk-chuk*. Female has weak quack.
- **BEHAVIOR** Eats aquatic plant seeds and insects, rice, corn, algae, snails, and crustaceans. Unlike other dabblers, skims water with bill or reaches below surface. Leaps into flight directly from water.
- **BREEDING** Monogamous. Solitary.
- **NESTING** Incubation 21–25 days by female. First flight after 49 days. 1 brood per year.
- **POPULATION** Fairly common to common from the Pacific Coast to the eastern Great Plains and south into Texas and west-central Mexico. Casual to accidental in the East in winter and spring migration.
- **CONSERVATION** Protected except for licensed seasonal hunting. Efforts made in last half of 20th century to increase nesting habitat. Declines due to loss of wetland habitat.

brown overall

blue mottling on forewing

FEMALE

Similar Birds

BLUE-WINGED TEAL ♀
Females almost identical • shorter, less spatulate bill; more distinct lore spot and eye line.

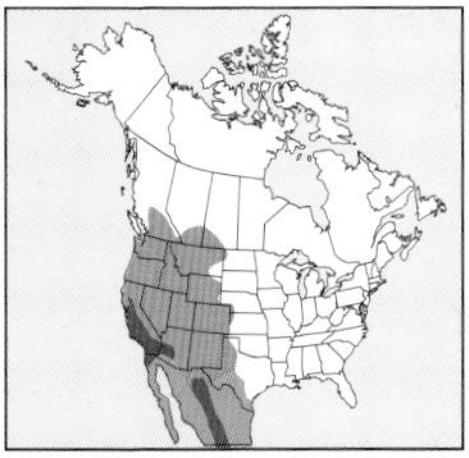

Flight Pattern
Swift direct flight with rapid wing beats.

Nest Identification	
Shape Location	On ground hidden in tall vegetation • in dense marsh grasses and reeds or in slight depression on bare ground • often 100 feet or more away from water • built by female • 9–12 pinkish buff or white eggs; subelliptical, 2 inches long.

Plumage Sexes differ	Habitat	Migration Migratory	Weight 14.4 ounces

DATE _____ TIME_____ LOCATION _____

Family ANATIDAE	Species *Anas clypeata*	Length 17–20 inches	Wingspan 27–33 inches

NORTHERN SHOVELER

No duck in North America has a bigger bill. The large, spatulate bill is longer than the head, giving the bird a front heavy look. In flight both sexes show large powder-blue patches on the forewing and a metallic green speculum. Both males and females have bright orange legs and feet.

black head with green gloss

MALE

large spoon-shaped black bill

white tail feathers (most)

black undertail and uppertail coverts

white flank spot

blue patch on folded wing

orange legs and feet

rich chestnut sides and belly

white breast

ECLIPSE MALE

grayish bill mottled orange

mottled brown

FEMALE

Similar Birds

MALLARD
Male has green head but has chestnut breast; white sides; lacks blue patch on forewing • female has smaller bill; lacks blue on front of wing.

BLUE-WINGED TEAL
Smaller; shows pale blue forewing patch in flight • male has brown body; gray head; white crescent on front of face; small black bill • female is brown overall; small black bill.

• **SONG** In courtship male utters guttural *who, who, who* or *took, took, took*. Female utters feeble quack and descending *WACK-wack-wack-wa-wa*.

• **BEHAVIOR** Frequently swims with head held low, bill partly submerged, straining water for small aquatic plants and animals through the comblike teeth along sides of bill. Animals make up approximately one-third of its diet. Swift flight into air by leaping off water. Rapid, sometimes darting, teal-like flight.

• **BREEDING** Monogamous. Solitary nester.

• **NESTING** Incubation 21–27 days by female. Precocial young leave nest within a few hours of hatching. First flight at 38–66 days. Tended by female. 1 brood per year.

• **POPULATION** Common to abundant. Increasing due to wet conditions in breeding range.

Flight Pattern
Strong direct flight with rapid wing beats.

Nest Identification	
Shape 〜 ⬬ Location ✱✱✱	Partly filled with dried grasses and weeds • lined with down • close to water, generally in area of short grass, or far from water on high dry ground of prairies • built by female • 6–19 olive-buff or greenish gray eggs; elliptical, 2 inches long.

Plumage Sexes differ	Habitat 〜 ≈ ⚊ ♦	Migration Migratory	Weight 1.4 pounds

DATE _____ TIME_____ LOCATION _____

Family ANATIDAE	Species *Anas acuta*	Length 21–29 inches	Wingspan 29–35 inches

NORTHERN PINTAIL

No other North American duck has the body shape of a pintail, either on the water or in the air. It holds its long slender neck erect and its long pointed tail at an upward angle on the water. In flight pintails are long and slender with a white trailing edge on the inner wing.

- **SONG** Female's low quacks more guttural than those of female Mallard. Male utters weak nasal *geeee* and double-noted whistle, *pruh* or *prripp*.
- **BEHAVIOR** Dabbling duck. Prefers shallows in freshwater, where it feeds primarily on vegetable material. Flocks of pintails have reputation of losing altitude rapidly, zigzagging in for a landing from considerable heights on wings that produce an audible "swish" and planing directly into a landing. Low-flying on breeding grounds, nesting individuals are sometimes killed by hitting utility wires and fences.
- **BREEDING** Monogamous. Solitary nester.
- **NESTING** Incubation 22–25 days by female. Young leave nest within a few hours of hatching. First flight at 36–57 days. Young tended by female but find own food. 1 brood per year.
- **POPULATION** Abundant in West; very common in East. Widespread and abundant, but some surveys show decline since 1960s.
- **CONSERVATION** As with other dabbling ducks, lead shot ingested from bottom ooze often leads to death.

chocolate head and hindneck

MALE

greenish brown speculum with white line on trailing edge

brownish gray back

gray bill

long white neck with white "finger" extended upward behind face

yellowish white at rear

white breast and underparts

long pointed feathers at center of tail

black uppertail and undertail coverts

gray legs and feet

vermiculated gray sides and flanks

gray bill

long neck

mottled brown

pointed brown tail not as long as that of male

FEMALE

ECLIPSE MALE

gray legs and feet

Similar Birds

Male is distinctive • female is somewhat similar to many other female dabbling ducks but the longer tail and longer neck make it distinctive.

Flight Pattern
Direct flight with fast wing beats on long pointed wings.

Nest Identification
Shape — Location

Lined with grasses, twigs, mosses, leaves, and added down • on dry ground among short vegetation near water • built by female • 3–12 olive-green, olive-buff, or cream eggs; elliptical to subelliptical or long oval, 2.2 inches long.

Plumage Sexes differ	Habitat	Migration Migratory	Weight 2.3 pounds

DATE _____ TIME_____ LOCATION _____

Family ANATIDAE	Species *Anas crecca*	Length 12–16 inches	Wingspan 20–25 inches

GREEN-WINGED TEAL

The smallest dabbling duck in North America, the Green-winged Teal is also one of the most agile and fastest on the wing. Small compact flocks of Green-winged Teals often wheel and bank like Rock Doves in flight. Flying birds show no pale wing patches but rather a metallic green speculum bordered in front with chestnut and behind with white.

- **SONG** In courtship a *KRICK-et* note, from which species name is derived; it has been likened to the voice of the Spring Peeper. Female makes a faint *quack*.
- **BEHAVIOR** Forages in shallows by tipping up. Walks easily on land. Feeds in fields, wood lots, and agricultural areas. Primarily feeds on vegetable materials.
- **BREEDING** Monogamous with forced extra pair copulation. Solitary nester.
- **NESTING** Incubation 20–24 days by female. First flight at about 34 days. Precocial young are tended by female but find their own food.

dark glossy green patch from eye to nape with narrow white border below

MALE

rich chestnut head

black bill

vermiculated gray sides and back

buff-white breast with dark spotting

yellowish undertail coverts

gray legs and feet

vertical white bar separates breast from side

dusky brown body with buff mottling

EURASIAN RACE MALE

whitish belly

FEMALE

white undertail coverts with brown mottling

Similar Birds

BLUE-WINGED TEAL ♂
In flight shows white belly and pale blue forewing patches
- female has longer bill. ♀

CINNAMON TEAL ♀
Female is darker brown with longer bill.

Flight Pattern

Swift, sometimes erratic, direct flight.

- **POPULATION** Common. Increasing.
- **CONSERVATION** Vulnerable to ingesting spent lead shot from bottom mud while feeding.

Nest Identification	
Shape Location	Grass, twigs, feathers, and leaves • lined with down • usually among grasses and weeds of meadows, sometimes in open woodlands or brush within 200 feet of water • built by female • 6–18 cream, light olive, buff, or dull white eggs; elliptical to subelliptical, 1.8 inches long.

Plumage Sexes differ	Habitat	Migration Migratory	Weight 12.8 ounces

DATE _____ TIME_____ LOCATION _____

Family ANATIDAE	Species *Aythya valisineria*	Length 19–24 inches	Wingspan 28–36 inches

CANVASBACK

A sloping profile from the front of its crown to the tip of its long dark bill distinguishes this bird. It is one of the largest and heaviest ducks in North America. At a distance the male appears white with a black rear and breast. The long neck and head are rich rust-red. The female is grayer with a rusty tint to the neck and head.

- **SONG** Male makes grunt or croak; female makes quack.
- **BEHAVIOR** A wary species that often rafts well away from the shoreline. Flies high, frequently in formations.

MALE

- sloping profile
- long dark bill
- rust-red neck and head
- black breast
- black tail and undertail coverts
- whitish sides and back

FEMALE

- rusty head and neck
- grayish back and sides

Dives deeply to feed on aquatic vegetation and mollusks.

- **BREEDING** Monogamous. Solitary nester.
- **NESTING** Incubation 23–29 days by female. First flight at about 56–60 days. Tended by female. 1 brood per year.
- **POPULATION** Common to uncommon but local. Declining for some time, but has dropped drastically in recent years because of drought and drainage of marshes where they breed. Currently stable.
- **CONSERVATION** Nesting habitat loss primarily blamed for decline. Releases from hunting pressures and development of nesting habitats may have stabilized populations.

Similar Birds

REDHEAD
Lacks sloping profile
- male has grayer sides • female is darker brown overall.

Flight Pattern

Strong direct flight with rapid wing beats. Flies in straight line or V formation.

Nest Identification

Shape ⬤ ◗ ◖   Location

Dead vegetation lined with down • in marsh in stands of vegetation above shallow water; sometimes on dry ground • built by female • 7–12 grayish or greenish olive eggs, 2.4 inches in diameter.

Plumage Sexes differ	Habitat	Migration Migratory	Weight 2.8 pounds

DATE _____ TIME_____ LOCATION _____

Family ANATIDAE	Species *Aythya americana*	Length 18–22 inches	Wingspan 29–35 inches

REDHEAD

A diving duck of freshwater marshes in summer, this bird congregates in large numbers on marine bays, estuaries, and big lakes in winter. The male's golden yellow eye is the most striking of North American waterfowl. In flight both sexes show a broad gray trailing edge to the wing.

round rufous-brown head

- **SONG** Silent most of year. During courtship male utters mewing sounds, *whee-ough* or *keyair*. Also makes low trilling *rrrrrr*. Female has grating *squak*.
- **BEHAVIOR** Diving duck. Crepuscular activities, including flight and feeding. Some feeding at night.

smoky gray upperparts and sides

black upper and lower tail coverts

black breast

MALE

blue-gray bill with black tip and white subterminal ring

pale at base of bill and on chin

rounded head

Primary diet of aquatic vegetation. Female appears to take initiative in courtship, often chasing males.

- **BREEDING** Monogamous. Brood parasite.

FEMALE

- **NESTING** Incubation 23–29 days by female. Young leave nest about 1 day after hatching. First flight at 56–73 days. Young tended by female but find own food. 1 brood per year.
- **POPULATION** Locally common. Declining in East. Far fewer than historical levels. Decrease due to loss of nesting habitat to agriculture, draining of wetlands, and drought.
- **CONSERVATION** Strictly regulated with hunting bag limits; some regions have no harvesting.

Similar Birds	
♂ ♂	CANVASBACK Male is whiter on sides and back; longer all-dark bill; sloping profile.
♀ ♂	GREATER SCAUP LESSER SCAUP Pale color on wings of female does not extend to primaries.
♀	RING-NECKED DUCK Female has peaked head.

Flight Pattern
Rapid direct flight with strong wing beats. Flies in V formation.

Nest Identification	
Shape 🦆 Location 🌾🌾	Dead vegetation and down anchored to standing growth • on bed of reeds and cattails connected to vegetation or set in thick marsh grasses above water • built by female • 9–14 pale olive, buff, or dull white eggs, 2.4 inches long • number of eggs hard to determine because Females lay eggs in nests of other Redheads.

Plumage Sexes differ	Habitat 🌾 〜〜	Migration Migratory	Weight 2.6 pounds

DATE _____ TIME_____ LOCATION _____

Family ANATIDAE	Species *Aythya collaris*	Length 14–18 inches	Wingspan 24–30 inches

RING-NECKED DUCK

This puffy-headed diving duck with a peaked crown prefers small freshwater ponds, wooded lakes, and swamps. On water the male appears dark with whitish gray sides separated from the black breast by a white crescent that is clearly discernible at a distance. Both sexes have a white ring on the bill, white bellies, bluish gray legs and feet, and show a gray wing stripe in flight. The cinnamon ring at the base of the neck, which gives the duck its name, is a poor field mark, seen only at close range in good light.

peaked black head with purplish gloss

MALE

blue-gray bill with black tip and broad white subterminal ring

pale gray sides and flanks

black tail and back

black breast and neck

peaked head

white eye ring and thin postocular stripe

FEMALE

pale face at base of bill, chin, and throat

- **SONG** Generally silent. Male makes a faint wheezy whistle; female makes harsh *deeeer*.
- **BEHAVIOR** Swims lightly with head up. Excellent diver. Aquatic plants more than 80 percent of diet. Feeds on bottom as deep as 40 feet below surface.
- **BREEDING** Monogamous. Solitary nester.
- **NESTING** Incubation 25–29 days by female. Young leave nest in 12–24 hours. First flight after 49–56 days. Young tended by female but find own food. 1 brood per year.
- **POPULATION** Fairly common and widespread. Stable or increasing.
- **CONSERVATION** As with other ducks that feed on the bottom, may ingest lead shot and be susceptible to lead poisoning.

Similar Birds

♂ ♀ **GREATER SCAUP LESSER SCAUP** White wing stripe • male has gray back • female has white ring around bill.

♂ ♀ **TUFTED DUCK** Males have white flanks • head rounded with tuft on back of crown; both sexes lack broad white band on bill • female lacks pale eye line; has shorter tuft on crown.

Flight Pattern	

Direct flight with rapid wing beats in loose flocks.

Nest Identification	
Shape 🥚 🥚 🥣 Location ✶✶✶ 🌾	Grasses, sedges, and weeds • lined with down and marsh plants • on dry hammock, clump of brush, or floating mat of vegetation, close to open water or just above water in marsh border of pond or slough • built by female • 6–14 olive, gray, olive-brown, or green-buff eggs; elliptical to oval, 2.3 inches long.

Plumage Sexes differ	Habitat 〰️ 〰️	Migration Migratory	Weight 1.6 pounds

Family ANATIDAE	Species *Aythya marila*	Length 15–20 inches	Wingspan 30–34 inches

GREATER SCAUP

Breeding farther north than related species, this large diving duck prefers ponds and lakes in summer. It winters primarily along the coast, often in floating flocks or "rafts" of tens of thousands. The color of the gloss on the male's head usually greenish. From a distance on the water males appear black in front, white in the middle, and black behind. In flight the white wing stripe extends onto the primaries.

rounded black head with greenish gloss

blue-gray bill

MALE

• **SONG** Usually quiet. Common note is loud *scaup*. Courting males make soft whistled *week-week-whew*; female makes low *harrrr*.

finely barred gray flanks and back

black neck and breast

black tail and tail coverts

• **BEHAVIOR** Diving duck. Often winters in huge flocks. Dives to 20 feet below surface to feed on variety of insects, plants, and vertebrates in summer. Diet at sea primarily mollusks and vegetable matter.

white around face at base of bill

white sides and belly

dark brown upperparts

JUVENILE

white belly

• **BREEDING** Monogamous. May nest in colonies.

• **NESTING** Incubation 24–28 days by female. Precocial young led to water shortly after hatching. First flight at 35–42 days. Young tended by female but find own food. 1 brood per year.

gray legs and feet

FEMALE

Similar Birds

♂ LESSER SCAUP
Smaller • male has grayer sides; more pointed head with usually purplish gloss
♀ • females similar; white on wing does not extend onto primaries.

• **POPULATION** Common to uncommon. Abundant in winter, with most individuals wintering along seacoasts.

• **CONSERVATION** Heavy winter concentrations in coastal bays may be vulnerable to oil spills and other pollution.

Flight Pattern
Direct flight with strong rapid wing beats.

Nest Identification	
Shape ⚬⚬ ⊷ Location ⊷⊷ ⊷	Lined with dead plant material and down • usually very close to water on an island, shoreline, or mats of floating vegetation • built by female • 5–11 dark olive-buff eggs, 2.5 inches long.

Plumage Sexes differ	Habitat 〰 〰	Migration Migratory	Weight 2.1 pounds

DATE _____ TIME_____ LOCATION _____

Family ANATIDAE	Species *Aythya affinis*	Length 15–18 inches	Wingspan 24–33 inches

LESSER SCAUP

Like the very similar Greater Scaup, at a distance the male appears dark in front, white in the middle, and dark behind. The Lesser Scaup has a more pointed head. The gloss on the male's head is usually purplish. In flight the white wing stripe confined to the secondaries. The Lesser Scaup is more commonly seen inland in winter than the Greater Scaup and is perhaps the most abundant diving duck in North America.

pointed black head with purple gloss

MALE

medium gray barring on back and flanks

bluish gray bill

- **SONG** Courting males utter low, whistled *whew*. Females make odd

black tail and tail coverts

white at base of bill

black breast and neck

rattling purr, *kwuh-h-h-h.*

dark brown head, neck, breast, and upperparts

mottled brown sides

- **BEHAVIOR** Diving duck. Behavior similar to closely related Greater Scaup. Diet varies with habitat but fairly evenly distributed between plant and animal materials.

FEMALE

- **BREEDING** Monogamous. Solitary nester.
- **NESTING** Incubation 21–28 days by female. Precocial young leave nest shortly after hatching. First flight after 45–50 days. Young tended by female but find own food.
- **POPULATION** Common. Slight decrease in 20th century.

Similar Birds

♂ **GREATER SCAUP**
Larger; white wing stripe extends through secondaries and onto primaries • male has whiter sides; more rounded head. ♀

- **CONSERVATION** Deaths due to fishing nets and lines may be significant. Like many other waterfowl, ingests lead shot on bottom while feeding, often resulting in death. Increased use of steel shot intended to eliminate this.

Flight Pattern
Swift direct flight with strong wing beats.

Nest Identification	
Shape	Location	Addition of some grasses • lined with down • on dry land close to water, often on islands, in tall prairie grass • built by female • 6–15 olive or olive-buff eggs; elliptical to nearly oval, 2.3 inches long.

Plumage Sexes differ	Habitat	Migration Migratory	Weight 1.9 pounds

DATE _____ TIME_____ LOCATION _____

Family ANATIDAE	Species *Melanitta perspicillata*	Length 17–21 inches	Wingspan 30–36 inches

SURF SCOTER

The male's black-and-white head pattern has given it the nickname "skunk head." The bill of both sexes is swollen at its base, and that of the male is a bright combination of red, orange, black, and white. The bill and forehead form a slope similar to that of the Canvasback. In flight the wings are dark and have no pattern.

- **SONG** Usually silent but sometimes makes low throaty notes. During courtship male whistles and has gurgling call.
- **BEHAVIOR** Very common along the coasts in winter, where it often feeds beyond the

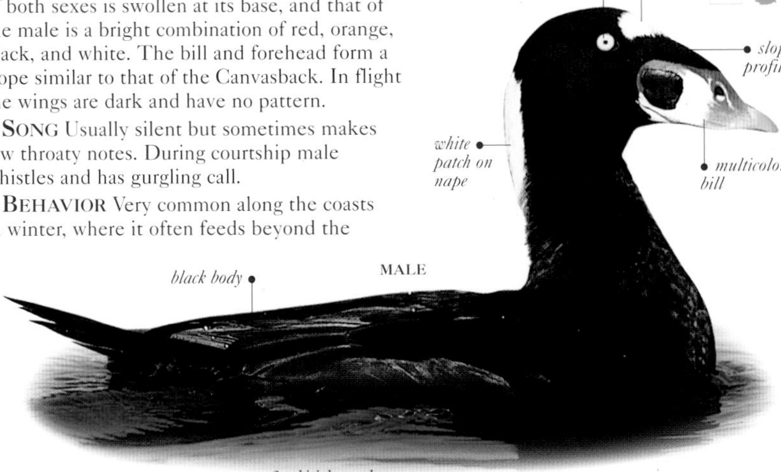

white patch on forehead

white eye

sloping profile

white patch on nape

multicolored bill

black body

MALE

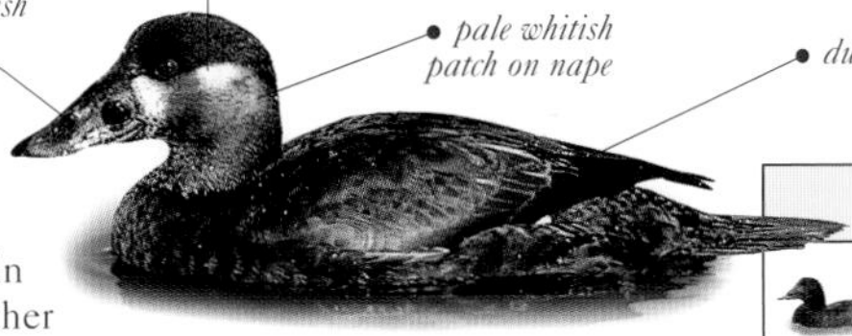

2 whitish patches on side of head

swollen greenish black bill

pale whitish patch on nape

dusky brown body

FEMALE

surf line by diving for food, primarily mollusks and crustaceans. Occurs in rafts offshore with other two scoters. Long strings of scoters may be seen as they move along the coast in winter.

- **BREEDING** Monogamous.
- **NESTING** Incubation by female. Precocial young leave nest shortly after hatching. First flight within 55 days. Fed by female. 1 brood per year.
- **POPULATION** Common to abundant. May have declined, but now stable and numerous. Declining in the West; the cause is unknown, but hunting is a possibility.

Similar Birds

WHITE-WINGED SCOTER ♀
Female has white wing patch.

BLACK SCOTER ♂ ♀
Lacks head pattern
- female has pale face and foreneck.

Flight Pattern

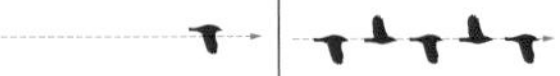

Rapid direct flight with strong wing beats. Flies in straight line formation.

Nest Identification

Shape — — Location — — —

Lined with down and weeds • on ground, often some distance from water, and well hidden under low tree branches or grass clumps • built by female • 5–8 pale buff, pinkish, or buff-white eggs, 2.4 inches long.

Plumage Sexes differ	Habitat	Migration Migratory	Weight 2.2 pounds

DATE _____ TIME_____ LOCATION _____

Family ANATIDAE	Species *Melanitta fusca*	Length 19–24 inches	Wingspan 33–41 inches

WHITE-WINGED SCOTER

The largest of the scoters is the only one with a white speculum, which is seen easily in flight but may show as a white patch in the folded wing or be concealed. Scoters may fly in bunched flocks, long lines, or V formations. Winter duck hunters along the Atlantic Coast discovered that when these ducks were flying too high overhead or too distant to shoot, they often would come closer when shouted at loudly.

white "swish" mark passes through eye

brownish wash on sides

black body MALE

white speculum may show as patch in folded wing

red, white, black, and orange bill with black knob at base

brownish gray bill with small knob at base

2 indistinct white spots on face

sooty brown body

FEMALE

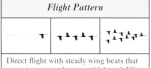

• **SONG** Both sexes utter whistle note in courtship; hoarse croak. In flight produces 6–8 bell-like notes.

Similar Birds

♂ SURF SCOTER
Lacks white wing patches • male has white forehead and patch on back of neck
♀ • female has 2 white patches on sides of face.

♂ BLACK SCOTER
Lacks white wing patches • male has solid black head • female has whitish-brown cheeks, chin, throat, and sides of neck.

♀

• **BEHAVIOR** Dives to depths of 40 feet. Feeds primarily on shellfish, which it swallows whole and breaks up with grinding action of powerful gizzard.

• **BREEDING** Monogamous. Solitary nester.

• **NESTING** Incubation 25–31 days by female. First flight at 63–75 days. Tended by female. 1 brood per year.

• **POPULATION** Common to abundant. Perhaps the most common scoter.

• **CONSERVATION** Sea ducks are vulnerable to pollution of wintering habitats and oil spills close to coasts.

Flight Pattern

Direct flight with steady wing beats that sometimes seem heavy and labored. Flies in straight line or V formation.

Nest Identification

Shape — Location

Lined with leaves, sticks, and down • on ground • built by female • 5–17 light ocher, pinkish, or creamy buff eggs; nearly elliptical, 2.6 inches long.

Plumage Sexes differ	Habitat	Migration Migratory	Weight 3.9 pounds

DATE _____ TIME_____ LOCATION _____

Family ANATIDAE	Species *Melanitta nigra*	Length 17–21 inches	Wingspan 30–35 inches

BLACK SCOTER

One of the large sea ducks, most birds of this species are seen on wintering grounds along both coasts. The male is the only all-black duck in North America. In flight both sexes show a silvery gray sheen on the flight feathers that contrasts with the black linings of the underwings. Wings make a whistling sound in flight. Males often winter further north than females, keeping in tight-knit flocks on the water. Adult males have brownish black feet and legs.

all-black plumage

yellow-orange knob on black bill

MALE

sooty brown cap

dark bill

center line to hindneck and body

pale brownish gray cheeks, sides of head, and foreneck

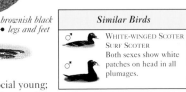

• **SONG** Usually silent. Male's melancholy mellow *cour-loo* thought by some to be the most musical duck call. In courtship male whistles; female has abrasive *cour-loo*.

• **BEHAVIOR** Diving duck. Usually feeds in shallower more protected waters about 25 feet deep. Primary diet is mollusks.

FEMALE

brownish black legs and feet

Similar Birds
♂ WHITE-WINGED SCOTER SURF SCOTER Both sexes show white patches on head in all plumages. ♂

• **BREEDING** Monogamous.

• **NESTING** Incubation 27–28 days by female. Precocial young; first flight at about 46 days. Female tends young but leaves after 7–21 days. 1 brood per year.

• **POPULATION** Common to fairly common; casual to uncommon in the winter in interior. Declining.

• **CONSERVATION** Vulnerable to coastal oil spills.

Flight Pattern
⊤ ⊤⊥⊤⊥⊤ ⊤⊥⊤⊥⊤⊥

Strong direct flight with rapid wing beats. Flies in straight line and V formation.

Nest Identification	
Shape 〰 ⬗ Location 🪹 🪺	Coarse grass • lined with feathers • on ground hidden in standing grass or under shrub • built by female • 5–8 buff to pink-buff eggs; elliptical to oval, 2.5 x 1.7 inches.

Plumage Sexes differ	Habitat ___ 〰〰 〰〰	Migration Migratory	Weight 2.4 pounds

DATE _____ TIME_____ LOCATION _____

Family ANATIDAE	Species *Clangula hyemalis*	Length 15–22 inches	Wingspan 26–31 inches

LONG-TAILED DUCK

Both the genus name and the former common name of Oldsquaw refer to the almost continuous chatter of this long-tailed sea duck. It is the only duck that undergoes two complete brilliant molts annually, plus an eclipse plumage. Winter males have a mostly white body with brownish black patches on the face, breast, and back, and a long black tail. Winter females appear similar but have a paler head. In flight both sexes show uniform dark wings without markings.

pale face patch

MALE

brownish black overall

stubby black bill with pinkish ring

long black tail

white sides and flanks

dark head

whitish postocular stripe curves behind ear to neck

dark upperparts

stubby gray bill

FEMALE

white underparts

WINTER PLUMAGE

• **SONG** Melodious *ow-ow-owdle-ow* calls that may be heard for a mile. Noisy at all seasons.

• **BEHAVIOR** Gregarious. This duck dives frequently and has been caught in fishermen's nets at 200 feet. Breeds on freshwater pools in tundra, but winters on very large lakes and ocean. Often flies close to water in tight bunched flocks.

• **BREEDING** Monogamous.

• **NESTING** Incubation 24–29 days by female. Precocial young leave nest shortly after hatching. First flight at 35–40 days. Young tended by female and frequently by an extra female but find own food. 1 brood per year.

• **POPULATION** Abundant; numbers in the millions.

• **CONSERVATION** Dense concentrations vulnerable to oil spills and other pollution of northern seas. Large numbers sometimes caught and drowned in fishing nets.

Similar Birds

NORTHERN PINTAIL ♂
Lacks face patches; greenish brown speculum; never pied.

Flight Pattern

Swift direct flight often with erratic side-to-side turns of body.

Nest Identification

Shape ↙ ⬤   Location ⚬⚬⚬ ⚘

Lined with available plant material and large amount of down • on dry ground close to water, partially hidden under low vegetation or rocks • built by female • 5–11 olive-buff, greenish yellow, or olive-gray eggs; 2.1 inches long.

Plumage Sexes differ	Habitat ▬ ≈ ⩘ ⩘	Migration Migratory	Weight 2.1 pounds

DATE _____ TIME_____ LOCATION _____

Family ANATIDAE	Species *Bucephala albeola*	Length 13–16 inches	Wingspan 20–24 inches

BUFFLEHEAD

The name of this large-headed duck, which means buffalo-headed or ox-headed, belies the Bufflehead's agility in flying, swimming, and diving. It is the smallest diving duck, but it is one of the best divers. In flight the male's pink legs and feet are bright against white underparts, and a white patch crosses the entire inner wing; female shows white in the secondaries only. These birds nest only in North America.

- **SONG** Squeaky whistle and low squealing or growling call.

large white patch from eye to crown

black back

large dark head with green to purple gloss in good light

In courtship makes loud grating or chattering noise. Female has a harsh quack, *ec-ec-ec* and buzzy *cuc-cuc-cuc*.

- **BEHAVIOR** Can take off directly from water unlike other diving ducks. Uses feet to swim underwater. Dives in groups for safety, leaving "lookouts" on surface. Eats aquatic insects, larvae, snails, small fish, and aquatic plant seeds. On saltwater eats shrimp and other crustaceans, shellfish, and snails. Male performs head-bobbing display in courtship.

MALE *mostly white body*   *small bill*

small white cheek patch

gray-brown body

white underparts   **FEMALE**

- **BREEDING** Monogamous. Solitary nester.
- **NESTING** Incubation 28–33 days by female. Precocial young leave nest by jumping out of tree cavity within 1 day of hatching. Tended by female. First flight at 50–55 days. 1 brood per year.

Similar Birds

HOODED MERGANSER ♂
Larger; brown sides; spikelike bill; large crest that can be fanned or lowered.

RUDDY DUCK ♂
Winter male resembles female Bufflehead
- longer bill and tail; large white cheek patch.

- **POPULATION** Common but has declined.
- **BIRDHOUSES** Will use nest boxes located near water.
- **CONSERVATION** Much less numerous now due to unrestricted shooting in the 20th century and loss of habitat.

Flight Pattern
Swift direct flight with rapid wing beats.

Nest Identification
Shape 🪶² Location 🌱🪺🐚📦

No material added to nest • will use wooden box placed in tree • 8–10 ivory-yellow, light olive-buff, or cream to pale buff eggs; elliptical to oval in shape, 2 x 1.5 inches.

Plumage Sexes differ	Habitat 〰️	Migration Migratory	Weight 1.0 pound

DATE _____ TIME _____ LOCATION _____

Family ANATIDAE	Species *Bucephala clangula*	Length 16–20 inches	Wingspan 25–32 inches

COMMON GOLDENEYE

In flight, on its whistling wings, the male shows more white plumage than any other North American duck except for the Common Merganser. Both sexes exhibit large white wing patches in flight. The small tight flocks often fly high.

• **SONG** During courtship male has grating *zee–zeee* or *zee-zee-at*, resembling call of Common Nighthawk. Female has abrasive low quack.

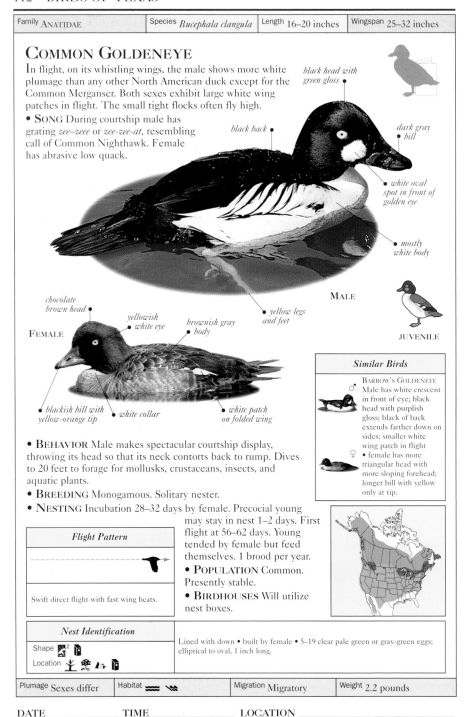

black head with green gloss

black back

dark gray bill

white oval spot in front of golden eye

mostly white body

MALE

chocolate brown head

yellowish white eye

brownish gray body

yellow legs and feet

FEMALE

JUVENILE

blackish bill with yellow-orange tip

white collar

white patch on folded wing

Similar Birds

BARROW'S GOLDENEYE
♂ Male has white crescent in front of eye; black head with purplish gloss; black of back extends farther down on sides; smaller white wing patch in flight
♀ • female has more triangular head with more sloping forehead; longer bill with yellow only at tip.

• **BEHAVIOR** Male makes spectacular courtship display, throwing its head so that its neck contorts back to rump. Dives to 20 feet to forage for mollusks, crustaceans, insects, and aquatic plants.

• **BREEDING** Monogamous. Solitary nester.

• **NESTING** Incubation 28–32 days by female. Precocial young may stay in nest 1–2 days. First flight at 56–62 days. Young tended by female but feed themselves. 1 brood per year.

• **POPULATION** Common. Presently stable.

• **BIRDHOUSES** Will utilize nest boxes.

Flight Pattern
Swift direct flight with fast wing beats.

Nest Identification	
Shape	Lined with down • built by female • 5–19 clear pale green or gray-green eggs; elliptical to oval, 1 inch long.
Location	

Plumage Sexes differ	Habitat	Migration Migratory	Weight 2.2 pounds

DATE _____ TIME_____ LOCATION _____

Family ANATIDAE	Species *Lophodytes cucullatus*	Length 16–19 inches	Wingspan 24–26 inches

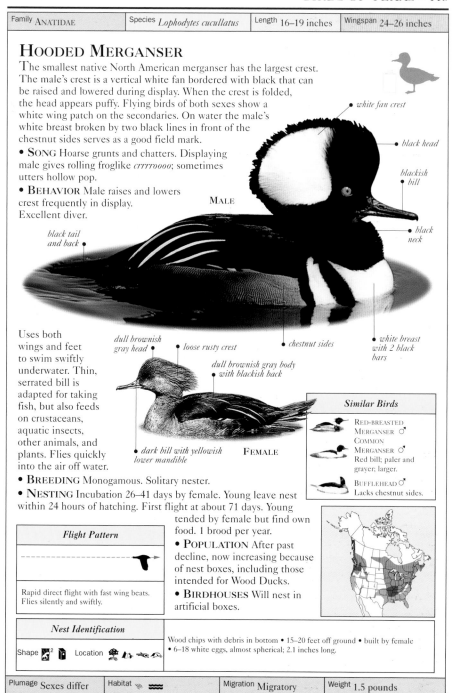

HOODED MERGANSER

The smallest native North American merganser has the largest crest. The male's crest is a vertical white fan bordered with black that can be raised and lowered during display. When the crest is folded, the head appears puffy. Flying birds of both sexes show a white wing patch on the secondaries. On water the male's white breast broken by two black lines in front of the chestnut sides serves as a good field mark.

• **SONG** Hoarse grunts and chatters. Displaying male gives rolling froglike *crrrroooo*; sometimes utters hollow pop.

• **BEHAVIOR** Male raises and lowers crest frequently in display. Excellent diver.

white fan crest

black head

blackish bill

black neck

MALE

black tail and back

Uses both wings and feet to swim swiftly underwater. Thin, serrated bill is adapted for taking fish, but also feeds on crustaceans, aquatic insects, other animals, and plants. Flies quickly into the air off water.

dull brownish gray head

loose rusty crest

chestnut sides

white breast with 2 black bars

dull brownish gray body with blackish back

dark bill with yellowish lower mandible

FEMALE

Similar Birds

RED-BREASTED MERGANSER ♂
COMMON MERGANSER ♂
Red bill; paler and grayer; larger.

BUFFLEHEAD ♂
Lacks chestnut sides.

• **BREEDING** Monogamous. Solitary nester.

• **NESTING** Incubation 26–41 days by female. Young leave nest within 24 hours of hatching. First flight at about 71 days. Young tended by female but find own food. 1 brood per year.

• **POPULATION** After past decline, now increasing because of nest boxes, including those intended for Wood Ducks.

• **BIRDHOUSES** Will nest in artificial boxes.

Flight Pattern

Rapid direct flight with fast wing beats. Flies silently and swiftly.

Nest Identification

Shape | Location

Wood chips with debris in bottom • 15–20 feet off ground • built by female • 6–18 white eggs, almost spherical; 2.1 inches long.

Plumage Sexes differ	Habitat	Migration Migratory	Weight 1.5 pounds

DATE _____ TIME_____ LOCATION _____

Family ANATIDAE	Species *Mergus merganser*	Length 22–27 inches	Wingspan 31–37 inches

COMMON MERGANSER

The Common Merganser is the largest merganser in North America. The male's mostly white body, dark head, and red bill easily distinguish it from the other mergansers at a distances or in flight. This is the only merganser in North America in which the female is crested and the male is not.

• **SONG** Male makes harsh croaks; female makes loud harsh *karr karr.*

• **BEHAVIOR** Expert diver pursues small fish under water. Also feeds on mollusks, crustaceans, aquatic insects, and some plants. In winter often stays as far north as open water will allow. Patters across water or land to build up speed for takeoff. Often flies low following stream courses.

• **BREEDING** Monogamous. Solitary nester.

• **NESTING** Incubation 28–35 days by female. Young remain in nest 1 day or more. First flight at 65–70 days. Young tended by female but find own food. 1 brood per year.

• **POPULATION** Fairly common. Stable in US; may be increasing in Europe.

• **BIRDHOUSES** Will use man-made nest boxes.

• **CONSERVATION** Some fishermen feel it competes for their catches and try to kill indiscriminately.

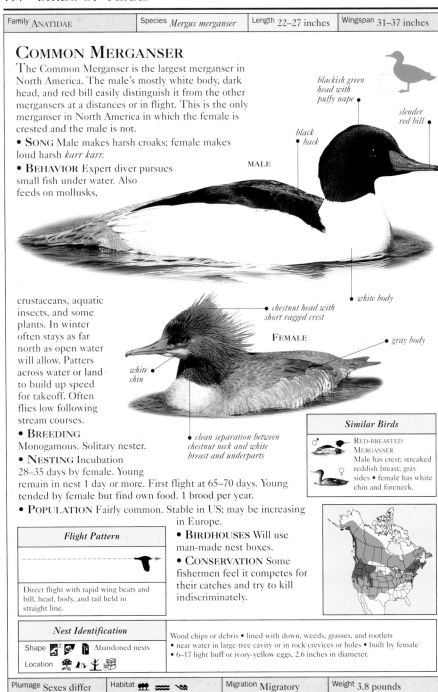

blackish green head with puffy nape

slender red bill

black back

MALE

white body

chestnut head with short ragged crest

FEMALE

gray body

white chin

clean separation between chestnut neck and white breast and underparts

Similar Birds

♂ RED-BREASTED MERGANSER Male has crest; streaked reddish breast; gray sides • female has white chin and foreneck.

Flight Pattern

Direct flight with rapid wing beats and bill, head, body, and tail held in straight line.

Nest Identification

Shape [symbols] Abandoned nests
Location [symbols]

Wood chips or debris • lined with down, weeds, grasses, and rootlets • near water in large tree cavity or in rock crevices or holes • built by female • 6–17 light buff or ivory-yellow eggs, 2.6 inches in diameter.

Plumage Sexes differ	Habitat [symbols]	Migration Migratory	Weight 3.8 pounds

DATE _____ TIME _____ LOCATION _____

Family ANATIDAE	Species *Mergus serrator*	Length 16–26 inches	Wingspan 31–35 inches

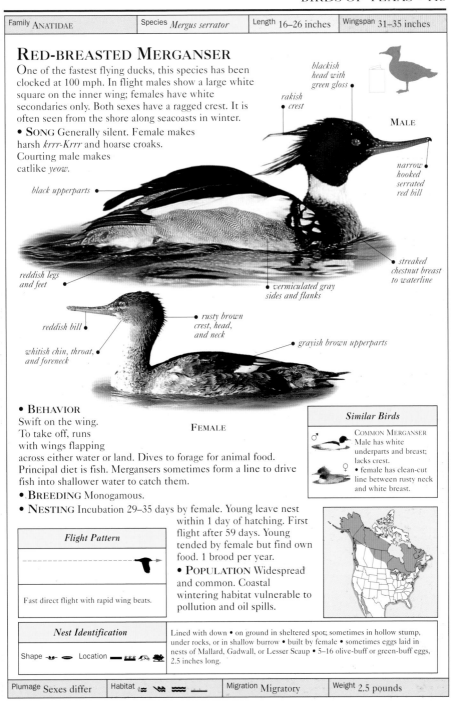

RED-BREASTED MERGANSER

One of the fastest flying ducks, this species has been clocked at 100 mph. In flight males show a large white square on the inner wing; females have white secondaries only. Both sexes have a ragged crest. It is often seen from the shore along seacoasts in winter.

- **SONG** Generally silent. Female makes harsh *krrr-Krrr* and hoarse croaks. Courting male makes catlike *yeow*.

blackish head with green gloss

rakish crest

MALE

narrow hooked serrated red bill

black upperparts

reddish legs and feet

streaked chestnut breast to waterline

vermiculated gray sides and flanks

reddish bill

rusty brown crest, head, and neck

whitish chin, throat, and foreneck

grayish brown upperparts

- **BEHAVIOR**
Swift on the wing. To take off, runs with wings flapping across either water or land. Dives to forage for animal food. Principal diet is fish. Mergansers sometimes form a line to drive fish into shallower water to catch them.

FEMALE

- **BREEDING** Monogamous.
- **NESTING** Incubation 29–35 days by female. Young leave nest within 1 day of hatching. First flight after 59 days. Young tended by female but find own food. 1 brood per year.
- **POPULATION** Widespread and common. Coastal wintering habitat vulnerable to pollution and oil spills.

Similar Birds

♂ COMMON MERGANSER Male has white underparts and breast; lacks crest.

♀ female has clean-cut line between rusty neck and white breast.

Flight Pattern
Fast direct flight with rapid wing beats.

Nest Identification	
Shape ⚬ ⚬ Location ▬ ▬ ⚬ ⚬	Lined with down • on ground in sheltered spot; sometimes in hollow stump, under rocks, or in shallow burrow • built by female • sometimes eggs laid in nests of Mallard, Gadwall, or Lesser Scaup • 5–16 olive-buff or green-buff eggs, 2.5 inches long.

Plumage Sexes differ	Habitat ⚬ ⚬ ⚬ ⚬	Migration Migratory	Weight 2.5 pounds

DATE _____ TIME _____ LOCATION _____

Family ANATIDAE	Species *Nomonyx dominicus*	Length 12–14 inches	Wingspan 20 inches

MASKED DUCK

A small, tropical duck that rarely wanders to, and even more rarely nests in, the southern United States. The Masked Duck is usually found in densely vegetated, warm freshwater pools and marshes. This is one of the "stiff-tailed" ducks closely related to the common and widespread Ruddy Duck. Both sexes show large white patches on the inner wing in flight.

black crown, forehead, and face

• SONG Courtship calls of *coo-coo-coo, ooo-ooo-ooo, du-du-du, kirroo-kirroo*. When alarmed male makes loud *kuri-kuroo*, often repeated. Female makes henlike clucking and hissing noises.

MALE

long spiked blackish tail

bluish bill

rich cinnamon-brown body with black mottling

brown bill

whitish brown face with blackish brown lines across cheek

brown body with buff mottling

• BEHAVIOR A shy and somewhat secretive duck that hides in the dense vegetation in water. Dives for food; diet consists primarily of aquatic plants, some insects, and crustaceans. Can sink slowly into the water. Takeoffs from water are often accomplished by first diving beneath the surface and bursting up in flight from below. As with other "stiff tails" often holds long stiff tail fanned on water or wrenlike over back.

brown neck

FEMALE

WINTER MALE

Similar Birds

♂ RUDDY DUCK Male has blackish cap; white cheeks • female has single dark stripe on cheek • both sexes lack white inner wing patch.

• BREEDING Monogamous.

• NESTING Incubation 28 days by female. Young tended by female but probably find own food. 1 brood per year.

• POPULATION Casual to rare; local. Does not seem to have large populations anywhere. Infrequent and local nesting in coastal Texas and Louisiana.

Flight Pattern

Direct flight, often close to water, with fast wing beats.

Nest Identification	
Shape ⬬ 🥥 🥚 Location 🌾 🌱	Roofed over, basketball-like • made of reeds and grasses • sparsely lined with down • among marsh vegetation in shallow water or near water • built by female • 4–10 white or buff eggs; subelliptical, 2.5 inches long.

Plumage Sexes differ	Habitat 〰	Migration Nonmigratory	Weight 12.8 ounces

DATE _____ TIME_____ LOCATION _____

Family ANATIDAE	Species *Oxyura jamaicensis*	Length 14–16 inches	Wingspan 21–24 inches

RUDDY DUCK

This big-headed chunky duck has a long stiff tail that is often cocked and fanned forward. Wings are uniform in color. In winter males become gray-brown with a gray bill. In breeding season found in pairs or small loose groups on freshwater lakes and ponds. After nesting, may occur in large flocks; in winter it can be found on salt bays.

blackish cap reaches below eye

long stiff black tail

blue bill

white cheeks

MALE

rust-red body

- **SONG** Usually silent. In courtship male utters continual *chuck-chuck-chuck-chuck-churrr*.
- **BEHAVIOR** Diving duck that can sink slowly beneath the surface like a grebe. When disturbed often swims away underwater instead of flying away. Gray legs and feet are placed so far beneath the body that it cannot walk upright. Primary diet of vegetable materials. A relatively tame bird.

whitish belly with light brown barring

blackish gray bill

white cheek with dark brown horizontal streak

brown-gray upperparts

WINTER PLUMAGE

FEMALE

pale underparts with fine brown barring

- **BREEDING** Monogamous.
- **NESTING** Incubation 23–26 days by female. Young leave nest within a day of hatching. First flight at 42–48 days. Young tended by female but feed themselves. 1 brood per year, sometimes 2 in the South.
- **POPULATION** Fairly common to common. Current levels are lower than in the past.
- **CONSERVATION** Reasons for decline unknown, but this bird is very tame and easily killed by hunters. Shallow-water nesting areas are subject to draining for agriculture and droughts.

Similar Birds

MASKED DUCK
Male lacks white cheek
- female has 2 dark lines across face
- population very local.

CINNAMON TEAL
Lacks stiff tail and white cheeks; large pale blue forewing patch in flight
- female lacks line through face.

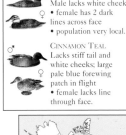

Flight Pattern

Jerky direct flight with rapid wing beats.

Nest Identification	
Shape Location	Grasses and cattails • lined with down • in dense marsh vegetation over shallow water • sometimes uses abandoned nests • built by female • 5–17 creamy white or nest-stained eggs, 2.5 inches long • eggs huge compared to body size and similar in size to those laid by much larger ducks.

Plumage Sexes differ	Habitat	Migration Migratory	Weight 1.3 pounds

DATE _____ TIME_____ LOCATION _____

Family ACCIPITRIDAE	Species *Pandion haliaetus*	Length 21–24 inches	Wingspan 54–72 inches

OSPREY

A kindred of other diurnal birds of prey, the Osprey is so distinctive it is sometimes placed in it own family. Its large size and uniquely curved claws allow the Osprey to carry a large fish a considerable distance to feed to its young in the nest. Occasionally an eagle dives upon an Osprey carrying a fish, forces a release, and catches the fish for itself before the fish hits the water.

dark brown upperparts with purplish gloss

mostly white head

broad black mark through cheeks and sides of neck

• **SONG** Series of loud whistled *kyews* or melodious whistle of *chewk-chewk-chewk* or *cheap-cheap-cheap*.

clear white belly

long tail with narrow black bars

toes equal in length on claws curved into one-third of a circle

• **BEHAVIOR** Eats mainly fish. Dives into water to catch prey from 30–100 feet above surface. Holds fish with both feet, stops to shake water out of feathers, points fish head forward to decrease wind resistance, and carries to perch or to feed young. Often flies with distinctive crook or kink in wing bent at wrist, which has a black patch.

• **BREEDING** Monogamous. Colonial or solitary nester.

• **NESTING** Incubation 32–43 days by both sexes; however, female does more, while male brings food. Semialtricial young stay in nest 48–59 days. Fed by both parents. 1 brood per year.

JUVENILE

• **POPULATION** Uncommon inland; species is fairly common in its coastal range.

• **BIRDHOUSES** Osprey will build nest on man-made cartwheel on pole or on platforms built in marshes.

Similar Birds

BALD EAGLE
Entirely white head and tail; crown held flat; dark underparts and underwings • juvenile has entirely dark head and patchy tannish white underwings.

• **CONSERVATION** Endangered in 1950s because of chemical pollution (especially DDT), but has since made a comeback, at least partly by transplanting young into areas where entire populations had been extirpated.

Flight Pattern
Deep, slow wing beats alternate with glides; sometimes soars on thermals.

Nest Identification	
Shape	Location

Sticks, sod, cow dung, seaweed, rubbish, and similar material • up to 200 feet above ground in dead or live trees near or over water, or atop telephone poles or bridges • built by both sexes • usually 3 white or pinkish eggs marked with brown and olive; 2.4 x 1 inches long.

Plumage Sexes similar	Habitat	Migration Migratory	Weight 3.1 pounds

DATE _____ TIME_____ LOCATION _____

Family ACCIPITRIDAE	Species *Chondrohierax uncinatus*	Length 16 inches	Wingspan 34–37 inches

HOOK-BILLED KITE

A native of South and Central America, this large kite sometimes makes its way to southern Texas. A heap of broken snail shells under a tree is a telltale sign of a nest or habitual perch in the branches above. A black morph exists, but it has not been seen in the United States. Males are slate-gray overall and have white eyes, which can be seen at close range. Females are brown with a barred reddish collar and reddish underparts with white barring. Juveniles have whitish underparts with brown barring, a white collar, and brown eyes.

- **SONG** Gives a musical, oriole-like 2–3 note whistle. Screams and chatters when disturbed, *weh keh-eh-eh-eh-eh-eh-eh.*
- **BEHAVIOR** Diet consists primarily of various types of snails, but it also eats frogs, salamanders, and insects. Its flight is distinctively floppy and loose, and the bird holds its paddle-shaped wings slightly raised and pushed forward.
- **BREEDING** Monogamous.
- **NESTING** Incubation by both sexes. Semialtricial young remain in nest 35–45 days and are fed by both sexes. 1 brood per year.
- **POPULATION** Uncommon.

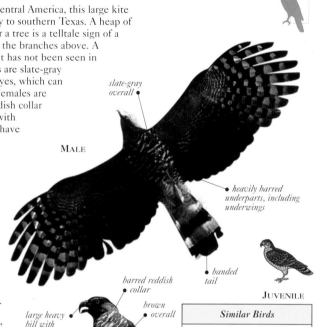

slate-gray overall

MALE

heavily barred underparts, including underwings

banded tail

JUVENILE

barred reddish collar

brown overall

large heavy bill with long hook

reddish underparts with white barring

FEMALE

Similar Birds

ZONE-TAILED HAWK
Larger; wings not paddle-shaped and are held in a dihedral while in flight; lacks barring on underparts.

CRANE HAWK
Larger; narrower blackish underwings; underparts lack barring; bright orange-red legs.

Flight Pattern

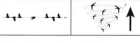

Distinctly loose floppy flight. Soars on thermals and updrafts.

Found in the US only in the lower Rio Grande Valley of southeastern Texas.
- **CONSERVATION** Some decline in the Tropics; West Indies population endangered.

Nest Identification

Shape ⬭ ⬬   Location 🐦

Dead twigs • built by both sexes • 2–3 buff-white eggs marked with reddish brown; 1.8 inches long.

Plumage Sexes differ	Habitat	Migration Nonmigratory	Weight 9.8 ounces

DATE _____ TIME_____ LOCATION _____

Family ACCIPITRIDAE	Species *Elanoides forficatus*	Length 19–25 inches	Wingspan 45–50 inches

SWALLOW-TAILED KITE

Flying swiftly with its wings cleaving the air and its forked tail opening and closing like scissors, the Swallow-tailed Kite is a breathtaking sight. The largest of the North American kites, this bird resembles a huge Barn Swallow. The black upperparts contrast sharply with the white head and underparts. Never taking time to hover, it will drop down to skim the surface of water to bathe or drink and then swoop suddenly up over the treetops. A tropical species that in North America is normally found only in the Southeast in the spring and summer, during spring migration individuals may "overshoot" and appear as far north as New England.

long pointed wings with black flight feathers and white wing linings

snow-white head and hind neck

snow-white underparts

black bill

15–16-inch-long black tail with deep fork

dark brown to red eyes

• **SONG** Utters shrill *ee-ee-ee* or *pee-pee-pee*. When several fly together they make sweet shrill cries of *peat, peat, peat; klee, klee, klee;* or soft whistles.

• **BEHAVIOR** Forms flocks in winter or migration. Catches and eats food while flying. Feeds on insects such as bees, dragonflies, crickets, cicadas, and beetles. Also consumes small snakes, lizards, frogs, and small birds, which often are taken from the treetops.

• **BREEDING** Monogamous. Forms loose colonies.

• **NESTING** Incubation 24–28 days by both sexes, but mostly by female. Semialtricial young stay in nest 36–42 days. Fed by both sexes. Probably only 1 brood per year.

• **POPULATION** Common.

• **CONSERVATION** Listed as endangered in South Carolina. Disappeared from many areas in early 20th century. Population now apparently stable and slowly expanding range.

Similar Birds

MISSISSIPPI KITE
Slightly notched black tail; gray underparts and head.

Flight Pattern

Buoyant flight with deep slow wing beats and glides; a master at soaring on thermals and updrafts.

Nest Identification	Sticks, twigs, moss, and pine needles • lined with leaves and lichen • usually in treetop, 60–130 feet above ground, concealed by thick foliage • built by both sexes • 2–3 white or creamy white eggs marked with brown, sometimes lavender, often concentrated at end; elliptical to short subelliptical, 1.8 x 1.25 inches long.
Shape	
Location	

Plumage Sexes similar	Habitat	Migration Migratory	Weight 15.6 ounces

DATE _____ TIME_____ LOCATION _____

Family ACCIPITRIDAE	Species *Elanus leucurus*	Length 15–17 inches	Wingspan 40–42 inches

WHITE-TAILED KITE

Sometimes called the white hawk, the White-tailed Kite soars and glides like a small gull. When seen from a distance, this gregarious bird appears completely white. Previously called the Black-shouldered Kite, the white linings of the underwing are broken distally by a black "thumb" mark on the wrist. It is the only North American kite to hover while hunting, with tail down and often with legs dangling, over savanna, riparian woodland, marshes, grassy foothills, or the cultivated fields it searches for food. It is a master at soaring on thermals and glides long distances after reaching considerable heights. Juveniles' underparts and head are lightly streaked with rufous.

orange to reddish brown eyes

black bill

pale gray upperparts

black patch on shoulders

white underparts

buff-yellow feet and legs

long white tail

JUVENILE

- **SONG** Brief whistled *keep, keep, keep.*
- **BEHAVIOR** Active hunter. Pauses to hover and study ground before swooping on prey. Eats voles, field mice, pocket gophers, ground squirrels, shrews, small birds, small snakes, lizards, frogs, grasshoppers, crickets, and beetles. Often roosts communally.
- **BREEDING** Monogamous. Nests built close together, sometimes in loose colonies.
- **NESTING** Incubation 30 days by female. Young stay in nest 35–40 days. Fed by both sexes. Male hunts for food and drives away crows and other hawks. Up to 2 broods per year.

Similar Birds

MISSISSIPPI KITE Lacks black shoulders and black "thumb" mark under wing; has black tail.

- **POPULATION** Common but local. Expanded in last half of 20th century.
- **CONSERVATION** Some concern about the spraying of pesticides and insecticides in open environments frequented by this species.

Flight Pattern
Hunts by flying slowly, gracefully, gull-like, with slow measured deep wing beats. Soars on thermals and updrafts.

Nest Identification	
Shape Location	Sticks and twigs • lined with grasses, dry stubble, weed stems, and rootlets • in oaks, cottonwood, or eucalyptus, about 15–60 feet above ground • built by both sexes • 3–6 white eggs, heavily blotched with rich brown; ovate to oval, 1.7 x 1.3 inches.

Plumage Sexes similar	Habitat	Migration Nonmigratory	Weight Undetermined

DATE _____ TIME_____ LOCATION _____

Family ACCIPITRIDAE	Species *Ictinia mississippiensis*	Length 13–17 inches	Wingspan 34–37 inches

MISSISSIPPI KITE

Far from shy, the Mississippi Kite has been seen chasing bats into caves and flying around horseback riders and cattle to catch insects. This bird is not territorial; several might perch together in trees, even during nesting season. They also gather at communal perches and foraging areas, and often soar communally while hunting insects. As many as 20 birds have been recorded following a herd of livestock for flushed insects. The Mississippi Kite never hovers and has a smooth graceful flight with its white secondary feathers showing.

deep red eyes

pale ash-gray head

gray overall

yellow to red legs

JUVENILE

solid black tail

- **SONG** Usually silent. Has alarm call of whistled *kee-e-e*. Also whistles *phee-phew*, *phee-phew*, resembling that of the Osprey.
- **BEHAVIOR** Gracefully catches large flying insects, often eating them in midair. Hunts with flock.
- **BREEDING** Monogamous. Colonial. Little courtship activity occurs on the US breeding grounds as the birds are already paired when they return from wintering in the neotropics.
- **NESTING** Incubation 31–32 days by both sexes. Young remain in nest 34 days, fed by both sexes. 1 brood per year.
- **POPULATION** Common to fairly common. Expanding range, particularly west of the Mississippi River. Regularly strays as far north as the southern Great Lakes region.

Similar Birds

WHITE-TAILED KITE Lighter tail; black shoulder patches; black "thumb" mark under wing.

NORTHERN HARRIER ♂ Male hovers and is larger; dark secondary feathers; white rump patch; facial disk.

Flight Pattern

Buoyant flight with steady wingbeats; sometimes alternates several wing strokes with short to long glides.

Nest Identification	
Shape Location	Sticks and twigs • lined with green leaves and Spanish moss (where available) • in upper branches, small forks, and occasionally on horizontal lines, 30–135 feet above ground • built by both sexes • 1–3 white or bluish white eggs, unmarked or faintly spotted, often nest-stained.

Plumage Sexes similar	Habitat	Migration Migratory	Weight 12.6 ounces

DATE _____ TIME_____ LOCATION _____

Family ACCIPITRIDAE	Species *Haliaeetus leucocephalus*	Length 34–43 inches	Wingspan 6–8 feet

BALD EAGLE

The national bird of the United States has an awe-inspiring wingspan and striking white head and tail that make adults easy to identify. Big concentrations of these huge birds can be seen perched in trees and resting on sandbars when salmon run in rivers of the Northwest. Juveniles can be recognized by their large size; dark brown head, tail, and body; mottled white patches on underwings and underparts; grayish eyes; and light yellow feet.

snow-white head and neck

bright yellow eyes

massive yellow bill and cere

dark brown body

JUVENILE

- **SONG** Both sexes utter gull-like squealing cackle of *kleek-kik-ik-ik-ik* or lower *kak-kak-kak*.
- **BEHAVIOR** Hunts for prey, primarily fish, especially in breeding season. Sometimes steals fish from Ospreys. Also eats carrion and injured or crippled waterfowl, squirrels, rabbits, and muskrats.

white tail

yellow feet and legs

Similar Birds

GOLDEN EAGLE
Similar to juvenile
- adult has less massive bill; less blotchy white on underwings and underparts; golden feathers on head
- juvenile has distinct white patches at base of primaries and base of tail; smaller head and bill; feathered legs.

STELLER'S SEA-EAGLE
Adult has long wedge-shaped white tail; white thighs and shoulders
- juvenile has long wedge-shaped white tail with dark tips
- Alaskan range.

- **BREEDING** Monogamous; thought to pair for life. Solitary nester.
- **NESTING** Incubation 31–46 days by both sexes. Semialtricial young stay in nest 70–98 days until first flight. Fed by both sexes. 1 brood per year.
- **POPULATION** Fairly common to common but local outside Florida and Alaska.
- **CONSERVATION** Protected by national wildlife refuges and legally with heavy fines. Made great comeback, especially in the United States, since the 1970s with widescale restoration programs, and the banning of DDT and other chemical pollutants. Moved from endangered status to threatened.

Flight Pattern

Several deep wing beats alternate with long glides; often flies direct with deep steady wing beats. Also soars on thermals.

Nest Identification

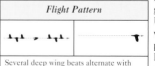

Shape ⌒⌒   Location 🌿 🍂 🪶 —

Made of large sticks and vegetation • deeply lined with fine material • in fork of tall tree or on ledge, 30–60 feet above ground • built by both sexes • 2 bluish white or dull white eggs, often nest-stained; 3 inches long.

Plumage Sexes similar	Habitat 〰️ 🦆	Migration Migratory	Weight 9.1 pounds

DATE _____ TIME_____ LOCATION _____

Family ACCIPITRIDAE	Species *Circus cyaneus*	Length 16–24 inches	Wingspan 38–48 inches

NORTHERN HARRIER

Its owl-like facial disk and white rump patch, which is prominent in flight, set the Northern Harrier apart from all other North American falconiformes. Males take several years to acquire their gray-plumaged upperparts. Their wings are long with black-tipped trailing edges, and the outermost four or five primaries are black.

- **SONG** Shrill calls *kek, kek, kek* or *keee, keee, keee*, especially around the nest.
- **BEHAVIOR** Hunts using low slow flight that consists of alternately flapping and gliding with the wings held in a shallow V above the back. Often quarters back and forth over low vegetation and can turn and drop rapidly on prey that it may detect initially by sound. Feeds on small mammals, especially rodents up to the size of a small rabbit, frogs, snakes, small birds, carrion, and large insects. Sometimes hunts the edges of grass fires to capture prey driven out by the flames. Courtship flight of males is thrillingly acrobatic.
- **BREEDING** Some pairs monogamous; some males are polygamous with up to 3 mates. Solitary nester. Both sexes very vocal with high-pitched screams when defending nest.
- **NESTING** Incubation 31–32 days by female. Semi-altricial young stay in nest 30–35 days, fed by both sexes. 1 brood per year.
- **POPULATION** Common but declining.

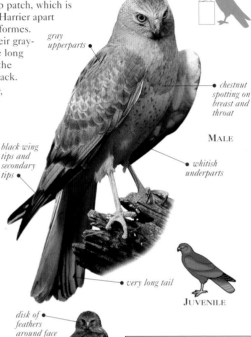

gray upperparts

chestnut spotting on breast and throat

MALE

black wing tips and secondary tips

whitish underparts

very long tail

JUVENILE

disk of feathers around face

brown upperparts

FEMALE

Similar Birds

ROUGH-LEGGED HAWK ♀
Base of tail (not rump) white; broad blackish subterminal band on tail • does not course low over fields but hunts from perch or by hovering.

- **CONSERVATION** Populations have declined everywhere on its breeding range because of the loss of marshland habitat as well as pesticides. Formerly, many were lost to shooting.

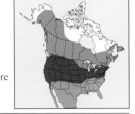

Flight Pattern

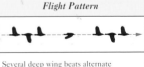

Several deep wing beats alternate with glides.

Nest Identification	
Shape 🦅 ➤　Location 🪹 🌿	Sticks and grass lined with fine material • usually placed on the ground • may be 5 feet above water or marshy terrain • built by both sexes, but female does most construction • 3–9 bluish white eggs, sometimes spotted with brown, 1.8 inches long.

Plumage Sexes differ	Habitat ___	Migration Some migrate	Weight 12.6 ounces

DATE _____ TIME_____ LOCATION _____

Family ACCIPITRIDAE	Species *Accipiter striatus*	Length 10–14 inches	Wingspan 20–28 inches

SHARP-SHINNED HAWK

A territorial bird, the Sharp-shinned Hawk occasionally strikes humans in defense of its nest. Its name describes its flattened, thin tarsus or shank. This is the smallest of the North American accipiters; the female is larger than the male. The head and neck seem small for its long, slender body. Its long tail has three to four narrow black crossbars, and is squared or notched on the tip. Juveniles have brown upperparts and white underparts with heavy brown streaking.

blue-gray upperparts

finely streaked red-brown throat

red-brown bars across chest and belly

white undertail coverts

long bright yellow legs with "sharp shins"

JUVENILE

square or slightly forked tail

narrow white tip on tail

- **SONG** When disturbed utters *kek-kek-kek* or *kik-kik-kik*. Call is melancholy cry.
- **BEHAVIOR** Eats mostly small birds, including songbirds, taken off ground or twigs, or in air. Also eats small mammals (including bats), reptiles, grasshoppers, and other larger insects.
- **BREEDING** Monogamous. Solitary nester.
- **NESTING** Incubation 32–35 days by female. Semialtricial young stay in nest 23–27 days. Fed by both sexes. 1 brood per year.
- **POPULATION** Common to fairly common.
- **FEEDERS** Often attracted to concentrations of small birds at bird feeders, especially in winter.
- **CONSERVATION** Decline during 1950s through 1970s due to pesticides and heavy metal pollutants in environment. Some comeback in 1980s but is perhaps declining again.

Similar Birds

COOPER'S HAWK
Rounded tail; larger (but female Sharp-shinned approach male Cooper's in size); larger head; more contrast between black crown and face; wide white band on tip of tail (can be tricky because of feather wear); sometimes lightly streaked undertail coverts.

Flight Pattern

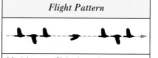

More buoyant flight than other accipiters with several rapid wing beats between glides.

Nest Identification

Shape — Location

Made of sticks and twigs • lined with strips of bark, grass, and coniferous needles • sometimes in deciduous trees but usually conifers, 10–60 feet above ground, next to trunk • 4–5 white or bluish eggs marked with browns, 1.5 inches long.

Plumage Sexes similar	Habitat	Migration Some migrate	Weight 3.6 ounces

DATE _____ TIME_____ LOCATION _____

Family ACCIPITRIDAE	Species *Accipiter cooperii*	Length 14–21 inches	Wingspan 27–36 inches

COOPER'S HAWK

Sometimes called the Blue Darter or Chicken Hawk by farmers; however, studies show poultry are only a small portion of the Cooper's Hawk's diet. It is named after William Cooper, who was the first person to collect one of these birds and have it identified. Like most hawks, the juvenile has heavily streaked underparts and brown upperparts, whereas adults show blue-gray upperparts. Females are larger than males, and both show a blue-gray back. In flight the long tail appears rounded.

JUVENILE

• **SONG** Alarm call is *kac-kac-kac* or *kuck, kuck kuck, kuck.*

• **BEHAVIOR** Territorial; will

dark gray or black on top of head

deep red to yellow eyes

yellow cere

white undertail coverts

rounded tail with dark bars and a white band on tip

reddish bars across breast and belly

yellow legs and feet

not allow similar Sharp-shinned Hawk in same woodland. Attacks poultry, other birds, small mammals, and takes songbirds out of nest. Occasionally eats fish. Sometimes carries prey to water and kills it by drowning. Hunts by waiting in ambush or by dashing in swift low flight through wooded lot; surprises prey and catches it with talons.

• **BREEDING** Monogamous. Solitary nester.

• **NESTING** Incubation 32–36 days by both sexes, but more by female. Semialtricial young stay in nest 27–34 days, fed by both sexes. 1 brood per year.

Similar Birds

SHARP-SHINNED HAWK
Shorter tail with notched or squared end; smaller head; less contrast between back and crown; narrower white band at tip of tail • male much smaller, but female approaches size of male Cooper's.

• **POPULATION** Uncommon to rare. Steadily increasing after bottoming out in 1970s.

• **CONSERVATION** Decline in mid-20th century principally due to pesticides. Stable or increasing in most areas.

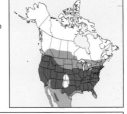

Flight Pattern

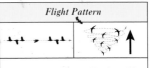

Rapid wing beats followed by short glide; often circles in flight on thermals.

Nest Identification	Sticks and twigs • lined with chips, outer bark strips, and occasionally green conifer needles • in crotch of conifer near trunk or in deciduous tree, 10–60 feet above ground • built by both sexes, but male does more • 4–5 bluish white or greenish white eggs, spotted with browns and usually nest-stained; elliptical to subelliptical, 1.5 inches long.
Shape Location	

Plumage Sexes similar	Habitat	Migration Some migrate	Weight 12.3 ounces

DATE _____ TIME_____ LOCATION _____

Family ACCIPITRIDAE	Species *Accipiter gentilis*	Length 19–27 inches	Wingspan 40–47 inches

NORTHERN GOSHAWK

An agile and proficient flier, the Northern Goshawk is not afraid to catch prey near humans when it is hungry. This bold hawk has been known to attack duck decoys. It appears pale gray at a distance, and in flight the shorter tail and longer, broad wings (for an accipiter) give the superficial appearance of a Red-tailed Hawk. The female is the larger and dominant partner in a pair.

• **SONG** Alarm call is harsher and deeper than Cooper's Hawk, *kac-kac-kac* or *kuk, kuk, kuk*. Female utters high-pitched melancholy whine, *kee-a-ah*, reminiscent of the Red-shouldered Hawk.

• **BEHAVIOR** Eats snowshoe hare, lemmings, and grouse; migrates south in irruptive numbers when their prey populations crash. Also eats small to medium mammals, large and small birds (including ducks and crows), and some large insects. Dives and kills prey on ground or in air with deadly grip of talons. Female very defensive of nest site to the point of attacking intruders, including humans.

• **BREEDING** Monogamous. Solitary nester.

• **NESTING** Incubation 36–42 days by both sexes, but female does more. Semialtricial young stay in nest 41–43 days. Fed by both sexes. First flight at 45 days. 1 brood per year.

distinct white eyebrow over each eye widens posteriorly

black crown

wedge-shaped black postocular stripe

orange-red eyes

blue-gray back

white underparts with gray mottling

relatively long rounded wings

JUVENILE

long rounded to wedge-shaped tail

fluffy white undertail coverts

Similar Birds

COOPER'S HAWK
Shorter wings; longer tail; darker blue-gray upperparts; barred rusty underparts.

• **POPULATION** Uncommon to rare.

• **CONSERVATION** Expanding range. Possible increase in the Northeast during recent decades. Southwestern mountain populations may be threatened by loss of habitat.

Flight Pattern

Several strong rapid wing beats interspersed with glides; soars on thermals.

Nest Identification

Shape Location

Sticks and twigs • lined with bark strips, evergreen sprigs, grass, and feathers • in fork of branch or trunk of tree, 20–75 feet above ground • built by both sexes, but male does more • 3–4 bluish or off-white eggs, occasionally nest-stained or spotted with brown; slightly elongate elliptical or oval, 2.3 inches long.

Plumage Sexes similar	Habitat	Migration Migratory	Weight 2.0 pounds

DATE _____ TIME_____ LOCATION _____

Family ACCIPITRIDAE	Species *Asturina nitida*	Length 16–18 inches	Wingspan 32–38 inches

GRAY HAWK

This stout little hawk is an uncommon and local resident of low-lying woodlands along streams in south Texas and a summer visitor to Arizona. It is not an accipiter as formerly thought but actually a small buteolike hawk. Juveniles are rusty or sooty brown with brown-streaked pale to buff underparts and have narrow dusky bars on the tail. In flight adults show whitish underparts with gray barring, rounded wing tips, a black tail with numerous white bands, and a white rump.

• **SONG** Loud descending mournful whistles, often in series of 3–7, *wheeeooo*; plaintive *cree-ee-ee*.

• **BEHAVIOR** Often perches conspicuously on roadside utility poles, wires, posts, and trees. Darts to ground for swift-running lizards. Picks up prey in talons. Also eats snakes, rabbits, small rodents, some birds, fish, and beetles.

yellow cere

JUVENILE

whitish underparts with gray barring

yellow legs and feet

white rump

broad black-and-white bands on tail

Similar Birds

BROAD-WINGED HAWK Barred reddish underparts, including underwing linings, dark trailing border of wing, and pointed wing tips; lacks white rump patch.

• **BREEDING** Monogamous. Solitary nester.
• **NESTING** Incubation 32 days by both sexes. Semialtricial young stay with female in nest 30 days. Male brings food for first 14 days. Then both parents feed. 1 brood per year.

• **POPULATION** Casual to rare. No more than 50 pairs known north of Mexico, but species is widespread in Tropics.

Flight Pattern
Graceful buoyant flap-and-glide flight; soars often but not to great heights.

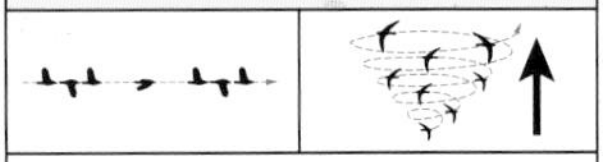

Nest Identification	
Shape	Location	Green twigs and sticks • lined with green leaves • 40–60 feet above ground concealed in treetops, especially sycamore or cottonwood • built by both sexes • 2–3 white to bluish white eggs, seldom marked (brown marks when present) but often nest-stained, 2 inches long.

Plumage Sexes similar	Habitat	Migration Some migrate	Weight Undetermined

DATE _____ TIME_____ LOCATION _____

Family ACCIPITRIDAE	Species *Buteogallus anthracinus*	Length 20–23 inches	Wingspan 48–50 inches

COMMON BLACK-HAWK

The Common Black-Hawk is chunky, gentle, and lethargic, except while nesting, when it will often plunge from great heights and snap off dead branches from trees during flight. They most frequently use large cottonwood trees in riparian stands along rivers as nest sites. These birds will abandon nest sites if there is too much human disturbance. In flight adults appear black with a single broad white tail band, a narrow white terminal tip on the very short fan-shaped tail, and a small white patch at the base of the outer primaries. Juveniles have a buff head and underparts and black-and-white bands on the tail.

white spotting on base of outer primaries

sooty black plumage

bright yellow cere

broad white band across middle of short mostly black tail

bright yellow feet and legs

white-tipped tail

wide wings

JUVENILE

- **SONG** Often calls when soaring and in display during breeding season. A triple-note ascending whistle and a drawn-out squealing *ka-a-a-ah, ka-a-a-ah.*
- **BEHAVIOR** Sits on open perch or walks on ground watching for fish and crabs washed up on sandbars. Eats frogs, fish, crabs, reptiles, small mammals, insects, and occasionally other birds. Soars often, especially in midday.
- **BREEDING** Monogamous. Solitary nester.
- **NESTING** Incubation 34 days by both sexes. Semialtricial young remain in nest 42–49 days, then move to nearby trees where parents continue to feed for another 35–42 days. 1 brood per year.
- **POPULATION** Rare, local.
- **CONSERVATION** Declining in North America, with an estimated 250 pairs remaining. Vulnerable to disturbance and loss of habitat.

Similar Birds

BLACK VULTURE
Larger whitish patch at base of primaries; lacks white bands on tail; grayish white feet, legs, and bill.

ZONE-TAILED HAWK
Narrower 2-toned wings with dark wing linings and barred silver-gray flight feathers; wings held in dihedral; more tail bands; less yellow-orange under eyes.

Flight Pattern

Deep steady and fairly slow wing beats alternate with short to long glides. Soars on thermals.

Nest Identification

Shape   Location

Dry sticks and mistletoe • in crotch of tree, usually cottonwood, sycamore, or large mesquite, 15–100 feet above ground • built by both sexes • 1–3 white eggs sometimes marked with brown; short ovate or nearly oval, 2.3 inches long.

Plumage Sexes similar	Habitat	Migration Some migrate	Weight 1.6 pounds

DATE _____ TIME_____ LOCATION _____

Family ACCIPITRIDAE	Species *Parabuteo unicinctus*	Length 17–24 inches	Wingspan 46 inches

HARRIS'S HAWK

Named after a friend of John James Audubon, Edward Harris, Harris's Hawk is rather tame. This dark sooty brown hawk has beautiful markings, including rufous-chestnut shoulders, underwing linings, and thighs, and a boldly marked black-and-white tail set off by a white rump and white tail coverts. Once called the Bay-winged Hawk, the juvenile has streaked underparts, a white rump, and rusty shoulders not as deeply colored as those of the adult.

• **SONG** Loud harsh nasal screams of *jaaahrr*, sounding similar to a Barn Owl.

• **BEHAVIOR** Often perches conspicuously near roads on utility

yellow cere

rufous-chestnut shoulders

dark sooty brown overall

rufous-chestnut thighs

white bands on tail base and tip

yellow legs and feet

JUVENILE

poles, fence posts, and trees. Hunts actively with low quartering flight similar to that of a Northern Harrier, or with rapid dashes like an accipiter. Gregarious; hunts cooperatively in small groups, and large prey is shared. Often 2–3 hunt together, chasing prey in turn until one makes the kill. Eats variety of small rodents, rabbits, ducks, herons, smaller birds, and reptiles.

• **BREEDING** Polyandrous. Solitary nester.

• **NESTING** Incubation 33–36 days by both sexes. Semialtricial young stay in nest 40–49 days, fed by both sexes. Often 2 broods per year.

• **POPULATION** Uncommon to fairly common but declining in some areas.

• **CONSERVATION** Disappeared from some former areas, such as lower Colorado River Valley and California; has been reintroduced to California. Threatened in some areas by illegal capture for falconry.

Similar Birds

RED-SHOULDERED HAWK
Lacks white patch at tail base but has multiple narrow white tail bands; barred rufous underparts; black-and-white barring in flight feathers.

Flight Pattern

Usually flies close to ground with several rapid wing beats followed by a short glide. Soars on thermals and updrafts.

Nest Identification	
Shape 🐚 Location 🌳	Sticks, twigs, and roots • lined with green mesquite, green shoots and leaves, grass, bark, and roots • in cactus 10–30 feet above ground • built by both sexes, but female does more • 2–4 white or bluish eggs, half marked with browns and lavender; short subelliptical to elongated, 2.1 inches long.

Plumage Sexes similar	Habitat	Migration Nonmigratory	Weight 1.6 pounds

DATE _____ TIME_____ LOCATION _____

Family ACCIPITRIDAE	Species *Buteo lineatus*	Length 17–24 inches	Wingspan 32–50 inches

RED-SHOULDERED HAWK

This bird uses the same territory for years, and even succeeding generations may return to the same territory. The longest recorded continuous use of the same territory is forty-five years. Five races (*lineatus*, *alleni*, *extimus*, *elagans*, and *texanus*) show variations in color and size but all have barred rusty underparts, reddish wing linings, and shoulders with banded tails. In flight the long black tail displays numerous narrow white bands on adults and juveniles. Flight feathers are spotted and barred black and white and show a pale "window" at the base of the outer primaries. Male is larger than female.

yellow cere

reddish shoulders

extensive pale spotting on upperparts

rust-red barring on underparts

- **SONG** Evenly spaced series of clear high loud and often rapidly repeated *kee-ah* or *clee-u clee-u clee-u* notes. Blue Jays can mimic the call perfectly.
- **BEHAVIOR** Stalks prey from perch. Catches and eats small to medium-sized mammals, small reptiles, amphibians, large insects, spiders, earthworms, snails, and an occasional bird. Prefers wet woodlands, often near water and swamps. Often perches low to hunt on posts, utility poles, and low to mid level in trees.

JUVENILE

FLORIDA RACE

yellow feet and legs

long black tail with numerous narrow white bands

- **BREEDING** Monogamous. Solitary nester.
- **NESTING** Incubation 28 days by both sexes. Semialtricial young stay in nest 35–45 days. Fed by both sexes. 1 brood per year.
- **POPULATION** Fairly common in range.
- **CONSERVATION** Some decline due to habitat loss and human encroachment particularly in West. Pesticides in Midwest interfered with reproduction during the 1970s.

Similar Birds

BROAD-WINGED HAWK Smaller; shorter tail; lacks barring in flight feathers; fewer, wider white tail bands; lacks reddish shoulders; lacks wing windows; peweelike call.

Flight Pattern

Flies with fairly rapid stiff wing beats; soars on flat wings and glides on slightly drooped wings. Soars on thermals.

Nest Identification	
Shape · Location	Made of sticks, twigs, inner bark strips, dry leaves, moss, lichen, and coniferous needles • usually by a tree trunk 10–200 feet above ground • built by both sexes • 2–6 white or bluish white eggs, often nest-stained and marked with brown; short elliptical, 2.1 inches long.

Plumage Sexes similar	Habitat	Migration Some migrate	Weight 1.1 pounds

DATE _____ TIME_____ LOCATION _____

| Family ACCIPITRIDAE | Species *Buteo platypterus* | Length 13–19 inches | Wingspan 32–39 inches |

BROAD-WINGED HAWK

The smallest of the North American buteos is similar in size to a stocky crow. These birds, which migrate in flocks of thousands, make up the bulk of hawk flights in September in the East. This peaceful bird is one of the tamest hawks. In flight the tips of the flight feathers appear dark, producing a black border along the trailing edge of the wing, and the underwing linings vary from white to rusty-buff. The black-and-white bands in the tail are approximately equal in width. Juveniles are similar to adults but appear more washed out and have fainter tail bands; underparts are pale with heavy dark streaking.

dark brown upperparts

red barring on underparts

large black-and-white bands on tail

JUVENILE

- **SONG** Thin shrill whistle, *peeteeee* or *peweeeeeeeeee*, often given in flight and similar to the high plaintive whistled note of an Eastern Wood-Pewee.
- **BEHAVIOR** Perches to watch for prey from utility poles and wires or near water along edge of woods. Hunts along wooded roads under the tree canopy. Swoops down to grab prey with talons. Eats amphibians, reptiles, small rodents, shrews, rabbits, some small birds, large insects, and insect larvae.
- **BREEDING** Monogamous. Solitary nester.
- **NESTING** Incubation 28–32 days by both sexes, but mostly by female. Semialtricial young stay in nest 29–35 days, fed by both sexes. 1 brood per year.
- **POPULATION** Common in eastern US and southern Canada west to a portion of eastern British Columbia. Rare in winter in California and Florida.
- **CONSERVATION** Large numbers once shot during migration, particularly along mountainous ridges in the East. Now protected by law. Neotropical migrant.

Similar Birds

RED-SHOULDERED HAWK
Larger in size; narrower, more rounded wings with barred and spotted black-and-white flight feathers; buff to rusty-red wing linings; longer, narrower tail with white bands much narrower than dark ones.

Flight Pattern	
Several rapid shallow wing beats followed by a glide. Soars on thermals and updrafts.	

Nest Identification	
Shape	Location

Sticks, twigs, and dead leaves • lined with inner bark strips with lichen, outer bark chips, evergreen sprigs, and green leaves • in crotch of deciduous tree, 30–50 feet above ground • built by both sexes in slow process that takes 3–5 weeks • 2–4 white or bluish white eggs sometimes marked with brown; short elliptical, 1.9 inches long.

| Plumage Sexes similar | Habitat | Migration Migratory | Weight 14.8 ounces |

DATE _____ TIME _____ LOCATION _____

Family ACCIPITRIDAE	Species *Buteo swainsoni*	Length 19–22 inches	Wingspan 46–58 inches

SWAINSON'S HAWK

Sometimes traveling in huge flocks, these birds migrate from North America to Argentina, about 11,000–17,000 miles each year. This large buteo lives in open rangeland, hill country, plains, and grasslands where trees are sparse. Swainson's Hawk is about the same size as the Red-tailed Hawk and has three different color morphs: light, rufous (intermediate), and dark. This variety provides for a confusing array of plumages: dark morphs are dark brown overall; the rufous morph is similar but with variegated medium brown underparts. In flight the narrow, slightly pointed wings are held in a slight dihedral, and the bird tilts from side to side like a Turkey Vulture.

uniformly dark brown upperparts

white wing linings

black bill with yellow cere

white throat

wide chestnut band on chest

JUVENILE

pale buff to white belly

RUFOUS MORPH

DARK MORPH

LIGHT MORPH

narrowly banded gray tail with wide dark subterminal band

- **SONG** Plaintive whistle, *kr-e-e-eeeeeer*, similar to that of the Broad-winged Hawk.
- **BEHAVIOR** Hunts, sometimes in flocks, for grasshoppers and crickets. Stalks ground squirrels at their burrows. Catches prey in talons. Also eats mice, rabbits, lizards, frogs, toads, and an occasional game bird. Frequents grasslands, agricultural grain fields, and open landscapes.
- **BREEDING** Monogamous. Solitary nester.
- **NESTING** Incubation 28–35 days by both sexes; female does more. Semialtricial young stay in nest 30–35 days. Fed by both sexes. First flight at 38–46 days. 1 brood per year.
- **POPULATION** Very common to common but numbers are recorded as declining.
- **CONSERVATION** Recent heavy losses in South American wintering grounds due to birds eating insects that have been poisoned by insecticides.

Similar Birds

SHORT-TAILED HAWK Shorter, broader wings and tail; wings with pale barring only in flight feathers • light morph has completely white underparts and white forehead • Florida range; casual to southeast Texas.

RED-TAILED HAWK Lacks breast band; pale flight feathers; reddish tail.

Flight Pattern

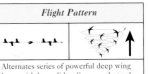

Alternates series of powerful deep wing beats with long glides. Soars on thermals, updrafts, wings bent upward in dihedral.

Nest Identification

Shape   Location 🪺

Large sticks, twigs, brambles, grass, and similar materials • lined with inner bark, fresh leaves, flower clusters, down, and feathers • in tree 6–70 feet above ground • 2–4 bluish greenish white eggs marked with pale brown; subelliptical to elliptical, 2.2 inches long.

Plumage Sexes similar	Habitat ___ 🌵 🌿	Migration Migratory	Weight 2.0 pounds

DATE _____ TIME_____ LOCATION _____

Family ACCIPITRIDAE	Species *Buteo albicaudatus*	Length 23–24 inches	Wingspan 48–54 inches

WHITE-TAILED HAWK

The White-tailed Hawk's yellow legs are the longest of any North American buteo. It can be seen flying with its wings held in a shallow V. Groups of ten to twenty or more may be attracted to grass fires from ten miles away to feed on prey escaping the flames. The female is similar to the male but has darker upperparts and more barring on the underparts. Adults in flight show light underparts, primaries with dusky barring, black-tipped flight feathers framing the trailing edge of the dark wing, white wing linings, and a short, broad white tail with a black subterminal band.

dark gray upperparts

rusty shoulder patches

long pointed wings project beyond tip of tail

white underparts

- **SONG** Usually silent. Near nest may give high-pitched alarm call, screaming *ke-ke-ke-ke* or *keh-eh, keh-eh, keh-eh, keh-eh.*
- **BEHAVIOR** Eats mostly rabbits; also small rodents, reptiles, frogs, grasshoppers, other large insects, and an occasional bird. Will eat carrion. Catches flying insects in the air. Spots prey from perch or while flying.
- **BREEDING** Monogamous. Solitary nester.
- **NESTING** Incubation 29–32 days mostly by female. Semialtricial young may stay with parents up to 7 months. First flight at 46–55 days. Not clear which sex feeds young in first couple of weeks, but both sexes hunt for food. 1 brood per year.
- **POPULATION** Rare to uncommon in southeastern Texas; casual in southwestern Louisiana.
- **CONSERVATION** On threatened list in Texas. Decline in Texas from 1950 to 1970 possibly due to pesticides and habitat loss.

JUVENILE LIGHT MORPH

JUVENILE DARK MORPH

Similar Birds

SWAINSON'S HAWK
Dark morph lacks reddish shoulder patch; uniformly dark upperparts and underparts.

FERRUGINOUS HAWK
Lighter-colored head; rufous thighs; feathered tarsus; larger reddish patch on shoulder and back; lacks dark subterminal tail band.

Flight Pattern	
Often flies close to ground with strong steady wing beats; soars with slight dihedral.	

Nest Identification	
Shape	Location	Uses same nest year after year and adds to it with sticks, twigs, grasses, and weeds • in top of low tree or shrub about 10 feet above ground • built by both sexes • 1–4 white eggs sometimes spotted with brown; oval, elliptical oval, ovate, or elliptical; 2.5 inches long.

Plumage Sexes similar	Habitat	Migration Nonmigratory	Weight 1.9 pounds

DATE _____ TIME_____ LOCATION _____

Family ACCIPITRIDAE	Species *Buteo albonotatus*	Length 18–21 inches	Wingspan 47–53 inches

ZONE-TAILED HAWK

Using what is called "aggressive mimicry," the Zone-tailed Hawk takes advantage of its similarity to the Turkey Vulture, a bird most animals perceive as harmless. This hawk resembles a Turkey Vulture in flight and appearance and even sometimes soars with them. This capable hunter glides slowly but plunges suddenly upon prey once it is spotted. In flight the wings are long, slender, and two-toned, and the banded tail is held partially spread. Juveniles have a grayish finely barred tail and white flecking on the breast.

barred flight feathers

bright yellow cere

body matte black overall

JUVENILE

3 narrow white or grayish tail bands

bright yellow feet and legs

- **SONG** Squeaking, peevish whistle similar to that of Red-tailed Hawk.

Similar Birds

TURKEY VULTURE Featherless head; no tail bands; no barring in flight feathers; grayish brown legs and feet; does not vocalize.

COMMON BLACK-HAWK Broader wings with dark flight feathers; shorter white-tipped tail with single broad white band.

- **BEHAVIOR** Circles like a Turkey Vulture on wings held in a dihedral. Eats small rodents and small birds, including nestlings, snatched with talons while in flight. Also takes lizards, frogs, and small fish.
- **BREEDING** Monogamous. Solitary nester. Screams and vigorously defends nest against intruders.
- **NESTING** Incubation 35 days by both sexes. Fed by both sexes. Semialtricial young leave nest in 35–40 days.
- **POPULATION** Uncommon.
- **CONSERVATION** Decline in population may be due to loss of nesting sites.

Flight Pattern
Flapping and gliding flight. Soars on thermals with wings lifted slightly above back and tilting from side to side.

Nest Identification	
Shape 🐾 Location 🪺	Made of large sticks • lined with twigs bearing green leaves • in tree, usually cottonwood or pine, 25–100 feet above ground • near stream • 2 white or bluish eggs dotted with lavender and yellowish brown, sometimes concentrated on one end, 2.2 inches long.

Plumage Sexes similar	Habitat 🌲 ___ 🏞 ⚊ 🌿 〰	Migration Migratory	Weight 1.4 pounds

DATE _____ TIME_____ LOCATION _____

Family ACCIPITRIDAE	Species *Buteo jamaicensis*	Length 19–25 inches	Wingspan 46–58 inches

RED-TAILED HAWK

This hawk is found in more habitats than any other North American buteo and, consequently, is the most common hawk on the continent. This species has five races: a pale pink-tailed Great Plains race known as "Krider's Red-tailed," *krideri;* the eastern *borealis*, the southwestern *fuertesi*; the western, *calurus*; and the rare "Harlan's Hawk" or *harlani*, once considered a separate species, which is very dark with a white-based tail. All adults show a dark brownish mantle in flight and dark brown bar on leading edge of underwing. All juveniles have a dark brown tail with a black band. Because it perches low on woodland edges and along roadsides this is one of the most conspicuous and easily observed hawks.

reddish tail ranges from pale buff-pink to deep rufous-red

whitish flight feathers with pale barring

pale wing linings

large bill with yellow cere

white belly with broad band of dark streaking

EASTERN ADULT
BOREALIS

• **SONG** Harsh descending slurred *keeeeer-r-r*. Also rasping hissing screamy, *p-s-s-s, kree-kree ree-e-e*.
• **BEHAVIOR** Across its vast range takes a wide variety of prey Eats small to medium mammals, reptiles, amphibians, grasshoppers, spiders, earthworms, crustaceans, some fish, and an occasional small bird or bat. Carries small prey to perch; partially eats large prey on ground.
• **BREEDING** Monogamous; may mate for life. Solitary nester.
• **NESTING** Incubation 28–35 days by both sexes; more by female. Semialtricial young stay in nest 42–46 days. Fed by both sexes. 1 brood per year.

HARLAN'S HAWK

KRIDER'S RED-TAILED

Similar Birds

ROUGH-LEGGED HAWK Smaller bill and feet; feathered legs; white rump; white tail with multiple dark bands; black belly (light morph).

SWAINSON'S HAWK Multiple tail bands; dark flight feathers; pale wing linings; brown chest (light morph).

• **POPULATION** Very common. Some decline due to habitat loss.
• **CONSERVATION** Some eggshell thinning. Many still killed illegally, and some are accidentally killed by cars.

Flight Pattern	

Several rapid strong wing beats followed by a glide. Soars well on thermals and sometimes hangs on updrafts.

Nest Identification	
Shape ⌣ Location 🌳🌲🌵🏚	Sticks and twigs • lined with inner bark strips, evergreen sprigs, and green leaves • in crotch of large tree, on cliff ledge, or on artificial structure, as high as 120 feet above ground • built by both sexes • 2–3 white or bluish white eggs sometimes spotted brown, 2.4 inches long.

Plumage Sexes similar	Habitat 🦅 🦆 ⚘ ﹍ ᴜ ⍦	Migration Migratory	Weight 2.3 pounds

DATE _____ TIME_____ LOCATION _____

Family ACCIPITRIDAE	Species *Buteo regalis*	Length 22–28 inches	Wingspan 56 inches

FERRUGINOUS HAWK

One of the largest and most powerful buteos, this hawk is true to its Latin species name, meaning kingly or royal. This bird has light, dark, and reddish morphs; the light morph is the most common. Dark morphs are dark rufous to dark brown overall. In flight all three hold the long pointed wings in a dihedral, and show a white patch at base of primaries from above. The light morph appears almost completely white from below except for the reddish legs, which form a rusty red V beneath the body.

rufous-streaked head

reddish brown upperparts

yellow cere

white underparts with light reddish brown spotting

JUVENILE

reddish leggings

yellow feet

DARK MORPH

pale tail with buff-gray tip

LIGHT MORPH

- **SONG** Alarm call of *kree-a* or *kaah kaah*.
- **BEHAVIOR** Eats mainly ground squirrels; spots them from perch, flies high in air, and swoops down to catch them. Also hunts prairie dogs, rabbits, small rodents, snakes, lizards, small to medium birds, and large insects. One of the few large hawks that hovers. Prefers open country, where it often hunts from low perches on fence posts, utility poles, or small trees.
- **BREEDING** Monogamous. Solitary nester.
- **NESTING** Incubation 31–33 days by both sexes, but female does more. Semialtricial young stay in nest 40–50 days; for first 21 days female stays on nest while male hunts, then both sexes hunt. First flight at 38–50 days. 1 brood per year.
- **POPULATION** Uncommon to fairly common. Rare to casual in migration or winter to states bordered by the Mississippi River and occasionally Florida.
- **CONSERVATION** Threatened and declining due to illegal shooting and loss of habitat. Some are accidentally killed by cars.

Similar Birds

ROUGH-LEGGED HAWK Dark morph has banded tail with broad dark subterminal band; no rusty leggings.

"KRIDER'S RED-TAILED" HAWK Juvenile is shorter; more rounded wings; dark subterminal tail band to tip; unfeathered tarsus.

Flight Pattern

Quarters back and forth close to ground; alternates several deep flaps with glides similar to Northern Harrier. Soars on thermals and hovers.

Nest Identification

Shape ☒   Location ✿ ⚘

Sticks and debris • lined with finer materials, including cow dung • usually on top of tree, 6–50 feet above ground; in treeless areas may build on cliffs or ground • built by both sexes • 2–6 pale bluish white eggs blotched with pale to dark browns and buffs; between spherical and elliptical, 2.5 inches long.

Plumage Sexes similar	Habitat ___ ▪ ▲	Migration Migratory	Weight 2.3 pounds

DATE _____ TIME_____ LOCATION _____

Family ACCIPITRIDAE	Species *Buteo lagopus*	Length 18–24 inches	Wingspan 48–56 inches

ROUGH-LEGGED HAWK

Named for the feathered shanks of its legs, this big high-soaring hawk of the open country often is seen perched on fence posts or dead trees. It flies low on long, thin pointed wings and is one of the few large hawks that regularly hovers. In flight the light morph's long grayish white tail with a broad dark subterminal band and white tail coverts contrast sharply with its black belly and dark back.

• **SONG** Usually silent in winter. Circling pairs in breeding season give melancholy whistle.

• **BEHAVIOR** Eats mostly small rodents and large insects. Usually catches prey on ground. Often hunts from low perch or by standing on ground on a mound or other elevation. When hunting in flight, flies low over open vegetation, quartering slowly back and forth, alternately flapping and gliding and hovering before plunging feet-first on prey. Irruptive flights when prey populations crash bring many south in winter.

• **BREEDING** Monogamous. Pairs have been recorded to remain together for many years.

• **NESTING** Incubation 28–31 days by female. Young leave nest at about 41 days and spend 21–42 days in Arctic after fledging and before migrating south for winter.

whitish head

LIGHT
MORPH
FEMALE

small bill with yellow cere

whitish underparts with dark brown streaking (heaviest on upper chest and belly)

thin feathered legs

small, dainty yellow feet

1-3 narrow dark marks on tail

LIGHT MORPH
JUVENILE

long grayish white tail with broad dark subterminal band

blackish brown overall

rarely, white mottling on head and chest

barred dark gray tail with broad dark subterminal band

DARK
MORPH
FEMALE

Similar Birds

RED-TAILED HAWK
Dark morph is dark brown overall; rufous tail; shorter wings and tails; smaller bill.

FERRUGINOUS HAWK
Dark morph has whitish carpal crescent on underwing; dark brown overall; brighter rufous on lesser upperwing coverts and tail coverts.

• **POPULATION** Common in breeding range; uncommon to fairly common with erratic numbers on wintering grounds.

• **CONSERVATION** Enormous numbers once were shot in western US because of tameness. In the West many killed while feeding on animal carcasses on highways.

Flight Pattern
Alternates powerful flaps with glides. Hangs in wind and hovers over one spot; somewhat floppy wing beats at times.

Nest Identification	
Shape Location	Small twigs and plant material; 24–30 inches in diameter • in river valleys, precipices, slopes in raised places • uses nest for several years; each pair can have several nests and use them alternately • 2–3 eggs when food is scarce; 5–7 eggs when food is abundant; blotched, white, or streaked with brown.

Plumage Sexes similar	Habitat	Migration Migratory	Weight 1.9 pounds

DATE _____ TIME_____ LOCATION _____

Family ACCIPITRIDAE	Species *Aquila chrysaetos*	Length 33–38 inches	Wingspan 6–8 feet

GOLDEN EAGLE

yellow cere

tawny-golden feathers on crown

black bill

tawny-golden feathers on nape and sides of neck

dark brown overall

feathered tarsus

yellow feet

JUVENILE

Like most other birds of prey, the female Golden Eagle is considerably larger than the male. This large dark eagle is fairly common in the West and rare to uncommon in the East. It has been clocked in a steep glide at 120 miles per hour and is estimated to swoop on prey in dives at more than 150 miles per hour. Juveniles in flight display "ringtail" plumage (a broad white tail band with a terminal band of black) and a broad white patch at the base of the primaries. Large birds of prey require large territories, and home ranges for a pair of this species have been recorded as large as 60 square miles.

• **SONG** Generally silent. Around nest makes yelping bark, *keya*, and whistled notes. During soaring courtship flight yelps or mews.

• **BEHAVIOR** Favors rabbit, ground squirrel, marmot, grouse, and ptarmigan. Also eats large insects, other small mammals, carrion, and reptiles, including turtles. Has been known to attack full-grown deer, antelopes, and birds as large as Great Horned Owls and cranes. Returns to the same nest yearly or every other year.

• **BREEDING** Monogamous; may pair for life. Solitary nester.

• **NESTING** Incubation 43–45 days by both sexes; female does more. Young stay in nest 66–70 days, dependent on parents for first 30 days. First flight at 65–70 days. Usually has 1 brood every 2 years.

• **POPULATION** Uncommon to rare in the East but fairly common in the West. A total of only 4,000–5,000 pairs were estimated in 1964. Circumpolar.

• **CONSERVATION** Protected by law. Thousands once killed by ranchers in efforts to protect livestock from potential predation. Also killed in collisions with aircraft. Protected areas established.

Similar Birds

BALD EAGLE
Juvenile has larger head; shorter tail; mottled white patches on underparts make tail more blotchy; underwing pattern; bare tarsus.

Flight Pattern

Alternates deep slow powerful wing beats with glides or rides easily on thermals.

Nest Identification

Shape 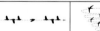 Location

Sticks woven with brush and leaves • lined with fine material • located 10–100 feet high in trees • 8–10 feet across and 3–4 feet deep • built by both sexes • 2 white or creamy buff eggs marked with brown or reddish brown, 2.9 inches long.

Plumage Sexes similar	Habitat 	Migration Some migrate	Weight 3.5 pounds

DATE _____ TIME_____ LOCATION _____

Family FALCONIDAE	Species *Caracara cheriway*	Length 20–25 inches	Wingspan 45–48 inches

CRESTED CARACARA

This large vulturelike raptor often walks on the ground on long legs in search of prey. Its black crown and short crest above the red to yellowish bare skin of the face are distinctive. In flight its flat profile, broad wings, and fanned tail are ravenlike. Flying birds also show white patches at the wing tips, a white head and breast, and a white tail with a broad black terminal band.

• **SONG** In breeding season makes loud *wick-wick-wick-wick-querrr*, throwing its head backward over its back on the last note. Harsh grating rattle. Usually silent.

• **BEHAVIOR** Makes head-throwing display. Only member of Falconidae that actually collects materials and builds nest. Often scavenges with vultures, where it may dominate the carcass. Feeds on variety of animal material, from large insects, reptiles, mammals, birds, amphibians, and fish to carrion.

• **BREEDING** Monogamous. Solitary nester.

• **NESTING** Incubation 28–33 days by both sexes. Semialtricial young stay in nest 30–60 days. Fed by both sexes. 1–2 broods per year.

• **POPULATION** Fairly common in Texas; rare to casual and local in Arizona; rare in Louisiana; fairly common and local in Florida. Has declined throughout its range. Florida and Arizona populations stable; Texas population increasing and expanding.

• **CONSERVATION** Considered threatened federally and in Florida.

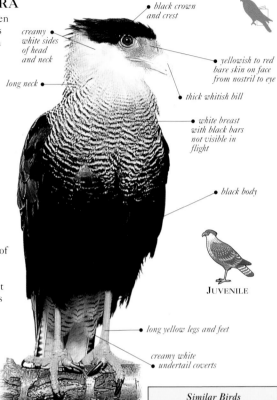

- black crown and crest
- creamy white sides of head and neck
- long neck
- yellowish to red bare skin on face from nostril to eye
- thick whitish bill
- white breast with black bars not visible in flight
- black body

JUVENILE

- long yellow legs and feet
- creamy white undertail coverts

Similar Birds

BLACK VULTURE
Black head and beak; only creamy white on wing tips.

Flight Pattern

Strong steady deep wing beats; often alternates series of wing beats with long to short glides. Sometimes soars on thermals.

Nest Identification	Sticks, vines, and twigs • lined with fine material • 15–30 feet above ground in palmetto or giant cacti • built by both sexes • 1–4 white or pinkish white eggs marked with browns, rarely unmarked; ovate to broadly oval or subspherical, slightly pointed at one end; 2.3 inches long.
Shape 🥚🍶 Location 🌿🌳🏔	

Plumage Sexes similar	Habitat ___ 🌿	Migration Nonmigratory	Weight 2.1 pounds

DATE _____ TIME _____ LOCATION _____

Family FALCONIDAE	Species *Falco sparverius*	Length 9–12 inches	Wingspan 20–25 inches

AMERICAN KESTREL

The smallest most common North American falcon is found all over the continent and north to the tree line in summer. It is sometimes called the Sparrow Hawk, a misnomer as the bird is neither a hawk nor does its diet include a significant amount of sparrows or other small birds. In flight it shows the typical long tail and long pointed wings of a falcon. A bird of the open country, it often is seen perched on wires along roadsides.

- **SONG** Alarm call a loud quick *klee-klee-klee* or *killy, killy, killy.*
- **BEHAVIOR** When perched bobs tail. Hunts rodents and insects from perch or hovers. Also eats bats, small birds, small reptiles, and frogs. Not dependent on drinking water in desert because it extracts water from its diet.
- **BREEDING** Monogamous. Solitary nester. During courtship male brings food and feeds female in the air.
- **NESTING** Incubation 29–31 days by both sexes, mostly by female. Semialtricial young stay in nest 30–31 days, fed by female. Male calls female from nest to feed. 1 brood per year, sometimes 2 in the South.
- **POPULATION** Common.
- **BIRDHOUSES** Readily nests in bird boxes built especially for kestrels. Occasionally attracted to bird feeders to prey on birds.

black-and-white pattern on head

rufous back with dark barring

2 vertical dark facial lines

spotted tawny-buff breast

MALE

blue-gray wings and wing coverts

long slender pointed wings

rufous-red tail without barring

2 vertical dark facial lines

streaked pale underparts

rufous tail with brown barring, black band, and narrow white tip

FEMALE

Similar Birds

SHARP-SHINNED HAWK Blue-gray upperparts; red-brown streaked and barred underparts; square or notched barred tail; short rounded wings.

MERLIN ♂ Larger; variegated head; lacks facial bars; blue-black tail and back; heavily streaked underparts • male has blue-black wings.

- **CONSERVATION** Migratory counts suggest recent decline in the Northeast; other populations seem stable. Expanded establishment of nest boxes in some areas, especially along highways, seems to have encouraged recovery.

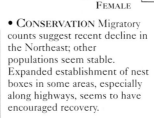

Flight Pattern
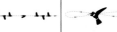
Several rapid wing beats followed by a glide; often hovers on rapidly beating wings. Also soars on thermals.

Nest Identification	
Shape  Location	Little, if any, nest material • in old flicker tree holes, niches in walls, and holes under gables, 12–80 feet above ground • 3–7 white to cream or pale pink eggs, heavily blotched with browns, sometimes unmarked; 1.4 inches long.

Plumage Sexes differ	Habitat	Migration Migratory	Weight 3.9 ounces

DATE _____ TIME _____ LOCATION _____

Family FALCONIDAE	Species *Falco columbarius*	Length 11–13 inches	Wingspan 23–26 inches

MERLIN

This medium-sized falcon of northern coniferous forests hunts the openings in parklike grasslands, bogs, and shrubby barrens. In flight it shows the distinctive falcon "jizz" of long pointed wings and a long tail with a big-headed, powerful look, and it displays impressive bursts of speed when in pursuit of prey. Geographic variation in color exists, from pale prairie birds to dark Pacific Northwest forms.

- **SONG** *Ki-ki-kee, kek-kek-kek* rapidly repeated.
- **BEHAVIOR** A relatively tame bird, allowing close approach. Defensive of nest; often attacks intruders, including humans. The Merlin flies close to the ground and catches prey with bursts of speed while in pursuit, rather than by diving or hovering. It is a bird that often hunts from an open perch. Primary diet of small birds, mammals, and large insects. May frequent cities in winter.
- **BREEDING** Monogamous. Solitary nester.
- **NESTING** Incubation 28–32 days mostly by female. Semialtricial young stay in nest 25–35 days. Fed by both sexes. 1 brood per year.
- **POPULATION** Uncommon.

blue-gray crown
yellow enlarged area at base of bill
white chin and throat with streaking
whitish buff head and nape
narrow black mustache
blue-gray back and wings
whitish buff underparts heavily streaked brown to black
yellow legs and feet

MALE

blue-black tail with gray barring and white tip

brown upperparts
more heavily streaked underparts

FEMALE

Similar Birds

AMERICAN KESTREL Smaller; bobs tail and hovers; barred rufous back and tail.

PEREGRINE FALCON Larger; indistinct barring on tail; dark hood on head extends beneath eye like broad sideburn.

- **CONSERVATION** Some declines attributed to pesticides and heavy metals in food chain.

Flight Pattern

Swift direct flight with rapid powerful wing beats.

Nest Identification

Shape

Location

Uses old tree nests of crows, magpies, and hawks, relined with bark and feathers • 15–35 feet above ground • built by female • 2–7 white eggs, some marked with reddish brown; short elliptical, 1.6 inches long.

Plumage Sexes differ	Habitat	Migration Most migrate	Weight 5.7 ounces

DATE _____ TIME_____ LOCATION _____

Family FALCONIDAE	Species *Falco femoralis*	Length 15–18 inches	Wingspan 40–48 inches

APLOMADO FALCON

This raptor is similar in size to the Prairie Falcon. The Aplomado Falcon formerly ranged into the southern US along the Mexican border from Texas to Arizona, and was fairly common in open desert and grasslands in the summer prior to the 1880s. By the early part of the 20th century it had all but disappeared. Continuing casual records probably represent birds from the population that still can be found near Chihuahua, Mexico. In flight this falcon shows dark underwings and cinnamon-orange thigh "britches" and undertail coverts.

- **SONG** Shrieking *keeh-keeh-keeh* and an abrasive single-note *keeh* or *kiih*.
- **BEHAVIOR** Found in open grasslands, savanna, and marshy habitats, where it often hunts from a perch on a pole, short tree, or shrub. Often lands on the ground. Hovers. Feeds primarily on large insects and small birds, both of which it often catches in flight. Sometimes this raptor will work grassfires, catching prey that is driven from its grassland cover by the flames.
- **BREEDING** Monogamous.
- **NESTING** Possibly 1 brood per year.
- **POPULATION** Casual to rare. Essentially extirpated from US range and declining in the northern part of Mexico.
- **CONSERVATION** Endangered subspecies. Restoration being attempted in southeast Texas, where introduced birds are successfully breeding.

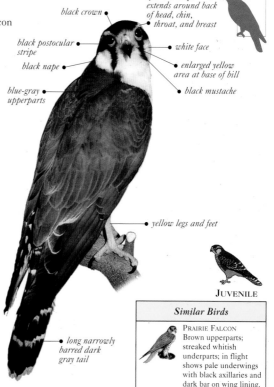

black crown
eyebrow stripe extends around back of head, chin, throat, and breast
black postocular stripe
white face
black nape
enlarged yellow area at base of bill
black mustache
blue-gray upperparts
yellow legs and feet
long narrowly barred dark gray tail

JUVENILE

Similar Birds

PRAIRIE FALCON Brown upperparts; streaked whitish underparts; in flight shows pale underwings with black axillaries and dark bar on wing lining.

AMERICAN KESTREL ♂ Much smaller; barred reddish brown back and tail; lacks black on belly and sides.

Flight Pattern
Fast swift direct flight with deep wing beats. Also hovers.

Nest Identification	
Shape ⌒ ⟶ Location 🌳 🌿 🌱	Uses nests of other birds • 7–25 feet above ground in yucca tree • 3–4 white to pink-white eggs, spotted or blotched with browns, 1.8 inches long.

Plumage Sexes similar	Habitat ___	Migration Nonmigratory	Weight 9.2 ounces

DATE _____ TIME_____ LOCATION _____

Family FALCONIDAE	Species *Falco peregrinus*	Length 16–20 inches	Wingspan 43–46 inches

PEREGRINE FALCON

A peregrine in a stoop is one of the fastest birds in the world, reaching speeds of 175 mph or more.

- **SONG** Usually silent. On breeding grounds makes loud *witchew, witchew, witchew.* When disturbed gives loud repeated *cack, cack, cack, cack.*
- **BEHAVIOR** Prefers open areas with good vantage points on which to perch, often near water. Feeds almost exclusively on birds it takes in the air after a steep swift dive from above them. Wanders widely after nesting season, following prey south as far as southern South America. Faithful to nesting sites and aeries, some of which have been used by generations of peregrines for centuries. Lives on buildings in large cities.
- **BREEDING** Monogamous. Solitary nester.
- **NESTING** Incubation 28–32 days mostly by female. Semialtricial young stay in nest 35–42 days. Fed by both sexes. 1 brood per year.
- **POPULATION** Common to fairly common on tundra; fairly common in migration; uncommon to rare as breeding bird in US. Increasing since continental lows suffered in 1960s and 1970s.
- **CONSERVATION** Federally listed as threatened. Regulation of DDT along with captive breeding and release program have sparked comeback.

fleshy yellow eye ring

black head from crown to below eye with "sideburns" gives helmeted look

slate-blue upperparts

white to buff chin

patch behind ear

white underparts with dark brown to black barring (except throat and chin)

yellow feet and legs

long slate-blue tail with dusky barring and white terminal tip

Similar Birds

MERLIN ♂
Smaller; heavily streaked underparts; pale face with narrow mustache mark.

GYRFALCON
Much larger; more uniform and paler coloration; pale head with thin mustache mark.

PRAIRIE FALCON
Paler overall; light brown upperparts; whitish underparts streaked with heavy brown spots; whitish face and supercilium; dark brown postocular stripe; thin mustache; brown barred tail; black axillars and inner wing linings.

Flight Pattern
Direct flight with rapid wing beats like a pigeon.

Nest Identification	
Shape	Made of debris on ledge • lined with grass • mostly on cliffs in southern US; also in hollows of old trees or open tops of cypress, sycamore, or cottonwood, 50–90 feet above ground • rarely uses old tree nest or cavity • built by female • 2–6 cream or buff eggs, heavily marked with brown and red, 2.1 inches long.
Abandoned nests	
Location	

Plumage Sexes similar	Habitat	Migration Some migrate	Weight 1.3 pounds

DATE _____ TIME_____ LOCATION _____

Family FALCONIDAE	Species *Falco mexicanus*	Length 15–19 inches	Wingspan 40–42 inches

PRAIRIE FALCON

Found on open prairies and grasslands with suitable cliffs, bluffs, and outcroppings for nesting sites, this bird's dusty sandy browns blend with the landscape. It is paler overall than the similar-sized Peregrine Falcon, whose range it overlaps in the West. In flight the "armpits" are blackish on axillaries and inner wing linings. Juveniles are darker above than adults and more heavily streaked below.

- **SONG** Mostly silent. Common alarm or territorial cackling call is shrill yelping *kik-kik-kik* or *kek-kek-kek*.
- **BEHAVIOR** Ledge display and spectacular aerial displays in courtship. Often perches on rocks, ledges, posts, or utility poles while scanning for prey. Overtakes birds in flight with rapid bursts of speed or in a dive from above. Eats primarily small birds, small mammals, and large insects. Nests in mountains as high as 10,000 feet and descends in winter to foothills and prairies.
- **BREEDING** Monogamous. Solitary nester.
- **NESTING** Incubation 29–33 days, mostly by female. Semialtricial young stay in nest 31–42 days. Fed by both sexes. 1 brood per year.
- **POPULATION** Uncommon to fairly common. Declining in Utah, western Canada, and agricultural California.
- **CONSERVATION** The Prairie Falcon has experienced some population declines which are for the most part attributed to disturbances from increasing human encroachment.

dark postocular stripe

white eyebrow

thin dark mustache

light brown upperparts edged with buff

yellow cere at base of bill

yellow bill with blue-gray tip

white throat, chin, and face

whitish underparts with heavy brown spots

yellow legs and feet

long dark brown tail with sandy bars

JUVENILE

Similar Birds

PEREGRINE FALCON
Adults slate-blue upperparts; darker head, helmeted appearance; in flight lacks black wing pits.

MERLIN ♂
Smaller • male has blue-gray back; more heavily streaked underparts; more contrasting barring in tail; lacks black in wing pits.

Flight Pattern
Swift flight with rapid wing beats. Sometimes alternates several rapid wing beats with glide.

Nest Identification	
Shape Location	On cliff ledge, occasionally in rock crevice • abandoned nests • always facing open habitat • 4–5 white eggs, heavily marked with brown and purple; short elliptical and subelliptical, 2.1 inches long.

Plumage Sexes similar	Habitat	Migration Nonmigratory	Weight 1.2 pounds

DATE _____ TIME _____ LOCATION _____

| Family CRACIDAE | Species *Ortalis vetula* | Length 22 inches | Wingspan 24–28 inches |

PLAIN CHACHALACA

The only chachalaca that reaches North America, this bird mostly lives in trees but flies to the ground for dust baths. Flocks of 4–20 feed together peacefully; however, when alarmed they half fly, half hop up through the trees with their crests raised high, tails spread wide, and small wings beating laboriously. This bird is noisy all year, but especially during breeding season and particularly at dawn and dusk, with multipitched choruses within and between flocks scattered across wooded thickets.

- **SONG** Cry of single bird is *cha-cha-lac*, but when flock joins chorus, "chachalaca" may be clearly heard over and over.
- **BEHAVIOR** Feeds mostly in trees but sometimes on ground. Eats berries, especially hackberries; fruits, including wild grapes and figs; seeds; green leaves; buds; and insects. Moves easily through dense vegetation and hops, glides, and flies from branch to branch within boll of trees. Glides between trees or across roads on short rounded wings with its long tail spread.
- **BREEDING** Monogamous. Social.
- **NESTING** Incubation 22–27 days by female. Precocial young stay in nest 3–4 days and flutter out of nest onto surrounding branches. Fed by regurgitation by both parents. 1 brood per year.
- **POPULATION** Common but somewhat secretive except for vocalizations in limited US range in lower Rio Grande Valley of Texas. Introduced on Sapelo Island, Georgia. Common and widespread in Mexico.
- **FEEDERS** Will come to feeders with fruits and seeds, also to water elements.
- **CONSERVATION** Killed for food in Mexico and other parts of its range south of the US–Mexico border.

gray orbital skin

small gray head

gray bill

gray neck

bare loose reddish throat skin (on breeding male only)

olive-brown upperparts

dusky cinnamon underparts and undertail coverts

blackish tail with green sheen and fairly broad pale tip

Flight Pattern
Several rapid stiff wing beats followed by a short glide on spread wings and fanned tail.

Nest Identification	
Shape ⌣ Location 🌳🌿	Frail structure of sticks and leaves • lined with green leaves • in fork in dense bush or tree, 4–20 feet above ground • 2–4 creamy or dull white eggs, 2.4 inches long.

| Plumage Sexes similar | Habitat 🌳 ▲ 🏔 | Migration Nonmigratory | Weight 1.3 pounds |

DATE _____ TIME_____ LOCATION _____

Family PHASIANIDAE	Species *Phasianus colchicus*	Length 21–36 inches	Wingspan 32 inches

RING-NECKED PHEASANT

First introduced as a game bird in California in 1857 and then in larger numbers elsewhere, the Asian Ring-necked Pheasant is one of the most widely distributed and most popular birds among hunters; thousands are harvested annually. The male has distinctive mottled brown plumage; a long, pointed tail; fleshy red eye patches; and a head that ranges in color from a glossy dark green to a purple hue.

- **SONG** When alarmed utters hoarse croaking notes. Male makes loud piercing double squawk *kok-cack*.
- **BEHAVIOR** Gregarious, forming flocks (sometimes large) in autumn and maintaining them into spring. Runs swiftly with tail cocked. Strong flight, rising off ground at steep angle with loud whirring takeoff.

red face wattles

short rounded wings

iridescent ear tufts

iridescent bronze overall

large body

brown, black, and green mottling

long pointed tail

MALE

In spring eats mostly plant-based diet, including grains, weed seeds, acorns, pine seeds, and wild berries. Also eats variety of insects and occasionally takes mice and snails. Roosts on ground or in trees. Adults often have short life span (males average 10 months; females average 20 months). Many young do not live beyond autumn.

- **BREEDING** Polygamous. Loosely colonial.
- **NESTING** Incubation 23–25 days by female. Precocial young can fly short distances at 7 days. Tended by female 35–42 days but feed themselves. 1 brood per year.
- **POPULATION** Common to fairly common. Some eastern populations decreasing.
- **FEEDERS** Drawn to feeders with corn or small grains scattered on ground.

FEMALE

mottled buff-brown overall

long pointed tail

Similar Birds

SHARP-TAILED GROUSE Similar to female but smaller body; shorter, pointed tail with white sides; barred whitish underparts; feathered tarsus.

- **CONSERVATION** Managed as game bird in North America. Some populations may not be self-sustaining, but occasional releases from captivity help maintain population. Never successfully established in the South despite many attempts.

Flight Pattern

Swift direct flight with shallow rapid wing beats. Often alternates several quick wing strokes with short glides.

Nest Identification

Shape ⟶ Location ⟶

Lined with grass and weeds • usually on ground in shallow natural depression or one made by female • in grasses, hedgerows, grain fields, and brushy ditches • built by female • 5–23 but usually 10–12 (large clutches occur when 2 hens lay in same nest) dark green-buff or rich brown-olive eggs; oval to short oval, 1.6 x 1.3 inches.

Plumage Sexes differ	Habitat	Migration Nonmigratory	Weight 2.9 pounds

DATE _____ TIME_____ LOCATION _____

Family PHASIANIDAE	Species *Tympanuchus cupido*	Length 17–18 inches	Wingspan 28 inches

GREATER PRAIRIE-CHICKEN

rounded dark tail

brown, buff, and white barring on upperparts

fleshy yellow-orange eye combs

straw-brown bill

elongated dark neck feathers

bare yellowish orange sacs (visible only during display)

heavily barred underparts

brown overall

Although both sexes of this chickenlike bird have elongated dark neck feathers, the male has longer ones, which he erects during courtship display. The yellowish orange sacs on the sides of the male's throat, called tympani, are inflated during courtship. Females have barred tails and also have neck sacs, but they are very small and lack color. Both sexes have feathered feet. Once common over most of its prairie grassland range this bird is now uncommon, declining, and local. Some races, like Attwater's prairie-chicken in southeastern Texas, are threatened with extinction. The Heath Hen, which lived along the Atlantic seaboard, became extinct in 1932.

• **SONG** Largely silent except during courtship. Male produces booming sound, *whhoo-doo-doooohh, zooooo … wooooo … youoo.*

• **BEHAVIOR** In summer eats insects, especially grasshoppers; also eats leaves, fruit flowers, shoots, grain seeds, and rose hips. In winter eats acorns, oats, rye, and wheat. Makes short flights.

• **BREEDING** Promiscuous. Males use leks. Dominant males mate with majority of females attracted to booming dances.

• **NESTING** Incubation 23–24 days by female. Precocial young leave nest soon after hatching. First flight at 7–14 days. Tended by female. 1 brood per year.

• **POPULATION** Uncommon to rare; local. Decreasing.

• **CONSERVATION** Endangered. Vulnerable to habitat loss caused by the agricultural plowing of the native grasslands it inhabits.

Similar Birds

LESSER PRAIRIE-CHICKEN Smaller; paler; less heavily barred underparts • male makes higher-pitched courting notes; reddish orange air sac • limited western range.

SHARP-TAILED GROUSE Spotted, scaled underparts; lacks elongated blackish neck feathers; long pointed tail with white borders.

Flight Pattern

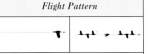

Strong rapid flight with series of rapid stiff wing beats alternating between glides on drooping wings.

Nest Identification

Shape ⟶ Location ▬ ▪▪▪ 🪺

Lined with grasses, dead leaves, and feathers • in hayfields, woods, or clearings • built by female • 7–17 olive eggs spotted with dark brown; ovate, 1.8 inches long.

Plumage Sexes similar	Habitat ▬ ▪	Migration Most do not migrate	Weight 2.2 pounds

Family PHASIANIDAE	Species *Tympanuchus pallidicinctus*	Length 16 inches	Wingspan 28 inches

LESSER PRAIRIE-CHICKEN

The Lesser Prairie-Chicken resembles the Greater Prairie-Chicken but is smaller in size, paler in color, and has dull red instead of orange air sacs. Having a more limited range than its relative, it chooses to live in short-grass prairies with scattered trees, especially shinnery oak, sagebrush, and other deciduous trees. Females are very similar in appearance to the males but have a barred brown tail instead of a black one, and they lack the male's yellow eyebrow combs and neck sacs.

dull red air sacs (visible only during display)

blackish tail

fine buff, brown, and white barring on upperparts

yellow eye combs

blackish neck feathers

brown overall

barred underparts

- **SONG** Booming often described as gobbling, bubbling, or even yodeling.
- **BEHAVIOR** Eats grasshoppers, other insects, leaves, flowers, shoots, seeds, grain, acorns, corn, oats, wheat, and rye. Males concentrate on leks during breeding season, booming and displaying to attract females. Dominant males breed with majority of females attending lek displays. Prefers short-grass prairies and more brushy cover than Greater Prairie-Chicken. Usually walks rather than flies. Makes relatively short flights.
- **BREEDING** Polygamous; promiscuous.
- **NESTING** Incubation 22–24 days by female. Precocial young leave nest soon after hatching. First flight at 7–10 days. Tended by female. 1 brood per year.
- **POPULATION** Uncommon to rare. Declining. Extirpated from much of former range.
- **CONSERVATION** Threatened due to conversion of habitat to farmland. Listed federally as a Threatened Wildlife species.

Similar Birds

GREATER PRAIRIE-CHICKEN
Larger; yellow-orange air sacs; heavier barring on underparts.

SHARP-TAILED GROUSE
Scaled, spotted underparts; pointed mostly white tail; has less prominent yellow-orange eye combs.

Flight Pattern
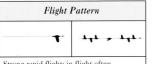
Strong rapid flight; in flight often alternates several rapid wing beats with short glides.

Nest Identification	
Shape ～ Location ✿✿✿ ❦	Lined with grasses • on ground often at base of sagebrush or concealed in grass or shrubs • built by female • 11–13 whitish to buff eggs, sometimes finely spotted with pale brown or olive; ovate, 1.6 inches long.

Plumage Sexes similar	Habitat ⤳ ⸺ ▲	Migration Nonmigratory	Weight 1.7 pounds

DATE _____ TIME _____ LOCATION _____

Family PHASIANIDAE	Species *Meleagris gallopavo*	Length 37–46 inches	Wingspan 4–5 feet

WILD TURKEY

The largest game bird in North America, the Wild Turkey once was so widespread it was considered for the US national emblem. Male turkeys gobble year round, but in spring they are easily startled and will gobble at any abrupt noise. Today this unmistakable symbol of a US national holiday is becoming common again due to conservation efforts and its own adjustments to changes in its original woodland habitat.

- **SONG** Gobbling may be heard up to a mile away and is easily imitated, with bird often responding to it. Several different clucking calls given by both sexes: *cluk, cluck, cut, putt,* and others.
- **BEHAVIOR** Powerful muscular gizzard can grind hardest foods. Eats nuts, seeds, large insects, frogs, lizards, wild fruits, and grapes. Flies to tree roosts for the night. Male displays by strutting with tail spread, wings drooped to ground, bare skin of head intensified in color, and frequent gobbling.
- **BREEDING** Polygamous.
- **NESTING** Incubation 27–28 days by female. First flight in about 14 days. Tended by female. 1 brood per year.
- **POPULATION** Rare to fairly common. Wild birds unlikely in areas of human habitation, though widely domesticated. Increasing.
- **CONSERVATION** Trap and transfer programs have helped reestablish some populations. Increased comeback of blocks of forest interspersed with agricultural areas, as well as wildlife management programs, have helped increase populations.

bare blue and pink head

large iridescent dark body glistens with greens and bronzes

red wattles

MALE

white-barred flight feathers

proportionally smaller head

blackish breast tuft or "beard"

lacks breast tuft (small "beard" present in some older females)

spurred pinkish legs

duller in color and less iridescent than male

smaller than male

FEMALE

medium-length broad tail

Flight Pattern
Swift powerful flight for short distances with rapid wing beats and deep strokes; often glides after several series of wing beats.

Nest Identification	
Shape ⚬ Location ▬	Lined with a few dead leaves and grass • on ground concealed under shrub or in grass • built by female • 8–20 white to cream or buff eggs, sometimes blotched or spotted with brown or red, 2.5 inches long.

Plumage Sexes differ	Habitat	Migration Nonmigratory	Weight 16.3 pounds

Family ODONTOPHORIDAE	Species *Callipepla squamata*	Length 10 inches	Wingspan 13–14 inches

SCALED QUAIL

This native of the Southwest is sometimes called "cotton top" because of its conspicuous white-tipped crest. When alarmed, flocks of these birds run into bushes for cover. The female resembles the male but has a smaller buffier crest. Even at a distance the bird's bluish gray breast and mantle and white-tipped crest make it easy to identify. A close view reveals the body feathers' tiny dark edging that gives the scaled appearance, upon which the common and scientific names are based. Juveniles are more rufous and appear more mottled than scaly. In southern Texas the male has a dark chestnut patch on the belly.

white-tipped crest

grayish overall

dark edges on mantle, neck, breast, and belly feathers give a scaled appearance

olive-brown wings

bluish gray breast

chunky, rounded body

white-streaked sides

- **SONG** Most common is a low nasal *chip-CHURR* or *pe-COS* or *wait-UP* with accent on second syllable. Also, other clucking notes.
- **BEHAVIOR** Eats insects; seeds from desert shrubs, cacti, weeds, grasses, and flowers; flower blossoms; and tender shoots. Found in pairs or small groups in spring and summer; at other times forms coveys of 7 to more than 100. Makes daily trips to waterholes or cattle tanks. Spends heat of day under shade of a shrub. Would rather walk or run than fly.
- **BREEDING** Monogamous. Breeding success correlates to amount of rain; may not nest when rainfall is scarce.
- **NESTING** Incubation 22–23 days mostly by female. Precocial young leave nest soon after hatching. Tended by both sexes. First flight at 14–16 days. 1 brood per year.
- **POPULATION** Fairly common in semidesert scrubland east to Texas. Local populations fluctuate. Adversely affected by drought years and exceedingly heavy rain.
- **FEEDERS** Uses stations where small seed is placed on ground. Attracted to permanent man-made water sources.
- **CONSERVATION** Moderate grazing improves habitat. Hunted as a game bird.

Similar Birds

NORTHERN BOBWHITE ♂
Rufous overall; short crest lacks white tip; white or buff pattern on face.

GAMBEL'S QUAIL ♂
Short dark head plume that tilts forward; lacks scaly feathers • inhabits desert scrublands of the Southwest.

Flight Pattern

Takes off on rapidly beating wings, then alternates between series of rapid stiff wing beats and short glides.

Nest Identification

Shape ⚬ Location ⚬⚬⚬ 🌿

Lined with dry grasses and feathers • sheltered by shrub or grassy tussock • sometimes in open field • built by female • 9–16 dull white to cream-white eggs, some thickly speckled with small spots or dots of light brown, 1.3 inches long.

Plumage Sexes similar	Habitat	Migration Nonmigratory	Weight 6.7 ounces

DATE _____ TIME_____ LOCATION _____

Family ODONTOPHORIDAE	Species *Callipepla gambelii*	Length 11 inches	Wingspan 14–16 inches

GAMBEL'S QUAIL

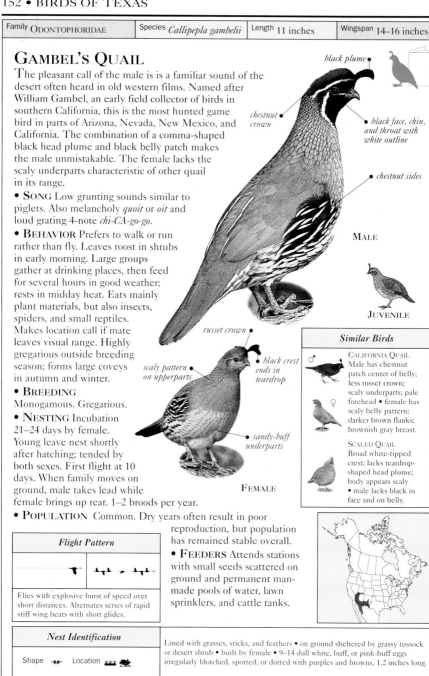

The pleasant call of the male is is a familiar sound of the desert often heard in old western films. Named after William Gambel, an early field collector of birds in southern California, this is the most hunted game bird in parts of Arizona, Nevada, New Mexico, and California. The combination of a comma-shaped black head plume and black belly patch makes the male unmistakable. The female lacks the scaly underparts characteristic of other quail in its range.

- **SONG** Low grunting sounds similar to piglets. Also melancholy *quoit* or *oit* and loud grating 4-note *chi-CA-go-go*.
- **BEHAVIOR** Prefers to walk or run rather than fly. Leaves roost in shrubs in early morning. Large groups gather at drinking places, then feed for several hours in good weather; rests in midday heat. Eats mainly plant materials, but also insects, spiders, and small reptiles. Makes location call if mate leaves visual range. Highly gregarious outside breeding season; forms large coveys in autumn and winter.
- **BREEDING** Monogamous. Gregarious.
- **NESTING** Incubation 21–24 days by female. Young leave nest shortly after hatching; tended by both sexes. First flight at 10 days. When family moves on ground, male takes lead while female brings up rear. 1–2 broods per year.
- **POPULATION** Common. Dry years often result in poor reproduction, but population has remained stable overall.
- **FEEDERS** Attends stations with small seeds scattered on ground and permanent man-made pools of water, lawn sprinklers, and cattle tanks.

black plume

chestnut crown

black face, chin, and throat with white outline

chestnut sides

MALE

JUVENILE

russet crown

scaly pattern on upperparts

black crest ends in teardrop

sandy-buff underparts

FEMALE

Similar Birds

♂ CALIFORNIA QUAIL
Male has chestnut patch center of belly; less russet crown; scaly underparts; pale forehead • female has scaly belly pattern; darker brown flanks; brownish gray breast.

SCALED QUAIL
Broad white-tipped crest; lacks teardrop-shaped head plume; body appears scaly • male lacks black in face and on belly.

Flight Pattern

Flies with explosive burst of speed over short distances. Alternates series of rapid stiff wing beats with short glides.

Nest Identification

Shape   Location

Lined with grasses, sticks, and feathers • on ground sheltered by grassy tussock or desert shrub • built by female • 9–14 dull white, buff, or pink-buff eggs irregularly blotched, spotted, or dotted with purples and browns, 1.2 inches long.

Plumage Sexes differ	Habitat	Migration Nonmigratory	Weight 6.0 ounces

DATE _____ TIME _____ LOCATION _____

Family ODONTOPHORIDAE	Species *Colinus virginianus*	Length 9–10 inches	Wingspan 14–16 inches

NORTHERN BOBWHITE

This familiar eastern quail, named for the male's loud call, inhabits farmlands, fields, lightly grazed pastures, and grasslands. The "Masked Bobwhite," a southwestern race with a black face and cinnamon-rufous underparts, formerly of Mexico and southeast Arizona, has been reintroduced into Arizona grasslands.

- **SONG** Rising clear whistle, *bob-WHITE!* or *bob-bob-WHITE!*, given most often by males in spring and summer. Also whistles *hoy*.
- **BEHAVIOR** Solitary or in pairs in spring; family groups in summer; coveys of 8–15 in fall and winter. Roosts on ground in groups of up to 30, tails pushed together and heads facing out of a tight wagon wheel–shaped circle. Eats seeds, insects, worms, and spiders.
- **BREEDING** Monogamous; some evidence of polygamy.
- **NESTING** Incubation 23–24 days by both sexes. Young leave nest soon after hatching; tended by both sexes. First flight at 12–14 days. 1 brood per year.
- **POPULATION** Uncommon to common in brushlands and open woodland. Introduced into northwestern US. Significantly declining over much of range.
- **FEEDERS** Scattered grains on ground or man-made permanent sources of water.
- **CONSERVATION** Hunted as a game bird; highly managed in some states. Decline may be due to habitat loss and changes in farming practices. Sensitive to cold winter weather; entire populations may be wiped out by hard freezes.

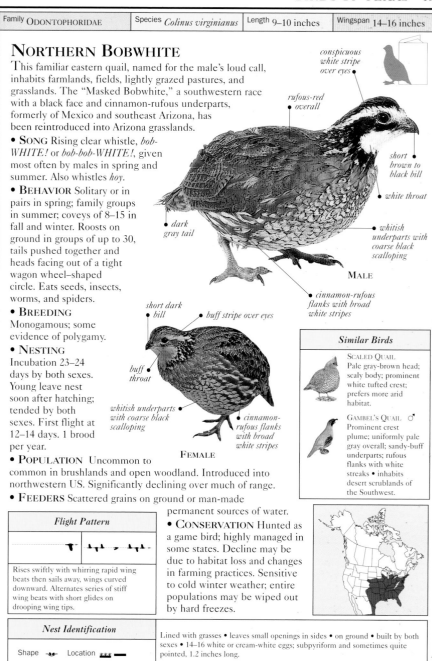

conspicuous white stripe over eyes

rufous-red overall

short brown to black bill

white throat

whitish underparts with coarse black scalloping

dark gray tail

MALE

cinnamon-rufous flanks with broad white stripes

short dark bill

buff stripe over eyes

buff throat

whitish underparts with coarse black scalloping

cinnamon-rufous flanks with broad white stripes

FEMALE

Similar Birds

SCALED QUAIL
Pale gray-brown head; scaly body; prominent white tufted crest; prefers more arid habitat.

GAMBEL'S QUAIL ♂
Prominent crest plume; uniformly pale gray overall; sandy-buff underparts; rufous flanks with white streaks • inhabits desert scrublands of the Southwest.

Flight Pattern

Rises swiftly with whirring rapid wing beats then sails away, wings curved downward. Alternates series of stiff wing beats with short glides on drooping wing tips.

Nest Identification

Shape ⌣ Location ⁙ ▬

Lined with grasses • leaves small openings in sides • on ground • built by both sexes • 14–16 white or cream-white eggs; subpyriform and sometimes quite pointed, 1.2 inches long.

Plumage Sexes differ	Habitat ⸺ 🌿 🌱	Migration Nonmigratory	Weight 6.3 ounces

DATE _____ TIME _____ LOCATION _____

Family ODONTOPHORIDAE	Species *Cyrtonyx montezumae*	Length 8–9 inches	Wingspan 12–14 inches

MONTEZUMA QUAIL

This quail's arched claws help it walk easily over steep rocky places in mountainous open oak grasslands. It is a plump, short-tailed, secretive quail. The male has a bold pattern with white spots on the sides and flanks, a dark chestnut breast, a striking black-and-white pattern on its "clown face," and a soft tan crest. Females are brown with white, black, and brown mottling and streaking. Juveniles are paler brown with heavy black mottling on the underparts.

• **SONG** Bold tremulous descending whistle resembling that of the Eastern Screech-Owl.

• **BEHAVIOR** Prefers grasslands in pine-oak or juniper-oak open forests in mountains and foothills. Scratches on ground to uncover plant bulbs. Eats nuts of oak and pine, fruits of juniper, seeds of grasses, weeds, buds, tender leaves, blossoms, and insects. Tame. Often sits low and explodes into flight practically beneath one's feet. Moves in pairs or families.

• **BREEDING** Monogamous.

• **NESTING** Incubation 25–26 days by both sexes. Precocial young leave nest soon after hatching. First flight at about 10 days. Tended by both sexes. 1 brood per year.

• **POPULATION** Uncommon to rare and local. Has disappeared or become scarce in parts of the Southwest due to overgrazing by livestock. This also may be occuring in Mexico, but the bird's status there is not well known.

• **FEEDERS** Attends feeders with small seeds scattered on ground and permanent man-made water sources in proper habitat.

• **CONSERVATION** Concern over population declines, though still considered a game bird in some areas.

soft tan crest extends back over neck

black mottling and spotting on back and wings

black-and-white facial pattern

brown and tan plump body

rounded wings

short tail

dark gray sides and flanks with numerous white spots

MALE

less distinct head markings

FEMALE

short tail

ocher-brown mottling on underparts

Similar Birds

NORTHERN BOBWHITE
♂ Rarely in same habitat; rufous-brown overall;
♀ scaly pale underparts.

GAMBEL'S QUAIL
♂ Teardrop-shaped head plume; gray-brown
♀ overall; longer tail.

SCALED QUAIL
White-tipped crest; scaly gray-brown body.

Flight Pattern
Rises in swift direct flight on rapidly beating wings, then alternates series of rapid stiff wing beats and short glides on drooping wings.

Nest Identification	
Shape Location	Lined and roofed with grass • in ground • built by female, sometimes with help from male • 6–14 white or cream eggs, unmarked but often nest-stained, 1.2 inches long.

Plumage Sexes differ	Habitat	Migration Nonmigratory	Weight 6.9 ounces

DATE _____ TIME _____ LOCATION _____

Family RALLIDAE	Species *Coturnicops noveboracensis*	Length 6–7.25 inches	Wingspan 10–13 inches

YELLOW RAIL

The sparrow-sized Yellow Rail is one of the least-known rails. It is so reluctant to fly that trained dogs can catch it. If flushed it flies weakly with its feet dangling, showing a white patch on the trailing edge of the inner wing before dropping back into cover. Its narrow body, strong toes, and flexible wings help it survive in dense marsh grasses. Adults have olive-gray legs, a buff chest, dark brown flanks with white bars, white-spotted wing coverts, and cinnamon undertail coverts. Juveniles are darker gray-black above with slight buffy striping; more white spotting on head, neck, breast, and sides; and more black barring on the flanks.

dark brown upperparts with broad buff stripes and narrow white crossbars

dark brown crown

broad dark smudge through eye

short yellowish to greenish gray bill

- **SONG** Like pebbles tapping, *tick-tick, tick-tick-tick.* Usually at night.
- **BEHAVIOR** Secretive; difficult to see in the open; sticks to thick grasses and marsh vegetation. Prefers to walk or run if disturbed. Flutters in air when flushed, then quickly drops and runs on the ground to escape. Averse to flying yet able to migrate great distances. Eats insects, small snails, seeds, tender leaves of clover, and grasses.
- **BREEDING** Monogamous. Solitary nester.
- **NESTING** Incubation 16–18 days by female. Precocial young leave nest shortly after hatching. Probably tended by female. May be independent of parents at 35 days. 1 brood per year.
- **POPULATION** Uncommon to rare and poorly known. Declining due to loss of habitat.
- **CONSERVATION** Draining and development of wetlands negatively impacting populations. Considered a game bird in some states.

Similar Birds

SORA
Juveniles are twice as large; bright yellow bill; lack buff stripes on upperparts; lacks white wing patch in flight.

Flight Pattern

Flutters weakly on floppy wings for short low flights. Direct flight when traveling longer distances.

Nest Identification

Shape ◡ ◖ Location ▬ ▬▬

Canopy of vegetation pulled to cover mat of fine dead grass • above damp soil on bare ground or flattened vegetation • a little above water of marsh or meadow and screened by small blades of grass • built by both sexes • 7–10 creamy buff eggs occasionally spotted with reddish brown and capped; ovate but often markedly elongated, 1.1 inches long.

Plumage Sexes similar	Habitat ⯗ ▬ ≈≈ ⑊	Migration Migratory	Weight 1.8 ounces

Family RALLIDAE	Species *Laterallus jamaicensis*	Length 6 inches	Wingspan 10.5–11.5 inches

BLACK RAIL

The smallest and perhaps most secretive member of the rail family, this bird was first recorded on the island of Jamaica and is extremely difficult to find. Its range is not well known, and small populations and individual records scattered widely across the United States provide our only information. If glimpsed, it appears like a rodent scampering. Its flight is faint and shaky with legs dangling,

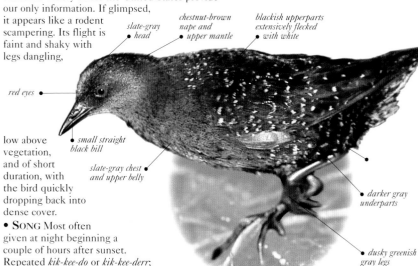

slate-gray head

chestnut-brown nape and upper mantle

blackish upperparts extensively flecked with white

red eyes

small straight black bill

slate-gray chest and upper belly

darker gray underparts

dusky greenish gray legs

low above vegetation, and of short duration, with the bird quickly dropping back into dense cover.

• **SONG** Most often given at night beginning a couple of hours after sunset. Repeated *kik-kee-do* or *kik-kee-derr*; sometimes gives 4 notes, *kik-kik-kee-do*.

• **BEHAVIOR** Remains in cover of vegetation; rarely stays exposed for long. Rarely flies. Lives in freshwater marshes and wet meadows or in shallow margins of saltwater marshes above the beach line. Sometimes found in grain fields and dry hay fields. Eats seeds of aquatic plants, grasses and grains, insects, and isopods (small marine crustaceans).

• **BREEDING** Monogamous. Solitary nester.

• **NESTING** Incubation 16–20 days by both sexes. Precocial young leave nest soon after hatching. Tended by both parents. Possibly 2 broods per year.

• **POPULATION** Generally uncommon to rare; although locally common in some places. Declining in most parts of North American range due to loss of habitat, especially coastal marshes. Population stable in protected habitat.

• **CONSERVATION** Wetland conservation important.

Similar Birds

YELLOW RAIL
Larger; buff; white wing patches visible in flight.

Flight Pattern
Weak fluttering floppy flight with legs dangling.

Nest Identification	Woven coil of soft grass blades, sedge, or other vegetation • in grass 18–24 inches tall on edge of marsh • built by both sexes • 4–13 white, pinkish white, or creamy white eggs dotted with brown; short subelliptical or elliptical, 1 inch long.
Shape ⌣ Location 🌱🌱🌱	

Plumage Sexes similar	Habitat	Migration Most migrate	Weight 1.2 ounces

DATE _____ TIME_____ LOCATION _____

| Family RALLIDAE | Species *Rallus longirostris* | Length 14–16 inches | Wingspan 19–21 inches |

CLAPPER RAIL

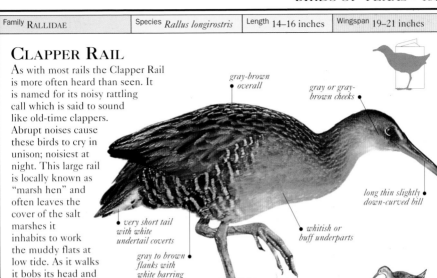

gray-brown overall

gray or gray-brown cheeks

long thin slightly down-curved bill

whitish or buff underparts

very short tail with white undertail coverts

gray to brown flanks with white barring

As with most rails the Clapper Rail is more often heard than seen. It is named for its noisy rattling call which is said to sound like old-time clappers. Abrupt noises cause these birds to cry in unison; noisiest at night. This large rail is locally known as "marsh hen" and often leaves the cover of the salt marshes it inhabits to work the muddy flats at low tide. As it walks it bobs its head and flips its short tail exposing white undertail coverts.

JUVENILE

• **SONG** A series of grating *kek-kek-kek* notes, accelerating then dropping off. Given most often at dusk on moonlit nights or when suddenly disturbed by loud noise. One call stimulates another; the calls travel like a wave through the marsh.

• **BEHAVIOR** Feeds mostly in the open at low tide on mudflats. At other times forages concealed in salt marsh vegetation. Eats crabs and other crustaceans, worms, amphibians, reptiles, mollusks, small fish, and aquatic insects.

• **BREEDING** Monogamous. Solitary nester.

• **NESTING** Incubation 20–23 days by both sexes. Precocial young abandon nest soon after hatching. Tended by both sexes. Independent after 35–42 days. First flight at 63–70 days. Possibly 2 broods per year.

• **POPULATION** Common in coastal salt marshes but declining on West Coast and in some places in the East. Casual on Atlantic Coast to the Maritimes.

Similar Birds

KING RAIL Favors freshwater marshes; bolder black-and-white bars on flanks; bright rufous-brown neck and chest; tawny-buff cheeks; buff-edged back feathers; brown wing coverts; voice differs.

VIRGINIA RAIL One-third the size; darker overall; blue-gray auriculars; bright rufous upperwing coverts.

• **CONSERVATION** The inland freshwater race on the lower Colorado River is considered endangered. Also endangered on the West Coast due to habitat loss and perhaps introduced predators.

Flight Pattern

Low fluttering flight over short distances with legs dangling.

Nest Identification	
Shape ⬱ Location 🪨 🌿 🌾	Basket of aquatic vegetation and tide-deposited materials • elevated on firm bank or under small bush • built by both sexes, but male does more • 5–12 buff or olive-buff eggs marked with brown; subelliptical to long subelliptical to ovate, 1.7 inches long.

| Plumage Sexes similar | Habitat 〰 ___ | Migration Migratory | Weight 11.4 ounces |

DATE _____ TIME_____ LOCATION _____

Family RALLIDAE	Species *Rallus elegans*	Length 15–19 inches	Wingspan 21–25 inches

KING RAIL

This large freshwater rail migrates through the Mississippi Valley and along the Atlantic Coast. Oddly, this bird's population seems tied to that of the muskrat, which creates open spaces in the marsh providing feeding and drinking areas for the rail. Widely

olive-brown upperparts with buff-edged back feathers

olive-brown head and hindneck

long slender, slightly down-curved bill

distributed in the East in summer, it is found in both freshwater and brackish marshes. Some consider it an inland freshwater race of the smaller Clapper Rail, but the King Rail is more rufous and has buff edging on the back feathers and brown to rufous wing coverts.

cinnamon-rufous foreneck and chest

blackish upper bill, orange to red lower bill, and dusky tip

dark blackish brown and white barring on flanks

JUVENILE

• **SONG** Series of less than 10 notes of *kek-kek-kek* or *jupe-jupe-jupe* deeper than those of Clapper Rail and not descending. Various other clucking and grunting notes.

• **BEHAVIOR** Sometimes feeds in open, mostly in shallow water or mudflats exposed at low tide. Variable diet of aquatic and semiaquatic foods includes plant parts, invertebrates, and vertebrates. Terrestrial, yet migrates long distances.

• **BREEDING** Monogamous. Solitary nester.

• **NESTING** Incubation 21–24 days by both sexes. Precocial young abandon nest soon after hatching; stay with parents about 63 days. Possibly 2 broods per year.

• **POPULATION** Fairly common to common in freshwater and brackish habitat near the Gulf Coast. Declined or disappeared in some areas due to loss of and/or contamination of habitat.

• **CONSERVATION** Considered a game bird in some states. Wetland management crucial inland and on coast.

Similar Birds

VIRGINIA RAIL
Much smaller; darker overall; blue-gray auriculars; bright rufous upperwing coverts.

CLAPPER RAIL
Slightly smaller; duller coloring; less barring on flanks; variable plumage, but grayish edge on brown-centered back feathers and olive-brown wing coverts; frequents salt marshes.

Flight Pattern
Slow floppy flight, often low above vegetation with feet dangling.

Nest Identification	
Shape ⌒⌒ Location ✴✴✴ ⱮⱮ	Dry aquatic vegetation • 6–8 inches above water amid aquatic vegetation • built by both sexes, but male does more • 6–15 buff eggs spotted with brown; ovate, 1.6 inches long.

Plumage Sexes similar	Habitat	Migration Migratory	Weight 14.6 ounces

DATE _____ TIME_____ LOCATION _____

Family RALLIDAE	Species *Rallus limicola*	Length 9–10 inches	Wingspan 13–14.5 inches

VIRGINIA RAIL

Like all rails, the Virginia Rail generally does not fly when it is being pursued but will run swiftly through the marsh grasses. Note its gray cheeks and the reddish bill and legs. Flanks, lower belly, and undertail coverts are barred with black and white. In flight the wings show chestnut in the leading edge. Although this bird prefers freshwater and brackish marshes, it often inhabits salt marshes in winter. Juveniles have dark blackish brown upperparts and black, gray, and white mottling and barring on underparts.

blue-gray face •

• blackish crown

• whitish to pale chin

reddish legs and feet •

cinnamon-rufous throat and breast •

slightly down-• curved, long, slender reddish bill

JUVENILE

- **SONG** Resembles the clicking of keys on an old typewriter, *kid-ick, kid-ick, kid-ick* or *tic-tic-tic*. Also makes *kik, kik, kik, ki-queea* "kicker" call and descending series of piglike grunts and other odd calls.
- **BEHAVIOR** Somewhat secretive and terrestrial. Feeds primarily on insects but also takes aquatic animals, including worms, spiders, crustaceans, and small fish. Diet is varied, especially in winter, with duckweed and seeds of marsh grasses, rushes, and sedges.
- **BREEDING** Monogamous.
- **NESTING** Incubation 18–20 days by both sexes. Precocial young leave nest soon after hatching. Tended by both parents. First flight at about 25 days. Possibly 2 broods per year.
- **POPULATION** Fairly common to uncommon. Declining but still widespread despite loss of wetland habitat.
- **CONSERVATION** Still hunted as a game bird in some states. Wetland protection and management is crucial.

Similar Birds

KING RAIL
About twice the size • olive-brown head; brown to gray cheeks; cinnamon-rufous underparts; black-and-white barring on flanks.

CLAPPER RAIL
Larger; grayish body; cinnamon to gray underparts; black-and-white barring on flanks; prefers salt marshes.

Flight Pattern

Weak brief fluttering flight with long legs dangling.

Nest Identification	
Shape ⬳ Location 🌾🌱	Pile of matted reeds and layers of coarse aquatic vegetation and grass • in tussock or clumped vegetation • built by both sexes • 5–13 off-white or buff eggs spotted with brown and often wreathed; oval to short oval, 1.3 inches long.

Plumage Sexes similar	Habitat 〰 ⌁	Migration Migratory	Weight 3.1 ounces

DATE _____ TIME_____ LOCATION _____

Family RALLIDAE	Species *Porzana carolina*	Length 8–10 inches	Wingspan 12–14.5 inches

SORA

In late summer large numbers of these birds gather in marshes to feed and build up fat reserves before migrating; they seem especially fond of smartweed seeds and wild rice. Like all rails, the Sora migrates at night, and for a group that hardly distinguishes itself in the air, this species may cover almost 3,000 miles between wintering and breeding grounds. It is identifiable by its short yellow bill framed with black feathers around its base, black throat, and black center in the upper breast. Small and plump, it is one of the most common North American rails. Juveniles lack the black on the face and underparts and, with their buff coloration, sometimes are confused with the much smaller Yellow Rail.

black-and-buff spots on wings and back

black patch on face and throat

short chickenlike yellow bill

irregular barring of thin white lines on gray underparts

yellow-green legs

JUVENILE   WINTER PLUMAGE

very long toes

• **SONG** Descending melodious whinny and abrasive high-pitched *keek*. Makes froglike whistle of *ker-wheer* on breeding ground.
• **BEHAVIOR** Small bill prevents it from probing into marsh mud for animals like the long-billed rails. Eats mainly plant life such as seeds, wild rice, and algae. Also feeds on insects, spiders, small crustaceans, and snails. Often found in the open where it walks slowly with head down and short tail cocked and flicked above white undertail coverts. Can show up in almost any moist habitat, especially in migration.
• **BREEDING** Monogamous.
• **NESTING** Incubation 19–20 days. Precocial young abandon nest soon after hatching. 2 broods per year.

Similar Birds

VIRGINIA RAIL
Long, slender, slightly down-curved reddish bill; gray face; rusty-red throat and breast.

YELLOW RAIL
Much smaller; checkered pattern of buff stripes and white bars on a blackish back on upperparts; lacks black on chin and throat; shows white wing patch in flight.

• **POPULATION** Common and widespread despite loss of wetland habitat.
• **CONSERVATION** Recent loss of habitat due to draining and development of marshes; also due to loss of wintering coastal habitat.

Flight Pattern

Weak labored floppy flight for short distances and low over vegetation with legs dangling.

Nest Identification

Shape ⬤   Location ⬆ 🌱

A bowl of cattails, dry leaves, grasses, and reeds • about 6 inches in diameter • connected to stems of marsh vegetation a few inches above water • in reeds, cattails, or grasses over deeper water • 10–12 rich buff eggs irregularly spotted with browns and grays; ovate, 1.2 inches long.

Plumage Sexes similar	Habitat 🌾 〰️ 〰️	Migration Migratory	Weight 2.6 ounces

DATE _____ TIME_____ LOCATION _____

Family RALLIDAE	Species *Porphyrula martinica*	Length 13–14 inches	Wingspan 22 inches

PURPLE GALLINULE

This beautiful brightly colored member of the rail family can be seen walking gracefully on lily pads on extremely long yellow feet or swimming in open water with its head pumping back and forth. Most often seen in protected areas in the south, such as the Everglades National Park, individuals have wandered as far north as New England. Gaudy in color, the hues blend with the greens of marsh vegetation and the reflections of blue sky on water, sometimes making the bird difficult to see if not for the flicking tail revealing white undertail coverts. Juveniles have chocolate-brown to bluish olive upperparts and paler underparts.

glossy brownish green back

pale blue frontal shield

red bill with yellow tip

bright purplish head and neck

bright purplish underparts

snow-white undertail coverts

yellow legs and feet

JUVENILE

- **SONG** Various abrasive shrieking calls and hoarse chatters: sharp *kr'lik'* or *kee-k'*, gruff *kruk kruk-kruk-kruk*, screaming *whiehrrr* or *w'heehrr*, series of rapid clucking *kahw cohw-cohw-cohw* or *keh-keh-keh*.
- **BEHAVIOR** Feeds on seeds, fruits, and other parts of wild rice; grasses; fruit of water lily; grains; insects; crustaceans; snails; eggs and sometimes nestlings of marsh birds; amphibians; and small fish. Pumps and bobs head. Flicks short cocked tail when walking. Climbs well in vegetation.
- **BREEDING** Cooperative.
- **NESTING** Incubation 22–25 days by both sexes. Precocial young abandon nest soon after hatching and drying off. Tended and fed by both sexes, often with help from other birds. First flight at about 63 days. Possibly 2 broods per year.
- **POPULATION** Fairly common in southern and coastal freshwater marshes, vegetated lakes, overgrown swamps, and lagoons. Decline due to loss of wetlands habitat.
- **CONSERVATION** Wetland conservation critical.

Similar Birds

COMMON MOORHEN
White line separates flanks from upperparts in juveniles and adults
- adults have red frontal shield; gray underparts; brownish upperparts.

AMERICAN COOT
Gray body; blackish head and neck; white bill and reddish brown frontal shield.

Flight Pattern
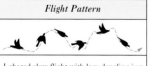
Labored slow flight with legs dangling just above water.

Nest Identification	
Shape Location	Green and dry stems with leaves • floating island of vegetation • built by both sexes • 5–10 cinnamon-pink or buff eggs marked with brown, 1.5 inches long.

Plumage Sexes similar	Habitat	Migration Migratory	Weight 9.1 ounces

DATE _____ TIME_____ LOCATION _____

Family RALLIDAE	Species *Gallinula chloropus*	Length 14 inches	Wingspan 20–23 inches

COMMON MOORHEN

This is a fairly tame chickenlike bird of freshwater marshes, ponds, and lakes with heavy stands of cattails, rushes, sedges, and other aquatic vegetation.

- **SONG** No musical sounds are produced. Vocalizations range from explosive, froglike *hups* to loud, chickenlike grunts, clucks, and squeaks along with drawn-out whines and rapid *thicket-thicket-thicket* calls.
- **BEHAVIOR** This noisy bird of the wetlands, unlike most of the rail family, is often seen in the open walking over or climbing through aquatic vegetation. It swims with a pumping back-and-forth motion of its head and neck. When walking it often flicks its tail up and down, flashing the white undertail coverts with their dark center. Usually found in medium to large groups in which individuals can be aggressive toward other members in disputes over food, mates, or nesting areas. Feeds on aquatic vegetation, snails, grasshoppers, and other invertebrates.
- **BREEDING** Monogamous. Solitary to semicolonial, some cooperative breeding.
- **NESTING** Incubation 18–22 days by both sexes. Precocial young stay in nest 40–50 days, fed by both parents and extra birds. 1–3 broods per year.
- **POPULATION** Common, but loss of wetlands has resulted in decline, especially in northern range. Still widespread; may be common in good marsh habitat.

blackish head and neck

red frontal shield

white "line" on side

brownish olive back

red bill with yellow tip

red garter

yellow-green legs

yellow feet

JUVENILE

WINTER PLUMAGE

Similar Birds

AMERICAN COOT
White bill; slate-gray back; no white band on flanks.

Flight Pattern

Swift and strong direct flight when moving long distance. Weak and fluttering flight when moving very short distance.

Nest Identification

Shape   Location

Often with ramp of vegetation • made of bleached aquatic vegetation lined with grass • on ground near water or low shrub over water • built by both sexes • 2–13 cinnamon or buff eggs spotted with reddish brown or olive and overlaid with scattered fine dots, 1.7 inches long.

Plumage Sexes similar	Habitat	Migration Some migrate	Weight 12.0 ounces

DATE _____ TIME _____ LOCATION _____

Family RALLIDAE	Species *Fulica americana*	Length 15 inches	Wingspan 23–28 inches

AMERICAN COOT

This close relative of the gallinules and moorhens lives on open water and is often mistaken for a duck. It pumps its small head back and forth like a chicken when walking or swimming and usually travels and feeds in flocks. A common and widely distributed species over much of North America, the American Coot is easily distinguished by its overall slate-gray plumage, which is

gray-black head and neck

reddish brown frontal shield

slate-gray body

short white bill

JUVENILE

blacker on the head and neck, its white bill, and small reddish brown frontal shield. Juveniles are similar to adults but paler, particularly on the underparts, with a darker bill.

• SONG Grunts, grating quacks, and hoarse chatters of *ke-yik* and *k-rrk!* or *krek!* Drawling *k-yew-r* and laughing *wah wahk* or *kuk-kuk-kuk-kuk-kuk*.

• BEHAVIOR Feeds by immersing head and neck in shallows with body and tail tipped up. May also pick food off surface. Dives 10–25 feet deep for fronds, leaves, seeds, and roots of aquatic plants, which make up most of diet. Also eats insects, amphibians, mollusks, and small fish. Runs with wings flapping rapidly to gain flight from water. Often aggressive toward other waterbirds, chasing them nosily from its vicinity.

• BREEDING Monogamous. Pairs display in front of each other on water in courtship. The male also chases the female across surface of water.

• NESTING Incubation 21–25 days by both sexes. Precocial young abandon nest shortly after hatching and drying off. Tended by both sexes. First flight at 49–56 days. 1–2 broods per year.

• POPULATION Common to abundant. Has decreased in the East in recent years.

Similar Birds

COMMON MOORHEN
Red shield; yellow-tipped red bill; brown back; white-tipped flank feathers form line between flank and back • juvenile paler with white flank stripe.

PURPLE GALLINULE
Dark bluish purple head, neck, and underparts; greenish brown back; yellow-tipped red bill; pale blue shield • juvenile has olive-brown upperparts; pale brown underparts; dull yellowish bill.

Flight Pattern

Fairly swift direct flight with rapid wing beats and feet protruding beyond tail.

Nest Identification

Shape 🪺   Location 🪺 🌾

Made of dead stems • lined with finer material • floating and anchored to vegetation • built by both sexes • 2–12 pinkish buff eggs marked with blackish brown, 1.9 inches long.

Plumage Sexes similar	Habitat 〰️ 〰️	Migration Migratory	Weight 1.6 pounds

DATE _____ TIME_____ LOCATION _____

Family GRUIDAE	Species *Grus canadensis*	Length 34–48 inches	Wingspan 73–90 inches

SANDHILL CRANE

The five North American subspecies of this crane (plus one in Cuba) differ in size and intensity of coloration. The small southern sedentary populations are the most threatened. On the ground cranes look stately with long necks, heavy straight bills, long legs, "bustle" of tertials drooping over the tail, and upright stance. In flight they are distinguished from herons because the neck and head are extended and the slow downward wing beat is jerked quickly upward. This bird may probe for food in mud that contains iron, which deposits on the bill and stains the feathers rusty-brown when the bird preens.

dull red skin on crown and lores

straight blackish gray bill

whitish cheeks, chin, and upper throat

long neck

gray body

long blackish gray legs and feet

black primaries

JUVENILE

• **SONG** Noisy trumpetlike *garoo-oo-a-a-a-a*; can carry more than a mile.

• **BEHAVIOR** Roosts communally at night in winter, standing on damp low land or in shallow water. Courtship dances in late winter and spring involve bounding 6–8 feet into air with wings half spread and calling loudly. Eats variety of plants and animals. In summer feeds in breeding marshes or nearby meadows. Walks great distances for food. May soar on thermals and migrate so high it is invisible from the ground.

• **BREEDING** Monogamous. Thought to mate for life.

• **NESTING** Incubation 28–32 days by both sexes. Precocial young leave nest soon after hatching. First flight at 65 days. 1 brood per year.

• **POPULATION** Common to fairly common and local. Stable or increasing, though vulnerable to habitat loss.

• **CONSERVATION** Killing and habitat loss to agriculture depleted southern numbers in the last two centuries. Degradation of habitat at major migration stopping points seriously impacting species. Mississippi Sandhill Crane National Wildlife Refuge houses most remaining Mississippi Sandhill Cranes, and there is an active propagation program.

Similar Birds

WHOOPING CRANE Rare; larger; white; reddish black mustache; black primaries visible in flight.

GREAT BLUE HERON Lacks "bustle"; gray upperparts; yellow bill; dull yellow-brown legs; white head; elongated black supercilium; flies with neck pulled back in S-curve on body.

Flight Pattern

Heavy, labored, steady wing beats with slow downstroke and rapid jerky upstroke. Flies in V or straight line formation.

Nest Identification

Shape ⬯   Location ••• — ⑃

Dead sticks, moss, reeds, and grass • built by both sexes • 2 buff eggs marked with olive or 2 olive eggs marked with brown; subelliptical to long oval, 3.7–3.8 x 2.3 inches.

Plumage Sexes similar	Habitat	Migration Some migrate	Weight 7.4 pounds

DATE _____ TIME_____ LOCATION _____

Family GRUIDAE	Species *Grus americana*	Length 52 inches	Wingspan 87 inches

WHOOPING CRANE

The stately Whooping Crane is the tallest bird in North America and one of the most endangered. By 1941 only fifteen individuals wintering on the Texas coast were left in the wild. The breeding grounds of these birds were unknown until 1954 when they were discovered in Wood Buffalo National Park in Alberta in central Canada. Intensive conservation and management programs have slowly increased this flock to more than one hundred fifty individuals. Juveniles are white with a rusty red head and neck and have rusty red feathers scattered over the rest of the body.

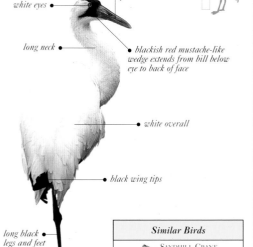

bright red bare skin on crown

long heavy dull yellow bill

white eyes

long neck

blackish red mustache-like wedge extends from bill below eye to back of face

white overall

black wing tips

long black legs and feet

• **SONG** Piercing trumpetlike *ker-loo ker-lee-loo* that can be heard for more than 2 miles. This volume is achieved by the 5-foot-long trachea coiled within the keel of the breast bone.

• **BEHAVIOR** Eats fish, frogs, small mammals, mollusks, crustaceans, corn, other grains, and roots of water plants.

• **BREEDING** Monogamous; mates for life. In courtship dance, one of pair begins by lowering head and flapping wings. Bird leaps 3 feet in air with head back, bill pointed skyward, neck arched over back, legs stiff, and wings flapping. Mate runs forward a few steps, pumping head up and down and flapping wings. Then both leap into air and bounce up and down. The silent dance ends as suddenly as it begins. On wintering grounds do not form flocks but maintain family groups of 3–4 birds and hold winter territory.

• **NESTING** Incubation 29–35 days by both sexes. Precocial young abandon nest soon after hatching; tended by both parents. First flight at approximately 80–90 days. 1 brood per year.

• **POPULATION** Increasing. Populations introduced in Idaho and Florida.

• **CONSERVATION** Endangered, but public education as well as intensive management and protection programs, slowly succeeding.

Similar Birds

SANDHILL CRANE
Smaller; lacks mustache; bare red skin also on forehead and lores; pale gray overall; black bill and legs; shows black primaries in flight.

AMERICAN WHITE PELICAN
Larger; white with black outer secondaries, primaries, and upper primary coverts; short legs; flies with neck folded and long yellow-orange bill resting on breast.

Flight Pattern

Typical crane flight of slow downward wing beat with powerful flick or jerk on upbeat. Flies in V formation in migration.

Nest Identification

Shape Location

Soft or coarse grass, reeds, or sod • built on a mound by both sexes • 1–3 cream-olive buff eggs marked with brown; ovate or elliptical ovate, 3.9 x 2.5 inches.

Plumage Sexes similar	Habitat	Migration Migratory	Weight 12.8 pounds

DATE _____ TIME_____ LOCATION _____

Family CHARADRIIDAE	Species *Pluvialis squatarola*	Length 11.5–13 inches	Wingspan 22–25 inches

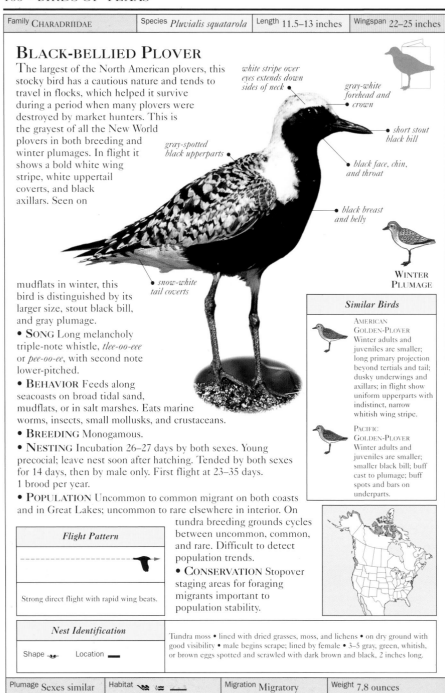

BLACK-BELLIED PLOVER

The largest of the North American plovers, this stocky bird has a cautious nature and tends to travel in flocks, which helped it survive during a period when many plovers were destroyed by market hunters. This is the grayest of all the New World plovers in both breeding and winter plumages. In flight it shows a bold white wing stripe, white uppertail coverts, and black axillars. Seen on

white stripe over eyes extends down sides of neck

gray-white forehead and crown

gray-spotted black upperparts

short stout black bill

black face, chin, and throat

black breast and belly

WINTER PLUMAGE

mudflats in winter, this bird is distinguished by its larger size, stout black bill, and gray plumage.

snow-white tail coverts

• **SONG** Long melancholy triple-note whistle, *tlee-oo-eee* or *pee-oo-ee*, with second note lower-pitched.

• **BEHAVIOR** Feeds along seacoasts on broad tidal sand, mudflats, or in salt marshes. Eats marine worms, insects, small mollusks, and crustaceans.

• **BREEDING** Monogamous.

• **NESTING** Incubation 26–27 days by both sexes. Young precocial; leave nest soon after hatching. Tended by both sexes for 14 days, then by male only. First flight at 23–35 days. 1 brood per year.

• **POPULATION** Uncommon to common migrant on both coasts and in Great Lakes; uncommon to rare elsewhere in interior. On tundra breeding grounds cycles between uncommon, common, and rare. Difficult to detect population trends.

• **CONSERVATION** Stopover staging areas for foraging migrants important to population stability.

Similar Birds

AMERICAN GOLDEN-PLOVER
Winter adults and juveniles are smaller; long primary projection beyond tertials and tail; dusky underwings and axillars; in flight show uniform upperparts with indistinct, narrow whitish wing stripe.

PACIFIC GOLDEN-PLOVER
Winter adults and juveniles are smaller; smaller black bill; buff cast to plumage; buff spots and bars on underparts.

Flight Pattern

Strong direct flight with rapid wing beats.

Nest Identification

Shape ⚲ Location ▬

Tundra moss • lined with dried grasses, moss, and lichens • on dry ground with good visibility • male begins scrape; lined by female • 3–5 gray, green, whitish, or brown eggs spotted and scrawled with dark brown and black, 2 inches long.

Plumage Sexes similar	Habitat 〜 ⪆ ⏚	Migration Migratory	Weight 7.8 ounces

DATE _____ TIME_____ LOCATION _____

Family CHARADRIIDAE	Species *Pluvialis dominica*	Length 10–11 inches	Wingspan 18–22.5 inches

AMERICAN GOLDEN-PLOVER

This expert long-distance migrant flies at a rate of sixty miles per hour and covers thousands of miles per year between Arctic tundra nesting grounds and winter quarters as far away as Argentina. Once an abundant bird, the American Golden-Plover was almost eradicted by market hunters during the late 1800s. Winter adults and juveniles are

short thin black bill

dark brown upperparts dappled profusely with golden spots

broad white stripe over eyes and forehead extends down sides of neck

black face and foreneck

black breast

WINTER PLUMAGE

brown overall with darker upperparts than underparts and lack the distinctive black-and-white markings. In flight in all plumages the uppertail coverts and back are the same color, the underwings are gray throughout, and there is an indistinct pale wing stripe. Primaries of standing birds extend well past the tail.

black underparts, including undertail coverts

- **SONG** Shrieking *ku-wheep* or *quee-dle*.
- **BEHAVIOR** Often flies in small swiftly moving flocks. Holds wings above back after alighting; often bobs head. Feeds on insects (mostly grasshoppers, crickets, and larvae), small mollusks, and crustaceans. On tundra often gorges on crowberry in preparation for autumn migration.
- **BREEDING** Monogamous.
- **NESTING** Incubation 26–27 days by both sexes in turn; male by day, female at night. Precocial young abandon nest soon after hatching. Tended by both sexes. First flight at 21–24 days. 1 brood per year.
- **POPULATION** Uncommon. May be limited because of habitat loss on South American winter range; perhaps never fully recovered from 19th-century market hunting.

Similar Birds

PACIFIC GOLDEN-PLOVER ♂ Longer tertials; shorter primary projection • juveniles and winter birds appear golden yellow overall with spangling and spotting on upperparts; less contrasting crown.

MOUNTAIN PLOVER Plainer overall without markings on lower breast or belly; pale legs.

BLACK-BELLIED PLOVER In winter plumage has black axillaries; white rump.

Flight Pattern

Swift strong direct flight on steady rapid wing beats. Flies in tight flocks that constantly change shape.

Nest Identification

Shape   Location

Lined with lichens, moss, grass, and leaves • on ground in tundra • built by male • 3–4 cinnamon to light buff or cream eggs marked with black and brown spots and blotches, 1.9 inches long.

Plumage Sexes similar	Habitat	Migration Migratory	Weight 5.1 ounces

DATE _____ TIME_____ LOCATION _____

Family CHARADRIIDAE	Species *Charadrius alexandrinus*	Length 6–7 inches	Wingspan 13.5 inches

SNOWY PLOVER

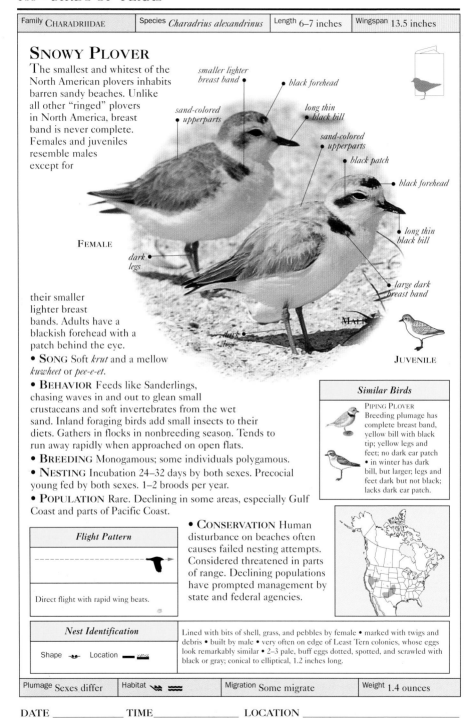

The smallest and whitest of the North American plovers inhabits barren sandy beaches. Unlike all other "ringed" plovers in North America, breast band is never complete. Females and juveniles resemble males except for

smaller lighter breast band

black forehead

sand-colored upperparts

long thin black bill

sand-colored upperparts

black patch

black forehead

long thin black bill

FEMALE

dark legs

large dark breast band

MALE

dark legs

JUVENILE

their smaller lighter breast bands. Adults have a blackish forehead with a patch behind the eye.

- **SONG** Soft *krut* and a mellow *kuwheet* or *pee-e-et.*
- **BEHAVIOR** Feeds like Sanderlings, chasing waves in and out to glean small crustaceans and soft invertebrates from the wet sand. Inland foraging birds add small insects to their diets. Gathers in flocks in nonbreeding season. Tends to run away rapidly when approached on open flats.
- **BREEDING** Monogamous; some individuals polygamous.
- **NESTING** Incubation 24–32 days by both sexes. Precocial young fed by both sexes. 1–2 broods per year.
- **POPULATION** Rare. Declining in some areas, especially Gulf Coast and parts of Pacific Coast.

Similar Birds

PIPING PLOVER
Breeding plumage has complete breast band, yellow bill with black tip; yellow legs and feet; no dark ear patch • in winter has dark bill, but larger; legs and feet dark but not black; lacks dark ear patch.

- **CONSERVATION** Human disturbance on beaches often causes failed nesting attempts. Considered threatened in parts of range. Declining populations have prompted management by state and federal agencies.

Flight Pattern
Direct flight with rapid wing beats.

Nest Identification	Lined with bits of shell, grass, and pebbles by female • marked with twigs and debris • built by male • very often on edge of Least Tern colonies, whose eggs look remarkably similar • 2–3 pale, buff eggs dotted, spotted, and scrawled with black or gray; conical to elliptical, 1.2 inches long.
Shape ⌣ Location ▬ ▨	

Plumage Sexes differ	Habitat ⌇ ≈	Migration Some migrate	Weight 1.4 ounces

DATE _____ TIME_____ LOCATION _____

Family CHARADRIIDAE	Species *Charadrius wilsonia*	Length 7–8 inches	Wingspan 14–16 inches

WILSON'S PLOVER

Like other plovers, if a human intrudes upon its nest, the female will dash around, pretending to scrape various nests, to distract the trespasser. Both sexes perform the "crippled bird" act to lure predators away from the nest. This coastal species flies effortlessly, yet if presented with danger on land it usually runs down the beach instead of flying. The duller-colored female is similar to the male but has a brown neck band, forecrown, and lores. Juveniles resemble females, but have scalier upperparts.

may have cinnamon-buff ear patch in breeding season

dark sandy brown crown

dark sandy brown upperparts

heavy long black bill

broad black to brown neck band (depending on season)

white underparts

pinkish legs and feet

- **SONG** Abrasive whistle, *wheet* or *whip*.
- **BEHAVIOR** Feeds on small crustaceans, marine worms, insects, small mollusks, and aquatic larvae. Lives primarily on beaches, shores, and mudflats and nests above high-tide line. Often found near river mouths and inlets.
- **BREEDING** Monogamous. Scrape-making is part of male's courtship performance. He scrapes a hollow and invites female to join him.
- **NESTING** Incubation 23–25 days by both sexes. Precocial young leave nest soon after hatching. First flight at 21 days. Young feed themselves; tended by both sexes. 1 brood per year.
- **POPULATION** Fairly common to uncommon. Declining because of habitat loss and increased human disturbances during nesting season.
- **CONSERVATION** Some efforts are being made to restrict public access to beach nesting areas.

Similar Birds

SEMIPALMATED PLOVER
Smaller; shorter, stubby bill; orange legs; shorter, narrower eye stripe; narrower breast band.

KILLDEER
Larger; red eye ring; slender black bill; 2 black bands across chest; gray-brown upperparts; bright rufous-orange rump and uppertail coverts; long rounded tail with black subterminal band.

Flight Pattern

Swift direct flight with rapid wing beats. Flocks fly in circles low over beach and water.

Nest Identification

Shape  Location

Sparse lining of pebbles, shell pieces, grass, and debris • on ground • male makes several scrapes; female chooses one • 2–3 buff eggs blotched with brown and black; 1.4 inches long.

Plumage Sexes similar	Habitat	Migration Migratory	Weight 1.9 ounces

DATE _____ TIME_____ LOCATION _____

Family CHARADRIIDAE	Species *Charadrius semipalmatus*	Length 7 inches	Wingspan 14–15.25 inches

SEMIPALMATED PLOVER

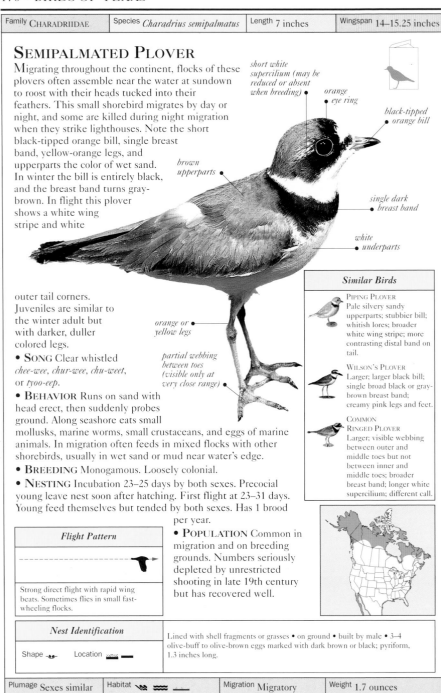

Migrating throughout the continent, flocks of these plovers often assemble near the water at sundown to roost with their heads tucked into their feathers. This small shorebird migrates by day or night, and some are killed during night migration when they strike lighthouses. Note the short black-tipped orange bill, single breast band, yellow-orange legs, and upperparts the color of wet sand. In winter the bill is entirely black, and the breast band turns gray-brown. In flight this plover shows a white wing stripe and white

short white supercilium (may be reduced or absent when breeding)

orange eye ring

black-tipped orange bill

brown upperparts

single dark breast band

white underparts

outer tail corners. Juveniles are similar to the winter adult but with darker, duller colored legs.

orange or yellow legs

partial webbing between toes (visible only at very close range)

• **SONG** Clear whistled *chee-wee, chur-wee, chu-weet,* or *tyoo-eep.*

• **BEHAVIOR** Runs on sand with head erect, then suddenly probes ground. Along seashore eats small mollusks, marine worms, small crustaceans, and eggs of marine animals. In migration often feeds in mixed flocks with other shorebirds, usually in wet sand or mud near water's edge.

• **BREEDING** Monogamous. Loosely colonial.

• **NESTING** Incubation 23–25 days by both sexes. Precocial young leave nest soon after hatching. First flight at 23–31 days. Young feed themselves but tended by both sexes. Has 1 brood per year.

• **POPULATION** Common in migration and on breeding grounds. Numbers seriously depleted by unrestricted shooting in late 19th century but has recovered well.

Similar Birds

PIPING PLOVER
Pale silvery sandy upperparts; stubbier bill; whitish lores; broader white wing stripe; more contrasting distal band on tail.

WILSON'S PLOVER
Larger; larger black bill; single broad black or gray-brown breast band; creamy pink legs and feet.

COMMON RINGED PLOVER
Larger; visible webbing between outer and middle toes but not between inner and middle toes; broader breast band; longer white supercilium; different call.

Flight Pattern

Strong direct flight with rapid wing beats. Sometimes flies in small fast-wheeling flocks.

Nest Identification

Shape ⚬ Location ⚬

Lined with shell fragments or grasses • on ground • built by male • 3–4 olive-buff to olive-brown eggs marked with dark brown or black; pyriform, 1.3 inches long.

Plumage Sexes similar	Habitat 〰〰 〰〰 ___	Migration Migratory	Weight 1.7 ounces

DATE _____ TIME_____ LOCATION _____

Family CHARADRIIDAE	Species *Charadrius melodus*	Length 7.25 inches	Wingspan 14–15.5 inches

PIPING PLOVER

This plover is difficult to spot until it moves, as its plumage blends in with the dry summer sand along the Atlantic Coast and south shores of the Great Lakes region. Endemic to central and eastern North America, and once common on beaches, this bird is now endangered because of human activity and disturbance during nesting season. Note the dry sand color of the upperparts, the yellow legs, and in flight the white wing stripe and white rump with contrasting black tail tip. Winter plumaged birds have a blackish orange bill, darker duller orange legs, and the sandy breast band may be broken. Juveniles are similar to winter adults.

white forehead and lores

sandy buff overall

orange bill with black tip

narrow blackish breast band (may be incomplete in females and East Coast birds)

white underparts

yellow-orange legs and feet

- **SONG** Clear *peep-lo*.
- **BEHAVIOR** Gregarious in post-breeding seasons, but territorial when nesting. Sprints, then stops to inspect sand with head cocked to one side; picks food off ground. Eats fly larvae, beetles, crustaceans, and marine worms. Often feeds higher on the beach (where upperparts more closely match sand) than other small plovers. In migration feeds in mixed flocks with other shorebirds.
- **BREEDING** Monogamous. Loosely colonial. Territorial during breeding season.
- **NESTING** Incubation 26–28 days by both sexes. Precocial young stay in nest 20–35 days. Fed by both sexes. Has 1 brood per year.
- **POPULATION** Uncommon to rare and declining in many parts of range, especially in Midwest and Great Lakes. Uncommon migrant inland.
- **CONSERVATION** Endangered; almost eliminated as a breeder in Great Lakes region due to human activity on beaches. Irregular pattern of water release from dams affects nesting on interior rivers.

WINTER PLUMAGE

Similar Birds

SEMIPALMATED PLOVER
Dark brown upperparts the color of wet sand; dark rump in flight.

SNOWY PLOVER
Smaller; long dark legs; slim dark bill; lateral dark breast patches; lacks white rump patch in flight.

Flight Pattern

Wild direct flight with twists and turns and rapid steady wing beats; often in small flocks.

Nest Identification	
Shape ⌣ Location ▨ ▬	Lined with broken shells, small stones, or driftwood • on sandy shore of lake or ocean well above high-water mark • built by both sexes • 3–4 pale buff eggs blotched with black and dark brown; short oval to short pyriform, 1.2 inches long.

Plumage Sexes similar	Habitat ▨ ▬	Migration Migratory	Weight 1.9 ounces

DATE _____ TIME_____ LOCATION _____

Family CHARADRIIDAE	Species *Charadrius vociferus*	Length 9–10.5 inches	Wingspan 19–21 inches

KILLDEER

Named for its distinctive call, this bird is the largest of the ringed plovers and the only double-banded plover within its range. Perhaps the most familiar shorebird in North America, in summer it is found across almost the entire continent south of the tundra. In flight note the long pointed wings with long white stripe and the rufous-gold rump and long tail with subterminal black tail band. Juveniles are similar in appearance but have only one black band across the chest.

red eye ring

gray-brown upperparts

long rounded tail with black subterminal band and white tip

slim black bill

bright rufous-orange rump and uppertail coverts

white underparts with 2 black bands across chest

creamy pink legs and feet

- **SONG** Loud cry, *kill-dee* or *kill-deear* or *kill-deeah-dee-dee*. And ascending *dee-ee*. Also long trilled *trrrrrrrr* during display or when young are threatened.

- **BEHAVIOR** Alternately runs, then stands still as though to look or listen, then dabs suddenly with bill at ground. More than 98 percent of food consists of insects from riverbanks, golf courses, fields, and even lawns. Runs well. Leads intruders away from nest and young with "broken wing" act, rapid calls, one or both wings dragging, tail spread, and often limping or listing to one side. Once lured far enough from the nest/young, the "crippled" bird suddenly "heals" and flies away, calling all the while.

- **BREEDING** Monogamous. Solitary nester. Often returns to same mate and breeding site.

- **NESTING** Incubation 24–28 days by both sexes. Precocial young leave nest soon after hatching and feed themselves, but are tended by parents. First flight at 25 days. 2 broods per year.

- **POPULATION** Abundant to common in the northernmost regions of the range.

Similar Birds

SEMIPALMATED PLOVER
Smaller; single breast band; rump and tail same color as back; yellow-orange legs.

WILSON'S PLOVER
Smaller; single breast band; brown back, rump, and tail; large black bill.

Flight Pattern
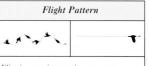
Flies in wavering erratic manner on territory. Capable of swift direct flight.

Nest Identification	
Shape ⬦ Location 〰 ••• ▬ ⊷	Unlined or lined with pebbles, grass, and twigs • on ground with good visibility • built by male • 3–5 buff eggs with black and brown blotches; oval to pyriform, typically quite pointed; 1.4 inches long.

Plumage Sexes similar	Habitat 〰 ⚊ ⚊ 〰 〰	Migration Migratory	Weight 3.2 ounces

DATE _____ TIME_____ LOCATION _____

| Family CHARADRIIDAE | Species *Charadrius montanus* | Length 9 inches | Wingspan 17.5–19.5 inches |

MOUNTAIN PLOVER

This fast-running pale brown plover is one of few shorebirds that lives in dry regions away from water. Its sand-colored back and buffy white underparts and breast help distinguish this large plover and also blend it perfectly into the arid grasslands it calls home. In flight note the black-tipped tail, thin white wing stripe, and the white undersides of the wings. In winter the sandy buff breast is more extensive.

black frontal crown bar

white forehead and stripe over eyes

black lores

sandy brown back

slim blackish or brownish bill

- **SONG** Variable. Slightly rasping dry *krehrr*, a clipped dry *kep*, and a slightly reedy *krrip* or *krreek*.
- **BEHAVIOR** Eats grasshoppers, beetles, flies, crickets, and other insects. Protective of its eggs. Will fly up into the face of cattle or other intruder or try to lure them away with the crippled-bird

sandy buff breast

fairly long pale brownish yellow legs

black tail band with white border

display. Forms small flocks on the wintering grounds.
- **BREEDING** Mostly monogamous; some polygamous.
- **NESTING** Incubation 28–31 days by both sexes. After laying first set of eggs, which are incubated by male, female lays and incubates second set. First flight at 33–34 days. Precocial young feed themselves, tended by both sexes. 2 broods per year.
- **POPULATION** Uncommon to casual.
- **CONSERVATION** Has disappeared from much of former breeding range due to the land's conversion to farmland and range land for cattle that often overgraze it. Decline also linked to decline of prairie dog population, because plovers use the mounds around the entrances to old prairie dog burrows for nests.

Similar Birds

AMERICAN GOLDEN-PLOVER
Winter adult and juvenile • slightly larger; darker legs; darker gray plumage conspicuously spotted and notched on upperparts; dull brownish gray underwings and auxiliaries; lacks black and white on tail.

Flight Pattern

Short flights on breeding grounds with few rapid wing flutters between short glides. Direct flight with rapid steady wing beats for longer distances or in migration.

Nest Identification

Shape — Location ▬

Scant lining of rootlets and dried grass, often added during incubation • flat open ground between hummocks, occasionally amid cacti or scattered shrubs • built by male • 2–4 olive-buff eggs, with many black marks and wreathed; blunt pyriform, 1.5 inches long.

| Plumage Sexes similar | Habitat | Migration Migratory | Weight 3.6 ounces |

DATE _____ TIME_____ LOCATION _____

Family HAEMATOPODIDAE	Species *Haematopus palliatus*	Length 18–20 inches	Wingspan 30–36 inches

AMERICAN OYSTERCATCHER

Like all oystercatchers, this bird uses its three- to four-inch, laterally compressed, sharp chisel-tipped bill to pry open shells for food, but it sometimes hammers and chips them open as well. The largest oystercatcher is coastal in all seasons; only vagrants are seen inland.

black head •
• yellow eyes
brownish back •
long red-orange bill
dark brown tail end •
• black neck
white wing patches •
long white wing stripe shows in flight •
• white underparts
• pink legs and feet

In flight it shows large white patches on the wings and base of the upper tail. Juveniles have a black-tipped dark red bill, brown head and neck, and scaly brown underparts.

JUVENILE

- **SONG** *Kleep*, *wheep*, or *peep*. Makes loud *crik, crik, crik* when it takes flight.
- **BEHAVIOR** Wary; usually does not allow close approach. Eats oysters, clams, and other bivalves; also small sea urchins, marine worms, and starfish. Usually solitary or in pairs or family groups; never in large flocks. Often feeds with other birds.
- **BREEDING** Monogamous. Solitary nester.
- **NESTING** Incubation 24–29 days by both sexes. Precocial young leave nest shortly after hatching. First flight at about 5 weeks. Tended by both sexes. 1 brood per year.
- **POPULATION** Uncommon or rare resident in most of coastal North America from southern California to Pacific Coast of Mexico and from Gulf Coast of Mexico to Maryland. In summer expanding breeding range in the Northeast to Cape Cod.
- **CONSERVATION** Declined in late 19th century principally because of overshooting; however, protection by law helped population recover and species currently is expanding back into some of its former range in the Northeast.

Similar Birds

EURASIAN OYSTERCATCHER Longer white wing patches; black upperparts; white back, rump, and tail; black tail band;
• juvenile has white patch on foreneck.

BLACK OYSTERCATCHER Smaller; entirely dark body; no white on wings.

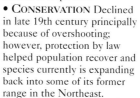

Flight Pattern
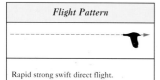
Rapid strong swift direct flight.

Nest Identification	
Shape 〜 Location ▬ 〜	Rimmed with shells • usually unlined • small hills of sand on dry flat beaches • above high-water line • built by both sexes • 1–4 buff-gray eggs often with dark brown speckles; ovoid, 2.2 inches long.

Plumage Sexes similar	Habitat 〜	Migration Most do not migrate	Weight 1.4 pounds

DATE _____ TIME_____ LOCATION _____

| Family RECURVIROSTRIDAE | Species *Himantopus mexicanus* | Length 14–15.5 inches | Wingspan 25–27 inches |

BLACK-NECKED STILT

Extremely protective of its nest, this stilt will try to attack an intruder or will splash water with its breast as a distraction. This bird's reddish legs, which are eight to ten inches long, may be the longest, in proportion to its body size, among all birds. The female is duller and has more brown on its back. In flight the black upperparts and wings contrast strongly with the white underparts, rump, and tail, and the long legs trail far behind.

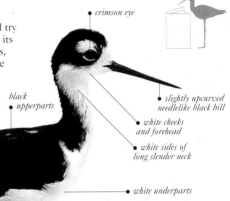

- crimson eye
- slightly upcurved needlelike black bill
- white cheeks and forehead
- white sides of long slender neck
- black upperparts
- white underparts

- **SONG** Loud *kek-kek-kek* or *yip-yip-yip*, sometimes with barking yelps.
- **BEHAVIOR** Actively feeds by walking, often rapidly, and picking up insects in shallow water along shores. Sometimes wades up to its belly. Prefers freshwater. Also eats small crustaceans, worms, small fish, and some seeds. Solitary, in pairs, or in small flocks.
- **BREEDING** Monogamous. Loosely colonial.
- **NESTING** Incubation 22–25 days by both sexes; done by female at night, by male during day. Precocial young leave nest after hatching and feed themselves, but are tended by both sexes. First flight at 4–5 weeks. 1 brood per year.
- **POPULATION** Fairly common to uncommon. Casual north of breeding range. May be increasing as range expands.

- long pink or red legs

Similar Birds

AMERICAN AVOCET
Black-and-white pattern on back and wings; white underparts and upper back; long, slender upturned bill • rusty cinnamon head and neck in breeding plumage • grayish buff head and neck in winter.

BLACK-WINGED STILT
Face entirely white; base of hind neck and shoulders white • male has black crown and hind neck in breeding plumage • female head and neck entirely white • male like female in winter • juveniles have brown upperparts • accidental on Aleutian Islands.

Flight Pattern

Strong swift direct flight with somewhat shallow wing beats.

| Nest Identification | Lined with stems, weeds, sticks, grasses, fragments of shells, small rocks, fish bones, and rubbish • on ground • sometimes hidden by grasses • built by both sexes • 3–5 yellow or buff eggs heavily blotched with black or brown; pyriform, 1.7 inches long. |
Shape  Location

| Plumage Sexes similar | Habitat 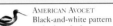 | Migration Most migrate | Weight 5.9 ounces |

DATE _____ TIME_____ LOCATION _____

Family RECURVIROSTRIDAE	Species *Recurvirostra americana*	Length 18–20 inches	Wingspan 27–38 inches

AMERICAN AVOCET

The tallest in its family, this graceful long-legged bird is the world's only avocet with distinct basic and alternate plumages. Winter (basic) plumage shows a gray head and neck, while breeding adults show rusty cinnamon on the head and neck. Females are similar to males but have a shorter and more upward-curved bill. In flight both sexes show a bold black-and-white pattern on the upperparts and black wing tips, primary coverts, and scapular bars.

rusty cinnamon head and neck

black-and-white upperparts

whitish scapulars

long slender upcurved black bill

- **SONG** Loud *wheet* or *pleeet*.

white underparts

long blue-gray legs

- **BEHAVIOR** Eats primarily insects, shrimp, and other crustaceans but also takes other aquatic invertebrates. Prefers to feed in flocks, sometimes with more than 100 birds walking shoulder to shoulder. Sometimes feeds in water up to its belly with bill in water. In shallow water brings food to surface by sweeping its open bill back and forth in the water. In deep water may feed like a dabbling duck by tipping over.

WINTER PLUMAGE

- **BREEDING** Monogamous. Loosely colonial. Pairs perform elaborate courtship display and group rituals.
- **NESTING** Incubation 22–29 days by both sexes. Precocial young leave nest soon after hatching. Tended by both sexes but feed themselves. First flight at 28–35 days. 1 brood per year.
- **POPULATION** The American Avocet is fairly common; stable and possibly increasing west of the Great Plains; uncommon and local in the East, where it is an uncommon transient in summer and a coastal species in winter.

Similar Birds

BLACK-NECKED STILT Slightly upcurved black bill; black upperparts; white underparts; long reddish legs and feet.

- **CONSERVATION** Protected by law and currently making a comeback after overhunting depleted numbers in the 19th and early 20th centuries.

Flight Pattern
Strong direct flight with neck extended slightly forward and long legs trailing behind tail.

Nest Identification	
Shape 🐦 Location ▬ ✹✹✹	Lined with dry grasses and mud chips • on flat ground or marsh near water • built by both sexes • 3–4 olive-buff eggs blotched with brown and black; pyriform to long pyriform, 2 inches long.

Plumage Sexes similar	Habitat ≋ ⚬ ⌇ ⌇	Migration Migratory	Weight 11.1 ounces

DATE _____ TIME_____ LOCATION _____

Family JACANIDAE	Species *Jacana spinosa*	Length 9 inches	Wingspan 17–18 inches

NORTHERN JACANA

An extremely territorial and aggressive bird, this jacana prefers freshwater ponds and marshes with heavy vegetation, a habitat for which it is well suited as it has extremely long toes with long nails to support it on the soft mud and delicate aquatic vegetation. During courtship display both sexes lift their wings and flaunt the green-yellow wing patches beneath them, revealing an unusual long yellowish spur at the bend of the wing. The female jacana is similar to the male, but larger. In flight the yellow flight feathers contrast with the dark brownish body, and the long legs trail or dangle behind. Juveniles have brown upperparts and white underparts with a black postocular stripe extending along the side of the neck.

leaf-shaped yellow wattle on forehead

glossy black head and neck

glossy black upper back

rich chestnut-maroon upperparts

ploverlike yellow bill with blue edge around base

glossy black chest

- **SONG** Noisy with loud shrills and a clicking chatter that resembles an old-fashioned telegraph or typewriter.
- **BEHAVIOR** Often walks over floating aquatic vegetation. Swims well. Dives to avoid enemies. Eats insects and seeds picked from vegetation in marsh or pond, or off wet ground. Often raises wings over back to reveal yellow flight feathers; also momentarily raises wings upon landing.

extremely long toes and nails

chestnut-maroon underparts

grayish green legs

JUVENILE

- **BREEDING** Polyandrous. Female may lay eggs fertilized by 1–4 mates; each male will incubate eggs alone and tend chicks.
- **NESTING** Incubation 22–24 days by male, which defends offspring from intruders. Precocial young leave nest 1–2 days after hatching; find own food but tended by male. First flight at 35 days. Multiple broods per year.
- **POPULATION** Very common in proper habitat in Mexico and Central America. Rare to casual and irregular visitor to southern Arizona and southern and central Texas.
- **CONSERVATION** Some declines in breeding ranges due to habitat loss.

Similar Birds
None in North America.

Flight Pattern
Weak fluttering mothlike flight, often low over vegetation.

Nest Identification	
Shape 🪺 ⬬ Location 🪺 ⱴⱴⱴ	Cattail leaves and other green leaves and grasses • on small floating pile of vegetation or leaves • built by male • 3–5 brown eggs with black lines; almost round, 1.2 inches long.

Plumage Sexes similar	Habitat 🌾 🌊 🏞	Migration Nonmigratory	Weight 2.8 ounces

DATE _____ TIME _____ LOCATION _____

Family SCOLOPACIDAE	Species *Tringa melanoleuca*	Length 14 inches	Wingspan 23–26 inches

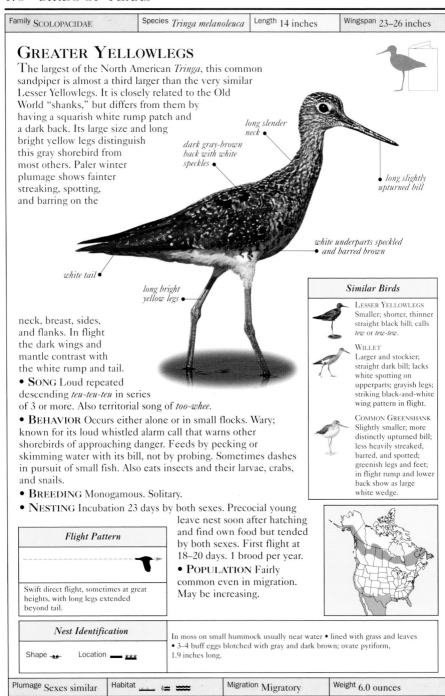

GREATER YELLOWLEGS

The largest of the North American *Tringa*, this common sandpiper is almost a third larger than the very similar Lesser Yellowlegs. It is closely related to the Old World "shanks," but differs from them by having a squarish white rump patch and a dark back. Its large size and long bright yellow legs distinguish this gray shorebird from most others. Paler winter plumage shows fainter streaking, spotting, and barring on the

long slender neck

dark gray-brown back with white speckles

long slightly upturned bill

white underparts speckled and barred brown

white tail

long bright yellow legs

neck, breast, sides, and flanks. In flight the dark wings and mantle contrast with the white rump and tail.

• **SONG** Loud repeated descending *teu-teu-teu* in series of 3 or more. Also territorial song of *too-whee*.

• **BEHAVIOR** Occurs either alone or in small flocks. Wary; known for its loud whistled alarm call that warns other shorebirds of approaching danger. Feeds by pecking or skimming water with its bill, not by probing. Sometimes dashes in pursuit of small fish. Also eats insects and their larvae, crabs, and snails.

• **BREEDING** Monogamous. Solitary.

• **NESTING** Incubation 23 days by both sexes. Precocial young leave nest soon after hatching and find own food but tended by both sexes. First flight at 18–20 days. 1 brood per year.

• **POPULATION** Fairly common even in migration. May be increasing.

Similar Birds

LESSER YELLOWLEGS
Smaller; shorter, thinner straight black bill; calls *tew* or *tew-tew*.

WILLET
Larger and stockier; straight dark bill; lacks white spotting on upperparts; grayish legs; striking black-and-white wing pattern in flight.

COMMON GREENSHANK
Slightly smaller; more distinctly upturned bill; less heavily streaked, barred, and spotted; greenish legs and feet; in flight rump and lower back show as large white wedge.

Flight Pattern

Swift direct flight, sometimes at great heights, with long legs extended beyond tail.

Nest Identification

Shape ⌣ Location ▬ ⁂

In moss on small hummock usually near water • lined with grass and leaves • 3–4 buff eggs blotched with gray and dark brown; ovate pyriform, 1.9 inches long.

Plumage Sexes similar	Habitat	Migration Migratory	Weight 6.0 ounces

DATE _____ TIME_____ LOCATION _____

Family SCOLOPACIDAE	Species *Tringa flavipes*	Length 10.5 inches	Wingspan 19–22 inches

LESSER YELLOWLEGS

Often seen walking gracefully on mudflats or shores, this sandpiper is tame and approachable. It is best distinguished from the Greater Yellowlegs by its smaller size and its bill, which is completely straight and only one-third the length of its cousin's bill, as well as by its different voice. Winter plumage is grayer and paler overall with little or no streaking. In flight the dark wings and back contrast sharply with the white tail and rump.

heavy brown streaks on head and neck

blackish grayish scapulars and mantle with white spots

long straight thin bill

blackish grayish tertials with white spots

heavy brown streaks on breast

sparse brown streaks on flanks

long orange-yellow legs

- **SONG** Harsh short *tew-tew* or *tew*. Alarm call is sharp *kip*. Also makes musical *pill-e-wee*.
- **BEHAVIOR** Gregarious; occurs in flocks, sometimes large, in winter and migration. Slowly picks food from surface of water. Feeds with a delicate high-stepping gait. Eats insects, small crustaceans, bloodworms, and small fish.
- **BREEDING** Monogamous. Loosely colonial. Noisy on nesting grounds.
- **NESTING** Incubation 22–23 days by both sexes. Precocial young leave nest soon after hatching and feed themselves, but are tended by both sexes for 18–20 days. 1 brood per year.
- **POPULATION** Common on breeding grounds. In migration, common in the East and the Midwest; uncommon in the far West. Fairly common in winter in Baja and on the Gulf Coast. Stable or slightly increasing.

Similar Birds

GREATER YELLOWLEGS Larger; longer, often slightly upturned bill; more heavily barred breast and flanks; makes descending whistled series of 3 or more, *teu-teu-teu*.

SOLITARY SANDPIPER Slightly smaller; darker brown upperparts; heavier brownish streaking on neck and breast; white eye ring; dull greenish yellow legs; dark rump; in flight shows barred dark tail edged with white.

Flight Pattern
Swift direct flight with rapid wing beats.

Nest Identification	
Shape ⏜ Location ⁙	In grass marshes and bogs surrounded by black spruce trees • on raised pile of leaves or vegetation near water • lined with small amount of grass and leaves • built by female • 3–4 buff to yellow or gray eggs with brown blotches; ovate pyriform, 1.7 x 1.2 inches.

Plumage Sexes similar	Habitat	Migration Migratory	Weight 2.9 ounces

DATE _____ TIME _____ LOCATION _____

Family SCOLOPACIDAE	Species *Tringa solitaria*	Length 8–9 inches	Wingspan 15–17 inches

SOLITARY SANDPIPER

As its name suggests, this sandpiper is often seen alone or in small loose groups in its habitat of freshwater lakes, ponds, marshes, and rivers. This shorebird is not wary around humans and often exhibits an up-and-down bobbing or jerking motion with its head and body similar to a Spotted Sandpiper's bobbing. In flight the dark

dark brown uppparts with dense whitish buff spotting

slender body

dark wings

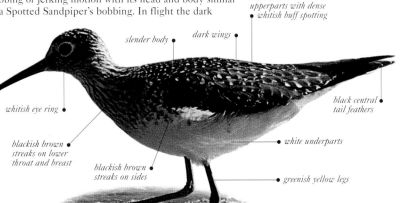

whitish eye ring

blackish brown streaks on lower throat and breast

blackish brown streaks on sides

black central tail feathers

white underparts

greenish yellow legs

rump patch and central tail feathers contrast with the white outer tail feathers, which have black bars. Also note the dark wings without a wing stripe, dark underwings.

- **SONG** High shrill *pit-peet-wheet* or *peet*.
- **BEHAVIOR** Searches for food by stirring up water, especially in stagnant pools, with bill and feet. Picks food from surface or probes with bill. Eats insects and insect larvae, small fish, small crustaceans, and other invertebrates. Somewhat aggressive toward other birds when feeding. Migrates singly or in small groups. Upon landing holds wings above back before folding.
- **BREEDING** Monogamous.
- **NESTING** Incubation 23–24 days by female. Precocial young leave nest soon after hatching and are tended by female. First flight at 17–20 days. 1 brood per year.
- **POPULATION** Fairly common on breeding grounds; fairly common and widespread in migration. Seems stable.

Similar Birds

SPOTTED SANDPIPER Smaller; less upright stance; teeters body; yellowish or creamy pink legs; pink bill with dark tip; white supercilium; white wing stripe; shallow stiff wing beats • spotted underparts in summer.

Flight Pattern

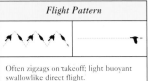

Often zigzags on takeoff; light buoyant swallowlike direct flight.

Nest Identification

Shape ◗   Location 🪺

Female strengthens abandoned nest with other material • most often in conifers, 4–40 feet above ground • 4–5 olive eggs marked with brown, usually in wreath shape; pyriform to oval, 1.5 x 1.1 inches.

Plumage Sexes similar	Habitat 🏞 🐾 🦆 🌿 🌊 〰	Migration Migratory	Weight 1.7 ounces

DATE _____ TIME_____ LOCATION _____

Family SCOLOPACIDAE	Species *Catoptrophorus semipalmatus*	Length 13–16 inches	Wingspan 24–31 inches

WILLET

This large gray sandpiper is named for its song of *pill-will-willet* given loudly and frequently on the breeding grounds. A rather nondescript shorebird, the Willet may initially thwart your efforts at identification as it sleeps standing on one leg with its head tucked in on its back or probes in mud with its long gray-black bill. But the moment it takes flight it is readily identified by the mostly white tail, white rump, bold black-and-white wing pattern, and loud call of its name. In winter the light upperparts lack the variegated/barred pattern.

white spectacles

variegated light brownish gray to light gray overall

light underparts

bold black-and-white wing pattern

blue-gray legs

WINTER PLUMAGE

- **SONG** Alarm or scolding call of *kip* or *wiek*. In flight makes *wee-wee-wee*. Well-known call of *pill-will-will*, *pill-o-will-o-willet*, or *pill-will-willet*.
- **BEHAVIOR** Generalist. Wades, probing for food with bill. In water eats aquatic insects, marine worms, crabs, mollusks, and small fish. On land eats seeds, fresh shoots, and rice. On breeding grounds often perches high on rocks, posts, shrubs, or other tall objects, from which it may scold intruders in its territory. Becomes noisy when alarmed. Mobs will attack interlopers, especially at nesting time.
- **BREEDING** Monogamous. Semicolonial. Nests are 200 or more feet apart.
- **NESTING** Incubation 22–29 days by both sexes (male at night; female at other times). Precocial young leave nest soon after hatching but tended by both sexes. Parents sometimes abandon unhatched eggs after first young leaves nest even though they have well-developed embryos. First flight at about 28 days. 1 brood per year.

Similar Birds

GREATER YELLOWLEGS Slimmer; grayer; thinner, more needlelike, often slightly upturned bill; yellow legs; in flight has white rump and tail with distal tail bands; no wing pattern.

- **POPULATION** Common. Has recovered from hunting in late 19th century and expanded into new or parts of ranges where it had been extirpated.
- **CONSERVATION** Habitat disturbance is beginning to negatively affect population.

Flight Pattern

Short low flight; series of rapid wing beats alternates with glides. Over long distances direct flight with steady rapid wing beats.

Nest Identification

Shape 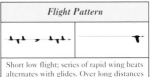   Location

Lined with dry grass • on sand away from shrubbery, tucked in cups of vegetation or tall grasses • 4–5 grayish to olive-buff eggs blotched with brown; 2.1 inches long.

Plumage Sexes similar	Habitat	Migration Migratory	Weight 7.6 ounces

DATE _____ TIME_____ LOCATION _____

Family SCOLOPACIDAE	Species *Actitis macularia*	Length 7.5 inches	Wingspan 13–14 inches

SPOTTED SANDPIPER

The most widespread and best-known sandpiper in North America is distinguishable on the ground by the way it constantly teeters its body as it stands with tail up and head down. Females are larger than their male counterparts and have more spotting. In flight it shows a short white wing stripe and the inner wing has a narrow white

olive-brown upperparts

WINTER PLUMAGE

white supercilium

dull yellow legs

short straight bill with pinkish to orange base and black tip

trailing edge. In winter Spotted Sandpipers can be found as close as the southern United States to as far away as southern South America.

large dark brown-black breast spots

Similar Birds

SOLITARY SANDPIPER
Similar on ground but slightly larger and more slender; darker greenish legs; white eye ring; barred tail with white sides; greater contrast between upperparts and belly; deep wing beats.

COMMON SANDPIPER
Barred darker brown upperparts provide greater contrast with white flanks and belly; duller grayish or straw-colored legs; dark bill with pale base; longer tail extends well beyond folded wings; streaked breast and sides of head • juvenile has tertials with strongly marked edges • rare in Alaskan range.

• **SONG** High shrieking *peet-weet*. Chirps repeated *weet* in flight.
• **BEHAVIOR** In summer found almost anywhere near water. Feeds primarily on invertebrates, especially insects and their larvae; sometimes takes small fish. When flushed its curious, jerky flight and *weet-weet* notes are distinctive.
• **BREEDING** Monogamous but often sequentially polyandrous. Usually solitary nester; sometimes loosely colonial.
• **NESTING** Incubation 20–24 days mostly by male. Female sometimes helps with final clutch of season. Young leave nest soon after hatching. Young feed themselves but tended solely by male. First flight at 13–21 days. 1–2 broods per year.
• **POPULATION** Widespread and common but some decline throughout range.

Flight Pattern

Direct flight low over water, wings flapping in shallow arcs, producing clipped, stiff beat on drooping wings.

Nest Identification

Shape   Location

Lined with moss, grass, feathers, and weeds • sometimes elevated in grass • built by both sexes • 3–5 brownish, greenish, pinkish, or buff eggs blotched with brown; ovate to pyriform, 1.3 x 0.9 inches.

Plumage Sexes similar	Habitat	Migration Migratory	Weight 1.4 ounces

DATE _____ TIME _____ LOCATION _____

Family SCOLOPACIDAE	Species *Bartramia longicauda*	Length 12 inches	Wingspan 17–20 inches

UPLAND SANDPIPER

The distinctive silhouette of the Upland Sandpiper is often seen perched on fences, utility poles, rocks, and stumps watching for intruders and predators in the grasslands and prairies it inhabits in summer. This large pale sandpiper has a long slender neck, small dovelike head, large dark eyes, and long tail. In winter the Upland Sandpiper migrates long distances to eastern South America.

small dovelike head

large dark brown eye

long slender neck

brown-streaked buff-edged upperparts

short thin yellow-brown bill slightly decurved toward tip

buff neck and breast with streaks, bars, and chevrons

• **SONG** Trilling *pulip pulip*. In low circling stiff-winged flight on breeding grounds, emits wolflike whistle *wheelooooooooo*. Usual flight call is piping *quip-ip-ip-ip*.

• **BEHAVIOR** Has ploverlike feeding patterns: runs, stops, then runs again. Not a bird of shores and wetlands like most sandpipers, it frequents hay fields, pastures, and prairies and often perches on poles. Feeds on insects, other invertebrates, and seeds of weeds, grasses, and grains. Upon landing often holds wings above body for 1–2 seconds before folding them.

dark rump

wedge-shaped tail with white border and thin black bars

whitish belly and undertail coverts

yellow-green legs and feet

• **BREEDING** Monogamous. Loose colonies. During courtship flight spreads wings and circles high in sky, singing a melodious song that can be heard up to a mile away.

• **NESTING** Incubation 21–27 days. Precocial young leave nest soon after hatching. First flight at about 30–31 days. Young feed themselves but are tended and protected by both sexes. 1 brood per year.

• **POPULATION** Mostly recovered since large decline in late 1800s. Common in parts of the Great Plains; some decline has been recorded in local populations throughout much of the East and the Northeast.

• **CONSERVATION** Eastern decline due to habitat loss and increased human disturbance.

Similar Birds

BUFF-BREASTED SANDPIPER
Smaller; black bill; short yellow legs; buff face and underparts; wings project beyond tail.

Flight Pattern

Swift direct flight when traveling some distance. In breeding display flies slowly with flickering wing beats.

Nest Identification

Shape Location

Lined with dry grass • built by both sexes • 4 creamy pale buff to pinkish buff eggs speckled red-brown; pyriform, 1.8 inches long.

Plumage Sexes similar	Habitat	Migration Migratory	Weight 4.8 ounces

DATE _____ TIME_____ LOCATION _____

Family SCOLOPACIDAE	Species *Numenius phaeopus*	Length 17–18 inches	Wingspan 31–33 inches

WHIMBREL

Easily identified by its large size, distinctive head stripes, and decurved bill, this bird is the most widespread of the curlews in North America. During migration it makes frequent stops at salt marshes, coastal shores, and inland lakes and rivers. In flight this bird can easily be distinguished from European and Asian races that occur on the East and West Coasts, respectively, by its dark rump and underwings.

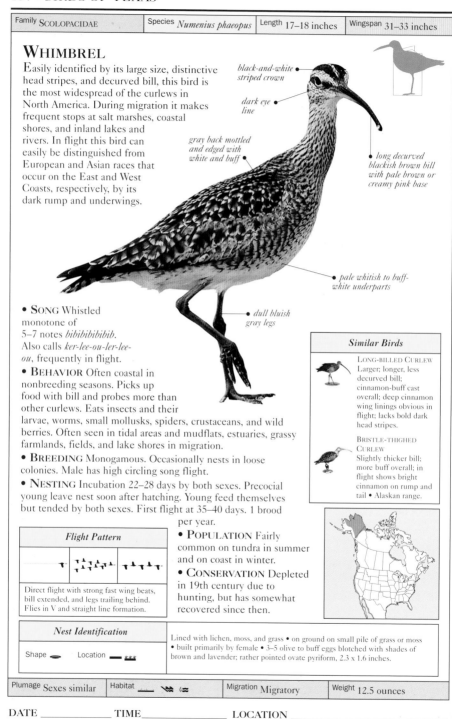

black-and-white striped crown

dark eye line

gray back mottled and edged with white and buff

long decurved blackish brown bill with pale brown or creamy pink base

pale whitish to buff-white underparts

dull bluish gray legs

- **SONG** Whistled monotone of 5–7 notes *bibibibibibib*. Also calls *ker-lee-ou-ler-lee-ou*, frequently in flight.
- **BEHAVIOR** Often coastal in nonbreeding seasons. Picks up food with bill and probes more than other curlews. Eats insects and their larvae, worms, small mollusks, spiders, crustaceans, and wild berries. Often seen in tidal areas and mudflats, estuaries, grassy farmlands, fields, and lake shores in migration.
- **BREEDING** Monogamous. Occasionally nests in loose colonies. Male has high circling song flight.
- **NESTING** Incubation 22–28 days by both sexes. Precocial young leave nest soon after hatching. Young feed themselves but tended by both sexes. First flight at 35–40 days. 1 brood per year.
- **POPULATION** Fairly common on tundra in summer and on coast in winter.
- **CONSERVATION** Depleted in 19th century due to hunting, but has somewhat recovered since then.

Similar Birds

LONG-BILLED CURLEW
Larger; longer, less decurved bill; cinnamon-buff cast overall; deep cinnamon wing linings obvious in flight; lacks bold dark head stripes.

BRISTLE-THIGHED CURLEW
Slightly thicker bill; more buff overall; in flight shows bright cinnamon on rump and tail • Alaskan range.

Flight Pattern

Direct flight with strong fast wing beats, bill extended, and legs trailing behind. Flies in V and straight line formation.

Nest Identification

Shape ⬬   Location ▬ ▬▬

Lined with lichen, moss, and grass • on ground on small pile of grass or moss • built primarily by female • 3–5 olive to buff eggs blotched with shades of brown and lavender; rather pointed ovate pyriform, 2.3 x 1.6 inches.

Plumage Sexes similar	Habitat ▬ ⋙ ⋎	Migration Migratory	Weight 12.5 ounces

DATE _____ TIME _____ LOCATION _____

Family SCOLOPACIDAE	Species *Numenius americanus*	Length 23 inches	Wingspan 36–40 inches

LONG-BILLED CURLEW

The largest North American member of the sandpiper family has a very long, slender decurved bill. The male claims and defends large territories with a flapping gliding flight. After courtship and mating, these birds usually nest in dry uplands often near rivers but sometimes rangelands or farmlands. As with other curlews the female is larger than the male. It is distinguished in flight by the long decurved bill and cinnamon underwing linings.

indistinct eye line

cinnamon-brown upperparts

long decurved bill

pinkish or grayish brown base on lower mandible

buff-brown underparts

dull blue-gray legs

- **SONG** Solid melodic ascending *cur-lee*. On breeding grounds gives bubbling warbled *curleeeeeeeeeuuu*.
- **BEHAVIOR** Feeds by probing mud with bill or dunking head under water. Eats adult insects, fly larvae, aquatic insects, mollusks, crustaceans, and small amphibians. Often flies in wedge-shaped flocks, especially in migration.
- **BREEDING** Monogamous. Colonial or semicolonial.
- **NESTING** Incubation 27–30 days by both sexes. Incubating bird sits motionless on nest even if approached. Precocial young leave nest soon after hatching. Tended by both sexes. First flight at 32–45 days. 1 brood per year.
- **POPULATION** Common and widespread in nesting area. Casual to rare on southeastern Atlantic Coast in winter.
- **CONSERVATION** Overgrazing in nesting areas has caused some decline.

Similar Birds

WHIMBREL
Smaller; grayer overall; gray-brown head with distinctive stripes; pale whitish gray underparts.

MARBLED GODWIT
Smaller; straight or slightly upturned bill; cinnamon secondaries; brighter inner primaries with fewer brown markings.

Flight Pattern

Steady strong wing beats in direct flight. Gliding flight in display on breeding grounds.

Nest Identification

Shape ⬛ Location ▬

Lined with a few bits of grass, weeds, and chips • on ground in open prairie • 3–5 pale to olive-buff eggs with brown and olive spotting, 2.6 inches long.

Plumage Sexes similar	Habitat	Migration Migratory	Weight 1.2 pounds

DATE _____ TIME_____ LOCATION _____

Family SCOLOPACIDAE	Species *Limosa haemastica*	Length 15 inches	Wingspan 27 inches

HUDSONIAN GODWIT

On the shores of James Bay in Canada, thousands of these birds can be seen migrating together in late August. The male godwit is quiet during migration but has a noisy, complex display flight during breeding. The female is larger and duller with less barring. Both sexes are distinctive in flight with a white rump, a black tail with white base, a white wing stripe, and dusky black wing linings and axillaries. In winter the bird has a gray back and neck and whitish underparts.

brownish black back with white-tipped feathers giving scaly appearance

long pointed slightly upcurved creamy pink bill with black tip

black barring overall

dark chestnut underparts

dark blue-gray legs

black-and-white tail

WINTER PLUMAGE

• **SONG** Sings a clear high-pitched *toe-wit, god-wit, whit,* or *toe-whit-ta.*

• **BEHAVIOR** Feeds by probing rapidly in mud with bill. Sometimes wades deep enough to immerse bill and head in water. Eats mollusks, marine worms, crustaceans, and insects. Wary. Only shorebird with undulating flight pattern. Flies in either long lines or V-formation in migration.

• **BREEDING** Monogamous. Gregarious.

• **NESTING** Incubation 22–25 days by female during day and male at night. Precocial young leave nest soon after hatching and feed themselves. Tended by both sexes. First flight at 30 days. Parents very aggressive in defense of young. 1 brood per year.

• **POPULATION** The Hudsonian Godwit is fairly common to uncommon on its breeding grounds (but total breeding range poorly known). Uncommon to casual migrant on the Great Plains in spring and on the East Coast in autumn migration. Casual on the Pacific Coast.

Similar Birds

MARBLED GODWIT
Larger; lacks black-and-white wing and tail pattern; grayish cinnamon overall; cinnamon wing linings; boldly spangled upperparts.

BLACK-TAILED GODWIT
Broad wing bar on tail reaches to outer primaries; bright white axillaries and underwing coverts; less white on rump and upperwing.

Flight Pattern

Swift powerful undulating flight. Flies in straight lines or V-formation.

Nest Identification

Shape ⌣ ⬬   Location ▬ ▪▪▪ ⱽⱽ

Sparsely lined with dead leaves and fresh grass • on tussock hidden under marsh grass or shrubs • built by both sexes • 3–4 olive-buff to olive-brown eggs sparsely marked with olive-brown, 2.2 inches long.

Plumage Sexes similar	Habitat ⤳ ▬ ♠♦ ≈≈ ⱽ	Migration Migratory	Weight 7.8 ounces

DATE _____ TIME_____ LOCATION _____

Family SCOLOPACIDAE	Species *Limosa fedoa*	Length 18–20 inches	Wingspan 32 inches

MARBLED GODWIT

Taking its name from its call of *godWHIT, godWHIT*, this buff-brown bird is distinguished by its long upturned bicolored bill. Very social and nesting in semicolonial groups, these shorebirds have no clear territorial boundaries. Most spend winters on the coast and migrate in flocks. In flight note the cinnamon wing linings and cinnamon-buff in the primary and secondary feathers.

• **SONG** Distinctive bold grating *cor-ack, terWHIT*, or *godWHIT*. Repetitive barking *rack-a* or *raddica* in display.

• **BEHAVIOR** Often feeds by wading into water. Probes with bill in tidal flats and mudflats for crustaceans, mollusks, and worms. Also eats insects, including grasshoppers, and vegetal materials, including seeds and berries. Often flocks in nonbreeding seasons. Prefers high plains and rangelands, often nesting in grassy meadows near water. In migration flocks fly in long lines with the front changing irregularly.

• **BREEDING** Monogamous. Loosely colonial. Generally noisy when breeding.

• **NESTING** Incubation 21–23 days by both sexes. Precocial young leave nest soon after hatching. Tended by both sexes. First flight at about 21 days. 1 brood per year.

• **POPULATION** Common to fairly common on interior breeding grounds. In winter common on the West Coast and fairly common on Texas Gulf Coast and in Florida. Rare but regular on tidal flats in the East.

• **CONSERVATION** Declining because of the conversion of habitat to farmland.

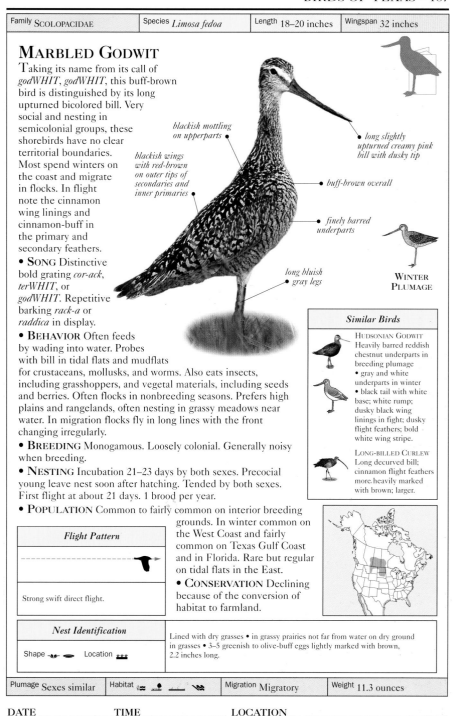

blackish mottling on upperparts

blackish wings with red-brown on outer tips of secondaries and inner primaries

long slightly upturned creamy pink bill with dusky tip

buff-brown overall

finely barred underparts

long bluish gray legs

WINTER PLUMAGE

Similar Birds

HUDSONIAN GODWIT Heavily barred reddish chestnut underparts in breeding plumage • gray and white underparts in winter • black tail with white base; white rump; dusky black wing linings in fight; dusky flight feathers; bold white wing stripe.

LONG-BILLED CURLEW Long decurved bill; cinnamon flight feathers more heavily marked with brown; larger.

Flight Pattern
Strong swift direct flight.

Nest Identification	
Shape ⌣ ⌐ Location ▪▪▪	Lined with dry grasses • in grassy prairies not far from water on dry ground in grasses • 3–5 greenish to olive-buff eggs lightly marked with brown, 2.2 inches long.

Plumage Sexes similar	Habitat	Migration Migratory	Weight 11.3 ounces

DATE _____ TIME _____ LOCATION _____

Family SCOLOPACIDAE	Species *Arenaria interpres*	Length 9–10 inches	Wingspan 17–18 inches

RUDDY TURNSTONE

The alarm cry of this stout little ploverlike shorebird alerts other birds to possible danger. It often is seen probing the drift line on beaches, even cleaning up leftovers from beach picnics. Some will take bread from a human hand. In flight the vividly patterned body and wings are unmistakable in bold rusty reds, blacks, and white. Winter plumage shows a brown-and-white face, dull brown wings and back, and a brown bib but retains the striking white stripes on the wings, back, and tail.

black-and-white face •

short pointed dark bill tilts up at tip •

black, white, and rusty red harlequin-patterned back and wings •

• black bib on breast

• *white underparts*

• *short orange-red legs (duller in winter)*

• **SONG** Low guttural rattle. Alarm call is *chick-ik* or *kewk.* Flight call is *ket-ah-kek* or *kit-it-it.* While feeding gives contact call of *tut.*
• **BEHAVIOR** Roots through seaweed and tips over stones, shells, and other things washed up onto shore. Feeds on insects, mollusks, crustaceans and their eggs, worms, and bird eggs. Sometimes eats discards of birds such as oystercatchers, including carrion. May eat coconut meat as well. Forages alone or in small flocks often mixed with other shorebirds. Other shorebirds may nest near Turnstones to gain protection from predators.
• **BREEDING** Monogamous.
• **NESTING** Incubation 21–24 days by both sexes, but female does more. Precocial young leave nest soon after hatching but feed themselves. Tended by both sexes, but female leaves before first flight at 19–21 days. 1 brood per year.
• **POPULATION** Common and widespread on tundra breeding grounds and on coasts in winter. Casual to rare inland in migration, except around the Great Lakes where the species is more common.

WINTER PLUMAGE

Similar Birds

BLACK TURNSTONE Dark chin; lacks chestnut or rust coloring; dark reddish brown legs • Alaskan and West Coast range.

Flight Pattern
Swift direct flight with rapid wing beats.

Nest Identification	
Shape ⚬ Location ☐ ▬	Lined with bits of dry plants, withered leaves, moss, grass, or seaweed • in open tundra • built by female • 2–4 olive-green to olive-buff eggs marked with browns and blacks, 1.6 inches long.

Plumage Sexes similar	Habitat ___	Migration Migratory	Weight 3.9 ounces

DATE _____ TIME_____ LOCATION _____

| Family SCOLOPACIDAE | Species *Calidris canutus* | Length 10–11 inches | Wingspan 20 inches |

RED KNOT

At one time the Red Knot was one of the most abundant shorebirds in North America, but 19th-century market hunters diminished its population by slaughtering it in both spring and autumn migrations. It can be distinguished by its chunky body, short bill, and short greenish legs. Known as classic high-arctic breeders and long-distance migrants, Red Knots winter mostly in the lower half of South America and may travel 19,000 miles per year. Dappled brown-black upperparts and chestnut underparts turn to pale gray upperparts and white underparts in winter.

buff-chestnut face

dappled brown-black upperparts

short, slightly curved black bill

buff-chestnut breast

WINTER PLUMAGE

finely barred pale grayish white tail and rump

short greenish legs

- **SONG** Generally silent. Feeding birds and flocks in flight emit harsh monosyllabic *knut*. Males on breeding grounds whistle a melodious *poor-me*.
- **BEHAVIOR** Generally feeds on beaches, tidal flats, and lagoons. Eats mollusks, crabs, and insects and their larvae. When feeding in mud probes for food with bill. Often migrates and winters in large flocks that wheel, bank, and roll together in tight, dashing formations. Breeding display flight involves high, circling flight on still or quivering wings, ending with a rapid, tumbling fall, and landing with wings upraised.
- **BREEDING** Monogamous. Gregarious.
- **NESTING** Incubation 21–23 days by both sexes. Precocial young leave nest soon after hatching. Tended by both sexes. First flight at 18–20 days. Female leaves before first flight. 1 brood per year.
- **POPULATION** Uncommon to fairly common on breeding grounds and in migration on Atlantic Coast. Uncommon transient on Pacific Coast. A rare transient inland.
- **CONSERVATION** Federal protection has helped increase populations of this bird.

Similar Birds

CURLEW SANDPIPER Slim and small; longer curved bill; pale rump • red underparts in breeding plumage.

GREAT KNOT Longer bill; large body; lacks robin-red face, neck, and underparts; heavily spotted white underparts; heavy black spotting on breast; black streaking on neck and head; more heavily barred pale rump and tail • spring migrant in western Alaska.

Flight Pattern
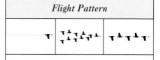
Swift direct flight with rapid wing beats. Flies in V or straight line formation.

Nest Identification	
Shape ⌣ Location ▬ ▨▨ ▨▨	Lined with leaves, lichen, and moss • hollow in clumps of lichens among rocks and scant plant life near water • built by both sexes, but male does most • 3–4 olive-buff eggs marked with brown-black spot; pyriform, 1.6 inches long.

| Plumage Sexes similar | Habitat ⌣ ⱳ | Migration Migratory | Weight 4.4 ounces |

DATE _____ TIME_____ LOCATION _____

Family SCOLOPACIDAE	Species *Calidris alba*	Length 8 inches	Wingspan 15 inches

SANDERLING

This sandpiper runs back and forth on the beach with the ebb and flow of the water, chasing receding waves to snatch up exposed invertebrates. It also stands on one leg for long periods. The palest of the sandpipers, this bird differs from others in its family by its lack of a hind toe. Its light-colored winter plumage blends in with dry sand. The Sanderling nests in the arctic of both hemispheres and winters to the southern end of both, traveling as far as eight thousand miles between its summer and winter homes. In flight the wings show a broad white stripe, black leading and trailing edges, and white underwings. Its white tail has black central tail feathers.

rusty wash over head and back

black shoulders

black bill

black legs and feet

white underparts

rusty wash over breast

- **SONG** Harsh *kree*. Also gives a *twick* or *kip* while in flight.
- **BEHAVIOR** Hunts for sand crabs and mollusks in the sand at the water's edge. Also eats other crustaceans, marine worms, amphipods, isopods, and insects. On arctic breeding grounds eats insects and insect larvae, some plants, leaves, and algae. In flight flocks often wheel and turn, changing direction with flashing wings and a change of color, first showing dark backs then light underparts.
- **BREEDING** Monogamous or polyandrous. Colonial.
- **NESTING** Incubation 24–31 days usually by male, while female often lays second clutch, incubating 1 while male incubates other. Some females take 2 mates, lay a clutch in each nest, then leave the males to tend the eggs and young in their respective nests. Precocial young leave nest soon after hatching; feed themselves but tended by at least 1 parent; female leaves if male is present. First flight at 17 days. 1–2 broods per year.
- **POPULATION** Common.
- **CONSERVATION** Decline due to destruction of habitat.

Similar Birds

RED KNOT
Larger; in breeding plumage rusty red underparts extend onto lower breast and upper belly; barred flanks and undertail coverts; barred rump; in nonbreeding lacks black in shoulders.

DUNLIN
Slightly larger; stout bill droops at the tip
• in winter has gray-brown upperparts, lores, and cheeks; grayish throat and upper breast with fine dusky streaking; lacks black in bend of wing.

Flight Pattern

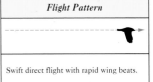

Swift direct flight with rapid wing beats.

Nest Identification

Shape ⌣ ◗   Location ▬ ▬

Lined with small leaves, grass, lichen, mosses, or willow leaves • on high, well-drained, rocky tundra • built by both sexes, but male does more • 3–4 dull olive-green or brown eggs sparsely spotted with brown and black, 1.4 inches long.

Plumage Sexes similar	Habitat ⋙ ≈ ⌐	Migration Migratory	Weight 4.2 ounces

DATE _____ TIME_____ LOCATION _____

Family SCOLOPACIDAE	Species *Calidris pusilla*	Length 6.5 inches	Wingspan 11–13 inches

SEMIPALMATED SANDPIPER

This coastal inhabitant gets its name from the partial webbing it has between its front toes. This bird often mingles with other shorebirds such as sanderlings and Semipalmated Plovers around the time of high tide. Like most shorebirds, Semipalmated Sandpipers will frequently sleep standing on one or both legs, with their bill tucked into their back feathers. Sometimes they will travel along the beach hopping on one leg. Grayer in all plumages than most peeps and have less streaking on the breast and no spotting on the flanks.

trace wash of rufous on crown, auriculars, and scapulars

dusky smudge across eye

gray-brown upperparts, crown, and nape

white face and throat

black semi-straight blunt-tipped bill, deep at base

dusky dark-brown-streaked chest side patches

thick short body

black legs and feet

white underparts

- **SONG** Short *churk* or *churp*. On breeding ground, song given in flight is a monotonous *kee-kee-kee-kee*.
- **BEHAVIOR** The bird is often seen running along the beach, pecking and occasionally probing the sand, searching for insects, worms, small mollusks, and small crustaceans. Generally feeds farther from the water's edge than other peeps. Often gathers in large flocks in migration.
- **BREEDING** Monogamous. Gregarious. Aggressive during breeding season.
- **NESTING** Incubation 18–22 days by both sexes. Precocial young leave nest on day of hatching and feed themselves, tended by both parents. Female abandons after few days. First flight at 14–19 days. 1 brood per year.
- **POPULATION** Fairly common to common on breeding grounds. Common migrant from Atlantic Coast to central Great Plains; rare migrant in the West, south of Canada. Casual to rare in Florida in winter.
- **CONSERVATION** Species still abundant but is being threatened due to diminishing stopover points.

WINTER PLUMAGE

Similar Birds

WESTERN SANDPIPER
Bright rufous on scapulars, back, ear patch, and crown; gray plumage, less uniformly brown; larger and lankier; longer legs; longer, slightly decurved bill (especially female).

Flight Pattern	

Swift flight on rapidly beating wings. Flushed birds rise in zigzag pattern. Flocks twist and turn as precise unit.

Nest Identification	
Shape	Location

Grass-lined with leaves and moss • nests generally built on grassy slope or mound surrounded by short vegetation • built by both sexes • 2–4 whitish to olive-buff eggs, blotched with brown, chestnut, or gray; ovate pyriform to subpyriform, 0.8 x 1.2 inches.

Plumage Sexes similar	Habitat	Migration Migratory	Weight 1.1 ounces

DATE _____ TIME _____ LOCATION _____

Family SCOLOPACIDAE	Species *Calidris mauri*	Length 6–7 inches	Wingspan 12–14 inches

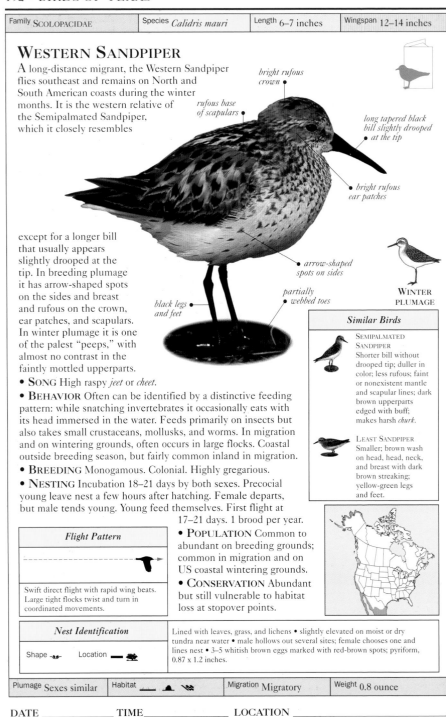

WESTERN SANDPIPER

A long-distance migrant, the Western Sandpiper flies southeast and remains on North and South American coasts during the winter months. It is the western relative of the Semipalmated Sandpiper, which it closely resembles

bright rufous crown

rufous base of scapulars

long tapered black bill slightly drooped at the tip

bright rufous ear patches

except for a longer bill that usually appears slightly drooped at the tip. In breeding plumage it has arrow-shaped spots on the sides and breast and rufous on the crown, ear patches, and scapulars. In winter plumage it is one of the palest "peeps," with almost no contrast in the faintly mottled upperparts.

arrow-shaped spots on sides

partially webbed toes

black legs and feet

WINTER PLUMAGE

• **SONG** High raspy *jeet* or *cheet*.

• **BEHAVIOR** Often can be identified by a distinctive feeding pattern: while snatching invertebrates it occasionally eats with its head immersed in the water. Feeds primarily on insects but also takes small crustaceans, mollusks, and worms. In migration and on wintering grounds, often occurs in large flocks. Coastal outside breeding season, but fairly common inland in migration.

• **BREEDING** Monogamous. Colonial. Highly gregarious.

• **NESTING** Incubation 18–21 days by both sexes. Precocial young leave nest a few hours after hatching. Female departs, but male tends young. Young feed themselves. First flight at 17–21 days. 1 brood per year.

Similar Birds

SEMIPALMATED SANDPIPER Shorter bill without drooped tip; duller in color; less rufous; faint or nonexistent mantle and scapular lines; dark brown upperparts edged with buff; makes harsh *churk*.

LEAST SANDPIPER Smaller; brown wash on head, head, neck, and breast with dark brown streaking; yellow-green legs and feet.

• **POPULATION** Common to abundant on breeding grounds; common in migration and on US coastal wintering grounds.

• **CONSERVATION** Abundant but still vulnerable to habitat loss at stopover points.

Flight Pattern

Swift direct flight with rapid wing beats. Large tight flocks twist and turn in coordinated movements.

Nest Identification

Shape ⌣ Location 🪺🌿

Lined with leaves, grass, and lichens • slightly elevated on moist or dry tundra near water • male hollows out several sites; female chooses one and lines nest • 3–5 whitish brown eggs marked with red-brown spots; pyriform, 0.87 x 1.2 inches.

Plumage Sexes similar	Habitat ▃▃ ▲ 🦆	Migration Migratory	Weight 0.8 ounce

DATE _____ TIME_____ LOCATION _____

Family SCOLOPACIDAE	Species *Calidris minutilla*	Length 6 inches	Wingspan 11–12 inches

LEAST SANDPIPER

During migration a small sandpiper on the edge of an inland pool or wet area is likely to be this species. The Least Sandpiper is the smallest of the native North American sandpipers and among the smallest waders

streaked dark neck

brown-gray upperparts

slender slightly decurved dark bill

streaked dark breast

white belly

pale green-yellow legs

white undertail coverts

WINTER PLUMAGE

in the world. These tame birds will walk close to humans along the shore. With a buff-brown wash on its streaked breast, it is one of the brownest and darkest of the "peeps." The legs and feet are dull yellowish or greenish yellow rather than black like those of most small North American sandpipers.

- **SONG** High *kneet* or *knee-eet*.
- **BEHAVIOR** Usually found in wet habitats where it obtains food by picking small animals from surface of mud and by probing mud for insects, insect larvae, and small crustaceans. Gregarious, occurring in small to large flocks. Often mixes and forages with other species of shorebirds, especially in migration and on wintering grounds. Relatively tame. Migrates at night. When flushed often rises quickly in zigzag fashion.
- **BREEDING** Monogamous. Colonial. Male announces territory by singing continuously, often for several minutes, while performing display flight.
- **NESTING** Incubation 19–23 days by both sexes (female at night; male during day; male does more). Precocial young leave nest day of hatching and feed themselves. Tended by both sexes. First flight at 14–16 days. 1 brood per year.
- **POPULATION** Common.

Similar Birds

SEMIPALMATED SANDPIPER
Slightly larger; straighter bill; whiter face, throat, and chest; black legs.

WESTERN SANDPIPER
Larger; long bill is heavier at base and slightly downcurved at tip; rustier back, ear patch, and crown; black legs • in breeding plumage has more heavily streaked breast.

Flight Pattern

Swift direct flight with rapid wing beats. When flushed often rises quickly in zigzag fashion.

Nest Identification	
Shape	Location

Lined with grass and dry leaves • on small pile of grass or moss near water • male begins building; female finishes • 3–4 olive, pinkish, or buff eggs with dark brown spots; ovate pyriform, 1.2 x 0.85 inches.

Plumage Sexes similar	Habitat	Migration Migratory	Weight 0.8 ounce

DATE _____ TIME _____ LOCATION _____

Family SCOLOPACIDAE	Species *Calidris fuscicollis*	Length 7–8 inches	Wingspan 14–16.5 inches

WHITE-RUMPED SANDPIPER

whitish face and throat

gray to gray-brown head

small streaks on head and neck

straight slightly tapered bill

gray to gray-brown upperparts

wingtips extend beyond tail

yellow or greenish brown spot often at base of lower mandible

small streaks on breast, sides, and flanks

blackish legs

whitish underparts

WINTER PLUMAGE

The white rump, best seen in flight, can sometimes be glimpsed on a standing bird when it spreads its wings slightly. At rest the wing tips extend well beyond the tail. In flight the rump is a distinctive field mark shared by only one other small sandpiper, the Curlew Sandpiper (a casual to rare Eurasian species). A long-distance champion flier, this bird migrates from the Canadian Arctic to southern South America, a distance of more than eight thousand miles. It appears larger in flight than it does on the ground. Crown and back are rusty.

• **SONG** High-pitched *jeet* described as insectlike, mouselike, or batlike.
• **BEHAVIOR** Gregarious. Often wades when foraging and may immerse entire head in water. Also probes with bill in mud for food. Feeds on marine worms, insects, weed seeds, snails, and crustaceans. Often forms single-species flocks or mixes with other shorebirds.
• **BREEDING** Polygamous. Male leaves breeding ground once eggs are laid.
• **NESTING** Incubation 21–22 days by female. Precocial young leave nest soon after hatching and feed themselves. Tended by female. First flight at 16–17 days. 1 brood per year.
• **POPULATION** Fairly common. Casual in the West.
• **CONSERVATION** Vulnerable to habitat destruction in staging areas.

Similar Birds

BAIRD'S SANDPIPER More brown overall; less-contrasting supercilium; buff edging on upperparts; buff wash on face and across streaked breast; lacks white uppertail patch.

WESTERN SANDPIPER Smaller; shorter wings do not extend past tail; dark-centered uppertail.

Flight Pattern

Strong direct flight with rapid wing beats.

Nest Identification

Shape ⌣ Location ⁘ ▬

Lichens, moss, and leaves, especially dry willow • on pile of grass or moss near water • built by female • 3–4 olive-buff to light green eggs marked with brown; pyriform to ovate, 0.9 x 1.4 inches.

Plumage Sexes similar	Habitat ⌐ ⚲ ≈ ≈	Migration Migratory	Weight 1.2 ounces

DATE _____ TIME_____ LOCATION _____

Family SCOLOPACIDAE	Species *Calidris bairdii*	Length 7.5 inches	Wingspan 15–16.5 inches

BAIRD'S SANDPIPER

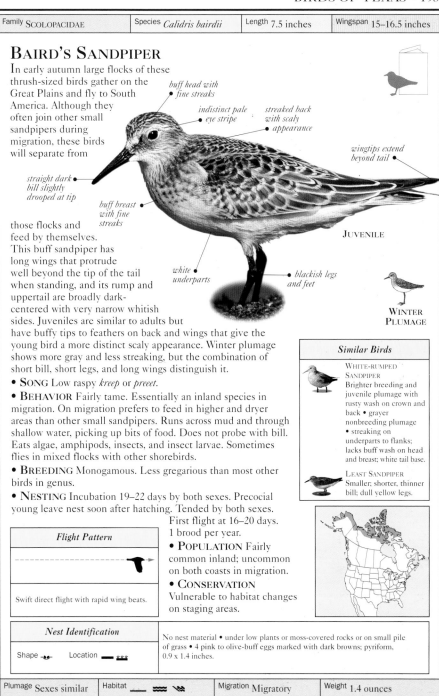

In early autumn large flocks of these thrush-sized birds gather on the Great Plains and fly to South America. Although they often join other small sandpipers during migration, these birds will separate from

buff head with fine streaks

indistinct pale eye stripe

streaked back with scaly appearance

wingtips extend beyond tail

straight dark bill slightly drooped at tip

buff breast with fine streaks

those flocks and feed by themselves. This buff sandpiper has long wings that protrude well beyond the tip of the tail when standing, and its rump and uppertail are broadly dark-centered with very narrow whitish sides. Juveniles are similar to adults but have buffy tips to feathers on back and wings that give the young bird a more distinct scaly appearance. Winter plumage shows more gray and less streaking, but the combination of short bill, short legs, and long wings distinguish it.

white underparts

blackish legs and feet

JUVENILE

WINTER PLUMAGE

- **SONG** Low raspy *kreep* or *preeet*.
- **BEHAVIOR** Fairly tame. Essentially an inland species in migration. On migration prefers to feed in higher and dryer areas than other small sandpipers. Runs across mud and through shallow water, picking up bits of food. Does not probe with bill. Eats algae, amphipods, insects, and insect larvae. Sometimes flies in mixed flocks with other shorebirds.
- **BREEDING** Monogamous. Less gregarious than most other birds in genus.
- **NESTING** Incubation 19–22 days by both sexes. Precocial young leave nest soon after hatching. Tended by both sexes. First flight at 16–20 days. 1 brood per year.
- **POPULATION** Fairly common inland; uncommon on both coasts in migration.
- **CONSERVATION** Vulnerable to habitat changes on staging areas.

Similar Birds

WHITE-RUMPED SANDPIPER
Brighter breeding and juvenile plumage with rusty wash on crown and back • grayer nonbreeding plumage • streaking on underparts to flanks; lacks buff wash on head and breast; white tail base.

LEAST SANDPIPER
Smaller; shorter, thinner bill; dull yellow legs.

Flight Pattern
Swift direct flight with rapid wing beats.

Nest Identification	
Shape	Location	No nest material • under low plants or moss-covered rocks or on small pile of grass • 4 pink to olive-buff eggs marked with dark browns; pyriform, 0.9 x 1.4 inches.

Plumage Sexes similar	Habitat	Migration Migratory	Weight 1.4 ounces

DATE _____ TIME_____ LOCATION _____

Family SCOLOPACIDAE	Species *Calidris melanotos*	Length 8–9 inches	Wingspan 15–16 inches

PECTORAL SANDPIPER

This bird is named for the two saclike structures under the neck and breast of the male. During courtship the male inflates these sacs, thus enhancing the appearance of the heavy streaking on its breast. The streaking ends abruptly in a sharp line, separating it from the snow-white belly. During flight the sacs pump up and down in rhythm with the bird's hooting calls. In flight this bird shows a blackish brown rump and tail. Males and females are similar but the male has darker brown streaking on the throat and breast with white mottling. Winter plumage is pale brown overall.

dark brown crown with black, chestnut, and pale olive-brown stripes

thin white stripes on back and scapulars

white stripe over each eye

slender black bill with greenish yellow base to lower mandible

streaked brown breast

scapular, tertial, and mantle feathers have blackish brown centers with chestnut to buff fringes

whitish underparts

greenish yellow legs

• **SONG** Low reedy *churk* or *churrrt*. Male has hooting courtship call; murmuring foghornlike *khoor, khoor*; or loud coarse *gr, gr, gr* repeated several times per second.

• **BEHAVIOR** Forages in vegetation. Feeds by pecking and shallow probing. Eats insects and larvae, small crustaceans, spiders, seeds, and amphipods. In migration prefers meadows, marshes, pond edges, tidal flats, and mudflats. Usually in small flocks of 20–40 birds. Relatively tame. May fly short distance, then pitch back into grass.

• **BREEDING** Promiscuous. Males mate several times. Females visit territories of other males. Males leave territories prior to hatching of eggs.

• **NESTING** Incubation 19–23 days by female. Precocial young leave nest soon after hatching and feed themselves, tended by female. First flight at 18–21 days. 1 brood per year.

• **POPULATION** Fairly common to common on breeding grounds and in migration on East Coast and in Midwest; uncommon from Great Plains to West Coast.

Similar Birds

SHARP-TAILED SANDPIPER
Lacks sharply defined streaked breast; buff wash across breast • in breeding plumage has streaking on crissum, sides, and flanks • juvenile has buff-orange breast and rusty crown.

RUFF ♀
Larger; longer neck; gray-brown breast with heavy spotting and blotches; in flight shows large white ovals on uppertail and stronger wing bars.

Flight Pattern

Swift direct flight with rapid wing beats. When flushed climbs with zigzag flight.

Nest Identification	
Shape	Location	Grass and leaves • on dry ground near water • built by female • whitish to olive-buff eggs splotched with dark browns; pyriform to oval, 1.5 x 1.0 inches.

Plumage Sexes similar	Habitat	Migration Migratory	Weight 3.5 ounces

DATE _____ TIME_____ LOCATION _____

Family SCOLOPACIDAE	Species *Calidris alpina*	Length 7.5–8.5 inches	Wingspan 14.5–15.75 inches

DUNLIN

Impressive fliers, these small brown sandpipers are able to migrate at speeds of more than a hundred miles per hour and travel in flocks that can be so large they look like a swarm of insects. Once known as the Red-backed Sandpiper, the breeding bird is unmistakable with its long sturdy droop-tipped bill, rusty red upperparts, and black belly patch. Females are similar to males but have brown napes. When feeding it often gives the appearance of being hunchbacked.

- *variegated chestnut cap*
- *whitish or light gray nape with brown streaks*
- *patterned reddish brown back and wings*
- *long stout black bill decurved toward tip*
- *white throat with brown streaking that increases toward breast*
- *tail with dark brown center, gray distal sides, and white basal sides*
- *black belly patch surrounded by white*
- *black legs and feet*

WINTER PLUMAGE

- **SONG** Nasal slurred reedy call of *cheezp, kreeep*, or *treezp*. Flocks make soft twittering noises at roost and on feeding grounds. Alarm call on breeding grounds is *quoi*.

- **BEHAVIOR** Eats insects and larvae, marine worms, small crustaceans, snails, and small fish. Wades in shallows and uses bill to probe and pick up food. Probes with rapid up-and-down stitching motion several times per second. Gregarious, often in large flocks in migration and winter. On tundra breeding grounds male makes territorial display of lifting one wing over its back when another male enters the breeding ground. Fly rapidly while performing synchronized maneuvers as a flock.

- **BREEDING** Monogamous.

- **NESTING** Incubation 20–23 days by both sexes. Precocial young leave nest day of hatching. Tended by both sexes, but primarily by male, for several days. First flight at 19–23 days. 1 brood per year.

- **POPULATION** Common on breeding grounds, both coasts, and inland to the Great Plains in migration. Rare on the Great Plains. Common on coastal wintering grounds. Has been declining since the 1970s for undetermined reasons.

- **CONSERVATION** Vulnerable to habitat loss in staging and wintering areas.

Similar Birds

ROCK SANDPIPER
Yellow-green base of bill, legs, and feet;
- in breeding plumage has black chest patch
- western range.

CURLEW SANDPIPER
Long decurved bill • in breeding plumage has bright rusty red underparts, neck, and head; white belly, undertail coverts, and rump patch • in winter plumage has white rump without black center line.

Flight Pattern

Swift direct flight with rapid wing beats.

Nest Identification

Shape ⬤ Location ✳✳✳

Leaves and grasses • hummock or raised dry area on wet, grass, or sedge tundra • both sexes make scrapes, but female chooses one and completes nest • 4 olive, bluish green, or buff eggs blotched with browns or gray; pyriform, 1.4 inches long.

Plumage Sexes similar	Habitat ___ 〰 〰 〰	Migration Migratory	Weight 1.9 ounces

DATE _____ TIME _____ LOCATION _____

Family SCOLOPACIDAE	Species *Calidris ferruginea*	Length 7.5–8.5 inches	Wingspan 14.5–16.5 inches

CURLEW SANDPIPER

This Eurasian species is a rare to casual, but regular, visitor to North America, and in 1962 it was found nesting in Alaska for the first time. A long-distance flier, this bird migrates from the arctic regions to Africa and Australia. Adults in breeding plumage are conspicuous with rich reddish chestnut head, neck, and underparts, and chestnut upperparts mottled black and white. The long bill is decurved, and the white rump, undertail coverts, and underwings are conspicuous in flight. The Curlew Sandpiper often associates with the Dunlin, which it resembles, in migration.

dark russet or chestnut head

russet pattern on upperwings

white undertail coverts and rump

black legs and feet

black bill slightly decurved along entire length

dark russet or chestnut breast and belly

WINTER PLUMAGE

In winter, this sandpiper displays a white chest lightly streaked with brown, a white belly, and gray upperparts.

• **SONG** Call is a pleasant liquid *chirrup* or *chirrip* in flight, or a *wick-wick-wick* in alarm. The male sings while flying on its breeding grounds.

• **BEHAVIOR** On tundra breeding grounds, feeds on insects, especially beetles. Outside breeding areas, also eats leeches, worms, crustaceans, and small mollusks. Probes rapidly with bill in mud, usually working away from others into the shallows and often wading belly deep – a behavior that is useful in picking them out of mixed feeding flocks.

• **BREEDING** Monogamous; solitary nester. Male chases female in courtship by running and flying around her in zigzag pattern, showing off his white rump. Male leaves after courtship before eggs hatch.

Similar Birds

DUNLIN
Winter plumage
• shorter legs; more streaking on breast; bill curved only at tip; dark brown center to rump.

RED KNOT
Breeding plumage
• larger and chunkier; shorter legs; shorter, straight bill; finely barred white rump.

Flight Pattern	
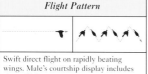	

Swift direct flight on rapidly beating wings. Male's courtship display includes zigzag flight pattern.

• **NESTING** Incubation 21 days by female. Precocial young tended by female. 1 brood per year.

• **POPULATION** Rare to casual, but regularly appears in North America.

Nest Identification	
Shape Location ▬▬	Reindeer moss, lined with moss, tender leaves, lichen, and willow leaves • dry hummock or on ledge of moist tundra • built by both parents • 4 cream, yellow, or olive-tinted eggs, with brown or blackish spots; pyriform, 1.4 inches long.

Plumage Sexes similar	Habitat 🪶 〰〰 〰	Migration Migratory	Weight 2.4 ounces

DATE _____ TIME_____ LOCATION _____

Family SCOLOPACIDAE	Species *Calidris himantopus*	Length 7.5–8.5 inches	Wingspan 15.5–17 inches

STILT SANDPIPER

This long-legged sandpiper can be seen during migration feeding in dense flocks in shallow waters along the Atlantic coast. It is unwary and approachable, attributes that were exploited by early nineteenth-century market hunters to the point that it became rare and irregular in New England, where it was once common. Today this slender, long-necked, long-legged shorebird seems to be increasing in numbers and is once again common. In flight it shows a white rump. In winter, the Stilt Sandpiper displays gray upperparts and white underparts.

rufous patch on cheeks

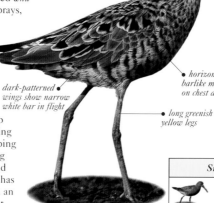

long, slender, slightly decurved black bill

- **SONG** Low hoarse whistled *whu* or rattling trill *querrp*. Also brays, whines, and utters guttural trills on breeding ground.

- **BEHAVIOR** Eats mostly insects and their larvae, but also takes small crustaceans and mollusks and some plant materials, including seeds. May wade belly-deep in water and feed by thrusting head underwater while probing mud with beak in a stitching motion. Usually tame around humans; however, this bird has been known to attack when an intruder approaches the nest.

dark-patterned wings show narrow white bar in flight

horizontal barlike marking on chest and belly

long greenish yellow legs

WINTER PLUMAGE

- **BREEDING** Monogamous. Male chases female in flight until he flies ahead, then male dives downward singing and raising wings over back.

- **NESTING** Incubation 19–21 days by both parents; male by day, female at night. Precocial young leave nest shortly after hatching, tended by parents for about 14 days. First flight at 17–18 days. 1 brood per year.

- **POPULATION** Common on breeding grounds and in the interior east of the Rockies during migration. Rare on West Coast, primarily in fall. Uncommon on East Coast in spring; common in fall. Rare in winter in coastal southern US.

- **CONSERVATION** Populations seem to be slowly on the increase.

Similar Birds

CURLEW SANDPIPER
Winter plumage • black legs; beak more curved.

LESSER YELLOWLEGS
Winter plumage • larger; darker gray upperparts with extensive white speckling; dusky lores; white supralorals; white eye ring; bright yellow legs and feet; long straight black bill.

Flight Pattern
Strong powerful direct flight on long, rapidly beating wings.

Nest Identification	
 Shape Location	On small piles of sedge or low well-drained rocky ledges • pair may return to former nest site from year to year • male scrapes, but female decides which nest to use • 4 pale green to olive-green or cream eggs with brown spots; pyriform, 1.4 inches long.

Plumage Sexes similar	Habitat	Migration Migratory	Weight 2.1 ounces

DATE _____ TIME_____ LOCATION _____

Family SCOLOPACIDAE	Species *Tryngites subruficollis*	Length 7.5–8.25 inches	Wingspan 16–17 inches

BUFF-BREASTED SANDPIPER

Birders can spot this shorebird during migration when it stops to forage in the wet fields, turf farms, and rice fields of inland North America; it also favors golf courses and airports. This species generally is approachable, but when frightened it usually runs from danger rather than flying. It has a short pigeonlike bill, and an upright stance like a plover. In flight the silvery white axillars and underwing linings contrast with the buff underparts and darker back. Juveniles have more scaly upperparts.

- short straight dark brown bill
- long buff neck
- buff head and face with streaked and spotted brown crown
- prominent dark eye with light eye ring
- streaked and spotted brown hindneck
- buff-edged brown upperparts appear scaly
- buff breast with streaked and spotted brown sides
- white belly and undertail coverts
- buff-edged brown tail
- yellowish orange legs and feet

- **SONG** During migration a soft hoarse call of *pr-r-r-reet*. During display makes quick clucking sounds. Otherwise mostly silent.

- **BEHAVIOR** Gregarious. Eats insects, fly larvae and pupae, some spiders, and seeds. Prefers short dry grasslands in migration. Travels in small flocks, often mixing with other species. Rarely forages beside water.

- **BREEDING** Promiscuous. Males display together at a communal area called a lek. During the display the male flash the silvery white undersides of its wings. Successful males may mate with several females. Males leave shortly after breeding.

- **NESTING** Female incubates 19–21 days; precocial young leave nest soon after hatching. First flight at about 21 days. 1 brood per year.

- **POPULATION** Uncommon to fairly common on breeding grounds and in interior during migration. Rare to casual or uncommon in autumn migration on both coasts.

- **CONSERVATION** Once abundant, but tameness and flock density have made it vulnerable to slaughter by market hunters. Protective laws have helped population recover from near extinction.

Similar Birds

UPLAND SANDPIPER Larger; streaked brown plumage with no conspicuous marks on upperparts; streaking on breast, sides, and flanks; long, thin neck; small dovelike head; short yellow bill with black tip.

RUFF Juvenile larger; smaller head; shorter, droopy bill; long neck; deep-bellied, hump-backed body; U-shaped white rump band • rare to casual.

Flight Pattern

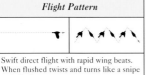

Swift direct flight with rapid wing beats. When flushed twists and turns like a snipe as it climbs away.

Nest Identification

Shape — Location

Lined with grasses or moss • on ground in pile of vegetation or in tree stump • built by female • 4 white, buff, or olive eggs with brown blotches; pyriform, 1.3 inches long.

Plumage Sexes similar	Habitat	Migration Migratory	Weight 2.5 ounces

DATE _____ TIME_____ LOCATION _____

Family SCOLOPACIDAE	Species *Limnodromus griseus*	Length 10.5–12 inches	Wingspan 18–22 inches

SHORT-BILLED DOWITCHER

This snipelike sandpiper is commonly seen in open marshes and mudflats during migration. Dowitchers are known by the long bill, a white wedge from the barred tail to the back that is only visible in flight, and a light belly. Although its call differs from that of the Long-billed Dowitcher, they are difficult to distinguish in the field because of the variety of breeding plumages in its three races and the overlap in bill length between the two species. Juveniles are the easiest to separate by plumage from August to October. Winter plumage is gray overall. The female is similar to the male but larger.

white supercilium

dark brownish upperparts with rufous-buff-edged feathers

whitish chin

long blackish brown bill

chunky body

white to cinnamon-red breast with heavy brownish spotting or barring

barred tail

short greenish legs

WINTER PLUMAGE

- **SONG** Generally silent. Utters clear mellow or abrasive *chi-too-too* or *kee-you*. Also sings *tiddle-whee*, especially in spring.
- **BEHAVIOR** Gregarious; feeds and roosts in large flocks and associates with other species. Eats mostly insects, also eggs of king or horseshoe crabs. Probes with fast up-and-down motion of bill. Often submerges head in water. May freeze in standing position when approached. Often flies at considerable heights.
- **BREEDING** Monogamous. Colonial. Male displays with a hovering flight song over breeding territory.
- **NESTING** Incubation 21 days by female, sometimes by both sexes. Precocial young leave nest soon after hatching. Tended by male but feed themselves. 1 brood per year.
- **POPULATION** Common.

Similar Birds

LONG-BILLED DOWITCHER
Slightly larger; longer legs; darker overall; darker tail with white bars narrower than dark bars; different voice
- females may have longer bill than males
- in breeding plumage lacks white underparts

Flight Pattern

Strong swift direct flight with rapid wing beats.

Nest Identification

Shape ⚬ Location ⚬⚬⚬ ▬

Sticks, leaves, and grasses * on ground in small pile of grass or moss • built by both sexes • 4 buff-green or brownish eggs speckled and blotched with brown; pyriform, 1.6 x 1.1 inches.

Plumage Sexes similar	Habitat ⚬ ⚬ ≈ ≈ ≈	Migration Migratory	Weight 3.8 ounces

DATE _____ TIME_____ LOCATION _____

Family SCOLOPACIDAE	Species *Limnodromus scolopaceus*	Length 11–12.5 inches	Wingspan 18–20 inches

LONG-BILLED DOWITCHER

Despite its name, only the female has a slightly longer bill than its cousin, the Short-billed Dowitcher. The Long-billed prefers freshwater habitats and migrates south later in the season than the Short-billed. Winter plumage shows gray overall. In breeding plumage birds show no white on the underparts, and the tail is darker than that of the Short-billed,

dense dark barring on throat and upper breast

bright white scapular tips

pale chestnut to buff supercilium

pale chestnut to buff chin

long straight bill

dark barring on lower breast and belly

reddish underparts

greenish yellow legs and feet

WINTER PLUMAGE

with smaller light bars than dark ones. Juveniles have darker upperparts and duller underparts than the juvenile Short-billed. The scapulars have narrow dark rust edges, while the tertials have narrow, very even pale edges. On the Short-billed these feathers are broadly edged with reddish buff, and many have internal markings.

• **SONG** Fast high-pitched thin nasal *keek* or *keek-keek-keek* usually uttered as a single or triple note. Also sings *peter-wee-too*.
• **BEHAVIOR** Gregarious. When feeding rapidly probes up and down with long bill. Often puts entire head in water to probe for insects. Eats mostly insects and insect larvae but also takes crustaceans, mollusks, and plant seeds. Favors freshwater mudflats in migration and winter. Often flies high in migration.
• **BREEDING** Monogamous. Small colonies. Male sings while performing hovering display flight.
• **NESTING** Incubation 20 days by both sexes in first week, then just by male. Precocial young leave nest day of hatching, then tended by male but feed themselves. 1 brood per year.
• **POPULATION** Varies from common to uncommon.

Similar Birds

SHORT-BILLED DOWITCHER
Slightly smaller; shorter legs; paler upperparts; some white in underparts; paler tail with white bars as wide or wider than dark bars; different call.

COMMON SNIPE
Long bill; boldly striped head; buff stripes on back; barred flanks; rusty red tail.

Flight Pattern

Swift direct flight with rapid wing beats.

Nest Identification

Shape — Location

Lined with leaves and grass • atop small pile of grasses or moss • built by female • 4 brown to olive eggs with brown and gray blotches; pyriform, 1.6 x 1.1 inches.

Plumage Sexes similar	Habitat	Migration Migratory	Weight 3.5 ounces

DATE _____ TIME_____ LOCATION _____

| Family SCOLOPACIDAE | Species *Gallinago gallinago* | Length 10–11 inches | Wingspan 17–20 inches |

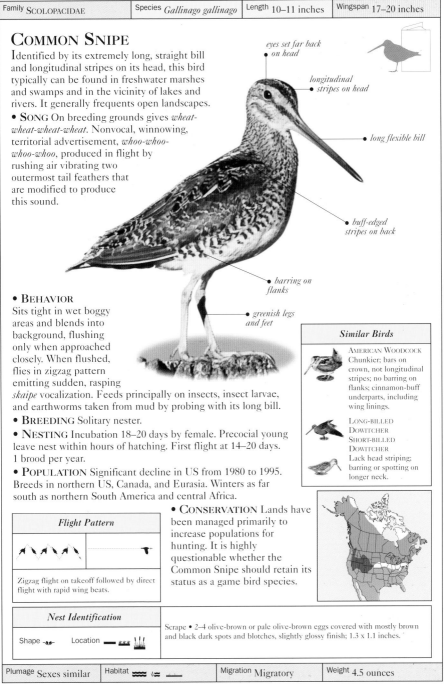

COMMON SNIPE

Identified by its extremely long, straight bill and longitudinal stripes on its head, this bird typically can be found in freshwater marshes and swamps and in the vicinity of lakes and rivers. It generally frequents open landscapes.

• **SONG** On breeding grounds gives *wheat-wheat-wheat-wheat*. Nonvocal, winnowing, territorial advertisement, *whoo-whoo-whoo-whoo*, produced in flight by rushing air vibrating two outermost tail feathers that are modified to produce this sound.

eyes set far back on head

longitudinal stripes on head

long flexible bill

buff-edged stripes on back

barring on flanks

greenish legs and feet

• **BEHAVIOR** Sits tight in wet boggy areas and blends into background, flushing only when approached closely. When flushed, flies in zigzag pattern emitting sudden, rasping *skaipe* vocalization. Feeds principally on insects, insect larvae, and earthworms taken from mud by probing with its long bill.

• **BREEDING** Solitary nester.

• **NESTING** Incubation 18–20 days by female. Precocial young leave nest within hours of hatching. First flight at 14–20 days. 1 brood per year.

• **POPULATION** Significant decline in US from 1980 to 1995. Breeds in northern US, Canada, and Eurasia. Winters as far south as northern South America and central Africa.

• **CONSERVATION** Lands have been managed primarily to increase populations for hunting. It is highly questionable whether the Common Snipe should retain its status as a game bird species.

Similar Birds

AMERICAN WOODCOCK
Chunkier; bars on crown, not longitudinal stripes; no barring on flanks; cinnamon-buff underparts, including wing linings.

LONG-BILLED DOWITCHER
SHORT-BILLED DOWITCHER
Lack head striping; barring or spotting on longer neck.

Flight Pattern

Zigzag flight on takeoff followed by direct flight with rapid wing beats.

Nest Identification

Shape — Location

Scrape • 2–4 olive-brown or pale olive-brown eggs covered with mostly brown and black dark spots and blotches, slightly glossy finish; 1.3 x 1.1 inches.

| Plumage Sexes similar | Habitat | Migration Migratory | Weight 4.5 ounces |

DATE _____ TIME _____ LOCATION _____

Family SCOLOPACIDAE	Species *Scolopax minor*	Length 10.5–11 inches	Wingspan 18 inches

AMERICAN WOODCOCK

The long bill of this upland shorebird is sensitive and flexible, allowing it to feel for worms in deep soil. Woodcocks are rarely seen during the day unless flushed and escaping straightaway in flight on twittering rounded wings. Chunky, short-necked, and short-legged, its plumage matches the dead leaves of the forest floor and old fields where it roosts by day.

• **SONG** Generally silent. In spring, male on display ground has nasal call of *peeant*, similar to that of the Common Nighthawk. During display flights male produces a musical twittering with wings and a liquid, bubbling song from high overhead.

• **BEHAVIOR** Crepuscular and nocturnal.

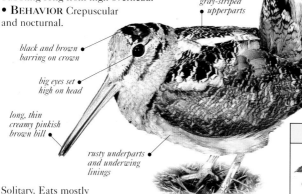

short black tail with silvery white terminal band

gray-striped upperparts

black and brown barring on crown

big eyes set high on head

overall black and brown barring and markings

long, thin creamy pinkish brown bill

rusty underparts and underwing linings

Solitary. Eats mostly earthworms, but also takes slugs, insects, and some seeds and berries. Before probing into soil with bill, often stamps foot on ground, causing earthworms to move. During feeding, walks slowly with a back and forth rocking motion.

• **BREEDING** Polygamous; loose colonies. Male has complex courtship flight: he flies from ground, circling as high as 300 feet, hovers, chirps, and glides earthward in a series of zigzags.

• **NESTING** Incubation 20–21 days by female. Precocial young leave nest 1–2 days after hatching to feed themselves, tended by female. First flight at 14 days; independent at 42–56 days. 1 brood per year.

• **POPULATION** Fairly common. Casual to eastern Colorado and eastern New Mexico; accidental to southeastern California.

• **CONSERVATION** Hunted and managed as a game bird.

Similar Birds

COMMON SNIPE
More slender overall; longer bill; striped head pattern; pointed wings; barred sides, flanks, and undertail coverts; streaked neck and upper breast; buffy white stripes on back; reddish tail with white terminal band; longer greenish legs and feet.

EURASIAN WOODCOCK
Accidental — no recent records • much larger; brown- and pale buff-barred underparts; pointier, longer wings.

Flight Pattern

Most often has swift direct flight; when flushed, flies low for short distance before dropping back into cover.

Nest Identification

Shape ⌣⌣   Location 🌾🌿🐚🌱

Lined with twigs and dried leaves • on ground, hidden in tall grasses, weeds, or near stump of tree • built by female • 4 buff or cinnamon eggs, with gray, purple, and brown spots; oval, 1.5 x 1.1 inches.

Plumage Sexes similar	Habitat 🌾🌾 🌿🌿 🏞️	Migration Migratory	Weight 6.2 ounces

DATE _____ TIME_____ LOCATION _____

| Family SCOLOPACIDAE | Species *Phalaropus tricolor* | Length 8–9.5 inches | Wingspan 14.5–16 inches |

WILSON'S PHALAROPE

Phalaropes have devised a terrific way to get plankton and other food to the water's surface for harvest. They spin like tops – as fast as 60 times per minute – creating small whirlpools that pull food to the surface where they can pick it up with their long slender bills. In flight, wings lack striping, and uppertail coverts are white.

This is the only phalarope confined to inland habitats and restricted to the Western Hemisphere.

brownish black upperparts are duller than female's

long needle-shaped bill

MALE

white underparts

white chin and cheeks

dull yellow legs and feet with narrow lateral membranes

JUVENILE

- **SONG** Generally silent. Breeding call of *nya* sounds like a toy whistle. Occasional flight call a low croaking *aangh*.
- **BEHAVIOR** Tame. Solitary, pairs, small flocks. Eats insects, larvae, crustaceans, marsh plant seeds. Probes mud in shallow water, sometimes with head submerged. Spins and dabbles. Seen following shoveler ducks to pick stirred-up prey from surface. Sometimes snags insects from air. Often walks in vegetation, picking prey from ground and plants.

pale gray crown

white mark above eye

broad black stripe extends down neck, fading to reddish chestnut

WINTER PLUMAGE

gray wing coverts and wings

orange wash forms partial necklace on pale gray neck

black legs and feet **FEMALE**

Similar Birds

LESSER YELLOWLEGS Larger; darker upperparts; streaked breast and belly; lightly barred tail; canary-yellow legs.

RED-NECKED PHALAROPE Smaller; shorter bill; black ear patch even in winter plumage; strongly streaked upperparts; dark gray rump; white wing stripe.

- **BREEDING** May be polyandrous. Loose colonies. Female courts male by swimming beside him and chasing off other females; eventually male makes sexual advances. Male develops incubation patches.
- **NESTING** Incubation 18–21 days by male. Precocial young leave nest day of hatching. Tended by male but feed themselves. First flight at 16–18 days. 1 or more broods per year.
- **POPULATION** Abundant to common in the West, although declining slightly. Uncommon to rare or casual in the East.
- **CONSERVATION** Drainage of marshes has caused loss of nesting areas; protection of such areas is needed.

Flight Pattern
Swift direct flight with rapid wing beats.

Nest Identification	
Shape ～ Location ▬ ⁂ ⋔	Lined with grass • female may start, but built mostly by male • 4 buff eggs with brown blotches; pyriform, 1.3 inches long.

| Plumage Sexes differ | Habitat ＿ ⧰ ≈≈ | Migration Migratory | Weight 2.4 ounces |

DATE _____ TIME _____ LOCATION _____

Family SCOLOPACIDAE	Species *Phalaropus lobatus*	Length 7.75–8 inches	Wingspan 14–15 inches

RED-NECKED PHALAROPE

Formerly called the Northern Phalarope, this bird is the smallest of the phalaropes, as well as the most abundant and widely distributed. Like all birds in its genus, the male is the only gender with brood patches with which to incubate the clutch. Male and female have similar plumage, but male looks more washed-out. White wing bars show in flight. In winter plumage both sexes have heavily streaked gray upperparts, whitish underparts, a black line through the eyes, and dark legs and feet.

streaked gray forehead and crown

straight, needlelike black bill

dark gray back with buff striping and feather edging

white throat

MALE

- **SONG** Flight call is soft *clipp* or *twit*, *tirric* or *twik*. Utters various insectlike alarm calls on breeding grounds.

white underparts

- **BEHAVIOR** Very tame. Gregarious in migration and winter; also pelagic in winter. Turns in circles while feeding in shallow water and picks up zooplankton stirred up to surface. Turns over rocks, picks larvae off water. Eats brine shrimp, aquatic vegetation, insect larvae, mollusks, and plankton. Female initiates courtship, selects scrape, and deserts male as soon as incubation begins; sometimes mates with a second male.

short blue-gray legs and feet

small white spot in front of eye

black face and crown

rufous-red on neck

JUVENILE

FEMALE

WINTER PLUMAGE

gray sides of breast

gray streaking on sides and flanks

- **BREEDING** Monogamous, or female serially polyandrous (at least 10 percent). Solitary or in pairs.

- **NESTING** Incubation 17–21 days by male. Precocial young leave nest soon after hatching and are able to swim immediately. Tended by male but feed themselves. First flight at 20–21 days. 1 brood by male and 1–2 broods by female per year.

Similar Birds

RED PHALAROPE
Larger; longer wings
- thicker yellowish bill in breeding season
- in winter has thicker blackish bill; more uniform pale gray upperparts without whitish streaking.

- **POPULATION** Abundant. Common off West Coast and inland in the West during migration; rare inland in the Midwest and the East; uncommon off Atlantic Coast; fairly common offshore in Maritimes and New England.

- **CONSERVATION** Vulnerable to marine pollution and oil spills.

Flight Pattern

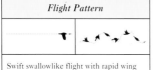

Swift swallowlike flight with rapid wing beats and quick movements and turns.

Nest Identification

Shape — Location

Lined with grasses, dried leaves, and stalks • in tussock of grasses or sunken in mosses, often sheltered by vegetation • built by male, often in company of female • 3–4 buff-olive eggs spotted with brown; oval to pyriform, 1.2 x 0.8 inches.

Plumage Sexes differ	Habitat	Migration Migratory	Weight 1.2 ounces

DATE _____ TIME_____ LOCATION _____

Family SCOLOPACIDAE	Species *Phalaropus fulicaria*	Length 8–9 inches	Wingspan 14–16 inches

RED PHALAROPE

Of all phalaropes, the Red is most pelagic, nests farthest north, and migrates farthest south. It breeds well north of the Arctic Circle and winters at sea off both Atlantic and Pacific Coasts. Its bill is shorter and thicker than that of other phalaropes. In flight it shows a white wing stripe, a uniformly gray back (in winter), and brownish legs and feet.

black wing tips

MALE

- **SONG** Bell-like *clink-clink*. Also a shrieking shrill *wit-wit* and *tink* or *tsik*.
- **BEHAVIOR** Tame. Solitary or in small flocks; at sea occasionally in very large flocks. Pelagic in winter. Swims readily. Wades into water to feed; finds food on surface and in shallow water. Swims and spins often, picking up planktonic food particles with its bill from the surface. Eats small insects, fish, and aquatic invertebrates.

white face

black crown and forehead

black at base of bill

dark gray upperparts have feathers fringed with rufous-buff

yellowish bill with black tip

JUVENILE

- **BREEDING** Female polyandrous; male promiscuous. Semicolonial. Female selects territory, leaves area shortly after laying eggs; and sometimes mates again.
- **NESTING** Incubation 18–20 days by male. Precocial young leave nest soon after hatching. Tended by male but feed themselves. First flight at 16–20 days. 1 brood per year by male and 2 broods by female.

chestnut-red underparts

WINTER PLUMAGE

more brightly colored

FEMALE

chestnut-red underparts

Similar Birds

♂ **RED-NECKED PHALAROPE** Thinner, needlelike bill; smaller • in winter plumage is darker with heavily striped back; blacker crown; more contrasting wing stripe.

- **POPULATION** Abundant on breeding grounds. In winter and migration fairly common off the West Coast; uncommon off the East Coast. Rare inland.
- **CONSERVATION** Accidents occur during migration, such as collisions with lighthouses. Storms at sea can blow birds inland. Vulnerable to oil spills.

Flight Pattern
Swift direct flight with rapid wing beats.

Nest Identification	
Shape	Location	Domed with grass • lined with grasses and other fine materials • on ground near water • built by male • 3–4 olive-green eggs blotched with black or brown; oval to pyriform, 1.2 x 0.9 inches.

Plumage Sexes differ	Habitat	Migration Migratory	Weight 1.8 ounces

DATE _____ TIME_____ LOCATION _____

Family LARIDAE	Species *Stercorarius pomarinus*	Length 20–23 inches	Wingspan 48 inches

POMARINE JAEGER

The largest and strongest jaeger is about the size of a Ring-billed or Heermann's Gull, with a bulky body, thick neck, and wide-based wings. Like many of the skuas, its nesting is related to lemming populations on the Arctic tundra. When the brown lemming is numerous these seabirds nest, and when the rodent is not abundant they may not breed at all.

It has a light color morph and a more rare dark morph. Adults

yellowish wash over nape and cheeks

chocolate-brown back, upperwing coverts, secondary flight feathers, and tail feathers

dark helmeted appearance

heavy hooked bill

2 long central tail feathers twisted 90 degrees

LIGHT MORPH

have 2 blunt central tail feathers with vanes twisted vertically. In flight this bird appears bulkier, with a slower wing beat, than other jaegers, and displays a larger white patch at the base of the primaries, often with a second smaller and fainter patch nearby.

dark band mottled across chest

chocolate-brown underwing coverts

white to pale base of primary flight feathers, darker toward tips

- **SONG** Often silent, except on breeding grounds. Sharp *which-yew* or *yeew*; high-pitched *week-week* or *yeew-eee*.
- **BEHAVIOR** Solitary or in pairs. Predatory. Eats small mammals, fish, birds, carrion, and refuse. Often steals from other seabirds. Picks up prey with bill, never talons. Found at sea outside breeding season.
- **BREEDING** Monogamous; small colonies. During courtship, male and female face one another and vibrate wings while singing.
- **NESTING** Incubation 25–27 days by both sexes. Semiprecocial young leave nest after a few days, but tended 42 days or more. First flight at 21–27 days after fledging nest. Average less than 1 brood per year.
- **POPULATION** Uncommon to fairly common on tundra breeding grounds. Common to uncommon far offshore on both coasts outside breeding season.

DARK MORPH

JUVENILE

Similar Birds

PARASITIC JAEGER
Smaller; more slender; two central tail feathers extended and pointed but not twisted; smaller bill; less white at base of primaries.

SOUTH POLAR SKUA
Bulky, heavy body; golden streaking on nape; hunchback appearance; short wedge-shaped tail with central tail feathers not extended.

Flight Pattern
Strong steady flight with slow deep wing beats like a large gull; may alternate several wing beats with long glide.

Nest Identification	
Shape	Location

Lined with plant material • on ground • built by both parents • 2 olive to brown eggs, with dark brown blotches; short elliptical, 2.6 inches long.

Plumage Sexes similar	Habitat	Migration Migratory	Weight 1.4 pounds

DATE _____ TIME_____ LOCATION _____

Family LARIDAE	Species *Stercorarius parasiticus*	Length 15–21 inches	Wingspan 36 inches

PARASITIC JAEGER

This skua can sometimes be seen from shore, intruding upon migrating flocks of terns and stealing food from other seabirds. It has two distinct color morphs, light and dark, and many intermediates. Falconlike in pursuit, it is about the size of a Laughing or Mew Gull and normally flies with quick wing beats broken by short glides. It is not known to breed until three to five years of age.

• **SONG** Usually silent when not on breeding grounds. Yelping notes and rising *skooo-a* or *ka-aaow*.

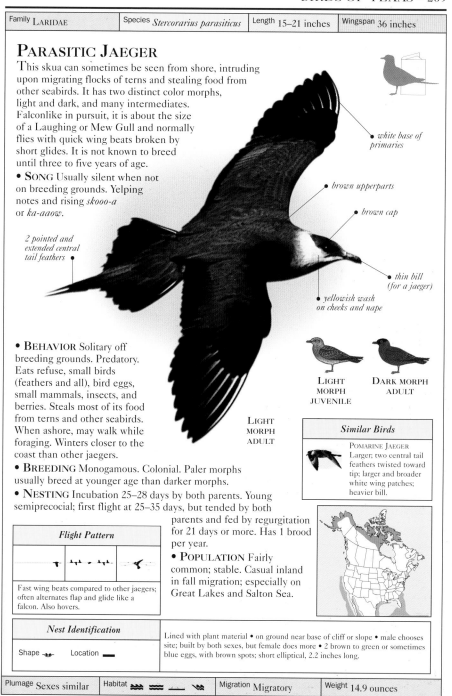

white base of primaries

brown upperparts

brown cap

2 pointed and extended central tail feathers

thin bill (for a jaeger)

yellowish wash on cheeks and nape

LIGHT MORPH JUVENILE

DARK MORPH ADULT

LIGHT MORPH ADULT

• **BEHAVIOR** Solitary off breeding grounds. Predatory. Eats refuse, small birds (feathers and all), bird eggs, small mammals, insects, and berries. Steals most of its food from terns and other seabirds. When ashore, may walk while foraging. Winters closer to the coast than other jaegers.

• **BREEDING** Monogamous. Colonial. Paler morphs usually breed at younger age than darker morphs.

• **NESTING** Incubation 25–28 days by both parents. Young semiprecocial; first flight at 25–35 days, but tended by both parents and fed by regurgitation for 21 days or more. Has 1 brood per year.

• **POPULATION** Fairly common; stable. Casual inland in fall migration; especially on Great Lakes and Salton Sea.

Similar Birds

POMARINE JAEGER Larger; two central tail feathers twisted toward tip; larger and broader white wing patches; heavier bill.

Flight Pattern

Fast wing beats compared to other jaegers; often alternates flap and glide like a falcon. Also hovers.

Nest Identification

Shape ⚬ Location ▬

Lined with plant material • on ground near base of cliff or slope • male chooses site; built by both sexes, but female does more • 2 brown to green or sometimes blue eggs, with brown spots; short elliptical, 2.2 inches long.

Plumage Sexes similar	Habitat 〰〰 ~~ _ ⌇	Migration Migratory	Weight 14.9 ounces

DATE _____ TIME_____ LOCATION _____

Family LARIDAE	Species *Larus atricilla*	Length 15–17 inches	Wingspan 40–42 inches

LAUGHING GULL

Named for its laughterlike call, this gull was threatened by the feather trade in the early 20th century. Now this coastal inhabitant forms colonies with thousands of nests. A distinguishing habit is its tendency to steal food from the Brown Pelican by snatching it out of the pelican's pouch after it surfaces with a catch. This three-year gull passes through two different winter plumages prior to attaining adult plumage. Adults have a white tail year round. In winter adults the black head is replaced by a gray smudge on the nape, and the bill, legs, and feet are dull blackish.

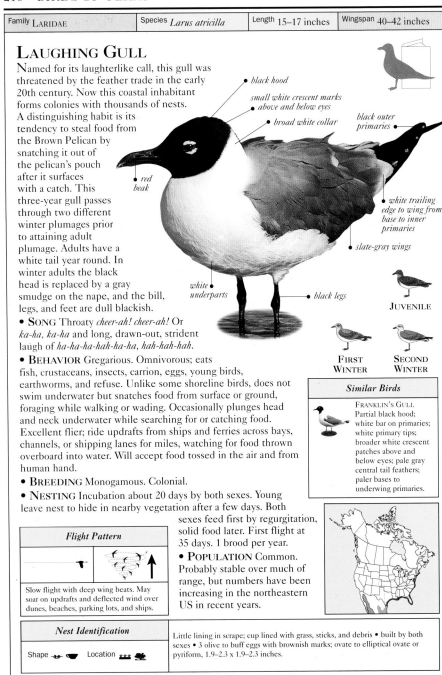

black hood

small white crescent marks above and below eyes

broad white collar

black outer primaries

red beak

white trailing edge to wing from base to inner primaries

slate-gray wings

white underparts

black legs

JUVENILE

FIRST WINTER

SECOND WINTER

- **SONG** Throaty *cheer-ah! cheer-ah!* Or *ka-ha, ka-ha* and long, drawn-out, strident laugh of *ha-ha-ha-hah-ha-ha, hah-hah-hah.*
- **BEHAVIOR** Gregarious. Omnivorous; eats fish, crustaceans, insects, carrion, eggs, young birds, earthworms, and refuse. Unlike some shoreline birds, does not swim underwater but snatches food from surface or ground, foraging while walking or wading. Occasionally plunges head and neck underwater while searching for or catching food. Excellent flier; ride updrafts from ships and ferries across bays, channels, or shipping lanes for miles, watching for food thrown overboard into water. Will accept food tossed in the air and from human hand.
- **BREEDING** Monogamous. Colonial.
- **NESTING** Incubation about 20 days by both sexes. Young leave nest to hide in nearby vegetation after a few days. Both sexes feed first by regurgitation, solid food later. First flight at 35 days. 1 brood per year.
- **POPULATION** Common. Probably stable over much of range, but numbers have been increasing in the northeastern US in recent years.

Similar Birds

FRANKLIN'S GULL Partial black hood; white bar on primaries; white primary tips; broader white crescent patches above and below eyes; pale gray central tail feathers; paler bases to underwing primaries.

Flight Pattern

Slow flight with deep wing beats. May soar on updrafts and deflected wind over dunes, beaches, parking lots, and ships.

Nest Identification

Shape Location

Little lining in scrape; cup lined with grass, sticks, and debris • built by both sexes • 3 olive to buff eggs with brownish marks; ovate to elliptical ovate or pyriform, 1.9–2.3 x 1.9–2.3 inches.

Plumage Sexes similar	Habitat	Migration Migratory	Weight 11.5 ounces

DATE _____ TIME_____ LOCATION _____

Family LARIDAE	Species *Larus pipixcan*	Length 13–15 inches	Wingspan 36 inches

FRANKLIN'S GULL

Often called the Prairie Dove, this three-year gull is sometimes spotted on farmland, following plows to feed on grubs and other insects. The bird has a characteristic black hood in summer, but in winter its head is white with the reduced dusky hood covering its eye and reaching from midcrown to nape. In flight, it differs from the similar Laughing Gull by a white bar and large white tips on primaries and a paler surface on the underwing primaries.

• **SONG** A shrill *kuk-kuk-kuk*, with *weeh-ah, weeh-ah* occasionally interjected.

white crescents above and below eyes

red bill

white underparts with pinkish highlights

white-tipped secondary flight feathers

white-tipped black primary flight feathers

white wing band between black tips and slate-gray bases

light slate-gray wings

red legs and feet

JUVENILE

• **BEHAVIOR** Gregarious. Terrestrial in summer; winters on Pacific Ocean from Central America southward. Forages for food while walking, wading, or swimming, sometimes spotting prey while hovering over water. Eats insects, fish, leeches, earthworms, crustaceans, and snails. Sometimes catches insects while flying. Attends agricultural cultivating machinery, taking exposed prey.

• **BREEDING** Monogamous. Colonial.

• **NESTING** Incubation 18–25 days by both sexes. Semiprecocial young fed by both sexes. First flight at 32–35 days. 1 brood per year.

FIRST WINTER   SECOND WINTER

Similar Birds

LAUGHING GULL
Fuller hood; smaller crescent patches around eyes; lacks white wing bar; darker primary tips above and below.

• **POPULATION** Common in breeding range, but local populations often fluctuate due to rainfall or drought patterns. Rare in migration on both coasts; rare in winter on Gulf Coast and in southern California.

• **CONSERVATION** Some loss of nesting habitat due to agricultural practices.

Flight Pattern

Strong direct flight with deep wing beats. Soars on thermals and updrafts.

Nest Identification

Shape   Location

Lined with bulrushes, cattails, and other plant material • built by both sexes • 3 dull buff, olive, or brown eggs blotched with brown or black; ovate to elliptical ovate or pyriform, 2.1 inches long.

Plumage Sexes similar	Habitat	Migration Migratory	Weight 9.9 ounces

DATE _____ TIME_____ LOCATION _____

Family LARIDAE	Species *Larus philadelphia*	Length 12–14 inches	Wingspan 33–36 inches

BONAPARTE'S GULL

This is one of the smallest gulls in North America and the smallest native species. It is named for French zoologist Charles Lucien Bonaparte, a nephew of Napoleon. In winter plumage it shows a plain white head without the black hood, leaving only a distinctive black spot between the eye and ear. In flight, note a white wedge on the leading edge of the outer wing, black tips on the primaries, and pale underwings. This is a two-year gull.

blackish hood

gray back and wings

black bill

black-tipped primaries

white wedge on wing

orange legs

white underparts

JUVENILE

- **SONG** Shrieking whistles and a call of *cheeer*.
- **BEHAVIOR** Gregarious. Eats mostly insects on summer breeding grounds, where it sometimes hawks flying insects. In winter eats fish, crustaceans, and marine worms. Catches fish by wading in water as well as by diving. Forages on ground for insects and also catches them in flight. Its habit of nesting in trees is most unusual among gulls.
- **BREEDING** Monogamous. Solitary or small colonial.
- **NESTING** Incubation 24 days by both sexes. Not known when semiprecocial young first fly, but known to be fed by both parents while in nest. 1 brood per year.
- **POPULATION** Stable. Common in migration and winter on Great Lakes and on Pacific, Atlantic, and Gulf Coasts. Uncommon migrant inland in the West.

WINTER PLUMAGE

Similar Birds

BLACK-HEADED GULL
Dark brown-black hood; red bill; dark underside of primaries.

Flight Pattern

Light and buoyant direct flight is ternlike, with rapid wing beats.

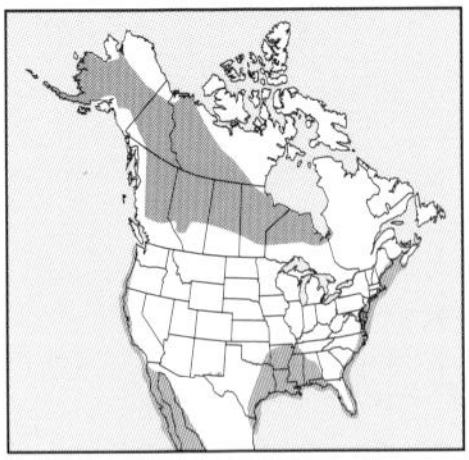

Nest Identification

Shape ⌒ Location ⌂

Sticks lined with moss and grasses; abandoned nests lined with hay and moss • coniferous tree, 4–20 feet above ground • built by both sexes • 2–4 olive to buff eggs, marked with brown blotches; ovate to elliptical-ovate, 2 inches long.

Plumage Sexes similar	Habitat	Migration Migratory	Weight 7.5 ounces

| Family LARIDAE | Species *Larus delawarensis* | Length 18–19 inches | Wingspan 48 inches |

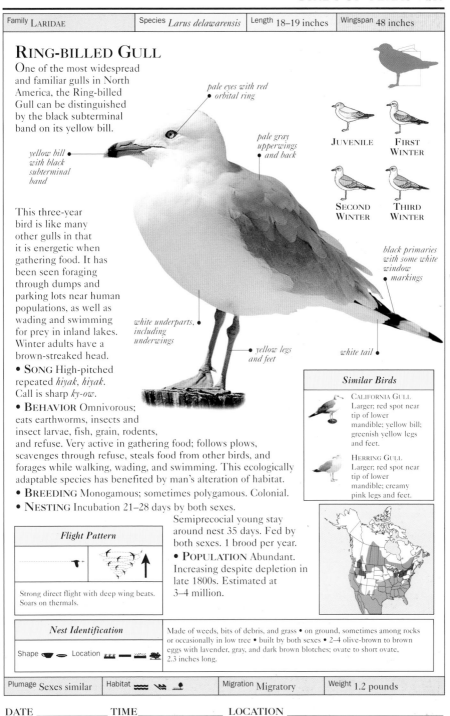

RING-BILLED GULL

One of the most widespread and familiar gulls in North America, the Ring-billed Gull can be distinguished by the black subterminal band on its yellow bill.

pale eyes with red orbital ring

yellow bill with black subterminal band

pale gray upperwings and back

JUVENILE   FIRST WINTER

SECOND WINTER   THIRD WINTER

black primaries with some white window markings

This three-year bird is like many other gulls in that it is energetic when gathering food. It has been seen foraging through dumps and parking lots near human populations, as well as wading and swimming for prey in inland lakes. Winter adults have a brown-streaked head.

white underparts, including underwings

yellow legs and feet

white tail

- **SONG** High-pitched repeated *hiyak, hiyak.* Call is sharp *ky-ow.*
- **BEHAVIOR** Omnivorous; eats earthworms, insects and insect larvae, fish, grain, rodents, and refuse. Very active in gathering food; follows plows, scavenges through refuse, steals food from other birds, and forages while walking, wading, and swimming. This ecologically adaptable species has benefited by man's alteration of habitat.
- **BREEDING** Monogamous; sometimes polygamous. Colonial.
- **NESTING** Incubation 21–28 days by both sexes. Semiprecocial young stay around nest 35 days. Fed by both sexes. 1 brood per year.
- **POPULATION** Abundant. Increasing despite depletion in late 1800s. Estimated at 3–4 million.

Similar Birds

CALIFORNIA GULL
Larger; red spot near tip of lower mandible; yellow bill; greenish yellow legs and feet.

HERRING GULL
Larger; red spot near tip of lower mandible; creamy pink legs and feet.

Flight Pattern

Strong direct flight with deep wing beats. Soars on thermals.

Nest Identification

Shape ⬛ ⬤   Location 🌿 ▬ 🪺

Made of weeds, bits of debris, and grass • on ground, sometimes among rocks or occasionally in low tree • built by both sexes • 2–4 olive-brown to brown eggs with lavender, gray, and dark brown blotches; ovate to short ovate, 2.3 inches long.

| Plumage Sexes similar | Habitat 〰️ 〰️ 🔱 | Migration Migratory | Weight 1.2 pounds |

DATE _____ TIME_____ LOCATION _____

Family LARIDAE	Species *Larus argentatus*	Length 22–26 inches	Wingspan 54–58 inches

HERRING GULL

After facing a serious decrease in population in the 19th century, the Herring Gull has recovered and is once again numerous along the Atlantic Coast. Its range continues to expand, making it the most widespread and best-known gull in North America. This four-year gull usually nests on the ground, but when humans intrude, it will

light yellow eyes

heavy yellow bill

red spot on lower mandible

white head and neck

light gray upperwings and back

DARK JUVENILE

black wing tips with white spots

white breast

SECOND WINTER

white tail

white underparts

THIRD WINTER

FOURTH WINTER

creamy pinkish legs and feet

choose choose trees or even rooftops. Winter adults have a white head, neck, and upper breast streaked with pale brown. Plumage is highly variable.

- **SONG** Noisy with various calls, including loud *cleew cleew*, strident *kyow*, or trumpetlike *kee-ou, kee-ou*. Also has alarm call of *kek-kek-kek* or *hyiah–hyak*.
- **BEHAVIOR** Opportunistic. Often follows ships in sea lanes to feed on refuse thrown overboard. Along seacoasts eats fish, wide variety of marine invertebrates, refuse, carrion, and algae. On land eats worms, insects and insect larvae, berries, rodents, and eggs and young of other birds. Active forager. Like other gulls, carries hard-shelled mollusks into the air, then drops them on hard surface to break open shells. Sometimes steals food from other birds. Frequents garbage dumps.
- **BREEDING** Monogamous. Colonial.

Similar Birds

CALIFORNIA GULL
Smaller; dark eye; red spot edged with black on lower mandible; darker gray mantle and wings; dusky trailing edge on underwing; yellow-green legs and feet.

RING-BILLED GULL
Smaller yellow bill has black subterminal ring; greenish yellow legs.

- **NESTING** Incubation 23–27 days by both sexes. Semiprecocial young stay around nest 24–49 days. Fed by both sexes. 1 brood per year.
- **POPULATION** Abundant. Today all gulls are protected by federal law.

Flight Pattern
Strong steady flight with deep wing beats. Soars on thermals and deflected updrafts.

Nest Identification	
Shape	Lined with weeds, grass, and seaweed • on ground sheltered by shrubs or rock, in tree, or on roof • 2–3 gray, green, bluish, or brown eggs with brown, lavender, and black streaks; ovoid, 2.6–3 x 1.8–2.2 inches.
Location	

Plumage Sexes similar	Habitat	Migration Migratory	Weight 2.7 pounds

DATE _____ TIME_____ LOCATION _____

Family LARIDAE	Species *Larus fuscus*	Length 21–22 inches	Wingspan 54 inches

LESSER BLACK-BACKED GULL

This European gull is wintering in increasing numbers in North America. It is similar to the Western Gull and the Great Black-backed Gull. Smaller than either of those gulls, it has yellow, not pink, feet and legs. Winter adults have a brown streaked head and neck. This four-year gull's behavior and voice resembles other gulls.

• **SONG** A loud *kyow* and a wide range of other calls, including *yuk-yuk-yuk-yuckle-yuckle* or *hiyak, hiyak, hiyak, hiyak-hiyak*.

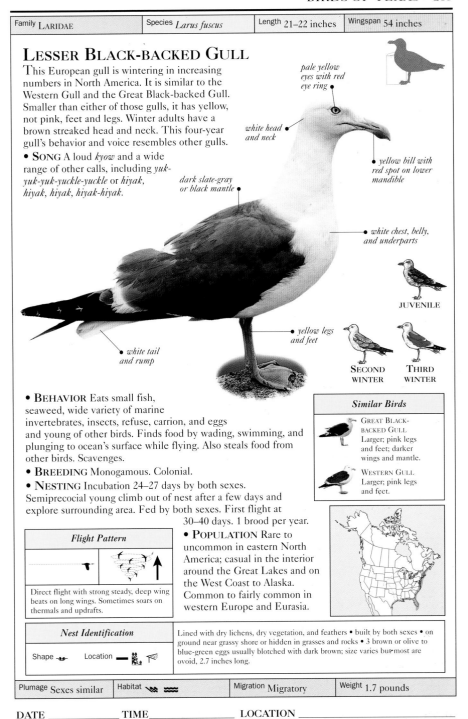

pale yellow eyes with red eye ring

white head and neck

yellow bill with red spot on lower mandible

dark slate-gray or black mantle

white chest, belly, and underparts

JUVENILE

white tail and rump

yellow legs and feet

SECOND WINTER   THIRD WINTER

• **BEHAVIOR** Eats small fish, seaweed, wide variety of marine invertebrates, insects, refuse, carrion, and eggs and young of other birds. Finds food by wading, swimming, and plunging to ocean's surface while flying. Also steals food from other birds. Scavenges.

• **BREEDING** Monogamous. Colonial.

• **NESTING** Incubation 24–27 days by both sexes. Semiprecocial young climb out of nest after a few days and explore surrounding area. Fed by both sexes. First flight at 30–40 days. 1 brood per year.

• **POPULATION** Rare to uncommon in eastern North America; casual in the interior around the Great Lakes and on the West Coast to Alaska. Common to fairly common in western Europe and Eurasia.

Similar Birds

GREAT BLACK-BACKED GULL Larger; pink legs and feet; darker wings and mantle.

WESTERN GULL Larger; pink legs and feet.

Flight Pattern

Direct flight with strong steady, deep wing beats on long wings. Sometimes soars on thermals and updrafts.

Nest Identification

Shape ⚬⚬⚬   Location ▬🪺🏴

Lined with dry lichens, dry vegetation, and feathers • built by both sexes • on ground near grassy shore or hidden in grasses and rocks • 3 brown or olive to blue-green eggs usually blotched with dark brown; size varies but most are ovoid, 2.7 inches long.

Plumage Sexes similar	Habitat 〰️ 〰️	Migration Migratory	Weight 1.7 pounds

DATE _____ TIME_____ LOCATION _____

Family LARIDAE	Species *Larus hyperboreus*	Length 26–30 inches	Wingspan 56–60 inches

GLAUCOUS GULL

The palest of the large gulls, this bird is also the most northerly breeder of the *Larus* gulls. It can be found nesting on the Arctic coasts of North America and Greenland. A heavy-bodied, stocky, barrel-chested gull, its short wings barely extend beyond the tail when standing. Winter adults show head and neck lightly streaked pale brown. This is a four-year gull.

massive yellow bill with red spot on lower mandible

white-tipped pale gray primaries

white head and neck

- **SONG** Usually silent. While flying, makes a prattling-like quack. Also has various shrieking cries, similar to those of Herring Gull.

yellow eyes with yellow orbital ring

white rump, uppertail coverts, belly, and chest

- **BEHAVIOR** Marine habits. Predatory and aggressive, especially in summer when it feeds primarily on eggs and young of other birds, especially ducks, alcids, shorebirds, and gulls. Also eats fish, marine invertebrates, refuse, insects, and berries. Major predator on lemmings and other small mammals during their peak population cycles. Steals food from other seabirds. Also finds food by wading in water and diving to surface while flying. Catches smaller birds and insects in air.

white tail and undertail coverts

pink legs and feet

JUVENILE

SECOND WINTER

THIRD WINTER

- **BREEDING** Monogamous. Colonial.
- **NESTING** Incubation 27–28 days by both sexes. Semiprecocial young leave nest within days of hatching, but remain in vicinity. Fed by both sexes. Independent soon after first flight at 45–50 days. Usually 1 brood per year.

Similar Birds

GLAUCOUS-WINGED GULL
Smaller; gray marks on primaries; slight red ring around dark eye; bill more slender.

ICELAND GULL
Smaller in size; pale gray primaries with translucent white tips (Kumlien's form has darker gray tips to translucent primaries); yellow eye with red orbital ring.

- **POPULATION** Common on breeding grounds. Closely tied to lemming population near its nesting grounds. Uncommon to fairly common in winter on the north Atlantic and north Pacific Coasts. Rare south and inland.

Flight Pattern

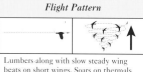

Lumbers along with slow steady wing beats on short wings. Soars on thermals and updrafts.

Nest Identification

Shape ⬡   Location ▬ 🪹 〰

Lined with seaweed, moss, feathers, and debris • on ground or set on ridges of cliffs, often on small pile of grass or moss • built by both sexes • 2–3 eggs, light brown or olive-buff, with dark brown blotches; subelliptical to ovate, 3.0 inches long.

Plumage Sexes similar	Habitat 〰 〰 🐚	Migration Migratory	Weight 3.4 pounds

DATE _____ TIME_____ LOCATION _____

Family LARIDAE	Species *Larus marinus*	Length 28–31 inches	Wingspan 60–66 inches

GREAT BLACK-BACKED GULL

This predatory and domineering bird is the largest
gull in North America. It is highly aggressive
toward other birds but will nest harmoniously
in colonies with other gulls. A four-year gull,
it frequents the northern Atlantic Coast
of North America. The adult is snow-
white below with a white tail and
black mantle and upperwings.
Winter adults have very little
streaking on the white head
and nape. In all
plumages
it has pink
legs and
feet. The
prevalence
of garbage
dumps in
coastal areas
has led to an
increase in population
of this species.

pale yellow eye

*massive
yellow bill*

*white head
and neck*

*black mantle and
upper wings*

*red spot
on lower
mandible*

*white primary
tips*

*white
underparts*

*white trailing
edge of wing*

*pale pink legs
and feet*

JUVENILE

- **SONG** Usually silent. On
breeding grounds utters low slow
screeching *keeeeeeee-aaaahh*. Also makes
throaty laughing call of *hah-hah-hah* or deep *owk, owk.*
- **BEHAVIOR** Pugnacious. Predatory and opportunistic. Eats
carrion, fish, refuse, eggs and young of other birds, mollusks,
crustaceans, rodents, berries, and insects. May take prey as large
as gulls, cormorants, and rabbits. Steals food from other birds and
scavenges on beaches. Wades in water to feed. Dives to surface
while flying to catch food.
- **BREEDING** Monogamous. Colonial but occasionally solitary.
- **NESTING** Incubation 26–29 days by both sexes. Fed by both
sexes. Semiprecocial young may wander from nest but stay close
to parents. First flight at 49–56 days. 1 brood per year.
- **POPULATION** Fairly common; has increased in number since

SECOND
WINTER

THIRD
WINTER

Similar Birds

LESSER
BLACK-BACKED GULL
Smaller; yellow legs.

1930s. Range expanding
southward along Atlantic Coast.
Fairly common on the eastern
Great Lakes but rare on the
western ones; casual inland in
the East in winter; accidental to
casual elsewhere.

Flight Pattern

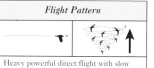

Heavy powerful direct flight with slow
deep wing beats. Soars on thermals or
deflected updrafts.

Nest Identification

Shape ⬯   Location 🏞️

Made of grasses, seaweed, moss, feathers, debris, and sticks • on ground atop
small pile of grasses or seaweed, often sheltered in ridges of cliff • built by both
sexes • 2–3 buff, olive, or brown eggs with brown spots; ovoid, 3.1 inches long.

Plumage Sexes similar	Habitat 〰️ 〰️	Migration Most do not migrate	Weight 4.0 pounds

DATE _____ TIME_____ LOCATION _____

Family LARIDAE	Species *Xema sabini*	Length 13–14 inches	Wingspan 33–36 inches

SABINE'S GULL

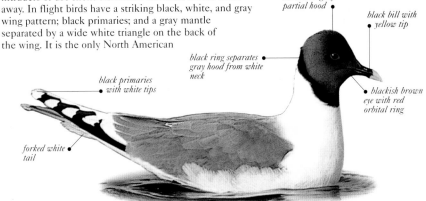

This two-year gull summers near the arctic coasts of North America, but after nesting season it is rarely spotted from shore because it spends most of its time at sea. Nesting in the tundra, parents are very protective of the nest and will attack intruders or use silent distraction methods to lure them away. In flight birds have a striking black, white, and gray wing pattern; black primaries; and a gray mantle separated by a wide white triangle on the back of the wing. It is the only North American

dark slate-gray partial hood

black bill with yellow tip

black ring separates gray hood from white neck

black primaries with white tips

blackish brown eye with red orbital ring

forked white tail

gull with a distinctly forked tail. Winter adults have a white head with dusky gray on the back of the crown and nape.

- **SONG** Short, harsh ternlike cry of *creeeeee*.
- **BEHAVIOR** Largely pelagic. Eats insects, fish, crustaceans, mollusks, and marine worms in breeding season; otherwise, eats mostly fish. Runs along mudflats like a plover searching for food. Also feeds by dipping to water's surface from flight and foraging while swimming.
- **BREEDING** Monogamous. Small colonies. Often in company of Arctic Terns.
- **NESTING** Incubation 23–26 days by both sexes. Semiprecocial young. Shortly after hatching, nestlings led to water by parents. Young feed themselves. First flight at about 35 days. 1 brood per year.

JUVENILE   WINTER ADULT

Similar Birds

BONAPARTE'S GULL
Black bill; black hood; orange legs and feet; white outer primaries form triangle at wing tip; square tail.

- **POPULATION** Common on breeding grounds. Winters at sea mainly in Southern Hemisphere. Common migrant well off West Coast; casual on and off East Coast. Rare to casual in migration in interior of the West and on Great Lakes.

Flight Pattern

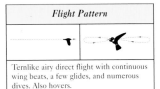

Ternlike airy direct flight with continuous wing beats, a few glides, and numerous dives. Also hovers.

Nest Identification

Shape ⌣   Location ▬ ✳✳

Seaweed, grasses, moss, and feathers • on ground atop pile of vegetation near water • may be built by both sexes • 1–3 olive-buff eggs spotted with darker olive-brown and occasionally wreathed; ovate to subelliptical, 1.8 inches long.

Plumage Sexes similar	Habitat ▬ 〰	Migration Migratory	Weight 7.2 ounces

Family LARIDAE	Species *Rissa tridactyla*	Length 16–17 inches	Wingspan 36 inches

BLACK-LEGGED KITTIWAKE

Named for its call of *kittiwake*, this pelagic three-year gull nests on high narrow cliffs on arctic and sub-arctic coasts. Unlike most gulls it does not scavenge at garbage dumps but spends most of its time at sea and drinks only saltwater. Adults have a white body, gray mantle and wings, pale whitish underwings, a square to slightly notched tail, and black legs and feet. The black tips of the outer primaries lack white spotting and produce a clean, straight-edged dark tip. Winter adults show a dark smudge across the nape. Juveniles have a black collar across the back of the neck, a black-tipped tail, and a black W stretching from wing tip to wing tip across the back.

- black-tipped outer primaries
- light gray wings with paler gray flight feathers
- light gray back
- white tail coverts and tail
- dark eyes
- unmarked thin pale yellow bill
- white head and neck

JUVENILE WINTER ADULT

- **SONG** Series of piercing *kittiwake*'s. Also makes quieter *ock-ock-ock*.
- **BEHAVIOR** Pelagic outside breeding season. Eats primarily small fish but also takes crustaceans, mollusks, squid, insects, and refuse from ships. Forages for food while swimming and dips while flying to snatch items from surface. Often hovers briefly above water before dropping on prey at surface.
- **BREEDING** Monogamous. Colonial.
- **NESTING** Incubation 25–32 days by both sexes. First flight at 34–58 days. Young return to nest at night after first flight and are fed by both sexes. 1 brood per year.
- **POPULATION** Abundant on breeding grounds. In migration and winter common to uncommon on open ocean; usually not seen from shore in the East, seen uncommonly in the West. Casual to accidental inland in winter.
- **CONSERVATION** Large nesting colonies vulnerable to human disturbance.

Similar Birds

SABINE'S GULL
Winter plumage
- notched white tail; wings black from "wrist" to tip, forming black triangle; inner primaries and secondaries white; black half-collar over nape; yellow-tipped black bill
- Pacific Coast range.

RED-LEGGED KITTIWAKE
Bright reddish coral legs; shorter broader bill; darker upperparts
- Pacific Coast range.

Flight Pattern

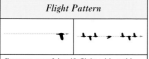

Buoyant graceful swift flight with rapid wing beats and shallow strokes alternating with several rapid wing beats and a glide.

Nest Identification

Shape ● Location

Mud, seaweed, moss, and sod • on cliff ledge, side of building, or in cave • built by both sexes with materials brought by male • 1–3 buff to olive or pale blue eggs with brown or gray speckles; subelliptical, 2.2 x 1.6 inches.

Plumage Sexes similar	Habitat	Migration Migratory	Weight 14.9 ounces

Family LARIDAE	Species *Sterna nilotica*	Length 13–14 inches	Wingspan 33–34 inches

GULL-BILLED TERN

The whitest of the North American tern species was almost exterminated in the early 1900s due to the demand for their eggs as a delicacy and their feathers to adorn women's hats. Gull-billed Terns are common summer residents in California and along the Atlantic Coast. Some remain on the Gulf Coast during winter months. In summer adults have a black cap that extends below the eyes and down the nape and pale gray upperparts that are darker at the wing tips. At a distance it appears white with rather broad, rounded wings, a heavy body, and a moderately forked tail. In winter the head is white with faint dusky streaking on the nape. Juveniles have dusky streaking on the pale upperparts and a brownish bill.

black crown and nape

pale gray upperparts

broad wings with darker tips

stout black bill

stocky body

long black legs and feet

white underparts

JUVENILE

WINTER PLUMAGE

• **SONG** Raspy sharp *ge-rek* or dry raspy *kay-tih-DID* or *kay-DID*. Young give faint high-pitched *peep peep* call.

• **BEHAVIOR** Flies over farm fields or marshes to catch insects, its main diet. Over water sometimes swoops to surface to catch small prey. Also eats earthworms, frogs, and crustaceans.

• **BREEDING** Monogamous. Colonial and/or solitary. Pairs sometimes nest at edge of other tern species' colonies.

• **NESTING** Incubation 22–23 days by both sexes. Semiprecocial young may leave nest a few days after hatching and hide in dense plant cover. Fed by both sexes. First flight at 28–35 days. Young may remain with parents for 90 days or more and migrate with them. 1 brood per year.

• **POPULATION** Fairly common but local. Less common on Atlantic Coast. Casual to accidental in interior except in Salton Sea.

• **CONSERVATION** Species has never recovered from near extermination in early 1900s.

Similar Birds

SANDWICH TERN
Slender black bill with yellow tip; deeper fork in tail; longer, more slender, more pointed wings with darker outer primaries; more slender body.

FORSTER'S TERN
White underparts; pale gray upperparts; more slender body; slender, more pointed wings; deeply forked tail; mostly orange bill, legs, and feet.

Flight Pattern

Direct flight with easy, graceful shallow wing beats.

Nest Identification	
Shape 🐛 Location ▬ 🔧 ⚓ 🎋	On open ground; often concealed in detritus among shells • lined with plant material and debris; rimmed with sand, shells, sticks, and grass • built by both sexes • 1–4 pink-buff to yellowish eggs lightly spotted with dark brown; oval and well-rounded at small end, 1.9 x 1.3 inches.

Plumage Sexes similar	Habitat ▬ 〰	Migration Migratory	Weight 8.2 ounces

DATE _____ TIME_____ LOCATION _____

Family LARIDAE	Species *Sterna caspia*	Length 19–23 inches	Wingspan 50–55 inches

CASPIAN TERN

The largest and least sociable tern is easily distinguished by its large size, stout red-orange bill, and tail forked to a quarter of its length. In flight the underside of the outer primaries are dark. Caspian Terns are known for their predatory feeding habits, sometimes stealing catches from other seabirds and eating eggs and young of other terns and gulls. Many Caspian Terns migrate to coastal regions during winter months, moving as far south as the West Indies and the northern regions of South America. Some remain in coastal locales year-round. Juveniles and winter adults have a streaked dusky-and-white cap that extends below the eye.

black cap covers head from bill to nape and extends below eye

pale gray upperparts

large thick red-orange bill often with black tip (sometimes tip is yellow or orange)

white underparts

forked tail

black legs and feet

dusky to dark gray undersides of primaries

WINTER PLUMAGE

- **SONG** Call is harsh deep *kaark* and *ka-arr*. Young whistle a distinctive *whee-you*.
- **BEHAVIOR** This common coastal inhabitant also visits inland wetlands in summer. Gull-like, it often feeds on water surfaces but sometimes dives into water for small fish, its principal food. When patrolling flies with bill pointed down. Often hovers before plunge diving into water for prey.
- **BREEDING** Monogamous. Colonial. Rarely solitary.
- **NESTING** Incubation 20–28 days by both sexes. Semiprecocial young may leave nest for nearby shore a few days after hatching. First flight at 28–35 days. Young may remain with parents up to 8 months. 1 brood per year.
- **POPULATION** Stable range; some populations increasing. Small colonies scattered over breeding range.
- **CONSERVATION** Vulnerable to disturbance of coastal nesting colonies and habitat loss on beaches and inland wetlands.

Similar Birds

ROYAL TERN Smaller; longer more deeply forked tail; lacks blackish wedge on underwing tips; mostly white forehead and anterior crown except early in breeding season, when entire crown is black; black crest on nape; less stout orange bill without black tip.

ELEGANT TERN Smaller; long thin red-orange bill without black tip; black crest; white underparts with pinkish tinge • western range.

Flight Pattern

Strong swift graceful flight. Bulk makes it appear gull-like. Sometimes hovers briefly over prey before dipping down to seize it.

Nest Identification

Shape ⚬ Location ▬ ⚬

Lined with seaweed, moss, grass, and occasional debris • sometimes concealed among shells, driftwood, and rubbish • built by both sexes • 1–3, sometimes 4–5, pinkish buff eggs with brown markings; ovate, elliptical ovate, or subelliptical, 2.5 x 1.8 inches.

Plumage Sexes similar	Habitat ≈≈ ⌂ ⌐	Migration Migratory	Weight 1.4 pounds

DATE _____ TIME _____ LOCATION _____

Family LARIDAE	Species *Sterna maxima*	Length 18–21 inches	Wingspan 42–44 inches

ROYAL TERN

The second-largest tern in North America sometimes is seen snatching food from the Brown Pelican's pouch. Briefly in spring and early summer adults have a shaggy black crown from bill to nape; the rest of the year the forehead and forecrown are white. In flight birds show a tail forked to about half its length, pale underwings to the tips of dusky outermost primaries, and an orange bill. Juveniles look like winter adults but have more faint streaking on the upperparts and yellowish or orange feet and legs.

pumpkin-orange to yellow-orange bill

black crest and head

pale gray mantle

white body

black legs and feet

WINTER PLUMAGE

• **SONG** Large repertoire of calls includes bleating *ee-ah* and melodic trilled whistle, *tourreee*. In nesting areas often squawks *quak*, *kak*, or *kowk*.

• **BEHAVIOR** Plunge dives, from a hover 40–60 feet above ocean or inlets, and goes below surface for a catch. Eats mostly fish but also takes marine invertebrates, including shrimp and squid. When not feeding often loafs on sandbars, beaches, or mudflats with other species of terns and gulls.

• **BREEDING** Monogamous. Colonial. Often nests in mixed colonies with other species of terns.

• **NESTING** Incubation 20–31 days by both sexes. Young semiprecocial; upon leaving nest a few days after hatching, young often gather in creche, where they recognize parents by voice and beg for food. First flight at 28–35 days. May remain with parents up to 8 months or longer and migrate with them.

• **POPULATION** Declining. Has declined in California since 1950. Fairly common in breeding range; uncommon to rare north of it in late summer on Atlantic Coast. Fairly common in winter in southern California; rare to accidental inland from coasts.

• **CONSERVATION** Vulnerable to disturbance on nesting beaches by humans and wild and domestic predators.

Similar Birds

ELEGANT TERN
Smaller body; more slender reddish orange bill that appears slightly drooped at tip; longer shaggy crest extends down nape;
• western range.

CASPIAN TERN
Larger body; black cap extends below eyes; lacks white forehead; thicker bright red bill; tail not as deeply forked; dark underside and pale upperside on primaries.

Flight Pattern
┬
Direct flight with deep, more rangy, continual slow wing beats. Hovers briefly before plunge diving for prey.

Nest Identification	
Shape ⬬ Location ⬯	Sometimes sparsely lined with debris • built by both sexes • 1–2, sometimes 3–4, whitish buff to brown eggs with reddish brown markings, occasionally wreathed; ovate to elliptical ovate; 2.5 inches long.

Plumage Sexes similar	Habitat 〰〰 〰	Migration Migratory	Weight 1.0 pound

Family LARIDAE	Species *Sterna sandvicensis*	Length 14–16 inches	Wingspan 34 inches

SANDWICH TERN

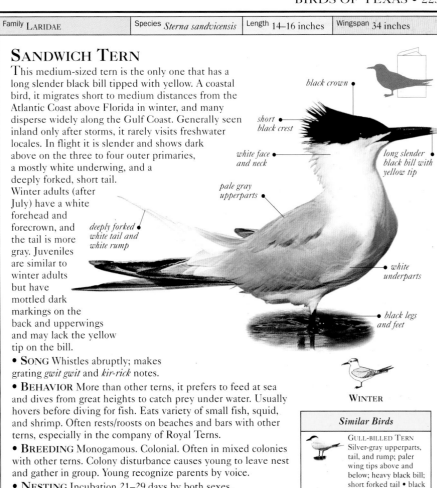

This medium-sized tern is the only one that has a long slender black bill tipped with yellow. A coastal bird, it migrates short to medium distances from the Atlantic Coast above Florida in winter, and many disperse widely along the Gulf Coast. Generally seen inland only after storms, it rarely visits freshwater locales. In flight it is slender and shows dark above on the three to four outer primaries, a mostly white underwing, and a deeply forked, short tail. Winter adults (after July) have a white forehead and forecrown, and the tail is more gray. Juveniles are similar to winter adults but have mottled dark markings on the back and upperwings and may lack the yellow tip on the bill.

black crown

short black crest

white face and neck

pale gray upperparts

long slender black bill with yellow tip

deeply forked white tail and white rump

white underparts

black legs and feet

- **SONG** Whistles abruptly; makes grating *gwit gwit* and *kir-rick* notes.
- **BEHAVIOR** More than other terns, it prefers to feed at sea and dives from great heights to catch prey under water. Usually hovers before diving for fish. Eats variety of small fish, squid, and shrimp. Often rests/roosts on beaches and bars with other terns, especially in the company of Royal Terns.
- **BREEDING** Monogamous. Colonial. Often in mixed colonies with other terns. Colony disturbance causes young to leave nest and gather in group. Young recognize parents by voice.
- **NESTING** Incubation 21–29 days by both sexes. Semiprecocial young fed by both sexes. First flight at 28–32 days. Remains with parents for 4 months after first flight. 1 brood per year.
- **POPULATION** Increasing but still uncommon. Casual spring and summer visitor to coastal southern California.
- **CONSERVATION** Vulnerable to disturbance and predation at nesting colonies.

WINTER

Similar Birds

GULL-BILLED TERN Silver-gray upperparts, tail, and rump; paler wing tips above and below; heavy black bill; short forked tail • black cap until early autumn.

Flight Pattern
Powerful direct flight heavier and less graceful than that of similar-sized terns. Usually hovers before diving for fish.

Nest Identification	
Shape ↘ Location ▬	Lined with debris or unlined • on ground in open above tidemark • built by both sexes • 1–3 pale cream to pinkish buff eggs with brown, black, and gray markings; subelliptical, 2 x 1.4 inches.

Plumage Sexes similar	Habitat 〰	Migration Migratory	Weight 7.3 ounces

DATE _____ TIME_____ LOCATION _____

Family LARIDAE	Species *Sterna hirundo*	Length 13–16 inches	Wingspan 30–31 inches

COMMON TERN

Often called the Mackerel Gull, the Common Tern is seen tending areas where large fish, such as mackerel and tuna, drive schools of smaller fish to the surface. By following the Common Tern, fishermen often find the best place to cast their nets. Although common throughout their range, today's northeastern populations of this tern are lower than previously recorded. Inland populations are suspected to be on the decline as well. The upperwings and mantle are a

black cap and nape

red bill, usually black-tipped

pale gray underparts

red legs and feet

dusky-tipped wings

forked white tail with dark outer margins and white rump

darker gray than most other similar-sized terns; the wing tips are dark; and the short tail is not as deeply forked. Winter adults have white foreheads and crowns past the eye, and also have dark bills.

• **SONG** Low piercing drawn-out *kee-ar-r-r-r*. Also rolling *tee-ar-r-r-r*, and high slightly grating *kik-kik-kik*.

• **BEHAVIOR** Coastal and widespread inland in breeding season. Hovering, it spots fish and plunges, knifing into water, earning the name "striker" on the mid-Atlantic shore. Principally eats small fish, generally between 3–4 inches, and some crustaceans.

• **BREEDING** Monogamous. Colonial. Often nests in mixed colonies with other terns.

• **NESTING** Incubation 21–27 days by both sexes. Young leave nest after a few days, but remain nearby. First flight at 22–28 days, but may remain with parents at least another 2 months. Fed by both sexes. 1–2 broods per year.

• **POPULATION** Common on breeding grounds and in migration on both coasts; rare in winter on southern California coast and Gulf Coast.

Similar Birds

FORSTER'S TERN
Similar in size; paler underparts and upperparts; heavier black-tipped orange bill; primaries often silver-white above, producing frosty wing tips; long forked tail, gray-edged on inner side.

ARCTIC TERN
Similar in size; shorter neck; darker gray underparts and upperparts; white cheeks; red bill without black tip; paler wing tips.

• **CONSERVATION** Almost completely extirpated in early 1900s by plume hunters for fashion markets. Has largely recovered since full protection established in 1913.

Flight Pattern
Direct flight is light and buoyant. Hovers when feeding prior to plunge-diving into water for prey.

Nest Identification	
Shape ⟋ Location ▬ ▨ ✦✦	Lined with vegetation and debris, including grass, shells, and seaweed • built by both sexes • 1–3 buff to cinnamon-brown eggs, generally heavily spotted and overlaid with shades of dark brown and black; generally wreathed; oval to subelliptical, 1.6 inches long.

Plumage Sexes similar	Habitat ▬ 🐟 ▨ ⤳	Migration Migratory	Weight 4.2 ounces

DATE _____ TIME_____ LOCATION _____

Family LARIDAE	Species *Sterna forsteri*	Length 14–15 inches	Wingspan 30–31 inches

FORSTER'S TERN

Frequenting inland marshes as well as the coast, this widespread tern feeds and flocks with other terns. It can be distinguished by its long tail and orange-red bill. In flight note the pale frosty wing tips, white rump, and deeply forked

black cap and nape

pale gray upperparts

orange-red bill with dark tip

snowy white underparts

orange-red legs and feet

long deeply forked gray tail with white-trimmed outer margins

gray tail with white outer margins. Winter plumage shows dull yellow feet, a dark bill, and a white head with a black patch through the eye and ear. Juveniles are like winter adults but have a shorter tail, a ginger crown, and darker upperwings.

JUVENILE

- **SONG** Throaty nasal *ki-arr, za-a-ap,* or *zrurrr,* with nighthawklike quality. Also gives piercing *kit, kit, kit* cry.
- **BEHAVIOR** Catches insects in flight. Eats dragonflies and other insects. Hovers above water, then plunge dives for small fish. Dips to water's surface to catch floating insects, keeping its feathers dry.

WINTER PLUMAGE

- **BREEDING** Monogamous. Loose colonies.
- **NESTING** Incubation 23–25 days by both sexes. Semiprecocial young leave nest after a few days but tended by both sexes until able to fly. 1 brood per year.

Similar Birds

COMMON TERN
Shorter legs and bill; dark wing tips; white tail with dark outer margins • winter adults and juveniles have white forehead and forecrown; dark shoulder; dark eye patch joins at nape; higher-pitched call.

ARCTIC TERN
Shorter red bill without dark tip; shorter legs; gray underparts; gray throat and chin contrast with white face; white tail with dark outer margins; pale underwing with black trailing margins.

- **POPULATION** Common. Declining in some areas because of loss of marshlands.
- **CONSERVATION** Vulnerable to habitat loss to agriculture and development in draining of wetlands.

Flight Pattern
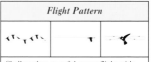
Shallow slow graceful strong flight with body moving up and down. Hovers over water prior to diving for prey.

Nest Identification	
Shape 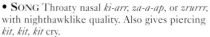 Location	Atop floating dried reeds and lined with grass and reeds; in mud or sand and lined with bits of shells and grass; sometimes uses old grebe nests or muskrat houses • built by both sexes • 1–4 olive or buff eggs with brown or olive splotches and sometimes marked with dark brown lines; oval to short elliptical, 1.7 inches long.

Plumage Sexes similar	Habitat	Migration Migratory	Weight 5.6 ounces

DATE _____ TIME_____ LOCATION _____

Family LARIDAE	Species *Sterna antillarum*	Length 8–9 inches	Wingspan 20 inches

LEAST TERN

The smallest North American tern has a graceful airy flight. Like other terns, it is very protective of its nest and will divebomb intruders, screeching and releasing droppings. The female is similar to the male but smaller. The small size; yellow-orange bill, legs, and feet; black lores, crown, and nape; and white forehead distinguish this species. In flight it shows a deeply forked tail. Winter adults show a dark bill and dusky-streaked whitish crown. Juveniles are similar to winter adults but have darker outer wings and a dusky carpal bar on the leading edge of the inner wings.

black cap and nape

white forehead

gray upperparts

black lores

orange-yellow bill with dark tip

white underparts

orange-yellow legs

black wedge on outer primaries

• **SONG** Piercing *kip, kip, kip* or rapid repeated *kid-ik, kid-ik*. Also makes a grating *zr-e-e-e-ep*.

JUVENILE   FIRST SUMMER

• **BEHAVIOR** Catches food in bill in flight by swooping down to surface or by diving. After catching prey often swallows it while flying or brings it to nest. Eats small fish, crustaceans, and sand eels. Hovers prior to plunge diving.

• **BREEDING** Monogamous. Colonial. Occasionally solitary.

• **NESTING** Incubation 20–25 days by both sexes (female begins incubation; male finishes it). Semiprecocial young leave nest a few days after hatching, hide nearby, and are fed and tended by both sexes for 60–90 days after first flight. First flight at 19–20 days. 1–2 broods per year.

• **POPULATION** Fairly common but local in the East and on the Gulf Coast. Some decline in interior, Mississippi Valley, and on southern California coast.

Similar Birds

BLACK TERN
Winter adults and juveniles have dark bill; dusky crown and ear patch; darker mantle; darker legs and feet; larger; tail not deeply forked.

• **CONSERVATION** Some populations considered endangered due to human disturbance of nesting areas.

Flight Pattern

Buoyant, graceful, fast, smooth flight with rapid airy wing beats; more rapid wing beats than any other tern in range. Hovers briefly before dipping down to seize prey.

Nest Identification

Shape ⌣ Location ▬▬ ⌐

Sometimes lined with pebbles, grass, and debris • on ground in sand or sometimes on roof • built by female • 1–3 buff to pale green eggs with black, gray, or brown markings; oval or subelliptical, 1 x 1.4 inches.

Plumage Sexes similar	Habitat ⌇⌇ ≈	Migration Migratory	Weight 1.5 ounces

DATE _____ TIME_____ LOCATION _____

Family LARIDAE	Species *Sterna fuscata*	Length 16–17 inches	Wingspan 32–34 inches

SOOTY TERN

For years, tuna fishermen have followed feeding flocks of Sooty Terns to locate schools of tuna. Sailors sometimes call this bird "wide-awake," because of its loud night call from the nesting colony, which sounds like *wide-a-wake*. These birds do not breed until they are at least four to eight years of age. Adults have clean-cut black upperparts and white underparts, wing linings, forehead, and short eye stripe.

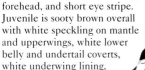

Juvenile is sooty brown overall with white speckling on mantle and upperwings, white lower belly and undertail coverts, white underwing lining, and forked tail.

blackish brown cap

white forehead patch

blackish brown upperparts

black bill

• **SONG** A high nasal *ker-wacky-wack* or *wide-a-wake*.

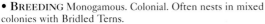

• **BEHAVIOR** Highly gregarious. Eats small fish and small squid. It is believed these birds sleep "on the wing," because they do not land on water and return to shore only when nesting. Banding in Dry Tortugas indicates adults are not highly migratory but that juveniles migrate as far as west Africa and may be gone 2–6 years before returning to the Florida Keys.

white underparts

black legs and feet

dark forked tail with white edges

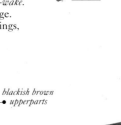

JUVENILE

• **BREEDING** Monogamous. Colonial. Often nests in mixed colonies with Bridled Terns.

• **NESTING** Incubation 27–30 days by both sexes. Semiprecocial young wander around nest shortly after hatching, but remain close to parents. First flight at 56–63 days. May not leave colony for another 14–21 days, fed by both sexes. 1 brood per year.

• **POPULATION** Abundant. Widespread throughout tropical oceans. Large nesting colony on the Dry Tortugas; also nests on islands off Texas and Louisiana and on barrier islands of North Carolina. Regular in summer in Gulf Stream to North Carolina; casual to southern coastal California. Storm-blown birds to Maritimes and Great Lakes.

• **CONSERVATION** Strict protection laws on the Tortugas and some Hawaiian colonies. Vulnerable to human disturbance and introduced predators on breeding islands.

Similar Birds

BRIDLED TERN White patch on forehead extends beyond eye; more pointed wings; paler lead-gray upperparts; white collar separates crown from back; forked tail paler with more white edging on tip.

Flight Pattern

Buoyant direct flight with strong, steady, shallow wing beats. Hovers above water before dipping to surface to pick up food.

Nest Identification

Shape · Location

Lined with leaves • built by both sexes • 1 white to buff egg, with brown, gray, lavender, or black markings; oval, 2.0 x 1.4 inches.

Plumage Sexes similar	Habitat	Migration Migratory	Weight 6.3 ounces

DATE _____ TIME_____ LOCATION _____

Family LARIDAE	Species *Chlidonias niger*	Length 9–10 inches	Wingspan 20–24 inches

BLACK TERN

A black-bodied tern that prefers to breed and nest in the inland marshes of the North American prairie country but winters at sea. It is distinguishable by its overall black breeding plumage, gray upperparts, and dark red legs and feet. Its head and underparts turn white in winter and produce a strange-looking pied bird in late summer as winter molt begins. Winter adults have a black crown with an attached ear patch, a white collar, and a dusky black side bar. Juveniles are similar to winter adults with brownish mottling on the back and a dark carpal bar.

black head and neck

broad wings

short notched dark gray tail

black bill

uniformly pale gray underwings

dark gray upperwings

black underparts

• **SONG**
Drawn-out squeaky *ka-sheek* and abrasive *kik-kik-kik*.

• **BEHAVIOR**
In summer prefers inland lakes and freshwater marshes. Hovers to spot insects. Catches insects in air or swoops down to water or ground to pick up with bill. Plunge dives on occasion. Eats mostly large flying insects but also takes spiders, small fish, crayfish, and small mollusks. Follows people tilling soil and feeds on disturbed insects.

• **BREEDING** Monogamous. Colonial.

• **NESTING** Incubation 17–22 days by both sexes. Semiprecocial young leave nest after 2–3 days but remain in nearby grasses. First flight at 19–25 days, but may be fed by both sexes for up to 2 additional weeks. 1 brood per year in most regions; 2 broods per year in the South.

JUVENILE

WINTER PLUMAGE

Similar Birds

WHITE-WINGED TERN
Dark red bill; black body and underwing linings; white upperwings and underwing flight feathers; white rump; slightly notched white tail.

• **POPULATION** Common to fairly common in the East; common in middle and western parts of range; uncommon to rare on the West Coast.

• **CONSERVATION** Has declined inland and on the East Coast from wetlands drainage.

Flight Pattern

Buoyant direct flight with deep rapid wing beats. Hovers for insects. Uneven foraging flight with much stopping and starting.

Nest Identification

Shape   Location

Dried reeds, stalks, and grasses • on floating dried vegetation • built by both sexes • 2–4 light buff to olive eggs with black, brown, and greenish buff blotches, usually wreathed; oval to long oval, 1.7 x 1.2 inches.

Plumage Sexes similar	Habitat	Migration Migratory	Weight 2.3 ounces

DATE _____ TIME_____ LOCATION _____

Family LARIDAE	Species *Anous minutus*	Length 12–13.5 inches	Wingspan 28–30 inches

BLACK NODDY

Sometimes called the White-capped Noddy, this tropical tern is similar to the Brown Noddy but smaller and darker, with a whiter cap and a longer thinner bill. It often feeds farther out on the open sea. Known to be very tame, this bird sometimes will allow physical human contact. Juveniles are similar to adults, but the white on their heads is more sharply defined and does not blend gradually into the surrounding dark plumage of the head.

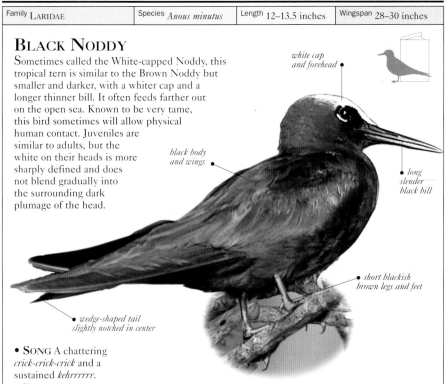

white cap and forehead

black body and wings

long slender black bill

short blackish brown legs and feet

wedge-shaped tail slightly notched in center

- **SONG** A chattering *crick-crick-crick* and a sustained *kehrrrrrr*.
- **BEHAVIOR** Feeds far out at sea, using its bill to scoop up prey from the water. Often feeds in flocks. Eats small fish and squid that it picks from the surface of the water; also swims in shallow water and dives beneath the surface to catch food. Flies close to water. More sedentary than Brown Noddy, with most populations roosting at breeding sites throughout the year, departing at dawn and returning at dusk.
- **BREEDING** Monogamous. Colonial.
- **NESTING** Incubation 34–39 days by both sexes. Young stay in nest 39–52 days, fed by both parents. 1 brood per year.
- **POPULATION** Nonbreeding individuals are uncommon to rare on the Dry Tortugas off the Florida coast with colony of Brown Noddies. Casual to Texas coast.

Similar Birds

BROWN NODDY
Lighter and more brown; larger; longer legs; shorter, thicker bill.

Flight Pattern

Strong, swift, and erratic, but more fluttering than Brown Noddy. Typically flies close to the surface of the ocean.

Nest Identification	
Shape 🐦 ➡ 🐦 Location 🏔 🌿 🌳	No nesting material if crevice is used; otherwise, dead tree branches and seaweed, lined with shells, rock, and bits of coral • cactus and bay cedar bushes, about 12 feet above ground • built by both sexes • 1 white to light red egg, tinted with buff; oval or short subelliptical, 1.7 x 1.2 inches.

Plumage Sexes similar	Habitat 〰 🌊 〰	Migration Migratory	Weight 4.2 ounces

DATE _____ TIME_____ LOCATION _____

Family LARIDAE	Species *Rynchops niger*	Length 18–19 inches	Wingspan 42–50 inches

BLACK SKIMMER

This crow-sized bird's Spanish name, *rayador*, is derived from the word *rayar*, for its habit of making lines in the ground by skimming sand around the nest with its long bill. The Black Skimmer is the largest of the world's three species and, like them, has unique compressed, knifelike mandibles, with the lower one one-third longer than the upper one. This long-winged bird has black upperparts, white underparts, a black rump and a slightly notched tail. Winter adults have a white collar. Juveniles are similar to winter adults but they have mottled brown upperparts. Nestlings are camouflaged by their buff coloring, which blends with the seashore. The lower and upper mandibles are similar in length until young are almost fully grown.

long pointed wings with
white trailing edge

black crown

white forehead

short forked white tail with black central tail feathers

bright red bill with black tip

long lower mandible

white underparts

short red legs and feet

JUVENILE

• **SONG** Low throaty bark of *kak-kak-kak*, *kuk-kuk-kuk*, or *yap-yap-yap*. Pairs sometimes sing together, *kow-kow* or *keow-keow*.

• **BEHAVIOR** Crepuscular and partially nocturnal. Often begins foraging in late evening when waters are calmer and prey rises to surface. Flies low and skims water with lower mandible to locate prey by touch, then snaps the bill shut. Grasps small fish and crustaceans with upper mandible, tilts head, and swallows while still flying. Spends much of day loafing on beaches.

• **BREEDING** Monogamous. Small colonies.

• **NESTING** Incubation 21–23 days by both sexes. Semiprecocial young remain in nest area 23–25 days. Fed by both sexes. 1 brood per year.

• **POPULATION** Common in coastal areas. Casual to accidental inland; birds are often driven there by storms.

• **CONSERVATION** Vulnerable to disturbance of nesting colonies. Eggs and young often trampled by dogs or humans, especially runners on beach.

Flight Pattern
Graceful buoyant direct flight with measured wing beats. In perfect synchrony flocks wheel, twist, and glide.

Nest Identification	
Shape ᵔ Location ▬ ᷟᷟᷟ ⤳	No materials added • on upper beach above high tidemark • built by both sexes • 4–5 bluish white or pinkish white eggs with brown, lilac, and gray blotches; round ovate to elongated ovate, 1.3 inches long.

Plumage Sexes similar	Habitat ᷟᷟᷟ ᷟᷟᷟ	Migration Some migrate	Weight 12.3 ounces

DATE _____ TIME_____ LOCATION _____

Family COLUMBIDAE	Species *Columba livia*	Length 13–14 inches	Wingspan 24–25 inches

ROCK DOVE

Introduced into North America by Europeans in the early 1600s, the Rock Dove is often called homing pigeon or carrier pigeon. Early Romans are said to have used the Rock Dove to carry the report of Caesar's conquest of Gaul back to Rome, and legend says the Rock Dove brought news of Napoleon's defeat at Waterloo to England days before messages sent via horses and ships. Although native to wild rocky habitats, today these birds are most common in urban and rural settings, and they are still raised in coops or pigeon lofts.

blue-gray overall

iridescent feathers on head and neck reflect green, bronze, and purple

2 thick broad bars across each wing

WILDTYPE

They can vary in color from wildtype to browns, grays, white-gray, mosaics, or pure white, but they always show a white rump pattern.

COLOR VARIATIONS

- **SONG** Sings a repetitive cooing *coo-a-roo, coo-roo-cooo* or *cock-a-war* or *coo-cuk-cuk.*
- **BEHAVIOR** In wild eats grass, weed seeds, grains, clover, and berries. In cities eats bread crumbs and garbage. Will take food from the hand, but when frightened claps wings over the back while flying up. Able to fly faster than 85 miles per hour.
- **BREEDING** Male displays by turning in circles while cooing. Monogamous.
- **NESTING** Incubation 16–19 days by both sexes. Altricial young remain in nest about 27–35 days. Fed by both parents. Young thrust bills into parents' mouths to eat regurgitated food. 5 or more broods per year.
- **POPULATION** Common, especially in urban settings.

Similar Birds

BAND-TAILED PIGEON
West • white bar on nape; broad gray tail band; lacks white rump.

MOURNING DOVE
Much smaller; long pointed tail; lacks white rump patch.

Flight Pattern

Swift direct flight with rapid wing beats.

Nest Identification

Shape — Location —

Unlined platform of sticks, twigs, leaves, grasses • building ledges, barn rafters, gutters, sheltered cliff edges, or rocks • built by female with materials gathered by male • 2 white eggs, about 1.6 inches long.

Plumage Sexes similar	Habitat	Migration Nonmigratory	Weight 13.0 ounces

DATE _____ TIME_____ LOCATION _____

| Family COLUMBIDAE | Species *Columba flavirostris* | Length 13–14 inches | Wingspan 24 inches |

RED-BILLED PIGEON

Appearing plain and dark at first glance, the Red-billed Pigeon is unusually attractive when bright sunlight hits its iridescent colors of purple, blue-gray, and olive-brown, which contrast with its brilliant red markings. In flight it shows a blue-gray rump. Small numbers of this shy native of Mexico and Central America nest in the dense woods of the lower Rio Grande Valley. Being fond of water, the Red-billed Pigeon makes frequent visits to sandbars in streams to drink and bathe.

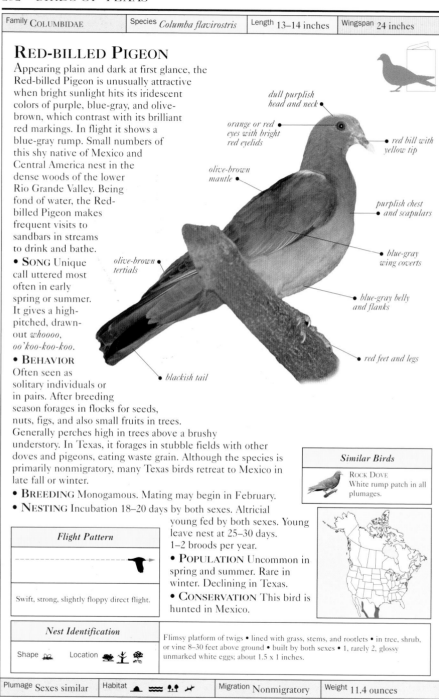

dull purplish head and neck

orange or red eyes with bright red eyelids

olive-brown mantle

red bill with yellow tip

purplish chest and scapulars

blue-gray wing coverts

olive-brown tertials

blue-gray belly and flanks

red feet and legs

blackish tail

• **SONG** Unique call uttered most often in early spring or summer. It gives a high-pitched, drawn-out *whoooo, oo'koo-koo-koo.*

• **BEHAVIOR** Often seen as solitary individuals or in pairs. After breeding season forages in flocks for seeds, nuts, figs, and also small fruits in trees. Generally perches high in trees above a brushy understory. In Texas, it forages in stubble fields with other doves and pigeons, eating waste grain. Although the species is primarily nonmigratory, many Texas birds retreat to Mexico in late fall or winter.

• **BREEDING** Monogamous. Mating may begin in February.

• **NESTING** Incubation 18–20 days by both sexes. Altricial young fed by both sexes. Young leave nest at 25–30 days. 1–2 broods per year.

• **POPULATION** Uncommon in spring and summer. Rare in winter. Declining in Texas.

• **CONSERVATION** This bird is hunted in Mexico.

Similar Birds

ROCK DOVE
White rump patch in all plumages.

Flight Pattern

Swift, strong, slightly floppy direct flight.

Nest Identification

Shape   Location

Flimsy platform of twigs • lined with grass, stems, and rootlets • in tree, shrub, or vine 8–30 feet above ground • built by both sexes • 1, rarely 2, glossy unmarked white eggs; about 1.5 x 1 inches.

| Plumage Sexes similar | Habitat | Migration Nonmigratory | Weight 11.4 ounces |

Family COLUMBIDAE	Species *Columba fasciata*	Length 14–15 inches	Wingspan 25 inches

BAND-TAILED PIGEON

Reduced in numbers by overhunting, the Band-tailed Pigeon has recovered as a result of bans on hunting in several states. It is generally is found in woods and wooded canyons in mountains, where it perches for long periods of time in the tops of leafless trees. Large flocks often gather at water holes and salt licks.

purplish head

narrow white band on nape of neck

yellow bill with dark tip

purplish wings and breast

yellow legs and feet

conspicuous wide dark gray terminal band across tail

• **SONG** An owl-like repetitive *oo-whoo* or *whoo-oo-whoo*. During nesting season male utters deep smooth tremulous *whoo-whoo-hoo* or two-syllable *whoo-uh*.

• **BEHAVIOR** Not as gregarious as some other species of doves and pigeons, these birds often perch in small groups high in trees on open branches. Small flocks may fly together to water holes or to forage. In winter these flocks may number several hundred birds, rarely thousands. Flutters among branches, to pick berries.

Also eats wild peas, grains, seeds, nuts, and insects.

• **BREEDING** Male calls to female from open perch in tree. Monogamous. Scattered pairs or occasionally small colonies.

• **NESTING** Incubation 18–20 days by both sexes. Young stay in nest 25–30 days. Tended by both parents. Young fed by regurgitation of seeds, fruits, berries, and pigeons' milk. 2–3 broods per year.

• **POPULATION** Uncommon to fairly common; local.

• **CONSERVATION** Nearly extirpated from overhunting, but has recovered with restraints on hunting.

Similar Birds

ROCK DOVE White rump; no contrasting gray band at end of tail.

Flight Pattern
Swift strong direct flight.

Nest Identification	
Shape 〰 Location 🌿 🌲	Flimsy platform of twigs • usually in tree branches or forks 8–40 feet above ground • built by female with materials gathered by male • 1–2 unmarked white eggs, 1.6 x 1 inches.

Plumage Sexes similar	Habitat 🌳 ⛰ 👥	Migration Migratory	Weight 12.5 ounces

DATE _____ TIME_____ LOCATION _____

Family COLUMBIDAE	Species *Streptopelia decaocto*	Length 12.5 inches	Wingspan 18–19 inches

EURASIAN COLLARED-DOVE

This large dove, a native of Eurasia, was introduced into the Bahama Islands in 1974. By the end of the 1970s, it had found its way to Florida, where it could be seen feeding in backyard gardens, towns, and parks. By the beginning of the new millennium this now established exotic had spread up the Atlantic Coast to North Carolina, across the Gulf Coast to Texas, and up the Mississippi River to Tennessee, with records in Oklahoma and Pennsylvania. Although similar to other doves

pale gray-pink head, neck, and breast

black bill

very pale buff upperparts

black "half-moon" trimmed with white on nape

pink legs and feet

in its habits, this dove is less shy around people and prefers life in and around human habitation. In flight, it shows a two-toned tail, gray base, and white-tipped blackish primaries.

- **SONG** Soft, continual cooing *hoo-hoooo-hoo* with emphasis on the second syllable; also a complaining *mair.*
- **BEHAVIOR** Solitary; pairs and family groups, but not in large flocks. Feeds close to houses; trusting of human contact. Eats mostly grain and seeds. Feeds on lawns, roadsides, feed mills, farms, and agricultural areas.
- **BREEDING** Monogamous. Male gives displays and coos while perched in tree or roof.
- **NESTING** Incubation 14–18 days by both sexes. Young stay in nest 15–20 days, fed and tended by both parents for an additional week. Up to 6 broods per year in Europe, possibly same in Florida.
- **POPULATION** Fairly common to common. Spreading quickly in southeastern US cities, villages, and gardens.
- **FEEDERS** Attracted to feeding stations, bird feeders, birdbaths, and garden pools.

Similar Birds

MOURNING DOVE Smaller; pinkish fawn head and underparts; pinkish iridescence on neck; black spot on auriculars; brownish gray upperparts and unmarked nape; long, pointed tail with white tips and black subteminal band on all but two central feathers; black spots on upper inner wing • wings make whistling sound in flight.

Flight Pattern

Swift strong direct flight on rapidly beating wings.

Nest Identification

Shape   Location

Twigs and dry stalks • in tree, shrub, and balconies or eves of houses, 6–7 feet above ground • male collects materials, female builds • 2 pure white eggs; oval to elliptical, 1.2 inches.

Plumage Sexes similar	Habitat	Migration Nonmigratory	Weight 5.4 ounces

| Family COLUMBIDAE | Species *Zenaida asiatica* | Length 11–12 inches | Wingspan 17–18 inches |

WHITE-WINGED DOVE

Its distinctive white wing patches set this dove apart from other doves and pigeons; when the bird perches the patch shows only as a narrow white line outlining the bottom of the folded wing. Often making its home in the desert, it will fly more than twenty miles for drinking water, using both natural and man-made sources. The female is smaller than the male and duller in color.

- **SONG** A low-pitched cooing *who-cooks-for-you; who koo-koo-koo.*
- **BEHAVIOR** Gregarious. Sometimes seen in flocks of thousands in the West. Eats seeds, grains, and fruits from trees, shrubs, and cacti. Feeds in flocks. Obtains drinking water

orange-red eyes surrounded by bare blue skin

reddish purple crown and nape

dark blue bill

iridescent greenish gold on sides of neck

brownish upperparts

black mark below ear coverts

rounded gray tail with white corners, black-trimmed inside

large white wing patches and dark gray flight feathers

red legs and feet

from streams and cacti, as well as from various man-made sources, such as reservoirs, irrigation canals, windmill troughs, and cattle tanks.

- **BREEDING** Monogamous. Small colonies. In display flight, male climbs with clapping wing beats, then glides down on stiff, slightly downward-bowed wings.
- **NESTING** Incubation 13–14 days by both sexes. Young stay in nest 13–16 days, tended by both sexes. 2–3 broods per year.
- **POPULATION** Common in the Southwest; locally fairly common in southern Florida; Casual elsewhere.
- **FEEDERS** Attracted to birdbaths, garden pools, and bird feeders and feeding stations providing small seeds.
- **CONSERVATION** Harvested and managed as a game species in the western United States.

Similar Birds

MOURNING DOVE Lacks white wing patch; longer, more pointed tail; gray-brown flight feathers.

Flight Pattern

Fairly fast direct flight, but slower and usually higher and without the zigzagging of the Mourning Dove.

Nest Identification

Shape   Location

Sticks, grasses, and stems of weeds • cactus, shrub, or low in tree, 4–30 feet above ground • built by both sexes; male gathers material, female builds • 2 creamy buff eggs; oval to elliptical, 1.2 inches.

| Plumage Sexes similar | Habitat | Migration Migratory | Weight 5.4 ounces |

Family COLUMBIDAE	Species *Zenaida macroura*	Length 12 inches	Wingspan 17–19 inches

MOURNING DOVE

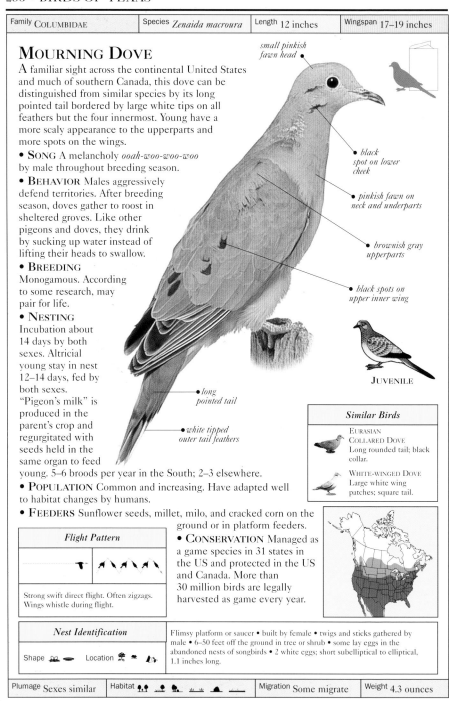

A familiar sight across the continental United States and much of southern Canada, this dove can be distinguished from similar species by its long pointed tail bordered by large white tips on all feathers but the four innermost. Young have a more scaly appearance to the upperparts and more spots on the wings.

- **SONG** A melancholy *ooah-woo-woo-woo* by male throughout breeding season.
- **BEHAVIOR** Males aggressively defend territories. After breeding season, doves gather to roost in sheltered groves. Like other pigeons and doves, they drink by sucking up water instead of lifting their heads to swallow.
- **BREEDING** Monogamous. According to some research, may pair for life.
- **NESTING** Incubation about 14 days by both sexes. Altricial young stay in nest 12–14 days, fed by both sexes. "Pigeon's milk" is produced in the parent's crop and regurgitated with seeds held in the same organ to feed young. 5–6 broods per year in the South; 2–3 elsewhere.
- **POPULATION** Common and increasing. Have adapted well to habitat changes by humans.
- **FEEDERS** Sunflower seeds, millet, milo, and cracked corn on the ground or in platform feeders.
- **CONSERVATION** Managed as a game species in 31 states in the US and protected in the US and Canada. More than 30 million birds are legally harvested as game every year.

small pinkish fawn head

black spot on lower cheek

pinkish fawn on neck and underparts

brownish gray upperparts

black spots on upper inner wing

JUVENILE

long pointed tail

white tipped outer tail feathers

Similar Birds

EURASIAN COLLARED DOVE
Long rounded tail; black collar.

WHITE-WINGED DOVE
Large white wing patches; square tail.

Flight Pattern

Strong swift direct flight. Often zigzags. Wings whistle during flight.

Nest Identification

Shape ⌒ Location 🌳 🌿 🪶

Flimsy platform or saucer • built by female • twigs and sticks gathered by male • 6–50 feet off the ground in tree or shrub • some lay eggs in the abandoned nests of songbirds • 2 white eggs; short subelliptical to elliptical, 1.1 inches long.

Plumage Sexes similar	Habitat	Migration Some migrate	Weight 4.3 ounces

DATE _____ TIME _____ LOCATION _____

Family COLUMBIDAE	Species *Columbina inca*	Length 7.5–8 inches	Wingspan 12–13 inches

INCA DOVE

During autumn large flocks of these small birds can be seen huddled together for warmth on clotheslines or fences. Choosing to make its home near human habitation, this tame dove feeds in parks, barnyards,

gray-buff upperparts

long square-ended tail

scaly grayish white underparts

gardens, and birdbaths. Its feathering makes the body appear distinctively scalloped, and the rufous wings often make a twittering noise while the bird is flying. In flight its long tail is brown centrally, black laterally with white edges, and tipped white on the outer tail feathers.

- **SONG** Monotonous fluted *coe-coo* or *whoo-oo-whoo*, "*no-hope*." Also conversational *cut-cut-ca-doo-ca-doo*.
- **BEHAVIOR** Pairs or small flocks; sometimes flocks and forages with other small doves. Huddles in tiers 2–3 high with birds standing on the back of other birds in a pyramid to keep warm on very cold days. A terrestrial species, it spends much time walking on the ground picking up seeds and grain. Sometimes feeds with chickens in barnyards. Prefers open ground near water sources.
- **BREEDING** Monogamous.
- **NESTING** Incubation 12–15 days by both sexes. Altricial young leave nest after 16 days but tended by parent for additional 7 days. Fed by both sexes. 2–5 broods per year.
- **POPULATION** Abundant. Expanding to the North.
- **FEEDERS** Birdbaths and man-made feeders.

Similar Birds

COMMON GROUND-DOVE Shorter, rounded black tail with white only on corners; not as scaly; black spots and streaks on folded wing.

Flight Pattern
Direct flight with rapid wing beats recorded as fast as 28 miles per hour.

Nest Identification	
Shape ⌐ ♋ Location 🌷 🌿 🌳	Twigs, stems, and leaves • sometimes lined with grass • built by female with material gathered by male • in tree or shrub 5–20 feet above ground • 2–7 white unmarked eggs, 0.9 inches long.

Plumage Sexes similar	Habitat ▲ ⤚ ⊥	Migration Nonmigratory	Weight 1.7 ounces

| Family COLUMBIDAE | Species *Columbina passerina* | Length 6–7 inches | Wingspan 8.75–10 inches |

COMMON GROUND-DOVE

The Common Ground-Dove is about the size of a sparrow and often can be seen perched on fences, roofs of buildings, and trees. Known as tame, this bird sometimes will not fly away until almost stepped upon. The female is grayer than the male and more uniformly colored. In flight this small dove has flashing rufous-red primaries and wing linings and a black tail with white corners.

scaly head

brown back

brown wings with brown-black spots

rounded wings show red-brown primaries and wing linings in flight

dusky black bill with pink base

scaly breast

pinkish brown underparts

stubby black tail

pink or yellow feet and legs

• **SONG** Continual soft melancholy *coo-oo* or *woo-oo*, rising on second syllable and often for hours at a time. Also soft *wah-up*.
• **BEHAVIOR** Terrestrial, walking on rapidly moving short legs with head bobbing. Eats seeds of grasses and weeds, waste grain in fields, insects, and small berries off ground. Often frequents quiet roadsides in early morning and late afternoon, where it may feed and pick up grit. Usually stays in pairs or small flocks.
• **BREEDING** Monogamous. Thought to mate for life.
• **NESTING** Incubation 12–14 days by both sexes. Altricial young fed by both sexes. Young leave nest as soon as they can fly, at about 11–12 days. 2–4 broods per year.
• **POPULATION** Declining in recent decades, especially in the southeastern states and along the Gulf Coast.
• **FEEDERS** Will feed on seeds scattered on ground or on platform feeders.

Similar Birds

INCA DOVE
Much larger; longer white-edged tail; scaly upperparts and underparts.

RUDDY GROUND-DOVE ♂
Rufous on upperparts; lacks scaling; dark bill.

Flight Pattern
Rapid direct flight with swift wing beats.

Nest Identification	Sometimes flimsy platform of twigs and plant fibers or slight depression on ground with little or no materials • on beach or floor of woods or fields; in low bush, stump, or vine; or on top of fence post or tree branch, 1–21 feet above ground • sometimes uses abandoned nest of songbird or other dove species • built by both sexes • 2–3 white eggs, 0.8 inches long.
Shape	
Location	

| Plumage Sexes similar | Habitat | Migration Nonmigratory | Weight 1.1 ounces |

DATE _____ TIME_____ LOCATION _____

Family COLUMBIDAE	Species *Leptotila verreauxi*	Length 11–12 inches	Wingspan 17–18 inches

WHITE-TIPPED DOVE

Sometimes called the White-fronted Dove or Wood Pigeon, this primarily Latin American bird lives in North America in the lower Rio Grande Valley of Texas. Its wings make a whistling sound similar to the wings of a woodcock when it flies straight up in the air. About the size of a Mourning Dove but lacking its pointed tail, a flying White-tipped Dove shows a white throat, forehead, belly, undertail coverts, and corners on the rounded tail. Wing linings and axillars are chestnut in color.

white forehead

brown upperwings

black bill

white throat

rounded tail

gray breast

white undertail coverts and belly

purple-red legs and feet

- **SONG** Resembling a small deep-sounding foghorn in the thicket, *oo-whooooo* or *hu' woo wooooo*.
- **BEHAVIOR** Feeds mainly from ground. Eats fallen tree seeds, prickly pear cacti, grasses, some cultivated grains such as corn and sorghum, and large insects such as grasshoppers and crickets. Prefers to walk on the ground in dense understory. Walks quickly away from intruders unless pressed into flight on whistling wings. Solitary or in pairs; never in flocks.
- **NESTING** Incubation 14 days by both sexes. Young brooded and fed by both sexes. Young fledge nest at 14–15 days. 2 or more broods per year.
- **POPULATION** Stable. Permanent resident of lower Rio Grande Valley of Texas.
- **FEEDERS** Comes to seeds scattered on ground or to platform feeders positioned near thick cover.

Similar Birds

MOURNING DOVE
Pinkish gray forehead and throat; gray underparts; long pointed tail with white tips on all but central tail feathers.

WHITE-WINGED DOVE
Gray tail with white-tipped feathers (except 2 sandy brown central tail feathers); white crescents across wings form white edge on folded wing.

Flight Pattern

Very swift direct flight with rapid wing beats.

Nest Identification

Shape ⌂ Location 🌳 🌿 ▬

Sticks and twigs or grass, fibers, and weed stems • in low branch or fork of tree, shrub, or tangle of vines; sometimes on ground • built by both sexes • 2 cream or buff unmarked eggs; elliptical to oval, 1.2 inches long.

Plumage Sexes similar	Habitat 🌾 🏞 ⛰	Migration Nonmigratory	Weight 5.4 ounces

DATE _____ TIME_____ LOCATION _____

Family PSITTACIDAE	Species *Myiopsitta monachus*	Length 11.5 inches	Wingspan 17–18 inches

MONK PARAKEET

Introduced as an escaped or intentionally released bird in North America, this parakeet has established itself primarily in and around cities from New England to the Midwest, southeast Texas, and Florida. The most widespread breeding populations are found in south Florida. Using sticks and twigs, Monk Parakeets build large condominium nests in trees and on man-made structures. The nests contain separate compartments for as many as twenty pairs. It is the only parrot in the world to build large communal nests. In its native South American temperate habitat, flocks of Monk Parakeet destroy crops, particularly corn and sunflowers, and the species is considered the foremost avian threat to agriculture.

gray face and forehead

green overall

dark eyes set in white eye ring

hooked creamy pink bill

gray chest

yellow-green belly

deep blue flight feathers

long pointed green-and-blue tail

bluish legs and feet

• **SONG** Garrulous. Wide range of high staccato shrieks and screams. Makes high-pitched chattering when feeding.

• **BEHAVIOR** Gregarious. Searches for food in flocks, often tearing apart crops. Eats legumes, grains, seeds, fruits, and insects. Frequents areas near human habitation. Builds large conspicuous domed nests of sticks with entrance on side. Pairs roost throughout the year in their chambers within.

• **BREEDING** Monogamous. Loosely colonial, often communal in a single large multichambered nest.

• **NESTING** Incubation 25–31 days by both sexes. Fed by both sexes. Altricial young stay in nest 38–42 days. 2 broods per year.

• **POPULATION** Exotic. Very popular and common caged bird. Found in Florida, Texas, southeastern cities, the Northeast, and the Midwest.

• **FEEDERS** Groups attend feeders, especially in the winter, and eat seeds, cracked corn, pine seeds, suet, acorns, grass seeds, apples, cherries, grapes, raisins, and currants.

• **CONSERVATION** Attempts to control and/or eliminate this exotic species in many areas of the US are destroying both birds and nests.

Similar Birds

WHITE-WINGED PARAKEET
In south Florida only
• also similar to Yellow-chevroned Parakeet
• smaller; yellow-green overall; yellow edge on folded wing shows as yellow patch at bend of wing in flight; dark green flight feathers; lacks gray on face, crown, and breast.

Flight Pattern

Swift direct flight with rapid wing beats, often in flocks. Sometimes slight undulating flight.

Nest Identification

Shape  Location

Sticks and twigs • in highest branches of tree or leaning against tree or any tall structure • built by both sexes, often with other birds in colony • 5–9 white eggs; short subelliptical ovate, 1.1 x 0.8 inches.

Plumage Sexes similar	Habitat	Migration Nonmigratory	Weight Undetermined

DATE _____ TIME_____ LOCATION _____

Family PSITTACIDAE	Species *Aratinga holochlora*	Length 12–13 inches	Wingspan 17–19 inches

GREEN PARAKEET

This parakeet is a tropical bird, but vagrants may find their way to the southern tip of Texas and join the flocks that have become established there. In its native habitat of Mexico, it frequents deciduous forests and plantations, but these birds are most often spotted in Texas in urban or suburban and agricultural areas, where they feed on flowers, fruits, seeds, and berries. In flight the tail appears long and pointed, and all the flight feathers on the underwing are bright metallic yellow. Juveniles are similar to adults but have a brown iris.

• **SONG** Calls are high, grating, and screaming. In flight gives a shrill metallic screech, rapidly repeated. Also gives much twittering.

orange-red eyes with bare whitish beige eye ring

bright green overall

hooked pale pinkish beige bill

scant red flecks on throat and neck of some birds

metallic yellow on underside of primaries and secondaries

paler and more yellowish underparts

brownish feet and legs

long pointed tail with yellowish undertail feathers

• **BEHAVIOR** In noisy flocks, except during nesting season when in pairs. Size of flocks may depend on food supply. Eats seeds, fruits, nuts, berries, blossoms, and buds taken from canopy or outer branches of shrubs. Raids corn crops. Sometimes uses feet to bring food to mouth. Uses bill and feet to climb among branches and foliage.

• **BREEDING** Monogamous. Solitary. Often semicolonial.

• **NESTING** Breeding biology poorly known. Estimated incubation 23–28 days by female; male roosts in nesting cavity with female at night but not known to incubate. Young altricial; brooded by female; stay in nest estimated 42–56 days, fed by both sexes. 1 brood per year.

• **POPULATION** Casual in North America. Fairly common to common in the lower Rio Grande Valley of Texas.

• **FEEDERS** Seeds and fruits.

• **CONSERVATION** Captured as cage bird in native Mexico and northern Central America.

Similar Birds

RED-CROWNED PARROT
Stocky; green overall; short fan-shaped tail with yellow terminal band; green wings with dark blue-tipped primaries and secondaries; red patch in secondaries; pale blue mottling on crown and nape; red forehead and crown (more extensive in male); gray feet and legs; tan to creamy pink bill • not that similar since body shape differs, but the only other established green parrot in range in southern Texas.

Flight Pattern
Very swift direct flight on rapidly beating wings, often high above the terrain.

Nest Identification	
Shape	Location	Adds only a few twigs • in natural tree hollow or abandoned hole or sometimes in rock crevices • in native range, pairs sometimes excavate arboreal termite nests • 2–5 white eggs; nearly spherical, 1.17 x 0.97 inches.

Plumage Sexes similar	Habitat	Migration Nonmigratory	Weight Undetermined

DATE _____ TIME_____ LOCATION _____

Family PSITTACIDAE	Species *Amazona viridigenalis*	Length 12–13 inches	Wingspan 19 inches

RED-CROWNED PARROT

Small groups of these birds, which are most likely descended from escaped caged birds, have established themselves in Texas, California, and Florida. In its native habitats in northeastern Mexico, it spends its time in the pine-oak ridges and tropical forests of canyons, often traveling in conspicuous highly vocal flocks between the treetops. In flight, note the stocky appearance, dark blue-tipped flight feathers, red patch in secondaries, and yellowish-tipped tail. The male has an entirely red crown, while the female and juvenile have only a red forehead.

red forehead, crown, and lores

pinkish straw-colored hooked bill

blue sides of head above eyes and on sides of nape

first 5 outer secondaries red with violet-blue tips (shows as red edge on folded wing)

green overall with paler yellow-green underparts

• **SONG** Noisy. Has a squawking harsh *kee-crah-crah-crah* and a smooth *rreeoo* or *heeeyo*.
• **BEHAVIOR** Gregarious. Usually in flocks of 10–20 or more, except during breeding season when it occurs in pairs. Feeds on a variety of fruit, seeds (including pine seeds), nuts, berries, buds, and flowers. Can be agricultural pests locally. Often wasteful, eating only a bite or two, then dropping food to take another. Holds food in feet and manipulates it to the beak.
• **BREEDING** Monogamous. Solitary. Courting males often offer tidbits to their mates.
• **NESTING** Incubation 25–31 days by female. Duration of nest and age at fledging undetermined. Altricial young fed by both sexes. 1 brood per year.
• **POPULATION** Exotic; escaped or released birds established in southern Texas, southern California, and southern Florida. Some Texas birds may be wild birds from Mexico.
• **CONSERVATION** Populations declining in native areas, probably threatened by habitat destruction as well as capture for cage trade.

Similar Birds

None in US range, although southern California, Texas, and south Florida have many large green parrots flying about its cities and suburban areas, where this species should be identified with care.

Flight Pattern

Swift direct flight on rapidly beating wings with shallow wing strokes.

Nest Identification

Shape ▨ Location 🌳 🪴 ⚘

No materials used • nest in preformed cavity • 2–5 white eggs; elliptical, 1.4 x 1.1 inches.

Plumage Sexes similar	Habitat 🌳🌿 🌵 🌱	Migration Nonmigratory	Weight 10.4 ounces

DATE _____ TIME _____ LOCATION _____

| Family CUCULIDAE | Species *Coccyzus erythropthalmus* | Length 11–12 inches | Wingspan 15–17 inches |

BLACK-BILLED CUCKOO

This shy bird spends most of its time skulking in deep wooded forests. In rare instances, instead of incubating its own eggs it will lay its eggs in the nests of Yellow-billed Cuckoos, Gray Catbirds, Wood Thrushes, Yellow Warblers, or Chipping Sparrows. In flight note the long tail, which has small crescent-shaped white spots on the tips of all but the two central tail feathers, and the uniformly grayish brown wings and back. Juveniles are similar to adults but have a buff eye ring, paler undertail, and buff wash on the underparts, especially the undertail coverts.

narrow red eye ring

decurved black bill

grayish brown upperparts

white underparts

gray legs and feet

long graduated brown tail

- **SONG** Generally silent. Repeated monotone *cu-cu-cu* or *cu-cu-cu-cu* in series of 3–4 notes. Also gives series of rapid *kowk-kowk-kowk* notes all on a single pitch. Sometimes sings at night.
- **BEHAVIOR** Skulks through thick vegetation in shrubs and trees. Often sits quietly on branch scanning in all directions before changing perches. Eats primarily caterpillars, especially hairy tent caterpillars, and other insects; occasionally eats small mollusks, fish, and some wild fruits. Often found in damp thickets and wet places. Engages in courtship feeding.
- **BREEDING** Monogamous.
- **NESTING** Incubation 10–14 days by both sexes. Altricial young stay in nest 7–9 days; fed by both sexes. Young leave nest before they can fly and climb around on nest tree or shrub for about 14 days. 1 brood per year.
- **POPULATION** Uncommon to fairly common. Somewhat dependant on caterpillar populations; larger clutches laid when food is plentiful.

Similar Birds

YELLOW-BILLED CUCKOO
Yellow bill with dark tip; rufous primaries contrast with wing coverts and upperparts; larger white spots on undertail.

Flight Pattern

Often flies low and makes short flights from one tree to the next.

Nest Identification	
Shape ᔔ ⬯ Location 🌳 🌲	Dried twigs • lined with fresh grass, leaves, pine needles, catkins, and vegetation • in tree or shrub 2–20 feet above ground • 2–5 blue-green eggs with dark blotches, 1.1 x 0.8 inches.

| Plumage Sexes similar | Habitat 🌾 ⛰ 🌿 | Migration Migratory | Weight 3.6 ounces |

DATE _____ TIME_____ LOCATION _____

Family CUCULIDAE	Species *Coccyzus americanus*	Length 11–13 inches	Wingspan 15–17 inches

YELLOW-BILLED CUCKOO

Like most of the cuckoos, this bird prefers to perch unobtrusively in thick forests or shrubs. Many rural people know this bird as the "Rain Crow." Sometimes it lays its eggs in nests of the Black-billed Cuckoo but rarely in nests of other birds. It is often a casualty at "tower kills" while migrating at night. In flight, note the long tail and the contrast of rufous primaries against gray-brown wing coverts and upperparts. The juvenile shows a paler undertail pattern, and the lower mandible may not be yellow.

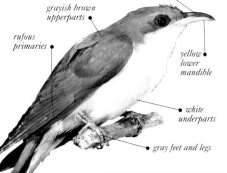

decurved bill with dark upper mandible and tip

grayish brown upperparts

rufous primaries

yellow lower mandible

white underparts

gray feet and legs

• **SONG** Often silent; song heard more often in summer. A monotonous throaty *ka-ka-ka-ka-kow-kow-kow-kow-kowlp—kowlp——kowl*, pruning down and slowing at the end.

• **BEHAVIOR** Slips quietly and somewhat stealthily through tangles; flies easily from tree to tree. Often sits motionless on an interior branch and slowly surveys the surrounding vegetation. Eats mostly hairy caterpillars; also insects, larvae, and small fruits and berries. Sometimes eats small frogs and lizards and the eggs of other birds. Engages in courtship feeding in which the male lands by perched female, climbs on her shoulder, and places food in her bill.

large white spots on black undertail

• **BREEDING** Monogamous. Solitary nester.

• **NESTING** Incubation 9–11 days by both sexes. Altricial young stay in nest 7–9 days, fed by both sexes. Young leave nest before able to fly but remain in vicinity, climbing in branches; fed by parent for about 14 more days. 1 brood per year.

• **POPULATION** Uncommon to common. Somewhat dependent on caterpillar population; species produces greater number of eggs when plentiful.

• **CONSERVATION** Neotropical migrant that has declined significantly over much of its range.

Similar Birds

BLACK-BILLED CUCKOO Entirely black bill; red eye ring; no rufous in wing; gray underside of tail with smaller crescent-shaped white spots; voice differs.

MANGROVE CUCKOO Gray-brown wings and coverts; black mask extends past eye; tawny-buff lower breast, sides, belly, flanks, and undertail coverts; decurved black bill, yellow at base of lower mandible • limited range in Florida; accidental on Gulf Coast.

Flight Pattern

Direct flight with slow light steady wing beats; often flies low from tree to tree with flash of rufous in wings.

Nest Identification	Small sticks, with lining of leaves, grasses, mosses, bits of fabric, and catkins from oaks and willow trees • so flimsy eggs can sometimes be seen from beneath • in tree or shrub, 2–12 feet above ground • built by both sexes • 1–5 pale bluish green eggs that fade to light greenish yellow, unmarked; elliptical to cylindrical, 1.2 x 0.9 inches.
Shape ⌒ ⌐ Location 🌳 🌿	

Plumage Sexes similar	Habitat 🌾 🌳 🌳 🌿	Migration Migratory	Weight 3.6 ounces

DATE _____ TIME_____ LOCATION _____

| Family CUCULIDAE | Species *Geococcyx californianus* | Length 20–24 inches | Wingspan 32 inches |

GREATER ROADRUNNER

Able to run up to 15 miles per hour, this bird generally seems to prefer sprinting rather than flying. Because this large slender member of the cuckoo family habitually stays on the ground, it can be difficult to see. Centuries ago, it was sometimes called the Ground Cuckoo because it would run along paths in front of horse-drawn carriages. This shy solitary bird is the state bird of New Mexico. Look for the large streaked body, shaggy crest, and long tail that shows white tips when it is spread. In flight, the short, rounded wings reveal a white crescent in the primaries. Sometimes visible is a patch of bare skin around and behind the eye that shades from blue proximally to red to orange distally.

- **SONG** A series of throaty descending dovelike *coooos*. Also a low, rolling *preeet-preeet*.
- **BEHAVIOR** Terrestrial. Often solitary. Eats insects, snakes, lizards, rodents, and small birds; some fruits and seeds. Runs on ground in pursuit of prey. Seldom flies. Pairs hold territory all year. Performs distraction display to lure intruders from nest.

shaggy crest

cinnamon, blackish, and white streaks overall

heavy black bill hooked at tip

short rounded wings

white crescent on wings shows in flight

long pale blue legs and feet

long tail

- **BREEDING** Monogamous. Solitary. May mate for life. Has unusual courtship display: male bows, alternately lifting and dropping its wings, while spreading its tail; parades in front of female with head held high on ridged neck and with tail and wings drooped.
- **NESTING** Incubation about 20 days by both sexes, but male does more. Altricial young stay in nest 17–18 days, fed by both sexes. 1–2 broods per year.
- **POPULATION** Fairly common to common. Local populations tend to decline after a severe winter.
- **CONSERVATION** Often persecuted based on belief that they make serious inroads on quail populations.

Flight Pattern

When flushed or crossing obstacles, alternates several shallow rapid wing beats with long glides.

Nest Identification

Shape ▭ Location 🌳 🌿 🌲

Twigs, with lining of grass, mesquite pods, leaves, feathers, snakeskin, and horse or cattle droppings • in shrub, tree, or cactus, 2–12 feet above ground • 2 white to pale yellow eggs; elliptical to cylindrical, 1.5 inches long.

| Plumage Sexes similar | Habitat | Migration Nonmigratory | Weight 13.2 ounces |

DATE _____ TIME_____ LOCATION _____

Family CUCULIDAE	Species *Crotophaga sulcirostris*	Length 12–14 inches	Wingspan 16–18 inches

GROOVE-BILLED ANI

Easily distinguished as an ani by its black plumage and its parrotlike bill, this member of the cuckoo family often sleeps at night in communal roosts in trees with as many as thirty to forty birds. During breeding season, three to four pairs of birds build and share one nest. The laterally compressed black bill has a series of three to four parallel grooves in the upper mandible that are difficult to see except at close range. It shows paler scalloping on the chest and back.

• **SONG** Sings a liquid *TEE-hoe* with first upslurred note

curved ridge on top of bill, lower than crown

parallel grooves on upper mandible

black overall with shimmering purple and green overtones

long tail

blackish gray legs and feet

emphasized, repeated 10–12 times. The vocalization has a flickerlike quality.

• **BEHAVIOR** Gregarious. Follows livestock to pick ticks off their backs or eat insects swarming around them. Eats mainly insects and spiders but also takes lizards, seeds, fruits, and berries. Lives in groups of 1–4 monogamous pairs and several additional "helpers" on permanent territories. All group members contribute to territorial defense, nest building, and rearing of young. Often dips and wags tail from side to side. Groups often fly 1 at a time from 1 spot to the next.

• **BREEDING** Monogamous. Communal.

• **NESTING** Incubation 13–14 days by both sexes and by alpha male at night. Altricial young remain in nest 6–7 days, fed by all adults. First flight at 10 days. 1–2 broods per year.

• **POPULATION** Common to fairly common. Stable and expanding in Gulf Coast range; increasing in the tropics. Casual to accidental elsewhere.

Similar Birds

SMOOTH-BILLED ANI
Larger bill with higher arched culmen reaching above level of crown; no grooves in upper mandible; voice differs • only in the East.

COMMON GRACKLE
Smaller long pointed bill; pale eyes • male has long keeled tail.

Flight Pattern

Flies low to the ground, alternating between rapid shallow wing beats and short glides.

Nest Identification		Sticks lined with fresh vegetation • in low tree or shrub, 5–15 feet above ground • built by both sexes and extra birds • nest may contain up to 16–20 eggs • 3–4 pale blue eggs per female; oval to long oval, 1.3 x 1.0 inches.
Shape	Location	

Plumage Sexes similar	Habitat	Migration Migratory	Weight 3.1 ounces

DATE _____ TIME_____ LOCATION _____

Family TYTONIDAE	Species *Tyto alba*	Length 14–20 inches	Wingspan 43–47 inches

BARN OWL

Associating more closely with man than any other owl, the nearly cosmopolitan Barn Owl often roosts and nests in buildings and hunts in areas cleared for agriculture, particularly meadows and pastures. It is perhaps the most distinctive looking owl with its long legs and heart-shaped "monkey" face. The unexpected gasping screech of this owl nearby in the darkness can raise the hair on the back of one's head. Like other species of owls it can locate and capture its prey in total darkness using its hearing alone. This is accomplished with asymetrically positioned ear openings, and the aid of the facial disks.

no ear tufts

dark eyes

heart-shaped face

golden tawny upperparts

white to cinnamon underparts with spots instead of streaks

barring in wings

long legs

• **SONG** Harsh hissing screaming grating whistling gasp, *eeeeeeSEEek.*

• **BEHAVIOR** Nocturnal. Feeds primarily on small mammals such as rodents and shrews, but occasionally takes small birds. May nest during any month of the year, and pairs are believed to mate for life. Many farmers encourage the presence of this excellent mouser in their barns.

barred tail

• **BREEDING** Monogamous.

• **NESTING** Incubation 29–34 days by female. Semialtricial young stay in nest 55–65 days. Fed by both sexes. 1–3 broods per year.

Similar Birds

SHORT-EARED OWL Yellow to orange eyes; short ear tufts; heavily streaked underparts; often diurnal.

• **POPULATION** Rare to uncommon. Stable in most areas, but some declines noted in the East.

• **BIRDHOUSES** Nest boxes.

• **CONSERVATION** Listed as threatened in some states.

Flight Pattern

Slow light silent mothlike flight.

Nest Identification	
Shape	Debris arranged into crude depression • in tree cavity, barn loft, building, nest box, crevice, mine shaft, or cave • 2–12 whitish eggs, sometimes nest-stained; short subelliptical, 1.7 inches long.
Location	

Plumage Sexes similar	Habitat	Migration Some migrate	Weight 1.1 pounds

DATE _____ TIME_____ LOCATION _____

Family STRIGIDAE	Species *Otus flammeolus*	Length 6–7 inches	Wingspan 13 inches

FLAMMULATED OWL

One of the smallest owls in North America, the Flammulated Owl is also the only small owl with dark, not yellow, eyes. This owl's ear tufts are minute and hardly noticeable. The Flammulated Owl has two color phases, reddish and gray, with the former being more common in the southeastern part of the bird's range. The natural history of this diminutive North American owl is poorly known.

reddish brown facial disk

tawny scapular bar

small ear tufts

dark eyes

grayish brown body

REDDISH FORM

• **SONG** *Boo-BOOT* with emphasis on the second note of the song. A series of single paired low hoarse hollow hoots is given repeatedly at intervals of 2–3 seconds.

• **BEHAVIOR** Little is known. The bird is nocturnal. It feeds primarily on insects, including moths taken in flight and arachnids such as spiders and scorpions gleaned from the ground or the foliage of trees in its habitat. Sometimes will take as its prey various small mammals or other birds. It frequents primarily open pine and oak forests and spruce-fir forests in mountains as high that are 8,000 feet.

• **BREEDING** Monogamous. Sometimes has been observed living in loose colonies.

• **NESTING** Incubation 21–26 days by female. Semialtricial young remain in nest about 25 days. Young are fed by both sexes. 1 brood per year.

• **POPULATION** Widespread and common in range, though slight declines are possible. Highly migratory; strays have made it to Florida and the Gulf Coast.

Similar Birds

NORTHERN PYGMY-OWL
Thinner; longer tail; white underparts with heavy streaking; lacks ear tufts; yellow eyes; black nape patches; chiefly diurnal.

WESTERN SCREECH-OWL
Yellow eyes; lacks brown bar in scapulars; has different voice.

WHISKERED SCREECH-OWL
Longer ear tufts; yellow eyes; different voice.

NOTE: These are all permanent residents of the woodlands in the West. There are no similar birds ranging in the East.

Flight Pattern
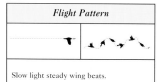
Slow light steady wing beats.

Nest Identification	
Shape ▨² Location ⚹ ▲ ❀	Old woodpecker hole • no lining • 15–40 feet above ground • 2–4 white or creamy white eggs; about oval, 1.1 inches long.

Plumage Sexes similar	Habitat 🌾 🌳 ⛰	Migration Migratory	Weight 1.9 ounces

DATE _____ TIME_____ LOCATION _____

| Family STRIGIDAE | Species *Otus kennicottii* | Length 8–10 inches | Wingspan 18–24 inches |

WESTERN SCREECH-OWL

This small tufted owl, the western counterpart of the Eastern Screech-Owl, is found in a wide variety of habitats, from wooded canyons, riparian thickets, and deserts to orchards and the suburbs. It is more often heard than seen. Over most of its range its plumage is generally gray, but Pacific Coast birds are more brownish in color.

ear tufts

gray to brown upperparts with vermiculations and streaking

yellow eyes

dark bill

large white spots on scapulars

heavily streaked and lightly barred underparts

- **SONG** Repeated brief whistles accelerating in tempo in the pattern of a dropped ball bouncing to a stop; a short trill followed by a drawn-out trill.
- **BEHAVIOR** Nocturnal; becomes active at dusk. Feeds on variety of small mammals, birds, reptiles, large insects, and arachnids, but the primary food is large insects. Small mammals carried to the nest to feed the young often are decapitated by the adults. Surplus food is cached in winter roosting cavities. Roosts by day in cavities or thick vegetation. Sedentary, often staying in the same home range throughout the year; males may defend a territory for as long as 10 months. Courtship begins as early as February when the male begins calling each night shortly after sunset to attract a mate. The calls cease when a pair is formed.
- **BREEDING** Monogamous.
- **NESTING** Incubation 21–30 days by female. Semialtricial young stay in nest about 28 days, fed by both sexes. 1 brood per year.
- **POPULATION** Common; widely distributed over range.
- **BIRDHOUSES** Will use man-made nest boxes.

Similar Birds

EASTERN SCREECH-OWL
May have rufous-red plumage; pale bill; different voice.

WHISKERED SCREECH-OWL
Pale bill; different voice; bolder streaking on underparts.

FLAMMULATED OWL
Dark eyes; brown bar in scapulars; different voice.

Flight Pattern

Buoyant silent flight with rapid wing beats.

Nest Identification

Shape

Location

Natural hole in tree or woodpecker hole • may use old magpie nests • no lining added • 5–35 feet off ground • 2–6 white eggs, 1.4 inches long.

| Plumage Sexes similar | Habitat | Migration Nonmigratory | Weight 5.4 ounces |

DATE _____ TIME_____ LOCATION _____

Family STRIGIDAE	Species *Otus asio*	Length 8–10 inches	Wingspan 18–24 inches

EASTERN SCREECH-OWL

Perhaps the best-known owl in eastern North America, this small tufted bird is found in a great variety of habitats, from wooded lots to urban gardens. It is able to flatten its ear tufts, which gives the head a rounded appearance. There are two distinct color phases, reddish brown and gray, plus there are brown intermediates. Its voice is not a screech but rather a mournful whinny familiar to many.

RED MORPH

tufted head

yellow eyes

pale bill

bright rusty brown to gray body

streaked underparts

• **SONG** Series of melancholy tremulous whistles descending in pitch; drawn-out trilling note. Simple to imitate.

• **BEHAVIOR** Nocturnal; becomes active at dusk. Feeds on wide variety of small vertebrates and invertebrates, including insects, arachnids, crayfish, mammals, amphibians, reptiles, birds, and fish. When using a cavity for a day roost, often will sit in the entrance. When approached on its roost, will flatten its body, erect its ear tufts, and close its eyes in an attempt to hide by blending into the background.

BROWN INTERMEDIATE

GRAY MORPH

white spots on scapulars

• **BREEDING** Monogamous.

• **NESTING** Incubation about 26 days mostly by female. Semialtricial young stay in nest about 28 days. Fed by both sexes. 1 brood per year.

• **POPULATION** Widespread and fairly common, but with gradual decline.

• **BIRDHOUSES** Will roost and nest in nesting boxes sized for wood ducks or flickers.

Similar Birds

NORTHERN SAW-WHET OWL
Smaller; lacks ear tufts; blackish bill; large white spots on upperparts; small white streaking on forehead, crown, and nape.

WESTERN SCREECH-OWL
Gray to brown; dark bill; different voice
• western range.

Flight Pattern

Buoyant flight with silent wing beats.

Nest Identification

Shape   Location

Lined with feathers and debris from food • 10–30 feet above ground in tree • 2–8 white eggs; round oval, 1.4 inches long.

Plumage Sexes similar	Habitat	Migration Nonmigratory	Weight 5.9 ounces

Family STRIGIDAE	Species *Bubo virginianus*	Length 18–25 inches	Wingspan 36–60 inches

GREAT HORNED OWL

The most widespread owl in North America and perhaps the most powerful, this owl often attacks animals much larger and heavier than itself, including domestic cats, skunks, and porcupines. Its color varies regionally from pale arctic birds to dark northwestern ones.

large "horns" on head

yellow eyes

rusty facial disks

white chin and throat

mottled barred brownish gray upperparts

- **SONG** Series of 3–8 bold deep hoots, with the second and third hoots often running together, *Whoo! Whoo-whoo-whoo! Whoo! Whoo!* Often described as "You awake? Me too!" Female's hooting is higher in pitch.
- **BEHAVIOR** Chiefly nocturnal; becomes active at dusk. Sometimes hunts during the day. Takes wide variety of vertebrates; primarily feeds on mammals, but also eats birds, reptiles, and amphibians. Often aggressively defends nest and young to the point of striking humans who venture too close.
- **BREEDING** Monogamous. One of the earliest nesting species, with eggs laid in winter.
- **NESTING** Incubation 28–35 days mostly by female. Young stay in nest 35–45 days. Fed by both sexes. 1 brood per year.
- **POPULATION** Fairly common to common. Widespread.
- **BIRDHOUSES** Accepts artificial nesting platforms.
- **CONSERVATION** Many are killed by hunters and farmers.

Similar Birds

LONG-EARED OWL
Smaller and thinner; ear tufts closer together; vertical streaking, not horizontal barring, on underparts.

GREAT GRAY OWL
Larger; lacks ear tufts; large grayish white facial disks ringed with dark brown concentric circles; brown upperparts barred with dark browns and white; whitish underparts barred and streaked with browns; yellowish bill; long brownish tail barred with dark browns and white.

Flight Pattern
Direct flap-and-glide flight with strong, silent wing beats.

Nest Identification	
Shape	Abandoned nest of larger bird • large cavities, broken-off snags, buildings, ledges • 20–60 feet above ground • 1–5 dull whitish eggs; elliptical, 2.7 inches long.
Location	

Plumage Sexes similar	Habitat	Migration Nonmigratory	Weight 3.0 pounds

DATE _____ TIME _____ LOCATION _____

| Family STRIGIDAE | Species *Nyctea scandiaca* | Length 20–27 inches | Wingspan 54–66 inches |

SNOWY OWL

A heavy-bodied, large-headed owl of open areas, this bird breeds on Arctic tundra and winters on grasslands, marshes, coastal beaches, and dunes. Regional crashes of Arctic lemming populations force these owls far south in some winters. This is our only all-white owl. Females and juveniles are similar, and show more dusky barring than males.

yellow eyes

large head without ear tufts

• **SONG** Piercing whistle and bold, growling bark, *krow-ow*, which can carry for more than a mile. Usually silent outside breeding season.

• **BEHAVIOR** Active in daylight and darkness. Often perches on ground or close to it on posts, rocks, dunes, ice, hay bales, or buildings. Eats primarily small mammals (voles and lemmings on breeding grounds), but takes some birds and fish. Male defends nest and young fearlessly; will give "crippled bird" act to lure predators away from nest.

• **BREEDING** Monogamous.

• **NESTING** Incubation 31–34 days by both sexes or female only. Young stay in nest 14–21 days, fed by both sexes. First flight at 43–57 days. 1 brood per year. Number of eggs depends on food supply; in poor lemming years, pairs may not breed.

more dusky barring

FEMALE

• **POPULATION** Fairly common on breeding grounds; rare to casual south of breeding range. Stable because of remoteness from human disturbance.

• **CONSERVATION** No issues reported, but many birds are killed when wintering south of normal range.

Similar Birds

BARN OWL
White to cinnamon-buff underparts; golden-buff upperparts; heart-shaped face; dark eyes.

Flight Pattern

Direct flap-and-glide flight with strong, deep wing beats.

Nest Identification

Shape — Location —

Simple depression • unlined or minimally lined with moss, lichen, and plucked grass • on raised site with good visibility • built by female • 3–11 whitish eggs that become nest-stained, short elliptical or subelliptical, 2.2 inches long.

| Plumage Sexes differ | Habitat | Migration Irregular | Weight 4.0 pounds |

DATE _____ TIME_____ LOCATION _____

Family STRIGIDAE	Species *Glaucidium brasilianum*	Length 6–7 inches	Wingspan 15 inches

FERRUGINOUS PYGMY-OWL

This very small long-tailed owl inhabits cottonwood riparian, mesquite thicket, and saguaro desert habitats. A bold little predator, it is often noisily mobbed by other birds. Its streaked head lacks ear tufts, and it often can be seen nervously flicking its long barred rufous tail. Like the Northern Pygmy-Owl, two black spots on the nape of its neck resemble a pair of eyes.

yellow eyes

streaked head without ear tufts

reddish brown upperparts

long barred reddish tail

whitish buff underparts with brown streaking

• **SONG** Fluted notes, *puk-puk-puk*; rapid, repeated *took* up to 50–60 times.

• **BEHAVIOR** Diurnal, but often most active at dusk and at dawn (crepuscular). Often roosts in dense cover. Frequently gets mobbed by songbirds, which attracts attention to the little owl. Feeds primarily on large insects and arachnids, also taking some small vertebrates. Male feeds female and young in nest cavity.

• **BREEDING** Monogamous.

• **NESTING** Incubation about 28 days by female. Young remain in nest 27–30 days. Fed by both sexes. 1 brood per year.

• **POPULATION** Uncommon. Endangered or threatened in limited range in US. Widespread in tropics.

• **CONSERVATION** Concern over small populations.

Similar Birds

ELF OWL
Smaller; short tail; no eye spots on nape; faint streaking on underparts; facial disk has black border.

NORTHERN PYGMY-OWL
Brown tail with white barring; heavy blackish brown streaking on underparts • inhabits denser forests at higher elevations; not found in deserts; inhabits montane and foothill woodlands in the West.

Flight Pattern

Rapid direct flight with unmuffled wing beats.

Nest Identification

Shape ◣ 2   Location 🌵 🌳

In tree cavity or cactus; usually in old woodpecker hole • no material added • 10–30 feet above ground • 3–5 white eggs, 1.1 inches long.

Plumage Sexes similar	Habitat ⸬	Migration Nonmigratory	Weight 2.2 ounces

DATE _____ TIME_____ LOCATION _____

Family STRIGIDAE	Species *Micrathene whitneyi*	Length 5–6 inches	Wingspan 15 inches

ELF OWL

At about the size of a chunky sparrow, this is the smallest owl in the world. It can be recognized by its size, small round head, lack of ear tufts, and short tail. This species is perhaps more often heard than seen.

• **SONG** Puppylike chuckling and yips; erratic series of high chirps, and chattering notes. Amazingly loud for such a small owl.

• **BEHAVIOR** Nocturnal; becomes active at dusk. Roosts and nests in woodpecker holes and in natural cavities in trees, saguaro, and utility poles. Feeds primarily on insects, arachnids

no ear tufts

yellow eyes

mottled grayish brown body

white spotting on scapulars

whitish underparts with ocher-brown streaking

short tail

(including scorpions), and some small vertebrates. Catches some insects in flight with its feet.

• **BREEDING** Monogamous.

• **NESTING** Incubation 24 days by female. Young stay in nest 28 days. Fed by both sexes. 1 brood per year.

• **POPULATION** Fairly common to common. Scarce along lower Colorado River and in southern Texas; still abundant in southern Arizona; almost eliminated in California.

• **BIRDHOUSES** Will occasionally roost and nest in man-made boxes.

Similar Birds

FERRUGINOUS PYGMY-OWL NORTHERN PYGMY-OWL Longer tails; black eyespots on nape; heavily streaked underparts; diurnal • Northern Pygmy-Owl inhabits montane and foothill woodlands in the West.

Flight Pattern

Mothlike flight with silent wing beats; sometimes hovers and hawks.

Nest Identification

Shape   Location

In old woodpecker hole in tree, utility pole, or cactus • no lining added • 15–50 feet above ground in sycamores or 10–30 feet above ground in saguaros • 1–5 white eggs, 1.1 inches long.

Plumage Sexes similar	Habitat	Migration Migratory	Weight 1.4 ounces

DATE _____ TIME_____ LOCATION _____

Family STRIGIDAE	Species *Athene cunicularia*	Length 9–11 inches	Wingspan 20–24 inches

BURROWING OWL

This long-legged, short-tailed little owl inhabits grassland and prairies, but in its range it also can be found in similar habitats near humans such as golf courses and airports. In the West the Burrowing Owl often is associated with prairie dog towns, and the historical poisoning of the prairie dogs also brought declines in the owl's populations. The owls use an abandoned burrow for their nest and daytime roost, usually after some additional digging to enlarge and reshape it.

white streaking on head

brown upperparts with white spotting

yellow eyes

white chin and throat

spotted white chest

white to buff underparts with brown barring

long legs

short tail

- **SONG** High melancholy cry, *coo-coo-roo* or *co-hoo;* twittering series of *chack* notes. If disturbed in nest, young give alarm that mimics the buzzing of a rattlesnake.
- **BEHAVIOR** Terrestrial. Primarily nocturnal and crepuscular. Perches on ground, fence posts, utility wires, rocks, or mounds near burrow during day. Inhabits open country where it feeds primarily on large insects, some of which it catches in flight, and small mammals.
- **BREEDING** Monogamous. Often colonial.
- **NESTING** Incubation 21–30 days by female. Semialtricial young remain in nest 28 days, fed by both sexes. Typically 1–2 broods per year.
- **POPULATION** Fairly common to common but local.
- **BIRDHOUSES** Will nest in artificial man-made burrows.
- **CONSERVATION** Endangered or threatened over much of its range. Declining because of prairie dog and ground squirrel poison-control programs and habitat loss. Many killed by automobiles. Some attempts at management being made due to declining local populations.

Similar Birds

SHORT-EARED OWL
Larger; long tail; short legs; buff-brown; heavily streaked upperparts and underparts.

Flight Pattern

Buoyant, sometimes erratic flight, with show silent wing beats; may hover briefly above prey.

Nest Identification

Shape ▨ ▯ Location ▬

Lined with cow manure, horse dung, food debris, dry grass, weeds, pellets, and feathers • built by both sexes, but male does more • 7–10 white nest-stained eggs (4–6 in Florida); round to ovate, 1.2 inches long.

Plumage Sexes similar	Habitat ▬ ▬	Migration Some migrate	Weight 5.3 ounces

DATE _____ TIME_____ LOCATION _____

Family STRIGIDAE	Species *Strix occidentalis*	Length 16–19 inches	Wingspan 45–48 inches

SPOTTED OWL

Although it is the western counterpart of the Barred Owl in shape, size, and habitat preference, this owl lacks the barring and streaking of that species. Its dark brown plumage is heavily spotted with white on the underparts and upperparts. This secretive bird inhabits dense, moist old-growth forests and deeply wooded canyons.

- **SONG** 3–4 barking notes, *Whoo-whoo-hoo-hoo.* Also gives low, hollow, ascending whistle, sounding like *coooo-wee.*
- **BEHAVIOR** Nocturnal and seldom seen. Perches inconspicuously in dense cover during the day. Feeds primarily on small mammals, some birds, and large insects. Hybridizes with Barred Owl, which is becoming more common in its northwestern range.
- **BREEDING** Monogamous.
- **NESTING** Incubation 28–32 days by female. Young stay in nest 34–36 days. Fed by both sexes. 1 brood per year.
- **POPULATION** Rare to uncommon. Listed as endangered in the Pacific Northwest and threatened in the Southwest. Does poorly in second-growth forests.
- **CONSERVATION** Federally protected. Affected by loss of old-growth forest habitat from logging and by hybridization with expanding populations of Barred Owl.

large, puffy head without ear tufts

dark eyes

rich dark brown and liberally spotted white overall

Similar Birds

BARRED OWL
Barred chest and upper breast; streaked underparts.

GREAT GRAY OWL
Larger; grayer; streaked underparts; yellow eyes.

Flight Pattern

Short flights with quick wing strokes; longer flights series of silent strong wing beats followed by short glides.

Nest Identification	
Shape	Simple scrape • hollow in tree, cave, or crevice • on cliff or in tree 30–160 feet above ground • sometimes uses abandoned nests • built by female • 1–4 white eggs with faint tinge of buff; elliptical, 2 inches long.
Location	

Plumage Sexes similar	Habitat	Migration Nonmigratory	Weight 1.3 pounds

DATE _____ TIME_____ LOCATION _____

Family STRIGIDAE	Species *Strix varia*	Length 17–24 inches	Wingspan 50–60 inches

BARRED OWL

The "hoot owl" of southern swamps, this puffy-headed owl can also be found in woodlands. It lacks ear tufts, is stoutly built, and is heavily streaked, spotted, and variegated brown, buff, and white. This is one of only three large owls with dark eyes in North America.

- **SONG** Usually 8 or more drawn-out notes, "*Who cooks for you; who cooks for you-all?*" Call is drawn-out, descending *hoooAwllll*. Group of 2 or more owls make a loud, excited caterwauling. Often heard in daytime. Responds readily to imitations of its call by coming closer and often calling back.
- **BEHAVIOR** Mostly nocturnal and crepuscular but often active in daylight. Prefers deep woods; inhabits conifer, riparian, and swampy habitats. Feeds on wide variety of animals, including small mammals, birds, frogs, salamanders, lizards, snakes, fish, large insects, crabs, and crayfish.
- **BREEDING** Monogamous. Thought to pair for life.
- **NESTING.** Incubation 28–33 days by female. Young stay in nest 42 days. Fed by both sexes. 1 brood per year.
- **POPULATION** Very common to common and widespread. Swamp habitat population in the South has diminished. Range increasing now in the Northwest, where hybridizes with Spotted Owl.

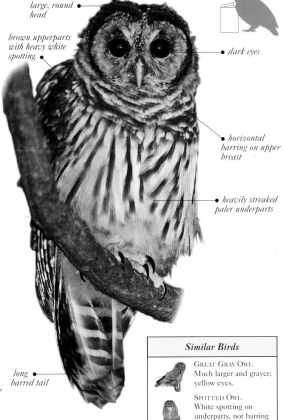

- large, round head
- brown upperparts with heavy white spotting
- dark eyes
- horizontal barring on upper breast
- heavily streaked paler underparts
- long barred tail

Similar Birds

GREAT GRAY OWL
Much larger and grayer; yellow eyes.

SPOTTED OWL
White spotting on underparts, not barring or streaking • western range.

Flight Pattern

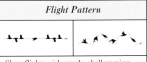

Short flights with steady, shallow wing beats, longer flights on silent rapid wing strokes followed by short glide.

Nest Identification

Shape [icons] Location [icons]

In the East uses abandoned nests • 15–80 feet above ground in tree • 2–3 white eggs, 2 inches long.

Plumage Sexes similar	Habitat [icons]	Migration Nonmigratory	Weight 1.4 pounds

DATE _____ TIME_____ LOCATION _____

Family STRIGIDAE	Species *Strix nebulosa*	Length 24–33 inches	Wingspan 54–60 inches

GREAT GRAY OWL

Although this is the largest North American owl, the Great Horned Owl is heavier. Long-tailed and large-headed, the Great Gray Owl has huge facial disks crossed by a series of dark gray concentric circles that make the yellow eyes seem small. It inhabits deep boreal forests and open muskeg bogs.

• **SONG** A bold, deep, booming *hoo-hoo-hooo*; also utters single-note hoots.

large facial disks with heavy concentric circles

no ear tufts

yellow eyes

white mustache

black chin

heavily streaked underparts

barred, vermiculated, mottled gray plumage

long tail

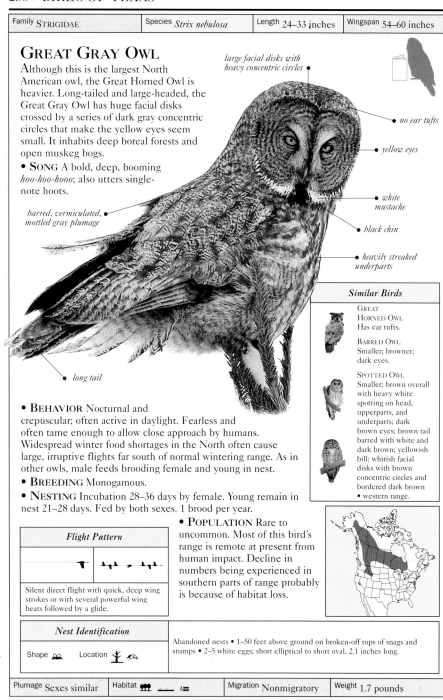

Similar Birds

GREAT HORNED OWL Has ear tufts.

BARRED OWL Smaller; browner; dark eyes.

SPOTTED OWL Smaller; brown overall with heavy white spotting on head, upperparts, and underparts; dark brown eyes; brown tail barred with white and dark brown; yellowish bill; whitish facial disks with brown concentric circles and bordered dark brown • western range.

• **BEHAVIOR** Nocturnal and crepuscular; often active in daylight. Fearless and often tame enough to allow close approach by humans. Widespread winter food shortages in the North often cause large, irruptive flights far south of normal wintering range. As in other owls, male feeds brooding female and young in nest.

• **BREEDING** Monogamous.

• **NESTING** Incubation 28–36 days by female. Young remain in nest 21–28 days. Fed by both sexes. 1 brood per year.

• **POPULATION** Rare to uncommon. Most of this bird's range is remote at present from human impact. Decline in numbers being experienced in southern parts of range probably is because of habitat loss.

Flight Pattern

Silent direct flight with quick, deep wing strokes or with several powerful wing beats followed by a glide.

Nest Identification

Shape ⌣⌣   Location ⚓ 🪶

Abandoned nests • 1–50 feet above ground on broken-off tops of snags and stumps • 2–5 white eggs; short elliptical to short oval, 2.1 inches long.

Plumage Sexes similar	Habitat 🌲 ▬ 〰	Migration Nonmigratory	Weight 1.7 pounds

DATE _____ TIME _____ LOCATION _____

Family STRIGIDAE	Species *Asio otus*	Length 13–16 inches	Wingspan 36–42 inches

LONG-EARED OWL

The most slender and most nocturnal of the large owls is perhaps the most overlooked. It is hard to detect because of its cryptic coloration, shy habits, and the ability to "freeze" against a perch with body flattened. This owl often uses the same winter perch day after day, resulting in a large accumulation of pellets and droppings beneath it; this telltale evidence can be used to locate the roosting owl above. Although the female is larger, both sexes appear similar. Frequents a wide range of habitats, from desert oases to riparian thickets to dense coniferous woodlands.

long close-set blackish ear tufts

yellow eyes

rusty facial disks

mottled brown

mottled buffy-white with heavy vertical streaking

• **SONG** Melodic low hoots, *quoo-quoo-quoo*, and long *hoos*. Sometimes sounds like a barking, whining puppy. Virtually mute outside breeding season.
• **BEHAVIOR** Nocturnal. Roosts perched close to tree trunk in thick cover during day. Hunts over open fields and marshes. Feeds primarily on mouse-size mammals; sometimes takes small birds. Often gregarious on roosts in winter. Accumulated pellet contents below roost can reveal local diet, as the undigested bones, teeth, and exoskeletons of its prey are compacted within them. Chooses abandoned nest of squirrel, crow, hawk, or heron as its own nesting site.
• **BREEDING** Monogamous.

long tail

Similar Birds

 GREAT HORNED OWL Much larger, stouter build; ear tufts farther apart on head; horizontal barring beneath (not vertical streaking).

 SHORT-EARED OWL Buffier below; shorter ear tufts; diurnal.

• **NESTING** Incubation 26–28 days by female. Semialtricial young stay in nest 23–26 days, fed by both sexes. 1 brood per year.
• **POPULATION** Uncommon to locally common; may be more common than suspected.

Flight Pattern

Buoyant silent wing beats. Ear tufts flattened back on head in flight.

Nest Identification

Shape | Location

Typically does not build nest • uses abandoned nests; sometimes tree cavity • suspected of sometimes evicting crow • 4–30 feet above ground in a tree • 2–10 white eggs; elliptical, 1.6 inches long.

Plumage Sexes similar	Habitat	Migration Northern birds migrate	Weight 8.6 ounces

DATE _____ TIME _____ LOCATION _____

Family STRIGIDAE	Species *Asio flammeus*	Length 13–17 inches	Wingspan 38–44 inches

SHORT-EARED OWL

A big-headed, short-necked owl of grasslands and marshes, this bird is often seen quartering low over vegetation during the day. With tawny to buff-brown plumage, it shows large buff wing patches on the upperwing and a dark "wrist" mark on the underwing in flight. The ear tufts are very small and difficult to see unless the bird is perched. It has a streaked buff to whitish belly and white undertail coverts with faint streaking. Its diurnal activities make it frequently visible.

dark facial disks that become paler farther from the center

short ear tufts

yellow to orange eyes

heavily streaked head

tawny to buff-brown overall

heavily streaked upper breast

• **SONG** On breeding grounds this owl gives a loud *eeee-yerp*; a high-pitched grating *waowk, waowk, waowk*, like the barking of a dog; or a *toot-toot-toot-toot-toot*. When on its wintering grounds, the Short-eared Owl usually remains silent.

• **BEHAVIOR** Nocturnal and crepuscular; may hunt in late afternoons or on overcast days. Flies back and forth low over the ground, dropping feet first with wings held high onto prey. May perch on post or shrub to watch for prey. Feeds primarily on small rodents but also takes some small birds of open habitats and large insects. Uses crippled-bird display to lure intruders away from the nest or young on the ground.

• **BREEDING** Monogamous. Sometimes forms small colonies.

• **NESTING** Incubation 24–37 days by female. Semialtricial young stay in nest 21–36 days. Fed by both sexes. Typically 1 brood per year.

• **POPULATION** Fairly common. It has disappeared in parts of its southern range because of habitat loss.

• **CONSERVATION** The main conservation concern for this owl is a degree of habitat loss to agriculture and also loss due to killing by shooting.

Similar Birds

LONG-EARED OWL Smaller buff upperwing and black wrist patches; heavily barred underparts; large ear tufts; nocturnal.

Flight Pattern

Buoyant erratic flight with flopping wing beats.

Nest Identification

Shape ⬤ ⬤ ⬤   Location ⁂ 𝖬

Shallow depression • lined with grass and feathers • on ground • built by female • 3–11 white eggs that become nest-stained; short elliptical, 1.5 inches long.

Plumage Sexes similar	Habitat ___	Migration Some migrate	Weight 11.1 ounces

DATE _____ TIME_____ LOCATION _____

Family STRIGIDAE	Species *Aegolius acadicus*	Length 7–8 inches	Wingspan 17–20 inches

NORTHERN SAW-WHET OWL

brown forehead and crown with liberal white streaking

pale buff to brownish facial disks

whitish eyebrows

white patch between eyes

blackish bill

chestnut-brown upperparts with heavy white and buff spotting

white underparts with reddish brown and dark brown blotches and streaks

unmarked white undertail coverts

The incessant call of the male Northern Saw-whet Owl during breeding season sounds like a saw being sharpened or whetted. Some winters numbers of this little owl are found well south of the normal breeding range. This species is one of the smallest owls. Note the lack of ear tufts, dark bill, and white eyebrows. Females are larger than males. Juveniles have tawny-cinnamon underparts, chocolate-brown upperparts with white spotting, and a bold white Y from beak to eyebrows.

• **SONG** Repeated 1-note whistle of *too, too, too, too, too* or *sch-whet, sch-whet,* sometimes for hours at a time. Sings during breeding season only; singing decreases after mate is attracted. Voice may carry 0.5 mile or more.

• **BEHAVIOR** Solitary or in pairs. Eats small rodents, large insects, birds, and bats. Hunts primarily at night. Perches low, searching for prey, then flies down and snatches it with talons. Territorial birds often respond to imitations of their call by speeding up the rate of their calling; often attracted to playbacks of their call.

• **BREEDING** Monogamous. Solitary.

• **NESTING** Incubation 26–29 days by female. Semialtricial young stay in nest 27–34 days. Fed by both sexes: Male brings food, then female feeds young for about first 18 days. 1 brood per year.

• **POPULATION** Fairly common. Declining.

JUVENILE

Similar Birds

BOREAL OWL
Larger; white face with blackish border; darker brown head with contrasting white spots; pale bill.

• **BIRDHOUSES** Uses nest boxes about the size of Wood Duck boxes.

• **CONSERVATION** Declining in parts of range due to habitat loss from logging, air pollution, and adelgid tree kills in high peaks of southern Appalachians.

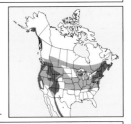

Flight Pattern
Silent buoyant direct flight with fluttering wing beats.

Nest Identification	
Shape	Location

No nest materials • in tree cavity, abandoned woodpecker hole, or nesting box, 14–60 feet above ground • 4–7 white eggs; oval to ovate, 1.2 inches long.

Plumage Sexes similar	Habitat	Migration Most do not migrate	Weight 2.6 ounces

DATE _____ TIME _____ LOCATION _____

Family CAPRIMULGIDAE	Species *Chordeiles acutipennis*	Length 8–9 inches	Wingspan 20–23 inches

LESSER NIGHTHAWK

Although it has a similar appearance to its larger cousin, the Common Nighthawk, this bird generally has a much lower flight and the male does not power dive during its mating display. The white primary bar, which is buffy on females, is slightly nearer the tip of the shorter rounder wing. The male also has a white tail band and buffy underparts with light barring. The female has a buffy throat. This cryptically colored bird of western arid and semiarid lowlands becomes torpid in cold weather when food is lacking. Juveniles are similar to females.

pale supercilium

pale gray, black, buff, and cinnamon pattern on crown, nape, and upperparts

white throat

rounded wing tips

white bar across primaries

long barred slightly notched tail

• **SONG** On breeding grounds the Lesser Nighthawk utters a quick low *chuck chuck*. It also has a soft froglike trill. In fact, one former name of this bird is the Trilling Nighthawk.

• **BEHAVIOR** This is a crepuscular and nocturnal bird. Insectivorous, it forages for food by flying near to the ground, catching insects in the air. Feeds late into the morning, unlike most other nighthawks. It is attracted to bright outdoor lights for feeding on flying insects. Wanders wildly for food; not territorial. Males perform an aerial courtship display.

• **BREEDING** Monogamous. Loosely colonial.

• **NESTING** Incubation 18–19 days, mostly or entirely by female. Young semiprecocial; first flight at 21 days, fed by both sexes. 1 brood per year.

• **POPULATION** The Lesser Nighthawk is fairly common in its habitat. While it is rare in migration on the Gulf Coast, it is casual in winter in Florida, Texas, and California.

Similar Birds

COMMON NIGHTHAWK
Longer, more pointed wings; longer tail; white band on primaries; darker overall; voice differs; power dives.

COMMON PAURAQUE
Long rounded tail; shorter rounder wings.

Flight Pattern

Darting flight with quick and erratic wing beats; often changing direction; buoyant.

Nest Identification	
Shape ♣ Location ▬ ▨ 🐾	No nest • on bare ground, atop sand or pile of pebbles, occasionally on flat gravel roofs • 2 white to pale gray eggs with small gray, brown, and lavender dots; oval to elliptical oval, 1.1 x 0.8 inches.

Plumage Sexes similar	Habitat 🌿 🌿 ⚥ ✈ ▬	Migration Migratory	Weight 1.8 ounces

DATE _____ TIME_____ LOCATION _____

Family CAPRIMULGIDAE	Species *Chordeiles minor*	Length 8–10 inches	Wingspan 21–24 inches

COMMON NIGHTHAWK

Like all members of the nightjar family, the adult bird flutters its gular pouch during intense heat to cool itself. The eggs and nestlings are sometimes carried to another location if temperatures become extreme. The female is similar to the male, but has a buffy, rather than white, throat and lacks the white tail band. Juveniles also lack this tail band. Note the long pointed wings with the white bar through the primaries, and the mothlike flight of the "bullbat," which is the colloquial name used for this nighthawk in the South. Although predominantly grayish brown overall, there is much color variation over the large North American range.

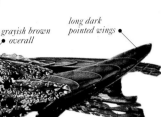

grayish brown overall

long dark pointed wings

white throat

notched tail with thick white band

distinctive white bar across primaries

- **SONG** Has raspy nasal somewhat froglike call of *peeant* or *beant*.
- **BEHAVIOR** Solitary or in small groups. Sometimes migrates in large flocks in fall. Crepuscular and nocturnal, but often feeds day or night, catching insects in flight. Eats a wide range of flying insects. Attracted to street lights and other outdoor lights at night to scoop up swarming insects. Bird species seen by many because of its habit of feeding over towns and cities. Skims over lakes and streams to drink water from surface.
- **BREEDING** Monogamous. Solitary. Male displays with a courtship power-dive, at the end of which the air rushes through his wings, making a loud *sw-r-r-r-oonk* sound like a rubber band or banjo string being plucked.
- **NESTING** Incubation 19–20 days, mostly by female. Young semiprecocial; first flight at 21 days, fed by both sexes. 1–2 broods per year.
- **POPULATION** Common but declining in parts of continent.
- **CONSERVATION** Neotropical migrant. Became common in towns and cities with the introduction of flat graveled roofs in mid-1800s as well as increased use of outside lighting, which attracts insects.

Similar Birds

LESSER NIGHTHAWK Shorter, more rounded wings; whitish bar across primaries slightly closer to tip; paler upperparts with more uniform mottling; generally flies closer to ground; does not power-dive; voice differs.

ANTILLEAN NIGHTHAWK Smaller; shorter wings; more fluttery flight; much more buffy overall; voice differs. • rare in eastern range.

Flight Pattern

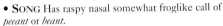

Darting flight on long pointed wings with erratic twists and turns and changes of direction. Wing beats slow and steady.

Nest Identification	
Shape	Lays eggs on rocks, small pebbles, abandoned fields, stumps, fence rails, and even on tarred or graveled roofs; 0–8 feet above ground • female chooses site • 2 creamy white to pale olive-buff eggs, with brown and gray speckles; oval to elliptical oval, 1.2 x 0.9 inches.
Location 	

Plumage Sexes similar	Habitat	Migration Migratory	Weight 2.2 ounces

DATE _____ TIME_____ LOCATION _____

| Family CAPRIMULGIDAE | Species *Nyctidromus albicollis* | Length 10–11 inches | Wingspan 21–23 inches |

COMMON PAURAQUE

A primarily tropical nightjar that reaches the northern limit of its range in south Texas, the Common Pauaque is very busy at night when it can be heard singing for hours. The name "pauraque" is an imitation of the Spanish rendering of its call. It flies low to the ground and sometimes feeds for insects in the beams of automobile headlights. In flight, note the white bar crossing the primaries and the

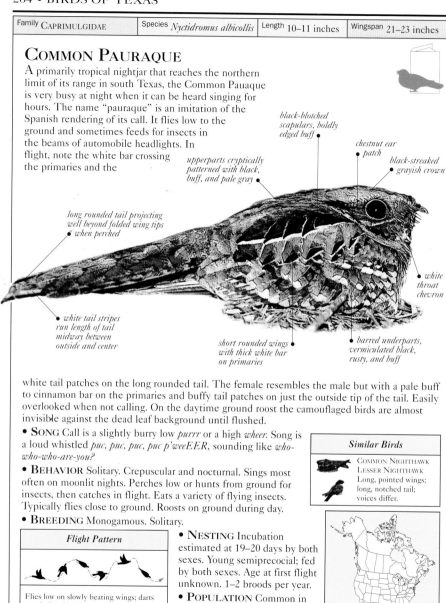

black-blotched scapulars, boldly edged buff

chestnut ear patch

black-streaked grayish crown

upperparts cryptically patterned with black, buff, and pale gray

long rounded tail projecting well beyond folded wing tips when perched

white throat chevron

white tail stripes run length of tail midway between outside and center

short rounded wings with thick white bar on primaries

barred underparts, vermiculated black, rusty, and buff

white tail patches on the long rounded tail. The female resembles the male but with a pale buff to cinnamon bar on the primaries and buffy tail patches on just the outside tip of the tail. Easily overlooked when not calling. On the daytime ground roost the camouflaged birds are almost invisible against the dead leaf background until flushed.

- **SONG** Call is a slightly burry low *purr* or a high *wheer*. Song is a loud whistled *puc, puc, puc, puc p'weeEER*, sounding like *who-who-who-are-you?*
- **BEHAVIOR** Solitary. Crepuscular and nocturnal. Sings most often on moonlit nights. Perches low or hunts from ground for insects, then catches in flight. Eats a variety of flying insects. Typically flies close to ground. Roosts on ground during day.
- **BREEDING** Monogamous. Solitary.

Similar Birds

COMMON NIGHTHAWK
LESSER NIGHTHAWK
Long, pointed wings;
long, notched tail;
voices differ.

Flight Pattern

Flies low on slowly beating wings; darts erratically, changing courses; buoyant.

- **NESTING** Incubation estimated at 19–20 days by both sexes. Young semiprecocial; fed by both sexes. Age at first flight unknown. 1–2 broods per year.
- **POPULATION** Common in south Texas and the tropics.

Nest Identification

Shape ♣   Location ▬ ✶✶✶

No nesting materials • on bare ground • 2 buff to pale pink eggs, marked with fine reddish brown dots; elliptical-oval, 1.2 inches long.

| Plumage Sexes similar | Habitat 🌳🌳 🏞 🏔 ⤳ | Migration Nonmigratory | Weight 1.8 ounces |

DATE _____   TIME_____   LOCATION _____

Family CAPRIMULGIDAE	Species *Phalaenoptilus nuttallii*	Length 7–8 inches	Wingspan 11–13 inches

COMMON POORWILL

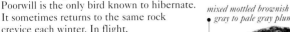

The smallest of the North American nightjars, this bird is the western counterpart of the eastern Whip-poor-will. It primarily feeds at night. Though all but its southernmost population migrates, the Common Poorwill is the only bird known to hibernate. It sometimes returns to the same rock crevice each winter. In flight, note its small size, short, rounded wings that

mixed mottled brownish gray to pale gray plumage

black throat and sides of face

broad white band over throat and dark breast

white-tipped black outer tail feathers

lack white patches, and the rounded tail with white tail corners. Male and female are similar, but the male has a larger bolder patch on its tail. This bird is more often heard than seen.

grayish underparts mottled dark gray and black

- **SONG** Has cry of *poor-will* or *poor-willy* or *poor-willow*, repeated 30–40 times per minute.
- **BEHAVIOR** Solitary. Nocturnal. During day, roosts hidden on ground in shrubs and grasses. Flies close to the ground at night searching for food or sits on ground watching for prey. Eats night-flying moths and other insects. Birds have been found in a state of hibernation during extremely cold weather.
- **BREEDING** Monogamous. Solitary.

Similar Birds

WHIP-POOR-WILL
Locally in Southwest
- larger longer tail with large white corners (male) or buffy tips (female); voice differs.

- **NESTING** Incubation 20–21 days by both sexes. Young semiprecocial; fed by both sexes; first flight at 20–23 days. 1–2 broods per year.
- **POPULATION** Fairly common; widespread, stable.

Flight Pattern

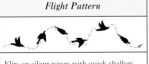

Flits on silent wings with quick shallow wing beats.

Nest Identification

Shape ♣ ⚬ Location ▬ ▨

On bare soil, pebbles, or atop small pile of leaves, usually shaded by bush or grasses • 2 white to pinkish white eggs, sometimes spotted or mottled with violet; oval to elliptical oval, 1.0 x 0.8 inches.

Plumage Sexes similar	Habitat ⤴ ⚊ ⚊ ▲	Migration Migratory	Weight 1.8 ounces

DATE _____ TIME_____ LOCATION _____

Family CAPRIMULGIDAE	Species *Caprimulgus carolinensis*	Length 11–13 inches	Wingspan 24.5–25.5 inches

CHUCK-WILL'S-WIDOW

True to its name, this bird can be heard singing *chuck-will's-widow* continuously in the early evening on a summer's night in the rural South. The largest North American nightjar is shy and will often flush at the slightest disturbance, fluttering away on silent wings like a huge brown moth. The female is similar to the male but has tan feathers on her throat and in her tail corners.

long grayish superctlium

- **SONG** A bold *chuck-will's-WID-ow* in 4 parts, with the *chuck* low-pitched (sometimes inaudible at a distance) and the other 3 notes clearly whistled, with emphasis on the *wid*. While hunting, may give low growl or croak in flight.

rounded wings

brownish red throat with white half-collar

long rounded tail

tawny buff-brown mottling overall

buff-tipped outer tail feathers have white inner webs

some whitish feathers form bar on tips of lesser wing coverts

- **BEHAVIOR** Solitary. Nocturnal feeder. While in flight, catches numerous insects at a time with its cavernous mouth, which has a 2-inch gap and rictal bristles in its corners to aid in trapping prey. Eats mainly insects and an occasional small bird, which it swallows whole. Roosts like other nightjars, perched parallel to the limb or on the ground, where its cryptic plumage makes it all but impossible to see unless it moves. Roosts on the same perch daily.
- **BREEDING** Monogamous. Solitary nester.
- **NESTING** Incubation 20–24 days by female, who will move eggs if nest is disturbed. Semiprecocial young brooded by female; remain in nest approximately 17 days, fed by female. Female tends young until independent. 1 brood per year.
- **POPULATION** Fairly common in pine-oak and live-oak woodlands, as well as in deciduous forests.
- **CONSERVATION** Neotropical migrant. May be declining due to habitat loss from lack of proper forest management.

Similar Birds

WHIP-POOR-WILL
Smaller; grayer; rufous bar on shoulder; voice differs • male has more white in tail and white crescent at lower edge of black throat • female has dark brown throat, buffy necklace, and pale buff tips to outer tail feathers.

Flight Pattern

Easy buoyant silent flight with flicking wing beats.

Nest Identification

Shape ♣ Location ▬

No nest materials • on ground atop dried leaves, shaded by dense trees or ground cover • 2 shiny pinkish cream or buff eggs, with brown, lavender, or gray markings; oval to elliptical, 1.4 x 1.0 inches.

Plumage Sexes similar	Habitat 🌿 🌾	Migration Migratory	Weight 4.2 ounces

DATE _____ TIME_____ LOCATION _____

Family CAPRIMULGIDAE	Species *Caprimulgus vociferus*	Length 9–10 inches	Wingspan 16–19.5 inches

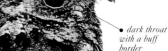

WHIP-POOR-WILL

The Whip-poor-will is best located and identified by its distinctive calls. It is nearly impossible to see because it tends to sit on the ground or lengthwise on a branch, and its pattern closely matches the leaf litter of the wood lots it frequents. "Whips" have rounded wings that when folded do not reach to the tip of the tail. Males are similar to females but the throat is bordered with white and the tail has large white patches.

white necklace

large eyes

• **SONG** A loud, clear *whip-poor-will* often repeated at night in eastern birds; call is more coarse among southwestern birds.

dark throat with a buff border

long tail with buff tips

FEMALE

• **BEHAVIOR** Incubating or perched birds often allow a close approach. They fly close to the ground at night and catch large flying insects, especially medium to large moths. Their large eyes, like those of other creatures active at night, reflect light with a red eye-shine. In rural areas, birds often sit along dirt or gravel roads in the open at night.
• **BREEDING** Monogamous.
• **NESTING** Incubation 19–20 days by female. Semiprecocial young stay in nest 20 days. Fed by both sexes. 1–2 broods per year.

• **POPULATION** Uncommon. Has declined in the East in recent decades because of habitat loss caused by forest fragmentation and development.
• **CONSERVATION** Species federally protected.

Similar Birds

CHUCK-WILL'S WIDOW
Lacks wing bars and black wing and tail
• breeds throughout much of North, Southwest.

COMMON NIGHTHAWK
Yellow undertail coverts
• ranges in Northwest, Rockies, and much of the Southwest.

Flight Pattern

Erratic mothlike flight. Male hovers during display, with slow smooth flight.

Nest Identification	
Shape ♣ Location ▬	Eggs laid on flat ground on leaf litter • 2 whitish eggs marked with brown and gray overlaid with brown, olive, and lavender; 1.2 inches long.

Plumage Sexes similar	Habitat	Migration Most migrate	Weight 2.0 ounces

DATE _____ TIME_____ LOCATION _____

Family APODIDAE	Species *Streptoprocne zonaris*	Length 8.75 inches	Wingspan 19–21 inches

WHITE-COLLARED SWIFT

This strong fast-flying bird soars in flocks over long distances, frequently feeding high in the sky with other swifts on swarms of insects just in front of rainstorms. A tropical species native to Central and South America, vagrants have visited North America in Texas, Florida, Michigan and California. The White-collared Swift is a very large swift with a white collar band that encircles the neck and a slightly notched tail that appears round or square when fully spread. Legs and feet are black. It soars with wings arched downward (the anhedral position). Juveniles are duller and sootier overall, with a much reduced or absent collar, grayish-edged belly feathers, and a reduced tail notch.

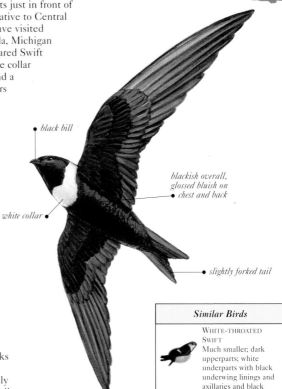

black bill

blackish overall, glossed bluish on chest and back

white collar

slightly forked tail

• **SONG** Loud screeching *chee-chee-chee.* Also much chattering. Often heard high overhead before it is seen.

• **BEHAVIOR** Gregarious. Catches food in flight; often high in the air column. Eats flying insects including ants, beetles, wasps, and bees. When foraging it circles and dives, seeming to barely flap wings. Roosts and nests in flocks of 50 or more, in caves or wet crevices in mountains, especially near waterfalls. Ranges many miles daily to feed, returning to roost at dusk.

• **BREEDING** Monogamous. Colonial.

Similar Birds

WHITE-THROATED SWIFT Much smaller; dark upperparts; white underparts with black underwing linings and axillaries and black patch extending onto sides; long forked tail.

• **NESTING** Incubation 16–28 days by both sexes (periods of cold weather prolong incubation). Altricial young stay in nest 45–60 days, fed by both sexes. 1 brood per year.

• **POPULATION** Accidental in North America.

Flight Pattern

Strong fast powerful flight. Alternates rapid shallow wing beats with long glides. Soars on thermals and updrafts.

Nest Identification

Shape ⌒ Location 🏠 ▬

Mud, moss, and insect exoskeletons • in caves, on cliff ledges behind waterfalls, rarely on an exposed cliff ledge • built by both sexes • 2 white eggs, may be nest-stained; oval to cylindrical, 1.3 inches long.

Plumage Sexes similar	Habitat 🌊 ⛰ 🏘 🏕 🏕	Migration Nonmigratory	Weight 3.5 ounces

DATE _____ TIME_____ LOCATION _____

Family APODIDAE	Species *Chaetura pelagica*	Length 5.5 inches	Wingspan 12–12.75 inches

CHIMNEY SWIFT

Often referred to as "a cigar with wings" because of its flight silhouette, this is the only swift normally found in eastern North America. Named for its habit of building nests inside chimneys or air shafts, it uses its gluelike saliva to attach its nest to the brick or concrete and to bind together the individual sticks. Adult birds feed their young until they are old enough to fly out of the chimney. In fall migration, hundreds may swirl above a large chimney at dusk before dropping into it to roost for the night. This bird has become so adapted to life in man-made structures that it now is a common summer species sweeping the skies over our towns, cities, and suburbs.

blackish gray bill

sooty gray overall

blackish gray legs and feet

short cigar-shaped body

long narrow curved wings

• **SONG** Bold chattering; rapid twittering calls cascade down from above.

• **BEHAVIOR** Gregarious. Eats flying insects and ballooning spiders in the air column. Catches food while flying. Roosted and nested in hollow trees before Europeans settled North America; now uses chimneys and air shafts. Almost always seen on the wing. Aerial courtship and mating with courtship V-ing display – pairs flying with wings held in extreme dihedral V above their backs.

• **BREEDING** Monogamous. Solitary or colonial. Sometimes with helpers at the nest.

• **NESTING** Incubation 19–21 days by both sexes, sometimes with the aid of helpers. Young altricial; stay in nest 30 days, fed by both sexes, but female feeds more. 1 brood per year.

• **POPULATION** Fairly common to common in range. Has increased dramatically with the abundance of artificial nesting sites created by European settlement of North America. Rare in southern California.

• **CONSERVATION** Neotropical migrant that winters in South America's Amazon Basin.

Similar Birds

VAUX'S SWIFT Smaller; shorter wings; paler underparts and rump; voice differs; soars less frequently.

Flight Pattern

Rapid batlike flight on stiff swept-back wings alternates with long sweeping glides. Darts erratically. Soars on thermal drafts.

Nest Identification	
Shape ⬖ Location 🏭 ⚲ 🧱 🕳🐟	Half saucer of sticks and saliva • hollow interior of tree, chimney, air shaft, vertical pipe, silo, barn, open well or cistern, fruit cellar, or side of building • nest built by both sexes • 2–7 white eggs, may be nest stained; long oval to cylindrical, 0.8 x 0.5 inches.

Plumage Sexes similar	Habitat 🌿🌲 🌾 〰	Migration Migratory	Weight 0.8 ounce

DATE _____ TIME_____ LOCATION _____

Family TROCHILIDAE	Species *Colibri thalassinus*	Length 4 inches	Wingspan 5–6 inches

GREEN VIOLET-EAR

This large dark hummingbird with shiny dark green upperparts and bluish green underparts is often noisy and first attracts attention when it is perched and giving its loud *chi-it, chi-I-it* notes. It vocalizes frequently and sometimes persistently. Generally associated with mountain forests, forest clearings, and the forest edge, it is common from Central Mexico southward into northern South America. However, vagrant individuals may show up almost anywhere, and there are numerous records from the eastern US and as far north as Alberta and Ontario, Canada. The blue-violet ear patch and large spot on the chest are difficult to see in some light, and often the dark green of the body appears black in shadow or strong backlighting. The broad dark blue tail is often fanned when the bird is hovering, revealing a wide subterminal black band. Females and juveniles are similar to males but appear more faded in color.

slightly decurved black bill

dark metallic green body

blue-violet ear patch

blue-violet patch on breast

bluish green underparts

squared blue-green tail with dark subterminal band

- **SONG** Repeated, loud *tsip-tsip*. Jerky, dry rattle, *t'-iiiissk, t'-iiiissk, t'-iiiissk.*
- **BEHAVIOR** Solitary. Feeds high to low in vegetation on nectar and insects. Often aggressive toward other hummers at feeding areas. Perches inside shrub or tree on exposed bare twigs and often calls from perch.
- **BREEDING** Solitary.
- **NESTING** Incubation 14–18 days by female. Altricial young fledge at about 18–23 days. 1–2 broods per year.
- **POPULATION** Accidental to casual in US; fairly common to common in native Mexico.
- **FEEDERS** Attracted to feeders with sugar water.

Similar Birds

BLUE-THROATED HUMMINGBIRD ♂
Larger; blue throat; white tips on tail feathers; 2 white lines on face.

Flight Pattern

Direct and hovering flight with very rapid wing beats.

Nest Identification

Shape ●   Location

Down, dry grass blades, and mosses; bound with cobwebs • decorated with bits of moss and lichen • on drooping twig or rootlet at forest edge, streamside, or on overhanging road bank • built by female • 2 white eggs; elliptical with one end more pointed, 0.5 x 0.33 inches.

Plumage Sexes similar	Habitat 🌳 🌿 🍃 🌾	Migration Nonmigratory	Weight 0.2 ounce

DATE _____ TIME_____ LOCATION _____

Family TROCHILIDAE	Species *Cynanthus latirostris*	Length 3–4 inches	Wingspan 5–6 inches

BROAD-BILLED HUMMINGBIRD

The Broad-billed Hummingbird frequents dry scrubby vegetation in the semidesert, low foothills, and canyons of the Southwest. The male's tail is blue-black and deeply forked, while that of the female is square-tipped to slightly forked with white-tipped outer tail feathers.

- **SONG** Chattering *je-dit* call is very similar to that of the Ruby-crowned Kinglet. In courtship male utters whining *zing.*
- **BEHAVIOR** Persistently wags and spreads tail when feeding. Feeds on nectar and insects taken high to low in vegetation. Often very aggressive at feeding stations toward other hummers, which it actively drives away with frequent power dives toward interlopers. Like other hummingbirds it is attracted to red and will often come seemingly from nowhere to inspect a person's red garments or red patterns and patches on clothing. Likewise, the red taillights and red reflectors on vehicles parked in its territory are also inspected as possible nectar sources.
- **BREEDING** Solitary.
- **NESTING** Incubation about 2 weeks by female. Altricial young stay near nest for 15–20 days. Often 2 broods per year.
- **POPULATION** Common to fairly common in southeast Arizona, southwest New Mexico, and southwest Texas; rare to casual elsewhere; casual in winter. Sometimes very common in limited US range and parts of Mexico. No evidence of decline in number.
- **FEEDERS** Attracted to feeders with sugar water.

red bill with black tip

glittery green upperparts

glittery blue throat

MALE

dark green underparts

white undertail coverts

forked blue-black tail

upperparts more washed out than male

FEMALE

thin white postocular stripe

gray throat

gray underparts

square to slightly notched dark tail with white-tipped outer tail feathers

Similar Birds

♂ WHITE-EARED HUMMINGBIRD Broad white postocular stripe • female has streaked throat. ♀

Flight Pattern
Direct and hovering flight with very rapid wing beats.

Nest Identification	
Shape  Location	Grasses • lined with plant down, parts of leaves, and bark; no lichen on outer nest • on branch of small tree, stalk of vine, or shrub, usually 3–9 feet above ground • built by female • 2 white eggs; elliptical, 0.5 x 0.3 inches.

Plumage Sexes differ	Habitat	Migration Migratory	Weight 0.1 ounce

DATE _____ TIME_____ LOCATION _____

| Family TROCHILIDAE | Species *Amazilia yucatanensis* | Length 4–5 inches | Wingspan 5.5 inches |

BUFF-BELLIED HUMMINGBIRD

Generally the only greenish hummingbird with buff underparts seen in the United States, this bird often visits gardens and feeders in southeast Texas, where it resides all year. The Buff-bellied is the largest hummingbird normally seen in the East and the only one with a red bill. The bill is slightly decurved, and the adult male's is red with a black tip, while the adult female has a black-tipped bill with a blackish upper mandible and a reddish lower one. In flight the rufous base and sides of the tail are often very noticeable.

- **SONG** High-pitched repeated *siik;* also gives hard *chip.*
- **BEHAVIOR** Feeds primarily on nectar but takes some insects. Inhabits open woodlands, shrub-scrub areas, and citrus groves.
- **BREEDING** Solitary.
- **NESTING** Incubation about 14 days by female. Fed by female only. Young fledge at 18–22 days. Possibly 2 broods per year.
- **POPULATION** Common to fairly common in southeast Texas; rare to casual elsewhere in the Southeast. US breeding population confined to year-round residents in Texas.

black-tipped bill has blackish upper and reddish lower mandible

green head

green throat and upper breast

bronzy green upperparts

cinnamon-buff lower breast and belly

FEMALE

cinnamon-buff undertail coverts

bronzy chestnut tail

Similar Birds

♂ RUFOUS HUMMINGBIRD Vagrant in winter range • straight black bill; lacks green head and breast. ♀

Flight Pattern
Direct and hovering flight with very rapid wing beats.

Decline in US in first half of 20th century due to conversion of habitat to agriculture.
- **FEEDERS** Attracted to feeders with sugar water.
- **CONSERVATION** Current population seems stable.

Nest Identification	Plant fibers, fine stems, shreds of bark, and spiderwebs • lined with plant down; outside covered with lichens and flower petals • in large shrub or small tree, saddled on horizontal or drooping branch • built by female • 2 white eggs.
Shape Location	

| Plumage Sexes similar | Habitat | Migration Nonmigratory | Weight 0.1 ounce |

DATE _____ TIME _____ LOCATION _____

Family TROCHILIDAE	Species *Lampornis clemenciae*	Length 5–5.5 inches	Wingspan 7 inches

BLUE-THROATED HUMMINGBIRD

One of the largest and most impressive hummingbirds in the southern United States is found in wooded canyons and mountains, especially along streams in southeastern Arizona, southwestern New Mexico, and western Texas. When hovering, it often fans its long, squared blue-black tail, which has large white tips.

- **SONG** Male's call is bold, high-pitched, repetitive *seep* given while perched at mid-level in trees or in flight. This loud, monotonous squeak is often the first evidence of the bird's presence.

- **BEHAVIOR** Dominant at feeders and feeding areas; easily drives away other hummingbirds. Is quick to investigate feeders; often they can be attracted to a campsite within hours by hanging red feeders. Also investigates anything red in the campsite or on hikers, including clothing, gear, and reflectors on vehicles. Feeds on nectar and insects at low to mid-level in vegetation.

- **BREEDING** Solitary.

- **NESTING** Incubation 17–18 days by female. Young stay in nest 24–29 days. Up to 3 broods per year.

- **POPULATION** Very restricted range in southwestern US; most birds found in Mexico. Fairly common in summer; rare to casual in winter. Accidental in southeastern US.

- **FEEDERS** Sugar water.

- **CONSERVATION** Vulnerable to loss of habitat in Mexican range.

white mustache border
white postocular stripe
black ear patch
long, slightly decurved black bill
blue throat
blue-gray underparts
greenish upperparts

MALE

long, squared, white-tipped blue-black tail

FEMALE

gray underparts
gray throat

Similar Birds

MAGNIFICENT HUMMINGBIRD
♂ Black body; notched tail lacks white-tipped feathers; glittering green throat; lacks ♀ white lines on face.

Flight Pattern

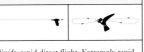

Swift, rapid direct flight. Extremely rapid wing beats when hovering.

Nest Identification

Shape

Location

Plant down and moss; bound by spider's silk with outer covering of moss • on stems of flowering plants and ferns; along streams; under eaves of houses, bridges, water towers; and inside buildings • 1–30 feet above ground; often sheltered from above • built by female • 2 white eggs.

Plumage Sexes differ	Habitat	Migration Some migrate	Weight 0.3 ounce

DATE _____ TIME_____ LOCATION _____

Family TROCHILIDAE	Species *Eugenes fulgens*	Length 4.5–5.25 inches	Wingspan 7 inches

MAGNIFICENT HUMMINGBIRD

Large for a hummingbird, it appears all black at a distance, but when the male turns in sunlight the crown flashes deep purple and the chin and throat glitter green. The bill is long and black, and the male's dark green tail is deeply forked. It is often found in deciduous woods along streams or on pine-oak mountain slopes.

• **SONG** Main call is grating *tcheep*. Also has squeaky scratchy twittering song.

• **BEHAVIOR** Aggressively defends feeding areas. Feeds on nectar, insects, and spiders. Hawks insects in flight and gleans them from foliage. Often sits on exposed, rather high perches. Attracted to the color red.

• **BREEDING** Solitary.

• **NESTING** Incubation about 16 days by female. Fed by female. Young fledge at 20–24 days. Probably 1 brood per year.

• **POPULATION** Common to fairly common in southwest Texas, southwest New Mexico, and southeast Arizona in summer; rare to casual elsewhere. Stable in restricted US range. Some declines in Mexico due to habitat loss.

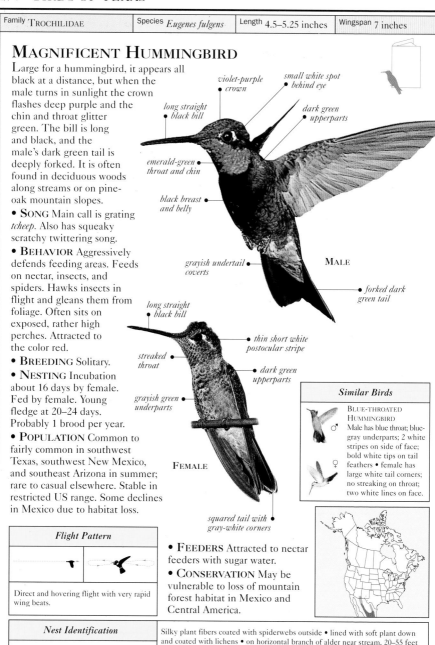

violet-purple crown

small white spot behind eye

long straight black bill

dark green upperparts

emerald-green throat and chin

black breast and belly

grayish undertail coverts

MALE

forked dark green tail

long straight black bill

thin short white postocular stripe

streaked throat

dark green upperparts

grayish green underparts

FEMALE

squared tail with gray-white corners

Similar Birds

BLUE-THROATED HUMMINGBIRD
♂ Male has blue throat; blue-gray underparts; 2 white stripes on side of face; bold white tips on tail feathers • female has large white tail corners; no streaking on throat; two white lines on face.

• **FEEDERS** Attracted to nectar feeders with sugar water.

• **CONSERVATION** May be vulnerable to loss of mountain forest habitat in Mexico and Central America.

Flight Pattern

Direct and hovering flight with very rapid wing beats.

Nest Identification

Shape ♥ Location 🐝 🪹

Silky plant fibers coated with spiderwebs outside • lined with soft plant down and coated with lichens • on horizontal branch of alder near stream, 20–55 feet above ground • also in walnut, pine, maple, and sycamore trees, 10–60 feet high • built by female • 2 white eggs.

Plumage Sexes differ	Habitat ▲ ⚊ 🌾	Migration Some migrate	Weight 0.3 ounce

DATE _____ TIME _____ LOCATION _____

Family TROCHILIDAE	Species *Calothorax lucifer*	Length 3–4 inches	Wingspan 4–5 inches

LUCIFER HUMMINGBIRD

The only small hummingbird in the West with a long strongly decurved bill, the Lucifer Hummingbird frequents arid slopes with agave and yucca, where it is often attracted to the blooming flowers. Adult birds have greenish upperparts and a buff wash on the sides. Male birds have a brilliant violet-purple to violet-red throat and a long deeply forked tail that looks spikelike when closed.

- **SONG** Can be heard emitting high squeaky and twittering *chip* sounds.
- **BEHAVIOR** This hummingbird feeds primarily on nectar but also takes insects and spiders. It often feeds at fairly low levels. It is very aggressive at feeding stations. In the presence of a female the male displays with a buzzing flight that has a wide pendulum motion.
- **BREEDING** Promiscuous. Solitary.
- **NESTING** Incubation 15 days by female. Altricial young stay in nest 19–24 days. Up to 2 broods per year.
- **POPULATION** The breeding population of the Lucifer Hummingbird barely reaches the western US, where the birds are fairly common in the Big Bend area of Texas. It is rare to casual in scrublands, arid slopes, and canyons in southwest New Mexico and southeast Arizona. Accidental elsewhere. Winters in Mexico.
- **FEEDERS** Attracted to feeders with sugar water.

glistening green crown

white postocular stripe

glistening green upperparts

decurved black bill

violet-purple throat

white underparts

MALE

deeply forked greenish tail

decurved black bill

greenish crown

white chin and throat

greenish upperparts

FEMALE

buff wash on sides and flanks

white underparts

rufous tail feathers at base

rounded tail with white-tipped feathers

Similar Birds

BLACK-CHINNED HUMMINGBIRD ♂
Purple throat; black face; no white postocular stripe; straight black bill; short notched tail.

COSTA'S HUMMINGBIRD ♂
Purple crown, head, and throat; straight bill; short rounded tail • western range.

Flight Pattern
Direct and hovering flight with very rapid wing beats.

Nest Identification	
Shape 🥣 Location 🪹	Plant fibers, flowers, lichen, and seeds held together with spider's silk • in shrubs 4–6 feet above ground; sometimes in open cholla cactus, on stem of ocotillo, or on agave stalk 2–10 feet above ground • built by female • 2 white eggs.

Plumage Sexes differ	Habitat	Migration Migratory	Weight 0.1 ounce

DATE _____ TIME_____ LOCATION _____

Family TROCHILIDAE	Species *Archilochus colubris*	Length 3–3.75 inches	Wingspan 4.25–4.5 inches

RUBY-THROATED HUMMINGBIRD

The only hummer known by most Easterners has a range that covers most of eastern North America. This is the hummingbird that frequents Eastern gardens and feeders. Both sexes have glittering green crown and upperparts, and the underparts are grayish white. Males have black faces and a deep red to orange-red throat, or gorget. The humming of its wings is clearly discernible from some distance.

straight black bill

green crown

green upperparts

greenish sides and flanks

MALE

grayish white underparts

forked dark green tail

- **SONG** Series of rapid squeaky *chipping* notes.
- **BEHAVIOR** Feeds primarily on nectar but takes some insects and spiders, also sap from sapsucker drill wells. In courtship flight male makes huge a 180-degree arc back and forth, emitting a buzzing sound at its lowest point. Males often arrive on breeding grounds well ahead of females. These birds are strongly attracted to the color red, as are many other hummers.

white chin and throat

FEMALE

JUVENILE

greenish upperparts

- **BREEDING** Solitary.
- **NESTING** Incubation 11–16 days by female. Altricial young stay in nest 20–22 days. Fed by female. 1–3 broods per year.

white underparts with buff wash on sides and flanks

- **POPULATION** Common to fairly common in breeding range. A few winter regularly in south Florida. Rare elsewhere.

rounded tail with white-tipped outer feathers

- **FEEDERS** Red columbine in spring; saliva, trumpet or coral honeysuckle, and bee balm later in year. Also jewelweed, phlox, petunias, lilies, trumpet creeper, Siberian peatree, nasturtium, cone-shaped red flowers (wild and domesticated), and sugar water.

Similar Birds

♂ ♀ **BLACK-CHINNED HUMMINGBIRD** Male has black chin; purple throat • female very similar to female Ruby-throated but with white to grayish sides and flanks.

- **CONSERVATION** Red food dyes added to sugar water may harm birds. Sometimes attracted to red supporting insulators on electrical fences, then killed.

Flight Pattern

Very rapid wing beats (up to 75 per second).

Nest Identification	
Shape 🥚 Location 🌳🌲	Soft plant down, fireweed, milkweed thistles, and leaves; bound with spider webs and cocoon material; trimmed with moss and lichens • looks like knot on a branch • 5–20 feet above ground, often on downsloping branch over brook and sheltered by leaves • built by female • 2 white eggs; elliptical, 0.5 x 0.3 inches.

Plumage Sexes differ	Habitat 🪶 🌿 🌱	Migration Migratory	Weight 0.1 ounce

DATE _____ TIME_____ LOCATION _____

Family TROCHILIDAE	Species *Archilochus alexandri*	Length 3.5–3.75 inches	Wingspan 4–5 inches

BLACK-CHINNED HUMMINGBIRD

Like others in its genus, this western hummingbird has a complex courtship display. While flying in a pendulum pattern, the male vibrates its wings to make a buzzing noise when diving downward past the perched female. The black throat and distinctive white collar set this bird apart from its close cousin, the Ruby-throated Hummingbird. In good light the lower throat glistens in a violet band. Juveniles resemble adult females, and juvenile males begin to show some violet on the lower throat in late summer.

• **SONG** Repetitive *teew* or *tchew*. When defending feeding territory or giving chase, combines *teew* note with high-pitched twitters and squeaks.

• **BEHAVIOR** Solitary. Eats nectar, pollen, and insects. Hovers by flowers to gather nectar or sallies from perch to catch tiny insects in midair. Often twitches tail while hovering. Prefers arid areas. Bathes in water or by hovering against wet foliage.

• **BREEDING** Polygamous. Solitary nester.

• **NESTING** Incubation 13–16 days by female. Young stay in nest 13–21 days. Fed by female. 2–3 broods per year.

• **POPULATION** Neotropical migrant. Common in lowlands and mountain foothills. Casual in the Southeast in winter.

• **FEEDERS** Visits feeders with sugar water.

greenish head

greenish upperparts

straight black bill

black throat

partial white collar

whitish underparts

dusky green sides and flanks

MALE

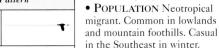

notched greenish tail with blackish outer tail feathers

FEMALE

whitish throat may show faint greenish streaking

dusky sides and flanks

whitish underparts

greenish upperparts

rounded green tail with white corners

Similar Birds

RUBY-THROATED HUMMINGBIRD ♀
Female twitches tail less while feeding; shorter bill; greener crown; buff wash on sides; different voice.

COSTA'S HUMMINGBIRD ♀
Smaller; generally grayer upperparts and whiter underparts; squared tail with white tips and black central tail feathers; different voice • does not stray to the Southeast.

Flight Pattern

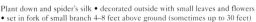

Swift direct flight. Hovers with rapid wing beats (approximately 75 times per second) to feed. Can fly backward.

Nest Identification

Shape 🐦 Location 🌳 🌿

Plant down and spider's silk • decorated outside with small leaves and flowers • set in fork of small branch 4–8 feet above ground (sometimes up to 30 feet) • built by female • 1–3 white eggs; elliptical, with 1 end slightly more pointed, 0.5 x 0.3 inches.

Plumage Sexes differ	Habitat 🌲 ✈ 🌱 🌊	Migration Migratory	Weight 0.1 ounce

DATE _____ TIME_____ LOCATION _____

Family TROCHILIDAE	Species *Calypte anna*	Length 3.5–4 inches	Wingspan 4.75 inches

ANNA'S HUMMINGBIRD

Able to adapt to suburban habitat, this hummingbird is expanding geographically and becoming more numerous. Although predominantly nonmigratory, some have been reported to migrate. It eats more insects and spiders than any other hummingbird. The male, which often vocalizes while perched, is the only North American hummingbird with rose-red crown and throat. Juveniles are similar to females, but juvenile males have some red on the crown as well as the throat.

rose-red head, throat, and sides of neck

short straight black bill

MALE

grayish underparts with greenish tint to sides, flanks, and belly

• **SONG** Sharp squeaky call, *chick*. Chase calls are rapid, high-pitched rattles. Song is garbled mixture of coarse squeaky notes, usually delivered from a perch.

• **BEHAVIOR** Solitary. Eats nectar, insects, spiders, and sap from sapsucker drill wells. Hovers to gather nectar from flowers. Catches insects in midair and plucks spiders and insects from spider webs. Often bathes by hovering against rain- or dew-covered foliage. Male displays for female in a high arc, making explosive *chirp* at the bottom after a rapid dive. Often found in gardens and attending ornamental plantings in yards.

straight black bill

red flecks or spot on throat

FEMALE

pale gray underparts

green crown, nape, and upperparts

JUVENILE MALE

slightly notched, dark green tail with blackish outer tail feathers

rounded green tail with white tips on outer three feathers

• **BREEDING** Polygamous. Solitary.

• **NESTING** Incubation 14–19 days by female. Altricial young stay in nest 18–23 days, fed by female. 2–3 broods per year.

Similar Birds

BLACK-CHINNED HUMMINGBIRD ♀
COSTA'S HUMMINGBIRD ♀
Smaller; whitish underparts; lack red markings on throat • Costa's winters only as far east as west Texas.

• **POPULATION** Abundant; increasing. Vagrants get to coastal Alaska in summer; casual to accidental in the East in winter.

• **FEEDERS** Sugar-water.

• **CONSERVATION** Neotropical migrant. Winters south to the central Baja Peninsula and northwestern Mexico.

Flight Pattern

Flies forward, backward, up, down, and side to side on rapidly beating wings as it feeds. Swift darting flight from place to place. Wing beats a blur.

Nest Identification

Shape 🥛 Location 🌳🌳

Plant down bound with spider silk and lined with plant down and feathers • on small tree branch, on ledge of cliff, or sometimes on utility wire • 1.5–30 feet above ground • built by female • 1–3 white eggs; elliptical oval or subelliptical, with similar curvatures at each end, 0.5 x 0.3 inches.

Plumage Sexes differ	Habitat 	Migration Nonmigratory	Weight 0.1 ounce

DATE _____ TIME_____ LOCATION _____

Family TROCHILIDAE	Species *Selasphorus platycercus*	Length 4–4.5 inches	Wingspan 5 inches

BROAD-TAILED HUMMINGBIRD

The male's wings produce a unique trilling sound when the bird is in flight. The buzzing whistle sound is produced by air rushing through the slots created by the finely tapered tips of the male's outer primaries. Dwelling in the Rocky Mountains and outlying mountain ranges, it can be seen bathing in the shallow waters of mountain streams or defending its territory of flower patches from other hummingbirds. When perched the wings extend beyond the tail tip.

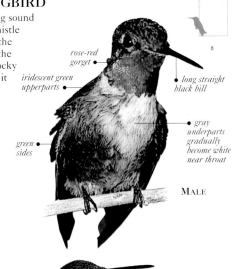

rose-red gorget

iridescent green upperparts

long straight black bill

gray underparts gradually become white near throat

green sides

MALE

• **SONG** Fairly sharp but not hard, repeated *chip; chitter chitter chitte*r; no song. In display makes high thin slurred *szzzzzziiuu*.
• **BEHAVIOR** Solitary. Feeds and perches at low to middle levels in open pine and pine-oak woodlands and edges. Eats nectar, insects, spiders, and sap. Hovers with tail closed, rarely flashed open or wagged, to feed on nectar and catch insects in flight. Plucks insects and spiders from spider webs. Like other hummers, eats sap from holes drilled by sapsuckers. In display flight male flies in U-shaped pattern in front of female, diving 30–50 feet; both sexes may ascend together to 90–100 feet, with one 4–5 feet beneath the other, before diving back down again.

green upperparts

FEMALE

bronze dots on throat

buff underparts

white-tipped outer tail feathers have rufous base

rufous sides

Similar Birds

CALLIOPE HUMMINGBIRD ♀ Female is smaller; wing tips extend beyond short tail; lighter rufous tint on sides; no rufous in bases of tail feathers; shorter bill.

• **BREEDING** Promiscuous. Solitary nester.
• **NESTING** Incubation 14–17 days by female. Young stay in nest 21–26 days. Fed by female. 1–2 broods per year.

• **POPULATION** Common in summer in mountains. Casual in autumn and winter in Gulf Coast states.
• **FEEDERS** Sugar water.
• **CONSERVATION** Neotropical migrant.

Flight Pattern

Hovers when feeding, moving in all directions in a blur of rapidly beating wings. Swift dashing direct flight from point to point.

Nest Identification

Shape 🥄   Location 🪺 🐦

Plant down and bound with spider webs; exterior made of lichens, bark shreds, and leaves • on horizontal tree branch or occasionally in fork; often near or over mountain streams; 4–15 feet above ground • built by female • 2 white eggs; elliptical-oval or subelliptical, 0.5 x 0.34 inches.

Plumage Sexes differ	Habitat 🌳 ⛰ 〰	Migration Migratory	Weight 0.1 ounce

Family TROCHILIDAE	Species *Selasphorus rufus*	Length 3.75 inches	Wingspan 4.75 inches

RUFOUS HUMMINGBIRD

This tenacious hummingbird aggressively defends its territory and will attack not only larger birds such as blackbirds and thrushes, but also chipmunks. At feeders it is intolerant of all other would-be visitors and spends much of its time driving them away from the nectar. Like most hummingbirds, highly attracted to the color red, it has been known to examine human clothing, magazine covers, and other items showing this color. This is the only hummingbird in North America with a rufous back, and the one most likely to be seen in the East in the fall and winter after the Ruby-throated Hummingbirds have migrated south. The male has green markings on his rufous back, a rufous tail, and his gorget sparkles copper-red in good light; the female also has small spots on her throat that appear red in certain light.

straight black bill

white chest, often extends as central streak on belly

rufous wash on underparts

rufous upperparts

MALE

white throat speckled with small spots

white breast and center of belly

rufous-buff on sides, flanks, and sides of belly

green upperparts

FEMALE

• **SONG** Call is sibilant *chewp chewp*; in defense chases, proclaims *zeee-chupppity-chup*.

• **BEHAVIOR** Solitary. A hardy hummer that nests as far north as southern Alaska. Strongly prefers red to any other color and hovers by red tubular flowers, such as columbine and tiger lilies, to gather nectar. Feeds and perches at low to middle levels. Catches insects in midair and eats sap from holes drilled by sapsuckers. Plucks spiders and insects from webs. Wings make buzzy whistle in flight. Male displays for female in U-shaped or oval pattern; ascends with back to female, then dives, turning toward her on whistling wings with orange-red gorget flashing.

• **BREEDING** Polygamous. Solitary in small loose semicolonies.

• **NESTING** Incubation 12–14 days by female. Altricial young stay in nest 20 days, fed by female. 1–2 broods per year.

Similar Birds

ALLEN'S HUMMINGBIRD
Male has green back
• females cannot be distinguished in the field
• in the hand, tail feathers more slender.

• **POPULATION** Abundant to common. Rare in the East in fall and winter.

• **FEEDERS** Sugar water.

• **CONSERVATION** Neotropical migrant. Possible decline in recent years; no noted cause.

Flight Pattern

Hovers while feeding; darts up and down, in and out, and backwards; swift and dashing flight on a blur of whirring wings.

Nest Identification

Shape   Location

Plant down, covered with lichen, moss, bud scales, leaves, shredded bark, and plant fibers; bound with spider silk and lined with plant down • most often on drooping limb; occasionally in fork of tree or shrub, 5–50 feet above ground • built by female • 2 white eggs; elliptical oval or subelliptical, 0.5 x 0.33 inches.

Plumage Sexes differ	Habitat	Migration Migratory	Weight 0.1 ounce

DATE _____ TIME_____ LOCATION _____

Family TROCHILIDAE	Species *Selasphorus sasin*	Length 3.75 inches	Wingspan 4.75 inches

ALLEN'S HUMMINGBIRD

When defending its territory this diminutive bird will attack many birds, including large hawks. Highly adaptable, it can be found in suburban gardens and parks in its range. Males appear similar to the Rufous Hummingbird but have a green back; females and juveniles are inseparable from the Rufous in the field. Allen's is often found in drier habitats, including chaparral and thickets, than the Rufous.

MALE

straight black bill

green crown

copper-red gorget

green upperparts

white below throat on breast extends in line onto center of belly

rufous sides, flanks, and sides of belly

rufous rump and tail

- **SONG** Utters sharp *chip* or series of *chips* similar to voice of Rufous Hummingbird.
- **BEHAVIOR** Solitary. Gathers nectar from flowers and catches insects in midair. Also plucks insects and spiders from webs. Eats sap from sapsucker holes. In courtship display male flies in J-shaped pattern: He ascends 75–80 feet and dives on whistling wings to the level of the perched female, then ascends about 25 feet on the other side of the arc and hovers, with his gorget glittering in the sun. Begins with pendulum-like, side-to-side display. Males may depart breeding areas a month or more before females depart.
- **BREEDING** Promiscuous. Solitary nester. Semicolonial, with nests often clustered.
- **NESTING** Incubation 15–22 days by female. Young stay in nest 22–25 days. Fed by female. 2 broods per year.
- **POPULATION** Common to

FEMALE

green upperparts

white throat with bronze dotted pattern

rufous-buff underparts with rufous wash on sides

rufous on base of tail feathers

Similar Birds

♂ RUFOUS HUMMINGBIRD Male has rufous back • female and juvenile have wider outer tail feathers, which can only be discerned in the hand • breeding range is more northern and further inland.

♀

fairly common. Casual to rare vagrant in the East in autumn migration and winter.
- **FEEDERS** Sugar water.
- **CONSERVATION** Declining because of habitat loss.

Flight Pattern

Hovers when feeding, moving in all directions in a blur of rapidly beating wings. Swift darting direct flight.

Nest Identification

Shape ◗   Location 🐦 🌿 🏠

Moss, stems, weeds, and plant down; covered with lichens and bound with spider's silk • lined with plant down • in shaded area on top of tree limb, shrub, or building • built by female • 2 white eggs, 0.5 x 0.33 inches.

Plumage Sexes differ	Habitat 🌿 ✈ 🏔	Migration Neotropical migrant	Weight 0.1 ounce

DATE _____ TIME_____ LOCATION _____

Family ALCEDINIDAE	Species *Ceryle torquata*	Length 16.5 inches	Wingspan 24–29 inches

RINGED KINGFISHER

This is the largest kingfisher in the Western Hemisphere. A strikingly colored bird, it is widely distributed in the Americas but barely reaches north of the US border with Mexico. Found along big rivers, this bird flies and perches high. The upperparts and most of the head are blue-gray, while the underparts are chiefly bright rufous. The black bill is large. In flight, males show white underwing and undertail coverts; females show rufous.

- **SONG** Drawling low-pitched harsh loud clattering rattle. In flight this bird gives a loud *cla-ak!*

- **BEHAVIOR** Largely solitary and somewhat noisy. Found along larger rivers, lakes, and lagoons, where it hunts from a perch and dives for fish and sometimes frogs and reptiles. Often wags or bobs its tail. Often perches high on overhanging branches, poles, and utility wires.

- **BREEDING** Monogamous and solitary.

- **NESTING** Incubation by both sexes. Altricial young remain in nest 35 days, fed by both sexes.

- **POPULATION** Uncommon and local but has gradually increased its range in the southeast Texas area since the mid-1960s. Widespread in the American tropics.

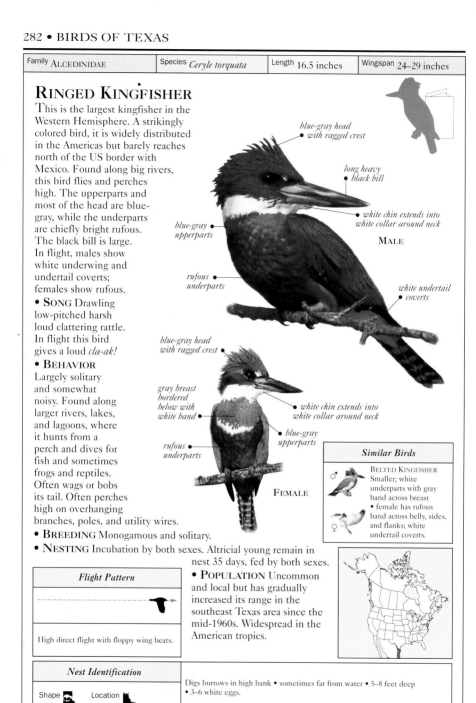

blue-gray head with ragged crest

long heavy black bill

white chin extends into white collar around neck

MALE

blue-gray upperparts

rufous underparts

white undertail coverts

blue-gray head with ragged crest

gray breast bordered below with white band

white chin extends into white collar around neck

blue-gray upperparts

rufous underparts

FEMALE

Similar Birds

BELTED KINGFISHER
Smaller; white underparts with gray band across breast
- female has rufous band across belly, sides, and flanks; white undertail coverts.

Flight Pattern

High direct flight with floppy wing beats.

Nest Identification

Shape ___   Location ___

Digs burrows in high bank • sometimes far from water • 5–8 feet deep • 3–6 white eggs.

Plumage Sexes differ	Habitat ~~~ ⋙	Migration Nonmigratory	Weight 11.1 ounces

DATE _____ TIME_____ LOCATION _____

Family ALCEDINIDAE	Species *Ceryle alcyon*	Length 11–14.5 inches	Wingspan 22–26 inches

BELTED KINGFISHER

Widely distributed and common along freshwater bodies of water as well as the coast, this is the only kingfisher across most of its range, except along the Mexican border. It is one of the few North American birds in which the female is more colorful than the male. The male has blue-gray upperparts with a blue-gray band across the breast and appears big-headed with its large bill and ragged crest. In flight it shows a white patch on the upperwing at the base of the primaries.

shaggy crest

MALE

white spot in front of eye

broad white collar

blue-gray upperparts

long thick black bill

blue-gray band across breast

white underparts

chestnut band across belly

chestnut on sides and flanks

FEMALE

- **SONG** Bold raspy rattle sounds like a heavy fishing reel.
- **BEHAVIOR** Generally solitary. Plunges headfirst into water from perch or a hover up to 20 feet or more above water to catch fish. Feeds primarily on fish but also takes amphibians, reptiles, insects, crustaceans, and mollusks. Frequents favorite perches along waterways for hunting. Pair digs burrow in bank 3–7 feet deep (can be up to 15 feet).
- **BREEDING** Monogamous; solitary nester.
- **NESTING** Incubation 23–24 days by both sexes. Altricial young stay in nest 27–29 days. Fed by both sexes. 1–2 broods per year.
- **POPULATION** Slight decline in North America.
- **CONSERVATION** Often viewed as problem at fish hatcheries; before regulation they were shot and killed at hatcheries and along trout streams. This may still occur at some hatcheries.

Similar Birds

BLUE JAY
Smaller; brighter blues; black band on breast forms collar.

RINGED KINGFISHER
In southeast Texas only • larger • male has bright rufous-chestnut underparts with no white; female has narrow white band.

Flight Pattern

Slow direct flight with somewhat erratic pattern. Hovers above water to search for prey.

Nest Identification	Horizontal burrow, occasionally slanted upward, in bank beside fresh water • usually no lining but debris and undigested fish bones and scales • may be far from water • 3–7 feet long • built by both sexes • 5–8 white eggs, about 1.3 x 1.0 inches.
Shape Location	

Plumage Sexes differ	Habitat	Migration Some migrate	Weight 5.2 ounces

DATE _____ TIME_____ LOCATION _____

Family ALCEDINIDAE	Species *Chloroceryle americana*	Length 8.75 inches	Wingspan 11–13 inches

GREEN KINGFISHER

Our smallest kingfisher has a very restricted US range. It has dark green upperparts with a white collar and a long black bill. The white outer tail feathers are conspicuous in flight, when the bird may call attention to itself with its high-pitched *cheep* notes. Since it hunts from low perches along quiet waterways, it is difficult to see.

• SONG Faint but abrasive *tick tick*, usually with a brief rattle at the end. In flight, the Green Kingfisher utters squeaky *cheep* notes.

• BEHAVIOR This bird prefers small clear streams, quiet pools, and backwaters, where it hunts from low perches along the edge of the water or from rocks in the water. It does not hover like larger kingfishers. Feeds primarily on small fish taken in a plunging dive and on aquatic insects and amphibians. Can be easily overlooked except for its sharp vocalizations.

• BREEDING Monogamous and solitary.

• NESTING Incubation 19–21 days by both sexes. Altricial young remain in the nest 22–26 days, fed by both sexes.

• POPULATION Uncommon and local in southern Texas; may have declined in parts of Texas with loss of streamside habitat. Rare to casual in southeastern Arizona; has recently begun nesting locally in south Arizona, spreading north from Mexico across the US border.

• CONSERVATION Water pollution and loss of streamside riparian habitats have negative impacts on the small populations of this kingfisher.

short crest

long straight black bill

wide rufous-chestnut breast band

dark green spots on sides and flanks

white underparts

white collar

dark green upperparts

wings flecked with white dots and streaks

MALE

broken collar of green spots and streaks on upper breast extends onto sides

dark green upperparts

white outer tail feathers

FEMALE

Similar Birds

BELTED KINGFISHER
RINGED KINGFISHER
Larger with blue-gray upperparts and head.

Flight Pattern

Rapid buzzing direct flight.

Nest Identification

Shape ▨ Location ◣

Horizontal burrow 2–3 feet deep in stream bank • built by both sexes • 3–6 white eggs, 1 inch in diameter.

Plumage Sexes differ	Habitat 〰 ⩩	Migration Nonmigratory	Weight 1.3 ounces

DATE _____ TIME_____ LOCATION _____

Family PICIDAE	Species *Melanerpes lewis*	Length 10–11.5 inches	Wingspan 20–21 inches

LEWIS'S WOODPECKER

Discovered by and named for Meriwether Lewis of the Lewis and Clark expedition of 1803–1806, this bird often is mistaken for a crow in flight because of its overall blackish appearance and its direct flight pattern, which is unlike most woodpeckers. It is the only North American woodpecker that is mostly black with iridescent green highlights and a pinkish belly. In flight it shows a blackish green crissum. The female is similar to the male but smaller. Juveniles have a brownish head and underparts and lack the gray collar, red face, and pink belly.

blackish green head

wide gray collar

dark red face patch

black back and upperparts with glossy green sheen

black bill

wide blackish green wings

black legs and feet

pinkish red belly

blackish green tail

- **SONG** Usually silent. Grating repetitive call of *churrr-churrr* or *chea-er*. Alarm call is *yick-yick*.
- **BEHAVIOR** Solitary or in pairs. May perch on wires to catch insects in flight, which is unusual for woodpeckers; also probes for insects in trees. Diet also includes nuts and fruits. Stores surplus food in crevice of tree in nonbreeding season, modifying acorns and nuts to fit the hole by removing the shell and shaping them. Defends cache from would-be robbers. Frequents logged areas, burns, riparian woodlands, and orchards.
- **BREEDING** Monogamous. Pairs may mate for life. Solitary nester.
- **NESTING** Incubation 13–14 days by both sexes (male at night, female during day). Altricial young stay in nest 28–34 days. Fed by both sexes. 1 brood per year.

JUVENILE

- **POPULATION** Uncommon to fairly common. Declined in recent years, especially on northwest coast. Some individuals are nomadic. Accidental in the East.
- **FEEDERS** Visits feeders with suet and other foods.
- **CONSERVATION** Listed as a species of special concern by the National Audubon Society, but populations have appeared stable in recent decades.

Flight Pattern
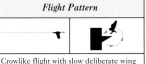
Crowlike flight with slow deliberate wing beats. Sallies from perch to take insects in flight, returning to same or nearby perch.

Nest Identification	
Shape ▨ Location 🐦 🌳	A few wood chips or pieces of bark • in trunks of dead or live trees or poles; often in snag of living tree • 2- to 3-inch entrance hole; 9- to 30-inch-deep cavity; 5–170 feet high • built by both sexes, but male does most of excavating • 4–9 white eggs; oval to elliptical, 1 inch in diameter.

Plumage Sexes similar	Habitat	Migration Some migrate	Weight 4.1 ounces

DATE _____ TIME _____ LOCATION _____

Family PICIDAE	Species *Melanerpes erythrocephalus*	Length 8.5–9.25 inches	Wingspan 16–18 inches

RED-HEADED WOODPECKER

The ecological eastern counterpart of Lewis's Woodpecker, this is the only woodpecker in the East with an entirely red head. Unlike many other woodpeckers, the Red-headed Woodpecker catches most of its food in flight, from the ground, or by gleaning it from tree trunks and limbs; it rarely bores holes in trees to probe for insects. The male does, however, vigorously drill its nest cavity with the aid of its mate. In flight the white underparts, white rump, and large white secondary patches contrast sharply with the black tail, wings, and back. Juveniles have brownish black upperparts and brown heads.

red head, neck, and throat

black bill

red upper breast

black back

black wing coverts and primaries

white underparts

- **SONG** Fairly noisy. In breeding season has bold grating *queark* or *queer, queer, queer*. Also sounds like a chicken clucking, *kerr-uck, kerr-uck*.
- **BEHAVIOR** Solitary or in pairs. Eats various insects, spiders, millipedes, and centipedes; sometimes takes eggs and young of other birds, mice, corn, grains, various nuts, and berries. Often hunts from low perches, flying to ground to pick up prey or nut. Caches acorns and nuts, removing shells and storing the meat for winter.
- **BREEDING** Monogamous. Solitary nester.
- **NESTING** Incubation 12–14 days by both sexes. Altricial young stay in nest 27–31 days. Fed by both sexes. 1–2 broods per year.
- **POPULATION** Uncommon and declining. Casual to accidental west of the Rocky Mountains.
- **FEEDERS AND BIRDHOUSES** Suet, sunflower seeds, cracked corn, raisins, nuts, and bread. Some will nest in birdhouse built for woodpeckers.
- **CONSERVATION** Listed as species of special concern by National Audubon Society. Decline in past century due to habitat loss, collisions with automobiles, and competition for nesting cavities with European Starling. Creosote-coated utility poles are lethal to eggs and young.

black tail

JUVENILE

Similar Birds

RED-BELLIED WOODPECKER Red crown and nape only; barred black-and-white upperparts; white patches at bases of primaries; grayish face and underparts.

Flight Pattern

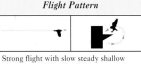

Strong flight with slow steady shallow wing beats. Sallies for flying insects, then returns to same or nearby perch.

Nest Identification

Shape 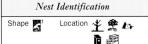   Location

In snag, limb of living tree, stump, or dead tree • 1.75-inch entrance; 8–24 inches deep; 8–80 feet above ground • drilled mostly by male • 4–7 white eggs; oval to elliptical, 1 inch in diameter.

Plumage Sexes similar	Habitat	Migration Some migrate	Weight 2.5 ounces

DATE _____ TIME_____ LOCATION _____

Family PICIDAE	Species *Melanerpes formicivorus*	Length 9 inches	Wingspan 17 inches

ACORN WOODPECKER

This noisy sociable woodpecker is found where oaks are plentiful in the southwestern US and along the Pacific Coast from Baja California to Washington. Its colorful face pattern is clownlike, with bright contrasting splashes of white, black, red, and yellow set around a pale yellow-white eye. In flight white patches show on each wing and the rump. In appearance, the females differ from the male only in their bicolor crown, which is black in front and red in the back.

whitish eye

white across forehead passes in front of eye and forms bib across throat

entirely red crown

black sides of head

black back

black patch around base of bill

black breast

white belly

white flanks and sides with black streaks

white undertail coverts

- **SONG** *Waka, waka, waka* repeated often.
- **BEHAVIOR** Clans of birds store acorns in individual holes drilled in a tree trunk in autumn, pounding nuts into each hole for winter food supply. The same granary tree is used year after year. The clan actively defends its stored larder from being stolen by squirrels and other birds, particularly other woodpeckers and jays. Diet includes insects it may catch in flight and tree sap from drill wells it excavates. Often lives in social groups that forage together and may act as helpers at the nest.
- **BREEDING** Cooperative in small groups of up to 16 birds. Communal; several females per nest.
- **NESTING** Incubation 11–14 days by both sexes and helper birds. Altricial young remain in nest 30–32 days. Fed by both sexes and helper birds. 1–2 broods per year.
- **POPULATION** Fairly common to common, and conspicuous.
- **CONSERVATION** Habitat is being lost due to overgrazing in montane riparian areas and pine-oak habitat where livestock destroy seedling generations needed to replace aging parent trees.

Similar Birds

The clown face with its white eye makes it unmistakable among North American woodpeckers.

Flight Pattern

Undulating flight with several rapid wing beats and a pause.

Nest Identification

Shape   Location

Wood chips in base of cavity • usually 5–60 feet above ground • built by both sexes and members of social group • 3–7 white eggs, about 1 x 0.75 inches.

Plumage Sexes differ	Habitat	Migration Few migrate	Weight 2.9 ounces

DATE _____ TIME_____ LOCATION _____

Family PICIDAE	Species *Melanerpes aurifrons*	Length 8.5–10 inches	Wingspan 16–18 inches

GOLDEN-FRONTED WOODPECKER

Working together for about 8 days, the male and female drill their nest cavity 12–18 inches deep in a snag, pole, or dead limb or top of a living tree. The female looks similar to the male but lacks the red cap on the gray crown. Very similar in appearance and behavior to the eastern Red-bellied Woodpecker, it also shows a white rump patch and white patches at the bases of the primaries in flight. Juveniles have a streaked breast and lack the golden patch at the upper mandible base, the golden yellow nape, and the male's red cap.

yellow feathers at base of upper mandible

bold red cap

black bill

grayish white face

grayish white underparts with dull buff wash

black feet and legs

golden yellow-orange nape

barred black-and-white back and wings

white rump

unbarred black tail

- **SONG** Noisy trill, *churrrrrrr-churrrrrrrr*; flickerlike *kek-kek-kek-kek-kek-kek* or *check, check.*

- **BEHAVIOR** Solitary or in pairs. Prefers dry forests, mesquite brushlands, and cottonwoods in riparian edges. Often forages low on tree and on ground. Eats insects, spiders, wild berries, fruits, nuts, acorns, corn, and grains. Caches food for winter in bark crevices.

- **BREEDING** Monogamous. Solitary nester.

- **NESTING** Incubation 12–14 days by both sexes (male at night, female during day). Altricial young stay in nest 30 days. Fed by both sexes. 1–2 broods per year.

- **POPULATION** Common to fairly common. Stable. Common in Texas towns. Accidental elsewhere. East Coast reports may be Red-bellied Woodpeckers with abnormal amounts of yellow.

- **FEEDERS** Suet, corn, nuts, and sunflower seeds.

- **CONSERVATION** Called a "pole pest" by utility and railroad companies, because it found the pine of poles easier to excavate than native trees; many were killed on sight.

Similar Birds

♂ **RED-BELLIED WOODPECKER**
Male has entirely red crown and nape
- female has red on nape only • both have lightly barred rump; barred tail; reddish wash on center of lower belly.

Flight Pattern

Alternates series of shallow rapid wing beats with short glides, producing a series of undulations as it progresses.

Nest Identification

Shape 〼¹ 〼² Location 🐜 ⚘ 🍂

Sometimes a few bark chips • in cavity of dead or live tree, stump, utility pole, fence post, or man-made structure 3–25 feet above ground • often uses same cavity year after year • built by both sexes • 4–7 white eggs; oval to elliptical, 1 inch long.

Plumage Sexes similar	Habitat 🌿 🌳 ▬	Migration Nonmigratory	Weight 3.0 ounces

DATE _____ TIME_____ LOCATION _____

Family PICIDAE	Species *Melanerpes carolinus*	Length 9–10.5 inches	Wingspan 15–18 inches

RED-BELLIED WOODPECKER

This noisy common woodpecker of eastern US forests and forest edges has adapted to different habitats, from southern pine forests to northern hardwoods, scattered trees, and urban parks. The bird's upperparts have black-and-white barring in a zebra pattern. The "red belly" that gives the bird its name is a reddish wash low on the belly and between the legs that is actually difficult to see in the field. In flight it shows a white rump, white patches at the base of the primaries, and white-barred central tail feathers. Juvenile birds are similar to adults but have a gray-brown head.

pale grayish tan face and chin

red crown and nape

MALE

black-and-white barring on upperparts

pale grayish tan underparts

gray crown

red nape

- **SONG** Quavering *churr-churr* or *querrr-querrr* and abrupt *chuck, chuck, chuck*, softer than Golden-fronted Woodpecker.
- **BEHAVIOR** Conspicuous, with noisy vocalizations and drumming in breeding season. Nests and roosts nightly in tree cavities. Eats wide variety of fare, including insects, fruits, vegetables, seeds, and sap from sapsucker drill wells.
- **BREEDING** Monogamous. Solitary nester.
- **NESTING** Incubation 11–14 days by both sexes; male at night, female during day. Young stay in nest 22–27 days. Fed by both sexes. 1 brood per year in the North; 2–3 broods per year in the South.

FEMALE

Similar Birds

GOLDEN-FRONTED WOODPECKER
Black tail without white barring; golden-orange nape; yellow patch at base of upper mandible; indistinct yellowish wash on belly • male has red cap.

- **POPULATION** Common to fairly common. Expanding northward in recent decades to southern border of Canada. Seems stable overall; may be increasing slightly.
- **FEEDERS** Nuts, sunflower seeds, peanut butter, and suet.

Flight Pattern

Undulating flight with fairly rapid wing beats interspersed with periods of roller-coaster flight with wings folded.

Nest Identification

Shape   Location

In tree 5–70 feet above ground • built by both sexes • sometimes uses abandoned holes of other woodpeckers • 3–8 white eggs, 1 inch in diameter.

Plumage Sexes differ	Habitat	Migration Nonmigratory	Weight 2.4 ounces

DATE _____ TIME_____ LOCATION _____

Family PICIDAE	Species *Sphyrapicus thyroideus*	Length 9 inches	Wingspan 17 inches

WILLIAMSON'S SAPSUCKER

The male and female plumages are so different that they once were thought to be of different species. This shy bird makes its home among the coniferous trees in the mountains of western North America. In strong sunlight the male's head, neck, back, breast, wings, and tail shine with a green iridescent sheen. Males in flight often appear entirely black with a white rump and white shoulder patches. Females in flight show brown upperparts with whitish barring and a white rump. Juveniles are similar to adults, but the juvenile male has a white throat, and the juvenile female lacks the black breast patch.

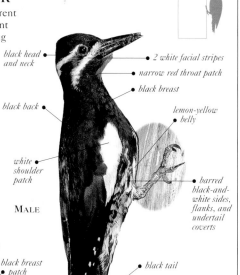

black head and neck

2 white facial stripes

narrow red throat patch

black breast

black back

lemon-yellow belly

white shoulder patch

MALE

barred black-and-white sides, flanks, and undertail coverts

- **SONG** Often quiet. Loud shrieking *cheeeeer* is similar to Red-tailed Hawk's call. Also makes trilling *k-k-r-r-r-r-r* and soft nasal *whang* or *wheather*. Males make staccato tapping sounds.

brown head

black breast patch

black tail

- **BEHAVIOR** Solitary or in pairs. Shy and wary. Bores holes in trees to drink sap, and picks insects off tree bark. Eats various insects and their larvae, spiders, berries, and cambium. Courtship involves mutual head bobbing, crest raising, holding wings above back, and fluttering mothlike flights.

brown-and-white barring on back

FEMALE

lemon-yellow belly

brown barring on sides, flanks, and undertail coverts

Similar Birds

YELLOW-BELLIED SAPSUCKER
Red forehead and forecrown; white shoulder patches; pale yellow belly.

RED-NAPED SAPSUCKER
Red forehead, forecrown, and nape; white shoulder patches; pale yellow belly
• only in the West.

- **BREEDING** Monogamous. Small, very loose colonies.
- **NESTING** Incubation 12–14 days by both sexes (male at night, female during day). Altricial young stay in nest 21–35 days. Fed by both sexes. 1 brood per year.
- **POPULATION** Fairly common to uncommon in western mountains. Accidental in eastern North America.
- **FEEDERS** Visits feeders filled with sugar water and suet.

Flight Pattern

Alternates between several rapid shallow wing beats and periods of short glides.

Nest Identification

Shape   Location 🐦 ⭐ 🌲

No lining except a few bark chips • in dead or live conifer or aspen 3–60 feet above ground; excavation takes 3–4 weeks; excavates new nest annually but often uses same tree as previous year • built by male • 3–7 porcelain-white eggs; oval to elliptical, 0.9 x 0.7 inches.

Plumage Sexes differ	Habitat 🌳 🏞 ⛰	Migration Migratory	Weight 1.7 ounces

DATE _____ TIME_____ LOCATION _____

Family PICIDAE	Species *Sphyrapicus varius*	Length 8–9 inches	Wingspan 16–18 inches

YELLOW-BELLIED SAPSUCKER

Eastern counterpart to the Red-naped Sapsucker, this is the most widespread of the four North American sapsuckers. In breeding season male and female perform continual loud drumming duets, including ritual tapping at the nest entrance. The female is similar to the male but has a white throat. In flight birds show a white rump and white shoulder patches. Juveniles have brown mottling on the chest, head, and upperparts, and a white shoulder patch but lack the bright head and throat colors.

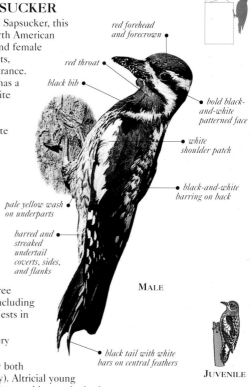

red forehead and forecrown

red throat

black bib

bold black-and-white patterned face

white shoulder patch

black-and-white barring on back

pale yellow wash on underparts

barred and streaked undertail coverts, sides, and flanks

MALE

black tail with white bars on central feathers

JUVENILE

- **SONG** Often silent. Low, growling nasal *mew* sounds somewhat catlike. Alarm call of *cheee-er, cheeee-er*. During courtship display cries *hoih-hoih*. Males make staccato drumming sounds.
- **BEHAVIOR** Solitary or in pairs. Bores series of small holes, often in horizontal rows, in trees to drink the sap that collects. Eats insects attracted to drill wells, plus fruits, berries, and tree buds. Guards wells from other birds, including hummingbirds, and small mammals. Nests in soft deciduous trees, often near water.
- **BREEDING** Monogamous. Small, very loose colonies.
- **NESTING** Incubation 12–13 days by both sexes (male at night, female during day). Altricial young stay in nest 25–29 days; fed mixture of sap and insects by both sexes. Taught sapsucking by both sexes. 1 brood per year.
- **POPULATION** Common to fairly common in deciduous and mixed forests. Accidental to rare in West during migration and winter.
- **FEEDERS** In winter, mixture of suet and sugar. Will eat sweets, like jelly or doughnuts. Drinks sugar water from hummingbird feeders.
- **CONSERVATION** People dislike the drill wells created in their shade and fruit trees; fearing the tree will be injured or diseased, they often kill sapsuckers, although the birds are protected by law.

Similar Birds

RED-NAPED SAPSUCKER
Red on nape.
- only in the West.

Flight Pattern

Alternates several rapid shallow wing beats with short glides, producing undulating flight as the bird progresses.

Nest Identification

Shape [symbols]   Location [symbols]

Usually no materials except bark chips • in dead or live tree (prefers live tree); 6–60 feet above ground • built by both sexes in 7–10 days • 1.25 x 1.6–inch entrance hole; 5 x 14–inch gourd-shaped cavity • 4–7 white eggs; oval to elliptical, 0.9 x 0.7 inches.

Plumage Sexes similar	Habitat [symbols]	Migration Migratory	Weight 1.8 ounces

DATE _____ TIME_____ LOCATION _____

Family PICIDAE	Species *Sphyrapicus nuchalis*	Length 8–9 inches	Wingspan 16–18 inches

RED-NAPED SAPSUCKER

South and west of the Rocky Mountains, this is the counterpart to the Yellow-bellied Sapsucker, which it very much resembles. Adept at drilling sap wells, these birds carry sap in their crops to feed their nestlings and teach them to "sapsuck" shortly after fledging. Its white rump patch is conspicuous in flight. Females are similar to males but usually have a whitish chin with variable amounts of red on the throat. Juveniles lack the red head and have brown-mottled upperparts and underparts, but do have the white shoulder patch.

red forehead, forecrown, and nape

2 white stripes on black face

2 converging, chainlike stripes on back

white shoulder patches

white underparts with yellow wash on breast and belly

black-and-white barring on back and wings

chevron-shaped spots and streaks on undertail coverts, sides, and flanks

black-and-white barring on central tail feather

- **SONG** Often silent. Low growling mewing *meeah*, similar to that of Yellow-bellied Sapsucker. Males make staccato drumming sounds.
- **BEHAVIOR** Solitary or in pairs. Bores small regularly spaced holes in trees to drink the sap that collects in them. Feeds mainly on sap, pine pitch, cambium, and some insects and berries. Males and females perform drumming duets during courtship and ritual tapping at nest hole. Important provider of preformed cavities for nests and dens of other species in its habitat, where it often is one of the only woodpecker species.
- **BREEDING** Monogamous. Small, very loose colonies.
- **NESTING** Incubation 12–13 days by both sexes; male incubates at night. Altricial young stay in nest 25–29 days, fed by both sexes. 1 brood per year.
- **POPULATION** Common in deciduous forest. Casual or accidental in southwest Canada, the Midwest, and in southeastern Louisiana.
- **FEEDERS** Mixture of sugar and suet.

Similar Birds

YELLOW-BELLIED SAPSUCKER
More obscure mottled pattern on back; lacks red nape; red on throat smaller and more confined by black borders at sides
- female lacks any red on throat.

RED-BREASTED SAPSUCKER
All-red head, neck, and breast; less mottling and barring on back.

Flight Pattern

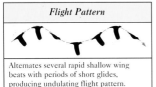

Alternates several rapid shallow wing beats with periods of short glides, producing undulating flight pattern.

Nest Identification	
Shape 🪹 Location 🌲🎋🪵	Usually no materials, except a few bark chips • in dead or live tree, more frequently live deciduous, 10–35 feet above ground • built by both sexes • gourd-shaped, 5 x 14 inches; entrance hole 1.25–1.65 inches • 5–6 white eggs; oval to elliptical, 0.9 x 0.7 inches.

Plumage Sexes differ	Habitat 🌿 🪵	Migration Migratory	Weight 2.4 ounces

DATE _____ TIME_____ LOCATION _____

Family PICIDAE	Species *Picoides scalaris*	Length 7.25 inches	Wingspan 11–12 inches

LADDER-BACKED WOODPECKER

This small bird the size of a Downy Woodpecker inhabits deserts, arid scrub, riparian woodlands, piñon-junipers, and pine-oaks – the arid woodlands and scrublands of the Southwest. It is the only small woodpecker in most of its range, and it is well adapted to smaller trees, shrubs, and cacti, the dominant woody plants in the rugged country it calls home. Note the black-and-white barred back, the profusion of white spotting and barring on the wings and shoulders, and the buffy gray underparts.

• **SONG** Call note is a clear high-pitched *pik*, similar to Hairy Woodpecker; descending whinny.

• **BEHAVIOR** Solitary or in pairs. Sexes forage differently. Males tend to forage lower and on the ground, probing for insects, especially ants; females forage higher in the vegetation and glean insects from bark. Both readily eat fruits of cactus. Often seen in towns and rural areas.

• **BREEDING** Monogamous.

• **NESTING** Incubation 13 days by both sexes. Young altricial; estimated to fledge nest at 20–25 days. Fed by both sexes. 1 brood per year.

• **POPULATION** Common in arid and semiarid brushlands.

• **FEEDERS** Attracted to birdbaths, pools, and other water elements, and feeders with suet, peanut butter, corn, and sunflower seeds.

straight black bill

black forehead and nape

red crown

buffy gray face outlined with black triangle

black-and-white barred upperparts, shoulders, and wings

black legs and feet

buffy gray, black-spotted underparts

MALE

black rump and tail

white-barred outer tail feathers

whitish gray face outlined with black triangle

black forehead, crown, and nape

black-and-white barred upperparts, shoulders, and wings

FEMALE

buffy gray underparts with black spotting on breast, sides, and flanks

outer tail feathers barred white

black rump and tail

Similar Birds

DOWNY WOODPECKER
White back; white underparts without spotting; white outer tail feathers with black spotting; black ear patch • male has red patch on back of head.

NUTTALL'S WOODPECKER
Black face with narrow white supercilium curving down behind auriculars and white mustache; white underparts; voice differs • male has red on back of crown only • south California range barely overlaps • limited range in the West.

Flight Pattern

Series of rapid shallow wing beats alternating with short glides.

Nest Identification

Shape Location 🌵🌳

Excavated cavity lined with chips • in upper part of agave, saguaro, or other huge cactus; in dead trees or branches; in top of woody shrub, 3–30 feet above ground • unknown which sex digs cavity • 2–7 white eggs; oval to elliptical, 0.8 x 0.6 inches.

Plumage Sexes differ	Habitat 🐾 ⚐ ⚐ ⚐ 🌲 🌿	Migration Nonmigratory	Weight 1.1 ounces

DATE _____ TIME_____ LOCATION _____

Family PICIDAE	Species *Picoides pubescens*	Length 6.75–7 inches	Wingspan 11–12 inches

DOWNY WOODPECKER

The smallest woodpecker in North America is found across most of the continent, ranging from coast to coast and from the northern tree line south to the Gulf and the deserts and dry grasslands just north of the Mexican border. The combination of small size, white back, and small stubby bill distinguishes this common woodpecker. The female differs from the male only in that it lacks the red occipital patch. In the Pacific Northwest these birds show pale brownish gray underparts and back.

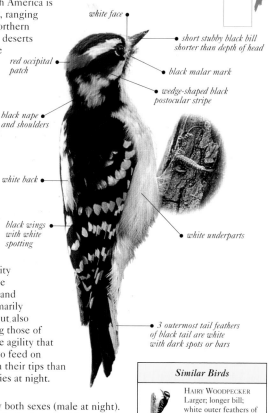

white face

short stubby black bill shorter than depth of head

red occipital patch

black malar mark

wedge-shaped black postocular stripe

black nape and shoulders

white back

black wings with white spotting

white underparts

3 outermost tail feathers of black tail are white with dark spots or bars

• **SONG** Downslurred soft high-pitched whinny. Call is flat *pik* or *pick* and not as high-pitched as that given by the Hairy Woodpecker.

• **BEHAVIOR** Both sexes drum on dead limbs or tree trunks with good resonating qualities or on utility poles, buildings, or other man-made objects to advertise their presence and proclaim territorial rights. Eats primarily insects and their larvae and eggs, but also takes seeds, nuts, berries (including those of poison ivy), spiders, and snails. The agility that comes with its small size allows it to feed on smaller branches and farther out on their tips than other woodpeckers. Roosts in cavities at night.

• **BREEDING** Monogamous.

• **NESTING** Incubation 12 days by both sexes (male at night). Young stay in nest 20–25 days. Fed by both sexes. 1 brood per year, possibly 2 in the South.

• **POPULATION** Widespread and common. Species can be found almost anywhere there are trees.

Similar Birds

HAIRY WOODPECKER Larger; longer bill; white outer feathers of black tail lack spots or bars; call is *peek*.

• **FEEDERS AND BIRDHOUSES** Will come to feeders for suet, peanut butter, sunflower seeds, and bread. Will nest in bird box designed for it.

Flight Pattern

Undulating flight with rapid wing beats alternating with pauses on folded wings, which produces bouncing flight.

Nest Identification

Shape | Location

Excavated in dead tree trunk or branch; pair usually leaves chips in bottom • usually 12–30 feet above ground, sometimes 5–60 feet • built by both sexes • 3–7 white eggs, 0.8 inch in diameter.

Plumage Sexes similar	Habitat	Migration Nonmigratory	Weight 1.0 ounce

DATE _____ TIME _____ LOCATION _____

Family PICIDAE	Species *Picoides villosus*	Length 8.5–10.5 inches	Wingspan 15–17.5 inches

HAIRY WOODPECKER

The Hairy Woodpecker and the Northern Flicker are the two most widely distributed woodpeckers in North America. This woodpecker is found almost anywhere forests exist. Similar in appearance to the smaller Downy Woodpecker, it is noisier but less confiding in humans and does not often allow a close approach before it flies away. Learning its high-pitched *peek* call note will make this shy bird easier to locate. Look for a white back when bird is in flight. The only difference between male and female birds is that the female lacks the red occipital patch. Birds in the Pacific Northwest show pale brownish gray underparts.

long black bill is nearly as long as head is deep

red occipital patch

black nape

white face with black malar mark and wedge-shaped postocular stripe

black shoulders

white underparts

black wings with white spotting/barring

black tail with 3 entirely white outermost feathers on each side

- **SONG** Loud downslurred whinny reminiscent of Belted Kingfisher's rattle. Call is bold, grating, sharp *peek*.
- **BEHAVIOR** Roosts in cavities at night. Feeds primarily on wood-boring insects and their larvae, other insects, nuts, seeds, and from the drill wells of sapsuckers. Both sexes drum to advertise presence and maintain territory.
- **BREEDING** Monogamous. Some individuals known to remain with same mate for at least 4 years.
- **NESTING** Incubation 11–15 days by both sexes (male at night). Altricial young remain in nest 28–30 days. Fed by both sexes. 1 brood per year unless nest is robbed or disturbed.
- **POPULATION** Fairly common, but sometimes local, over most of range. Sometimes more common in northern hardwood and boreal forests; rare in the Deep South and in Florida.
- **FEEDERS** Sometimes comes for sunflower seeds, nuts, fruits, peanut butter, and suet.

Similar Birds

DOWNY WOODPECKER Smaller; shorter, stubby bill (length much less than depth of head); white outer tailfeathers with dark spots/bars.

THREE-TOED WOODPECKER Black-and-white barring on back; dark barred sides • male has yellow crown.

Flight Pattern

Undulating flight with rapid wing beats alternating with pauses on folded wings, which produces bouncing flight.

Nest Identification

Shape ▨ Location ⚓ 🐝 🐦

4–60 feet above ground • built by both sexes • 3–6 white eggs, 1 inch in diameter.

Plumage Sexes differ	Habitat 🌲🌳	Migration Most do not migrate	Weight 2.5 ounces

DATE _____ TIME_____ LOCATION _____

| Family PICIDAE | Species *Picoides borealis* | Length 8.5 inches | Wingspan 16 inches |

RED-COCKADED WOODPECKER

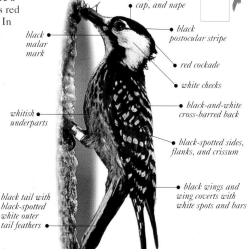

black forehead, cap, and nape

black postocular stripe

black malar mark

red cockade

white cheeks

black-and-white cross-barred back

whitish underparts

black-spotted sides, flanks, and crissum

black wings and wing coverts with white spots and bars

black tail with black-spotted white outer tail feathers

The white cheeks of this woodpecker are a more accurate field mark than the male's red cockade, which is indistinct in the field. In summer, the male begins drilling a large roosting and nesting cavity, which takes more than a year to complete. These cavities may be used for forty to fifty years. The Red-cockaded is unique among North American woodpeckers because it requires a living pine tree for its nesting cavity. When the cavity is drilled, sap and resins flow around the entrance, serving as a predator guard. Females lack the small red cockade.

• **SONG** Noisy. Call is *yank, yank,* somewhat like White-breasted Nuthatch. Also has hoarse *sripp* and high-pitched *tsick.*

• **BEHAVIOR** Gregarious. In clans of 3–7, consisting of mated pair, current young, and unmated adult helper(s). Forages and drills for insects on trunks of pine trees, sometimes circling tree as it climbs. In summer may feed on earworms in corn. Also eats berries and nuts. Nesting and roosting holes are marked by long strands of sap and resin oozing from inch-wide drill holes in rows above and below them; drill holes are maintained by clan who may remove bark from around hole.

• **BREEDING** Monogamous. Cooperative breeding in small colonies or clans. Mates for life.

• **NESTING** Incubation 10–15 days by both sexes. Young altricial; stay in nest 22–29 days, fed by both sexes and helpers. 1 brood per year.

• **POPULATION** Uncommon. Declined in 20th century.

• **FEEDERS AND BIRDHOUSES** Comes to mixture of suet and water. Will accept artificial nest cavities inserted into pine trees.

Similar Birds

HAIRY WOODPECKER
Black ear patch; white back; unmarked white underparts; unmarked white outer tail feathers; voice differs
• male has red occipital patch.

DOWNY WOODPECKER
Smaller in size; black ear patch; white back; unmarked white underparts; voice differs
• male has red occipital patch.

• **CONSERVATION** Has been designated an endangered species as a result of the over-cutting of mature pine forests as well as by fire suppression in the fire-maintained ecosystem of the Southeast.

Flight Pattern

Alternates several rapid wing beats with short glide with wings partially folded to sides, producing up-and-down flight.

Nest Identification

Shape Location

Dried wood chips • in live mature pine tree, often infected with heart fungus, 12–70 feet above ground • built by male and extra birds with some help from female • 2–5 white eggs; oval to elliptical, 1.0 x 0.75 inches.

| Plumage Sexes similar | Habitat | Migration Nonmigratory | Weight 1.6 ounces |

DATE _____ TIME _____ LOCATION _____

Family PICIDAE	Species *Colaptes auratus*	Length 12.75–14 inches	Wingspan 19–21 inches

NORTHERN FLICKER

This large woodpecker is often found in open spaces where it spends considerable time on the ground foraging for ants. Two distinct geographical groups, which were considered separate species until the early 1980s, occur: in the East and Northwest, Yellow-shafted Flicker has yellow underwings and undertail, and a black mustache; and, in the West, Red-shafted Flicker has bright salmon-red to red-orange underwings and undertail, and a red mustache. Although the two forms have similar bodies, the Red-shafted form shows a different pattern on its head with colors that are basically reversed from those of the Yellow-shafted form: a gray face and brown forehead, crown, and nape with no red crescent. Females are similar to males, lacking only the mustache. All birds have brown backs and wings with dark barring, a black crescent bib, buff to grayish underparts with heavy spotting, and a white rump patch.

red crescent on back of crown

gray nape

brown back and upperwings with black barring

gray crown and forehead

tan face

black mustache

YELLOW-SHAFTED MALE

buff-white underparts with heavy black spotting

RED-SHAFTED MALE

- **SONG** In breeding season, long bold repeated *wick-er, wick-er, wick-er* notes. Year-round, makes single loud *klee-yer* or *clearrrr*.
- **BEHAVIOR** Most terrestrial North American woodpecker. An analysis of the contents of a single flicker stomach revealed 3,000 ants. Spring courtship displays are noisy and animated, as pair bonds are established and rivals are driven away.
- **BREEDING** Monogamous. Solitary nester.
- **NESTING** Incubation 11–16 days by both sexes. Altricial young stay in nest 4 weeks, fed by both sexes. Usually 1 brood per year, sometimes 2 in the South.
- **POPULATION** Yellow-shafted form common. Red-shafted form is fairly common to common. Both thought to be declining.
- **BIRDHOUSES** Nests in houses and boxes.
- **CONSERVATION** Declining. Introduced European Starlings successfully compete for nest sites.

Similar Birds

GILDED FLICKER Limited range but overlaps with Red-shafted form; like a smaller, more washed out Red-shafted Flicker; yellow wash under wings and tail • only in the West.

Flight Pattern

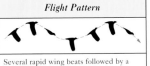

Several rapid wing beats followed by a pause with wings folded at sides produces up-and-down flight pattern.

Nest Identification	
Shape  Location	In snag, poles, posts, buildings, nest boxes, and banks (sometimes driving out the kingfisher or Bank Swallow tenants) • 6–20 feet above ground, sometimes higher • built by both sexes • sometimes uses same nest hole for second season • 3–12 white eggs; oval to short-oval; 1.1 x 0.8 inches.

Plumage Sexes differ	Habitat	Migration Most do not migrate	Weight 4.8 ounces

DATE _____ TIME_____ LOCATION _____

Family PICIDAE	Species *Dryocopus pileatus*	Length 16.5–19.5 inches	Wingspan 27–30 inches

PILEATED WOODPECKER

These crow-sized woodpeckers drum on trees to claim territory and attract a mate; the loud heavy sound is as if the tree is being hit with a wooden mallet. Each member of a mated pair excavates several roosting cavities and may retire for the evening in one of them. The male roosts in the current nesting cavity before the eggs are laid and afterward incubates them there at night. In flight both sexes show a large white patch at the base of the primaries as well as white underwing linings.

red crest extending from forehead to nape

large black bill

white chin

scarlet mustache

white line from base of bill crosses face to back of neck and extends down neck to side

solid black back

MALE

black forehead

black mustache

FEMALE

• **SONG** Location call to mate is a deliberate loud *cuck, cuck, cuck*. Both sexes have a call of *yucka, yucka, yucka*, similar to a flicker, that changes in pitch, loudness, and in its cadence.

• **BEHAVIOR** Solitary or in pairs. Loud and often conspicuous. Bores deep into trees and peels off large strips of bark for food. Also digs on ground and on fallen logs. Eats ants, beetles, and a variety of other insects, especially tree-boring ones, acorns, beechnuts, seeds of tree cones, nuts, and various fruits.

• **BREEDING** Monogamous.

• **NESTING** Incubation 15–18 days by both sexes, mostly male. Young altricial; brooded by female; stay in nest 26–28 days, fed by both sexes. 1 brood per year.

• **POPULATION** Common to fairly common in the Southeast; uncommon and local elsewhere.

• **FEEDERS** Mixture of melted suet, pecans, and walnut meats.

Similar Birds

♂ IVORY- BILLED WOODPECKER
Probably extinct
• larger; 2 white stripes on back extending from sides of neck; white secondaries make white patch on back when wings fold; black chin; ivory-white bill; in flight, shows white secondaries and tips of inner primaries; white lining onedge of underwing • female has black crest.

• **CONSERVATION** Vulnerable to habitat loss and forest fragmentation. Sharp decline in early 20th century, but has adapted to habitat changes. Competes for excavated nesting cavities with European Starlings.

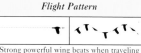

Flight Pattern

Strong powerful wing beats when traveling distances; alternates rapid wing strokes with brief periods of wings folded to sides on short flights beneath the canopy.

Nest Identification

Shape   Location 🪨 🪺 🌳

Few wood chips • dead or live tree in shaded area, 15–85 feet above ground • excavated by both sexes; female sometimes does more • 3–8 white eggs; oval to elliptical, 1.3 x 1.0 inches.

Plumage Sexes differ	Habitat 🌳 🌿 🍂	Migration Nonmigratory	Weight 10.9 ounces

DATE _____ TIME_____ LOCATION _____

Family TYRANNIDAE	Species *Camptostoma imberbe*	Length 4.5 inches	Wingspan 7 inches

NORTHERN BEARDLESS-TYRANNULET

As it is difficult to spot, this bird is best located by its high, thin voice. The male tends to sing from high perches in tall trees. Once spotted, this little flycatcher can be somewhat difficult to identify, especially if the crest is not raised and apparent. In conjunction with its voice, crest, and small size, other characteristics are the bird's fairly upright posture and wagging tail.

crown with bushy crest

faint whitish eyebrow

indistinct eye ring

small slightly curved bill with dusky tip and creamy-pink base

nape sometimes lighter than crown

gray-olive upperparts

2 buff-colored wing bars

dull white or pale yellow underparts

- **SONG** Clear notes with a whistled, slightly nasal *peeert* or *pee-yerp*. Also 3–5 or more brief melancholy downslurred notes, *dee-dee-dee-dee*.
- **BEHAVIOR** Solitary or in pairs. Easily overlooked. Forages low to high. In summer months, often seen hawking insects in midair in the manner of other flycatchers. In winter, forages for insects by gleaning from twigs and leaves like a kinglet, warbler, or vireo. Also feeds on small berries.
- **BREEDING** Monogamous.
- **NESTING** Breeding biology poorly known. Incubation time undetermined, but known to be performed by female. Young altricial; fed by both sexes. Age at first flight undetermined. 1–2 broods per year.
- **POPULATION** Uncommon in southeast Arizona and southern Texas, although can be locally common within range.
- **CONSERVATION** Neotropical migrant. Resident from northern Mexico through Central America. May have declined with the loss of streamside habitat.

Similar Birds

RUBY-CROWNED KINGLET
Rounder head; lacking crest; bold white eye ring; two distinct whitish wing bars; short notched tail; tiny dark bill; nervous habit of flicking wings as it hops through foliage.

BUFF-BREASTED FLYCATCHER
Slightly larger; pale brownish upperparts and head; cinnamon-buff breast; belly and undertail coverts washed pale yellowish white to buff-white; 2 whitish wingbars; white eye ring forms "teardrop"; white webs on outer tail feathers
- more limited Southwest range.

Flight Pattern	

Rather weak direct flight on rapidly beating wings. Often flies out from perch to take flying insect and returns.

Nest Identification	
Shape Location	Size and shape of baseball, with high entrance on one side • grass- and weed-lined, with vegetation, down, and feathers • outer branches of deciduous tree, 4–50 feet above ground; often built in the stems of a clump of mistletoe • built by female • 1–3 white eggs, finely marked with brown, olive, or gray spots at larger end; oval to long oval, 0.6 inch long.

Plumage Sexes similar	Habitat	Migration Migratory	Weight 0.3 ounce

DATE _____ TIME_____ LOCATION _____

Family TYRANNIDAE	Species *Contopus cooperi*	Length 7.5 inches	Wingspan 13 inches

OLIVE-SIDED FLYCATCHER

This is a stout large-headed flycatcher with dark olive sides and flanks and distinctive white rump side tufts, which are often concealed or obscured by the folded wings. The Olive-sided Flycatcher is often observed perched high on an exposed dead limb in a tree or on lookout in the tops of dead or living trees. Populations are on the decline in many regions, believed to be the result of disappearing winter habitats. Migration begins in late spring and early fall; these birds spend the winter as far away as Central and South America.

proportionally short neck

brownish olive upperparts

large mostly black bill with center and base of lower mandible a dull orange

dull white throat, center breast strip, belly, and undertail coverts

brownish olive sides of breast, streaked sides, and flanks

large stout body

black legs and feet

proportionally short tail

• **SONG** Call sounds like *quick three beers* with second note higher. Other calls include a trebled *pip*.

• **BEHAVIOR** Solitary. Reclusive. Often perched on high exposed branches. Hawks a wide variety of flying insects in midair, often taking larger insects the size of, and including, honeybees, beetles, and cicadas. Characteristic tendency is to vigorously defend nesting areas against predators and humans. Frequents open montane and boreal coniferous forests, burns, bogs, swamps, and areas around mountain lakes; uses dead trees for hunting perches.

• **BREEDING** Monogamous. Solitary.

• **NESTING** Incubation 14–17 days by female. Young altricial; fed by both sexes; first flight at 21–23 days. 1 brood per year.

• **POPULATION** Fairly common; casual in winter in coastal mountains of southern California. Declining; one factor may be deforestation and loss of habitat on wintering grounds.

• **CONSERVATION** Neotropical migrant.

Similar Birds

GREATER PEWEE
Longer tail; tufted crest; more uniform gray plumage overall; white chin and throat; dark upper mandible and bright orange lower mandible; lacks rump tufts; voice differs • casual in winter in Arizona and California.

EASTERN WOOD-PEWEE
Smaller, sparrow-sized body; pale whitish to olive-gray underparts; lacks rump tufts; 2 narrow white wing bars; voice differs.

Flight Pattern

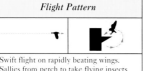

Swift flight on rapidly beating wings. Sallies from perch to take flying insects with audible snap of bill; returns to perch.

Nest Identification	
Shape 🥣 Location 🐦	Lined with lichen, grass, roots, twigs, weeds, and pine needles • in conifer, usually on horizontal branch, 5–70 feet above ground • built by female • 3–4 white to pinkish buff eggs with brown and gray spots concentrated at larger end; oval to short oval, 0.9 x 0.6 inches.

Plumage Sexes similar	Habitat ⛰ 🌲	Migration Migratory	Weight Undetermined

DATE _____ TIME_____ LOCATION _____

Family TYRANNIDAE	Species *Contopus pertinax*	Length 8 inches	Wingspan 13.5 inches

GREATER PEWEE

Also known as Coues's Flycatcher, the Greater Pewee is commonly seen year-round in most of the Mexican range, migrating only short distances northward into limited US montane breeding ranges in southeast to central Arizona and extreme southwest New Mexico. In summer months the Greater Pewee's plumage is grayish olive on its upperparts and yellowish white on its underparts. This species can be distinguished by its slender crest, which gives the head a slightly tufted appearance, and the long slender bicolored bill that is dark above and orange below.

slender tufted crest

grayish olive head and upperparts

dark upper mandible and orange lower mandible

pale wing bars

grayish white chin and throat

pale grayish breast and underparts with yellowish wash on belly

blackish legs and feet

long tail appears slightly notched when folded

- **SONG** A whistled *ho-sa, ma-re-ah*. Calls also include a mellow *pip-pip-pip*, which at times is steadily repeated.
- **BEHAVIOR** Solitary or in pairs. Often perched on dead branches midway up pine trees. Swoops down to catch insects in midair, often with an audible snap of its mandibles. Defends territory aggressively against intruders, including hawks, squirrels, snakes, and other birds.
- **BREEDING** Monogamous. Solitary.
- **NESTING** Period of incubation unknown. Young altricial; fed by both sexes; age at fledging undocumented. 1 brood per year.
- **POPULATION** Stable. Fairly common in montane pine-oak woodlands and sycamores. Casual in central and southern California and southern Arizona in winter.
- **CONSERVATION** Neotropical migrant, vulnerable to habitat loss because of timber harvesting.

Similar Birds

OLIVE-SIDED FLYCATCHER Proportionally bigger head and shorter tail; lacks pointed crest; heavy dark bill; creamy pink lower mandible with dark tip; dark grayish underparts with pale chin, throat, and central breast strip; dark grayish olive head and upperparts; white rump tufts; voice differs.

WESTERN WOOD-PEWEE Smaller, sparrow-sized body; dusky; 2-toned bill is dark above and yellow-orange on the base of the lower mandible; lacks tufted crest; voice differs.

Flight Pattern

Short flights with rapid shallow wing beats. Sallies out to take insects in air, often returning to same or nearby perch.

Nest Identification	
Shape	Location	Lined with fine grass, weeds, leaves, lichen, and other vegetation, often attached to branch by spider web • fork of horizontal branch, 10–40 feet above ground, in conifer or sycamore • built by female • 3–4 dull white to creamy white eggs, brown and gray markings mostly near larger end; oval to short oval, 0.8 inch long.

Plumage Sexes similar	Habitat	Migration Migratory	Weight 1.0 ounce

DATE _____ TIME_____ LOCATION _____

Family TYRANNIDAE	Species *Contopus sordidulus*	Length 6.25 inches	Wingspan 10.5 inches

WESTERN WOOD-PEWEE

The western counterpart to the Eastern Wood-Pewee is similar in appearance but has a different call. Like other pewees, its wings quiver when it lands, but it does not wag its tail. This sparrow-sized flycatcher is dark and dusky overall and inhabits riparian woodlands and open, mixed conifer and hardwood forests in the mountains. Note the two thin wing bars and the lack of an eye ring.

dark grayish brown overall

dark bill

yellow-orange on base of lower mandible

2 thin white bars on wings

paler underparts

blackish feet and legs

• **SONG** On breeding grounds sings *tswee-tee-teet*. Also has soft, nasal whistle *peeer* or *peeyee*, given throughout the year. Often vocalizes before daylight; in evenings sometimes sings until after dark.

• **BEHAVIOR** Solitary. Stays quietly hidden in trees or perched in open view until it spots food, then flies out and snatches insect. Eats wide variety of small to medium flying insects, some spiders, and a few wild berries.

• **BREEDING** Monogamous.

• **NESTING** Incubation 12–13 days by female. Altricial young. Fed by both sexes. First flight at 14–18 days. 1 brood per year.

• **POPULATION** Common to abundant in some areas but declining in parts of California. Casual in the East in migration.

• **CONSERVATION** Neotropical migrant. This bird is vulnerable to deforestation on its wintering grounds.

Similar Birds

GREATER PEWEE
Tufted crest; larger; larger bill; dark upperparts; yellow-orange underparts; indistinct wing bars; different call • casual in winter in Arizona and California.

EASTERN WOOD-PEWEE
More olive upperparts; less dusky underparts; pale bill; different voice.

Flight Pattern
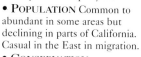

Weak fluttering direct flight with shallow wing beats. Sallies from perch to catch insects, returning to same or nearby perch.

Nest Identification	
Shape Location	Grass, plant fibers, and plant down • decorated outside with gray moss, leaves, and sometimes lichen • bound to branch with spider webs • in trees, usually conifer, on horizontal branch 15–75 feet above ground • built by female • 2–4 whitish to creamy eggs blotched with brown and lavender, often concentrated toward larger end; oval to short oval, 0.7 inch long.

Plumage Sexes similar	Habitat	Migration Migratory	Weight 0.5 ounce

DATE _____ TIME_____ LOCATION _____

Family TYRANNIDAE	Species *Contopus virens*	Length 6.25 inches	Wingspan 10.5 inches

EASTERN WOOD-PEWEE

Although this bird is very difficult to distinguish visually from its western counterpart, the Western Wood-Pewee, their ranges barely overlap and their voices differ. Like most flycatchers, it tends to perch on an open lookout among thick trees or shrubs, sailing into the open only to feed. It is often first detected by its voice, because it often calls its distinctive *pee-a-wee* while perched, awaiting its next chance at a flying insect. Juveniles are similar to adults but both upper and lower mandibles showing dark coloration.

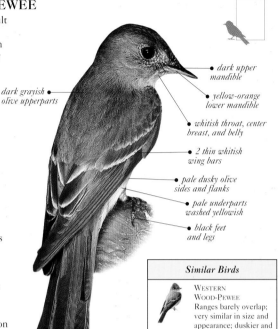

dark grayish olive upperparts

dark upper mandible

yellow-orange lower mandible

whitish throat, center breast, and belly

2 thin whitish wing bars

pale dusky olive sides and flanks

pale underparts washed yellowish

black feet and legs

- **SONG** During the day whistles distinctive, slow plaintive *pee-a-wee*, with second note lower; on second or third repeat, often followed by *pee-yeer*; second note lower. At dusk and early dawn, sings *ah-de-deee*.
- **BEHAVIOR** Solitary. Perches on open and/or dead branches in trees to spot prey; flies out to catch food. Eats a wide variety of flying insects, including beetles, flies, moths, wasps, and bees. Takes some spiders and a few berries. Like other flycatchers, it often defends its territory even from larger birds by flying at them and pecking at their backs.
- **BREEDING** Monogamous.
- **NESTING** Incubation 12–13 days by female. Young altricial; stay in nest 14–18 days, fed by both sexes. 1 brood per year.

Similar Birds

WESTERN WOOD-PEWEE
Ranges barely overlap; very similar in size and appearance; duskier and darker overall; darker lower mandible; voice is different.

EASTERN PHOEBE
Slightly larger; paler whitish to yellow underparts; lacks wing bars; both mandibles dark; pumps tail up and down while perched, especially upon landing; voice differs.

- **POPULATION** Fairly common and widespread. Casual in the West in migration.
- **CONSERVATION** Neotropical migrant. Infrequent host to cowbird's eggs. Decline due to possible loss of South American wintering habitat.

Flight Pattern

Rather slow fluttering direct flight on shallowly beating wings. Sallies forth to catch insects in midair, returning to perch.

Nest Identification

Shape ⬤ Location 🪺 🐦

Grass, plant fibers, and spider web, covered with thick layer of lichens • fork of tree or saddled on horizontal branch, 15–50 feet above ground • built by female • 2–4 whitish eggs, with brown blotches and purple, often wreathed at large end; oval to short ovate, 0.7 x 0.5 inches.

Plumage Sexes similar	Habitat 🌳 🪵	Migration Migratory	Weight 0.5 ounce

Family TYRANNIDAE	Species *Empidonax flaviventris*	Length 5.5 inches	Wingspan 8.5 inches

YELLOW-BELLIED FLYCATCHER

Once you spot this small bird, its yellowish underparts from chin to undertail coverts make it easy to identify because it is the only eastern Empidonax with a yellow throat. Voice and habitat also are key to clinching the identification. It usually stays hidden low in trees, shrubs, or thickets, but making various squeaking or kissing sounds on the back of your hand may lure it from its hiding place. This flycatcher is credited with eating more ants than any other empid.

large head

broad yellow eye ring

olive upperparts

pale orange lower mandible

yellow throat

olive wash on breast

2 whitish wing bars

yellow underparts

short tail

- **SONG** Often silent in migration. Slurred and explosive *pse-ek*! Also makes a *per-WEE*, reminiscent of a pewee's short song, and a shrill *chiu*.

- **BEHAVIOR** Secretive and quiet. Stays low in thickets near the ground and inside foliage in wet swampy woods. Eats a variety of insects, including beetles, moths, tent caterpillars, flies, ants, and some spiders. May subsist on mountain ash during severe weather. As it gives its single strong note it flutters its wings and jerks its head and tail as if the vocal effort was so strenuous as to cause the shudder.

- **BREEDING** Monogamous. Solitary.

- **NESTING** Incubation 12–14 days by female. Altricial young fed by both sexes. First flight at 13–14 days. 1 brood per year.

- **POPULATION** Common to fairly common. Stable.

- **CONSERVATION** Neotropical migrant. Occasionally parasitized by Brown-headed Cowbird.

Similar Birds

CORDILLERAN FLYCATCHER
Teardrop-shaped eye ring; less contrasting wings and wing bars; darker brown upperparts; proportionally longer tail; different voice.

ACADIAN FLYCATCHER
Whitish gray throat; buff to white wash on wing bars; larger bill is yellowish below; yellow wash on belly and undertail coverts; proportionally longer tail; different voice.

Flight Pattern

Weak fluttering flight with shallow rapid wing beats. Sallies from perch to hawk insects and returns to same or nearby perch.

Nest Identification

Shape 🍵 Location ━ 🪹 🪺

Twigs, rootlets, weeds, and moss • lined with thin rootlets, grass, and fresh leaves • atop hillock of moss or on upturned stumps among roots of fallen trees, 0–2 feet above ground • built by female • 3–5 white eggs with light brown dots that become heavier near larger end; oval to short oval, 0.7 by 0.5 inches.

Plumage Sexes similar	Habitat 🌳 🌲 🌿 ⛰	Migration Migratory	Weight 0.4 ounce

DATE _____ TIME _____ LOCATION _____

Family TYRANNIDAE	Species *Empidonax virescens*	Length 5.75 inches	Wingspan 8.75 inches

ACADIAN FLYCATCHER

Its scientific genus name, which means "mosquito king," widely misses the mark in describing this bird's feeding habits, but it is an apt description of the small size of a flycatcher that lords over a realm of small insects. It is the only Empidonax flycatcher to breed in the deep southern states of North America, where it rules in heavily wooded deciduous bottomlands, swamps, and riparian thickets, and in the wooded ravines of drier uplands. Like other empids it is best known by its voice.

• **SONG** Soft call of *peace* or *peeet*. Its explosive *PIZ-zza!!* sounds like a bird sneezing. On territory, males utter a mechanical *ti, ti, ti, ti* as they move from one perch to the next beneath the canopy.

• **BEHAVIOR** Solitary. Easily overlooked except for its occasional vocalizations. Perches in shade on lower to mid-level branches in thick trees to search for food, then dashes out to snatch insect. Eats wide variety of flying insects. Frequents wet areas in open woodlands where it aggressively drives away larger birds and other intruders from the breeding territory.

• **BREEDING** Monogamous.

• **NESTING** Incubation 13–15 days by female. Young altricial; fed by both sexes, but more by female. First flight at 13–15 days; male may feed fledglings while female starts second clutch. 2 broods per year.

• **POPULATION** Common; range expanding in Northeast.

• **CONSERVATION** Neotropical migrant. Frequently nest parasitized by Brown-headed Cowbird.

pale yellow eye ring

olive upperparts

2 buffy or whitish wing bars

long broad-based bill with yellow lower mandible

pale grayish throat

white lower breast

yellowish undertail coverts and belly

long primary projection

Similar Birds

LEAST FLYCATCHER Smaller bill; more brownish olive upperparts; grayish white underparts; bright white wingbars and eye ring; shorter primary projection • voice and breeding habitat differ.

WILLOW FLYCATCHER ALDER FLYCATCHER Less distinct eye ring, less contrasting wings with dull wingbars; and more brown upperparts • voice and breeding habitat differ.

Flight Pattern

Weak fluttering flight with shallow wing beats on rapidly beating wings. Sallies out from perch and takes insects in flight, then returns to same or nearby perch.

Nest Identification

Shape Location

Sticks, grass, dried stems, and bits of bark and cobweb; lined with grass, hair, and plant down • sloppy/messy-looking with long streamers of grasses hanging beneath cup • in fork of horizontal limb well out from trunk • 3–25 feet up • built by female • 2–4 creamy white eggs, with sparse brown spots; oval to short oval; 0.7 x 0.6 inches.

Plumage Sexes similar	Habitat	Migration Migratory	Weight 0.5 ounce

DATE _____ TIME_____ LOCATION _____

Family TYRANNIDAE	Species *Empidonax alnorum*	Length 5.75 inches	Wingspan 8–9 inches

ALDER FLYCATCHER

Perhaps the most green-brown of the eastern empids, this bird was formerly known as Traill's Flycatcher, from which both it and the Willow Flycatcher were split into separate species in the 1970s. This shy bird is easily overlooked; during nesting season it stays hidden within the thick trees and shrubs of its alder swamp and wet meadow-thicket habitat. Occasionally it can be spotted dashing out of hiding to catch passing insects or perching conspicuously on an exposed branch to sing.

brownish olive head

white eye ring

brownish olive upperparts

blackish bill with pinkish orange lower mandible

whitish throat

dusky wash on chest

pale yellow wash on sides and flanks

2 white bars on wings

whitish belly

darker wings

whitish undertail coverts

blackish legs and feet

darker tail

- **SONG** Raspy *fee-bee-o* or *way-bee-o* on breeding grounds. Also has call of bold *pep*.
- **BEHAVIOR** Male sings repeatedly for first 2 weeks after returning to territory in late spring, but after he bonds with female is largely silent. Stays low in thick vegetation, often hunting inside umbrella of thicket canopy. Perches in shrubs to spot prey, then catches it in flight. Eats wide variety of flying insects; gleans some from vegetation, including spiders and millipedes. Also feeds on some types of small berries.
- **BREEDING** Monogamous.
- **NESTING** Incubation 12–14 days by female. Altricial young. Fed by both sexes. First flight at 13–14 days. 1 brood per year.

Similar Birds

WILLOW FLYCATCHER
Different call; more brown overall; less-prominent wing bars and eye ring; *whit* call note • different breeding habitat.

ACADIAN FLYCATCHER
Greener upperparts; longer tail; yellowish eye ring; yellow wash on belly and undertail coverts; different voice and habitat.

- **POPULATION** Common and considered stable.
- **CONSERVATION** Neotropical migrant. Occasionally nest parasitized by Brown-headed Cowbird.

Flight Pattern

Weak fluttering direct flight with shallow wing beats. Sallies to hawk flying insects, often returning to same or nearby perch.

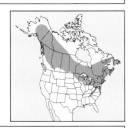

Nest Identification	Grass, weeds, bark strips, small twigs, and rootlets • lined with plant down or other soft materials • in horizontal or upright fork of shrub or low tree 1–4 feet (sometimes as high as 30 feet) above ground • built by female • 3–4 white eggs dotted with brown on larger end; oval, 0.7 x 0.55 inches.
Shape ☕ Location 🌳 🌲 🌿	

Plumage Sexes similar	Habitat 🌿 🌲	Migration Migratory	Weight 0.5 ounce

DATE _____ TIME_____ LOCATION _____

Family TYRANNIDAE	Species *Empidonax traillii*	Length 5.75 inches	Wingspan 8–9 inches

WILLOW FLYCATCHER

This bird can be distinguished from other Empidonax flycatchers by its voice and breeding habitat preference, plus it is perhaps the most brown of the eastern Empidonax and lacks a prominent eye ring. Much variation occurs in overall color: northwestern races have dark heads, while southwestern races are very pale. The compact, intricate nests of these birds often have streamers hanging underneath. Formerly this species was lumped together with the Alder Flycatcher as the Traill's Flycatcher.

brownish to brownish green head

brownish green upperparts

thin pale eye ring

pale lores

blackish bill with yellowish pink lower mandible

dark wings with buff to yellow wing bars

whitish center of belly and undertail coverts

pale yellow trim on tertials and secondaries

dusky flanks and sides tinged with yellow

blackish legs and feet

dark tail

- **SONG** Often silent in migration. Utters harsh, burry *fitz-bew* or *fritz-be-yew*, resembling a sneeze with accent on first syllable. Call a loud, thick *whit!*
- **BEHAVIOR** Inhabits swamps and willow thickets along streams. Often perches low below crown of vegetation; when singing uses exposed perch. Males chase females in courtship flights similar to those of other empids. Perches to spot prey, then catches it in flight. Eats wide variety of flying insects and those gleaned from foliage; also takes spiders and some berries.
- **BREEDING** Monogamous.
- **NESTING** Incubation 12–15 days by female. Altricial young. Fed by both sexes. First flight at 12–14 days. 1 brood per year.
- **POPULATION** Fairly common and expanding southern range in the East; uncommon to rare in parts of the West; declining on West Coast. Decline due to loss of streamside habitat.
- **CONSERVATION** Neotropical migrant. Nests parasitized by Brown-headed Cowbird. Populations increase with reduced cattle grazing in breeding habitats and cessation of killing and removing streamside willow thickets.

Similar Birds

ALDER FLYCATCHER
Shorter bill; more prominent eye ring; more olive-gray to olive-brown back; bolder buff wing bars • different voice and habitat.

Flight Pattern

Weak fluttering flight with shallow rapid wing beats. Sallies from perch to hawk flying insects, returning to perch.

Nest Identification

Shape   Location

Bark, grass, rootlets, and bits of plants • lined with plant down and other soft vegetation • in fork of deciduous tree or shrub 2–15 feet above ground • built by female • 2–4 pale buff to whitish eggs with brown spots that become thicker on the larger end; oval to short oval, 0.7 x 0.55 inches.

Plumage Sexes similar	Habitat	Migration Migratory	Weight 0.5 ounce

DATE _____ TIME _____ LOCATION _____

Family TYRANNIDAE	Species *Empidonax minimus*	Length 5.25 inches	Wingspan 7.5–8.5 inches

LEAST FLYCATCHER

large head

short triangular bill

white eye ring

whitish throat

pale lower mandible with dusky tip

gray wash on breast

olive-green to brown upperparts

paler underparts

white wing bars

short primary projection

pale yellow belly

pale yellow undertail coverts

A common summer breeding resident in North America and the smallest of the eastern empids, the Least Flycatcher is perhaps the most often-encountered small flycatcher in the East. During breeding season the male makes a noisy territorial display, calling *chee-BECK* more than sixty times per minute while chasing other flycatchers in its territory. Note its small size, small bill, brown to olive wash on the upperparts, and conspicuous eye ring and wing bars.

• **SONG** Sings raspy repetitive *chee-BECK*. Call is piercing *whitt-whitt-whitt*.

• **BEHAVIOR** Active, often changing perches. Flicks tail and wings a lot; jerks tail strongly upward. Chases female in courtship; chases ecologically similar American Redstart out of nesting territory. Perches to spot prey, then catches it in the air while flying. Also gleans insects from branches and foliage. Eats wide variety of insects, some spiders, and a few berries and seeds.

• **BREEDING** Monogamous. Sometimes in loose colonies.

• **NESTING** Incubation 13–15 days by female. Altricial young stay in nest 12–17 days. Fed by both sexes. 1–2 broods per year.

• **POPULATION** Common and widespread but declining in parts of range.

• **CONSERVATION** Neotropical migrant. Uncommon host to cowbird. Declining population noted by National Audubon Society.

Similar Birds

WILLOW, ALDER, AND ACADIAN FLYCATCHERS
Larger; larger bills; greener upperparts; longer primary extensions; different voices • Willow Flycatcher has less prominent eye ring but similar *whit* call note.

DUSKY FLYCATCHER
Slightly longer, narrower bill; longer tail; grayer throat; less contrast in wings; more narrow eye ring; different song.

HAMMOND'S FLYCATCHER
Small narrow bill; part of lower mandible is orangish; gray throat; darker olive-gray breast; more distinct teardrop-shaped eye ring; long primary projection; different voice.

Flight Pattern

Weak fluttering direct flight with shallow wing beats. Sallies to take insects in flight and returns to same or nearby perch.

Nest Identification	
Shape ◗ Location 🌳 🌿 🪶	Grass, bark strips, twigs, lichens, and plant fibers; bound by spider or caterpillar webs • in fork of tree or shrub 2–60 feet above ground • built by female • 3–6 creamy white eggs; ovate, 0.6 x 0.5 inches.

Plumage Sexes similar	Habitat 🌱 🌲	Migration Migratory	Weight 0.4 ounce

Family TYRANNIDAE	Species *Empidonax hammondii*	Length 5.5 inches	Wingspan 9 inches

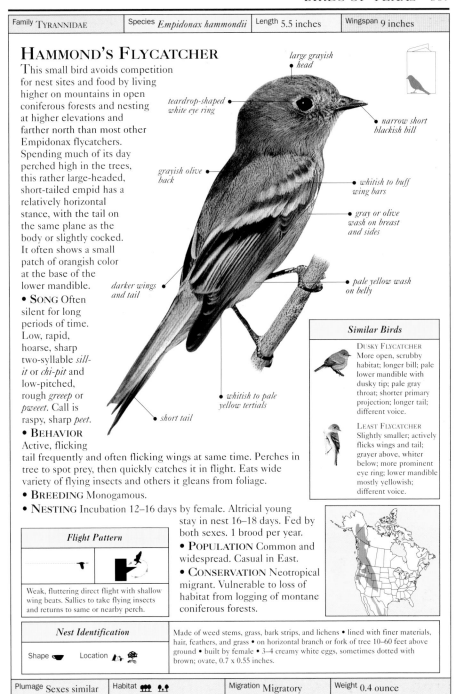

HAMMOND'S FLYCATCHER

This small bird avoids competition for nest sites and food by living higher on mountains in open coniferous forests and nesting at higher elevations and farther north than most other Empidonax flycatchers. Spending much of its day perched high in the trees, this rather large-headed, short-tailed empid has a relatively horizontal stance, with the tail on the same plane as the body or slightly cocked. It often shows a small patch of orangish color at the base of the lower mandible.

large grayish head

teardrop-shaped white eye ring

narrow short blackish bill

grayish olive back

whitish to buff wing bars

gray or olive wash on breast and sides

darker wings and tail

pale yellow wash on belly

• **SONG** Often silent for long periods of time. Low, rapid, hoarse, sharp two-syllable *sill-it* or *chi-pit* and low-pitched, rough *greeep* or *pweeet*. Call is raspy, sharp *peet*.

whitish to pale yellow tertials

short tail

• **BEHAVIOR** Active, flicking tail frequently and often flicking wings at same time. Perches in tree to spot prey, then quickly catches it in flight. Eats wide variety of flying insects and others it gleans from foliage.

• **BREEDING** Monogamous.

• **NESTING** Incubation 12–16 days by female. Altricial young stay in nest 16–18 days. Fed by both sexes. 1 brood per year.

• **POPULATION** Common and widespread. Casual in East.

• **CONSERVATION** Neotropical migrant. Vulnerable to loss of habitat from logging of montane coniferous forests.

Similar Birds

DUSKY FLYCATCHER
More open, scrubby habitat; longer bill; pale lower mandible with dusky tip; pale gray throat; shorter primary projection; longer tail; different voice.

LEAST FLYCATCHER
Slightly smaller; actively flicks wings and tail; grayer above, whiter below; more prominent eye ring; lower mandible mostly yellowish; different voice.

Flight Pattern

Weak, fluttering direct flight with shallow wing beats. Sallies to take flying insects and returns to same or nearby perch.

Nest Identification

Shape ⬤ Location 🌿🌳

Made of weed stems, grass, bark strips, and lichens • lined with finer materials, hair, feathers, and grass • on horizontal branch or fork of tree 10–60 feet above ground • built by female • 3–4 creamy white eggs, sometimes dotted with brown; ovate, 0.7 x 0.55 inches.

Plumage Sexes similar	Habitat 🌳 🌿	Migration Migratory	Weight 0.4 ounce

DATE _____ TIME_____ LOCATION _____

Family TYRANNIDAE	Species *Empidonax wrightii*	Length 6 inches	Wingspan 9.5 inches

GRAY FLYCATCHER

This shy bird is at home in the Great Basin spending most of its day in arid, open woodland, perched on piñon or juniper trees or in sagebrush. When frightened, it dives for cover and stays hidden in thick bushes until the intruder has passed. Its gray coloration and long tail, which it slowly bobs like a phoebe, make it the easiest empid to identify visually. By late fall, its whitish underparts show a pale yellow wash. Juveniles display two buffy rather than whitish wing bars.

pale gray face

small rounded head

bold white eye ring

gray upperparts with pale olive wash

long bill with black tip and dark upper mandible

pinkish orange lower mandible

whitish throat

2 thin whitish wing bars

whitish underparts

blackish feet and legs

long tail

• **SONG** Sings an energetic irregular low-pitched *chee-whipp* or *chuwip*. Call note is a *whipp*.

• **BEHAVIOR** The tail-dipping trait is the most distinctive of any empid and differs from the upward tail jerks of several other species. The long tail is quickly twitched, then slowly lowered, and finally raised back to the original position. Tends to perch low and fly down, taking insects on or near the ground. Eats grasshoppers, beetles, wasps, bees, moths, and other small insects.

• **BREEDING** Monogamous.

• **NESTING** Incubation 14 days by female. Young altricial; stay in nest 16 days, fed by both sexes. First flight at 16 days. 1 brood per year.

• **POPULATION** Fairly common in semiarid habitat of the Great Basin. Casual to uncommon migrant in coastal California; accidental in the East.

• **CONSERVATION** Neotropical migrant. Vulnerable to habitat loss due to development and overgrazing.

Similar Birds

DUSKY FLYCATCHER Frequents arid to semiarid scrub habitat • shorter bill with dark orange base; pale throat; olive-gray upperparts; fairly conspicuous eye ring; voice differs, but call note is similar.

Flight Pattern

Weak fluttering flight on shallow wing beats. Sallies forth to hawk insects in flight, often returning to same perch.

Nest Identification

Shape ☕ Location 🌿 🌲

Weeds, bark, grasses, and twigs, lined with plant down, fine bark fibers, animal fur, and feathers • fork of shrub or conifer, 2–9 feet above ground • female builds; male sometimes helps • 3–4 creamy white eggs; oval to short oval, 0.7 x 0.6 inches.

Plumage Sexes similar	Habitat 🏔 🌿 🏚	Migration Migratory	Weight 0.4 ounce

DATE _____ TIME_____ LOCATION _____

Family TYRANNIDAE	Species *Empidonax oberholseri*	Length 5.75 inches	Wingspan 8–9 inches

DUSKY FLYCATCHER

This bird prefers to breed and nest in the open woodlands and brushlands of high mountain chaparrals of western North America. It is similar to Hammond's Flycatcher but stays lower in elevation and less sheltered in trees, outside the dense spruce-fir forests preferred by Hammond's. It is intermediate between the Hammond's and Gray Flycatchers in body size, bill size, and tail length, and sometimes shows a yellowish wash on its underparts.

pale lores more conspicuous than other empids

white eye ring

grayish olive upperparts

bill has orange-based lower mandible fading into dark tip

whitish throat

pale olive wash on upper breast

- **SONG** Song is variable in pattern. On breeding grounds, sings a melancholy *dee-hick* or *sill-it*, given in late evening or early morning. Also has songs of a rough *grrreeep* and a clear high-pitched *pweet*. Call note is a dry *whit*.
- **BEHAVIOR** Solitary. Occasionally flicks tail upward while perched, but only flicks wings irregularly. Usually builds nests below 12 feet high, unlike Hammond's, which usually builds higher than 12 feet. Often perches in trees to sing. Feeds by gleaning insects from foliage and by hawking sallies; eats moths and other flying insects.
- **BREEDING** Monogamous.
- **NESTING** Incubation 12–16 days by female. Young altricial; stay in nest 15–20 days, fed by both sexes, but female does more. Parents tend young another 21 days after leaving nest. 1 brood per year.
- **POPULATION** Common and increasing. Accidental in the eastern US.
- **CONSERVATION** Neotropical migrant.

Similar Birds

GRAY FLYCATCHER Frequents more open desert scrub and piñon-juniper • longer bill; long tail; overall gray coloration; gray-white throat; dips tail down like a phoebe.

HAMMOND'S FLYCATCHER Frequents higher-elevation dense conifer forests • narrow, short bill with flesh-orange basal half to lower mandible; long primary extension; call differs.

Flight Pattern	

Weak fluttering flight with shallow wing beats. Sallies forth and picks off flying insects, often returning to the same perch.

Nest Identification	
Shape	Location 

Grasses, weeds, and bark, lined with plant down, soft grasses, feathers, and animal hair • fork of tree or shrub, 3–7 feet above ground • built by female • 3–4 chalky white eggs; ovate, 0.7 inch long.

Plumage Sexes similar	Habitat	Migration Migratory	Weight 0.4 ounce

DATE _____ TIME_____ LOCATION _____

Family TYRANNIDAE	Species *Empidonax occidentalis*	Length 5.5 inches	Wingspan 8.5 inches

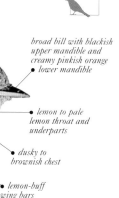

CORDILLERAN FLYCATCHER

At one time the Cordilleran Flycatcher and the Pacific-Slope Flycatcher were considered the same species, called the Western Flycatcher. Visually inseparable from the Pacific-Slope in the field, the Cordilleran is only reliably distinguished by the male's song, a double-note *pit peet*, and by its range during the breeding season. In September the Cordilleran Flycatcher migrates to Mexico, settling in foothills and mountains, where it is also a resident. The bird arrives in May on its breeding grounds.

teardrop-shaped pale lemon eye ring

broad bill with blackish upper mandible and creamy pinkish orange lower mandible

olive to brownish upperparts and olive head

lemon to pale lemon throat and underparts

dusky to brownish chest

dark brownish wings and tail

lemon-buff wing bars

blackish gray feet and legs

lemon-buff to pale lemon tertial edges, panel on secondaries

• **SONG** Male's song is a double-noted *pit peet*. Call is a thin high-pitched sharp *seet*.

• **BEHAVIOR** Solitary. Often perches in conspicuous place, but frequents shady spots rather than open places. Hawks flying insects and gleans insects from branches and foliage; insects include ants, bees, wasps, moths, caterpillars, and beetles. Sometimes eats berries and seeds.

• **BREEDING** Monogamous.

• **NESTING** Incubation 14–15 days by female. Altricial young remain in nest 14–18 days, fed by both sexes. 1 brood per year, perhaps 2.

• **POPULATION** Widespread and common in montane coniferous forests and wooded canyons. Casual on the Great Plains in migration.

• **CONSERVATION** Neotropical migrant. Sometimes parasitized by cowbirds. Vulnerable to habitat loss caused by logging operations.

Similar Birds

PACIFIC-SLOPE FLYCATCHER
Smaller body; paler brownish green upperparts and head; bright yellowish and olive underparts; brownish breast; broad pale eye ring is pointed behind eye; breeding range differs; voice of male differs.

Flight Pattern

Weak fluttering flight with shallow wing beats. Hawks insects by flying forth to take them in air and returning to perch.

Nest Identification

Shape ⬤   Location 🪹 🪺 🪵 🏚️ 🌿

Lined with lichen, leaves, bark, moss, grass, and roots • variety of locations such as stream banks, roots of upturned trees, cliff ledges, buildings, tree branches • 0–30 feet above ground • built by female • 3–5 whitish eggs, with brown blotches concentrated near larger end; oval to short-oval, 0.7 x 0.55 inches.

Plumage Sexes similar	Habitat 	Migration Migratory	Weight 0.4 ounce

DATE _____ TIME_____ LOCATION _____

Family TYRANNIDAE	Species *Sayornis nigricans*	Length 6–7 inches	Wingspan 10.5–11 inches

BLACK PHOEBE

An increasingly common bird, the Black Phoebe is often sighted pumping its tail, watching for prey from treetops and other perches. Because it nests, forages, and perches near water, a proliferation of artificial ponds and other bodies of water in its western range has ensured this species' survival. This is our only black flycatcher with a juncolike white pattern on its belly and undertail coverts. Juveniles show more brown and have a cinnamon rump and two indistinct cinnamon wing bars.

- *black body*
- *straight black bill with slight hook at tip*
- *white belly*
- *black legs and feet*
- *white undertail coverts*
- *black tail*

- **SONG** Most common call is a sharp *seek!* Typical song is in 4 parts, beginning with a rising scale followed by 2 descending notes, *pee-wee, pee-wee*; usually given at dawn but also often during the day, repeated many times, and often given while circling in flight. Also occasionally makes loud *tseee*.
- **BEHAVIOR** Solitary or in pairs. Found near streams, rivers, cattle tanks, ponds, lakes, and towns – wherever there is much water. Pumps tail up and down. Often hunts from a low, shaded perch where it watches for insects and swoops down to catch them in midair. Occasionally catches food from water's surface, ground, or vegetation. Coughs up indigestible insect parts in the form of pellets. Sometimes eats small fish caught at water's surface.
- **BREEDING** Monogamous. Solitary nester.
- **NESTING** Incubation 15–17 days by female. Altricial young stay in nest 14–21 days. Fed by both sexes. 2–3 broods per year.
- **POPULATION** Common near water. Accidental in East.
- **CONSERVATION** Artificial ponds are contributing to an increasing population.

Similar Birds

EASTERN PHOEBE Olive-gray on breast and sides; brownish gray on upperparts darkest on head; mostly white underparts • in fresh fall molt has yellow wash on underparts • emphatic *FEE-be!* voice.

EASTERN KINGBIRD Black head; blackish gray upperparts and wings; black tail with white terminal band; white underparts from chin to undertail coverts; black bill, legs, and feet; does not bob tail.

Flight Pattern

Weak fluttering buoyant flight with shallow wing beats. Sallies from perch to catch insects in air with audible snap of bill, returning to same or nearby perch.

Nest Identification

Shape ◣ Location ⌇⌇ 🪹 🏚

Adherent • made of mud pellets and moss • lined with vegetation, including grass, weeds, and roots, as well as bark and hair • attached to vertical surface or on shelf or beam • built by female • 3–6 white eggs with occasional reddish brown spots; ovate to short ovate, occasionally short subelliptical, 0.7 x 0.6 inches.

Plumage Sexes similar	Habitat 〰〰 🐚 ⚘	Migration Most do not migrate	Weight 0.7 ounce

DATE _____ TIME_____ LOCATION _____

| Family TYRANNIDAE | Species *Sayornis phoebe* | Length 7 inches | Wingspan 11.5 inches |

EASTERN PHOEBE

An early migration makes the Eastern Phoebe a common harbinger of spring north of the Mason-Dixon Line. It is easily identified by its wagging tail and distinctive, harsh *fee-be* calls. The subject of the first bird-banding experiment in North America, by John James Audubon in 1840, the Eastern Phoebe has provided researchers with much information about longevity, site fidelity, dispersal, and migratory movements. Phoebes are hardy birds that often winter near water as far north as the Ohio River. This is the only species of flycatcher to winter in the eastern United States. In the bird's nesting range it seems almost every concrete bridge and culvert over small to medium streams has a phoebe nest beneath it.

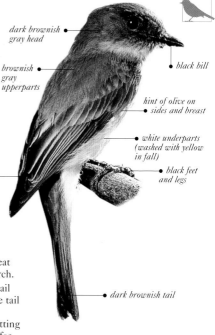

dark brownish gray head

black bill

brownish gray upperparts

hint of olive on sides and breast

white underparts (washed with yellow in fall)

black feet and legs

dark brownish wings

dark brownish tail

- **SONG** Sharp *chip* is one of most common calls. Also issues brusque pointed *FEE-be* accented on first syllable. Song often repeated, especially when male establishes territory and attempts to attract mate; may repeat many times per minute from high, exposed perch.
- **BEHAVIOR** Solitary or in pairs. Often bobs tail when perched, especially after landing with the tail swept downward, then raised upward, and sometimes pushed sideways in an arc. While sitting atop tree branches and other perches, watches for insects and sallies to catch them in midair. Also catches food in foliage and on ground. In addition to insects, also eats small fish, berries, and fruit.
- **BREEDING** Monogamous. Solitary nester.
- **NESTING** Incubation about 16 days by female. Altricial young stay in nest 15–16 days. Fed by both sexes. 2 broods per year, sometimes 3 in the South.
- **POPULATION** Common and increasing.

Similar Birds

EASTERN WOOD-PEWEE Darker underparts; yellowish lower mandible; 2 whitish wing bars; does not pump tail; different voice.

- **BIRDHOUSES** Accepts nesting ledges glued to vertical walls under concrete bridges.
- **CONSERVATION** Neotropical migrant. Parasitized by cowbirds. Buildings, dams, bridges, and culverts have provided more nesting areas.

Flight Pattern

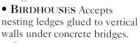

Weak buoyant fluttering flight with shallow wing beats. Hawks insects by flying from perch and taking insect in flight with audible pop of the mandibles.

Nest Identification

Shape   Location

Mud pellets covered with moss • lined with grass, weeds, leaves, hair, and feathers • often built on top of remains of old nest • attached to a vertical wall or on a shelf or beam • built by female • 2–8 white eggs with occasional reddish brown spots; oval, 0.8 x 0.6 inches.

| Plumage Sexes similar | Habitat | Migration Most migrate | Weight 0.7 ounce |

DATE _____ TIME_____ LOCATION _____

Family TYRANNIDAE	Species *Sayornis saya*	Length 7.5 inches	Wingspan 12.5 inches

SAY'S PHOEBE

Unlike other phoebes, Say's Phoebe is not as commonly tied to habitats near water but inhabits semiarid regions such as savannas, farmlands, and open brushlands. This active bird is rarely sedentary and is often spotted darting for insects and wagging its tail. Its gray-brown upperparts and rusty underparts make it superficially resemble the American Robin, but its upright posture and aerial acrobatics quickly reveal its identity as a flycatcher.

brownish gray upperparts

black bill

pale grayish brown throat and breast

tawny buff belly and undertail coverts

black legs and feet

blackish brown tail

Similar Birds

AMERICAN ROBIN
♂ Larger body; gray-brown upperparts; dark gray-brown or black head; chestnut-orange underparts; white lower belly and undertail coverts; black-and-white-streaked throat; broken white eye ring; yellow-orange bill with dark tip; largely terrestrial.

♀

VERMILION FLYCATCHER
♀ Female is smaller; gray-brown upperparts and crown; gray-brown lores and auriculars; white supercilium; blackish tail; white chin; white neck and breast with dusky streaking; salmon-peach belly and undertail coverts.

• **SONG** Often sings at dawn. Repertoire includes plaintive downslurred whistled *phee-eur* or *chu-weer*, often repeated many times. In fluttering flight also issues abrupt *pit-tse-ar*.

• **BEHAVIOR** Solitary or in pairs. Conspicuous. Perches at low to middle levels on branches, wires, posts, buildings, etc. From perch or while hovering watches for insects and swoops down to catch them in midair with an audible snap of the mandibles. This bird rarely eats berries. Sometimes regurgitates pellets of insect exoskeletons.

• **BREEDING** Monogamous. Solitary nester.

• **NESTING** Incubation 12–14 days by female. Altricial young stay in nest 14–16 days. Fed by both sexes. 1–2 broods per year, sometimes 3 in the Southwest along the Mexican border.

• **POPULATION** Stable and fairly common. Casual in eastern US.

• **CONSERVATION** Neotropical migrant. Rare host to cowbird parasitism.

Flight Pattern

Weak fluttering buoyant flight with shallow wing beats. Hawks from perch to catch flying insects; also hovers.

Nest Identification

Shape ☕   Location 🐦 🏠 〰️ 🏚️

Adherent • mud pellets, moss, and grass • lined with grass, weeds, moss, spider webs, and wool • attached to vertical walls • built by female • 3–7 white eggs with occasional brown or reddish spots; ovate to short ovate, 0.8 x 0.6 inches.

Plumage Sexes similar	Habitat	Migration Migratory	Weight 0.7 ounce

DATE _____ TIME_____ LOCATION _____

Family TYRANNIDAE	Species *Pyrocephalus rubinus*	Length 6 inches	Wingspan 9.5 inches

VERMILION FLYCATCHER

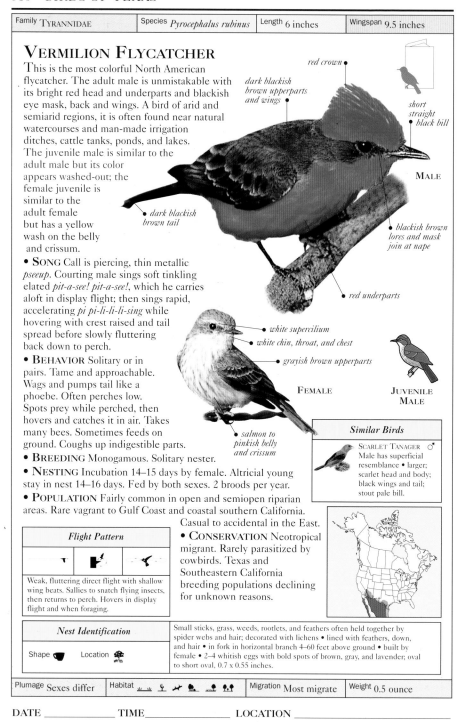

This is the most colorful North American flycatcher. The adult male is unmistakable with its bright red head and underparts and blackish eye mask, back and wings. A bird of arid and semiarid regions, it is often found near natural watercourses and man-made irrigation ditches, cattle tanks, ponds, and lakes. The juvenile male is similar to the adult male but its color appears washed-out; the female juvenile is similar to the adult female but has a yellow wash on the belly and crissum.

red crown

dark blackish brown upperparts and wings

short straight black bill

MALE

dark blackish brown tail

blackish brown lores and mask join at nape

red underparts

- **SONG** Call is piercing, thin metallic *pseeup*. Courting male sings soft tinkling elated *pit-a-see! pit-a-see!*, which he carries aloft in display flight; then sings rapid, accelerating *pi pi-li-li-li-sing* while hovering with crest raised and tail spread before slowly fluttering back down to perch.

white supercilium

white chin, throat, and chest

grayish brown upperparts

FEMALE

JUVENILE MALE

- **BEHAVIOR** Solitary or in pairs. Tame and approachable. Wags and pumps tail like a phoebe. Often perches low. Spots prey while perched, then hovers and catches it in air. Takes many bees. Sometimes feeds on ground. Coughs up indigestible parts.

salmon to pinkish belly and crissum

- **BREEDING** Monogamous. Solitary nester.
- **NESTING** Incubation 14–15 days by female. Altricial young stay in nest 14–16 days. Fed by both sexes. 2 broods per year.
- **POPULATION** Fairly common in open and semiopen riparian areas. Rare vagrant to Gulf Coast and coastal southern California. Casual to accidental in the East.
- **CONSERVATION** Neotropical migrant. Rarely parasitized by cowbirds. Texas and Southeastern California breeding populations declining for unknown reasons.

Similar Birds

SCARLET TANAGER ♂ Male has superficial resemblance • larger; scarlet head and body; black wings and tail; stout pale bill.

Flight Pattern

Weak, fluttering direct flight with shallow wing beats. Sallies to snatch flying insects, then returns to perch. Hovers in display flight and when foraging.

Nest Identification

Shape   Location

Small sticks, grass, weeds, rootlets, and feathers often held together by spider webs and hair; decorated with lichens • lined with feathers, down, and hair • in fork in horizontal branch 4–60 feet above ground • built by female • 2–4 whitish eggs with bold spots of brown, gray, and lavender; oval to short oval, 0.7 x 0.55 inches.

Plumage Sexes differ	Habitat	Migration Most migrate	Weight 0.5 ounce

DATE _____ TIME_____ LOCATION _____

Family TYRANNIDAE	Species *Myiarchus tuberculifer*	Length 6.5–7 inches	Wingspan 11 inches

DUSKY-CAPPED FLYCATCHER

Imitating this bird's descending, mournful call can often draw it out of hiding for observation. Otherwise, this wary bird spends most of its time unnoticed in the thick trees and shrubs of the dry pine-oak and juniper canyons where it feeds and nests. Often its voice is the first clue to its presence. This phoebe-sized flycatcher has brown upperparts; a gray chin, throat, and breast; bright yellow underparts; and just a hint of rufous in the tail. It was formerly known as the Olivaceous Flycatcher.

small crest

long, slender black bill with creamy base to lower mandible

brown upperparts

gray chin, throat, and breast

rufous-edged secondaries

2 whitish to rufous wing bars

lemon-yellow belly and undertail coverts

brown tail with a hint of rufous

- **SONG** Sorrowful, descending, whistled *peeur* or *wheeeeeu* is higher-pitched in the middle. Often one of the only bird sounds heard in the heat of midday in its range.

- **BEHAVIOR** Solitary or in pairs. Perches to watch for flying or crawling insects; hovers over foliage or ground to pick up prey or catch it in flight. Eats insects and some fruits and berries. Vigorously defends young in nest.

- **BREEDING** Monogamous. Solitary nester.

- **NESTING** Incubation 14 days by female. Altricial young stay in nest 14 days. Fed by both sexes. 1–2 broods per year.

- **POPULATION** Fairly common in dry wooded canyons and on mountain slopes. Casual in west Texas; rare to accidental in south and central California in autumn and winter. Numbers fluctuate widely year to year.

- **CONSERVATION** Neotropical migrant.

Similar Birds

ASH-THROATED FLYCATCHER
Larger; rusty tail; paler gray throat; paler yellow underparts; white wing bars; pale yellow to pale fawn edging on the secondaries; rufous edging on the primaries.

Flight Pattern

Fairly rapid flight with shallow wing beats. Sallies to snatch insect in flight, then returns to perch. Hovers over ground or foliage before dipping to pick up prey.

Nest Identification

Shape | Location

Lined with weeds, feathers, grass, twigs, bark strips, hair, plant fibers, and leaves • in cavity of tree, large cactus, stump, post, or pole 4–50 feet above ground; often use woodpecker holes • 4–5 creamy white eggs with brown, lavender, and olive-gray blotches; oval to short oval, 0.8 x 0.6 inches.

Plumage Sexes similar	Habitat 	Migration Migratory	Weight 0.7 ounce

DATE _____ TIME_____ LOCATION _____

Family TYRANNIDAE	Species *Myiarchus cinerascens*	Length 8.5 inches	Wingspan 14 inches

ASH-THROATED FLYCATCHER

This bird inhabits a wide range of habitats, from desert scrub below sea level to mountain regions of oak and piñon-juniper more than 9,000 feet high. It has the typical color pattern of *Myiarchus* flycatchers, with grayish brown upperparts, gray from the chin to lower breast, yellowish underparts, and rufous in the long tail. The visual key to its identity lies in the paleness of the underparts, which include a whitish throat and pale yellowish belly and undertail coverts.

grayish brown head

grayish brown upperparts

grayish brown wings

stout black bill

silvery white throat

pale gray breast

2 white wing bars

pale yellowish belly and undertail coverts

- **SONG** Most often a coarse *pwrrit*, like a referee's whistle, and a short *puip* or *huit*. On breeding grounds sings a rolling nasal *ka-brik, ka-brik*. Dawn song is varied arrangement of the calls.

- **BEHAVIOR** Solitary or in pairs. Seeks prey while perched, then hovers above and drops down on it or sallies from perch to catch it in flight. When hawking often does not return to same perch. Sometimes feeds from ground. Eats variety of insects, spiders, and caterpillars; also fruit, berries, and small lizards. Occasionally defends territory from large birds passing through, including hawks. Sometimes usurps nesting cavities from woodpeckers, forcing them to begin another hole elsewhere.

black legs and feet

rufous wash on inner webs of tail

- **BREEDING** Monogamous. Solitary nester.

- **NESTING** Incubation 15 days by female. Altricial young stay in nest 14–16 days. Fed by both sexes. 1–2 broods per year.

- **POPULATION** Common to fairly common in wide variety of habitats. Rare to accidental in fall and winter in the East.

Similar Birds

NUTTING'S FLYCATCHER Darker yellow belly; more olive-brown upperparts; dark color on outer webs of outer tail feathers does not extend across tips; orange mouth lining; different voice • accidental in winter in southeastern Arizona.

DUSKY-CAPPED FLYCATCHER Smaller; brighter lemon-yellow underparts; rufous-edged secondaries; tail largely lacks rufous; different voice • only in the West.

- **BIRDHOUSES** Uses bluebird nesting boxes and other nesting boxes with sufficient-sized openings to allow them access.

- **CONSERVATION** Stable and increasing in some areas. Neotropical migrant.

Flight Pattern

Fairly strong flight with shallow wing beats. Sallies from perch to snatch insects in flight. Sometimes hovers above foliage or ground before dipping to catch prey.

Nest Identification

Shape ⬛ 🔲   Location 🌳 🔲

Made of weeds, grass, twigs, and rootlets • often lined with hair and feathers • in tree cavity, man-made boxes, and woodpecker holes in trees, poles, and posts 3–20 feet above ground • built by both sexes • 3–7 creamy white eggs blotched with brown and lavender; oval to short oval, 0.9 x 0.7 inches.

Plumage Sexes similar	Habitat 〰 〰 ⚘ ✦ ♣ ♠	Migration Migratory	Weight 1.0 ounce

DATE _____ TIME_____ LOCATION _____

Family TYRANNIDAE	Species *Myiarchus crinitus*	Length 8.5 inches	Wingspan 12–14 inches

GREAT CRESTED FLYCATCHER

This big eastern flycatcher with a rusty tail and shaggy crest stays hidden in tall trees, but its coarse song is heard throughout the forest. Although similar in size to the Eastern Kingbird, the Great Crested Flycatcher prefers thickly wooded areas. Males defend their large territories by battling in the air with other males, clawing one another and sometimes pulling out feathers. Like some other members of its genus, it often tops off the nest with a discarded snakeskin, but in today's throwaway society it more readily finds cellophane and plastic. Upperparts are olive-green, and the bird shows two white wing bars.

darker gray crown

heavy black bill

gray throat and upper breast

lemon-yellow belly and undertail coverts

primaries show cinnamon-rufous edges

rufous inner webs on tail feathers

- **SONG** Bold melodic whistle of *wheeep!* and rolling *prrrrrrrrrreeeet.* *Wheeep* notes often given in rapid succession in series of 3 or more.
- **BEHAVIOR** Solitary or in pairs. Often ranges high in the canopy, sitting on exposed limbs in the crown of a tall tree or on top of a dead snag. Catches prey higher above ground than most flycatchers. Sallies from perch to snatch insects from foliage and catch them in midair, often returning to same or nearby perch. Eats variety of larger insects, including beetles, crickets, katydids, caterpillars, moths, and butterflies. Also eats some fruits and berries. Male chases female in courtship flight close to possible nesting cavity.
- **BREEDING** Monogamous. Solitary nester.
- **NESTING** Incubation 13–15 days by female. Altricial young remain in nest 12–21 days. Fed by both sexes. 1 brood per year.
- **POPULATION** Common in open wooded lots and on forest edge. Rare on California coast in autumn migration.
- **BIRDHOUSES** Sometimes uses nest boxes placed on trees or buildings 6–50 feet high.
- **CONSERVATION** Neotropical migrant. Vulnerable to habitat loss.

Similar Birds

ASH-THROATED FLYCATCHER
Smaller bill; paler underparts with whitish throat and pale gray breast; pale yellow belly and crissum; brown-tipped outer tail feathers; different voice.

BROWN-CRESTED FLYCATCHER
Bigger heavier bill; paler gray throat and breast; paler yellow belly; different voice.

Flight Pattern

Fairly swift buoyant direct flight. Hawks insects in flight, returning to perch. Hovers over foliage or ground then dips for food.

Nest Identification

Shape   Location

Filled and lined with grass, weeds, bark strips, rootlets, feathers, fur, snakeskin, onion skin, cellophane, and clear plastic • in cavity, abandoned holes of other birds, or bird boxes • built by both sexes • 4–8 creamy white to pale buff eggs marked with brown, olive, and lavender; ovate to short ovate, sometimes elliptical ovate or elongate ovate, 0.9 x 0.67 inches.

Plumage Sexes similar	Habitat	Migration Migratory	Weight 1.2 ounces

DATE _____ TIME_____ LOCATION _____

Family TYRANNIDAE	Species *Myiarchus tyrannulus*	Length 8.75 inches	Wingspan 12–14 inches

BROWN-CRESTED FLYCATCHER

This flycatcher makes its home in the sycamore canyons, mountain woodlands, saguaro desert, or any arid country where the trees are large enough for its nesting holes. Like other flycatchers the males aggressively defend their territory during breeding season, often attacking other birds with their claws and pulling out feathers. Their victims may be other flycatchers, woodpeckers, or wrens, all potential threats to take over the nesting cavity. When excited it may raise its bushy crest.

darkest coloring is on head

bushy crest

long thick dark bill is often creamy at base

olive-brown upperparts

pale grayish throat and chest

2 white wing bars

rufous in primaries

pale lemon-yellow belly and undertail coverts

- **SONG** Rough loud *come HERE, come HERE* or *whit-will-do, whit-will-do!* Also makes sharp calls of *bew, pwit,* or *purreeet.*

- **BEHAVIOR** Solitary or in pairs. Hawks flying insects or gleans them from foliage or ground. Occasionally catches and eats hummingbirds. Also takes small lizards, berries, and fruits. Hovers and plucks prey from trees and shrubs. Perches to eat fruits and berries.

rufous on inner webs of outer tail feathers

- **BEHAVIOR** Monogamous. Solitary nester. Very defensive around nest cavity, driving other birds away.

- **NESTING** Incubation 13–15 days by female. Altricial young stay in nest 12–21 days. Fed by both sexes. 1 brood per year.

- **POPULATION** Fairly common. Casual to the Gulf Coast and Florida.

- **CONSERVATION** A neotropical migrant that winters in Mexico.

Similar Birds

ASH-THROATED FLYCATCHER
Smaller; smaller bill; paler yellow underparts; less olive on back; dusky brown of outer tail feathers crosses tip of tail; different voice.

GREAT CRESTED FLYCATCHER
Deeper, brighter yellow belly and crissum; darker gray throat and chest; different voice.

Flight Pattern

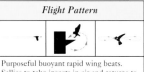

Purposeful buoyant rapid wing beats. Sallies to take insects in air and returns to perch. Also hovers and dips for prey.

Nest Identification

Shape ²　Location 🌵🌳

Lined with plant fibers, animal hair, and feathers; often adds snakeskin, onion skin, or clear plastic • in holes in giant cactus, tree, man-made structure, or abandoned woodpecker holes, 5–30 feet above ground • built by both sexes • 3–6 white to pale buff eggs with brown and lavender blotches; oval to short oval, 1 x 0.8 inches.

Plumage Sexes similar	Habitat 🌲🌿 ⚊ ⚊ ⚘ 🌿 ⚘	Migration Migratory	Weight 1.5 ounces

DATE _____ TIME_____ LOCATION _____

Family TYRANNIDAE	Species *Pitangus sulphuratus*	Length 9.75 inches	Wingspan 16 inches

GREAT KISKADEE

Inhabiting wet woodlands and riparian habitats, this bird can be spotted sunning itself on an open perch to dry its feathers after a series of dives into the water for aquatic insects or small fish on the surface. This large stout energetic flycatcher is named for its loud raucous screaming call of *kiss-ka-dee* or *k-reah*! Its voice carries a long way, so the bird often is heard long before it is seen. It is the only flycatcher north of Mexico with a bold black-and-white-striped head pattern. It also has a yellow crown patch, which usually is concealed. In flight the bright yellow underparts and underwing linings contrast sharply with the rufous wings and tail.

white forehead and eyebrows

black crown

wide black eye line

brown back and rump

rich reddish brown wings

stout black bill

white chin, cheeks, and throat

bright yellow chest and belly

- **SONG** Slow clear loud raucous *kiss-ka-dee*. Also makes bold screaming *cree-ah*.

bright yellow crissum

rich reddish brown tail

black legs and feet

- **BEHAVIOR** Solitary or in pairs. Conspicuous. Sits on perch to spot prey, then dives into water to catch fish and tadpoles. Sallies to catch prey, then returns to perch and often beats the victim on the branch several times before eating it. Catches insects in flight. Eats a variety of crawling and flying insects. Also catches frogs, small lizards, baby birds, and mice. Will eat fruits and berries when insects are not available. Noisy and aggressive; actively drives away much larger birds entering its territory.
- **BREEDING** Monogamous. Solitary nester.
- **NESTING** Breeding biology poorly known. Incubation by female estimated at 13–15 days. Altricial young estimated to stay in nest 12–21 days. Fed by both sexes. 2–3 broods per year.
- **POPULATION** Fairly common in southern Texas in lower Rio Grande valley. Casual vagrant to coastal Louisiana and in southeastern Arizona.
- **CONSERVATION** Some decline from habitat loss in US. Common throughout tropics.

Similar Birds
None in North America.

Flight Pattern

Slow fluttering direct flight with shallow wing beats. Sallies to catch prey, then returns to perch.

Nest Identification

Shape 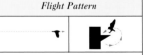 Location

Grass, weeds, bark strips, Spanish moss, and other plant fibers • in thorny tree, palm tree, or shrub or on metal braces on utility poles 6–50 feet above ground • sometimes refurbish old nest • built by both sexes • 2–5 creamy white eggs dotted with dark brown and lavender; oval to short oval, 1.1 inches long.

Plumage Sexes similar	Habitat	Migration Nonmigratory	Weight 2.1 ounces

DATE _____ TIME_____ LOCATION _____

Family TYRANNIDAE	Species *Tyrannus couchii*	Length 8–9.25 inches	Wingspan 15–16 inches

COUCH'S KINGBIRD

This bird is very similar to the Tropical Kingbird but has subtle differences in plumage and bill size. In fact, it was once considered a race of the Tropical Kingbird, but in the 1980s it was declared a separate species. Tropical and Couch's Kingbirds do not readily hybridize. Its breeding range in the United States is restricted to southern Texas, and it is best distinguished in the field by voice. Although primarily nonmigratory, birds in the northernmost parts of the breeding range are migratory.

light gray face and nape

dark gray ear patch

long stout black bill

whitish throat

greenish gray back

dark grayish brown wings

bright yellow underparts

black feet and legs

- **SONG** A high, trilled, nasal *breeeear* and a single-note or repeated *kip*. Predawn song is a series of rich whistles with abrupt inflections, *s'wee-s'wee-s'wee s'wee-I-chu*.
- **BEHAVIOR** Solitary or in pairs. Sometimes gregarious in winter. Perches and forages in middle to high levels. Sits on perch to spot prey. Sallies out to catch insects in midair. Hovers over foliage or ground, dipping down to pick up insects or berries. Eats various flying and crawling insects, also berries and fruits.

dark grayish brown tail, slightly notched

- **BREEDING** Monogamous. Solitary.
- **NESTING** Breeding biology poorly known. Incubation by female estimated at 14–16 days. Young altricial; fed by both sexes. First flight at 18–20 days. 1 brood per year.

Similar Birds

TROPICAL KINGBIRD
Grayer back; longer, thinner bill; unevenly staggered tips of primaries; voice differs.

WESTERN KINGBIRD
CASSIN'S KINGBIRD
Smaller thinner bills; indistinct, lighter gray ear patches; squared tips of tails; voices differ.

- **POPULATION** Common in lower Rio Grande Valley in summer; uncommon in winter. Casual to the Gulf Coast in fall and winter.
- **CONSERVATION** Neotropical migrant. Increasing in range and in numbers.

Flight Pattern

Slow fluttering flight on shallow wing beats. Sallies to take insects in flight, returns to perch. Hovers down for insects.

Nest Identification

Shape 🥄   Location 🌳 🐦

Twigs, leaves, Spanish moss, weeds, and bark strips, with lining of finer materials • on tree limb, 8–25 feet high • built by female • 3–5 pinkish to warm buff eggs, with brown and lavender blotches; ovate to long ovate, subelliptical to long elliptical; 1.0 x 0.7 inches.

Plumage Sexes similar	Habitat 🌳 🌿 🌱	Migration Northern birds migrate	Weight 1.6 ounces

DATE _____ TIME_____ LOCATION _____

Family TYRANNIDAE	Species *Tyrannus vociferans*	Length 8–9 inches	Wingspan 15–16.5 inches

CASSIN'S KINGBIRD

The loud morning song of the male can be heard through the canyons in the foothills covered with oak-piñon and pine-juniper-sycamore woodlands on the lower slopes of the mountains where this bird makes its home. This flycatcher eats more berries and fruit, in addition to its diet of insects, than any other North American kingbird. Darker on the head, back, and breast than the very similar and more widespread Western Kingbird, this bird has a pale tip on its squared tail. Cassin's Kingbird often inhabits higher altitudes than the Western Kingbird.

dark gray head and nape

short black bill

darker gray ear patch

white throat

dark olive-gray back

dark gray breast

dull yellow underparts

dark grayish brown tail with buff-white feather tips

black feet and legs

• **SONG** Bold burry 2-syllable call of *chi-BEW* with accent on the second syllable. Also sings a noisy high-spirited *ki-dear, ki-dear, ki-dear* in the morning.

• **BEHAVIOR** Solitary or in pairs. Perches at middle to high levels to spot prey, sallies to catch it, then returns to perch to eat. Hawks insects as far as 65 feet away from its perch. Hovers over ground or foliage and picks off insects, insect larvae, berries, and fruit. In courtship male can be seen flying in series of rushed zigzags.

• **BREEDING** Monogamous. Solitary nester.

• **NESTING** Incubation 18–19 days by female. Altricial young stay in nest 14–17 days. Fed by both sexes. 1 brood per year, 2 in southern part of US range.

• **POPULATION** Fairly common in variety of habitats. Accidental elsewhere in western, eastern, and southern US in migration and winter.

• **CONSERVATION** Neotropical migrant.

Similar Birds

WESTERN KINGBIRD Lighter gray head and nape; paler less-contrasting throat and chest; white-edged tail; different voice.

TROPICAL KINGBIRD COUCH'S KINGBIRD Larger longer bill; darker ear patch; olive breast; dusky brown tail has slightly notched tip and no whitish edging; different voice.

Flight Pattern

Buoyant fluttering flight with shallow wing beats. Hovers to take insects, berries, and fruit from foliage/ground. Also hawks.

Nest Identification

Shape ⬱   Location 🪹

Twigs, weed stems, rootlets, leaves, feathers, and hair • lined with fine plant fibers • on horizontal tree branch 20–50 feet above ground • built by both sexes • 3–5 creamy white eggs with brownish mottling concentrated at larger end; oval to long oval, 0.9 x 0.6 inches.

Plumage Sexes similar	Habitat 🌿 🌾 🌱 ⛰	Migration Migratory	Weight 1.6 ounces

DATE _____ TIME_____ LOCATION _____

Family TYRANNIDAE	Species *Tyrannus verticalis*	Length 8.75 inches	Wingspan 15–16 inches

WESTERN KINGBIRD

The most common and well-known kingbird in the West has easily adapted to the ongoing development of its habitat. It even takes advantage of it by using telephone poles and other artificial structures as nesting areas and fences and utility wires as hunting perches. Often found in urban areas, it is more gregarious than any other kingbird, with two or more pairs occasionally nesting in the same tree. Aggressive, it also is known for its tenacity for chasing hawks, crows, ravens, and other large birds away from its nesting territory. It can be distinguished from other large flycatchers and kingbirds by the black tail with white edging on each side. A red-orange crown patch usually is concealed.

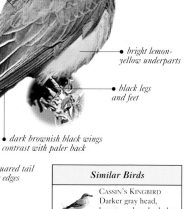

pale ashy gray head, neck, and breast

dark thin gray eye patch

olive-green tinted back

small black bill

bright lemon-yellow underparts

black legs and feet

dark brownish black wings contrast with paler back

black squared tail with white edges

- **SONG** Call is a rather quiet clipped *bek*. Has an abrasive and bickering chatter of *ker-er-ip, ker-er-ip, pree pree pr-prrr*.
- **BEHAVIOR** Solitary or in pairs or small groups. Gregarious in winter. Conspicuous. Hunts from open perches at low, middle, and high levels. Sits on perch to spot prey, flies out to catch in midair, and returns to perch to eat. Often hovers above foliage or ground and dips down to pick up food. Feeds on various insects, fruits, and berries. Male performs hectic courtship flight, darting upward into air, fluttering, vibrating feathers, and delivering trilling song.
- **BREEDING** Monogamous. Solitary. Sometimes can be found in loose semicolonies.
- **NESTING** Incubation 18–19 days by female. Young stay in nest 16–17 days, fed by both sexes. 1–2 broods per year.
- **POPULATION** Common in semiarid open country. Range has expanded during the 20th century as expansion of agriculture has created more suitable nesting and foraging areas. Some winter in southern Florida. Accidental in fall migration to New England and the Atlantic Coast.
- **CONSERVATION** Neotropical migrant.

Similar Birds

CASSIN'S KINGBIRD Darker gray head, breast, and neck; darker olive-brown back; pale buffy white tips on dusky brown tail feathers; whiter throat; voice differs.

TROPICAL AND COUCH'S KINGBIRDS Larger, longer bills; darker ear patches; darker upperparts; yellow of underparts extends upward to throats; slightly notched tails; voices differ.

Flight Pattern

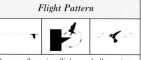

Buoyant fluttering flight on shallow wing beats. Sallies for insects in flight, returns to perch. Hovers over prey and dips down.

Nest Identification	
Shape 🥣 Location 🌳 🏠 🐦 🏭	Grass, weeds, twigs, and plant fibers, lined with finer materials, including hair, plant down, and cotton • near trunk on horizontal limb or fork of tree, 8–40 feet above ground • sometimes on brace or cross-arm of utility pole, church steeple, or other man-made structure • built by both sexes • 3–7 whitish eggs, heavily blotched with brown, lavender, and black; oval to short oval, 1.0 x 0.6 inches.

Plumage Sexes similar	Habitat 〰 〰 🌿	Migration Migratory	Weight 1.4 ounces

DATE _____ TIME_____ LOCATION _____

Family TYRANNIDAE	Species *Tyrannus tyrannus*	Length 8.5 inches	Wingspan 14–15 inches

EASTERN KINGBIRD

True to its name, this kingbird is the only one nesting in the East north of southern Florida. It has an extensive breeding range that covers most of North America: from the Atlantic Coast north almost to the treeline in the southern Yukon. Its Latin name means "king of the tyrants," and when defending its nest this aggressive bird sometimes will land on the backs of hawks, crows, and vultures, pecking and pulling their feathers. In winter flocks fly to South America and survive on a diet of mostly berries. This species is fashionably decked with blackish upperparts, white underparts, and a distinctive white terminal tail band. A red stripe on its crown, usually concealed, is seen only when the bird is displaying.

black cap, forehead, and sides of face

black bill

white throat

charcoal-gray back and rump

grayish wash on breast

charcoal-gray wings

white underparts

- **SONG** Utters grating buzzing high-pitched *dzeet* note combined with a rapid *tzi, tzeet, tzi, tzeet, tzi, tzeet.*
- **BEHAVIOR** Solitary or in pairs. Gregarious in migration and winter. Often sits on exposed, low- to mid-level perches and high on trees, shrubs, weed stalks, fences, utility wires, etc. Sits on perch to spot prey, hawks insects in air, and returns to perch to eat them. Also hovers to pick food off leaves or ground. Eats various insects, fruits, and berries. Male performs erratic courtship flights, hovering, circling, and tumbling with tail spread and crown patch revealed.

black feet and legs

black tail with white terminal band

- **BREEDING** Monogamous. Solitary nester.
- **NESTING** Incubation 16–18 days mostly by female. Altricial young stay in nest approximately 16–18 days. Fed by both sexes. 1 brood per year.
- **POPULATION** Common, widespread, and conspicuous. Has expanded its range and increased its numbers along with agricultural expansion.
- **CONSERVATION** Neotropical migrant. Common cowbird host, but often damages cowbird eggs.

Similar Birds

GRAY KINGBIRD
Pale gray upperparts; white underparts; black mask through eyes; forked tail lacks white terminal band • limited US range.

Flight Pattern

Fluttering stiff-winged direct flight with shallow wing beats. Sallies to snatch insects in flight, then returns to perch.

Nest Identification	Weed stalks, twigs, and grass • lined with fine grass, sometimes animal hair • far to midway out on horizontal tree branch or shrub; sometimes on post or stump; 7–60 feet above ground, usually near water • built by female with help from male • 3–5 white to pinkish white eggs with heavy brown, lavender, and gray blotches; long and pointed to very round, but most ovate, 0.9 x 0.7 inches.
Shape 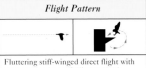 Location	

Plumage Sexes similar	Habitat	Migration Migratory	Weight 1.5 ounces

DATE _____ TIME_____ LOCATION _____

Family TYRANNIDAE	Species *Tyrannus forficatus*	Length 11.5–15 inches	Wingspan 14.25–15.5 inches

SCISSOR-TAILED FLYCATCHER

Unmistakable, graceful, and beautiful, the Scissor-tailed Flycatcher, often seen darting above grasslands, is named for the way it opens and closes its tail like a pair of scissors. During courtship the male performs a spectacular sky dance. From about a hundred feet above the ground, the male suddenly plunges, flies in a zigzag pattern with a trilling cackle, then flies straight up and falls over backward in two or three backward somersaults, displaying his long streaming tail. He repeats this courtship flight, sometimes until the eggs are hatched. In flight the salmon-pink and red axillaries can be seen. Juveniles are paler overall with a yellow to salmon wash on the underparts and a short tail.

pale gray head

black bill

white throat

pale gray upperparts

dark brown wings with white edges

white underparts

salmon-pink sides and flanks

black legs and feet

- **SONG** A harsh sharp *bik* or *kew*. Calls also include a dry, buzzing chattering *ka-quee-ka-quee* or repeated *ka-lup*.

- **BEHAVIOR** Solitary or in pairs. At night roosts communally (except nesting females) in groups that may number more than 200. Gregarious in migration and winter; often in spectacular flocks.

long scissorlike tail is black above with white outer edges and white below with black inner edges

Perches on branches, utility wires, and fences; often sits for hours to spot bees, wasps, and other flying insects, then catches them in midair. Often hunts from low perches, searching for grasshoppers and crickets on the ground. Can perform very acrobatic flight.

- **BREEDING** Monogamous. Solitary nester.

- **NESTING** Incubation 14–17 days by female. Altricial young stay in nest 14–16 days. Fed by both sexes. 1 brood per year.

- **POPULATION** Common in open country with scattered trees, prairies, scrublands, farmlands. Accidental to casual across much of North America. Small wintering population in central to south Florida.

- **CONSERVATION** Neotropical migrant. Rare host to cowbirds.

Similar Birds

FORK-TAILED FLYCATCHER Casual to accidental vagrant • black head; long, deeply forked black tail; white underparts and wing linings.

WESTERN KINGBIRD Similar to juvenile with short tail but has olive-green–tinted back; bright lemon-yellow underparts; squared tail.

Flight Pattern

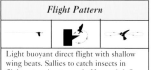

Light buoyant direct flight with shallow wing beats. Sallies to catch insects in flight, returning to perch. Hovers briefly over prey before dipping to pick it up.

Nest Identification	
Shape 🥣 Location 🌿 🪵 🌳 🏠	Lined with twigs, weeds, rootlets, grass, and hair • on horizontal limb or fork in tree or shrub or utility pole, post, building, or other man-made structure 7–40 feet above ground • built by female • 3–6 whitish eggs with reddish, brown, olive, and gray blotches; ovate to rounded ovate, 0.9 x 0.6 inches.

Plumage Sexes similar	Habitat	Migration Migratory	Weight 1.5 ounces

DATE _____ TIME _____ LOCATION _____

| Family TYRANNIDAE | Species *Pachyramphus aglaiae* | Length 6.5–7.25 inches | Wingspan 11.5 inches |

ROSE-THROATED BECARD

The brilliant rose-colored throat of the male helps distinguish this stocky big-headed flycatcher. Often nesting on or very near the same site year after year, it may take weeks to build its huge globular nest, which is 1–2.5 feet in size and hangs from the tip of a drooping tree branch high above the ground or over water. A native of Mexico and Central America, its range includes parts of southeast Arizona and southeast Texas. The race occurring in Texas is darker overall; males have blackish upperparts and dark gray underparts, and the rose patch on the throat is much reduced or absent. Texas females have a sooty black crown and deeper buff to tawny cinnamon underparts. Juveniles are similar to adult females.

blackish cap and nape, extending down to eyes

gray upperparts

rose or rose-pink patch on lower throat and upper breast

MALE

pale gray underparts

gray to dark gray crown

ocher-buff hind collar

grayish brown or cinnamon upperparts

pale buff underparts

FEMALE

• **SONG** Call is a sad downslurred whistled *tseeoou*, often preceded by a reedy chatter. Alarm note is a soft *peek*. Has a rarely heard song at dawn, which is plaintive, reedy, and long-continued, *wheeuu-whyeeeuur, wheeuu-whyeeeuur*.

• **BEHAVIOR** Solitary or in pairs. After nesting season may join mixed-species foraging flocks. Sits quietly, almost motionless, hidden in foliage on branch at middle levels in clearing, opening, or forest edge, watching for insects. Easily overlooked. Catches insects in flight. Eats insects, their larvae, and some wild fruits and berries. Also frequents canopy.

• **BREEDING** Monogamous. Solitary.

• **NESTING** Breeding biology poorly known. Estimated incubation 15–17 days by female. Young altricial; brooded by female; stay in nest 19–21 days, fed by both sexes. Has 1 brood per year.

• **POPULATION** Casual to rare in southeastern Arizona and in the lower Rio Grande Valley area of Texas.

• **CONSERVATION** Neotropical migrant. Rare host to cowbird parasitism.

Similar Birds
None in North American range.

Flight Pattern
Weak flights, often of short duration, with rapid shallow wing beats. Sallies forth to take insects in flight or off foliage.

Nest Identification	
Shape 🪺 Location 🐦	Lichen, bark, vine, pine needles, spider web, and feathers, lined with finer materials • hangs from branch of tree, 13–70 feet above ground • built by both sexes, but female does most • 2–6 white or creamy white eggs, with brown blotches; short subelliptical, 0.9 x 0.7 inches.

| Plumage Sexes differ | Habitat | Migration US birds migrate | Weight 1.1 ounces |

DATE _____ TIME_____ LOCATION _____

Family LANIIDAE	Species *Lanius ludovicianus*	Length 9 inches	Wingspan 12.5–13 inches

LOGGERHEAD SHRIKE

This large-headed bird with whitish underparts is one of two shrike species that nest and breed in North America. Known as the "Butcher Bird" across its range, this adept hunter usually perches in the open to watch for prey. It has the unusual behavior of caching the bodies of its prey by suspending them impaled on a plant spine or the barbed wire of a fence. The caches may serve as larder for future use, to soften the food for easier rendering, or to passively advertise the presence of the territory and its owner. Juveniles have brownish upperparts and more distinct barring on their underparts.

- large head
- black hooked beak
- black mask meets in a slender line over beak
- bluish gray upperparts
- black wings with white patch
- grayish to whitish rump

JUVENILE

- slender black tail with white outer feathers

- **SONG** Variety of squeaking notes and low warbles, delivered in slow deliberate phrases, often repeated, *queedle, queedle.* Call is a grating *shak-shak.*
- **BEHAVIOR** Solitary. Pairs in breeding season. Often sits immobile, hawklike, watching for prey for long periods. Flies down to catch prey with bill or sharp claws; also catches insects in flight. Eats small rodents, birds, reptiles, amphibians, and insects. Pair defends territory in breeding season but defend separate territories in winter.
- **BREEDING** Monogamous. Solitary nester.
- **NESTING** Incubation 16–17 days by female. Young altricial; brooded by female; stay in nest 17–21 days, fed by both sexes. 2 broods per year (occasionally 3 in the South).
- **POPULATION** Fairly common in habitats with open fields and scattered trees. Now rare over much of central part of range.
- **CONSERVATION** Some are neotropical migrants. Declining seriously in coastal California, the Northeast, and the eastern Midwest due to habitat loss and insecticide/pesticide use.

Similar Birds

NORTHERN SHRIKE
Larger; paler head and back; narrower mask does not meet above bill; larger, more deeply hooked bill, often pale at base of lower mandible; barred underparts; bobs tail
• juvenile much browner in color.

NORTHERN MOCKINGBIRD
Longer thinner straighter bill; lighter wings with larger white patches; paler tail with more extensive white in outer feathers; head proportionally smaller.

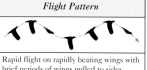

Flight Pattern

Rapid flight on rapidly beating wings with brief periods of wings pulled to sides. Often flies low across the ground.

Nest Identification

Shape ◖   Location 🌳 🪹 🌲

Twigs lined with grasses, string, feathers, and hair • in bush or tree, 8–15 feet above ground (but as high as 50 feet) • built by female or sometimes both sexes • 4–7 white to grayish buff eggs, marked with grays, browns, or blacks, often concentrated near large end; oval to long oval, 1.0 x 0.74 inches.

Plumage Sexes similar	Habitat 🌾 🪨 🦌 🌲 ___	Migration Migratory	Weight 1.7 ounces

DATE _____ TIME_____ LOCATION _____

Family LANIIDAE	Species *Lanius excubitor*	Length 9–10 inches	Wingspan 13.5–16.5 inches

NORTHERN SHRIKE

Perched high in the treetops, this robin-sized bird acts as a sentry, often uttering loud warning calls to other birds as it scans the landscape for prey. The larger and more northerly distributed of the two shrikes that nest and breed in North America, it is aggressive and will attack Blue Jays or other birds larger than itself, especially in defending its caches. Irruptive movements south in the winter seem to be correlated with the availability of prey species, especially small mammals. In flight the white wing patches, white rump, and white outer tail feathers contrast against the black wings and tail. The female is similar to the male but duller and sometimes more brown. Young birds are browner than adults and have heavier barring on their underparts.

white feathering above bill

black eye patch

pale gray upperparts and head

large hooked bill, often with pale base to lower mandible

whitish underparts with faint barring

FIRST WINTER

JUVENILE

• **SONG** Sings a low disjointed jerky thrasherlike song of clear notes and phrases, some musical, interspersed with grating shrieks. Call is a *shak-shak*. Also imitates calls of other birds.

• **BEHAVIOR** Solitary. Pairs in breeding season. Hunts in daytime. Perches in prominent lookout to spot prey; catches prey with beak, stuns it, and often impales it on sharp thorns or branches until ready to eat. Caches food for later use in this manner. Feeds on small mammals, mostly rodents, small birds, and insects. Aggressive in pursuit of prey. White in tail and white wing patches flash in flight.

• **BREEDING** Monogamous. Solitary nester.

• **NESTING** Incubation 15–16 days by female. Young altricial; brooded by female; stay in nest 20 days, fed by both sexes. First flight at about 20 days, but fed by both sexes for 10 more days or longer. 1 brood per year.

• **POPULATION** Uncommon in taiga (boreal forest) in clearings, open areas, and edges.

• **FEEDERS** Raw hamburger, suet. Also hunts feeder visitors.

Similar Birds

LOGGERHEAD SHRIKE Smaller; darker head and back; gray to white rump; wider mask extending above eye and across bill; smaller and less strongly hooked black bill; gray underparts with very faint or no barring • juveniles are gray-brown and lightly barred.

Flight Pattern
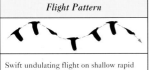
Swift undulating flight on shallow rapid wing beats, often low to the ground.

Nest Identification	
Shape ◗ Location 🌿 🌳	Sticks lined with feathers, hair, and fine materials • in tree or shrub, 12–20 feet above ground • built by both sexes • 4–9 grayish or greenish white eggs, heavily blotched with olive, brown, and lavender; oval to long oval, 1.1 x 0.8 inches.

Plumage Sexes similar	Habitat 🌾🌱 🏞 〜 🌿 ⛰	Migration Migratory	Weight 2.3 ounces

DATE _____ TIME_____ LOCATION _____

Family VIREONIDAE	Species *Vireo griseus*	Length 5 inches	Wingspan 8 inches

WHITE-EYED VIREO

Preferring to hide in the dense foliage of brushy thickets, this bird is known for uttering an explosive jumble of phonetic sounds and phrases, typically beginning and ending the song with a sharp *chick!* Sometimes it will mimic the songs and calls of other birds by incorporating their vocalizations into the jumbled middle portion of its rather unvireo-like song. Its white iris can be seen only at close range. Juveniles are paler overall with gray to brown irises.

distinctive white iris

yellow spectacles

grayish olive upperparts

short black bill with slightly hooked tip

2 whitish wing bars

pale yellow sides and flanks

gray legs and feet

• **SONG** Abrasive *chik, ticha wheeyo chik.* Mnemonics for the variable song differ from region to region, but the standard generic one is *quick-with-the-beer-check!* Individuals vary their songs and often omit either the introductory or the ending *chick.* Call is a wrenlike mewing note, a rasping rattle, and a sharp *tick!*

white underparts

• **BEHAVIOR** Solitary or in pairs. May join mixed foraging flocks in fall migration. Usually remains hidden close to the ground in blackberry thickets, thick brushy tangles, thick forest undergrowth, or the forest edge. Perches higher to sing. Often sings in winter. Gleans food from stems, branches, and foliage. Eats insects, snails, spiders, fruits, berries, and small lizards.

• **BREEDING** Monogamous. Solitary nester. Courting male postures before female with whining calls of *yip, yip, yah* while puffing up his feathers and spreading his tail.

• **NESTING** Incubation 12–16 days by both sexes. Altricial young stay in nest 10–12 days. Fed by both sexes. 1 brood per year, 2 in the South.

• **POPULATION** Fairly common to common. Casual vagrant to the West.

• **CONSERVATION** Neotropical migrant. Parasitized frequently by cowbirds.

Similar Birds

BELL'S VIREO
Smaller; greenish back; yellowish underparts; grayish face, crown, and nape; faint white spectacles; 1 bold and 1 faint white wingbar; dark brown eye.

YELLOW-THROATED VIREO
Yellow chin, throat, and breast; gray rump; bright yellow spectacles; lacks white iris; different song.

Flight Pattern

Relatively rapid direct flight on short, rounded wings.

Nest Identification

Shape | Location

Twigs, rootlets, bark strips, coarse grass, and leaves; bound with silk • lined with fine grass and fibers • hangs between fork in twigs at the end of a branch of shrub or small tree 1–8 feet above ground • built by both sexes • 3–5 white eggs spotted with brown and black; oval, 0.74 x 0.55 inches.

Plumage Sexes similar	Habitat	Migration Migratory	Weight 0.4 ounce

DATE _____ TIME_____ LOCATION _____

Family VIREONIDAE	Species *Vireo bellii*	Length 4.75 inches	Wingspan 7–8 inches

BELL'S VIREO

This small plain bird is the western counterpart of the White-eyed Vireo. It is a frequent victim of the Brown-headed Cowbird, which often lays eggs in its nest – the vireo often responds by building a new floor in the nest, covering the cowbird's eggs and its own. Although these birds actively forage during the day they are most often detected by their frequent singing. Overall plumage varies across its range, from the eastern and midwestern birds, which have greenish upperparts and yellowish underparts, to the West Coast race, which has gray upperparts and whitish underparts.

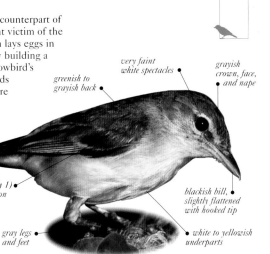

greenish to grayish back

very faint white spectacles

grayish crown, face, and nape

2 (sometimes only 1) faint white bars on each wing

gray legs and feet

blackish bill, slightly flattened with hooked tip

white to yellowish underparts

• **SONG** Male sings husky rapid jumble of question-and-answer-sounding phrases such as *cheadle cheadle chee? cheadle cheadle chew!* Often a phrase with rising inflection, followed by one that ends with a descending note. An active singer, may sing 8–17 songs a minute. Incubating males may sometimes sing from the nest. Call notes are harsh and scolding.

• **BEHAVIOR** Secretive and active. Often pumps tail. Sings often, revealing its presence in the thickets (particularly riparian), hedgerows, and scrub that it frequents. Eats variety of insects gleaned from the stems, branches, and foliage; also some fruits and berries. Courting male actively chases female, spreading tail, fluttering wings, and constantly singing.

• **BREEDING** Monogamous. Solitary.

• **NESTING** Incubation 14 days by both sexes. Young altricial; stay in nest 11–12 days, fed by both sexes. 2 broods per year.

• **POPULATION** Uncommon; declining in some regions. Some western riparian populations endangered.

• **CONSERVATION** Declining in Midwest and California from habitat loss, especially riparian habitat in arid and semiarid landscapes; frequent cowbird parasitism. Neotropical migrant.

Similar Birds

GRAY VIREO
Larger; gray overall; paler underparts; 1 or 2 faint wing bars; distinct eye ring; different song.

WHITE-EYED VIREO
Juvenile • dark eyes; grayish olive upperparts; whitish underparts with wash of yellow on sides and flanks; yellow spectacles; 2 white wing bars; voice differs.

Flight Pattern
Relatively rapid direct flight with shallow wing beats.

Nest Identification	
Shape  Location	Dry leaves, shredded bark, plant fibers, and spider cocoons, lined with fine grass, down, and hair • hung from fork in tree or shrub or suspended by rim between two limbs • 1–5 feet above ground • built by both sexes • 3–5 white eggs, usually dotted with black or brown; oval, 0.7 x 0.5 inches.

Plumage Sexes similar	Habitat	Migration Migratory	Weight 0.3 ounce

DATE _____ TIME_____ LOCATION _____

Family VIREONIDAE	Species *Vireo atricapillus*	Length 4.5 inches	Wingspan 8 inches

BLACK-CAPPED VIREO

The Black-capped Vireo is a federally listed endangered species. Difficult to spot because it forages among oak-scrub and dense thickets, it is a persistent singer often detected by its song. The male's black cap and broken white spectacles are distinctive. Females can be identified by the slate-gray cap; juvenile females have more buff-colored plumage. In the fall, this bird migrates southwest, wintering along the western coast of Mexico.

- **SONG** Persistent hurried series of twittering insistent 2- or 3-note phrases suggestive of *come here, right-now-quick!* Call note is *ji-dit*, similar to Ruby-crowned Kinglet.
- **BEHAVIOR** Solitary or in pairs. Secretive. Searches restlessly for food in deep cover among trees and thickets, looking for insects, their eggs, and larvae. Also eats small spiders and small fruits and berries. During fluttering display flight, male sings courtship song to female or follows her, singing and spreading tail.
- **BREEDING** Monogamous. Solitary.
- **NESTING** Incubation 14–17 days by both sexes; female at night and both sexes alternating during day. Young altricial; stay in nest 10–12 days, fed by both sexes. 2 broods per year.
- **POPULATION** Endangered. Uncommon to fairly common and local. Extirpated over much of its former range.
- **CONSERVATION** Cowbird brood parasitism a factor, with more than 90 percent of vireo nests parasitized in some areas, such as the Edwards Plateau in Texas. An additional known factor is the loss of oak-juniper habitat, primarily due to the development of land.

broken white spectacles

glossy black cap

blackish bill

olive upperparts

reddish eyes

yellowish white wing bars

white underparts

yellow flanks

blue-gray legs and feet

MALE

slaty-gray to bluish gray head

white spectacles

olive upperparts

pale lemon-yellow wing bars

buffy white underparts

yellowish wash on sides and flanks

FEMALE

Similar Birds

BLUE-HEADED VIREO
Female or juvenile
- larger; gray hood; white spectacles and throat; olive-green back; yellowish white wing bars and edging on tertials; greenish yellow edging on secondaries.

Flight Pattern

Somewhat weak fluttering direct flight on rapidly beating wings.

Nest Identification

Shape Location

Vegetation, including twigs, bark, and leaves, bound with silk and lined with fine grasses, 1–15 feet in scrub oak or other short deciduous tree • built by both sexes • 3–5 white eggs, unmarked; oval, 0.7 x 0.5 inches.

Plumage Sexes differ	Habitat	Migration Migratory	Weight 0.3 ounce

DATE _____ TIME_____ LOCATION _____

Family VIREONIDAE	Species *Vireo vicinior*	Length 5.5 inches	Wingspan 8.75 inches

GRAY VIREO

The Gray Vireo is most often found in arid thorn scrub, chaparral, and piñon-juniper or oak-juniper on the slopes in mountainous regions. It forages in low undergrowth. This bird is distinguished from other vireos by its plain gray plumage, narrow white eye ring, and two indistinct wing bars (sometimes only the lower one can be seen from a distance). The Gray Vireo also is identified by its unique tendency among vireos to flick its long tail gnatcatcher-like. A short-distance migrant, the Gray Vireo winters in Mexico.

white eye ring
gray back
black bill
whitish underparts
brownish wings
gray feet and legs

- **SONG** Song musical; a hesitant and slightly jerky, patchy *chu-wee, chu-wee, che-weet, chee, ch-churr-weet*, similar to Plumbeous Vireo but less throaty. Males often sing with varying inflections. In alarm, scolds wrenlike, issuing a low harsh *churr* or *schray*.
- **BEHAVIOR** Solitary or in pairs; small family groups in nesting season. Hops and flicks tail with jerky movements from low- to mid-level perches 1–12 feet above ground. Often stays concealed in dense foliage of trees and brush, including junipers and sagebrush. Feeds on variety of insects, which it gleans from branches, foliage, or ground.
- **BREEDING** Monogamous. Solitary.
- **NESTING** Incubation 13–14 days by both sexes. Young altricial; remain in nest 13–14 days and are fed by both sexes. 2 broods per year.
- **POPULATION** Fairly common. Mostly stable. Some decline in California. Accidental in Wisconsin.
- **CONSERVATION** Frequent victim of brood parasitism by cowbirds; often covers eggs with new nest.

Similar Birds

PLUMBEOUS VIREO Heavier body; shorter tail, not pumped or flicked; bold white spectacles; two bold wing bars; olive-gray wash and streaking on sides and flanks.

BELL'S VIREO Smaller; two faint wing bars; faint white spectacles; olive to gray upperparts; yellow to whitish underparts; does not wag or flick tail; voice differs.

Flight Pattern

Weak somewhat fluttering direct flight on rapidly beating wings.

Nest Identification

Shape   Location

Grasses, twigs, shredded bark, leaves, spider webs, and insect cocoons; lined with fine grass • 2–6 feet above ground in shrub • built by both sexes • 3–5 rose-colored eggs, with brown spots, especially near large end; oval, 0.7 x 0.5 inches.

Plumage Sexes similar	Habitat	Migration Migratory	Weight 0.5 ounce

DATE _____ TIME _____ LOCATION _____

Family VIREONIDAE	Species *Vireo flavifrons*	Length 5.5 inches	Wingspan 9.5 inches

YELLOW-THROATED VIREO

Considered the most brilliantly colored vireo, this bird is most often observed in deciduous forests. Its characteristic song is a series of short phrases similar in pattern to several other vireos in its range but with long pauses between phrases and a coarse quality.

• **SONG** Burry series of 2-note or sometimes 3-note phrases with hesitantly long pauses between them sounding like *three-EIGHT, three-EIGHT . . . three-EIGHT*, repeated with the pattern and quality of a Blue-headed Vireo with a sore throat. Calls harsh, nasal, accelerating, rapid series of *cheh, cheh, cheh* notes.

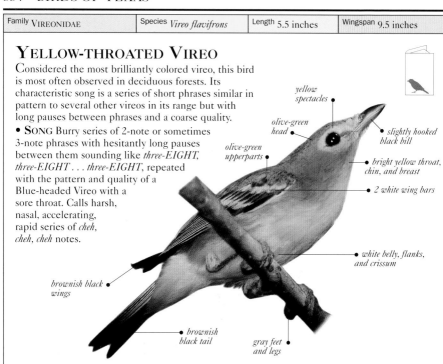

yellow spectacles

olive-green head

slightly hooked black bill

olive-green upperparts

bright yellow throat, chin, and breast

2 white wing bars

white belly, flanks, and crissum

brownish black wings

brownish black tail

gray feet and legs

• **BEHAVIOR** Solitary or in pairs. In autumn migration may form mixed foraging flocks. Generally forages in treetops, eating mostly insects. Also eats some small fruits and berries. In courtship male performs nest-building display, singing and crouching before female. He often begins several nests in his territory before pairing.

• **BREEDING** Monogamous. Solitary nester.

• **NESTING** Incubation 14 days by both sexes. Altricial young stay in nest 14 days. Fed by both sexes. 1 brood per year.

• **POPULATION** Fairly common and stable overall but declining in the Northeast (particularly in areas with insecticide spraying of shade trees) and increasing in the upper Midwest. Rare vagrant in the West; casual in winter in south Florida.

• **CONSERVATION** Neotropical migrant. Common brood parasite host for Brown-headed Cowbird; sometimes builds second floor to cover its own eggs as well as cowbird's.

Similar Birds

PINE WARBLER
Slender, pointed bill; slightly notched tail; yellow chin and throat; yellow breast and sides with dusky streaking; thin, broken yellow eye ring; narrow yellow superciliary mark; thin, straight black bill; white tail spots.

Flight Pattern

Relatively weak fluttering direct flight with rapid wing beats.

Nest Identification

Shape 🌰   Location 🪺

Grass covered with lichens • lined with grass, shredded bark, spider webs, and cocoons • in deciduous trees 3–60 feet above ground • built by both sexes • 3–5 white to pinkish white eggs with brown spots, especially near large end; oval, 0.7 x 0.5 inches.

Plumage Sexes similar	Habitat 🌳🌲	Migration Migratory	Weight 0.6 ounce

DATE _____ TIME_____ LOCATION _____

Family VIREONIDAE	Species *Vireo plumbeus*	Length 5.25 inches	Wingspan 8.5 inches

PLUMBEOUS VIREO

Formerly considered the grayest inland western race of the Solitary Vireo, this species was recently split from that complex. A bird of the Rocky Mountain environs, it breeds at almost ten thousand feet and frequents pines and pine-oak forests. It is much grayer than its two sibling species, with an olive-gray rump and mostly devoid of any yellow, which, if present, shows as a wash on the gray-streaked flanks.

• SONG Varied; hesitant pauses and coarse nasal phrases much like a hoarse Blue-headed Vireo or a Cassin's Vireo, *chureeh, ch-ireet', ch-reeh cg-ireet*, often repeated. Calls a chattering *cheh-cheh-cheh, cheh*, often accelerating.

• BEHAVIOR Solitary or in pairs. Forages and perches from mid to high levels in trees. Deliberately searches for insects, which it gleans from the foliage or bark surfaces. Takes a few fruits and berries, especially in fall. Male performs nest-building courtship display, crouching low in front of female and spreading tail. May chase female in courtship flight. Incubating and brooding birds sit tightly on the nest, sometimes allowing themselves to be touched by humans.

• BREEDING Monogamous. Solitary.

• NESTING Incubation 14–15 days by both sexes. Young altricial; brooded by female and fed by both sexes, but mostly by male. Fledge at 14–15 days. 1 brood per year.

• POPULATION Fairly common in varied pine and pine-oak woodland habitats. Accidental in Louisiana; other eastern records are unconfirmed.

• CONSERVATION Neotropical migrant. Fairly common victim of cowbird parasitism. Vulnerable to habitat loss due to logging.

gray head and upperparts

blackish bill

bold white spectacles broken by dusky lores

olive-tinged gray sides of breast

whitish throat and underparts

2 white wing bars and white-edged flight feathers

dusky wash on flanks

blackish brown wings and tail

blue-gray feet and legs

white-edged outer tail feathers

Similar Birds

CASSIN'S VIREO
Smaller; less gray overall; greenish gray head and upperparts; olive wash on sides and flanks.

GRAY VIREO
Not as heavily built; paler upperparts; long tail that it flicks and pumps; more faint wing bars (lower one more prominent); lacks spectacles; has white eye ring.

Flight Pattern

Somewhat weak fluttering direct flight on rapidly beating wings.

Nest Identification

Shape   Location

Bark, grasses, plant fibers, and spider web, lined with fine grasses and plant down • suspended between fork near tip of branch in tree or bush • 4–30 feet above ground • built by both sexes • 3–5 white eggs, spotted at larger end with reddish brown; oval, 0.7 x 0.5 inches.

Plumage Sexes similar	Habitat	Migration Migratory	Weight Undetermined

DATE _____ TIME_____ LOCATION _____

Family VIREONIDAE	Species *Vireo cassinii*	Length 5 inches	Wingspan 8.5 inches

CASSIN'S VIREO

Until the 1990s this bird and the Blue-headed and Plumbeous Vireos were classified as one species – the Solitary Vireo. Although similar to the Blue-headed Vireo, Cassin's differs in range and is duller in color with less white edging on flight feathers and tail. The male catches the female's attention by fluffing out

olive-washed grayish head

dusky lores break ring of white spectacles

grayish olive to olive upperparts

blackish brown wings with grayish olive trim on secondaries

blackish bill

grayish white throat and underparts

2 thick white to pale yellow wing bars and narrow tertial edgings

blackish brown tail with white-trimmed outer feathers and olive-trimmed central feathers

lemon feathers on flanks

olive wash on sides

blue-gray legs and feet

his bright yellow flank feathers and bowing up and down to her. Juvenile Cassin's females sometimes have greenish heads.

• **SONG** A mixed jumble of hesitant phrases, punctuated by short deliberate pauses, such as *chreu ... ch'ree ... choo'reet* or *ch-ree ... ch-ri'chi-roo*, often repeated.

• **BEHAVIOR** Solitary or in pairs. Forages high in trees by gleaning food from bark, branches, or foliage; sometimes hovers briefly to pick food off vegetation or catch insects in flight. Eats insects, larvae, and various fruits. Frequents open coniferous, coniferous-deciduous, pine-oak, or oak woodlands. Male performs nest-building display for female with no nesting material in mouth. Fairly tame on nest, allowing close approach.

• **BREEDING** Monogamous. Solitary.

• **NESTING** Incubation 11–12 days by both sexes, but female does more. Young altricial; stay in nest 12–14 days, fed by both sexes. 1–2 broods per year.

Similar Birds

PLUMBEOUS VIREO
Slightly larger; thicker bill; gray head and upperparts; more contrast between white throat and head and sides of breast; grayish sides and flanks with grayish streaking and without strong yellow wash.

HUTTON'S VIREO
Smaller; white eye ring breaks above eye; pale lores; grayish olive upperparts; different voice • only in the West.

• **POPULATION** Fairly common. Casual in winter in northwest California. Accidental in southeast Alaska, Oklahoma, New York, and New Jersey.

• **CONSERVATION** Neotropical migrant. Vulnerable to habitat loss due to logging.

Flight Pattern

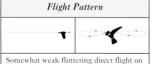

Somewhat weak fluttering direct flight on rapidly beating wings. May hover briefly to pick insect or fruit off vegetation.

Nest Identification

Shape 🥚 Location 🌿🌳🌲

Twigs, fine grasses, and stems, lined with finer grasses and hair • in fork of twig of tree or bush or set in middle of conifer, 4–30 feet above ground • built by both sexes • 3–5 white to creamy white eggs, with black and brown speckles; oval, 0.7 x 0.5 inches.

Plumage Sexes similar	Habitat 🌳 🌿 🌾	Migration Migratory	Weight Undetermined

Family VIREONIDAE	Species Vireo solitarius	Length 5.25 inches	Wingspan 8.5 inches

BLUE-HEADED VIREO

This bird makes its home in the thick coniferous and mixed coniferous-deciduous forests of Canada and the eastern United States, where it breeds southward through the southern Appalachians. The Appalachian race is larger, with a bluish gray back and the

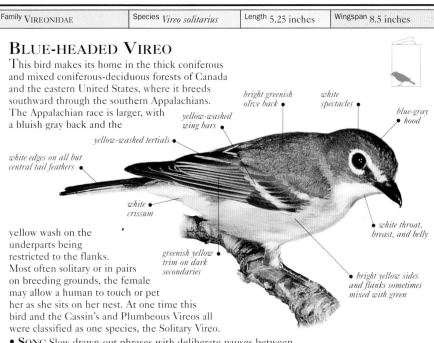

bright greenish olive back •

white spectacles •

blue-gray hood

yellow-washed wing bars •

yellow-washed tertials •

white edges on all but central tail feathers •

white crissum •

white throat, breast, and belly

yellow wash on the underparts being restricted to the flanks. Most often solitary or in pairs on breeding grounds, the female may allow a human to touch or pet her as she sits on her nest. At one time this bird and the Cassin's and Plumbeous Vireos all were classified as one species, the Solitary Vireo.

greenish yellow trim on dark secondaries •

bright yellow sides and flanks sometimes mixed with green

- **SONG** Slow drawn-out phrases with deliberate pauses between them, *cherry-o-wit . . . cheree . . . sissy-a-wt*, repeated frequently throughout the day. High, clear, sweet, sometimes piercing notes. Call notes resemble a husky chatter.
- **BEHAVIOR** Solitary or in pairs. Early spring migrant in the Southeast; the first vireo back in the woods in spring. Gleans insects, its principal food, from treetops and branches. Sometimes catches insects in midair or hovers briefly to pick them off foliage or branches. Eats some fruits, especially in winter. Male courts female with much bobbing, singing, and fluffing of yellowish flank feathers. Fairly tame.
- **BREEDING** Monogamous. Solitary nester.
- **NESTING** Incubation 12–14 days by both sexes. Altricial young stay in nest 12–14 days. Fed by both sexes. Occasionally 2 broods per year, particularly in the Southeast.
- **POPULATION** Common in mixed woodlands and at higher elevations in southern Appalachians. Casual to accidental in southwestern US.
- **CONSERVATION** Neotropical migrant. Frequent host to brood parasitism by Brown-headed Cowbirds.

Similar Birds
 BLACK-CAPPED VIREO ♀ Smaller • shorter, slimmer bill; glossy black cap; red eye • juvenile similar to female but has more buff underparts.

Flight Pattern
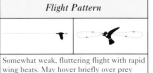
Somewhat weak, fluttering flight with rapid wing beats. May hover briefly over prey and dip to pick it off branch or foliage.

Nest Identification	Twigs, fine grass, shredded bark, stems, spider webs, and cocoons; decorated with lichens • lined with finer materials, including grasses and hair • in fork of tree or bush or in middle of conifer 4–30 feet above ground • built by both sexes • 3–5 white eggs with black and brown markings, especially near large end; oval, 0.8 x 0.6 inches.
Shape ▮ Location	

Plumage Sexes similar	Habitat	Migration Migratory	Weight 0.6 ounce

DATE _____ TIME_____ LOCATION _____

Family VIREONIDAE	Species *Vireo huttoni*	Length 4.75–5 inches	Wingspan 7–8 inches

HUTTON'S VIREO

This small, kingletlike vireo actively forages high in the treetops, where it can be easily overlooked save for its very vocal nature. It may rapidly repeat the same song hundreds of times within a short period. Its olive-tinged plumage serves as a camouflage in the southwestern mountains and Pacific coastal woodlands where this bird makes its home. The West Coast race has greener upperparts than the interior southwestern race, which has grayer plumage.

white eye ring broken above eye

large whitish loreal spot between eyes and bill

grayish olive upperparts

2 thick white bars on each wing

blackish brown wings and tail

dull buffy olive underparts

blue-gray legs and feet

pale yellow-washed belly and undertail coverts

• **SONG** A monotonously repetitive *siree, chi-ree* or *chi-weesu*. Call is a quiet *kip-kip-kip* or whining, scolding *jehr!*
• **BEHAVIOR** Solitary or in pairs or small groups. Often joins mixed-species foraging flocks. Frequents pine-oak and oak woodlands. Active; forages for food at middle to upper levels in trees, and sometimes catches insects in flight. Eats mostly insects, some spiders, and fruit, with almost all gleaned from foliage, bark, or branches. Fearless around the nest.
• **BREEDING** Monogamous. Solitary.
• **NESTING** Incubation 14 days by both sexes. Altricial young remain in nest 14 days, fed by both sexes. 1 brood per year, perhaps 2.
• **POPULATION** Fairly common in woodlands.
• **CONSERVATION** Rare brood parasite host for cowbirds.

Similar Birds

RUBY-CROWNED KINGLET
Smaller; slimmer bill; dark area below lower wing bar; when foraging, flicks wings open often; complete white eye ring.

CASSIN'S VIREO
Larger; more stoutish black bill; gray cap with white spectacles; white underparts with yellowish wash on sides and flanks.

Flight Pattern

Weak fluttering direct flight over short distance; longer flights with rapid wing beats followed by wings briefly folded in at sides, creating undulation.

Nest Identification

Shape   Location

Mosses, grasses, and lichen, bound with spider web and cocoon material, lined with fine dry grass • hanging between a fork toward end of branch, 7–35 feet above ground • built by both sexes • 3–5 white eggs, usually spotted with brown, mostly near large end (occasionally unmarked); oval, 0.7 x 0.5 inches.

Plumage Sexes similar	Habitat	Migration Nonmigratory	Weight 0.4 ounce

DATE _____ TIME_____ LOCATION _____

Family VIREONIDAE	Species *Vireo gilvus*	Length 5–5.5 inches	Wingspan 8.75 inches

WARBLING VIREO

Wintering in Mexico and Central America, this bird has the largest breeding range of any vireo in the woodlands of North America. Although common over most of its range, it is not well known by many people other

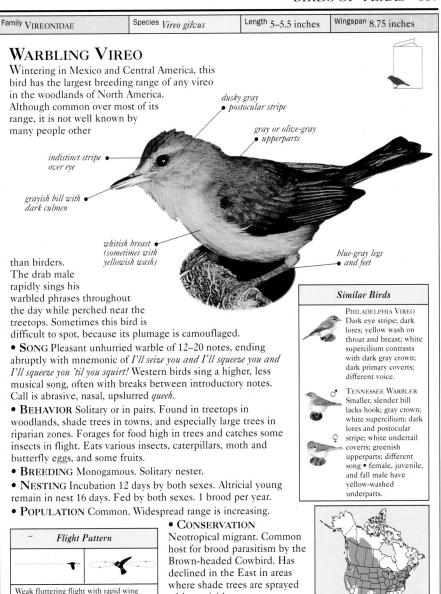

dusky gray postocular stripe

gray or olive-gray upperparts

indistinct stripe over eye

grayish bill with dark culmen

whitish breast (sometimes with yellowish wash)

blue-gray legs and feet

than birders. The drab male rapidly sings his warbled phrases throughout the day while perched near the treetops. Sometimes this bird is difficult to spot, because its plumage is camouflaged.

• **SONG** Pleasant unhurried warble of 12–20 notes, ending abruptly with mnemonic of *I'll seize you and I'll squeeze you and I'll squeeze you 'til you squirt!* Western birds sing a higher, less musical song, often with breaks between introductory notes. Call is abrasive, nasal, upslurred *queeh.*

• **BEHAVIOR** Solitary or in pairs. Found in treetops in woodlands, shade trees in towns, and especially large trees in riparian zones. Forages for food high in trees and catches some insects in flight. Eats various insects, caterpillars, moth and butterfly eggs, and some fruits.

• **BREEDING** Monogamous. Solitary nester.

• **NESTING** Incubation 12 days by both sexes. Altricial young remain in nest 16 days. Fed by both sexes. 1 brood per year.

• **POPULATION** Common. Widespread range is increasing.

• **CONSERVATION** Neotropical migrant. Common host for brood parasitism by the Brown-headed Cowbird. Has declined in the East in areas where shade trees are sprayed with pesticides.

Similar Birds

PHILADELPHIA VIREO Dark eye stripe; dark lores; yellow wash on throat and breast; white supercilium contrasts with dark gray crown; dark primary coverts; different voice.

TENNESSEE WARBLER Smaller, slender bill lacks hook; gray crown; white supercilium; dark lores and postocular stripe; white undertail coverts; greenish upperparts; different song • female, juvenile, and fall male have yellow-washed underparts.

Flight Pattern

Weak fluttering flight with rapid wing beats. Sometimes hovers briefly over foliage or branch, dipping for insect.

Nest Identification

Shape   Location

Bark strips, leaves, vegetation fibers, and grass • hangs between fork toward end of branch, twig, or sometimes shrub, usually 4–15 feet above ground • built by both sexes • 3–5 white eggs spotted with brown and black; oval, 0.8 x 0.5 inches.

Plumage Sexes similar	Habitat	Migration Migratory	Weight 0.5 ounce

DATE _____ TIME_____ LOCATION _____

Family VIREONIDAE	Species *Vireo philadelphicus*	Length 4.75–5.25 inches	Wingspan 8–9 inches

PHILADELPHIA VIREO

First discovered near Philadelphia in the 1840s, this quiet bird is the least known of the East Coast vireos. A late spring migrant, it is easily overlooked in the company of warblers, with which it often travels. Furthermore, it seldom sings in migration, a characteristic that serves to draw even less attention to it. Superficially similar to the Red-eyed Vireo in appearance and voice,

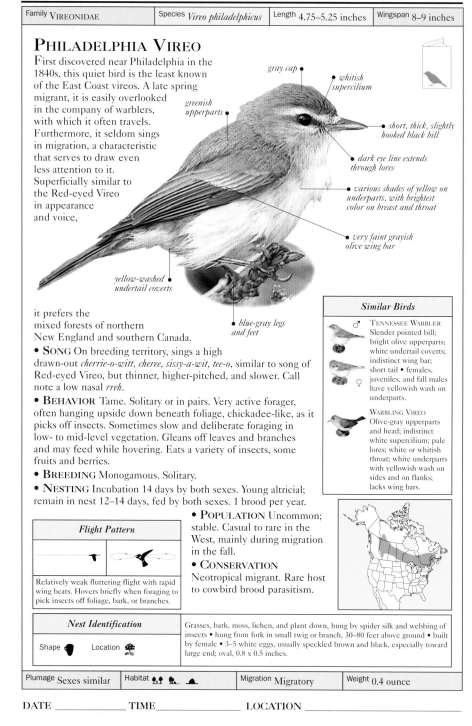

gray cap

whitish supercilium

greenish upperparts

short, thick, slightly hooked black bill

dark eye line extends through lores

various shades of yellow on underparts, with brightest color on breast and throat

very faint grayish olive wing bar

yellow-washed undertail coverts

blue-gray legs and feet

it prefers the mixed forests of northern New England and southern Canada.

• **SONG** On breeding territory, sings a high drawn-out *cherrie-o-witt, cheree, sissy-a-wit, tee-o*, similar to song of Red-eyed Vireo, but thinner, higher-pitched, and slower. Call note a low nasal *rreh*.

• **BEHAVIOR** Tame. Solitary or in pairs. Very active forager, often hanging upside down beneath foliage, chickadee-like, as it picks off insects. Sometimes slow and deliberate foraging in low- to mid-level vegetation. Gleans off leaves and branches and may feed while hovering. Eats a variety of insects, some fruits and berries.

• **BREEDING** Monogamous. Solitary.

• **NESTING** Incubation 14 days by both sexes. Young altricial; remain in nest 12–14 days, fed by both sexes. 1 brood per year.

• **POPULATION** Uncommon; stable. Casual to rare in the West, mainly during migration in the fall.

• **CONSERVATION** Neotropical migrant. Rare host to cowbird brood parasitism.

Similar Birds

TENNESSEE WARBLER
Slender pointed bill; bright olive upperparts; white undertail coverts; indistinct wing bar; short tail • females, juveniles, and fall males have yellowish wash on underparts.

WARBLING VIREO
Olive-gray upperparts and head; indistinct white supercilium; pale lores; white or whitish throat; white underparts with yellowish wash on sides and on flanks; lacks wing bars.

Flight Pattern

Relatively weak fluttering flight with rapid wing beats. Hovers briefly when foraging to pick insects off foliage, bark, or branches.

Nest Identification

Shape ● Location ▩

Grasses, bark, moss, lichen, and plant down, hung by spider silk and webbing of insects • hung from fork in small twig or branch, 30–80 feet above ground • built by female • 3–5 white eggs, usually speckled brown and black, especially toward large end; oval, 0.8 x 0.5 inches.

Plumage Sexes similar	Habitat	Migration Migratory	Weight 0.4 ounce

DATE _____ TIME _____ LOCATION _____

Family VIREONIDAE	Species *Vireo olivaceus*	Length 6 inches	Wingspan 10 inches

RED-EYED VIREO

One of the most abundant in North American deciduous forests, this bird sings almost nonstop from dawn to dusk and often all night. It delivers its brief trilled phrases as it sits on the nest, forages for food, even as it swallows insects. A researcher once totaled the number of song repetitions uttered by an individual in one summer day as a remarkable 22,197 songs. These "sermons" have lent it the handle of "preacher bird." The black-bordered white eyebrow stripe distinguishes this bird from other vireos. The red iris is not visible at a distance; juveniles have a brown iris. Juveniles and autumn birds may have a yellowish wash on the flanks.

white eyebrow outlined in black
greenish olive upperparts
blue-gray crown
stout blackish bill
ruby-red iris
white underparts
darker olive-green tail
darker olive-green wings
blue-gray feet and legs

- **SONG** Repeated phrases and pauses, *look up! . . . see me? . . . over here . . . this way! . . . higher still!* Individuals sing many different repertoires. Call is whining nasal *chewy!*
- **BEHAVIOR** Solitary or in pairs. Picks food off leaves and twigs. Sometimes hovers to snatch food off foliage, bark, or branch. Eats mostly insects; in fall migration lots of fruits and berries. Defensive at nest. Responds readily to pishing and squeaking noises. In migration often joins mixed feeding flocks.
- **BREEDING** Monogamous. Solitary nester.
- **NESTING** Incubation 11–14 days by female. Altricial young stay in nest 10–12 days. Fed by both sexes. 1–2 broods per year.
- **POPULATION** Common in eastern woodlands. Some decline due to clearing of forests in the East. Rare vagrant in migration in the Southwest and on the Pacific Coast.
- **CONSERVATION** Neotropical migrant. Frequent cowbird brood parasitism. Vulnerable to poisoning by ingesting insects sprayed with pesticides and Gypsy Moth control programs.

Similar Birds

BLACK-WHISKERED VIREO
Larger bill; lacks dark border on upper side of eyebrow; dull green upperparts; black mustache mark; different song • only in the Southeast.

YELLOW-GREEN VIREO
Olive-green upperparts; whitish throat and underparts; bright yellow sides, flanks, and undertail coverts; pale gray or whitish supercilium; gray crown; pale olive auriculars; dusky lores; red eyes.

Flight Pattern

Alternates series of rapid wing beats with short glides within forest. Also hovers briefly to pick insects or berries off foliage.

Nest Identification

Shape  Location

Grapevine bark, fine grasses, rootlets, paper from wasp nests, lichens, spider webs, and cocoons • hanging on fork of tree branch or shrub 2–60 feet above ground • built by both sexes, but mostly by female • 3–5 white eggs, most often with fine brown and black dots, especially toward large end; oval, 0.8 x 0.55 inches.

Plumage Sexes similar	Habitat	Migration Migratory	Weight 0.6 ounce

DATE _____ TIME_____ LOCATION _____

Family VIREONIDAE	Species *Vireo flavoviridis*	Length 6 inches	Wingspan 10 inches

YELLOW-GREEN VIREO

Very similar to the Red-eyed Vireo and recently split from it to restore it as a separate species, this native of Mexico has become a rare breeding bird in southern Texas and is being seen more often in southern California in the fall and along the Gulf Coast in spring. It shows extensively yellow-green upperparts (including a face with strong yellow sides), flanks, and undertail coverts, as well as a dull olive crown with more obscure head striping than the Red-eyed Vireo and inconspicuous or absent dark bordering lines.

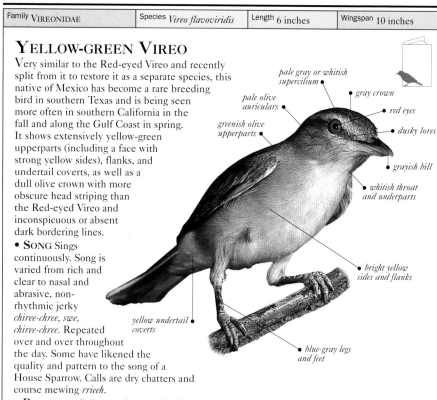

pale gray or whitish supercilium

gray crown

red eyes

pale olive auriculars

dusky lores

greenish olive upperparts

grayish bill

whitish throat and underparts

bright yellow sides and flanks

yellow undertail coverts

blue-gray legs and feet

- **SONG** Sings continuously. Song is varied from rich and clear to nasal and abrasive, non-rhythmic jerky *chiree-chree, swe, chiree-chree*. Repeated over and over throughout the day. Some have likened the quality and pattern to the song of a House Sparrow. Calls are dry chatters and course mewing *rrieeh*.

- **BEHAVIOR** Solitary or in pairs. Deliberate in its movements, foraging in the middle to upper levels of the vegetation. Sometimes joins mixed-species foraging flocks. Picks food off twigs and leaves; may hover briefly to take insect or fruit. Eats a wide variety of insects and spiders; minor part of diet is various seeds and berries.

- **BREEDING** Monogamous. Solitary.

- **NESTING** Incubation 13–14 days by female. Young altricial; stay in nest 12–14 days, fed by both sexes. 1–2 broods per year.

- **POPULATION** Rare to casual in North America; regular in summer in lower Rio Grande Valley of Texas. Casual in spring on Gulf Coast and increasingly regular in fall in coastal southern California.

Similar Birds

RED-EYED VIREO
Blackish lores; black border around white eyebrow; whitish underparts; dark gray cap; olive back and upperparts.

Flight Pattern

Relatively fast direct flight on rapidly beating wings.

Nest Identification

Shape

Location

Grasses, plant fiber, lichen, moss, cobwebs, and strips of papery bark • hanging between fork from thin branch, 5–40 feet above ground • built by female • 2–4 white eggs with fine dots of brown; oval, 0.8 x 0.5 inches.

Plumage Sexes similar	Habitat	Migration Migratory	Weight 0.6 ounce

DATE _____ TIME_____ LOCATION _____

Family CORVIDAE	Species *Cyanocitta stelleri*	Length 11.5 inches	Wingspan 17 inches

STELLER'S JAY

Recognized as the only crested jay in the West, Steller's Jay is named after Arctic explorer Georg Wilhelm Steller, who discovered this bird on the Alaska coast in 1741. The darkest jay in North America, it has a black head and crest and a sooty black back and breast. The extent of black on the body is variable among local populations, as is the amount of blue or white striping on the head or throat.

black crest and head

white striping on head

sooty black neck and breast

sooty black back

- **SONG** Variety of calls, including harsh *shaack, shaack, shaack* and *shooka, shooka* notes; a mellow *klook klook klook*; and shrill hawklike vocalizations. Often mimics calls of other birds, including loons and hawks.

cobalt or purple upperparts

long straight black bill

smoky blue belly and underparts

- **BEHAVIOR** Bold around campgrounds but somewhat shy in woods. Often travels in flocks of more than a dozen birds, which include family groups, after breeding season. Most often feeds in treetops and on ground. Omnivorous; eats wide variety of animal fare, including frogs, snakes, eggs and young of other birds, many kinds of insects, and carrion, but approximately 70 percent of annual diet (90–99 percent in winter) is comprised of pine seeds, acorns, and fruit. Caches seeds and acorns for winter larder.

narrow black-barred "ripple" on tail and wings

black feet and legs

- **BREEDING** This species is known to be monogamous. It is known as a solitary nester. Courtship feeding is done by the male Steller's Jay.

- **NESTING** Incubation 16–18 days mostly by female. Altricial young remain in nest 17–21 days. Fed by both sexes. 1 brood per year.

- **POPULATION** Steller's Jay is common in pine-oak and coniferous woodlands. Its population is both stable and increasing. Casual at lower elevations during the winter season. Accidental in the East.

- **FEEDERS** In winter family groups often frequent feeders.

Similar Birds

BLUE JAY
Purple-gray crest and back; grayish white underparts; black collar extends around body from breast to nape; white spots, bars, and patches in wings and tail; blue wings and tail with fine black barring.

Flight Pattern

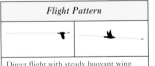

Direct flight with steady buoyant wing beats. Often glides between perches in or among trees, or from tree to ground.

Nest Identification

Shape ◥   Location 🐦 🌲

Cemented with mud • includes pine needles, twigs, dry leaves, roots, and grass • on horizontal limb near trunk or in crotch of conifer; occasionally in deciduous tree; 8–100 feet above ground • built by both sexes • 2–6, but most often 4, pale greenish blue or bluish green eggs with brown markings; subelliptical to short subelliptical, 1.2 x 0.9 inches.

Plumage Sexes similar	Habitat 🌳 🌾 🌲 ⛰	Migration Nonmigratory	Weight 4.5 ounces

DATE _____ TIME_____ LOCATION _____

| Family CORVIDAE | Species *Cyanocitta cristata* | Length 11 inches | Wingspan 16 inches |

BLUE JAY

Once considered primarily a forest dweller, the Blue Jay has adapted to cities, parks, gardens, and forest fragmentation. Some populations remain in locales year-round, while more northern ones migrate south in flocks of 50–100. Common despite clear-cutting in eastern forests, its range is expanding northwest. It is easily recognized by its large size; blue-purple upperparts, wings, and tail; and jaunty bluish purple crest.

purplish crest and back

black collar line extends from breast to nape

bright blue wings

long black bill

grayish white face, chin, and throat

grayish white underparts

white spots and fine black-barred "ripples" on wings

black feet and legs

fine black-barred "ripples" and white spots on bright blue tail

• **SONG** Sharp penetrating *jay jay jay* or *thief, thief, thief!* Also musical *weedle-weedle,* like the squeaking of a farm pump that needs oil. Variety of other vocalizations, some musical; mimics several hawk species.

• **BEHAVIOR** Usually in pairs or flocks; especially gregarious after nesting season. Lives in oak and beech trees. Noisy; shrieks alone or in groups at cats, snakes, owls, hawks, and hunters. Omnivorous, but over 70 percent of diet is plant matter, especially acorns, pine seeds, corn, fruits, and berries. Animal fare includes insects, carrion, eggs and young of other birds, snails, fish, frogs, small reptiles, and small mammals. Stores acorns in the ground for winter, a major factor in establishing and distributing oak forests, as many seeds are not found and thus germinate.

• **BREEDING** Monogamous. Solitary nester. Male feeds during courtship. May keep several mates for several years.

• **NESTING** Incubation 16–18 days by both sexes but most often by female. Altricial young stay in nest 17–21 days; brooded by female; fed by both sexes. 1 brood per year in the North, 2–3 in the South.

• **POPULATION** Common and widespread in woodlands and residential areas with big shade trees. Casual in the Northwest in autumn and winter.

• **FEEDERS** Suet, sunflower seeds, peanuts, cracked nuts; birdbaths.

Similar Birds

STELLER'S JAY
Black crest; smoky black back, neck, and breast; cobalt blue upperparts; no white spots in wings or tail.

WESTERN SCRUB-JAY FLORIDA SCRUB-JAY
Lacks crest; lacks white spotting on wings and tail; lacks black collar; grayish underparts contrast with gray-streaked white throat • Florida Scrub-Jay restricted to Florida.

Flight Pattern

Direct flight with steady, buoyant wing beats. Often glides between perches within or between trees, or to ground.

Nest Identification	
Shape	Location	Twigs, bark, moss, lichens, grass, and sometimes paper and string • built by both sexes • on horizontal branch near trunk or in crotch or vines 5–20 feet above ground; sometimes up to 50 feet • 3–7 pale greenish blue or bluish green eggs with dark brown markings; subelliptical, 1.1 x 0.85 inches.

| Plumage Sexes similar | Habitat | Migration Migratory | Weight 3.0 ounces |

DATE _____ TIME_____ LOCATION _____

Family CORVIDAE	Species *Cyanocorax yncas*	Length 10.5 inches	Wingspan 15 inches

GREEN JAY

Also known as the Rio Grande Jay, this brightly colored tropical bird is restricted to southern Texas in the US, although it also ranges south through Mexico, Central America, and northern regions of South America. Look for it in thickets and dense riparian growth along the river in the lower Rio Grande Valley. Nonmigratory, the Green Jay rarely wanders far from its nesting sites but may travel in foraging flocks to nearby ranch country after nesting season. Its bright colors blend remarkably well with sun-dappled foliage, but once it has been seen this green bird with its blue-and-black head and bright yellow outer tail feathers is unmistakable.

blue-white band on forehead and above and underneath eyes

blue nape and crown

dark green upperparts

black bill

black throat, face, and chest

light green to greenish yellow underparts

- **SONG** Dry harsh series of *cheh-cheh-cheh* notes; loud ringing *chink, chink, chink*; and froglike croaking of *ahrrrrrrrr*.
- **BEHAVIOR** Gregarious and noisy. Inquisitive. In pairs and small family groups; family groups of 4–9 remain on permanent territories. Inhabits heavily wooded areas and thickets. May occasionally forage in open country after nesting season; generally forages at low to middle levels. Omnivorous; eats insects, spiders, small vertebrates (including eggs and young of other birds), fruits, berries, and seeds of grass, weeds, and trees.

bluish green tail with yellow outer tail feathers

black legs and feet

- **BREEDING** Monogamous. Solitary nester; cooperative breeder with helpers at nest. Only 1 pair in each flock breeds.
- **NESTING** Incubation 17–18 days by female. Altricial young stay in nest 19–22 days. Brooded by both sexes. Fed by both sexes and helpers. 1 brood per year.
- **POPULATION** Common in restricted US range. Stable. Range expanding west and northwest.
- **FEEDERS** Suet, corn, nuts, and sunflower seeds.
- **CONSERVATION** Small US population is vulnerable to loss of riparian habitat due to human development and agriculture.

Similar Birds

None in North American range.

Flight Pattern

Direct flight with steady buoyant wing beats. Glides between perches within trees, between trees, or from tree to ground.

Nest Identification	Large platform supports cup of thorny twigs • lined with leaves, roots, vines, moss, and grass • in deciduous trees or shrubs 5–30 feet above ground • built by both sexes and sometimes other birds • 3–5, most often 4, grayish white, green-white, or buff eggs with brown, gray, and lavender markings; oval to short oval, 1.1 x 0.8 inches.
Shape 🥄 Location 🌿 🌳	

Plumage Sexes similar	Habitat 🌿🌱 🪨 ⛰	Migration Nonmigratory	Weight 2.7 ounces

DATE _____ TIME_____ LOCATION _____

Family CORVIDAE	Species *Cyanocorax morio*	Length 15–17 inches	Wingspan 30 inches

BROWN JAY

Large and noisy with a long graduated tail and short brushy crest, the Brown Jay is considered a cooperative bird and is often observed helping other parents and guarding their young. A young Brown Jay can be distinguished by its yellow bill and eye rings. In the US the species is restricted to the lower Rio Grande Valley of Texas in the vicinity of Falcon Dam, but in Mexico and Central America the Brown Jay is widespread and fairly common.

• **SONG** Harsh nasal call of *jay! jay! jay!* or *kyeeeah, kyeeeah, kyeeeah!* is similar to a Blue Jay or Red-shouldered Hawk but louder. Also makes steadily repeated soft mewing.

• **BEHAVIOR** Noisy and gregarious. Forms flocks of 6–15 birds composed mostly of

dark sooty brown body and wings

short brushy crest on forehead

black bill

cream belly and undertail coverts

long sooty brown tail

family members in which 1 monogamous pair may nest with young fed by several members of flock, or several females may lay eggs in a communal nest with young fed by helpers. New flocks are formed by young birds splitting off from original flock. Omnivorous; eats wide variety of insects, small vertebrates, eggs, seeds, nuts, fruits, and berries. Feeds from low to high and sometimes on ground.

• **BREEDING** Monogamous. Solitary nester but sometimes communal; cooperative with helpers at nest.

• **NESTING** Incubation 18–20 days by female and other birds. Altricial young stay in nest 22–31 days. Fed by both parents and other adult birds. 1–2 broods per year.

• **POPULATION** Uncommon to rare and local in lower Rio Grande Valley of southern Texas.

Similar Birds
None in North American range.

• **FEEDERS** Fruit, nuts, sunflower seeds, and suet.

• **CONSERVATION** Vulnerable to loss of riparian woodland habitat due to human development and agriculture, particularly in the lower Rio Grande Valley.

Flight Pattern

Steady buoyant, somewhat bouncy wing beats. Glides between perches among trees, and from trees to ground.

Nest Identification

Shape ⬗   Location 🪺 🌳

Lined with twigs and other vegetation • on horizontal limb far from trunk 23–70 feet above ground • built by both sexes and other birds • 1–8 blue-gray eggs with brown markings; oval, 1.3 x 0.9 inches.

Plumage Sexes similar	Habitat 👫 🐦 ✈	Migration Nonmigratory	Weight 7.2 ounces

DATE _____ TIME_____ LOCATION _____

Family CORVIDAE	Species *Aphelocoma californica*	Length 11 inches	Wingspan 16 inches

WESTERN SCRUB-JAY

Until recently the Western, Island, and Florida Scrub-Jays were considered races of one species, the Scrub Jay. The Western Scrub-Jay has a large range over varying habitats, and the several races currently accepted show some differences in plumage, including intensity of blue upperparts, color of crissum, and size of bill. This tame, bold bird serves as a major disperser of oak forests because of its habit of caching acorns in the earth for winter stores. Found near urban areas, it will sometimes take food from the hand of a human.

white eyebrow over dark eye patch

dark blue upperparts

smoky brown back

white throat outlined with blue necklace

blue band on chest

long blue tail

variable whitish, buff, and grayish underparts

- **SONG** Noisy. Call is a hoarse repeated *shreep* or *quay-quay-quay.*
- **BEHAVIOR** Often in pairs or small flocks. Perches in the open on trees, shrubs, or wires. Forages on ground and in trees for food. Eats insects, various grains, small lizards, frogs, various fruits, and eggs and young of other birds. Courting male hops around female with upright posture, head erect, and spread tail dragging the ground. Unlike the eastern Florida Scrub-Jay, pairs hold individual territories and have no helpers at the nest.
- **BREEDING** Monogamous. Solitary.
- **NESTING** Incubation 15–17 days by female; male feeds female during incubation. Altricial young stay in nest 18–19 days, brooded by female, but fed by both sexes. 1 brood per year.
- **POPULATION** Fairly common to common in scrub vegetation and in pine-oak-juniper woodlands.
- **FEEDERS** Attracted to feeder with nuts, sunflower seed, and fruit.

Similar Birds

PINYON JAY
Blue overall; white-streaked throat; short tail • western range.

MEXICAN JAY
Chunkier; lacks white supercilium; lacks white throat with blue necklace; grayer breast and throat without strong contrast between them • limited range in the Southwest.

Flight Pattern
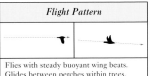
Flies with steady buoyant wing beats. Glides between perches within trees, between trees, and from tree to ground.

Nest Identification	Twigs, grass, and moss, lined with finer rootlets and sometimes animal hair • in tree or shrub, 5–30 feet above ground • built by both sexes • 2–7 light green or gray eggs, with brown, reddish brown, or olive spots; oval to long oval, 1.1 x 0.8 inches.
Shape ◥ Location 🌳 🌿 🌲	

Plumage Sexes similar	Habitat 🔺 🌿 🏔 ⚘ 🌲	Migration Nonmigratory	Weight 2.8 ounces

DATE _____ TIME_____ LOCATION _____

Family CORVIDAE	Species *Aphelocoma ultramarina*	Length 11 inches	Wingspan 15 inches

MEXICAN JAY

Traveling in clamoring flocks of 6–20 birds, Mexican Jays are often observed mobbing hawks and occasionally snakes or less common predators such as bobcats and foxes. Offspring often live with relatives for several years and help care for the young, which usually are produced in only one or two nests of the clan. Considered one of the most sedentary birds in North America, the Mexican Jay rarely journeys beyond its immediate breeding territory. It is a fairly common resident of oak and pine-oak forests in foothills, canyons, and mountains from 2,000 to 9,000 feet. The Arizona race has pale blue plumage, while the Texas race shows medium blue plumage. Juveniles have grayish blue upperparts, gray underparts, and a yellow bill. It was formerly known as the Gray-breasted Jay.

blackish lores and around eyes

light to medium blue upperparts

stout black bill

gray back with brown central patch

grayish white underparts

black legs and feet

long blue tail

• **SONG** Raucous ringing *weenk*, often heard in a series. Calls also include a *wait-wait-wait* and a soft *coo*.
• **BEHAVIOR** Gregarious. Tame. Travels in flocks of 5–20 or more birds, many of whom are related. Flocks made up of 2 breeding pairs and others that assist in nest building, feeding young, and territorial defense. Eats acorns as staple food but also takes wild fruit, various insects, carrion, and eggs and young of smaller birds.
• **BREEDING** Monogamous. Gregarious. Cooperative.
• **NESTING** Incubation 16–18 days by female. Altricial young remain in nest 24–25 days. Young are fed by both sexes as well as by other birds. 1 brood per year.

Similar Birds

WESTERN SCRUB-JAY White throat outlined by blue necklace; white eyebrow; more slender body • deeper blue upperparts than Arizona race of Mexican Jay.

• **POPULATION** Fairly common to common in montane pine-oak canyons of the Southwest.
• **CONSERVATION** Depends on mature pine-oak forests; vulnerable to habitat loss.

Flight Pattern

Slow steady buoyant wing beats. Glides between perches within trees, between trees, and from trees to ground.

Nest Identification

Shape ◖   Location 🪺 🐦

Lined with fine grass, hair, twigs, and roots • on horizontal branch or in crotch of oak, or sometimes conifer, 6–30 feet above ground • built by both sexes and other birds • 4–7 pale green eggs with green markings; subelliptical to long, 1.2 x 0.8 inches.

Plumage Sexes differ	Habitat 🌾 🌳 ⛰ ✈	Migration Nonmigratory	Weight 4.3 ounces

Family CORVIDAE	Species *Gymnorhinus cyanocephalus*	Length 10.5 inches	Wingspan 15 inches

PINYON JAY

Flying in huge flocks sometimes numbering into the hundreds, or as many as a thousand, in spring, autumn, and winter, these birds appear to be migrating but are traveling from the desert 9,000 feet up the mountains in search of piñon nuts and other food. In the highly organized colonies, feeding flocks leave several birds to act as sentries, which sound warning calls when an intruder approaches. Adults are proportioned like a small blue crow with a long bill and short tail. Juveniles are similar to adults but duller overall.

long pointed black bill

blue throat with white streaks

blue overall

black legs

blue tail

- **SONG** Noisy. Warning call of *crauk-crauk*. High nasal caw, *kaa-eh*, with lower second note. Also makes various high-pitched jaylike mews, caws, and chatters.
- **BEHAVIOR** Gregarious. Crowlike in behavior; walks, hops, and forages on ground as well as in trees. Nests in colonies of up to 150 birds, travels in large foraging flocks of up to a thousand birds, and roosts communally in nonbreeding season. Mostly forages in mountains in bands of conifers, especially piñon pines, at elevations of 3,000–8,000 feet. Eats piñon nuts and other pine seeds, grass seeds, berries, fruit, grain, insects, and eggs and young of small birds. Will boldly approach human habitations for food scraps.
- **BREEDING** Monogamous. Colonial.
- **NESTING** Incubation 16–17 days by female. Altricial young stay in nest 21 days. Fed by both sexes. 1–2 broods per year.
- **POPULATION** Common in piñon-juniper habitat in high plateaus and interior mountains. Stable, though numbers drastically fluctuate.
- **CONSERVATION** Dependent on piñon-juniper woodlands; vulnerable to habitat loss.

Similar Birds

WESTERN SCRUB-JAY Longer tail; grayish white underparts; white throat outlined with blue necklace; brown back patch.

STELLER'S JAY Crested; blackish underparts; blue upperparts.

Flight Pattern
Buoyant, steady direct flight with deep wing beats.

Nest Identification	
Shape ◀ Location 🐦 🌿	Sticks, crumbled bark, grasses, stems, roots, bits of hair, and paper • sometimes 3 nests in 1 tree; on branch or fork of tree 3–25 feet above ground • built by both sexes • 3–5 bluish white or greenish white eggs; subelliptical to long oval, 1.2 x 0.8 inches.

Plumage Sexes similar	Habitat 🔺 👫 ▬▬	Migration Nonmigratory	Weight 3.6 ounces

DATE _____ TIME_____ LOCATION _____

Family CORVIDAE	Species *Nucifraga columbiana*	Length 12.5 inches	Wingspan 18 inches

CLARK'S NUTCRACKER

Far from shy, this fearless bird can be seen chasing coyotes, barging into tents of campers, or flying toward the sound of an imitation owl call. It is named after Captain William Clark of the Lewis and Clark expedition. An avid forager, this bird gathers and stores its surplus pine nuts and seeds in caches in the ground by tens of thousands per year. They become its principal food from late winter to early summer, and those that germinate become important for the distribution of conifers. In flight the white tail with black central tail feathers and white secondary patch on the black wings contrast with the pale gray body. It resides in coniferous forests in the mountains between three- and thirteen-thousand feet near the timberline.

long black bill

stocky pale gray body

black wings with white secondaries forming patch on back of inner wing

white tail with black central tail feathers

black legs and feet

• **SONG** Noisy. Gives a very nasal rasping drawling dragged-out caw or *kra-a-a*.

• **BEHAVIOR** Gregarious; tame; curious. Eats insects and nuts, including the shell. Can carry 70–95 pine seeds at a time in sublingual pouch in mouth for winter cache. Sometimes invades human habitation, campgrounds, or picnic tables for scraps. Forages for food by walking or hopping on ground, or by pecking trees, woodpecker-style, for insects; may hawk flying insects like a flycatcher. Also takes bird eggs, nestlings, lizards, small mammals, and carrion. Can find thousands of buried seeds annually by memory.

• **BREEDING** Monogamous. Colonial.

• **NESTING** Incubation 16–18 days by both sexes. Altricial young stay in nest 18–21 days. Brooded by female. Fed by both sexes. 1 brood per year.

• **POPULATION** Common. Fluctuates from year to year but remains stable. Eruptions to desert and lowlands every 10–20 years. Accidental in East.

• **FEEDERS** Sunflower seeds.

• **CONSERVATION** Vulnerable to habitat loss due to logging operations in mountain coniferous forests.

Similar Birds

GRAY JAY
Slimmer; longer, uniformly gray tail; lacks white in wings; uniformly dark gray wings; black nape; short black bill.

Flight Pattern

Crowlike flight with slow steady deep deliberate wing beats. Sometimes alternates several rapid wing beats with long glides.

Nest Identification

Shape ⌣ ⌣   Location 🐦

Platform of small sticks and pieces of bark • lined with pine needles, leaves, and grass • on far end of horizontal branch of conifer 8–50 feet above ground • built by both sexes • 2–6 pale green or gray-green eggs marked with brown, olive, or gray; long oval pointed at small end; vary from ovate to elliptical ovate, 1.3 inches long.

Plumage Sexes similar	Habitat 🌳 🪨 ⛰	Migration Nonmigratory	Weight 5.0 ounces

DATE _____ TIME_____ LOCATION _____

| Family CORVIDAE | Species *Pica hudsonia* | Length 17.5–22 inches | Wingspan 24 inches |

BLACK-BILLED MAGPIE

The Black-billed Magpie is one of four songbirds that has a tail more than half the length of its body; one other is a magpie and two are flycatchers. As part of courtship, the male and female build large intricate structures for their nest, which they use year after year, producing a mud-based domed structure of sticks with a side entrance that may be two to four feet high. Other birds often seek shelter from storms in used magpie nests or nest in them themselves. In flight this bird appears black and white with large flashing white patches in the short rounded wings and a long dark green tail trailing behind.

- **SONG** Noisy. Call is plaintive nasal *mag.* Also utters bold raspy repetitive *chuck-chuck-chuck* and has melodic whistle.

- **BEHAVIOR** Gregarious. Travels in family flocks of 6–10 birds; in winter joins flocks of up to 50 or more birds. Forages for food on ground, walking or hopping. Eats insects, larvae, and carrion. Also picks ticks off backs of elk, deer, and livestock. Caches food when plentiful. Frequents open country with brushy thickets and scattered trees, especially riparian groves. Roosts communally.

- **BREEDING** Monogamous. Small colonies. Pairs may stay together all year and form long-term bonds.

- **NESTING** Incubation 16–21 days by female. Altricial young brooded by female but fed by both sexes. First flight at 25–32 days. 1 brood per year.

- **POPULATION** Common and widespread in rangeland and scrubland with open woodlands and thickets, especially near water. Casual in the East and the Southwest in winter. Some eastern birds may be escapees.

- **CONSERVATION** Thousands have been killed by accidentally ingesting poisoned bait intended for predators in rangeland.

black head
heavy black bill
black back and rump
black breast
white wing patches
white tertials
white sides and belly
black undertail coverts
graduated iridescent blackish green tail is 9.5–12 inches long
black legs and feet

Similar Birds

YELLOW-BILLED MAGPIE
Yellow bill; yellow patch of bare skin below or around eye; smaller
- western range, but Black-billed may casually wander into Yellow-billed's range.

Flight Pattern
Direct flight with slow, steady deliberate somewhat shallow wing beats. Often glides between perches or from perch to ground.

Nest Identification	
Shape ◉ Location 🌳 🪹 🌲	2–4-foot-high outside platform and roof made of sticks, mud, and thorny material • inside cup made of stems, rootlets, and horsehair • on limb of tree or shrub, typically no more than 25 feet above ground but up to 50 feet • built by female with materials brought by male • 7–13 greenish gray eggs marked with browns; usually subelliptical but sometimes long oval, 1.3 inches long.

| Plumage Sexes similar | Habitat 🏞️ 🌾 ✈️ 🌳 | Migration Nonmigratory | Weight 6.6 ounces |

DATE _____ TIME_____ LOCATION _____

Family CORVIDAE	Species *Corvus brachyrhynchos*	Length 17.5 inches	Wingspan 33–40 inches

AMERICAN CROW

One of the most widely distributed and recognized birds in North America, the American Crow is entirely black from beak to toe to tail with a glossy violet sheen. Studies of these intelligent birds have shown that they can count, solve puzzles, learn symbols, and retain information. They often are seen chasing and mobbing owls and hawks. Huge flocks from a few hundred to as many as 200,000 birds may assemble in winter to roost, travel, and feed together. Often persecuted, shot, poisoned, and even bombed on its roost in the past, this crow still lives among us by its intelligence and adaptability and is common throughout its range.

brown eyes

black bill

black overall with iridescent violet gloss on body

iridescent blue-violet and green-blue gloss on wings

black feet and legs

fan-shaped tail

- **SONG** Familiar loud call of *caw-caw* with many variations. Nasal begging call like *uh-uah* of the Fish Crow.
- **BEHAVIOR** Gregarious. Omnivorous; eats insects, many other small invertebrates from millipedes to snails, small amphibians, small reptiles, small mammals, eggs and young of other birds, waste corn and other grains, fruits, field crops, garbage, and carrion. Mobs avian predators, calling gangs of crows together to harass a large hawk or owl on a perch or drive it out of the area. Catches up to a soaring hawk and repeatedly dives on it from above, often forcing it down into the shelter of trees below. Breaks mollusk shells by dropping them on rocks from above.
- **BREEDING** Monogamous. Solitary nester. Sometimes known to be cooperative.
- **NESTING** Incubation 18 days by both sexes. Altricial young stay in nest 28–35 days. Brooded by female. Fed by both sexes and extra birds. 1 brood per year, 2 in the South.

Similar Birds

COMMON RAVEN
Larger; heavier stout bill; shaggy throat feathers; wedge-shaped tail; different voice.

FISH CROW
Smaller; more pointed wings; proportionally smaller more slender bill and longer tail; nasal, higher-pitched call
• eastern range.

- **POPULATION** Abundant. Adapting as habitat developed by humans.
- **CONSERVATION** Widely persecuted in the past by farmers and hunters. Still legally hunted for sport in many states.

Flight Pattern

Slow steady deliberate direct flight with deep wing beats. Glides with slight dihedral from altitude to perch or ground, between perches, and from perch to ground.

Nest Identification	Made of twigs and branches • lined with tree material, grass, feathers, moss, leaves, and hair • in fork of tree or shrub or cross arms of utility pole 0–100 feet above ground; sometimes on ground in prairie • built by both sexes and sometimes extra birds • 3–7 bluish green to olive-green eggs marked with brown and gray; oval, 1.6 x 1.1 inches.
Shape ⌒ ⌔ Location 🌲 🌿 🌳 🏚	

Plumage Sexes similar	Habitat 🌿 🌾 🌱 🏞	Migration Some migrate	Weight 1.0 pound

DATE _____ TIME_____ LOCATION _____

Family CORVIDAE.	Species *Corvus imparatus*	Length 14–15 inches	Wingspan 25–28 inches

TAMAULIPAS CROW

Historically an endemic of northeastern Mexico, this species has settled in the winter in the Lower Rio Grande Valley of Texas, especially near the city of Brownsville, where the species has been recorded since 1968. Once called the Mexican Crow, this gregarious small-bodied bird is highly adaptable. The most dependable place to see the bird in Texas has been the municipal dump in Brownsville. It is the smallest crow that has nested in the US, and it is possible to mistake it for a Great-tailed Grackle, but in flight note that this crow's tail is short and squared.

iridescent purple sheen on head

iridescent purple sheen on upperparts

slender black bill

glossy black overall

glossy blue to blue-green underparts

squared tail

black legs and feet

- **SONG** Utters a throaty *craw* or *khurr*, or sometimes a shrieking *creow*. Also has a low guttural croaking similar to the croaking of a frog.
- **BEHAVIOR** Solitary or in pairs or flocks; gregarious after breeding season. Eats insects, grains, carrion, refuse, eggs and young of other birds, and some fruits. Walks and hops on ground as it forages for food. Frequents open and semiopen areas with trees, brush, and thickets. Often found scavenging around towns, garbage dumps, and in agricultural areas. Often in large foraging flocks after the breeding season; roosts in communal roosts.
- **BREEDING** Monogamous. Colonial.
- **NESTING** Incubation 17–18 days by female. Young altricial; stay in nest 30–35 days, brooded by female and fed by both sexes. 1 brood per year.
- **POPULATION** Uncommon to fairly common and local. Some declines have occurred in southern Texas in recent years. Common to fairly common in northeastern Mexico. Adaptable to habitat changes.

Similar Birds

GREAT-TAILED GRACKLE ♂ Whitish yellow eyes; longer, keel-shaped tail; glossy black overall with purplish sheen.

CHIHUAHUAN RAVEN Larger; heavy bill; wedge-shaped tail; croaking voice; plumage not glossy.

Flight Pattern

Rapid direct flight on steadily beating wings. Glides from altitude to perch; glides between perches and from perch to ground.

Nest Identification

Shape ⌒⌒ ⬗   Location 🌳 🌳

Sticks and plant fibers, lined with softer materials • in fork of tree • built by both sexes • 4–5 pale blue to blue-gray eggs, with brown or olive-buff streaks; subelliptical to long oval, 1.1 inches long.

Plumage Sexes similar	Habitat 🪶 ⛰ ⛰	Migration Nonmigratory	Weight Undetermined

DATE _____ TIME_____ LOCATION _____

Family CORVIDAE	Species *Corvus ossifragus*	Length 15 inches	Wingspan 30–40 inches

FISH CROW

An active scavenger, the Fish Crow frequently harasses gulls and terns in attempts to force them to surrender their prey. It also raids the unguarded nests of other birds, particularly shorebirds, egrets and herons, or turtles, flying away with their eggs in its bill. In the winter, sometimes thousands of these crows can be seen roosting together. Smaller than the similar American Crow, the Fish Crow is never far away from water, living along the coast and penetrating inland mainly along major rivers. Although primarily nonmigratory, birds in the northwestern part of the range are migratory inland.

pointed wings

slender black bill

slender black body

fan-shaped tail

black feet and legs

• **SONG** Call is a high-pitched nasal *ca-hah* or *aw-uk*.
• **BEHAVIOR** Gregarious and sociable. Will feed inland but usually feeds in shallow waters along coastline and salt marshes. Omnivorous. Sometimes a major nest predator at heronries. Eats a wide variety of crustaceans, carrion, eggs of other birds, insects and insect larvae, fish, ticks from livestock, various berries, and some fruits. Drops mollusks from the air to break them on rocks, highways, or wharves. Often hovers over water or land, searching for prey before dropping down to grab it.
• **BREEDING** Monogamous. Small colonies.
• **NESTING** Incubation 16–18 days by both sexes. Young altricial; brooded by female; stay in nest at least 21 days, fed by both sexes. 1 brood per year.
• **POPULATION** Common especially along the coast. This bird's range is increasing and expanding to the north as well as inland.

Similar Birds

AMERICAN CROW
Slightly larger; larger bill; proportionally larger head; shorter tail; call is a lower clearer *caw*.

Flight Pattern

Flies with somewhat stiff wing beats, alternating several quick wing strokes with long glides. Hovers when foraging.

Nest Identification	Dried twigs with lining of bark chips, pine needles, feathers, horse and cattle hair, and soft grasses • set fairly high in fork of shrub or topmost
Shape  Location	crotch of deciduous tree or conifer, 6–90 feet above ground • built by both sexes • 4–5 bluish or grayish green eggs marked with brown and gray spots; oval, 1.5 inches long.

Plumage Sexes similar	Habitat	Migration Nonmigratory	Weight 10.6 ounces

DATE _____ TIME_____ LOCATION _____

Family CORVIDAE	Species *Corvus cryptoleucus*	Length 19.5 inches	Wingspan 38 inches

CHIHUAHUAN RAVEN

Sometimes called the White-necked Raven, this bird has white bases on the back of the neck and lower throat feathers that show only when ruffled by the wind or when the bird becomes agitated. Highly adventuresome, these birds sometimes dive into rotating air masses or dust devils and allow themselves to be taken for an upward ride. A small raven of arid grasslands, scrublands, and desert, it uses the endless strings of utility poles crossing the barren landscapes it inhabits as lookout stations, resting places, and nesting locations, placing nests high on the cross-arms of the poles.

black overall with purple gloss

heavy bill

black legs and feet

wedge-shaped tail

- **SONG** Call is drawling *crooaak*. Utters guttural *quark, quark* as a warning call.
- **BEHAVIOR** Gregarious. Active forager and scavenger. Eats wide variety of insects, insect larvae, spiders, worms, snails, earthworms, small mammals, lizards, eggs and young of other birds, carrion, grains, nuts, corn, cactus fruit, and scraps of human food. Breeds late in season, timing nesting with food availability. Forms flocks soon after nesting season that may become enormous, numbering in the thousands before winter. Male ruffles neck feathers in courtship display and engages in acrobatic aerial display for female. Then male and female sit next to each other and rub bills, bow to one another, and raise wings.
- **BREEDING** Monogamous. Colonial.
- **NESTING** Incubation 18–21 days by both sexes. Altricial young stay in nest 30 days. Brooded by female. Fed by both sexes. 1 brood per year.
- **POPULATION** Common to fairly common in arid to semiarid grassland, rangeland, and desert.

Similar Birds

COMMON RAVEN
Larger; heavier bill; longer tail; pale gray bases on upper neck and throat feathers.

AMERICAN CROW
Smaller; smaller bill; fan-shaped tail; dark gray bases on neck and throat feathers; different call.

- **CONSERVATION** Formerly highly persecuted by ranchers and farmers who considered them pests or threats to livestock; they were systematically shot and poisoned by the thousands in control programs.

Flight Pattern	

Alternates between several deep wing beats and short to long glides; glides from altitude to ground or perch. Soars effortlessly on thermals and updrafts.	

Nest Identification	
Shape Location	Prickly sticks and sometimes barbed wire • lined with bark chips, grass, hair, and bits of refuse • in fork of tree or shrub 9–40 feet above ground; sometimes on man-made structures such as windmills or utility poles • built by female • 3–8 pale or grayish green eggs with lilac and brown markings; subelliptical to long oval, 1.8 x 1.3 inches.

Plumage Sexes similar	Habitat 	Migration Most do not migrate	Weight 1.2 pounds

DATE _____ TIME _____ LOCATION _____

Family CORVIDAE	Species *Corvus corax*	Length 24–26 inches	Wingspan 46–56 inches

COMMON RAVEN

This magnificent flier is the aerial equal of hawks and falcons and is the largest passerine, or perching bird, in North America. If any bird truly enjoys flying to the point of playing in the air, it must be this raven. Intelligent resourceful hunters and scavengers, groups of these birds have been observed working together to capture prey that is too large for one bird to conquer. It is a revered totem and spirit to many Native Americans. Adults are glossy black overall, with a huge "Roman nose," and shaggy throat feathers that can be elevated or sleeked down. The female is similar to the male but smaller.

nostrils hidden by stiff tufts of feathers extending about a third of the way out the bill

black overall with iridescent purple and violet sheen

long wedge-shaped tail with long central tail feathers

long heavy bill

black legs and feet

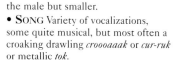

• **SONG** Variety of vocalizations, some quite musical, but most often a croaking drawling *croooaaak* or *cur-ruk* or metallic *tok*.

• **BEHAVIOR** Tame. Quick learner. Solitary or in pairs or small groups. Gregarious in winter, when it may occur in large foraging flocks and nightly communal roosts. Active forager, scavenger, and hunter. Omnivorous; eats wide variety of small invertebrates, from tadpoles and shellfish to worms and insects. Also takes many small vertebrates, including minnows, eggs and young of other birds, and rodents, as well as carrion and refuse. Elaborate courtship flight with great display of acrobatics and pair flying, male above female, wing-tip to wing-tip and heads touching.

• **BREEDING** Monogamous. Solitary; small, loose colonies in the North. Mates for life.

• **NESTING** Incubation 18–21 days by female. Altricial young stay in nest 38–44 days. Brooded by female. Fed by both sexes. 1 brood per year.

Similar Birds

AMERICAN CROW
Smaller; smaller bill; lacks shaggy throat feathers; fan-shaped tail; different call.

CHIHUAHUAN RAVEN
Smaller; shorter bill and wings; nasal bristles extend farther out on culmen; white-based neck and throat feathers.

• **POPULATION** Common. Expanding in California; also in Appalachians into areas where birds had been extirpated.

• **CONSERVATION** In past was shot, trapped, and poisoned for alleged damage to wild game and domesticated animals.

Flight Pattern

Strong flight, often rising in circles. Alternates deep wing beats with long glides or soaring on flat wings like a hawk. Soars on thermals and updrafts.

Nest Identification

Shape   Location

Branches and sticks on outside; cup made of small sticks • lined with bark chips, animal hair, sheep's wool, lichens, moss, seaweed, and grass • on cliff near water, in mountains, or in fork of tree 45–80 feet above ground • built by both sexes • 3–7 greenish or gray-green eggs with brown or olive spots; subelliptical to long oval, 2 x 1.4 inches.

Plumage Sexes similar	Habitat	Migration Nonmigratory	Weight 2.7 pounds

DATE _____ TIME_____ LOCATION _____

Family ALAUDIDAE	Species *Eremophila alpestris*	Length 7–8 inches	Wingspan 12.5–14 inches

HORNED LARK

The Horned Lark is one of the most widespread songbirds in North America. The spectacular display flight of the male bird begins with an ascending flight as high as 800 feet. Singing, he then circles, closes his wings, and drops headfirst almost to the ground, where he opens his wings at the last second. He then struts around the female with his wings drooped and horns erect. The female appears similar to the male but is duller in color and lacks the black crown. In flight note the white underparts, including the wings and wing linings, the black tail with white outer tail feathers, and black legs and feet.

hornlike black tufts on head connected by black-bordered forecrown

black "sideburns" and lores

brown back and rump

brown wings

yellowish to white face and forehead

black bill

pale yellow to white throat

black bib

whitish underparts with sandy buff wash on sides and flanks

black tail with white outer feathers

• **SONG** Given from ground or in high, circling flight. Sings series of bell-like, tinkling notes *pit-wit, wee-pit, pit-wee*. Call is *tsee-tete* or *zeet*.

• **BEHAVIOR** Pairs; gregarious in winter, forming large flocks sometimes mixed with Snow Buntings and longspurs. Walks and runs rather than hops. Forages on ground, often in open fields with bare soil, pebbles, or short, sparse vegetation. Eats mostly seeds, grains, insects, and small mollusks. Often found in agricultural areas, to which it has adapted for nesting and foraging, on country roadways and farm roads standing and walking on pavement or gravel. This bird nests as early as February in the South. In courtship males perform display flights and skylark.

• **BREEDING** Monogamous. Solitary to gregarious.

• **NESTING** Incubation 11–12 days by female. Altricial young stay in nest 9–12 days. Brooded by female. Fed by both sexes. 1 brood per year in the North, 2 in the South.

• **POPULATION** Common. Has expanded eastern range since early 1800s because of agricultural development.

Similar Birds

AMERICAN PIPIT
Gray upperparts; brown-streaked whitish underparts; dark grayish brown tail with white outer tail feathers; bobs tail continuously; lacks horns, face pattern, and black bib • cinnamon-buff underparts in summer.

Flight Pattern

After each wing beat folds wing feathers close to body.

Nest Identification	
Shape 〰️ 🐦 Location ▬ ⚋⚋	Grass • lined with feathers and soft materials • in shallow depression, natural or dug by female, often near clumps of dirt or animal manure • built by female • 2–5 gray or greenish eggs dotted with browns; subelliptical, 0.8 x 0.6 inches.

Plumage Sexes differ	Habitat ⚋⚋ ⚊🌱	Migration Migratory	Weight 1.1 ounces

DATE _____ TIME_____ LOCATION _____

Family HIRUNDINIDAE	Species *Progne subis*	Length 7.25–8.5 inches	Wingspan 15.5–16.75 inches

PURPLE MARTIN

Colonies once nested in holes in tall dead trees and saguaro cacti. Today the largest North American swallow usually nests in man-made multidwelling martin houses, sometimes with hundreds of pairs nesting together. Martin houses were inspired by the Native American custom of placing empty gourds on tall poles to attract the Purple Martin for aesthetic reasons and to reduce the insect population around villages and crops. Juvenile males have browner upperparts with whitish bellies and some purple sheen to their bodies. Juvenile females are brown overall with whitish bellies. A long-distant migrant, it winters from Venezuela to southeastern Brazil.

MALE

• dark iridescent purplish blue overall

FIRST SPRING MALE

• **SONG** A variety of rich low-pitched liquid gurgling notes and chirruping, mixed with cackling and varying in pitch. Songs often given predawn and in flight.

• **BEHAVIOR** In pairs or colonies. In fall, communal migratory and roosting flocks may number in the tens of thousands. Mostly catches and eats insects in flight, but also forages on ground. Nesting birds will eat broken eggshells placed for them. Frequents open country, rural agricultural areas, especially near water, and urban/suburban areas.

forked tail •

bluish gray upperparts •

grayish to whitish lower breast and belly •

• forked tail

FEMALE

Similar Birds

TREE SWALLOW Smaller; entire underparts are bright white with no grayish tone; dark glossy blue-green upperparts. • juveniles and first spring adults have browner upperparts.

GRAY-BREASTED MARTIN ♂ Smaller; gray-brown face, throat, and flanks; dusky gray-brown underparts; dark bluish upperparts; cleft tail • eastern range.

• **BREEDING** Monogamous. Colonial.

• **NESTING** Incubation 15–18 days by female. Young altricial; brooded by female; stay in nest 26–31 days, fed by both sexes. 1–3 broods per year.

• **POPULATION** Common; declining, especially in the West.

• **BIRDHOUSES** Man-made martin houses and gourds.

• **CONSERVATION** Neotropical migrant. National Audubon Society Blue List. Practice of removing dead cavity-filled trees, especially in riparian areas, has reduced nesting sites. Introduced European Starling and House Sparrow compete for nesting cavities.

Flight Pattern

Strong graceful flight with few rapid wing beats followed by long glides. Often flies in circles while gliding.

Nest Identification	
Shape	Grasses, leaves, mud, feathers, and bits of debris • in martin houses, old woodpecker holes in trees and cacti, or in ridges in cliffs or large rocks • 5–20 feet above ground • built by both sexes • 3–8 plain white eggs; oval to long oval, 0.96 x 0.68 inches.
Location	

Plumage Sexes differ	Habitat 	Migration Migratory	Weight 1.7 ounces

DATE _____ TIME_____ LOCATION _____

Family HIRUNDINIDAE	Species *Tachycineta bicolor*	Length 5.75 inches	Wingspan 12.5 inches

TREE SWALLOW

The Tree Swallow is equally common in open fields, marshes, or towns. This bird's ability to adapt to its ever-changing environment has led to its abundant and widespread population. Migrating in huge flocks during the day, it is one of the first swallows to travel to its summer home in upper North America. Many winter on the southern Atlantic Coast, Gulf Coast, and in Florida. In flight it shows dark upperparts, white underparts, triangular wings with greenish underwing linings, and a notched tail. Juveniles have dusky brown upperparts and often a dusky wash on the breast.

dark iridescent greenish blue upperparts

white cheek patch stops below eye

white underparts

blackish flight feathers

slightly notched tail

JUVENILE

- **SONG** Utters quick repetitious *silip* or *chi-veet*. In flight makes pleasant liquid gurgling chatter.
- **BEHAVIOR** Gregarious in migration and winter; often occurs in huge flocks. Feeds in mixed flocks with other swallow species. Catches insects in flight; sometimes forages on ground. Eats mainly flying insects but also may take small crustaceans and spiders. Often eats berries and seeds during cold snaps on wintering grounds or in spring migration. Inhabits open country and woodland edges near water. Male displays for female with series of aerial gymnastics.
- **BREEDING** Most often polygamous. Loose social colonies. Males may have 2 mates simultaneously and different mates each year.
- **NESTING** Incubation 13–16 days by female. Altricial young remain in nest 16–24 days. Fed by both sexes. 1 brood per year (rarely 2).
- **POPULATION** Abundant and increasing.

Similar Birds

VIOLET-GREEN SWALLOW
White rump patches extend onto sides of rump; white on cheek extends up to, behind, and above eye; purple-green gloss on upperparts • sympatric only in the West.

- **BIRDHOUSES** Uses man-made bird boxes and gourds.
- **CONSERVATION** Some are neotropical migrants. Forestry practice of removing dead trees eliminates many potential nesting sites.

Flight Pattern

Swift graceful flight with slow deep wing beats alternated with long to short glides. Turns back sharply on insects it passes.

Nest Identification

Shape  Location

Abandoned Nests

Dried stems and grass • lined with down and feathers • in tree cavity, abandoned nest, bird box, or other man-made structure • built by both sexes, but female does more • 4–6 white eggs; oval to long oval, 0.8 x 0.5 inches.

Plumage Sexes similar	Habitat	Migration Migratory	Weight 0.7 ounce

DATE _____ TIME_____ LOCATION _____

Family HIRUNDINIDAE	Species *Tachycineta thalassina*	Length 5–5.25 inches	Wingspan 11–12 inches

VIOLET-GREEN SWALLOW

The gloss of brilliant greens and purples that shows on its head, back, and rump in bright sunlight and the white patches on the sides of its rump that show in flight set this bird apart from its cousin, the Tree Swallow, with which it often closely associates. Its historical choice for nesting sites is in dead trees of partially cleared forests or abandoned woodpecker holes. Females show duller upperparts than males. Juveniles have gray-brown

white cheek marks extend above eye

notched greenish black tail

greenish black wings

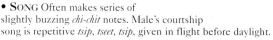

upperparts without the green-purple gloss and grayish or mottled underparts.

white underparts

JUVENILE

- **SONG** Often makes series of slightly buzzing *chi-chit* notes. Male's courtship song is repetitive *tsip, tseet, tsip,* given in flight before daylight.
- **BEHAVIOR** Gregarious. Usually feeds in flocks and catches insects, its principal diet, in flight. Rarely takes insects from ground. Usually feeds by flying close to the ground or low over water; sometimes feeds at great heights on insects that have risen high in the air column. Defends nest cavities from other swallows. Has been documented helping feed Western Bluebird nestlings, then taking over the nesting cavity when they fledge. Often perches high in trees, on fences, or on utility wires.
- **BREEDING** Monogamous. Occasionally found in loose colonies of up to around 20 pairs.
- **NESTING** Incubation 13–14 days by female. Altricial young remain in nest 16–24 days. Fed by both sexes, but female does more. 1 brood per year.
- **POPULATION** Common in various woodland habitats in range, often found at higher elevations in mountains. Stable. Casual in the East.
- **BIRDHOUSES** Will nest in man-made bird boxes.
- **CONSERVATION** Neotropical migrant. Has declined where forestry practices include removal of dead trees.

Similar Birds

TREE SWALLOW
Snowy white underparts; steely blue-green upperparts, including cap to below eye; blue-green rump; blackish flight feathers • juvenile has brownish upperparts; white underparts.

WHITE-THROATED SWIFT
Black upperparts; white underparts with black side patches; longer more slender wings; long forked tail; more fluttering flight.

Flight Pattern

Swift graceful flight, alternating several rapid wing beats with long glides. Soars on thermals and updrafts along cliff faces and canyon walls.

Nest Identification

Shape

Location

Grass and weed stems • lined with feathers • in natural cavity, abandoned woodpecker hole, or crevice in dead tree; on rock ridges or in bird box • built by both sexes • 4–6 unmarked white eggs; oval, 0.8 x 0.55 inches.

Plumage Sexes similar	Habitat	Migration Migratory	Weight 0.6 ounce

DATE _____ TIME_____ LOCATION _____

Family HIRUNDINIDAE	Species *Stelgidopteryx serripennis*	Length 5.5 inches	Wingspan 11–12 inches

NORTHERN ROUGH-WINGED SWALLOW

This bird is named for the tiny hooks found on its outer primary feathers. Their function is unknown, but they may produce a sound during courtship display. The male and female use their feet to dig nesting burrows, some as long as six feet, depending on the nature of the soil, but most are nine to twenty-eight inches deep. Since it is highly adaptable this bird has a wide breeding range. Juveniles are similar to adults but show more cinnamon tones in their upperparts and have cinnamon wing bars.

short black bill

light gray-brown wash on chin, throat, and upper breast

medium brown upperparts

- **SONG** Usually remains silent, but sometimes utters harsh, buzzing *quiz-z-zeeitp* or *zzrrit.*
- **BEHAVIOR** Solitary or in pairs or small flocks. Gregarious during migration. Catches and consumes a variety of flying insects while in flight. Also occasionally takes insects from ground. Often feeds low over open landscapes or water and sometimes feeds along with other species of swallows. Quickly adapted nesting to utilize crevices in rock cuts along interstate highways. During courtship male chases female, flying with white undertail coverts spread along sides of tail.

dark brownish black wings and wing linings

dull white underparts

slightly forked dark brownish black tail

- **BREEDING** Monogamous. Solitary or in small colonies.
- **NESTING** Incubation 12 days by female. Altricial young remain in nest 19–21 days. Fed by both sexes. 1 brood per year.
- **POPULATION** Common and increasing.
- **BIRDHOUSES** Will nest in some types of man-made structures but has not been recorded to use nest boxes.
- **CONSERVATION** Neotropical migrant.

Similar Birds

BANK SWALLOW
Smaller; darker brown upperparts; dark brown breast band; snow-white underparts; faster wing beats with quick changes of direction.

Flight Pattern

Swift graceful flight with several deep slow wing beats, pulling back wings after each stroke, then a short to long glide.

Nest Identification

Shape [icons]   Location [icons]

No nest materials except a few bark chips, grass, and leaves • on bank, sides of rough cliff, highway/railroad rock cuts, or building or in abandoned burrows, drain pipes, or sewer pipes • dug by both sexes • 4–8 plain white eggs; long oval, 0.7 x 0.5 inches.

Plumage Sexes similar	Habitat [icons]	Migration Migratory	Weight 0.6 ounce

DATE _____ TIME_____ LOCATION _____

Family HIRUNDINIDAE	Species *Riparia riparia*	Length 4.75 inches	Wingspan 10–11 inches

BANK SWALLOW

The smallest member of the North American swallow family is an aerial gymnast that twists and turns in the air over its breeding territory. Males and females take turns digging burrows into vertical banks with their bills. Once a hole is made, they use their feet to finish the tunnel, which sometimes is as long as five to six feet. The scientific name refers to their association with rivers during migration and their predilection for nesting along sandy gravelly river banks. The dark narrow breast band is difficult to see when the bird is in flight, but the combination of an erratic flight pattern, chocolate-brown upperparts, paler brown rump, dark brown wing linings, and snowy white underparts serve to identify this bird. Juvenile wing coverts and tertials are edged cinnamon and the throat and upper breast are washed pale cinnamon.

chocolate-brown upperparts

snowy white chin

blackish brown flight feathers

brownish gray breast band, sometimes extending down midline of upper breast

snowy white underparts

slightly forked tail

- **SONG** Dry chattering, *zzzrt orzzzrt, zzzrtt.*
- **BEHAVIOR** Gregarious. Often migrates and feeds with other swallows. Gathers in large premigratory and communal roosts. Catches insects while flying. Occasionally takes insects from ground or water's surface. Courtship includes dropping and catching feathers in the air, as if playing, by each member of pair; copulation in the nest burrow often follows such "play" and many feathers are used in the nest lining.
- **BREEDING** Monogamous. Colonial.
- **NESTING** Incubation 14–16 days by both sexes. Altricial young stay in nest 18–24 days, fed by both sexes. 1–2 broods per year.
- **POPULATION** Common and widespread; often near water. Numbers are stable overall, but species is declining in California due to river bank alteration for flood control.
- **CONSERVATION** Neotropical migrant.

Similar Birds

NORTHERN ROUGH-WINGED SWALLOW Larger; paler brown upperparts; lacks brown chest band; dusky white underparts; light gray-brown wash on chin, throat, and upper breast; slower deeper wing beats.

TREE SWALLOW Juvenile is larger; white underparts from chin to undertail coverts; often with dusky breast band; greenish blue upperparts.

Flight Pattern

Swift erratic fluttering flight on shallow wing beats; often alternates several rapid wing beats with short to long glides.

Nest Identification

Shape ▨   Location ▥ ▩

Lined with grass, rootlets, weed stems, horsehair, and feathers • in sandy or rocky bank, gravel pit, or man-made embankment, such as a highway road cut • dug by both sexes • 3–7 plain white eggs; oval to short oval, 0.7 x 0.5 inches.

Plumage Sexes similar	Habitat 〰 🔺	Migration Migratory	Weight 0.5 ounce

Family HIRUNDINIDAE	Species *Petrochelidon pyrrhonota*	Length 5.5 inches	Wingspan 12 inches

CLIFF SWALLOW

Hundreds of gourd-shaped "mud jugs" plastered to the side of a barn or under a bridge or highway overpass are a typical nesting territory for these highly adaptable birds. Farmers heartily welcome this resident because it eats numerous flying insects that are harmful to crops. Nesting colonies may number from eight hundred to more than one thousand birds. Note the dark rusty brown throat, and in flight the brown underwing linings, cinnamon buff rump, square tail, dusky cinnamon undertail coverts with dark centers, and whitish buff edged feathers of back and tertials. Juveniles have dusky brown upperparts and paler underparts. This swallow has successfully expanded its range in the Southeast and the West. The southwestern race displays a cinnamon forehead similar to the Cave Swallow.

squared blackish tail with slight cleft

chestnut sides of face extend to sides of nape

blue-black crown

whitish forehead

short black bill

black center patch on chestnut throat

blue-black wings and back

whitish underparts with dusky gray-brown sides and flanks

JUVENILE

- **SONG** Utters a dry guttural *churr* or *zarp*. Alarm call is burry *keeer*. During breeding, a chattering, squeaking, sputtering warble.
- **BEHAVIOR** Gregarious. Catches food in flight; sometimes forages on ground. Eats variety of flying insects and some berries and fruit. Constructs one of the most complex swallow nests: a sphere of mud pellets with a tubular entrance on one side. Colonies are source of foraging information for other birds; birds follow members who are successfully feeding young back to food sources.
- **BREEDING** Monogamous. Large colonies.
- **NESTING** Incubation 14–16 days by both sexes. Altricial young in nest 21–24 days, fed by both sexes. 1–3 broods a year.
- **POPULATION** Common in open country, especially near water. Range is expanding and numbers are increasing.
- **CONSERVATION** Neotropical migrant. Previously listed as being of special concern, but successful adaptation to nesting on man-made structures such as buildings, highway bridges and overpasses, railroad bridges, dams, and other vertical walls has greatly expanded populations and range.

Similar Birds

CAVE SWALLOW
Pale cinnamon-buff throat; cinnamon forehead; richer cinnamon-rust rump.

Flight Pattern

Swift graceful flight alternating several deep rapid wing beats with long elliptical glides with sharp sweeping upturns at the end. Soars on thermals and updrafts.

Nest Identification

Shape

Location

Pellets of clay or mud, with lining of grasses, down, and feathers • usually under eaves of buildings or under dams or bridges; sometimes on ridges of canyons; rarely on trunk of conifer tree under overhanging branch • built by both sexes • 3–6 white, cream, or pinkish eggs, marked with browns; oval to long oval, 0.8 x 0.5 inches.

Plumage Sexes similar	Habitat	Migration Migratory	Weight 0.8 ounce

DATE _____ TIME _____ LOCATION _____

Family HIRUNDINIDAE	Species *Petrochelidon fulva*	Length 5.5 inches	Wingspan 12 inches

CAVE SWALLOW

This bird plasters its cuplike nests to the sides of caves, but it has adapted to man-made structures and now also uses buildings, bridges, culverts, and even drainage pipes. A native of Mexico and the West Indies, in North America two races nest, one in the Southwest and one in Florida. One of the most visited colonies is established in the entrance to Carlsbad Caverns. Similar in appearance to the Cliff Swallow, it

cinnamon forehead

blue-black upperparts with whitish buff streaks on back

whitish buff edging to tertials

cinnamon-buff throat extends around neck as a collar

chestnut rump

blackish flight feathers

whitish underparts with rufous wash on breast and sides

squared tail

dusky cinnamon undertail coverts with dark centers

often nests with them, and with Barn Swallows. In flight it shows brownish underwing linings. The southwestern race of the Cliff Swallow has the cinnamon forehead but has a dark throat.

JUVENILE

- **SONG** Series of dry warbling buzzy chatters; sometimes calls *chu-chu* or *zweih*.
- **BEHAVIOR** Gregarious. Eats insects caught in flight. Builds a complex nest: a sphere constructed of mud pellets with a tubular entrance on one side. Colonies often active on same site year after year and may repair and reuse old nests.
- **BREEDING** Monogamous. Colonial.
- **NESTING** Incubation 15–18 days by both sexes. Young altricial; remain in nest 21–33 days, fed by both sexes. Has 2 broods per year.
- **POPULATION** Fairly common but somewhat local. Expanding range and increasing in number. Casual in Northeast.
- **CONSERVATION** Neotropical migrant.

Similar Birds

CLIFF SWALLOW
Pale whitish to buff forehead; dark rusty brown throat with black center patch; pale cinnamon-buff rump
• southwestern race has cinnamon forehead.

Flight Pattern

Swift graceful flight, alternating several rapid deep wing beats with long elliptical glides ending on sharp sweeping upturns. Soars on winds and thermals.

Nest Identification

Shape

Location

Pellets of clay and mud with lining of grasses and a few feathers • plastered to sides of caves, sinkholes, bridges, culverts, buildings, or even drainage pipes • built by both sexes • 3–5 white eggs, marked with browns; oval to long oval, 0.8 x 0.5 inches.

Plumage Sexes similar	Habitat	Migration Migratory	Weight 0.7 ounce

DATE _____ TIME_____ LOCATION _____

Family HIRUNDINIDAE	Species *Hirundo rustica*	Length 6.75–7.5 inches	Wingspan 12.5–13.5 inches

BARN SWALLOW

Since early colonial times this bird has been a welcome presence on farms because it eats many crop-destroying insects. Usually nesting inside of barns or other buildings, it is the only North American swallow with buffy to cinnamon underparts and underwing linings and a white-spotted deeply forked tail. The female is similar to the male but most often is duller in color. Juveniles have shorter forked tails and creamy white underparts. The most wide-ranging swallow in the world, it is cosmopolitan, found breeding or wintering on almost all continents.

rusty forehead

dark bluish black breast band

FEMALE

dark rusty brown throat

blackish flight feathers

dark iridescent blue-black upperparts

deeply forked blackish tail with white spots

JUVENILE

- **SONG** Utters a repetitive clipped *chi-dit, chi-dit* or *wit-wit*. Song is a prolonged twittering warble with liquid guttural notes interspersed.
- **BEHAVIOR** Gregarious. Often feeds close to ground or water. Eats a wide variety of flying insects, and follows farm machinery, even riding lawnmowers, to feed on stirred-up insects. Courtship flights may include pairs dropping and catching feathers in midair; upon landing pairs may engage in mutual preening. Individuals show strong site fidelity, and colonies may exist over long periods on the same site, with the same individuals sometimes building nests on the same site used the previous year. Has adapted to nesting in and on man-made structures.
- **BREEDING** Monogamous. Small colonies. During courtship, male chases female, flying over acres of land.
- **NESTING** Incubation 13–17 days by both sexes, but female does more. Young altricial; stay in nest 18–23 days, fed by both sexes. 2 broods per year.

Similar Birds

CLIFF SWALLOW
Blue-black upperparts; rusty cinnamon rump; pale forehead; short squared tail without white spots.

CAVE SWALLOW
Blue-black upperparts; chestnut rump; short, squared tail without white spots.

- **POPULATION** Abundant and widespread in open country, agricultural lands, and savanna, especially near water. Increasing. Eurasian races are accidental to casual in Alaska.
- **CONSERVATION** Neotropical migrant.

Flight Pattern

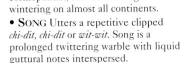

Swift and graceful with deep wing beats and wing-tips pulled back at the end of each stroke; glides are short and infrequent.

Nest Identification

Shape Location

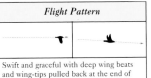

Clay or mud, dried stems, grasses, and straw, with thick lining of horsehair, down, and feathers • inside barn or other building, in ridges of cliff, under bridge, under culvert, or attached to bank • built by both sexes • 4–7 white eggs, marked with browns; oval to long oval, 0.8 x 0.5 inches.

Plumage Sexes similar	Habitat	Migration Migratory	Weight 0.6 ounce

DATE _____ TIME_____ LOCATION _____

Family PARIDAE	Species *Poecile carolinensis*	Length 4.75 inches	Wingspan 7.5 inches

CAROLINA CHICKADEE

Readily attracted to feeders supplying sunflower
seeds, this little chickadee is a familiar bird to many
who operate feeding stations in its range, where
it is the only songbird with a black bib and
black cap. This energetic bird, a common
inhabitant of the southeastern United
States primarily south of the zone of
glaciation, ranges north to New
Jersey and west into Ohio,
Indiana, Illinois, and to the
100th meridian in
eastern Texas. When
disturbed in the
nest cavity during
incubation, it will
hiss and strike
intruders,
behaving similarly to
copperheads and other snakes.

white cheeks

gray upperparts

black cap

narrow grayish white edging on wings

short black bill

black bib

short slightly notched tail

white underparts with buff-gray wash on lower belly, crissum sides, and flanks

blackish gray feet and legs

• **SONG** Calls include a higher-pitched rapid *chick-a-dee-dee-dee* and a 4-note whistled *fee-bee-fee-bay*, an octave
higher than that of the Black-capped Chickadee, with
lower-pitched 2nd and 4th notes. Also makes variety of
high-pitched thin squeaky notes when foraging with others.
Call notes are more complex than song.

• **BEHAVIOR** Pairs or small groups. After breeding often
joins mixed feeding flocks with titmice, nuthatches, kinglets,
warblers, Downy Woodpeckers, and others. Eats moths,
caterpillars, and a wide variety of other insects when available;
in winter and spring eats mostly seeds and some berries. May
excavate own nest or enlarge cavity if wood is soft enough.

• **BREEDING** Monogamous. Very early nester.

• **NESTING** Incubation 11–12 days by both sexes. Altricial
young stay in nest 13–17 days. Brooded by female. Fed by both
sexes, mostly larval insects. 1–2 broods per year.

• **POPULATION** Common in open deciduous forests, woodland
clearings, forest edges, and suburban areas.

Similar Birds

BLACK-CAPPED CHICKADEE Larger body; white-edged greater wing
coverts; broad white markings on edge of
secondaries; more boldly edged tertials
with darker centers; black bib extends
farther down chest; olive flanks; lower,
slower *chick-a-dee-dee-dee* call; typically gives 2-
to 3-note *fee-bee* or *fee-bee-be* song.

• **FEEDERS AND BIRDHOUSES** Suet,
doughnuts, and sunflower
seeds. Nests in birdhouses.

• **CONSERVATION** Sometimes
competes for nest sites with
House Wren, especially in
suburban areas.

Flight Pattern

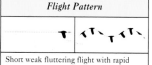

Short weak fluttering flight with rapid
beats; sometimes in longer flights folds
wings to sides after several quick strokes.

Nest Identification	
Shape	Location

Lined with plant material, including grass and moss, as well as feathers and hair
• in tree or snag 1–23 feet above ground or in man-made nest box • built by
both sexes • 5–8 white eggs with reddish brown markings; oval to short oval,
0.6 x 0.45 inches.

Plumage Sexes similar	Habitat	Migration Nonmigratory	Weight 0.4 ounce

Family PARIDAE	Species *Poecile gambeli*	Length 5.5 inches	Wingspan 7.5 inches

MOUNTAIN CHICKADEE

Easily identified by its white eyebrow, the Mountain Chickadee is a common inhabitant in mountainous regions of the West from southern Yukon to California and western Texas. During the fall months, some Mountain Chickadees leave the higher mountainous areas entering territory further downslope and outside the mountains that are normally inhabited by the Black-capped Chickadee. Birds of the Rocky Mountain race are washed with buff on their grayish sides, flanks, and back. Although primarily nonmigratory, some birds wander in winter outside the breeding range.

black cap joins black postocular stripe

white eyebrow

grayish upperparts

short black bill

white cheeks and lores

black bib

paler gray underparts

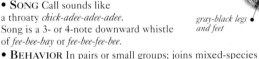

pale gray or gray-buff sides and flanks

gray-black legs and feet

- **SONG** Call sounds like a throaty *chick-adee-adee-adee*. Song is a 3- or 4-note downward whistle of *fee-bee-bay* or *fee-bee-fee-bee*.

- **BEHAVIOR** In pairs or small groups; joins mixed-species feeding flocks after breeding season. Clings under branches and pine cones when foraging and gleans food from trunk, branches, and foliage; occasionally feeds on ground. Primary diet of insects in breeding season and summer; conifer seeds, other plant seeds, spiders, and insect or spider eggs are also taken throughout year. Tame. When disturbed, incubating female hisses like snake and lunges toward nest entrance.

- **BREEDING** Monogamous.

- **NESTING** Incubation 14 days by female. Young altricial; brooded by female; stay in nest 21 days, fed by both sexes. 1–2 broods per year.

- **POPULATION** Common resident in coniferous and mixed montane woodlands.

- **FEEDERS AND BIRDHOUSES** Eats baby chick scratch feed and sunflower seeds. Will nest in man-made birdhouses.

- **CONSERVATION** Vulnerable to habitat loss due to logging operations.

Similar Birds

BRIDLED TITMOUSE Sharp pointed crest; white face with black line through eye, outlining ear and passing forward to connect with black bib; lacks black cap.

BLACK-CAPPED CHICKADEE Lacks white eyebrow; lower edge of black bib more ragged; olive-buff wash on sides, flanks, and crissum; vocalizations differ.

Flight Pattern

Short slow weak flitting flights on rapidly beating wings. Often folds wings to sides after several quick wing beats; repeats.

Nest Identification

Shape ▲² ▲¹ Location 🌿 🌳 ⚘ 🏠

Moss-lined with animal fur, feathers, and shredded bark • 4–8 feet above ground in conifer, deciduous tree, nest box, or snag • built by both sexes, but female does most • 5–12 white eggs, unmarked, with occasional reddish brown spots; oval to short oval, 0.6 x 0.45 inches.

Plumage Sexes similar	Habitat ▲ 🌿 ⚘ 🌾	Migration Nonmigratory	Weight 0.4 ounce

Family PARIDAE	Species *Baeolophus griseus*	Length 5.5 inches	Wingspan 8 inches

JUNIPER TITMOUSE

Formerly the Juniper Titmouse and the very similar Oak Titmouse were lumped together as one species, the Plain Titmouse. The two "new" titmice's ranges overlap only in one small area of northern California. Only two other gray crested birds occur in the range of the Juniper Titmouse in the mountains of southeast Arizona and southwest New Mexico: the much larger female Phainopepla and the Bridled Titmouse, distinctively marked with its black-and-white face pattern. As its name implies, look for this plain titmouse in juniper or piñon-juniper woodlands, as well as in riparian woodlands and suburban shade trees.

white patch above bill

pale gray body

darker gray wings and tail

straight black bill

paler whitish gray underparts

gray-black legs and feet

- **SONG** Call sounds like a raspy *tschick-adee*. Song is a varying rolling series of notes sung in the same pitch; all phrases in a series are alike.

- **BEHAVIOR** Sociable; in pairs or small groups. Does not form large flocks. Mates often stay together throughout year. Joins mixed-species foraging flocks after breeding season, especially in winter. Gleans insects from trunk, branches, and foliage; eats berries and seeds from twigs and ground. Often clings beneath limbs or cones to extract seeds; places large seeds or nuts either under feet or in crevice and pounds open with bill in jackhammer fashion.

- **BREEDING** Monogamous. Solitary.

- **NESTING** Incubation 14–16 days by female. Young altricial; brooded by female; stay in nest 16–21 days, fed by both sexes. 1–2 broods per year.

- **POPULATION** Stable. Uncommon to fairly common.

- **FEEDERS AND BIRDHOUSES** Attracted to feeders with suet, peanut butter, and sunflower seeds. Will use nest boxes.

- **CONSERVATION** Some habitat lost to development.

Similar Birds

OAK TITMOUSE
Slightly smaller; mousy gray-brown overall; slightly shorter bill; different voice; frequents different habitat of dry oak woodlands.

BRIDLED TITMOUSE
Darker gray upperparts; longer crest outlined blackish; white face with black line through eye and outlining ear patch; black bib.

Flight Pattern

Short weak fluttering flights with rapid shallow wing beats. May take several quick wing strokes and tuck wings to sides before repeating another series of strokes.

Nest Identification

Shape

Location

Lined with moss, grass, weeds, bark, feathers, and hair • in a natural cavity, abandoned woodpecker hole excavated by pair, or nest box • built by both sexes • 3–9 white eggs, unmarked, or marked faintly with reddish browns; oval to long oval, 0.6 x 0.5 inches.

Plumage Sexes similar	Habitat	Migration Nonmigratory	Weight Undetermined

DATE _____ TIME_____ LOCATION _____

Family PARIDAE	Species *Baeolophus bicolor*	Length 6.5 inches	Wingspan 10.75 inches

TUFTED TITMOUSE

Undaunted by the presence of people, this lively bird sometimes will swoop down and pluck out a human hair to use for its nest. The largest titmouse, it will fly toward people making squeaking or pishing sounds to attract birds. It is intelligent and may learn to eat food out of a human hand. Often it can be seen digging in the ground, where it stores surplus sunflower seeds. Adapted to wooded residential areas with large shade trees and to bird feeders and nesting boxes, it has become a familiar yard bird with its jaunty crest and large black eyes set against gray plumage. The black-crested form in southern and western Texas was formerly considered a separate species, the Black-crested Titmouse.

medium gray upperparts

tufted dark gray head

straight black bill

gray tail

rusty sides and flanks

whitish gray underparts

gray-black feet and legs

BLACK-CRESTED FORM

- **SONG** Bold, high-pitched, whistled *peter, peter, peter* or *peto, peto, peto*. Sometimes females sing but not as much as males. Calls vary from high-pitched, thin squeaky notes to low, harsh, fussy scolding notes.

- **BEHAVIOR** Relatively tame; social. Pairs or small family groups; joins mixed foraging flocks after nesting season. Inspects and forages in trees and shrubs for food, sometimes clinging upside down on trunk or branch tips. Uses bill to pound open nut, while anchoring it with feet. Eats insects and their larvae, spiders, snails, various berries, acorns and other nuts, and seeds. Male feeds female during courtship.

- **BREEDING** Monogamous. Solitary nester. Mates for life.

- **NESTING** Incubation 13–14 days by female. Altricial young stay in nest 15–18 days. Brooded by female. Fed by both sexes. 1 brood per year, 2 in the South.

Similar Birds

PHAINOPEPLA ♀
Small range overlap in Big Bend area of Texas with black-crested form • larger; medium sooty gray overall; crested; darker gray wing edges; white on wing coverts and tertials; whitish gray patch at base of primaries flashes in flight; long, rounded tail.

- **POPULATION** Abundant to common in forests, parks, and shaded suburbs.

- **FEEDERS AND BIRDHOUSES** Feeders with sunflower seeds, suet, cornmeal, and peanut butter. Will nest in man-made birdhouses.

Flight Pattern
Weak fluttering short flights with shallow rapid wing beats. Flitting flight with several quick wing beats alternating with wings drawn to sides, then repeated.

Nest Identification	
Shape	Location

Lined with bark, leaves, soft grass and moss, snakeskin, and bits of animal fur and hair • in natural cavity, bird box, or woodpecker hole 3–90 feet above ground • built by female • 4–8 white to creamy white eggs speckled with browns, occasionally wreathed; short subelliptical, 0.7 x 0.55 inches.

Plumage Sexes similar	Habitat	Migration Nonmigratory	Weight 0.8 ounce

Family REMIZIDAE	Species *Auriparus flaviceps*	Length 4.5 inches	Wingspan 7 inches

VERDIN

Sometimes using as many as two thousand twigs, this tiny bird builds an elaborate sphere-shaped nest up to eight inches in diameter. The spherical nest has thick walls to insulate it from the hot desert sun and the cold desert nights. Nests built early in the season have their side entrances facing away from the cooling winds to conserve heat; those built later in the nesting season face the direction of the wind for its cooling breezes. As it often nests ten or more miles away from any water source, this bird eats fruit and insects to obtain needed moisture. Brownish gray juveniles lack the yellow head and chestnut shoulder patch of the adults and, except for their shorter tail, could be mistaken for a Bushtit.

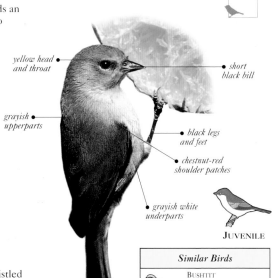

yellow head and throat

grayish upperparts

short black bill

black legs and feet

chestnut-red shoulder patches

grayish white underparts

JUVENILE

- **SONG** Song is a melancholy whistled *tswee-swee, tswee*, 3 notes with the second note higher. Call is a quick *tea-nip*.
- **BEHAVIOR** Solitary or in pairs; small family groups after breeding season. May join mixed-species foraging flocks in winter. Actively forages for food among twigs and leaves. Sometimes hangs upside down, clinging to limb or trunk like a chickadee. Eats insects, their larvae and eggs, spiders, wild berries, and fruit. Male builds several nests in his territory; female selects one, which may be used several times for nesting, even in succeeding years. Nests often are used for night roosts and as shelters from noonday sun, and some are constructed for just that purpose.
- **BREEDING** Monogamous. Solitary nester.

Similar Birds

BUSHTIT
Juveniles • grayer upperparts; longer tail; brownish cheek patch or crown; usually in staggered flocks; prefer oak scrub to desert basins • only in the West.

LUCY'S WARBLER
Pale gray overall • male has rusty red crown and rump patch • female and juvenile have chestnut or buffy rump patch respectively.

- **NESTING** Incubation 10 days by female. Young altricial; brooded by female; stay in nest 21 days, fed by both sexes. 2 broods per year.
- **POPULATION** Common in desert and arid scrub, especially mesquite and creosote bush.

Flight Pattern

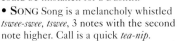

Somewhat weak fluttering flight with several fast shallow wing strokes followed by wings pulled in to sides; repeated. Flights often short duration, bush to bush.

Nest Identification

Shape   Location

Mass of sticks, leaves, and grasses held together with spider web and cocoon material, with lining of grasses, feathers, and plant down • well out toward tip of branch or in fork of shrubby tree, cactus, or bush, 2–20 feet above ground • built by male • 3–6 bluish green to greenish white eggs, with reddish brown speckles; oval to short oval, 0.6 inch long.

Plumage Sexes similar	Habitat	Migration Nonmigratory	Weight 0.2 ounce

DATE _____ TIME_____ LOCATION _____

Family AEGITHALIDAE	Species *Psaltriparus minimus*	Length 4.5 inches	Wingspan 7 inches

BUSHTIT

Often observed traveling in flocks, the Bushtit is sociable toward other Bushtits and other birds, often joining mixed-species flocks or letting other groups of Bushtits forage through their nesting territories. Females have cream to yellowish eyes, distinguishing them from male and juvenile birds, which have dark brown eyes. Coastal birds have brown crowns; interior populations have gray crowns and brown cheeks. Southwest populations, in which some adult males have black masks, were formerly considered a separate species, the Black-eared Bushtit. Some birds may move downslope to lower elevations during winter months.

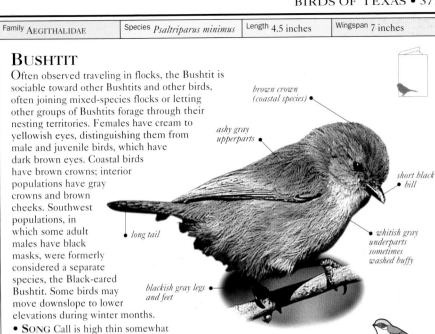

brown crown (coastal species)

ashy gray upperparts

short black bill

whitish gray underparts sometimes washed buffy

long tail

blackish gray legs and feet

• **SONG** Call is high thin somewhat buzzy excited twittering, given by many members of flocks. Also a thin, trilled *sir-r-r-rrrrrr*.

JUVENILE

• **BEHAVIOR** Gregarious, except when breeding. Forages in groups of 6–30 or more, often with other species, among trees and shrubs for food; gleans from foliage, branches, and twigs. Eats insects, their larvae and eggs, and spiders; also some fruit and berries. During the spring months, young often leave territory to establish their own colonies. Groups huddle together in tight mass on nightly roosts to conserve body heat and reduce energy loss on cold desert nights. If pair is disturbed while building nest or laying or incubating eggs, they often leave nest site, sometimes changing mates, and build a new nest.

Similar Birds

JUNIPER TITMOUSE
OAK TITMOUSE
Larger; head tufts; larger bills; smaller flocks; much less active.

VERDIN
Juvenile • shorter tail; gray-brown upperparts; gray-brown wash on sides, flanks, and belly.

• **BREEDING** Monogamous. Solitary.

• **NESTING** Incubation 12 days by both sexes; both roost in nest on eggs at night. Altricial young brooded by female; stay in nest 14–15 days, fed by both sexes. 2 broods per year.

• **POPULATION** Common in woodlands, scrub, chaparral, suburbs, parks, and gardens.

Flight Pattern
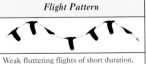
Weak fluttering flights of short duration, with rapid wing strokes alternating with wings pulled to sides; repeated.

Nest Identification	Jug-shaped hanging pouch • lined with vegetation, including flowers, grass, twigs, moss, lichen, leaves, insect cocoons, hair, and feathers • often secured by spider web • 4–25 feet above ground in deciduous tree or shrub • built by both sexes • 5–7 white eggs, unmarked; oval to short oval, 0.6 inch long.
Shape Location	

Plumage Sexes similar	Habitat	Migration Nonmigratory	Weight 0.2 ounce

DATE _____ TIME_____ LOCATION _____

Family SITTIDAE	Species *Sitta canadensis*	Length 4.5 inches	Wingspan 8 inches

RED-BREASTED NUTHATCH

This bird often will eat from the human hand. To protect young from predators, male and female smear pine pitch around the nest entrance. Females differ from males by the dark gray cap and nape and lighter underparts. The blue-gray tail spread in display or flight shows a white subterminal band. Winter range varies yearly, particularly in the East; this sedentary species remains in its breeding range as long as winter food supplies can support it.

black eye line from beak to back of head

black cap and nape

blue-gray back, shoulders, wings, and rump

white eyebrow

white cheeks

rust-colored underparts

short blue-gray tail

MALE

- **SONG** Calls are nasal and high pitched, resembling the sound of a tiny tin horn, *ank, ink,* or *enk,* often repeated in a rapid series.
- **BEHAVIOR** Solitary or in pairs. May join mixed-species feeding flocks after breeding season. Climbs up and down tree trunks, often headfirst, and walks on the underside of limbs. Forages for conifer seeds, nuts, and some insects by gleaning them from bark or foliage; wedges food in tree bark crevices and pounds with bill to break shell or exoskeleton.

blue-gray upperparts

dark gray crown and nape

FEMALE

lighter buff underparts are rustier on flank and crissum

Male courts female by feeding her, also by turning his back to her and lifting his head and tail, raising his back feathers and drooping his wings, swaying from side to side. Irruptive migrant.

- **BREEDING** Monogamous. Solitary.
- **NESTING** Incubation 12 days by female. Young altricial; brooded by female; stay in nest 14–21 days, fed by both sexes. 1 brood per year.
- **POPULATION** Fairly common to common in boreal and subalpine conifer forests and mixed conifer-deciduous northern montane forests. Stable. Eastern breeding range currently expanding southward.
- **FEEDERS** Sunflower seeds, peanut butter, and suet.
- **CONSERVATION** Vulnerable to habitat loss due to logging operations.

Similar Birds

WHITE-BREASTED NUTHATCH
Larger; white face lacks black eye line; white underparts with rusty wash on flanks and crissum; blue-gray tail with black outer tail feathers edged and tipped white; voice differs.

Flight Pattern

Somewhat weak fluttering flight of short duration, with rapid wing strokes followed by brief folding of wings to sides; repeated.

Nest Identification

Shape

Location

Lined with shredded bark, grass, and roots • usually 5–40 feet above ground (but up to 120 feet) in conifer • built by both sexes, but female does most of work • 4–7 white to pinkish white eggs, marked with reddish browns; oval to short oval, 0.6 x 0.46 inches.

Plumage Sexes differ	Habitat	Migration Some migrate	Weight 0.4 ounce

DATE _____ TIME_____ LOCATION _____

| Family SITTIDAE | Species *Sitta carolinensis* | Length 5–6 inches | Wingspan 9–11 inches |

WHITE-BREASTED NUTHATCH

The largest and most widespread of the North American nuthatches, this nimble bird can balance upside down on tree trunks, catch a falling nut in midair, and rapidly hop down skinny branches. In winter it joins mixed-species flocks and often feeds together in the same tree with chickadees, Downy Woodpeckers, and Brown Creepers. It is quick to accept bird feeders, and will often attempt to intimidate other avian visitors by spreading its wings and tail and swaying back and forth. Females in the Northeast have dark blue-gray crowns.

black cap and nape extend onto hindneck as partial collar

long black bill with slightly upturned tip

blue-gray upperparts

blackish blue tertials, secondaries, primaries, and wing coverts with white edging

white face and breast

white patches in blue-black tail

white underparts with rusty wash on flanks, lower belly, and crissum

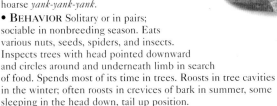
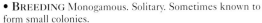

- **SONG** Sings an ascending *wee-wee-wee-wee-wee-wee-wee*. Call is a hoarse *yank-yank-yank*.

- **BEHAVIOR** Solitary or in pairs; sociable in nonbreeding season. Eats various nuts, seeds, spiders, and insects. Inspects trees with head pointed downward and circles around and underneath limb in search of food. Spends most of its time in trees. Roosts in tree cavities in the winter; often roosts in crevices of bark in summer, some sleeping in the head down, tail up position.

black feet and legs

- **BREEDING** Monogamous. Solitary. Sometimes known to form small colonies.

- **NESTING** Incubation 12 days by female. Young altricial; brooded by female; stay in nest 14 days, fed by both sexes. 1 brood per year.

- **POPULATION** Common in deciduous woodlots and in mixed coniferous-deciduous woods in the North and West.

- **FEEDERS AND BIRDHOUSES** Comes to feeders for suet and/or seeds; will nest in nest boxes.

- **CONSERVATION** Vulnerable to habitat loss due to logging operations.

Similar Birds

RED-BREASTED NUTHATCH Smaller; white face broken by long, black eye stripe; uniform rusty chestnut underparts; smaller bill; voice differs.

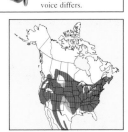

Flight Pattern

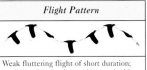

Weak fluttering flight of short duration; several rapid wing beats alternated with wings drawn to sides; repeated.

Nest Identification

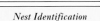

Shape ▨² ▯   Location ✿ ▯ ❦ ⚘

Lined with bark shreds, hair, and feathers • natural cavity, knothole, woodpecker's hole, or bird box, 10–60 feet above ground • built by both sexes; female does more • 3–10 white to pinkish eggs, with brown, gray, purple, and red blotches; oval to short oval, 0.8 x 0.56 inches.

| Plumage Sexes similar | Habitat ♠♦ ♣♣ ♠. | Migration Nonmigratory | Weight 0.7 ounce |

Family SITTIDAE	Species *Sitta pygmaea*	Length 4.25 inches	Wingspan 8 inches

PYGMY NUTHATCH

In the fall and winter, these nuthatches work through the treetops in loud flocks along with chickadees and titmice. At night, groups of as many as 100 birds will roost in a single cavity. This is the smallest of the North American nuthatches, and like all birds in its genus, it has long toes with sharp claws, allowing it to cling to tree trunks. Its small size, gray-brown cap, and a white spot on its

gray-brown cap

dark eye line bordering cap

blue-gray upperparts

creamy buff underparts

white chin, cheeks, and throat

nape serve to separate it from other nuthatches in its western range.

- **SONG** Has a noisy ongoing high rapid call of *tee-dee, tee-dee* and also a flutelike *wee-bee, wee-bee*.

- **BEHAVIOR** Social; gregarious. Often travels in small groups of 2–5, with some of the members being young unmated males that assist the mated pair with digging the nest cavity and feeding the young. Forages for food by climbing up, down, and around trunk and branches, often turning sideways and upside down. Gleans various insects, caterpillars, moths, and seeds of coniferous trees. Pairs bond long-term. Joins mixed-species feeding flocks after the nesting season. Roosts communally.

- **BREEDING** Monogamous. Cooperative.

- **NESTING** Incubation 15–16 days by female. Young altricial; brooded by female; stay in nest 20–22 days, fed by both parents and other birds. 1 brood per year.

- **POPULATION** Fairly common in pine forests and piñon-juniper woodlands. Accidental to the Midwest.

- **FEEDERS AND BIRDHOUSES** Nuts and seeds. Will nest in birdhouses.

- **CONSERVATION** Vulnerable to habitat loss due to logging activities.

Similar Birds

♂ RED-BREASTED NUTHATCH
Larger; black cap; black eye line; white eyebrow; rusty chestnut underparts; voice differs.
♀

Flight Pattern

Short flights, weak and fluttering, with several rapid wing beats, followed by wings pulled to sides; repeated.

Nest Identification

Shape

Location

Lined with leaves, shredded pinecones, plant down, fur, and feathers • in dead tree, old post, abandoned woodpecker hole, or nest box, 8–60 feet above ground • built by both parents and other birds • 4–9 white eggs, sparsely flecked with reddish brown; oval to short oval, 0.6 x 0.45 inches.

Plumage Sexes similar	Habitat	Migration Nonmigratory	Weight 0.4 ounce

DATE _____ TIME_____ LOCATION _____

Family SITTIDAE	Species *Sitta pusilla*	Length 4.5 inches	Wingspan 8.5 inches

BROWN-HEADED NUTHATCH

The only North American songbird to use a tool while foraging, this nuthatch lives in the southern woodlands, especially in open stands of pine. It sometimes holds a piece of bark in its bill and uses it to pry up another bark chip, uncovering insects. This bird travels in small flocks of family groups. Often foraging high in the trees and well out toward the tips of the branches, it would be easily overlooked but for its constant peeping calls and twittering.

buffy brown cap and nape with white spot on nape

blue-gray upperparts

thin dark eye line borders cap

straight black bill

white chin, cheeks, and throat

buffy whitish underparts

black legs and feet

• **SONG** Has various squeaky *bit-bit-bit* calls and a *dee-dee-dee*. During courtship, sings *pri-u, de-u, de-u*, like a squeaky toy.

• **BEHAVIOR** In pairs or small family groups, often including an unmated male helper that helps excavate the nesting cavity and feed female and young. Forages over, around, and up and down branches, small twigs, and trunks, even hanging upside down. Picks seeds from pinecones. Eats insects and their larvae and spiders. Caches pine seeds. Forms mixed-species foraging flocks with chickadees, titmice, kinglets, warblers, woodpeckers, and others.

• **BREEDING** Monogamous. Cooperative.

• **NESTING** Incubation 14 days by female. Young altricial; brooded by female; stay in nest 18–19 days, fed by both sexes and extra birds. 1 brood per year.

• **POPULATION** Fairly common in mature open pine forests and mixed pine-deciduous woodlands along the coastal plain.

• **FEEDERS AND BIRDHOUSES** Will come to eat at bird feeders and will nest in birdhouses built for them.

• **CONSERVATION** Vulnerable to habitat loss due to the cutting of pine forests and the replacement with pine plantations that are on short harvest rotations.

Similar Birds

♂ ♀ **RED-BREASTED NUTHATCH** Larger; black cap; white face with long black eye stripe; rusty chestnut underparts; black nape; voice differs.

WHITE-BREASTED NUTHATCH Larger; black cap; completely white face, breast, and underparts; rusty-washed flanks and crissum.

Flight Pattern

Weak fluttering flight of short duration, with series of rapid wing beats followed by wings pulled in to sides; repeated.

Nest Identification	
Shape	Soft bark shreds, wood chips, grasses, wool, hair, and feathers • in dead or live tree, bird box, stump, or old post, usually 2–12 feet above ground (but up to 90 feet) • built by both sexes and extra birds • 3–9 white or off-white eggs, with reddish brown speckles; short subelliptical to short oval, 0.6 x 0.45 inches.
Location	

Plumage Sexes similar	Habitat	Migration Nonmigratory	Weight 0.4 ounce

DATE _____ TIME _____ LOCATION _____

Family CERTHIIDAE	Species *Certhia americana*	Length 5.25 inches	Wingspan 7–8 inches

BROWN CREEPER

This tree-dwelling bird roosts by hanging onto a tree trunk or the side of a house with its sharp claws. Unlike the nuthatches, it does not move sideways or upside down when foraging for insects. Rather, it circles the tree in an upward direction, as if it were ascending a spiral staircase, or it takes a straighter path up, then drops to the base of a nearby tree and starts working its way up again. The long decurved bill is an efficient tool for picking insects out of bark crevices, and the stiff tail feathers prop the bird upright just as a woodpecker's tail does.

slender decurved pointed bill

white line over eyes

sharp claws

buff-streaked brown upperparts

white underparts

- **SONG** Call is a soft musical *see-see-titi-see*, similar to that of the Golden-crowned Kinglet, but thinner. Call note is a soft thin *seee*.
- **BEHAVIOR** Solitary or in pairs. Tame. Often joins mixed-species foraging flocks in winter. Forages for food by spiraling up tree, but does not move down or sideways. Hops back occasionally, but then moves on up. Eats various insects, larvae, seeds, and some nuts. Well camouflaged and difficult to spot; often escapes predators by pressing its body tightly against tree, spreading wings and tail, and remaining motionless. Fledglings roost in tight circle with heads in center of ring.

wings and coverts edged and tipped with buff and white

- **BREEDING** Monogamous. Solitary nester.
- **NESTING** Incubation 13–17 days by female. Young altricial; brooded by female; stay in nest 13–16 days. Fed by both sexes. 1 brood per year.

long rufous tail with stiff pointed tail feathers at end

- **POPULATION** Fairly common in pine, spruce-fir, mixed coniferous-deciduous, swampy forests; declining in some areas.

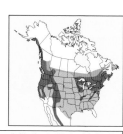

- **FEEDERS** Will come to feeders for mixture of nuts, peanut butter, suet, and cornmeal. Mixture can be put directly on tree trunk.
- **CONSERVATION** Nesting area threatened due to cutting of forest habitat.

Flight Pattern

Strong direct flights of short duration with rapid shallow wing beats.

Nest Identification	Twigs, moss, conifer needles, pieces of bark, and silk, lined with shredded bark and feathers • in cavity of dead tree, or beneath piece of bark against tree, 5–50 feet above ground • built by both sexes; female does more • 4–8 white eggs, sparsely flecked with reddish brown and often wreathed; oval to short oval, 0.6 x 0.46 inches.
Shape Location	

Plumage Sexes similar	Habitat	Migration Migratory	Weight 0.3 ounce

DATE _____ TIME_____ LOCATION _____

Family TROGLODYTIDAE	Species *Campylorhynchus brunneicapillus*	Length 8.5 inches	Wingspan 10.75 inches

CACTUS WREN

The Arizona state bird often builds its domed nest in the heavily barbed cholla cactus, where its nestlings and eggs are protected from predators. Once the young leave the cactus, the old nests are maintained and used for a roosting area by the adult birds. The largest of the North American wrens, with its large size, long tail, and long, slightly decurved bill, actually is more suggestive of a small thrasher

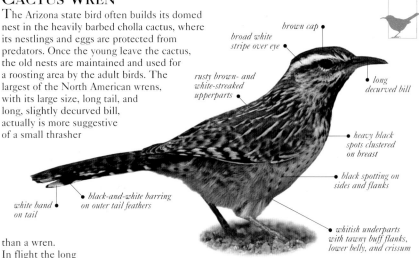

brown cap

broad white stripe over eye

rusty brown- and white-streaked upperparts

long decurved bill

heavy black spots clustered on breast

black spotting on sides and flanks

black-and-white barring on outer tail feathers

white band on tail

whitish underparts with tawny buff flanks, lower belly, and crissum

than a wren.
In flight the long tail is spread, revealing a striking banded pattern.

- **SONG** A quick low guttural *guah guah guah guah guah*, etc., gaining in speed toward the end.
- **BEHAVIOR** Pairs or small family groups. Forages for food on ground by probing and lifting up objects with bill. Gleans foliage and branches for insects, spiders, small frogs, small reptiles, nectar, and some fruits. More than other wrens, 15–20 percent of diet is fruit, mostly from cactus. When disturbed, sometimes runs on ground like a thrasher, rather than flying.
- **BREEDING** Monogamous. Solitary.
- **NESTING** Incubation 16 days by female. Young altricial; brooded by female; stay in nest 19–23 days, fed by both sexes. 2–3 broods per year.
- **POPULATION** Common and widespread in semidesert and desert communities with large cactus, arid hillsides, and gravelly bottomed valleys. Declining in parts of Texas and California.
- **FEEDERS** Will come to feeders for pieces of bread and slices of potato or raw apple.
- **CONSERVATION** Development of desert communities for housing, golf courses, and agriculture decrease and fragment the available habitat.

Similar Birds

SAGE THRASHER Grayer; unstriped barring on wings and back; brown-streaked underparts; spots not clustered on breast; white on tail corners only; shorter almost straight bill.

Flight Pattern

Weak direct flight. Holds tail partially spread when flying.

Nest Identification

Shape ⬚ Location 🌿 🌳 🏢 🌳

Stems, plant fibers, and grass, lined with feathers and fur • most often in cholla cactus; sometimes in prickly bush, old woodpecker hole, orange tree, or side of man-made structure • built by male • 2–7 pinkish eggs, speckled with brown; oval, 0.9 inch long.

Plumage Sexes similar	Habitat	Migration Nonmigratory	Weight 1.4 ounces

---

DATE _____ TIME_____ LOCATION _____

| Family TROGLODYTIDAE | Species *Salpinctes obsoletus* | Length 6 inches | Wingspan 9 inches |

ROCK WREN

This bird frequents more arid and barren terrain than its cousin, the Canyon Wren. Its grayish brown color serves as a camouflage, but the male often can be spotted when he hops to the top of a boulder to sing or to admonish intruders. The nest is built in a rock crevice, but a trail of tiny rocks leading to the opening is a clue to its location.

buffy white supercilium

grayish brown upperparts with white flecking

long slender bill

Individual males sing many variations of their songs and of those of neighboring males; some have more than a hundred songs in their repertoire. When the black-barred cinnamon tail is flicked open it reveals a thick blackish subterminal band and buffy tips.

lightly barred undertail coverts

cinnamon rump

fine-streaked white breast

cinnamon-buff wash on flanks

• **SONG** Sings a mix of buzzy trills, *keree-keree-keree, chair, chair, chair, deedle, deedle, deedle, tur, tur, tur, keree.* Call is a raspy *tic-keer.*

• **BEHAVIOR** Solitary or in pairs. Hops around, among, and between rocks. Bobs body and frequently cocks tail upward. Sings from conspicuous perches on rocks; forages for food around and between rocks. Eats insects, spiders, and various larvae. Often lines pathways to nests with hundreds of small pebbles and small animal bones.

• **BREEDING** Monogamous. Solitary nester.

• **NESTING** Breeding biology poorly known, but incubation estimated at 12–14 days by female. Young altricial; brooded by female; remain in nest estimated 14 days, fed by both sexes. 1–2 broods per year.

• **POPULATION** Fairly common in canyons, cliffs, and valleys with rocky outcroppings in arid and semiarid regions. Casual to accidental in fall and winter in the East.

Similar Birds

CANYON WREN
Bright white throat and upper breast; rich red-brown belly and underparts; rusty red upperparts; long slightly decurved bill.

Flight Pattern
Weak fluttering direct flight, often short, on shallowly beating wings.

Nest Identification	Rootlets, grasses, and various stems, with lining of feathers, various hair, and fur • in ridges of rock, crevices, burrows, banks, or even buildings • usually hidden by pile of rocks • built by both sexes • 4–10 white eggs, lightly flecked with reddish brown; oval, 0.7 inch long.
Shape	
Location	

| Plumage Sexes similar | Habitat | Migration Migratory | Weight 0.6 ounce |

DATE _____ TIME_____ LOCATION _____

Family TROGLODYTIDAE	Species *Catherpes mexicanus*	Length 5.75 inches	Wingspan 7.5 inches

CANYON WREN

True to its name, this energetic bird historically makes its home among the canyons, rocks, and caves in western North America. Adapting to man and his buildings, this wren now often builds its nest in or on them, especially those made of stone. Often staying hidden, its bold white breast showing through the crevices

reddish brown upperparts with dark barring and white flecking

long decurved bill

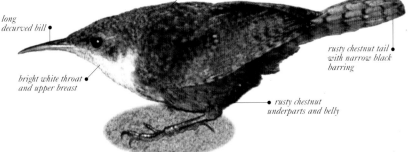

rusty chestnut tail with narrow black barring

bright white throat and upper breast

rusty chestnut underparts and belly

and ridges can be a clue to this bird's presence; but it is more often heard than seen, for the male's loud happy-sounding song cascades and bounces along canyon walls.

• **SONG** A descending gushing liquid rain of notes, *peup, peup, peup tew tew tew tew tew*, ending with a buzzy *mew*. Call is an abrasive nasal *jeet*.

• **BEHAVIOR** Solitary or in pairs. Thoroughly investigates rocks to look for food; hopping over, around, under, and between, then singing, it gleans food from rock surfaces and crevices. Often bobs body like a Rock Wren and cocks tail over back. Very tame; will enter houses and ranch buildings. Eats mainly spiders and insects.

• **BREEDING** Monogamous. Solitary nester.

• **NESTING** Incubation 12–18 days by female. Young altricial; brooded by female. Not known how long young stay in nest, but fed by both sexes. 2 broods per year; sometimes 3 in the South.

• **POPULATION** Common in arid and semiarid rocky canyons, rocky outcroppings, and cliffs, often near water; also around stone buildings and stone chimneys.

Similar Birds

ROCK WREN
Gray-brown upperparts barred dark brown and flecked white; cinnamon rump; barred tail with rufous-tipped corners and black subterminal band; dark streaking on white breast; whitish underparts washed buff; slender, shorter, barely curved bill.

Flight Pattern

Weak and fluttering direct flight, often of short duration, on shallowly beating wings.

Nest Identification

Shape | Location

Sticks, leaves, mosses, and finer material, with lining of feathers and fur • hidden in ridges of rocks or crevice, under stones, in holes, or sometimes in buildings • built by both sexes • 4–7 white eggs, lightly flecked with reddish brown; oval, 0.7 inch long.

Plumage Sexes similar	Habitat	Migration Nonmigratory	Weight 0.5 ounce

DATE _____ TIME_____ LOCATION _____

Family TROGLODYTIDAE	Species *Thryothorus ludovicianus*	Length 5.5 inches	Wingspan 7.75 inches

CAROLINA WREN

South Carolina's state bird is sensitive to cold weather. Mild winters allow Carolina Wrens to expand their range northwards but most will not survive the next hard winter. Energetic, loud, and conspicuous, the largest wren in eastern North America is equally at home in moist deciduous woodlots, on the farm, or in shaded suburbs. Pairs stay together on their territories all year, and the male may sing at any time of day, any day of the year. The female often responds with a quick "growl" of *t-shihrrr*.

bold white stripe above eye

rusty brown upperparts with dark brown bars on wings and tail

long slightly decurved bill

white chin, throat, and upper breast

rich buffy underparts

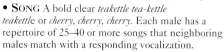

• **SONG** A bold clear *teakettle tea-kettle teakettl*e or *cherry, cherry, cherry.* Each male has a repertoire of 25–40 or more songs that neighboring males match with a responding vocalization.

• **BEHAVIOR** Most often in pairs. Sings from exposed perch. Usually stays hidden in undergrowth, but will emerge if it hears squeaking noises. Pokes into every nook and cranny, hopping with tail cocked over back. Eats mostly insects, larvae, and insect eggs, but will take small vertebrates, snails, berries, and some fruits. Common around human habitation; enters open buildings to inspect dark recesses for insects or spiders. Builds its bulky nest in any container large enough to hold it, from coat pockets and boots to buckets, flower baskets, and mailboxes.

• **BREEDING** Monogamous. Solitary nester.

• **NESTING** Incubation 12–14 days by female. Altricial young brooded by female; stay in nest 12–14 days, fed by both sexes but often tended by the male while female begins another clutch. 2 broods per year, often 3 in the South.

• **POPULATION** Common. Numbers decrease in northern range after harsh winters, but overall population stable except in the Northeast and Midwest where it is recorded as declining.

Similar Birds

BEWICK'S WREN
Whitish underparts; long rounded tail edged with white spots; reddish brown to gray-brown upperparts; long white eye stripe; frequently flips long tail; voice differs.

MARSH WREN
White-striped back; long white eye stripe; white underparts washed rufous-buff on sides and flanks; habitat and voice differ.

• **FEEDERS AND BIRDHOUSES** Suet and peanut butter. Will use nest boxes, often filling several with dummy nests.

• **CONSERVATION** Declines are of some concern.

Flight Pattern

Direct flight somewhat weak and fluttering with shallow rapid wing beats.

Nest Identification

Shape  Location

Stems, leaves, grasses, bark pieces, mosses, feathers, and snakeskin • cavity of tree, stump, or bank; sometimes old woodpecker hole, rafter, mailbox, bird box, or almost any cavity • built by both sexes • 4–8 white or light pink eggs, marked with brown; oval, 0.8 x 0.6 inches.

Plumage Sexes similar	Habitat	Migration Nonmigratory	Weight 0.7 ounce

DATE _____ TIME_____ LOCATION _____

Family TROGLODYTIDAE	Species *Thryomanes bewickii*	Length 5.25 inches	Wingspan 7.25 inches

BEWICK'S WREN

This bird ranges across most of the western United States eastward to the Appalachians. It usually builds its nest in natural cavities, but also will nest in mailboxes, baskets, cow skulls, or almost anything that provides shelter. A tame bird, it often resides near farms, homes, and small towns. For reasons still largely unknown, the Bewick's Wren is now rare in areas where it was once common. Since at least the 1960s, populations have seriously declined east of the Mississippi River. Color varies geographically from mousy gray-brown in the West to rusty brown in the East.

fine, dark brown or black barring on tail

white eye stripe

reddish or grayish brown upperparts with barring on wings

long slightly decurved bill

long rounded tail, with white spots on tips of feathers

whitish to grayish underparts

• **SONG** Male sings *chip, chip, chip, de-da-ah, tee-dee*, similar to the pattern of a Song Sparrow, but high, thin, buzzing, and variable, often ending in a thin trill. Call is a flat *jipp*.

• **BEHAVIOR** Often in pairs. Noisy and conspicuous; rather tame and bold. Holds tail high above back as it hops, often flicking it from side to side. Sings with head thrown back and tail depressed downward. Feeds mostly on ground or gleans food from trees. Eats mostly insects, but takes some spiders. Male builds several "dummy" nests in his territory; female chooses one and helps construct it.

• **BREEDING** Monogamous. Solitary.

• **NESTING** Incubation 12–14 days by female. Young altricial; brooded by female; stay in nest 14 days, fed by both sexes. 1 brood per year; possibly 2 in the South.

• **POPULATION** Common in the West in open woodland, scrubland, and around farms and suburbs. Declining east of the Rocky Mountains with most dramatic reductions happening east of the Mississippi River.

• **BIRDHOUSES** Will accept nest boxes.

• **CONSERVATION** Of special concern, especially in the East.

Similar Birds

CAROLINA WREN
Larger; rusty brown upperparts; buff underparts; shorter tail without white tips; song differs.

MARSH WREN
White-streaked back; rich brown upperparts; buff-washed sides and flanks; tail lacks white tips; different habitat and song.

Flight Pattern
Somewhat weak fluttering direct flight on shallow wing beats; often of short duration.

Nest Identification	
Shape / Location	Twigs, mosses, bits of snakeskin, and grass, lined with feathers • in cavity of almost anything; often tree, man-made structure, hollow log, post, basket, etc. • built by both sexes • 4–11 white eggs with flecks of purple, brown, and gray; oval, 0.7 x 0.5 inches.

Plumage Sexes similar	Habitat	Migration Eastern birds migrate	Weight 0.4 ounce

DATE _____ TIME _____ LOCATION _____

Family TROGLODYTIDAE	Species *Troglodytes aedon*	Length 4.75 inches	Wingspan 6–7 inches

HOUSE WREN

This plain bird has a wide range, breeding from southern Canada to Mexico. However, even though its range spread southward in the East throughout most of the 20th century, it is not currently found nesting in southeastern states. Despite its size, the House Wren is highly competitive when searching for nesting territory. It often invades nests of other wrens and songbirds, puncturing their eggs and killing their young. When it comes to selecting a nesting site, the male begins building dummy nests in almost any available cavity in his territory, from natural cavities and nesting boxes to boots, cans, buckets, toolboxes, coat pockets, and mailboxes. Birds in southeastern Arizona mountains have a buff supercilium, throat, and breast.

pale streak above eyes

narrow black barring on tail

grayish brown upperparts

narrow pale eye ring

narrow black barring on wings

thin slightly decurved bill

pale gray underparts

narrow black barring on sides, lower belly, and crissum

• **SONG** Sings beautiful, trilling, energetic flutelike melody delivered in a gurgling outburst and repeated at short intervals. Call is rough scolding *cheh-cheh*, often run into a scolding chatter.

• **BEHAVIOR** Solitary or in pairs. Loud and conspicuous. Relatively tame and bold. Often cocks tail upward. Eats various insects, spiders, millipedes, and some snails. Male starts several dummy nests in territory as part of courtship; when female joins him to inspect them and selects one to complete for nest. Highly migratory except in extreme southwestern US.

• **BREEDING** Usually monogamous but sometimes polygamous. Males occasionally have 2 mates at same time.

• **NESTING** Incubation 13–15 days by female. Altricial young stay in nest 12–18 days. Brooded by female. Fed by both sexes or female only. 2–3 broods per year.

• **POPULATION** Common in open woodlands, shrubs, farmlands, suburbs, gardens, and parks.

Similar Birds

WINTER WREN
Smaller; darker; heavier black barring on tail, flanks, and underparts; shorter tail; different voice.

• **FEEDERS** Will nest in man-made bird boxes.

• **CONSERVATION** Neotropical migrant. Nestlings sometimes are affected by bluebottle fly larvae and may die in nest.

Flight Pattern
Weak fluttering direct flight with rapid shallow wing beats.

Nest Identification	Base made of sticks • lined with hair, feathers, cocoons, and fine material • almost anywhere in cavity of tree, bird box, abandoned hole or nest, cow skull, pipes, watering cans, etc. • male builds platform; female lines • 5–9 white eggs with brown flecks, occasionally wreathed; short rounded ovate to oval, 0.6 x 0.5 inches.
Shape 🐦 Location 🌳 🕯 🦅 🐦 🏤 📦	

Plumage Sexes similar	Habitat 🏕 ✈ 🏔	Migration Most migrate	Weight 0.4 ounce

DATE _____ TIME_____ LOCATION _____

Family TROGLODYTIDAE	Species *Troglodytes troglodytes*	Length 4 inches	Wingspan 6 inches

WINTER WREN

One of the smallest songbirds in North America, this short-tailed wren nests primarily in the coniferous forests of Canada and the northern US, but it also resides along the Pacific Coast from central California to the Aleutians, and in the Appalachians south to northern Georgia. It usually hides in thick undergrowth, but when excited it will fly up, perch, bob its head up and down, and deliver an alarm call or a rapid, cascading song that may last six to seven seconds and contain more than a hundred notes. This is the only member of the wren family found in Europe.

gray to brown superciliary stripe

stubby tail

dark brown upperparts with faint barring

dark brown underparts

heavy, dark brownish black barring on flanks, underparts, and tail

- **SONG** Male sings warbling melody of varied up-and-down notes with rapid trills; some notes high, thin, and silvery. Also has whisper song. Call is abrasive *chirr* or *tik-tik-tik*.
- **BEHAVIOR** Often solitary; pairs in breeding season. Scampers on ground and in low trees while foraging, ducking in and out of root wads, in and around logs, into brush piles, and any opening or cranny large enough. Gleans food from surfaces, mostly insects, caterpillars, and berries. Sometimes will approach humans for bread crumbs. Bobs head and body and flicks tail, which is often cocked over back. Frequents habitats near water.
- **BREEDING** Polygamous.
- **NESTING** Incubation 12–16 days by female. Altricial young stay in nest 16–19 days, fed by female or both sexes. 1–2 broods per year.
- **POPULATION** Abundant. West Coast, northwest montane, and southern Appalachian populations permanent; others highly migratory.
- **BIRDHOUSES** Will roost in bird box.
- **CONSERVATION** Vulnerable to habitat loss caused by logging operations.

Similar Birds

HOUSE WREN
Larger; longer tail; less prominent barring on belly, sides, and flanks; faint eye stripe; voice differs.

Flight Pattern

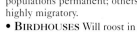

Weak fluttering flights of short duration on rapidly beating wings.

Nest Identification

Shape 🐦 🕊 📷

Location 🌿 🐦 🏚

Cavity filled with platform of sticks, covered with moss and grass, lined with hair and feathers • in cavity of log or stump, under tree roots, and sometimes in building • 0–6 feet above ground • male builds 1–5 nests; female chooses • 4–7 white eggs with brown flecks concentrated at large end; oval, 0.65 x 0.5 inches.

Plumage Sexes similar	Habitat 🌲 🌳 ⛰	Migration Most migrate	Weight 0.3 ounce

DATE _____ TIME_____ LOCATION _____

Family TROGLODYTIDAE	Species *Cistothorus platensis*	Length 4.5 inches	Wingspan 5.5–6 inches

SEDGE WREN

Camouflaged by its plumage, this wren stays hidden in dense marsh grasses, except when it perches to sing, which it sometimes does at night. The female chooses one of several rather well-concealed nests built by the male, then lines it with materials of her choice. This wren ranges over much of the grasslands and marshlands of the central and north-central United States and south-central Canada, often going where the habitat is most suitable and often changing nesting areas from year to year.

brownish black streaking on crown
brown upperparts
short slender bill
brownish black and white streaking on back and scapulars
whitish eyebrow
short barred tail
buff to whitish underparts

• **SONG** Sings a bold melody of single disconnected notes, followed by a rapid chatter of dry notes. Has call of *chip-chip*.

• **BEHAVIOR** Solitary on wintering grounds; often in pairs in small habitats; in small colonies in larger more favorable habitats. Secretive, staying down in the foliage except while singing, when it often ascends to a more exposed perch. Scampers on ground in wet meadows and in low brush, foraging for food. Eats mostly insects and spiders. Male builds several dummy nests and female chooses one; males will often destroy other bird's eggs when they discover them, including those of other Sedge Wrens.

• **BREEDING** Polygamous.

• **NESTING** Incubation 12–16 days by female. Young altricial; stay in nest 12–14 days. Fed by both sexes, but female does more. 2 broods per year.

• **POPULATION** Common in range but often very local; numbers may change from year to year. Rare in winter in New Mexico and casual to California in fall migration.

• **CONSERVATION** Neotropical migrant with some birds wintering in northeast Mexico. Vulnerable to habitat loss caused by agriculture.

Similar Birds

MARSH WREN
Larger; longer bill; dark crown; darker and more brown overall; unbarred rufous rump • western birds have duller, paler plumage with less distinct white streaking on back • eastern birds have richer browns and distinct back streaking.

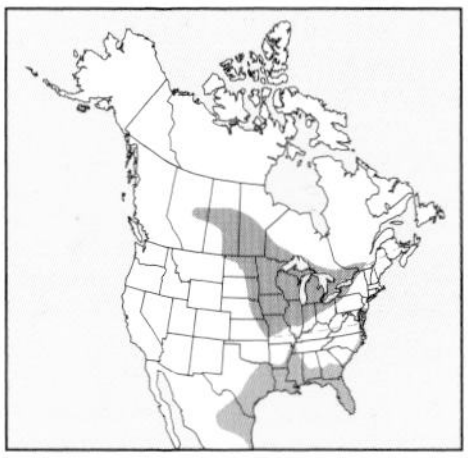

Flight Pattern

Weak fluttering flight with shallow, rapid wing beats; alternating several wing strokes with wings being drawn to sides; repeated.

Nest Identification	
Shape Location	Stems, grasses, and sedges • lined with plant down, feathers, and fur • on grasses or reeds, usually near water or marshy area • 0–2 feet above ground in grass • male builds several nests; female selects one and lines • 4–8 white eggs; oval to pyriform, 0.6 x 0.47 inches.

Plumage Sexes similar	Habitat	Migration Migratory	Weight 0.3 ounce

DATE _______________ TIME _______________ LOCATION _______________

Family TROGLODYTIDAE	Species *Cistothorus palustris*	Length 4.5–5 inches	Wingspan 5.5–7 inches

MARSH WREN

This bird usually stays hidden, but its song can be heard over the reeds and cattails of the marshlands. The male builds several intricate globular-shaped nests, which have side doors; the female chooses one and adds the lining of shredded plants and feathers. The male often roosts in one of the dummy nests. Some males have more than one mate, with each one occupying a small section of his territory. The black-and-white streaking on the back of the Marsh Wren is less distinct in western birds.

black cap

bold white eye stripe

brown upperparts with black-and-white streaking

black barring on wings

rufous-brown rump

long slender bill

whitish underparts with rufous-buff sides, flanks, and undertail coverts

black barring on tail

• **SONG** Sings a gurgling trilling melody, with western birds singing a harsher song than eastern birds. Call is an abrasive *te-suk-te-suk*. Western birds may have more than 200 songs in their varied repertoire, while eastern males may have only around 70.

• **BEHAVIOR** Solitary; in pairs or small colonies, depending on the size and quality of the habitat. Often secretive, foraging for food in tall marsh grasses and reeds, where it gleans aquatic insects, larvae, caterpillars, snails, and sometimes other bird's eggs. Males often sing from exposed perches or even skylark before dropping back into the cover of the thick vegetation; sometimes sing at night. Often enters the nests of other birds and destroys their eggs, sometimes having its own eggs destroyed in turn.

• **BREEDING** Polygamous. Colonial.

• **NESTING** Incubation 12–16 days by female. Young altricial; stay in nest 11–16 days, fed by both sexes, but female does more. 2 broods per year.

• **POPULATION** Common despite loss of freshwater wetlands. Most populations are migratory, but some in the West and on the coasts, are nonmigratory year round residents.

• **CONSERVATION** Neotropical migrant; vulnerable to habitat lost to development, agriculture, wetland drainage.

Similar Birds
 **SEDGE WREN** Smaller; shorter bill; buffy brown head and upperparts; dark streaking on cinnamon rump; less distinct eye stripe; voice differs.

Flight Pattern

Weak fluttering flights, often of short duration; alternates several quick wing beats with brief pause and wings at sides.

Nest Identification

Shape 🐦 Location 🌾

Reeds, grass, sedge, bulrushes for outer layer; grasses, reeds, and cattails for central cavity, lined with shredded soft materials • about 1–3 feet above water (but up to 15 feet) • male builds several nests, female selects and completes • 3–10 brown eggs, flecked with darker brown and sometimes wreathed; usually ovate, 0.7 x 0.55 inches.

Plumage Sexes similar	Habitat	Migration Migratory	Weight 0.4 ounce

DATE _____ TIME_____ LOCATION _____

Family REGULIDAE	Species *Regulus satrapa*	Length 4 inches	Wingspan 6.5–7 inches

GOLDEN-CROWNED KINGLET

Living in dense coniferous forests, this tiny bird's baseball-sized sphere-shaped nest is so small that its clutch of half-inch eggs must be laid in two layers. A tame bird, it will sometimes enter human habitations and not try to escape if held. It often feeds in mixed-species foraging flocks with woodpeckers, creepers, chickadees, nuthatches, and others. Females and juveniles have a yellow crown bordered by black.

orange patch on crown bordered by yellow

broad whitish stripe above eye

olive-green upperparts

black yellowish-edged tertials and secondaries

short straight black bill

2 whitish wing bars

pale buff to whitish underparts

MALE

- **SONG** Sings a song beginning with 3–4 high-pitched *tsee, tsee, tsee* notes, followed by a rapid trill. Call is a series of 3–4 high-pitched *tsee* notes.

- **BEHAVIOR** Solitary or in pairs. Tame. Flits wings as it hops along branches. Forages through dense foliage of trees to pick off food. Eats mainly insects, their eggs, and larvae; takes some seeds. Drinks tree sap, sometimes taking it from sapsucker drill wells. May hawk insects or hover briefly to glean them from trunk, branch, or foliage.

- **BREEDING** Monogamous. Solitary nester.

- **NESTING** Incubation 14–15 days by female. Young altricial; stay in nest 14–19 days, fed by both sexes. 1–2 broods per year.

- **POPULATION** Common in coniferous woodlands. Populations may drop after harsh cold seasons on winter range; long-term stable, with range expanding to northeast. Many populations nonmigratory.

yellow crown patch bordered by black

FEMALE

Similar Birds

RUBY-CROWNED KINGLET
♂ White eye ring instead of white stripe over eye; underparts are darker, dusky greenish yellow; olive-green crown and upperparts; different call • only male has concealed red crown patch.

- **CONSERVATION** Neotropical migrant. Vulnerable to habitat loss caused by logging, especially of mature coniferous forests.

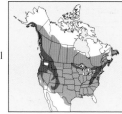

Flight Pattern

Weak fluttering flight, alternating rapid shallow wing strokes with a brief pull of wings to sides. Hovers over food before dipping down to pick it up with beak.

Nest Identification	
Shape Location 	Lichen and moss, with lining of bark chips, rootlets, and feathers • in branch of conifer, 30–60 feet above ground • built by female • 5–11 creamy white to muddy cream eggs splotched brown or gray, usually wreathed; elliptical ovate, 0.5 inch long.

Plumage Sexes differ	Habitat	Migration Migratory	Weight 0.2 ounce

DATE _____ TIME_____ LOCATION _____

Family REGULIDAE	Species *Regulus calendula*	Length 4.25 inches	Wingspan 6.75–7.5 inches

RUBY-CROWNED KINGLET

This small bird often is seen in mixed-species foraging flocks with creepers, nuthatches, titmice, warblers, and other kinglets. The red patch on the male's crown usually is not visible, unless he becomes excited, at which time he flashes it open and the whole crown seems to be gushing blood. The female and juvenile are similar to the male but lack the red patch. This species is widely distributed in the boreal zone across northern and western North America as a breeding bird, it is highly migratory.

small, often concealed, red patch on crown

white eye ring

short black bill

dusky buff to whitish underparts

olive-green upperparts

MALE

- **SONG** Series of high-pitched *tsee, tsee* notes, followed by several *tew* notes, followed by a 3-note trill of *liberty-liberty-liberty;* an impressively long and loud song for such a small bird. Calls are emphatic *je-ditt* and *cack-cack*.

- **BEHAVIOR** Solitary or in pairs. Tame and active. Picks food off tree trunks, branches, and dense foliage; may hawk or hover to take food. Eats mainly insects, their eggs, and larvae. Also eats some fruits and seeds. Drinks tree sap, especially from the drill wells of sapsuckers. Has "nervous" habit of flicking wings when foraging, perhaps to startle insects into flinching and revealing themselves.

2 white wing bars

yellowish edged secondaries and tertials

FEMALE

- **BREEDING** Monogamous. Solitary nester.
- **NESTING** Incubation 12–14 days by female. Altricial young leave nest at 10–16 days, fed by both sexes. 1 brood per year.
- **POPULATION** Common and widespread in coniferous and mixed conifer-deciduous forests. Studies indicate that populations may be regulated by conditions on the wintering grounds.
- **CONSERVATION** Neotropical migrant. Vulnerable to habitat lost to logging operations. Rare cowbird host.

Similar Birds

♂ GOLDEN-CROWNED KINGLET
White stripe above eye; paler underparts; song differs • male has orange crown patch with yellow and black border
♀ • females and juveniles have yellow crown patch with black border.

HUTTON'S VIREO
Stockier; larger head; stout bill; pale lores; olive-gray upperparts; secondaries and tertials lack yellow edging; does not flick wings; white eye ring broken above eyes; voice differs • western range.

Flight Pattern

Weak fluttering flight with shallow wing beats, alternating several quick strokes with brief periods of wings folded to sides. Hovers over branches to pick off food.

Nest Identification

Shape [symbols] Location [symbols]

Moss, lichen, down, twigs, and dead leaves, lined with finer materials, including feathers • hanging from tree branch, 2–100 feet above ground • built by female • 5–11 creamy white to muddy cream eggs, splotched with brown or gray, usually wreathed; elliptical ovate to oval, 0.5 inch long.

Plumage Sexes differ	Habitat ♠♦	Migration Migratory	Weight 0.2 ounce

DATE _____ TIME_____ LOCATION _____

Family SYLVIIDAE	Species *Polioptila caerulea*	Length 4.25 inches	Wingspan 5.75–6.5 inches

BLUE-GRAY GNATCATCHER

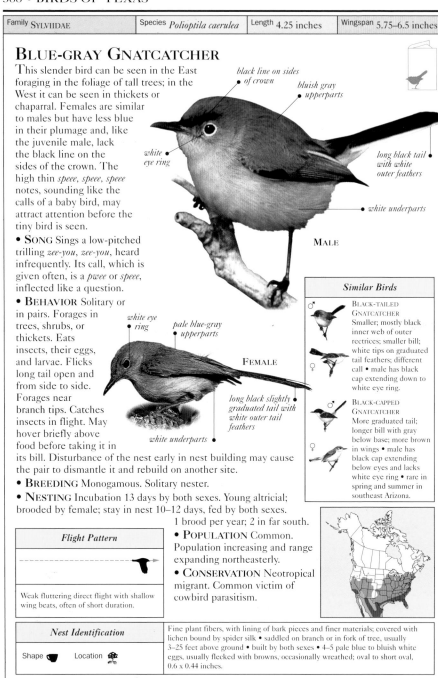

This slender bird can be seen in the East foraging in the foliage of tall trees; in the West it can be seen in thickets or chaparral. Females are similar to males but have less blue in their plumage and, like the juvenile male, lack the black line on the sides of the crown. The high thin *speee, speee, speee* notes, sounding like the calls of a baby bird, may attract attention before the tiny bird is seen.

black line on sides of crown

bluish gray upperparts

white eye ring

long black tail with white outer feathers

white underparts

MALE

- **SONG** Sings a low-pitched trilling *zee-you, zee-you*, heard infrequently. Its call, which is given often, is a *pwee* or *speee*, inflected like a question.

- **BEHAVIOR** Solitary or in pairs. Forages in trees, shrubs, or thickets. Eats insects, their eggs, and larvae. Flicks long tail open and from side to side. Forages near branch tips. Catches insects in flight. May hover briefly above food before taking it in its bill. Disturbance of the nest early in nest building may cause the pair to dismantle it and rebuild on another site.

white eye ring

pale blue-gray upperparts

FEMALE

long black slightly graduated tail with white outer tail feathers

white underparts

- **BREEDING** Monogamous. Solitary nester.

- **NESTING** Incubation 13 days by both sexes. Young altricial; brooded by female; stay in nest 10–12 days, fed by both sexes. 1 brood per year; 2 in far south.

- **POPULATION** Common. Population increasing and range expanding northeasterly.

- **CONSERVATION** Neotropical migrant. Common victim of cowbird parasitism.

Similar Birds

♂ **BLACK-TAILED GNATCATCHER** Smaller; mostly black inner web of outer rectrices; smaller bill; white tips on graduated tail feathers; different call • male has black cap extending down to white eye ring.

♀ **BLACK-CAPPED GNATCATCHER** More graduated tail; longer bill with gray below base; more brown in wings • male has black cap extending below eyes and lacks white eye ring • rare in spring and summer in southeast Arizona.

Flight Pattern
Weak fluttering direct flight with shallow wing beats, often of short duration.

Nest Identification	
Shape	Location

Fine plant fibers, with lining of bark pieces and finer materials; covered with lichen bound by spider silk • saddled on branch or in fork of tree, usually 3–25 feet above ground • built by both sexes • 4–5 pale blue to bluish white eggs, usually flecked with browns, occasionally wreathed; oval to short oval, 0.6 x 0.44 inches.

Plumage Sexes differ	Habitat	Migration Migratory	Weight 0.2 ounce

DATE _____ TIME_____ LOCATION _____

Family SYLVIIDAE	Species *Polioptila melanura*	Length 4 inches	Wingspan 5.5–6 inches

BLACK-TAILED GNATCATCHER

This bird lives near desert gulches and scrub growth. The male's black cap sets it apart from similar gnatcatchers, with the exception of the Black-capped Gnatcatcher, which is rare and local in southeastern Arizona. Males have white outer webs on outer tail feathers and white terminal spots on graduated tail feathers. Females have a brown wash on their blue-gray upperparts, especially on the back, and, like the nonbreeding males, lack the black cap.

glossy black cap
blue-gray upperparts
MALE
long mostly black tail
black bill
white eye ring
white underparts

- **SONG** Sings a quick repeated *jeh-jeh-jeh*. Has calls of *cheeh*, a breathy *sseheh*, and a *mew*.
- **BEHAVIOR** Solitary or in pairs. Active. Forages for food in shrubs and in foliage and branches of trees. Eats mostly insects but some spiders and seeds. Gleans prey from foliage; hovers over prey and takes it with small bill or sometimes sallies out like a small slender flycatcher and takes insects in midair. Flicks tail from side to side or open and up and down.
- **BREEDING** Monogamous. Solitary nester.
- **NESTING** Incubation 14 days by both sexes. Young altricial; brooded by female; stay in nest 9–15 days, fed by both sexes. 1–2 broods per year.

blue-gray upperparts washed brownish
white eye ring
white underparts
long, graduated black tail with white outer webs on outer tail feathers, white tips on each tail feather
FEMALE

Similar Birds

♂ **BLUE-GRAY GNATCATCHER**
Blue-gray upperparts, including crown; white eye ring; black tail with white outer tail feathers; white under tail with black central feathers; voice differs
• male has black line on sides of crown.

♂ **BLACK-CAPPED GNATCATCHER**
Long graduated black tail with white outer webs on outer tail feathers; mostly white undertail; longer bill; voice differs • rare and local in southeastern Arizona.

- **POPULATION** Fairly common in mesquite creosote bush and in other semidesert to desert shrub.
- **CONSERVATION** Vulnerable to habitat loss due to development and grazing. Host to cowbird parasitism.

Flight Pattern
Weak fluttering direct flight with shallow wing beats, often of short duration.

Nest Identification	
Shape 🐦 Location 🌿	Plant down and similar materials bound with spider silk, with lining of fine materials • in bush, usually 2–3 feet above ground • built by both sexes • 3–5 pale blue or green eggs with brown markings; oval to short oval, 0.6 x 0.44 inches.

Plumage Sexes differ	Habitat 🌿 ⚹ ⚹⚹	Migration Nonmigratory	Weight 0.2 ounce

DATE _____ TIME_____ LOCATION _____

| Family TURDIDAE | Species *Sialia sialis* | Length 7–7.75 inches | Wingspan 11.5–13 inches |

EASTERN BLUEBIRD

This brightly colored bird inhabits open woodlands, meadows, and fields. Its population has been in serious decline due to competition from other birds for its nesting holes, as well as occasional severe snowstorms in the South that kill them in great numbers. Juveniles show gray-brown upperparts with white spotting on the back, a brownish chest with white scalloping, a white belly and crissum, a white eye ring, and a bluish tail and wings.

MALE

bright blue upperparts

reddish brown chin, throat, and sides of neck

reddish brown breast, sides, and flanks

white belly and undertail coverts

• **SONG** Sings melodic *chur chur-lee chur-lee.* Male gives call of *true-a-ly, true-a-ly.*

• **BEHAVIOR** Pairs, family groups, or small flocks. Gregarious in winter, often forming large flocks and roosting communally in natural cavities or nest boxes at night. Forages in open from low perches. Flies from perch to ground and forages for food. Eats mostly insects, earthworms, and spiders but also takes snails, lizards, and frogs. In winter eats mostly berries and seeds.

• **BREEDING** Monogamous. In pairs and small groups.

• **NESTING** Incubation 12–14 days by female. Altricial young stay in nest 15–20 days; brooded by female, fed by both sexes. 2–3 broods per year.

gray upperparts

white eye ring

pale chestnut throat, breast, sides, and flanks

JUVENILE

• **POPULATION** Fairly common, but declined by more than 90 percent in 20th century. Adversely affected by severe winters.

white belly and undertail coverts

FEMALE

blue wings, rump, and tail

• **FEEDERS AND BIRDHOUSES** Peanut butter–cornmeal mixture and commercial bluebird food. Nests in man-made bird boxes.

Similar Birds

WESTERN BLUEBIRD
Blue throat and sides of neck; chestnut-red breast, sides, and flanks; pale grayish belly and crissum; rusty brown back • female has gray-rusty brown tinge on nape and back • western range.

Flight Pattern	
Relatively slow direct flight with shallow, somewhat jerky wing beats. Sallies from perch to catch insect in air.	

• **CONSERVATION** European Starling, House Sparrow, and other's intrude on nesting sites. Many nesting sites lost to cutting cavity trees. Bird boxes have helped recovery, especially those with proper hole sizes and predator guards.

Nest Identification	
Shape	Grass, weed stems, pine needles, twigs, and occasionally hair or feather • in abandoned woodpecker hole, natural hollow in tree or stump, or bird box 2–50 feet above ground • built by female • 2–7 light blue or white eggs; subelliptical to short subelliptical, 0.8 x 0.64 inches.
Location 	

| Plumage Sexes differ | Habitat | Migration Some migrate | Weight 1.1 ounces |

Family TURDIDAE	Species *Sialia mexicana*	Length 7–7.75 inches	Wingspan 11.5–13 inches

WESTERN BLUEBIRD

The Western Bluebird's brilliant blue throat distinguishes it from the Eastern Bluebird, and its chestnut-red underparts distinguish it from the Mountain Bluebird. In recent years its population has declined due to loss of habitat, especially large old trees, which it uses for nesting cavities. Bird boxes have been helpful but have not kept up with the loss of trees. Juveniles are brownish gray with white-spotted upperparts and underparts and bluish wings and tails.

- **SONG** Male's song is *f-few, f-few, faweee*. Also calls *pa-wee* or *mew*.
- **BEHAVIOR** In pairs or small family groups. More gregarious in winter. Often hunts from low perches from which it drops down on prey or hawks insects. Forages for food on ground and catches insects in flight. Eats insects, earthworms, spiders, and snails; in winter, principally feeds on various berries. Defends nesting cavity from other birds. Often roosts communally in winter, with many individuals sharing the same cavity for the night.
- **BREEDING** Monogamous. Solitary or small colonies.
- **NESTING** Incubation 13–14 days by female. Young altricial; brooded by female; leave nest in 15–22 days, fed by both sexes. 2 broods per year.
- **POPULATION** Common in open woodlands, riparian woodlands, cut-over woodlands, and farmlands; common in winter in deserts and semideserts.
- **FEEDERS AND BIRDHOUSES** Mealworms, peanut butter and suet mixture, cornmeal mixes, and commercial bluebird mixes. Currants, raisins, and soaked raisins are also favorites. Will nest in bird boxes.
- **CONSERVATION** Population declining due to loss of habitat and nesting sites because of competition from other songbirds.

MALE

blue throat and head

touch of chestnut on upper back and shoulders

chestnut breast, sides, and flanks

bright blue upperparts, including wings

grayish white belly and crissum

bright blue tail

conspicuous white eye ring

brownish gray upperparts

FEMALE

pale gray throat

chestnut-tinged breast, sides, and flanks

grayish white belly and crissum

Similar Birds

♂ **EASTERN BLUEBIRD**
Reddish brown throat and breast; white belly and undertail coverts;
♀ blue back.

Flight Pattern	
Relatively slow flight with shallow wing beats and somewhat jerky motion. Sallies forth to take insects in flight, returning to perch; sometimes hovers briefly over prey.	

Nest Identification	
Shape	Grass, weeds, stems, pine needles, and twigs, occasionally with hair or feathers • in natural cavity of tree or in bird box • 2–50 feet above ground • built by both sexes • 3–8 pale blue to bluish white eggs; oval to short oval, 0.8 x 0.64 inches.
Location	

Plumage Sexes differ	Habitat	Migration Northern birds migrate	Weight 1.0 ounce

DATE _____ TIME_____ LOCATION _____

Family TURDIDAE	Species *Sialia currucoides*	Length 7–7.25 inches	Wingspan 11–12.75 inches

MOUNTAIN BLUEBIRD

The overall brilliant blue coloring of the male sets it apart from other birds in its genus. Most often making its home in the tree-covered mountains and open landscapes of western North America, generally above seven thousand feet, it is considered to be at risk by conservationists due to its declining nesting habitat. In winter it descends to open lowlands and deserts. Juveniles are similar to females but with pale whitish streaking and spotting on the breast and sides.

• **SONG** Often silent. A low warbling *tru-lee*. Call is a *phew*.

• **BEHAVIOR** Solitary or in pairs or small family groups. Hovers more than other bluebirds, dropping on prey from above or pouncing on it from low perches. Catches insects in flight and forages on ground. Eats insects, caterpillars, and some fruits and berries. Eats mostly insects in summer.

• **BREEDING** Monogamous. Solitary nester.

• **NESTING** Incubation 13–14 days by female. Altricial young brooded by female first 6 days; stay in nest 22–23 days, fed by both sexes. 2 broods per year.

• **POPULATION** Fairly common but declined over much of its range in the 1900s due to loss of nesting cavities to other species. Casual in the East during migration and winter to north Atlantic seaboard.

• **BIRDHOUSES** Will nest in bird boxes.

• **CONSERVATION** Habitat loss is a concern.

turquoise-blue overall

MALE

pale blue underparts

white eye ring

white belly and undertail coverts

white-edged wing coverts, tertials, and secondaries

FEMALE

dull brownish gray overall

white undertail coverts and belly

Similar Birds

♂ **WESTERN BLUEBIRD** Male is darker blue-purple with chestnut-red breast, sides, and flanks; pale grayish belly and crissum; rusty brown back • female is tinged gray-rusty brown on nape and back; chestnut-red on breast, sides, and flanks • western range.

Flight Pattern
Relatively slow direct flight with shallow, somewhat jerky wing beats. Often hovers over prey before dipping down to seize it.

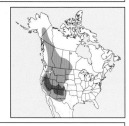

Nest Identification	
Shape ...	Grass, weed stems, pine needles, and twigs, occasionally with hair or feathers • in natural tree cavity, ridges of buildings, abandoned nest of swallow, or nest box • built by both sexes • 4–8 pale blue to bluish white eggs, rarely white; subelliptical to oval, 0.8 x 0.64 inches.
Location ...	

Plumage Sexes differ	Habitat	Migration Migratory	Weight 1.1 ounces

DATE _____ TIME_____ LOCATION _____

Family TURDIDAE	Species *Myadestes townsendi*	Length 8.5–9 inches	Wingspan 13–14.5 inches

TOWNSEND'S SOLITAIRE

white eye ring

gray overall

buffy wing patch near base of blackish flight feathers

Its beautiful prolonged song, given from high up in the trees, is in marked contrast with the rather plain-looking plumage of this gray bird. Although it makes its home in the high mountains most of the year, during the winter season Townsend's Solitaire moves into the canyons, where it maintains a winter territory and protects a critical food supply. In flight the white outer tail feathers contrast with the inner black ones, and the bird shows white axillaries and a long buffy wing patch. Juveniles are dark brownish gray, with buffy and white scalloping on both the upperparts and underparts, as well as a buffy crissum and wing patch.

black tail with white outer tail feathers that show in flight

• **SONG** A pleasant trilling and rich warble. Often sings in flight. Call is a squeaking *eek* or a plaintive whistled *whee.*

• **BEHAVIOR** Solitary or in pairs. Forms small groups in winter. Perches upright and remains still for long periods of time, thus is easily overlooked. Perches on exposed branch to spot insect, then sallies out to catch in midair and returns to perch. Also forages on ground. Feeds on various insects, worms, and caterpillars in summer; winter diet consists principally of juniper berries. In summer, frequents mountainous coniferous forests around 3,000 feet below the timberline; in winter, descends to canyons with open juniper forests on lower slopes.

JUVENILE

• **BREEDING** Monogamous. Solitary or small family groups.

• **NESTING** Incubation 14 days by both sexes, but female does more. Altricial young brooded by female; remain in nest 15–16 days, fed by both sexes. 1 brood per year (possibly 2 broods in the South).

• **POPULATION** Fairly common in montane coniferous forests. Casual to rare in winter in eastern North America.

Similar Birds

NORTHERN MOCKINGBIRD
Superficial resemblance • paler gray overall; 2 whitish wing bars; white wing patch; faint eye stripe; longer bill.

Flight Pattern

Rather slow flight; several slow wing beats followed by short glides. Often irregular in flight pattern, changing directions quickly. Sallies from perch to snatch insects in air.

Nest Identification

Shape   Location ▬ ⟋ ⟍

Grass, roots, and moss, lined with fine materials • on ground, sheltered by overhanging branches, rocks, or natural overhang • built by both sexes • 3–8 pale blue eggs, usually unmarked, occasionally flecked with red-brown; oval, varying from short oval to long oval, 0.8 x 0.6 inches.

Plumage Sexes similar	Habitat 🌳 ▲ 🌿 🏞 🌾	Migration Migratory	Weight 1.2 ounces

Family TURDIDAE	Species *Catharus fuscescens*	Length 7–7.5 inches	Wingspan 11–11.5 inches

VEERY

This bird is named for the lovely ethereal downward-slurring song of the male, which is heard at sunset, a repeated *veer-u*. It is one of the most splendid songs of any bird in North America. Its tawny and buff plumage serves as camouflage in the forest it calls home. The Veery is the least spotted of North America's brown-backed thrushes, with the western populations slightly more spotted than the eastern ones. This bird haunts shaded moist woodlands with dense to scattered understory.

tawny reddish brown upperparts

indistinct grayish eye ring

black upper mandible

creamy pink lower mandible with black tip

creamy pink legs and feet

buff breast with pale tawny brown spotting

white underparts

• **SONG** Sings pleasant liquid descending *veer-u, veer-u, veer-u*, with each note sung lower, repeated frequently with variation in phrasing. Call is harsh down-slurred *veer.* Summer evenings, woodlots and forests fill with the song of one singer cascading into that of another; the chorus at twilight is one of the truly beautiful sounds of nature in the Northwoods.

• **BEHAVIOR** Solitary or in pairs. Somewhat shy and retiring. Forages on ground and in trees; swoops from low perch to take prey on ground, or gleans food from branches, foliage, or ground. Eats various insects, caterpillars, spiders, berries, and fruit. Agitated birds flick wings and raise small crest. Both sexes guard and defend young.

• **BREEDING** Monogamous. Solitary nester.

• **NESTING** Incubation 10–12 days by female. Young altricial; brooded by female; remain in nest 10 days, fed by both sexes. 1 brood per year (sometimes 2 in the South).

• **POPULATION** Fairly common but numbers declining due to habitat loss on breeding and wintering grounds.

• **CONSERVATION** Neotropical migrant. Common nest host to Brown-headed Cowbird. Vulnerable to habitat loss due to deforestation.

Similar Birds

WOOD THRUSH
Larger; dark spotting on breast, sides, and upper belly; rufous on upperparts, brightest on nape and crown; black streaking on face; white eye ring.

HERMIT THRUSH
Olive- to russet-brown upperparts; pale grayish white underparts with blackish brown spots and speckles; reddish brown tail and rump; white eye ring.

Flight Pattern

Relatively swift direct flight with somewhat hesitant motion on rapidly beating wings.

Nest Identification

Shape ⌣ 🏺   Location 🔲 🌳 🌲

Grass, bark strips, weed stems, twigs, and moss, with lining of soft bark and dry leaves • atop platform on dry ground, sheltered by shrubs, grasses, or weeds; sometimes in low tree or shrub, 0–6 feet above ground • built by female • 3–5 pale blue eggs, usually unmarked; subelliptical to short subelliptical, 0.9 x 0.65 inches.

Plumage Sexes similar	Habitat 🌳🌿 🌾	Migration Migratory	Weight 1.1 ounces

DATE _____ TIME_____ LOCATION _____

Family TURDIDAE	Species *Catharus minimus*	Length 7–7.75 inches	Wingspan 11.5–13.5 inches

GRAY-CHEEKED THRUSH

This bird is a truly long-distance migrant. Each spring some of its population fly from southern Brazil to Alaska, across the Bering Strait, and on to their nesting grounds in eastern Siberia. Others spread across the arctic tundra and northern taiga from Alaska to Newfoundland. It has the most northern nesting range of any spotted thrush. In migration it can be found in almost any habitat from woodlots to city parks. The Newfoundland race has warmer-toned upperparts with a sepia back.

inconspicuous gray eye ring

olive-gray brown upperparts

black upper mandible

black lower mandible with yellowish pink base

gray cheeks

pale buff wash on breast and throat, with black-brown spots

- **SONG** Male sings thin oboelike phrases, somewhat

grayish white underparts

pink legs and feet

like the Veery, but middle phrases rise and first and last ones drop, *wheeoo-titi-wheeoo*. Call is a thin high abrasive *phreu*. Vocal at dawn and especially at dusk.
- **BEHAVIOR** Solitary or in pairs. Shy and retiring, often staying in the dense understory and thickets. More heard than seen. Feeds on spiders, caterpillars, earthworms, various insects, and even small crayfish. In fall migration, feeds more on berries and some fruits.
- **BREEDING** Monogamous. Solitary nester.
- **NESTING** Incubation 13–14 days by female. Young altricial; brooded by female; stay in nest 11–13 days. Fed by female. 1–2 broods per year.
- **POPULATION** Common; southern breeding populations declining due to loss of habitat.
- **CONSERVATION** Neotropical migrant. Vulnerable on both breeding grounds and wintering areas to habitat loss from logging operations and forest fragmentation.

Similar Birds

SWAINSON'S THRUSH Conspicuous eye ring; browner upperparts; buffy lores, cheeks, throat, and upper breast; buffy underwing linings; different voice.

BICKNELL'S THRUSH Formerly considered subspecies of Gray-cheeked Thrush
- smaller; warmer brown tones on upperparts, especially on tail and rump; more extensive yellow on lower mandible
- limited range in extreme northeast US
- best separated by voice.

Flight Pattern

Relatively swift direct flight with somewhat jerky wing strokes.

Nest Identification

Shape ⬩   Location 🪹 🌿 🌱

Grass, sedge, bark, weed stems, twigs, and moss, with lining of grass, leaves, and fine rootlets • on low branch of tree or shrub, usually 0–10 feet above ground (but as high as 20 feet) • built by female • 3–6 greenish blue to pale blue eggs, most often speckled brown; oval to short oval, 0.9 x 0.65 inches.

Plumage Sexes similar	Habitat 🌳 🌾	Migration Migratory	Weight 1.2 ounces

DATE _____ TIME_____ LOCATION _____

| Family TURDIDAE | Species *Catharus ustulatus* | Length 7 inches | Wingspan 11.5 inches |

SWAINSON'S THRUSH

Named for 19th-century British ornithologist William Swainson, this bird migrates through North America from its nesting grounds in Canada and mountainous eastern and western US to its winter home in the tropics. Migrating at night, flocks of these birds give plaintive, Spring Peeper-like calls in the darkness as they pass overhead. It often travels in mixed flocks with other thrushes, vireos, and wood warblers. In flight these birds show buff underwing linings.

prominent buff eye ring

black bill with pinkish yellow base to lower mandible

buff-olive-brown upperparts

buff chin, cheeks, and throat

buff breast with brownish spots

whitish gray underparts

pink legs and feet

• **SONG** Sings upward series of thin, musical, varied whistling notes repeated at intervals without change. Call is liquid *whit* similar to the dripping sound of a leaky faucet.

• **BEHAVIOR** Solitary or in pairs. Shy and retiring. Feeds more in trees than other spotted brown thrushes. Picks food off leaves, catches some insects in air, and forages for food on ground. Eats insects, snails, and earthworms. In fall migration eats more fruits and berries. A habitat generalist during migration; prefers conifers and mixed conifer-deciduous forests for nesting. In agonistic displays flicks wings and raises crest. More often heard than seen.

• **BREEDING** Monogamous. Solitary nester.

• **NESTING** Incubation 12–14 days by female. Altricial young stay in nest 10–13 days. Brooded by female. Fed by both sexes. 1 brood per year.

• **POPULATION** Fairly common in most woodlands as well as coniferous forests. Abundant in boreal forests.

• **CONSERVATION** Neotropical migrant. Vulnerable to habitat loss from logging and deforestation on breeding and wintering grounds.

Similar Birds

GRAY-CHEEKED THRUSH Larger; gray cheeks; buff-gray wash on spotted breast; gray wash on sides and flanks; olive-gray upperparts; indistinct eye ring; different voice.

BICKNELL'S THRUSH Smaller; more brown upperparts; tawny brown on rump and tail; more extensive yellow on lower mandible; different voice • northeastern range.

Flight Pattern

Relatively swift direct flight with rapid wing beats.

Nest Identification

Shape ◣   Location 🌿🌳🌲

Sticks, moss, leaves, plant fibers, and bark with occasional middle layer of mud • lined with lichens, dried leaves, and rootlets • on branch close to trunk of conifer, or occasionally in other trees or shrubs, 0–40 feet (usually 4–20 feet) above ground • built by female • 3–5 pale blue eggs usually flecked with browns; oval to short oval, 0.8 x 0.6 inches.

| Plumage Sexes similar | Habitat 🌿 🌱 🌳 ⛰ | Migration Migratory | Weight 1.1 ounces |

DATE _____ TIME_____ LOCATION _____

Family TURDIDAE	Species *Catharus guttatus*	Length 6.75 inches	Wingspan 11.5 inches

HERMIT THRUSH

Often considered to have one of the most beautiful songs of all North American birds, the Hermit Thrush lives in habitats with coniferous and deciduous trees and along forest edges. It is Vermont's state bird and the only brown-backed spotted thrush to winter in the US. Color variations exist across its broad breeding range: northern Pacific Coast races are smaller and darker with gray flanks; western mountain races are larger and paler also with gray flanks; and eastern races are brownish gray with buff-brown flanks.

distinct white eye ring

blackish upper mandible

olive-brown to russet-brown upperparts

black-tipped lower mandible with pinkish yellow at base

buff wash on breast and throat

- **SONG** Song begins with long clear low flutelike note and then rises with delicate ringing tones ending in thin, silvery notes; each phrase is repeated, and the pitch differs from that of the previous song. Call note is *chuck*, often doubled; also gives upslurred *whee*.

reddish brown tail and rump

pale grayish white underparts with blackish brown spots and speckles

pinkish legs and feet

- **BEHAVIOR** Solitary or in pairs. Often curious and approachable. Responds to pishing sound or imitations of Eastern Screech-Owl by coming close, flicking wings, raising crest, and raising and lowering tail. Often slightly raises and lowers tail upon landing. Sometimes hovers above food on branch or foliage and picks it off with beak. Forages on ground for various insects, insect larvae, and other small invertebrates, including earthworms and snails. Also eats berries and some fruit, especially in autumn migration and winter.
- **BREEDING** Monogamous. Solitary nester.
- **NESTING** Incubation 12–13 days by female. Altrical young remain in nest 12 days; brooded by female, fed by both sexes. 2–3 broods per year.

Similar Birds

VEERY
Reddish brown upperparts; lacks dark spotting on breast; inconspicuous eye ring; different voice.

WOOD THRUSH
Reddish brown upperparts; brightest on crown and nape; heavy black spotting on underparts; different voice.

- **POPULATION** Fairly common. Breeding range is extending southward in southern Appalachians.
- **CONSERVATION** Neotropical migrant. Uncommon host to cowbirds.

Flight Pattern

Rather swift direct flight with rapid wing beats. Sometimes hovers briefly over prey before dipping to pick it up.

Nest Identification	Weeds, rotted wood, twigs, mud, and other fine materials • lined with moss and grass • on ground or low on branch of tree 0–8 feet above ground • occasionally nests in rafters of mountain buildings • built by female • 3–6 greenish blue eggs usually unmarked but sometimes with black flecks; oval to short oval, 0.8 x 0.6 inches.
Shape 🥄 Location 🌳 🌿	

Plumage Sexes similar	Habitat 🌳 🌿 🪨	Migration Most migrate	Weight 1.1 ounces

DATE _____ TIME_____ LOCATION _____

Family TURDIDAE	Species *Hylocichla mustelina*	Length 7.75–8 inches	Wingspan 13–14 inches

WOOD THRUSH

In early spring, the peaceful flutelike songs of the males are heard throughout the nesting territory, announcing their arrival. It frequents moist forests or large woodlots, but also can be seen in parks, towns, and country gardens. When this heavy-bodied big-eyed short-tailed thrush is agitated, it lifts the feathers on its head like a crest. The song, one of the most beautiful thrush songs, is given before daybreak, but is most prolonged at dusk, when the singer perches high above ground and delivers it in leisurely fashion, rising and falling, until darkness silences him.

bright russet nape and crown

white eye ring surrounds large dark eye

reddish brown upperparts

black bill with creamy pink base to lower mandible

black streaking on white face

large black spots on breast, sides, and flanks

creamy pink legs and feet

- **SONG** A serene flutelike series of triple phrases, the middle note lower than the first, the last note highest and trilled, *ee-o-lee, ee-o-lay.* Call is an abrasive *quirt* or rapid *pit, pit, pit.*
- **BEHAVIOR** Solitary or in pairs. Somewhat shy and retiring but may feed in the open on wooded lawns. Feeds on ground or in trees close to ground, gleaning food from ground or from branches and foliage. Eats various insects, spiders, and fruits; feeds largely on fruits and berries in fall migration. In courtship, male chases female in series of fast twisting circling flights within the male's territory. Territorial in winter.
- **BREEDING** Monogamous. Solitary.
- **NESTING** Incubation 13–14 days by female. Young altricial; brooded by female; remain in nest 12 days, fed by both sexes. 1–2 broods per year.
- **POPULATION** Common in moist deciduous or mixed deciduous-conifer woodlands, often near water. Casual in the West during migration.
- **CONSERVATION** Neotropical migrant. Population declining in recent decades due to nest parasitism by cowbirds, forest fragmentation on breeding grounds, and habitat loss on wintering grounds in Central America.

Similar Birds

VEERY
Smaller; uniform reddish brown upperparts; lacks black spotting of underparts; longer tail; voice differs.

HERMIT THRUSH
Smaller; rich brown to gray-brown upperparts; buff wash on breast; dark spotting confined to throat and upper breast; rufous rump and tail; voice differs.

Flight Pattern

Relatively swift direct flight on rapidly beating wings. Flights in woodlots often of short duration.

Nest Identification	
Shape ⬲ Location 🌳 🪻 🌿	Moss, mud, and dried leaves, with lining of fine rootlets • in fork of tree or shrub, usually 6–50 feet above ground (but generally 6–12 feet) • built by female • 2–5 unmarked pale blue or bluish green eggs; short oval to short subelliptical, slightly pointed at end, 1.0 x 0.75 inches.

Plumage Sexes similar	Habitat 🌿 🌱 🍂	Migration Migratory	Weight 1.7 ounces

DATE _____ TIME_____ LOCATION _____

Family TURDIDAE	Species *Turdus grayi*	Length 9 inches	Wingspan 14.75 inches

CLAY-COLORED ROBIN

This native of Mexico and South and Central America makes rare visits to North America and has bred on occasion in southern Texas. It is most often seen in the lower Rio Grande Valley. Very similar in its habits to our American Robin, this bird has adapted to a wide variety of habitats, including dwelling in towns, villages, and cities, but it still is wary around humans. It is a yellow-billed robin with

brownish olive upperparts

greenish yellow bill

whitish buff throat with olive-brown streaking

brownish olive wings and tail

tawny buff underparts with brownish olive upper chest and flanks

olive-brown upperparts, buffy brown underparts, and a pale streaked throat. Juveniles are similar to adults but with some buffy spots on the upperwing coverts.

brownish gray legs and feet

• **SONG** Slow long continuous caroling of various musical phrases such as *cheerily-cheer-up-cheerio*. Calls include a throaty *tock*, a slurred *reeur-ee*, and a clucking note.

• **BEHAVIOR** Solitary or in pairs. Small flocks in fruiting trees. Somewhat shy and retiring. Upon alighting, spreads and closes tail while flipping it up and down. Hops and runs on the ground to forage, pushing litter aside with its bill; gleans food from branches and foliage low in trees. Eats insects, caterpillars, and some berries and fruits. Sometimes takes snails and small amphibians and reptiles. Defensive around nest and young.

• **BREEDING** Monogamous. Solitary nester.

• **NESTING** Incubation 12–14 days by female. Young altricial; brooded by female; stay in nest 13–15 days, fed by both sexes. 2 broods per year.

• **POPULATION** In North America, species is rare in southeastern Texas. Common to very common in Mexican range.

• **FEEDERS AND BIRDHOUSES** Comes to feeders for bananas and plantains; will visit birdbaths.

Similar Birds

AMERICAN ROBIN
Brick-red breast; white belly and crissum; grayish brown upperparts; white throat with black streaking; broken white eye ring; white corners on blackish brown tail; yellow bill.

Flight Pattern
Swift direct flight with rapid wing beats.

Nest Identification	
Shape 🐦 Location 🌳 🌿	Mud, grasses, and twigs • on low branch of tree or shrub • built by female • 2–4 pale blue eggs, with brown, gray, and reddish dots; oval to long oval, 1.1 x 0.8 inches.

Plumage Sexes similar	Habitat 🌿🌾 🌳 🏞️ 🌱	Migration Nonmigratory	Weight 2.6 ounces

DATE _____ TIME_____ LOCATION _____

Family TURDIDAE	Species *Turdus migratorius*	Length 10 inches	Wingspan 14–16 inches

AMERICAN ROBIN

In many areas this bird is considered a sign of spring, though it is a year-round resident in most of its US range. It is among the most common, widely distributed, and most well-known birds in North America. Juveniles are similar to adults but have heavily spotted underparts and white spotting and edging on the back and shoulders.

- **SONG** A bold gurgling leisurely *sing-song cheerily cheer-up cheerio*, with phrases often repeated. Has rapid call of *tut-tut-tut* or *hip-hip-hip*.

- **BEHAVIOR** Solitary or in pairs. Gregarious after breeding season; in winter often in flocks and roosts communally with other species. Eats earthworms, insects, and berries. Berries and fruits are principal diet in winter. Defensive of nest site and young. Adapted to human disturbance, especially agricultural areas and the combination of shade trees and lawns. Running-stopping foraging style in fields and lawns.

- **BREEDING** Monogamous. Solitary. Sometimes observed in loose colonies.

- **NESTING** Incubation 12–14 days by female. Altricial young brooded by female; stay in nest 14–16 days; female does more feeding. Male often tends first brood while female begins to incubate second clutch. 2–3 broods per year in south; fewer in north.

- **POPULATION** Abundant and widespread in variety of habitats, including forests, woodlands, gardens, and parks.

- **FEEDERS AND BIRDHOUSES** Will come to feeders for breadcrumbs. Attracted to birdbaths. Uses nesting shelves.

- **CONSERVATION** Neotropical migrant. Becoming more common in the Midwest and onto the Great Plains with planting of shelter belt trees and irrigation. Vulnerable to pesticide poisoning in the food chain.

blackish head

broken white eye ring

dark brownish gray upperparts

yellow bill

white throat with black striping

brick red breast

MALE

white lower belly and undertail coverts

blackish tail has white outer corners

dark brownish gray head

dark brownish gray upperparts

yellow bill

chestnut-orange breast

JUVENILE

FEMALE

Similar Birds

RUFOUS-BACKED ROBIN Rufous chest, back, and wing coverts; gray head and tail; heavy streaking on throat; yellow bill; yellow eye ring
- southwestern range.

Flight Pattern

Swift rapid direct flight on strongly beating wings.

Nest Identification

Shape | Location

Grasses and mud, with lining of fine grass • in all areas of tree, but with shelter from rain, or in building or nest shelf • female does more building • 3–7 pale blue eggs, occasionally white, usually unmarked, but occasionally flecked with brown; oval to short oval, 1.1 x 0.8 inches.

Plumage Sexes differ	Habitat	Migration Migratory	Weight 2.7 ounces

Family MIMIDAE	Species *Dumetella carolinensis*	Length 8.5–9 inches	Wingspan 11–12 inches

GRAY CATBIRD

Its black cap, long tail, and gentle mewing calls are helpful in identifying this tame gray bird. Frequenting thick undergrowth and bushes, it will reside in summer in the ornamental shrubs, thickets, and hedges in farmyards and towns. An accomplished songster with the quality of the other members of the mimic thrush family, it patterns its song with phrases, some squeaky, some melodious, but none repeated. The song is often interrupted with catlike mewing notes. This bird migrates at night. Although primarily migratory, birds on the coastal plain are nonmigratory.

slate-gray upperparts

black tail

black cap

reddish chestnut undertail coverts

short dark bill

pale gray underparts

• **SONG** A mixture of sweet to melodious, thin to squeaky, and sometimes abrasive pharases mixed with pauses. Does not repeat phrases like other eastern mimic thrushes. Some individuals mimic sounds of other birds, amphibians, and machinery, and incorporate them into their song. Distinctive *mew* notes often included in the phrases. Has call of quiet *mew*. Also a harsh *quit* or *chack*.

• **BEHAVIOR** Solitary or in pairs. Often stays low in thick bush and is easily overlooked. Relatively tame, frequently allowing a close approach. Sings from an exposed perch; sometimes sings at night. Often cocks tail upward and flicks from side to side. Gleans food from branches and foliage and picks it from ground. Eats mostly insects, spiders, berries, and fruits. Strongly defends nest and nestlings from predators and intruders. Uncommon cowbird host; recognizes their eggs and ejects them from nest. Often in loose flocks with other species in winter.

• **BREEDING** Monogamous. Solitary nester.

• **NESTING** Incubation 12–13 days by female. Young altricial; brooded by female; stay in nest 10–11 days, fed by both sexes but more by male. 2 broods per year.

• **POPULATION** Common.

• **FEEDERS** Cheese, bread, raisins, cornflakes, milk, cream, currants, peanuts, and crackers.

• **CONSERVATION** Neotropical migrant. Uncommon cowbird host.

Similar Birds

No other bird in its range is slate gray above and below with a long tail.

Flight Pattern

Swift direct flight on rapid wing beats over some distance; short flights often with several rapid wing beats and a short period with wings pulled to sides.

Nest Identification

Shape · Location

Grass, stems, twigs, and leaves, lined with fine materials • in shrub or tree, 3–10 feet above ground (as high as 50 feet) • built by both sexes but female does more • 2–6 dark blue-green eggs; subelliptical, 0.9 x 0.7 inches.

Plumage Sexes similar	Habitat	Migration Most migrate	Weight 1.3 ounces

DATE _____ TIME_____ LOCATION _____

Family MIMIDAE	Species *Mimus polyglottos*	Length 10 inches	Wingspan 13–15 inches

NORTHERN MOCKINGBIRD

True to its scientific name, *polyglottos*, meaning "many tongued," this bird imitates dozens of other birds, as well as other animals, insects, machinery, and even musical instruments. Traditionally considered a southern bird, it has adapted to a wide range of habitats, from lush southern plantation gardens to dry cactus land. Although nonmigratory over most of its range, northernmost populations do migrate. When sparring with a rival or when in flight, the large white wing patches and the white outer tail feathers flash conspicuously. Juveniles have underparts spotted with gray-browns.

medium gray upperparts

2 white wing bars

short blackish bill

long blackish gray tail with white outer feathers

large white wing patches on blackish wings

gray-white underparts

- **SONG** Perches to sing a variety of original and imitative sounds, each repeated 3–5 (or more) times. Also has an evening "whisper song." Call is a bold abrasive *check*. Often flutters skyward while singing and tumbles back to perch. May sing well into the night or, on moonlit nights or under the glow of a security light, may sing all night.

JUVENILE

- **BEHAVIOR** Solitary or in pairs. Conspicuous. Forages on ground and in bushes and trees. Lifts wings straight up with a jerky snap to bring insects out of hiding. Eats various insects and fruit. Very defensive during breeding season, especially close to the nest or young. Will attack larger birds and mammals that come too near. Sexes defend separate winter feeding territory. Has adapted well to disturbed habitats created by man and thrives in suburbs, towns, villages, and farmlands.

- **BREEDING** Monogamous. Solitary nester. Long-term pair bonds. Males perform display where they face one another and hop sideways, trying to keep other birds out of territory.

- **NESTING** Incubation 12–13 days by female. Young altricial; brooded by female; stay in nest 11–13 days, fed by both sexes. 2–3 broods per year.

Similar Birds

BAHAMA MOCKINGBIRD Larger; lacks white wing patches; browner upperparts; streaking on neck and flanks; white-tipped tail • eastern range.

TOWNSEND'S SOLITAIRE Darker gray; white eye ring; buff wing patches; shorter bill; white outer tail feathers.

- **POPULATION** Common. Range is expanding north, particularly to the Northeast. Casual north of the mapped distribution range, sometimes as far north as Alaska.

- **FEEDERS** Will come for bread, suet, and raisins.

Flight Pattern

Long flight is swift and strong on steadily beating wings. Shorter flights with several quick wing strokes alternated with wings pulled to sides; repeated.

Nest Identification

Shape ● Location 🌳 🌿 🌱

Sticks, stems, bits of fabric, dead leaves, and string, lined with finer materials • set in fork on branch of tree or shrub, usually 3–10 feet above ground • built by both sexes • 2–6 blue-green eggs, with splotches of brown; oval to short oval, occasionally short subelliptical, 1.0 x 0.8 inches.

Plumage Sexes similar	Habitat 🌿 🌳 🌱 〰️ ⚊ ⚘ ⚘	Migration Nonmigratory	Weight 1.7 ounces

DATE _____ TIME_____ LOCATION _____

| Family MIMIDAE | Species *Oreoscoptes montanus* | Length 8.5 inches | Wingspan 11.5 inches |

SAGE THRASHER

At dawn the male Sage Thrasher flies to a high perch and sings its pleasant song over the sagebrush plains. Slightly smaller than a robin, its short bill, ashy brown upperparts, and striped breast set it apart from other thrashers in its range. This shy bird quickly flies away when approached and slips into the thick sagebrush or runs off on the ground. Its streaking may be very faded and faint on individuals with worn plumage. The juvenile has a streaked head and back.

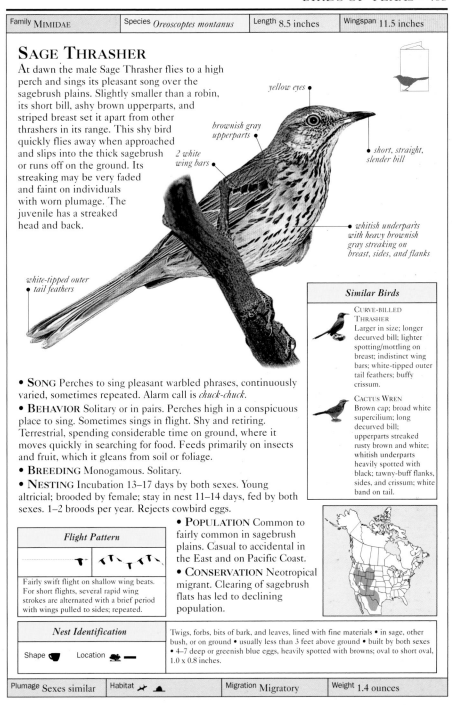

yellow eyes

brownish gray upperparts

2 white wing bars

short, straight, slender bill

whitish underparts with heavy brownish gray streaking on breast, sides, and flanks

white-tipped outer tail feathers

- **SONG** Perches to sing pleasant warbled phrases, continuously varied, sometimes repeated. Alarm call is *chuck-chuck*.
- **BEHAVIOR** Solitary or in pairs. Perches high in a conspicuous place to sing. Sometimes sings in flight. Shy and retiring. Terrestrial, spending considerable time on ground, where it moves quickly in searching for food. Feeds primarily on insects and fruit, which it gleans from soil or foliage.
- **BREEDING** Monogamous. Solitary.
- **NESTING** Incubation 13–17 days by both sexes. Young altricial; brooded by female; stay in nest 11–14 days, fed by both sexes. 1–2 broods per year. Rejects cowbird eggs.
- **POPULATION** Common to fairly common in sagebrush plains. Casual to accidental in the East and on Pacific Coast.
- **CONSERVATION** Neotropical migrant. Clearing of sagebrush flats has led to declining population.

Similar Birds

CURVE-BILLED THRASHER
Larger in size; longer decurved bill; lighter spotting/mottling on breast; indistinct wing bars; white-tipped outer tail feathers; buffy crissum.

CACTUS WREN
Brown cap; broad white supercilium; long decurved bill; upperparts streaked rusty brown and white; whitish underparts heavily spotted with black; tawny-buff flanks, sides, and crissum; white band on tail.

Flight Pattern

Fairly swift flight on shallow wing beats. For short flights, several rapid wing strokes are alternated with a brief period with wings pulled to sides; repeated.

Nest Identification

Shape   Location

Twigs, forbs, bits of bark, and leaves, lined with fine materials • in sage, other bush, or on ground • usually less than 3 feet above ground • built by both sexes • 4–7 deep or greenish blue eggs, heavily spotted with browns; oval to short oval, 1.0 x 0.8 inches.

| Plumage Sexes similar | Habitat | Migration Migratory | Weight 1.4 ounces |

DATE _____ TIME_____ LOCATION _____

Family MIMIDAE	Species *Toxostoma rufum*	Length 11.5 inches	Wingspan 12.5–14 inches

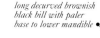

BROWN THRASHER

This shy bird becomes highly aggressive when defending its young, often charging toward the head of any intruder. The male bird sings from an exposed perch, sometimes quite high. It is able to imitate other birds but most often sings its own song, which is a curious mixture of musical phrases. Its bright rufous upperparts and heavily streaked underparts distinguish this species from all other thrashers in its range. Although primarily migratory, birds in the South do not migrate.

long decurved brownish black bill with paler base to lower mandible

reddish brown upperparts

deep yellow eyes

- **SONG** Male sings conversation-like phrases of *hello, hello, yes, yes, who is this? Who is this? I should say, I should say*, with the varied phrases being given in two's and three's. Reported to have the largest song repertoire of all North American birds with more than 1,100 song types recorded. Call is a bold *smack* or *churr.*

2 white wing bars

pale buff to white underparts with heavy streaking

- **BEHAVIOR** Solitary or in pairs. Highly terrestrial; forages on or near ground for food. Finds insects by digging with bill. Eats mainly insects, small amphibians, fruit, and some grains. Runs quickly on ground; turns over leaves and moves debris with bill. Frequents dense brush, early successional stage woodlots, and forest edges. Has adapted to living in shrubby ornamental vegetation of suburbs and gardens.

long reddish brown tail

- **BREEDING** Monogamous. Solitary nester.
- **NESTING** Incubation 11–14 days by both sexes. Young altricial; brooded by female; stay in nest 9–13 days, fed by both sexes. 2–3 broods per year.

Similar Birds

LONG-BILLED THRASHER
More brownish gray upperparts; darker streaking on creamy white underparts; 2 white wing bars; longer, more decurved bill; reddish orange eye; long gray-brown tail.

- **POPULATION** Common to fairly common. Rare in the Maritimes and in the West.
- **FEEDERS** Will sometimes tend feeders for raisins, suet, and bread.

Flight Pattern

Rather fast flight on shallow wing beats. Short flights are made with several rapid wing beats alternated with brief periods with wings pulled to sides; repeated.

Nest Identification	
Shape 🥣 Location 🪹 — 🌳 🔼	Sticks, grasses, and dried leaves, lined with fine grasses • in bush, on ground, or in low tree, usually 1–10 feet above ground • built by both sexes • 2–6 pale bluish white or white eggs, with pale brown specks, occasionally wreathed; oval to short oval, 0.1 x 0.8 inches.

Plumage Sexes similar	Habitat 🌾 🌳 🌲	Migration Migratory	Weight 2.4 ounces

DATE _____ TIME_____ LOCATION _____

Family MIMIDAE	Species *Toxostoma longirostre*	Length 11.5 inches	Wingspan 12.5–13.5 inches

LONG-BILLED THRASHER

This native of eastern Mexico and southern Texas is similar to the Brown Thrasher in habit and appearance, but it has a longer, more decurved bill. Its plumage is more gray, although the time of year and the extent of the bird's molt of the feathers also can affect color. Highly terrestrial, foraging on or near the ground, it flies to a high open perch to sing. This bird is most at home in the dense undergrowth of river-bottom forests but also is found in the cactus and mesquite of drier uplands.

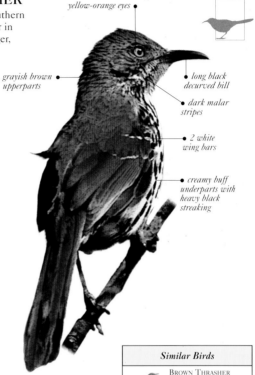

yellow-orange eyes

grayish brown upperparts

long black decurved bill

dark malar stripes

2 white wing bars

creamy buff underparts with heavy black streaking

• **SONG** Male perches to sing conversation-like phrases, similar to the Brown Thrasher, in doubles and triples. Various calls of *tsuck*, a soft *kleak*, and a bold flutelike *cheeooep*.

• **BEHAVIOR** Solitary or in pairs. Terrestrial. Somewhat shy, retreating when approached. Runs on ground; forages for food on ground and low in trees and shrubs. Often finds insects by digging in ground with bill. Eats mostly insects, small amphibians, and fruit. Maintains interspecific winter territories with Brown Thrasher when both are present.

• **BREEDING** Monogamous. Solitary.

• **NESTING** Incubation 13–14 days by both sexes. Altricial young brooded by female for just 2 days; leave nest at 12–14 days, fed by both sexes. 1–2 broods per year.

• **POPULATION** Common in brush and scrubland, bottomland willows, and dense forest habitat. Rare in western Texas. Accidental in New Mexico and Colorado.

• **CONSERVATION** Declining in southern Texas due to clearing of brushlands for development and agriculture. Common host to cowbird eggs.

Similar Birds
 **BROWN THRASHER** Shorter bill is not as decurved; more rusty brown upperparts; brown streaking on buffy underparts; white wing bars; long rufous-red tail; yellow eye.

Flight Pattern
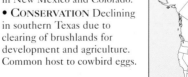
Long flights are relatively swift on rapidly beating wings. Shorter flights with several fast shallow wing strokes alternated with brief periods with wings pulled to sides.

Nest Identification	
Shape 🥄 Location 🌿 🌳	Prickly sticks, with lining of straw and soft grasses • in middle of shrub, bush, or small tree, 4–10 feet above ground • built by both sexes • 2–5 blue-green or greenish white eggs, speckled with reddish brown, occasionally wreathed; ovate to short oval, 1.1 x 0.8 inches.

Plumage Sexes similar	Habitat 🔺 🌳 🌿 ✈	Migration Nonmigratory	Weight 2.4 ounces

DATE _____ TIME_____ LOCATION _____

Family MIMIDAE	Species *Toxostoma curvirostre*	Length 11 inches	Wingspan 14 inches

CURVE-BILLED THRASHER

orange to yellow-orange eyes

long curved black bill

gray-brown upperparts

faintly spotted breast

buff-gray underparts

white- to gray-buff-tipped tail

Fond of water, the Curve-billed Thrasher is often observed in birdbaths, near dripping faucets, and near other water sources, which often are in scant supply in the desert and semiarid brushlands this bird inhabits, especially those with cholla cactus and mesquite. A nonmigratory bird, the Curve-billed Thrasher is a year-round resident that rarely wanders from its range, centered in the southwestern United States and Mexico. The most common of the desert thrashers, it displays a curved black bill, spotted underparts, buffy undertail coverts, and bright orange eyes in the adult. Some individuals have thin white wing bars. The westernmost race has indistinct spotting. Juveniles have straighter bills and yellow eyes.

• **SONG** Calls include a sharp *whit-wheet*, which sometimes includes 3 notes. Song is melodic, varied, and intricate, often with low trills and warbles, often with 2–3 repetitions of phrases.
• **BEHAVIOR** Solitary or in pairs. Terrestrial. Often conspicuous and noisy. Searches for insects by digging vigorously into the ground with bill. Also eats spiders, small reptiles, snails, fruits (especially cactus fruits), seeds, and berries. Mates remain paired throughout the year, often reusing the same nest. May build roosting platform in winter that becomes nest in spring.
• **BREEDING** Monogamous. Solitary.
• **NESTING** Incubation 12–15 days by both sexes, but mostly by female; female incubates at night and also trades off with male during the day. Young altricial; brooded by female (often to shade them from sun); remain in nest 11–18 days, fed by both sexes. 2 broods per year.

Similar Birds

BENDIRE'S THRASHER Smaller and more slender; shorter, less straight bill; yellow eyes; triangular or arrowhead-shaped markings on underparts; different call note.
• only in the West.

SAGE THRASHER Smaller; yellow eyes; short straight slender bill; whitish underparts; heavy brownish gray streaks on breast, sides, and flanks; 2 white wing bars; white-tipped outer tail feathers.

• **POPULATION** Common. Small declines in Texas but still abundant farther west. Casual in southeast California and north and east of its permanent range.
• **FEEDERS** Will come to water and to feeders with fruit.

Flight Pattern

Long flights are swift and direct on rapidly beating wings. Shorter flights are several rapid shallow wing beats followed by brief periods of wings at sides or short glide.

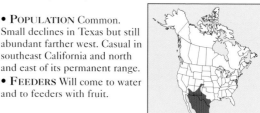

Nest Identification

Shape ❤ Location 🪹

Lined with fine materials, including twigs and grass • often found 2–8 feet above ground in shrub, cactus, or tree • built by both sexes • 1–5 pale blue-green eggs, with pale brown spots, rarely wreathed; ovate to short ovate or elliptical ovate, 1.2 x 0.8 inches.

Plumage Sexes similar	Habitat 🌳 ⚘ ⚘ ⚘	Migration Nonmigratory	Weight 2.8 ounces

DATE _____ TIME_____ LOCATION _____

Family MIMIDAE	Species *Toxostoma crissale*	Length 11.5 inches	Wingspan 13.5 inches

CRISSAL THRASHER

A common resident of southwestern deserts, the Crissal Thrasher is shy and stays hidden in dense underbrush. Like other thrashers, the male sings a musical varied song, often delivered from a high perch, concealed in vegetation. The common name refers to the crissal area or crissum, the rich chestnut undertail coverts, which helps distinguish this thrasher from other thrashers, along with the

straw-yellow eyes

long decurved black bill

olive-brown upperparts

blackish malar mark

grayish white throat

gray underparts without markings

rufous-chestnut crissum

straw-colored eyes, lack of chest spotting, and long decurved bill. Although primarily nonmigratory, some birds wander casually beyond mapped range in winter.

• **SONG** Call is a repeated *chideery*, a rich warbled *cheeoo-ree-eep*, or a *toit-toit-toit*. Song is varied and musical, often with phrases repeated 2–3 times. Does not mimic other birds.

• **BEHAVIOR** Solitary or in pairs. Secretive and terrestrial, running on ground and often staying in dense cover. Often works its way up through the interior of bushes. Diet is little studied, but eats insects, small lizards, spiders, fruits, and berries. Pairs often stay together throughout the year and remain on their territory. Discriminates between cowbird eggs and its own and ejects cowbird eggs from nest.

• **BREEDING** Monogamous. Solitary.

• **NESTING** Incubation 14 days by both sexes. Young altricial; brooded by female; stay in nest 11–13 days, fed by both sexes. 2 broods per year.

• **POPULATION** Fairly common in desert scrub, especially in washes, riparian brush, and mountain foothills and lower slopes to 6,000 feet.

• **CONSERVATION** Vulnerable to habitat loss due to development, agriculture, and grazing of livestock.

Similar Birds

CALIFORNIA THRASHER Larger; heavier bodied; darker olive-brown upperparts; darker cinnamon-brown underparts; cinnamon crissum; pale lores and supercilium; dark brown eye; black bill longer and more strongly decurved.

LE CONTE'S THRASHER Slender bodied; long, decurved black bill; dark brown eyes; pale gray-brown upperparts; pale whitish buff underparts; dusky black tail; tawny-ocher undertail coverts.

Flight Pattern

Longer flights are swift on rapidly beating wings; shorter flights alternate several quick shallow wing strokes and short glides.

Nest Identification

Shape ⬗ Location 🐾

Grass-lined with bark and other vegetation • 3–8 feet above ground in shrub, especially stands of mesquite or saltbush • built by both sexes • 1–4 blue-green eggs, unmarked; oval to long oval, 1.0 x. 0.8 inches.

Plumage Sexes similar	Habitat 🌱 🌿 🦅	Migration Nonmigratory	Weight 2.2 ounces

Family STURNIDAE	Species *Sturnus vulgaris*	Length 8.5 inches	Wingspan 15.5 inches

EUROPEAN STARLING

This chunky Eurasian species was introduced to North America in 1890 in New York City's Central Park and has become so well established that large flocks have in some cases become a nuisance, roosting in cities and towns from coast to coast and north into Canada to the tree line. Tenacious in nature, this bird competes with native species such as woodpeckers, flycatchers, and bluebirds for nesting holes. This bird's winter plumage shows white specks and its yellow bill becomes a dull gray. Juveniles are sooty gray-brown overall with pale streaking on the underparts and a dull brown bill.

buffy tips and edging to mantle feathers

short tail

long pointed yellow bill

black overall with iridescent sheen of green and purple

• **SONG** Sings various trilling melodies, clear whistles, clatters, and twitters in groups. Imitates songs of other birds, including Eastern Wood-Pewee and Northern Bobwhite, as well as mechanical sounds. Also has a flutelike *pheeEW*. Singing male often stands erect and flaps wings vigorously in display.

• **BEHAVIOR** Solitary or in pairs in breeding season. Juveniles form foraging flocks. Gregarious after breeding season, forming flocks with juveniles for foraging and roosting. Joins other species in winter roosts, which may number more than a million birds. Most often feeds in open areas, primarily on the ground. Eats various insects, fruits, and grains. The muscles that open its bill are stronger than those that close it, a unique trait that allows this bird to insert its bill in vegetation or into the ground and then pry it open to reveal food.

JUVENILE

• **BREEDING** Monogamous. Often forms loose colonies. Some individual males polygynous. Aggressive in claiming nesting chambers.

• **NESTING** Incubation 12–14 days by both sexes, but female does more. Young altricial; brooded by female; stay in nest 18–21 days, fed by both sexes. First flight at about 26 days. 2–3 broods per year.

• **POPULATION** Common. Stable over most of continent; perhaps still expanding range north and south.

• **FEEDERS AND BIRDHOUSES** Bread, peanut butter, suet, and small seeds. Uses bluebird-sized or larger nest boxes.

• **CONSERVATION** US laws do not protect nongame, non-native species.

Similar Birds
No native species of blackbird has yellow bill; short tail; chunky body; buffy streaking on back and wing coverts; and a notched tail.

Flight Pattern
Strong swift direct flight on rapidly beating wings.

Nest Identification	
Shape	Grass, twigs, forbs, rootlets, and straw • in natural hollow of tree, bird box, crevice in man-made structure, or abandoned woodpecker hole, 10–25 feet above ground (but up to 60 feet) • built by both sexes • 4–8 pale bluish or greenish white eggs, usually unmarked, but sometimes marked with browns; short oval to long oval, 1.2 x 0.8 inches.
Location	

Plumage Sexes similar	Habitat	Migration Northern birds migrate	Weight 3.0 ounces

DATE _____ TIME _____ LOCATION _____

Family MOTACILLIDAE	Species *Anthus rubescens*	Length 6.5 inches	Wingspan 10–11 inches

AMERICAN PIPIT

This sparrow-sized bird spends most of its time on the open ground, where it runs and walks, rather than hops. Like many of the pipits, the male has a dramatic song flight in which he flies to a height of fifty to two hundred feet then floats down with feet dangling below and tail cocked upward, all the while continuing to sing. The American Pipit's breeding ranges extend from alpine tundra in the high mountains of the western US to arctic tundra across the top of the continent. Winter birds have browner upperparts and they have more heavily streaked underparts.

slim blackish bill

grayish brown upperparts

buffy wing bars on dark gray wings

buff underparts with faint brown streaking

- **SONG** A repetitive rapid series of notes, *chee-chee-chee* or *cheedal-cheedal-cheedal*. Call sounds like *wit, wit* or *pip-pit* and is most often given in flight.

- **BEHAVIOR** Solitary or in pairs; gregarious after breeding season, forming flocks that may be very large and mixed with other species, including Horned Larks and longspurs. Walks on ground, often bobbing its head while pumping tail up and down or wagging it. Forages in foliage, grass, and soil. Also wades into shallow waters to pick food from surface. Eats insects and their larvae, seeds, small mollusks, and crustaceans. Alpine species may escape severe weather by moving down mountain slopes to warmer valleys.

white outer tail feathers

black legs and feet

- **BREEDING** Monogamous. Solitary nester. Male has courtship song flight.

- **NESTING** Incubation 13–15 days by female. Young altricial; brooded by female; stay in nest 13–15 days, when they can make short flight. Fed by both sexes. 1 brood per year.

- **POPULATION** Common and widespread in tundra and alpine tundra; in winter, in fields and on beaches.

- **CONSERVATION** Neotropical migrant. Vulnerable to habitat loss on wintering grounds as well as foraging areas used during migration.

Similar Birds

SPRAGUE'S PIPIT
Buff- and blackish-streaked upperparts; dark eye on pale buff face with pale eye ring; pinkish to yellow legs and feet; slender yellowish bill; white underparts with deeper buff on lightly streaked breast; does not pump tail.

Flight Pattern

Swift flight on series of rapidly beating wings, alternated with wings pulled to sides; repeated.

Nest Identification

Shape ~•~ 🥄   Location ▬ ✷✷✷

Often no nest materials; sometimes sticks and grass, occasionally with lining of small amount of mammal hair • sheltered by bank, rocks, or hillock • built by female • 3–7 grayish white eggs, with brown splotches; subelliptical, 0.8 x 0.6 inches.

Plumage Sexes similar	Habitat ⸜⸜ ▲ ⸜⸜ 〰	Migration Migratory	Weight 0.8 ounce

DATE _____ TIME_____ LOCATION _____

Family MOTACILLIDAE	Species *Anthus spragueii*	Length 6.5 inches	Wingspan 10–11 inches

SPRAGUE'S PIPIT

Because its plumage serves as camouflage in the prairie grasses, this bird is hard to spot. When frightened, it often chooses to run or freeze, rather than fly. Olive-tan upperparts are edged with buff on the coverts, flight feathers, and back, creating a scaly appearance. Dark eyes encircled by thin eye rings stand out in sharp contrast to a buffy face. In flight, white outer feathers are evident on the mostly black tail. Unlike the American Pipit, it does not bob or wag its tail when it walks.

buff- and black-streaked upperparts

dark eyes

thin pale bill

pale buff face

buff to whitish underparts with dark streaking

• **SONG** In display flight sings tinkling downward series of clear musical notes, *tzee, tzee-a*. Call is high-pitched *squeet-squeet-squeet*, mostly given in flight.

white outer tail feathers

creamy pink to yellowish feet and legs

• **BEHAVIOR** Solitary or in pairs; gregarious after breeding season, forming flocks, often with other species. Secretive. Walks and runs on ground as it forages in tall grasses and grain fields. Eats insects and seeds. When flushed, flies an extended erratic pattern before dropping back into the grasses. Female sits tightly on the nest; she often flies up to meet the male as he descends from his aerial courtship flight.

• **BREEDING** Monogamous. Solitary. Courting male flies in spirals as high as 500 feet, circles and sings, then closes his wings and falls earthward, opening his wings just above ground.

• **NESTING** Incubation unknown but estimated at 12–14 days by female. Altricial young brooded by female; stay in nest 10–11 days, fed by female. 1–2 broods per year.

• **POPULATION** Uncommon in short-grass prairies and grassy agricultural fields. Rare in fall and winter in California; accidental in East.

• **CONSERVATION** Neotropical migrant. Declining due to habitat loss on breeding and perhaps wintering ranges.

Similar Birds

AMERICAN PIPIT
Darker and grayer back without stripes; deeper buff breast; brown to black legs and feet; dark bill; buffy wing bars; dark grayish face; bobs and wags tail continuously.

VESPER SPARROW
Stockier; short conical bill; less extensive white on outer tail feathers; white-bordered dark ear patch; chestnut patch in bend of wing.

Flight Pattern

Swift flight on series of rapidly beating wing strokes, alternated with wings pulled in to body.

Nest Identification	
Shape 🐦 Location ▬ ★★★	Grasses • on ground, sometimes on grassy tussock • built by female • 4–6 pale buff or grayish white eggs, splotched with browns or gray, often with fine dark brown lines at larger end; subelliptical, 0.8 x 0.6 inches.

Plumage Sexes similar	Habitat ⚘	Migration Migratory	Weight 0.9 ounce

DATE _____ TIME_____ LOCATION _____

Family BOMBYCILLIDAE	Species *Bombycilla garrulus*	Length 8.25 inches	Wingspan 13–14 inches

BOHEMIAN WAXWING

True to its name, this bird is highly nomadic and travels in flocks over a wide range in search of abundant food sources, particularly berries, which make up its principal diet. In winter it often is attracted to berries and fruits produced by ornamental plantings in towns and residential areas, and flocks may appear as if from nowhere, lingering until the larder is stripped. Gray underparts with cinnamon undertail coverts distinguish it from the smaller Cedar Waxwing. Like that more widespread relative its tail is yellow tipped. In flight it shows a white patch at the base of the primaries. Juveniles have heavily streaked underparts and whitish throats.

long grayish cinnamon crest

narrow black mask with white lower border

grayish upperparts with more brown on the back and head

black chin

usually waxy red tips on secondaries

gray underparts

white markings on grayish wings with red and yellow borders

cinnamon undertail coverts

blackish gray tail with yellow trim

JUVENILE

• **SONG** While flying, utters continuous twittering and chatter. Call is an abrasive *scree* or *zirrrr*.

• **BEHAVIOR** In pairs or small groups during breeding season; gregarious rest of year, forming flocks. Usually feeds close to other birds on ground and in trees. Perches to spot insects, then hawks them in flight. Eats fruit, berries, and insects. Drinks sap. Very tame. Southward eruptions are unpredictable and varied, often tied to crashes in food sources in breeding range.

• **BREEDING** Monogamous. Colonial.

• **NESTING** Incubation 14–15 days by female. Young altricial; brooded by female; stay in nest 13–18 days, fed by both sexes. 1 brood per year.

• **POPULATION** Fairly common to uncommon in mixed conifer and open coniferous woodlands and muskeg; widespread in range during winter.

• **FEEDERS** Comes to feeders for dried fruits and berries.

• **CONSERVATION** Vulnerable to habitat loss due to logging in coniferous forests.

Similar Birds

CEDAR WAXWING Smaller; browner upperparts; yellow on belly; white undertail coverts; lacks yellow and white bars and spots on wings.

Flight Pattern

Strong rapid flight with a series of rapid wing beats alternating with wings pulled briefly to sides. Hawks for insects.

Nest Identification	
Shape ⌒ ⬤ Location 🪹	Sticks, lichen, stems, and grass; lined with mosses and fine materials • far out on horizontal limb, 4–50 feet above ground • built by both sexes • 2–6 pale bluish gray eggs, splotched and marked with black, especially at larger end; oval, 1.0 x 0.7 inches.

Plumage Sexes similar	Habitat 🌲🐾 🌳	Migration Migratory	Weight 2.0 ounces

DATE _____ TIME _____ LOCATION _____

Family BOMBYCILLIDAE	Species *Bombycilla cedrorum*	Length 7 inches	Wingspan 11–12.25 inches

CEDAR WAXWING

Named for the red waxlike tips on its secondaries, this social bird travels in large flocks in the nonbreeding season and may even nest in loose colonies. The purpose of the "red wax" is long-debated, but younger birds do not have it and the older birds do often choose each other as mates and produce more young than the younger pairs. At times this bird may become so intoxicated on overripe fruit that it cannot fly. Females are similar to males but show a brownish rather than a blackish throat (a difficult field mark that can be observed only at close range). Juveniles have streaked upperparts and underparts.

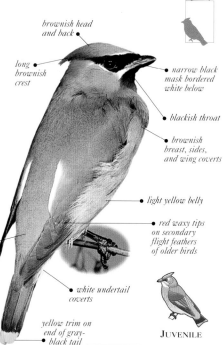

brownish head and back

long brownish crest

narrow black mask bordered white below

blackish throat

brownish breast, sides, and wing coverts

light yellow belly

red waxy tips on secondary flight feathers of older birds

gray rump and uppertail coverts

white undertail coverts

yellow trim on end of gray-black tail

JUVENILE

- **SONG** Call is thin, high-pitched warbled *zeeee* or *zeeeet*, more protracted just before leaving perch; may call constantly in flight.
- **BEHAVIOR** In pairs or in small to large flocks. Gregarious, especially in migration and winter. Tame and sociable. Feeds close to other birds in trees or on ground. Eats fruit, flower petals, and insects; drinks sap. Several may sit on a wire or branch and pass a piece of fruit back and forth, beak to beak. Hawks insects, particularly mayfly hatches and those of similar species, especially along streams.
- **BREEDING** Monogamous. Solitary to colonial. During courtship, male and female will sit together and pass flower petals back and forth, share food, and rub bills.
- **NESTING** Incubation 12–16 days by both sexes. Young altricial; brooded by female; stay in nest 14–18 days, fed by both sexes. 1–2 broods per year.
- **POPULATION** Fairly common to uncommon in woodland, forest edge, farmlands with fruit trees, towns, and suburbs.
- **FEEDERS** Raisins and berries; attracted to birdbaths.
- **CONSERVATION** Neotropical migrant. Not a common cowbird host; often rejects or damages its eggs.

Similar Birds

BOHEMIAN WAXWING
Larger; grayer; cinnamon undertail coverts; white and yellow spots and bars on wings; white bar at base of primaries on folded wing shows as white patch in flight.

Flight Pattern

Strong rapid flight with several quick wing strokes alternating with brief periods of wings pulled to sides.

Nest Identification

Shape  Location

Sticks, mosses, and grass, lined with fine grass, moss, rootlets, hair, and pine needles • on limb or in fork of conifer or deciduous tree, 6–60 feet above ground • built by both sexes • 2–6 pale bluish gray eggs, dotted with black and brown; oval, 0.8 x 0.6 inches.

Plumage Sexes similar	Habitat	Migration Migratory	Weight 1.1 ounces

DATE _____ TIME _____ LOCATION _____

Family PTILOGONATIDAE	Species *Phainopepla nitens*	Length 7.75 inches	Wingspan 11.5 inches

PHAINOPEPLA

This may be the only North American bird that nests in two different regions during the same breeding season. The early nest of the breeding season is usually in the desert. Then, as the desert warms with the season, the Phainopepla moves to a higher, more moist habitat and nests again. These highly nomadic birds survive by following the crops of mistletoe and other berries. The glossy black-crested males flash a white wing patch at the base of the primaries in flight; the slate-gray juveniles and females show a pale gray one.

- **SONG** Sings a short trilling somewhat liquid whistle of *tlee-oo-eee*, which is not often heard. Has mellow call of *whew* or *werp?*
- **BEHAVIOR** Solitary or in pairs or loose groups. Forages for food in trees, bushes, and, rarely, on ground. Catches insects in flight, similar to flycatcher. Eats mistletoe and various other berries; defends food trees and shrubs from other birds. Also eats spiders and flower petals. May hover over food and pick it up. Male has courtship display in which he flies 300 feet or so and zigzags or circles above his territory; sometimes other males join in above their own territories. Sometimes wanders beyond breeding range after nesting season.
- **BREEDING** Monogamous. Solitary or in small colonies.
- **NESTING** Incubation 14 days by both sexes. Young altricial; brooded by female; stay in nest 19–20 days, fed by both sexes. 1–2 broods per year.
- **POPULATION** Fairly common to common in desert scrub, mesquite brushland, and semiarid and riparian woodland and oak foothills. Accidental in the East.
- **CONSERVATION** Vulnerable to habitat loss due to development and agriculture, also cutting of mesquite for charcoal in Mexico.

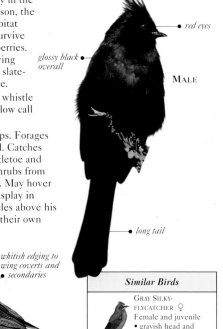

tall ragged crest on head

red eyes

glossy black overall

MALE

long tail

whitish edging to wing coverts and secondaries

slaty gray overall

FEMALE

Similar Birds

GRAY SILKY-FLYCATCHER ♀
Female and juvenile
- grayish head and breast; dusky gray upperparts; blackish gray wings and tail; gray uppertail coverts; dull gray-brown throat and underparts; whitish belly; yellowish undertail coverts.

Flight Pattern
Direct flight is high and fluttery, with shallow jerky wing strokes; sallies from perch to snatch insects in midair; returns.

Nest Identification	Sticks and plant down, bound with spider silk and lined with down and hair • in fork of tree or bush, often shaded by foliage, 4–50 feet above ground • mostly built by male, who may build several nests • 2–4 grayish eggs, dotted and splotched with browns and black; oval, 0.8 x 0.6 inches.
Shape Location	

Plumage Sexes differ	Habitat 	Migration Northern birds migrate	Weight 0.8 ounce

DATE _____ TIME_____ LOCATION _____

Family PARULIDAE	Species *Vermivora pinus*	Length 4.75 inches	Wingspan 6.75–7.5 inches

BLUE-WINGED WARBLER

Except when the male perches high to sing, this unobtrusive, deliberate bird usually forages low, amid brushy overgrown fields and thickets. It often interbreeds with the Golden-winged Warbler, producing the fertile hybrids known as Lawrence's Warbler and Brewster's Warbler. The female is similar to the male but duller in color and has less yellow on her crown. When its range overlaps that of the Golden-winged Warbler, it tends to displace it.

black eye line
olive-green upperparts
bold yellow crown
blue-gray wings with 2 white wing bars
yellowish to white undertail coverts and white underside of tail
long slim bill
bold yellow underparts

• **SONG** Sings a breathy descending *beeee-buzzzz*. A dry *buzz* followed by a lower *buzz* is the typical song. The alternate song sounds similar to that of the Golden-winged Warbler's *beee-buzz, buzz, buzz*. Call note is a sharp *tisk*.

• **BEHAVIOR** Solitary or in pairs. Somewhat tame, but also somewhat inconspicuous. Feeds low in trees and close to ground, often hanging upside down in the manner of a chickadee. Often probes into curled dead leaves with long bill. Eats insects and spiders. Sometimes hover gleans. More generalized in habitat requirements than Golden-winged Warbler, it lives in a wide variety of early successional stages from old fields to young clear-cuts to power line right-of-ways.

• **BREEDING** Monogamous. Solitary or small loose colonies.

• **NESTING** Incubation 10–12 days by female. Young altricial; brooded by female; stay in nest 8–11 days, fed by both sexes. 1–2 broods per year.

• **POPULATION** Uncommon to fairly common in second growth and early successional habitat. Expanding in northern and northeastern portions of range. Casual in West on migration.

• **CONSERVATION** Neotropical migrant. Host to cowbird parasitism. Decreasing in the Midwest due to habitat lost to agriculture.

Similar Birds

YELLOW WARBLER ♀
Female and juvenile • yellow wing bars, tail spots, and undertail coverts; lacks bluish wings, black eye stripe.

PROTHONOTARY WARBLER ♂
Golden yellow head, neck, and underparts; white undertail coverts; blue-gray wings and tail; large white tail patches; olive green back; long black bill; no wing bars or eyeline. ♀

BREWSTER'S WARBLER
Blue-winged/Golden-winged hybrid • yellow or whitish underparts tinged with yellow; whitish to yellowish wing bars.

Flight Pattern

Weak fluttering flight with wings briefly pulled to sides; repeated. Sometimes hovers to glean insects from foliage or branches.

Nest Identification

Shape ◗   Location ▬ ✳✳

Grasses, dried leaves, and bits of bark, with lining of fine grasses, vines, and hair • on ground, usually in vines or grasses and sheltered by shrub • built by female, perhaps aided by male • 4–7 white eggs, with flecks of brown and gray; oval to short oval, 0.6 x 0.49 inches.

Plumage Sexes similar	Habitat ▲ ≈ ♠	Migration Migratory	Weight 0.3 ounce

DATE _____ TIME_____ LOCATION _____

Family PARULIDAE	Species *Vermivora chrysoptera*	Length 4.75–5 inches	Wingspan 7.75–8.25 inches

GOLDEN-WINGED WARBLER

This bird feeds chickadee-style, often hanging upside down, to find its favorite food, leaf-eating caterpillars. Its combination of a yellow wing patch and a black throat sets it apart from other similar warblers. The female is similar to the male but is duller in color, and her throat and eye patch are gray. The Golden-winged Warbler hybridizes with the Blue-winged Warbler, producing two hybrid forms known as Brewster's Warbler and the very rare Lawrence's Warbler. The hybrids generally cross back with the parent species.

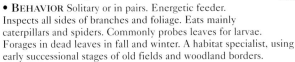

bright yellow crown

white supercilium

black patch through eyes

pearl gray upperparts

black throat

white malar mark

blackish wings

white underparts washed gray on flanks

BREWSTER'S WARBLER

blackish tail

- **SONG** Primary song is an insectlike *bee-buz-buz-buz*; gives second song of *bee-buzzz*, similar to that of Blue-winged Warbler.
- **BEHAVIOR** Solitary or in pairs. Energetic feeder. Inspects all sides of branches and foliage. Eats mainly caterpillars and spiders. Commonly probes leaves for larvae. Forages in dead leaves in fall and winter. A habitat specialist, using early successional stages of old fields and woodland borders.
- **BREEDING** Monogamous. Solitary nester.
- **NESTING** Incubation 10 days by female. Young altricial; brooded by female; stay in nest 9–10 days, fed by both sexes. 1 brood per year.
- **POPULATION** Uncommon to rare. Numbers are declining.
- **CONSERVATION** Neotropical migrant. Declining with loss of habitat primarily due to later stages of succession and to competition with increasing Blue-winged Warbler, which displaces it when ranges are sympatric. Vulnerable to nest parasitism by Brown-headed Cowbird.

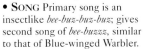

Flight Pattern
Weak fluttering flight with rapid wing beats, alternating with brief periods of wings drawn to sides; repeated.

Nest Identification	
Shape 🥄 Location ▬ ✶✶✶	Bark pieces and grass, lined with hair and a few bark chips • on ground at base of shrub or tree or hidden in tall grass; sometimes set on pile of stems • built by female • 4–7 white or cream-white eggs, with brown splotches and dots; oval to short oval; 0.7 x 0.5 inches.

Plumage Sexes similar	Habitat 🌾 ▲ 🍂	Migration Migratory	Weight 0.3 ounce

Family PARULIDAE	Species *Vermivora peregrina*	Length 4.75 inches	Wingspan 7.5–8 inches

TENNESSEE WARBLER

Despite its name, this short-tailed plump-bodied warbler nests almost entirely in Canada and is found in Tennessee only during migration. Fall adults and juveniles are similar to females but have a yellowish wash on the underparts, except for the undertail coverts, which are almost always white.

long straight bill

gray head

bold white stripe over eyes

bright olive-green upperparts

thin black eye line

short tail

grayish white underparts

white undertail coverts

MALE

pale yellow-tinged supercilium and auriculars

olive-gray crown, forehead, and nape

olive upperparts

grayish white face

grayish white underparts with pale yellow wash

FEMALE

FALL PLUMAGE

Similar Birds

ORANGE-CROWNED WARBLER Duller; often has streaking on throat and chest; less distinct face pattern; yellow or greenish yellow undertail coverts.

WARBLING VIREO Larger; heavier hooked bill; slower actions; duller and paler upperparts; indistinct pale arc beneath eye.

PHILADELPHIA VIREO Larger; indistinct pale arc below eye; heavier hooked bill; sluggish actions; duller, paler upperparts; yellowish undertail coverts.

• **SONG** Male sings often with a loud staccato 3-part song of *ticka-ticka-ticka-ticka*, *chip-chip-chip*, *sit-sit-sit-sit-sit-sita-sita-sita*; third part is faster and has a dry clattering similar to the twitter of Chimney Swift. Call is sharp *tsit*.

• **BEHAVIOR** Solitary when nesting; postbreeding birds form small groups, often in mixed-species flocks. Active, nervous. Creeps along branches, foraging at all levels. Eats mostly insects (especially spruce budworm), flower nectar, fruit, and some seeds. More active than similar vireos.

• **BREEDING** Monogamous. Solitary.

• **NESTING** Incubation 11–12 days by female. Altricial young brooded by female; stay in nest 9–11 days, fed by both sexes. 1 brood per year.

• **POPULATION** Fairly common; rising in coniferous and mixed deciduous-coniferous woodlands. Uncommon in West in fall. Rare in winter in California.

• **FEEDERS** Mixture of suet, peanut butter, and ripe banana.

• **CONSERVATION** Neotropical migrant. Rare cowbird host. Vulnerable to habitat loss.

Flight Pattern

Weak, somewhat fluttering flight with brief periods of wings pulled to sides.

Nest Identification

Shape 🍵

Location ━ ✸✸ ⑈ 🌿

Dried grasses and moss, with lining of fine grasses, stems, and hair • above bog in moss, on ground, or in base of shrub • built by female • 4–7 white or creamy white eggs, with brown splotches; ovate to short ovate, subelliptical to short subelliptical, 0.62 x 0.48 inches.

Plumage Sexes differ	Habitat 🐦 🐦 〰 〰	Migration Migratory	Weight 0.4 ounce

DATE _____ TIME_____ LOCATION _____

Family PARULIDAE	Species *Vermivora celata*	Length 4.75–5 inches	Wingspan 7–8 inches

ORANGE-CROWNED WARBLER

The brownish orange head patch for which this warbler is named is rarely noticeable unless the bird is frightened or agitated. It most often lives and nests in thick foliage close to the ground, but the male perches at the tops of tall trees to sing. Considerable color variation in this widely distributed species ranges from dull greenish birds in the East to brighter yellow birds in the West. The female

pale yellowish supercilium

indistinct dark eye line

thin slightly decurved bill

olive-green upperparts

faint streaking on sides of breast

small yellowish patch on marginal wing coverts

paler yellowish green underparts

yellow undertail coverts

sometimes lacks the crown patch. Juveniles are similar to adults but may show indistinct wing bars.

- **SONG** Male sings a high-pitched abrupt trill, which changes pitch toward the end, often slowing and dropping, *chip-ee, chip-ee, chip-ee*. Call note is a rough *stic*.
- **BEHAVIOR** Solitary. Vocal. Slow deliberate actions. Forages for food along branches and in foliage low in trees, shrubs, and grasses. Probes curled dead leaves. Eats mainly insects, flower nectar, and some fruits. Feeds from sapsucker drill wells. Hardy species, wintering farther north than most other warblers. Inquisitive; will respond to pishing and squeaking by birders.
- **BREEDING** Monogamous. Solitary.
- **NESTING** Incubation 12–14 days by female. Young altricial; brooded by female; stay in nest 8–10 days, fed by both sexes. 1 brood per year.

Similar Birds

YELLOW WARBLER ♀ Female and juvenile • pale edging to tertials, flight feathers, and wing coverts; yellow tail spots; dark eye on pale face.

NASHVILLE WARBLER Clear yellow underparts with no streaking; clear white eye ring; shorter tail.

TENNESSEE WARBLER Fall plumage • greener upperparts; shorter tail; unstreaked underparts; white undertail coverts.

- **POPULATION** Common in the West; rarer in the East.
- **FEEDERS** Mixture of peanut butter and suet. Also eats doughnuts.
- **CONSERVATION** Neotropical migrant. Rare cowbird host.

Flight Pattern

Somewhat weak flight with series of wing beats followed by brief period of wings pulled to sides.

Nest Identification

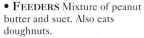

Shape ◗ Location ▬ ✦✦✦ ⟱

Bark pieces, grass, leaves, and plant fibers, with lining of hair, feathers, and grass • on ground, usually sheltered by shrub or grasses • built by female • 3–6 white eggs, with dark red and brown blotches; short ovate, 0.65 x 0.5 inches.

Plumage Sexes similar	Habitat	Migration Migratory	Weight 0.3 ounce

DATE _____ TIME_____ LOCATION _____

Family PARULIDAE	Species *Vermivora ruficapilla*	Length 4.75 inches	Wingspan 7.25–7.75 inches

NASHVILLE WARBLER

First collected while migrating near Nashville, Tennessee, this is the only North American warbler with a yellow throat, no wing bars, a white eye ring, and a blue-gray head. It also has a chestnut crown that is rarely noticeable. It has two breeding populations: one in the Pacific Coast states that often wags its tail, and another in northeastern and midwestern North America that does not wag its tail. The female is similar to the male but is duller in color and often lacks the chestnut crown.

white eye ring

blue-gray head

olive-green upperparts

bright yellow throat

yellowish underparts

white area between yellow belly and yellow undertail

- **SONG** High-pitched and loud, in 2 parts, *see-bit, see-bit, see-bit, titititititit* in the eastern birds, similar to that of the Tennessee Warbler. Western bird's songs begin the same way, but the second part is more musical, richer, and generally without the trill at the end. Call note is a sharp *pink*.
- **BEHAVIOR** Solitary. Frequent singer on territory. Sometimes gives song in flight. Sings from high exposed perch. Forages low in trees and in undergrowth for food, but often at the tips of branches or stems. Eats mostly insects.
- **BREEDING** Monogamous. Solitary.
- **NESTING** Incubation 11–12 days by both sexes; female does more. Young altricial; brooded by female; stay in nest 11 days, fed by both sexes but mostly by female. 1 brood per year.
- **POPULATION** Common to fairly common in riparian woodlands and bogs, deciduous or coniferous woodlands, and thickets.
- **CONSERVATION** Neotropical migrant. Rare cowbird host. Vulnerable to habitat loss.

Similar Birds

VIRGINIA'S WARBLER
Grayer overall; yellow underparts restricted to chest and undertail coverts; white eye ring; shorter tail • ranges do not overlap.

CONNECTICUT WARBLER
Larger; gray head; grayish throat; white eye ring; pink legs and feet; yellow underparts, including belly; sluggish behavior walking on limbs and on ground.

Flight Pattern

Rather weak flight with series of rapid wing strokes alternating with brief periods of wings pulled to sides.

Nest Identification	
Shape 🐦 Location ▬ ✱✱✱	Plant stems, pine needles, mosses, and rabbit fur, with lining of finer materials • on ground, sheltered by shrub or small tree, or sometimes placed on grassy or mossy tussock • built by female • 4–5 white or cream-white eggs, with fine dots of brown; ovate to short ovate, 0.6 x 0.47 inches.

Plumage Sexes similar	Habitat 🐦 🐦🐦 🔺 〰	Migration Migratory	Weight 0.3 ounce

DATE _____ TIME _____ LOCATION _____

| Family PARULIDAE | Species *Vermivora virginiae* | Length 4.5–4.75 inches | Wingspan 7.25–7.75 inches |

VIRGINIA'S WARBLER

This bird most often builds its nest in arid coniferous forests in mountains and chaparral between six thousand and nine thousand feet. It is named for the wife of Dr. William W. Anderson, an assistant army surgeon who first recorded the bird in New Mexico. It is closely related and very similar to the Nashville Warbler, although their ranges do not overlap. This shy and active warbler almost constantly bobs its tail up and down. Females are similar to males but have duller coloring, with both the rufous crown patch and the yellow breast patch being much reduced.

ashy gray head and upperparts

greenish yellow rump

bright lemon-yellow undertail coverts

white eye ring

yellow patch on breast

pale gray-buff underparts

JUVENILE

- **SONG** Sings a 2-part song of slurred notes, with first 2-syllabled part of *chee-wee, chee-wee, chee-wee, cheah, cheah, chee.* Call is a sharp abrasive *chink.*
- **BEHAVIOR** Solitary or in pairs. Rather shy and retiring. May join mixed-species foraging flocks after nesting season. Male often sings from high exposed perch. Forages in low trees, shrubs, and sometimes on ground. Eats mostly insects and their caterpillars. Gleans prey from branches and foliage and sometimes hover gleans. Catches some insects in flight.
- **BREEDING** Monogamous. Solitary nester.
- **NESTING** Breeding biology poorly known. Estimated incubation 11–12 days by both sexes, but mostly by female. Young altricial; brooded by female; stay in nest estimated 11 days, fed by both sexes. 2 broods per year.
- **POPULATION** Common in mountain brushlands with adjacent pines or oaks. Rare migrant and wintering bird to coastal California. Casual in the East during migration.
- **CONSERVATION** Neotropical migrant. Rare to uncommon host to cowbird parasitism. Some range expansion in California since the 1960s.

Similar Birds

LUCY'S WARBLER
Shorter tail; white underparts with white undertail coverts • male is smaller and has chestnut crown and rump • female and juvenile have cinnamon rumps.

COLIMA WARBLER
Larger; more brown on upperparts and flanks; brighter yellow rump; yellow undertail coverts.

Flight Pattern
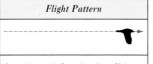
Somewhat weak fluttering direct flight on rapidly beating wings.

Nest Identification	
Shape ◣ Location ▬	Bark pieces, grasses, moss, lichens, and stems, with lining of same materials and hair • on ground, near grassy tussock or base of tree, or hidden in pile of leaves • built by female • 3–5 white eggs, flecked with brown; oval to short oval, 0.6 x 0.5 inches.

| Plumage Sexes differ | Habitat ▲ ⌁ ♣ | Migration Migratory | Weight 0.3 ounce |

DATE _____ TIME_____ LOCATION _____

Family PARULIDAE	Species *Vermivora crissalis*	Length 5.5 inches	Wingspan 8.5 inches

COLIMA WARBLER

This large warbler is a native of Mexico but has a breeding range in southwestern Texas and makes its summer home in the high mountain canyon oak forests of the Chisos Mountains in Big Bend National Park. This trusting bird is similar to Virginia's Warbler but is larger, longer tailed, has browner upperparts and underparts, and rarely bobs its tail. The female is similar to the male, and juveniles are similar to adults but have buffy wing bars, pale yellow uppertail coverts, and little or no rufous on the crown.

rufous crown

white eye ring

pale gray chin, throat, breast, and belly

grayish brown to olive-brown upperparts

brownish wash on sides of flanks and breast

bright yellow rump and uppertail coverts

bold tawny yellow undertail coverts

• **SONG** A high-pitched warbling staccato trill, with slight changes in pitch within each song, similar to that of the Orange-crowned Warbler. Has a sharp loud call of *plisst*. Males sing often throughout the day.

• **BEHAVIOR** Solitary or in pairs. Somewhat tame, allowing fairly close approach. Responsive to pishing by birders. Forages for food in trees, gleaning from branches, twigs, foliage, and flowers. Eats insects and their larvae. Occasionally catches insects in flight. Frequents moist mountain canyons above 6,000 feet with woodland overstory of oaks, juniper, piñon pines, and madrone.

• **BREEDING** Monogamous. Solitary nester.

• **NESTING** Breeding biology poorly known; virtually unstudied in the field. Estimated incubation is 10–12 days by both sexes. Young altricial; brooded by female; stay in nest estimated 11 days, fed by both sexes. 1 brood per year.

• **POPULATION** Common in limited US range and habitat in Chisos Mountains of Texas. Accidental in southeast Texas.

• **CONSERVATION** Neotropical migrant and habitat specialist. Vulnerable to habitat loss due to fire. Also vulnerable to habitat loss in Mexico from overgrazing and logging. US range is fully protected. Extent of cowbird parasitism unknown.

Similar Birds

VIRGINIA'S WARBLER Smaller; paler and grayer overall; large yellow breast patch; clear lemon-yellow undertail coverts; smaller rufous crown patch; lacks brown tones on upperparts, breast, and flanks.

Flight Pattern

Somewhat weak fluttering direct flight on rapidly beating wings.

Nest Identification	Dry leaves, dry grasses, pieces of bark, and moss, with lining of fur and hair • on ground, sheltered by grassy tussock, rocks, or stream bank • built by both sexes • 4 creamy white eggs, with brown wreath at larger end; oval, 0.72 x 0.53 inches.
Shape  Location ▬	

Plumage Sexes similar	Habitat ▲ ♠♦	Migration Migratory	Weight 0.4 ounce

DATE _____ TIME_____ LOCATION _____

Family PARULIDAE	Species *Vermivora luciae*	Length 4.25 inches	Wingspan 7 inches

LUCY'S WARBLER

Distinguished from similar birds by its reddish rump, Lucy's Warbler is the only wood warbler to nest in the desert of southwestern North America and the only western warbler to nest in crevices and tree cavities. It was named for the daughter of Spencer F. Baird, secretary of the Smithsonian Institution. A small pale plain gray bird, it is kinglet-sized and has a chestnut crown, chestnut uppertail coverts, and a habit of constantly bobbing its tail.

reddish brown patch on crown

pale ashy gray upperparts

white eye ring

whitish underparts

tawny to chestnut uppertail coverts

- **SONG** Sings a loud sweet persistent song of 2–3 parts on different pitches, *tea-tea-tee-tee-tee, wheat-wheat-wheat.* Call is sharp *chink.*
- **BEHAVIOR** Solitary or in pairs. After nesting season, forms small family groups and may join mixed-species foraging flocks. Active. Constantly on the move. Bobs tail habitually. Forages for food in foliage of trees, flowers, and shrubbery. Eats mostly insects and moths. Probes blossoms of cacti. Among North American warblers, only it and the Prothonotary are hole nesters.
- **BREEDING** Monogamous. Solitary nester.
- **NESTING** Breeding biology poorly known. Estimated incubation 10–12 days by both sexes. Young altricial; brooded by female; stay in nest estimated 10–11 days, fed by both sexes. 2 broods per year.
- **POPULATION** Fairly common in desert riparian thickets with willows and cottonwood and in stands of mesquite. Declining over much of range.
- **CONSERVATION** Declining due to clearing of riparian woodlands. Occasional host to cowbird parasitism. Neotropical migrant. Accidental in the East.

JUVENILE

Similar Birds

VIRGINIA'S WARBLER
Juvenile • larger; greenish yellow rump; yellowish undertail coverts; prominent white eye ring.

BELL'S VIREO
Larger; big-headed; white spectacles; 2 whitish wing bars; greenish gray cast to upperparts; also habitually bobs tail.

Flight Pattern
Rather weak fluttering direct flight on rapidly beating wings.

Nest Identification	
Shape ▨² ◨ Location ⚹ ❀ ▮	Pieces of bark, leaf stems, and weeds, lined with hair, fur, and fine bark chips • abandoned woodpecker holes, other birds' nests, or tree hollows • built by both sexes • 3–7 white to creamy white eggs, flecked with browns, usually concentrated at larger end; ovate to short ovate, 0.57 x 0.45 inches.

Plumage Sexes similar	Habitat ⚹ ⚹ ⚹ ↗	Migration Migratory	Weight 0.2 ounce

DATE _____ TIME_____ LOCATION _____

Family PARULIDAE	Species *Parula americana*	Length 4.25 inches	Wingspan 7 inches

NORTHERN PARULA

The male often can be heard singing its buzzy song during migration and from the tops of tall trees on its nesting ground. Nesting in the Deep South, it most often is associated with Spanish moss-covered trees, while more northern nests are in trees laced with the lichen *Usnea*. Both are important for construction of the nest. Females lack the chestnut/slate breast bands.

broken white eye ring

bold yellow chin, throat, and breast

bluish gray upperparts

chestnut and slate to blackish bands across upper breast

2 bold white wing bars

white belly and undertail coverts

short blue-gray tail with white spots in outer tail feathers

- **SONG** Ascending insectlike buzzy trill of *zeeeeeeee-yip*, which rises and trips over the top; the equivalent of the bird filling a cup with its song and running it over the rim. Secondary song is series of slow rising buzzy notes ending in a trill, reminiscent of the Cerulean Warbler. Regional variation; western birds often lack the abrupt downward ending note. Call note is a sharp *chip*.
- **BEHAVIOR** Solitary or in pairs. Allows close approach. Active, acrobatic forager; sometimes upside down to hunt for insects on trunk, cluster of leaves, or branch tip; hover gleans and hawks flying insects. Eats insects, caterpillars and larvae, and spiders. One of the smallest warblers, often dominated by other birds, including other warbler species.
- **BREEDING** Monogamous. Solitary.
- **NESTING** Incubation 12–14 days by both sexes; more by female. Altricial young brooded by and fed mostly by female. 1–2 broods per year.
- **POPULATION** Common in boreal forest, mixed hardwoods, bottomland forests, riparian corridors, and swamps. Rare in the West in migration.
- **CONSERVATION** Neotropical migrant. Rare cowbird host. Vulnerable to habitat loss due to logging, clearing of bottomland hardwoods for agriculture. Declining in Great Lakes region and on Atlantic Coast due to loss of *Usnea* lichen as a result of air pollutants.

Similar Birds

TROPICAL PARULA
More extensive yellow on underparts; orange wash on breast; lacks chestnut and gray-black chest bands; lacks white eye ring; often has dark mask.

Flight Pattern

Relatively swift flight of short duration on rapidly beating wings. Sallies forth to take insects in midair, returning to perch.

Nest Identification	
Shape ◗ ● Location 🪺 🌿	Lined with fine grasses, moss, and plant down • in Spanish moss, *Usnea* lichen, or tangled vine, hanging from tree, 0–55 feet above ground • built by female • 3–7 white to creamy white eggs, splotched and flecked with browns; subelliptical to short subelliptical, 0.64 x 0.47 inches.

Plumage Sexes differ	Habitat 🌳 🌿 🍂 〰️ 〰️	Migration Migratory	Weight 0.3 ounce

DATE _____ TIME_____ LOCATION _____

Family PARULIDAE	Species *Parula pitiayumi*	Length 4.5 inches	Wingspan 7 inches

TROPICAL PARULA

This warbler is a rare to uncommon nesting bird in southern Texas. It was more common along the lower Rio Grande before increasing development and intensified agriculture brought increased use of pesticides and clearing of riparian forests. It still can be found in thick riparian woods festooned with Spanish moss and bromeliads along the river, lagoons, and *resacas*. Its dark mask and lack of a white eye ring set it apart from its close relative, the Northern Parula. In flight it shows an olive-green patch on the center of its back and flanks often washed with cinnamon. Females are similar to males but show duller coloring and often lack the black mask. Although nonmigratory, some retreat from the northern part of the range in winter.

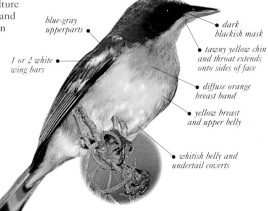

blue-gray upperparts

1 or 2 white wing bars

dark blackish mask

tawny yellow chin and throat extends onto sides of face

diffuse orange breast band

yellow breast and upper belly

whitish belly and undertail coverts

• **SONG** A buzzy insectlike trill of *zeeeee-yip* or *zzzzzzzzzirrr* and varied thin buzzy notes. Has a sharp call of *chik, chik*.

• **BEHAVIOR** Solitary or in pairs. Similar habits to Northern Parula. Forages in lower to middle levels of trees. Eats mostly insects and berries, which it gleans from branches and foliage. Sometimes hovers over food before dipping down to pick it off. Sallies forth from perch to hawk insects in flight. Frequents stands of trees with heavy growths of Spanish moss, which is important for nest construction and concealment.

• **BREEDING** Monogamous. Solitary.

• **NESTING** Incubation period and length of stay in nest undetermined. Altricial young brooded by female, fed by both sexes. 1–2 broods per year.

• **POPULATION** Uncommon in North America along lower Rio Grande Valley of Texas.

• **CONSERVATION** Neotropical migrant. Rare to casual north of the Rio Grande in Texas and adjacent Mexico; has declined significantly during 20th century due to habitat loss.

Similar Birds

NORTHERN PARULA
Dark chestnut breast band; less extensive yellow underparts not extended as far onto belly or sides of face; broken white eye ring.

CRESCENT-CHESTED WARBLER
White supercilium widens behind eye; lacks wing bars and crescent-shaped chestnut spot on chest • western range.

Flight Pattern	
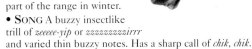	

Weak fluttering flight with brief periods of wings pulled to sides. Flies forth to snatch insects in flight, returning to perch.

Nest Identification	
Shape Location	Bits of bark, mosses, roots, grasses, and hair, with lining of plant down and feathers • set into pocket of Spanish moss or hanging vine, 8–40 feet above ground • sex of nest-builder undetermined • 3–4 white to creamy white eggs, usually wreathed at larger end; ovate to short ovate, 0.64 x 0.48 inches.

Plumage Sexes similar	Habitat	Migration Nonmigratory	Weight 0.1 ounce

DATE _____ TIME_____ LOCATION _____

Family PARULIDAE	Species *Dendroica petechia*	Length 5 inches	Wingspan 7.75 inches

YELLOW WARBLER

This plump-bodied bird has a wider range than any other North American warbler, nesting from Canada to Mexico and from the Pacific to the Atlantic Coasts. A habitat generalist, like many warblers, it feeds harmful leaf-eating caterpillars to its nestlings. When a cowbird invades and lays eggs in this warbler's nest, the female builds a roof over all of the eggs, both hers and the brood parasite's, and often lays a new set on the "new" nest floor. As many as six stories have been found in a single nest, each floor containing entombed cowbird eggs. Bright red streaking on the male's underparts distinguishes him from the female and all other North American warblers. Females may have faint reddish streaking on their underparts. Juveniles resemble adult females.

bright yellow head

dark eye contrasts with yellow face

short tail with yellow edging on feathers

yellowish overall

MALE

bright yellow underparts with reddish streaking

- **SONG** Sings a swift warbling *sweet-sweet, I'm-so-sweet* or *tseet-tseet-tseet-titi-deet*, bouncy and variable. Similar to some songs of Chestnut-sided Warbler and American Redstart.
- **BEHAVIOR** Solitary or in pairs. Tame and conspicuous. Active. Forages in bushes, shrubs, or trees. Gleans food from branches and foliage; sometimes hawks insects. Eats mostly insects, larvae, and some fruit.
- **BREEDING** Monogamous. Solitary.
- **NESTING** Incubation 11–12 days by female. Altricial young brooded by female; stay in nest 9–12 days, fed by both sexes. 1–2 broods per year.
- **POPULATION** Common and widespread in riparian thickets, second-growth woodlands, gardens, orchards, and wetlands.
- **CONSERVATION** Neotropical migrant. Common host to cowbird parasitism. Vulnerable to habitat loss, especially in riparian areas, and to herbicide spraying of willow thickets for grazing.

yellowish olive back, wings, and tail

yellow wing bars and edging

FEMALE

Similar Birds

WILSON'S WARBLER ♀
Female and juvenile • longer darker tail; lacks yellow tail spots; more uniform olive-green coloring on upperparts; no wing bars; female may show trace of dark cap.

ORANGE-CROWNED WARBLER
Olive-green overall; paler underparts with dusky streaking; uniform dark tail without pale edging or spots; lacks wing bars.

Flight Pattern
Weak, fluttering flight with brief periods of wings drawn to sides. Sallies out to snatch insects in air and returns to perch.

Nest Identification	
Shape 🥄 Location 🌳🌲	Strongly built from plant material, grasses, moss, lichen, and fur, bound with spider's silk and cocoon material; lined with fine materials • in fork of tree or bush, 6–14 feet high (but up to 60 feet) • built mostly by female; male watches • 3–6 grayish, green, or bluish white eggs, splotched with grays, olives, and browns, wreathed at large end; oval to short oval, 0.7 x 0.5 inches.

Plumage Sexes differ	Habitat 🐦 ▲ 🌱	Migration Migratory	Weight 0.3 ounce

DATE _____ TIME _____ LOCATION _____

Family PARULIDAE	Species *Dendroica pensylvanica*	Length 5–5.25 inches	Wingspan 7.5–8.25 inches

CHESTNUT-SIDED WARBLER

The only North American warbler with pure white underparts in all seasons, this bird most often lives in second-growth deciduous woodlands. An active feeder, it often cocks its tail high above its back, exposing a white crissum. Birds in fall plumage have a white eye ring on a gray face, a green crown, and creamy yellow wing bars; males have chestnut on the sides and black streaking on a green back.

light olive-green upperparts with black streaking

yellow crown

black lores and eye stripe

2 pale yellow wing bars

black malar mark

MALE

rich chestnut sides

slate-blue legs and feet

white underparts

- **SONG** High-pitched *please-please-pleased-to-meetcha.* Alternate or "second" song lacks strong up-and-down slurred notes at the end and is similar to that of the Yellow Warbler, *deet-deet-deet-titi-deet.* Call is a husky slurred *chip.*
- **BEHAVIOR** Solitary or in pairs. Tame and active. Singing male is conspicuous on territory. Eats insects, caterpillars, seeds, and berries. Picks food off leaves of trees and forages on ground. Catches insects in flight.
- **BREEDING** Monogamous. Solitary.
- **NESTING** Incubation 11–13 days by female. Altricial young brooded by female; remain in nest 10–12 days, fed by both sexes. 1–2 broods per year.

2 yellowish white wing bars

greenish upperparts with black streaking

yellow-green crown and forehead

FALL PLUMAGE

FEMALE

less chestnut on sides

blackish gray lores, malar, and postocular stripe

Similar Birds

All plumages are distinctive and if seen well are not likely to be confused with any other warbler.

- **POPULATION** Fairly common to common in brushy thickets, second-growth deciduous woodlands, brushy old fields, and young clear-cuts. Rare migrant in West.
- **CONSERVATION** Neotropical migrant. Vulnerable to habitat loss through natural succession processes. Rare in the early 1800s, but became increasingly common as eastern forests were cut, and brushy, early succession-stage woody habitats emerged. Declining in some areas as current forests mature.

Flight Pattern

Weak fluttering flight with brief periods of wings drawn to sides. Sallies forth to snatch insects in air, returning to perch.

Nest Identification

Shape   Location

Bark chips, vines, and plant material, with lining of animal hair and grasses • in fork of small tree or shrub, or in blackberry thicket, 1–4 feet above ground • built by female • 3–5 white to greenish white or creamy white eggs, with purple and brown blotches; oval to short oval, 0.66 x 0.5 inches.

Plumage Sexes differ	Habitat	Migration Migratory	Weight 0.4 ounce

DATE _____ TIME_____ LOCATION _____

Family PARULIDAE	Species *Dendroica magnolia*	Length 5 inches	Wingspan 7.75 inches

MAGNOLIA WARBLER

Often fanning its tail to show its broad white subterminal band and yellow rump, this bird nests in damp coniferous forests. The tail from below is white at the base with a black terminal band. From above, the white band is interrupted in the middle. Females are similar but show two white wing bars and sometimes a white eye ring during their first spring; a black loral mask may extend onto auriculars. Juveniles and fall-plumaged birds have gray heads with white eye rings, greenish gray upperparts with black streaking on the males, black streaking on the sides and flanks of males, and faint streaking on the flanks of females.

• **SONG** Brief high-pitched *wee-o, wee-o, wee-chew* or *weety-weety-weeteeo*, 2 or 3 slurred phrases with an ending note higher in pitch, emphatic and down-slurred. Call is distinctive nasal dry chip *tzek*.

• **BEHAVIOR** Solitary or in pairs. Tame and active. Males sing from conspicuous perches or while foraging. Often spreading tail, busily gleans insects from branches and foliage; occasionally hawks them in flight. Eats insects, larvae, caterpillars, and spiders.

• **BREEDING** Monogamous. Solitary.

• **NESTING** Incubation 11–13 days by female. Altricial young brooded by female; stay in nest 8–10 days, fed by both sexes. 1 brood per year.

• **POPULATION** Fairly common to common; slight decline in parts of Appalachians, increase in southern Appalachians and in New England. Casual in winter in Florida. Rare migrant in West.

• **CONSERVATION** Neotropical migrant. Vulnerable to habitat loss. The loss of eastern spruce-fir forests to adelgids and air pollution is causing a decline in numbers.

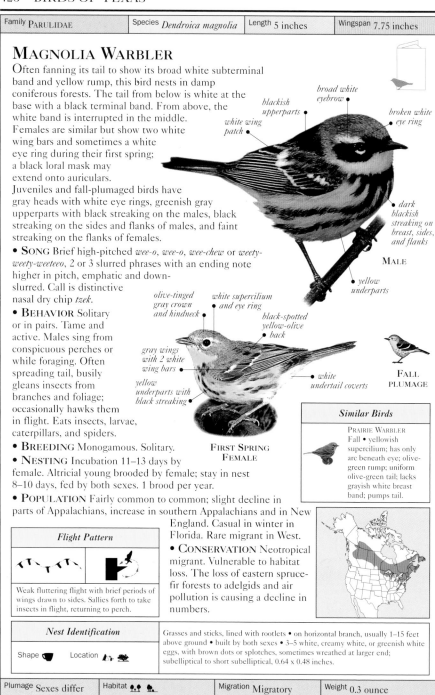

blackish upperparts
white wing patch
broad white eyebrow
broken white eye ring
dark blackish streaking on breast, sides, and flanks
MALE
yellow underparts

olive-tinged gray crown and hindneck
white supercilium and eye ring
black-spotted yellow-olive back
gray wings with 2 white wing bars
yellow underparts with black streaking
white undertail coverts
FALL PLUMAGE

FIRST SPRING FEMALE

Similar Birds

PRAIRIE WARBLER
Fall • yellowish supercilium; has only arc beneath eye; olive-green rump; uniform olive-green tail; lacks grayish white breast band; pumps tail.

Flight Pattern

Weak fluttering flight with brief periods of wings drawn to sides. Sallies forth to take insects in flight, returning to perch.

Nest Identification

Shape [icon]   Location [icons]

Grasses and sticks, lined with rootlets • on horizontal branch, usually 1–15 feet above ground • built by both sexes • 3–5 white, creamy white, or greenish white eggs, with brown dots or splotches, sometimes wreathed at larger end; subelliptical to short subelliptical, 0.64 x 0.48 inches.

Plumage Sexes differ	Habitat [icons]	Migration Migratory	Weight 0.3 ounce

DATE _____ TIME_____ LOCATION _____

Family PARULIDAE	Species *Dendroica tigrina*	Length 4.75 inches	Wingspan 7 inches

CAPE MAY WARBLER

Identifiable by its chestnut cheek patches, this bird is named after Cape May, New Jersey, where it was discovered in 1811. This fairly common inhabitant of northern spruce forests is known for its aggressive behavior of chasing other birds from treetop foraging areas. Females are duller but are easily identified by the yellow rump and patches on the side of the neck. Juveniles and fall-plumaged birds are similar to females, but many have faint gray streaking on pale yellow to whitish underparts.

blackish-streaked crown

olive-green upperparts with black stripes

large white wing patch

yellow on face and neck

chestnut cheek patch

heavily black-streaked yellow underparts

yellow or greenish rump

MALE

short tail

dark gray legs and feet

JUVENILE FEMALE

- **SONG** Sounds like *seet seet seet seet*, high-pitched, wiry, and upslurred, usually in series of 5–6 notes. Call is high thin *seet*.

- **BEHAVIOR** Solitary or in pairs. Forages in thickets or high in trees, particularly in conifers on breeding grounds. Hawks insects and spruce budworms. Sometimes drinks tree sap, juice from grapes, and flower nectar.

dusky gray postocular stripe

pale yellow patch on neck behind auriculars

yellow supercilium

dull olive-green upperparts

yellowish throat, breast, and sides with dusky streaking

2 narrow white wing bars

FEMALE

Similar Birds

YELLOW-RUMPED WARBLER ♀
Larger; browner upperparts; coarse dusky streaks on underparts; yellow patch on sides of chest; yellow rump; lacks yellow on neck; distinct facial pattern; longer tail; *chip* or *check* notes distinctive.

PALM WARBLER
Fall • distinct pale supercilium; yellow undertail coverts; usually found at ground level; wags tail.

- **BREEDING** Monogamous. Solitary.

- **NESTING** Breeding biology poorly known. Incubation about 11–13 days by female. Altricial young brooded by female; fed by both sexes; stay in nest estimated 10–12 days. 1 brood per year.

- **POPULATION** Uncommon in spruce fir forests; may become locally common during spruce budworm outbreaks. Declining short-term populations. Very rare to casual in West during migration.

- **CONSERVATION** Neotropical migrant. Vulnerable to loss of breeding and wintering grounds due to deforestation and forest fragmentation.

Flight Pattern
Weak fluttering flight with brief periods of wings pulled to sides; sometimes sallies from perch to take insects in flight.

Nest Identification	
Shape Location	Thickly lined with fine materials, including moss, vines, and weed stalks • 30–60 feet above ground on branch of spruce or fir • built by female • 6–9 creamy white eggs, with gray or brown spots; ovate to short ovate, 0.66 x 0.5 inches.

Plumage Sexes differ	Habitat	Migration Migratory	Weight 0.4 ounce

DATE _____ TIME_____ LOCATION _____

Family PARULIDAE	Species *Dendroica caerulescens*	Length 5.25 inches	Wingspan 7–7.5 inches

BLACK-THROATED BLUE WARBLER

Easily identified by its deep blue-gray back, white underparts, and white wing patch, this common migratory bird can be seen across eastern North America every spring and fall. Its nesting ranges from southern Canada through the Appalachians to northern Georgia. Females differ from their mates more than any of the wood warblers, with brownish olive to gray upperparts, whitish supercilium, and small white patch at the base of the primaries. Juvenile females sometimes lack the white patch.

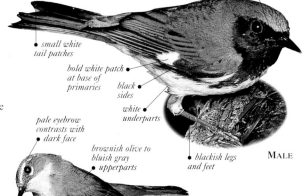

dark blue-gray upperparts

black lores, cheeks, chin, and throat

small white tail patches

bold white patch at base of primaries

black sides

white underparts

blackish legs and feet

MALE

pale eyebrow contrasts with dark face

brownish olive to bluish gray upperparts

buff underparts

smaller white wing patch

FEMALE

- **SONG** A breathy buzzy *zwee-zwee-zwee-zweeeee,* "*I am lazy,*" or *zur-zurr-zree.* Call is abrasive *dit.*
- **BEHAVIOR** Solitary or in pairs. Tame and trusting. Forages in low and middle level trees and underbrush. Sometimes hawks insects in flight. Eats insects and their larvae. In migration and winter, also takes fruit and seeds and may feed from sapsucker drill wells.
- **BREEDING** Monogamous. Solitary nester.
- **NESTING** Incubation 12–13 days by female. Young altricial; brooded by female; stay in nest 1–12 days, fed by both sexes. 1 brood per year.
- **POPULATION** Common in deciduous and mixed coniferous forests with dense undergrowth, rhododendron thickets, and bogs, often on mountain slopes. Western vagrant in migration. Uncommon in winter in Florida.
- **FEEDERS** Suet and peanut butter in migration and winter.
- **CONSERVATION** Neotropical migrant. Uncommon host to cowbird parasitism. Vulnerable to habitat loss due to deforestation.

Similar Birds

 TENNESSEE WARBLER ♀ Unbroken whitish supercilium; lacks white wing patch; bright greenish olive back; grayish white underparts with white crissum; short tail.

 ORANGE-CROWNED WARBLER Yellow to greenish olive upperparts; yellow-green underparts; yellowish crissum; indistinct supercilium.

Flight Pattern

Relatively weak flight with series of rapid wing beats alternating with brief periods of wings pulled to sides. Sallies from perch to snatch insect in air; returns to perch.

Nest Identification

Shape   Location

Bark pieces, dried grasses, stems, and leaves, with lining of fur, hair, mosses, and rootlets • built by both sexes • 0.5–3 feet above ground • 3–5 white to creamy white eggs, flecked or marked with grays and browns; ovate to short ovate, rarely tending to elongate ovate, 0.66 x 0.5 inches.

Plumage Sexes differ	Habitat	Migration Migratory	Weight 0.4 ounce

DATE _____ TIME_____ LOCATION _____

Family PARULIDAE	Species *Dendroica coronata*	Length 5.5 inches	Wingspan 8.5 inches

YELLOW-RUMPED WARBLER

In the East this is the most prevalent migrating warbler, and in winter it is the most abundant in North America. Plumage varies with geography. In the West the group known as Audubon's Warbler has a yellow throat and broken white eye ring. The northern and eastern group known as the Myrtle Warbler has white eyebrows, a white arc beneath the eye, and white on the throat and both sides of the neck. Until recently these groups were considered two species, but they interbreed where their ranges overlap and have been classified as geographic races of one species. Juveniles are similar to winter adults.

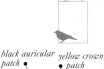

gray upperparts
2 white wing bars
black auricular patch
yellow crown patch
black streaking on breast, sides, and flanks
yellow rump

MALE MYRTLE WARBLER

white underparts

- **SONG** Variable slow warble that often slows in the middle then speeds up and ends on rising or falling notes. Some have musical trill. Call is loud *check, chup,* or *chip.*

black-streaked gray-brown upperparts
gray-brown wings
white arc below eye

FEMALE MYRTLE WARBLER

white underparts with gray streaks on breast and sides

yellow side patches

AUDUBON'S BREEDING MALE

WINTER PLUMAGE   **FALL MYRTLE**

- **BEHAVIOR** Solitary or in pairs. Gregarious in winter, often joins mixed feeding flocks. Gleans or hover-gleans on ground and in bushes and trees; also hawks. Able to live for long periods on berries and seeds. Also eats insects and spiders, and drinks tree sap and juice from fallen oranges.
- **BREEDING** Monogamous. Solitary.
- **NESTING** Incubation 12–13 days by female. Altricial young brooded by female; stay in nest 10–12 days, fed by both sexes. 2 broods per year.
- **POPULATION** Abundant in coniferous or mixed forests; wooded and brushy habitats in winter. In winter Myrtle form common in East, fairly common on West Coast; Audubon's form casual in East in winter.
- **FEEDERS** Suet, doughnuts, and peanut butter.
- **CONSERVATION** Neotropical migrant. Myrtles are common cowbird hosts.

Similar Birds
PALM WARBLER Juvenile • yellow undertail coverts; white spots in tail corners; pumps tail.
CAPE MAY WARBLER Juvenile • smaller; yellow on sides of neck; shorter tail; dull green rump; pale yellow wash on center of breast.

Flight Pattern

Fairly rapid flight with quick wing strokes, alternating with brief periods of wings pulled to sides. Sallies forth and takes insects in flight, returning to perch.

Nest Identification

Shape   Location

Shredded bark, weed stalks, twigs, and roots, lined with feathers • 4–50 feet above ground in conifer • built by female • 3–5 white to creamy eggs, with brown and gray markings, occasionally wreathed; oval to short oval, 0.7 x 0.53 inches.

Plumage Sexes differ	Habitat	Migration Migratory	Weight 0.5 ounce

DATE _____ TIME_____ LOCATION _____

Family PARULIDAE	Species *Dendroica nigrescens*	Length 4.75–5 inches	Wingspan 7.5–8 inches

BLACK-THROATED GRAY WARBLER

Its streaked plumage serves as camouflage in the coniferous forests and scrub-oak woodlands where this bird makes its home. The female is similar to the male but has a white throat and shows mostly gray coloring where the male bird shows black. Its pattern is very similar to that of a Townsend's Warbler but with the grays replaced by yellow-greens and the whites by yellow. The only yellow in the plumage of this bird is the small dot on the supralorals.

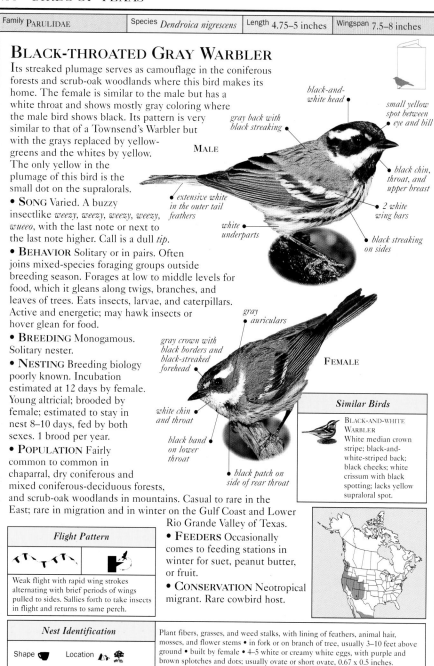

MALE

- black-and-white head
- small yellow spot between eye and bill
- gray back with black streaking
- black chin, throat, and upper breast
- extensive white in the outer tail feathers
- 2 white wing bars
- white underparts
- black streaking on sides

- **SONG** Varied. A buzzy insectlike *weezy, weezy, weezy, weezy, wueeo*, with the last note or next to the last note higher. Call is a dull *tip*.
- **BEHAVIOR** Solitary or in pairs. Often joins mixed-species foraging groups outside breeding season. Forages at low to middle levels for food, which it gleans along twigs, branches, and leaves of trees. Eats insects, larvae, and caterpillars. Active and energetic; may hawk insects or hover glean for food.
- **BREEDING** Monogamous. Solitary nester.
- **NESTING** Breeding biology poorly known. Incubation estimated at 12 days by female. Young altricial; brooded by female; estimated to stay in nest 8–10 days, fed by both sexes. 1 brood per year.
- **POPULATION** Fairly common to common in chaparral, dry coniferous and mixed coniferous-deciduous forests, and scrub-oak woodlands in mountains. Casual to rare in the East; rare in migration and in winter on the Gulf Coast and Lower Rio Grande Valley of Texas.
- **FEEDERS** Occasionally comes to feeding stations in winter for suet, peanut butter, or fruit.
- **CONSERVATION** Neotropical migrant. Rare cowbird host.

- gray auriculars
- gray crown with black borders and black-streaked forehead
- **FEMALE**
- white chin and throat
- black band on lower throat
- black patch on side of rear throat

Similar Birds

BLACK-AND-WHITE WARBLER
White median crown stripe; black-and-white-striped back; black cheeks; white crissum with black spotting; lacks yellow supraloral spot.

Flight Pattern

Weak flight with rapid wing strokes alternating with brief periods of wings pulled to sides. Sallies forth to take insects in flight and returns to same perch.

Nest Identification

Shape 🥄   Location 🌿🕊

Plant fibers, grasses, and weed stalks, with lining of feathers, animal hair, mosses, and flower stems • in fork or on branch of tree, usually 3–10 feet above ground • built by female • 4–5 white or creamy white eggs, with purple and brown splotches and dots; usually ovate or short ovate, 0.67 x 0.5 inches.

Plumage Sexes differ	Habitat 🌿 🌾 ✦	Migration Migratory	Weight 0.3 ounce

Family PARULIDAE	Species *Dendroica chrysoparia*	Length 4.75–5 inches	Wingspan 7.5–8 inches

GOLDEN-CHEEKED WARBLER

Now endangered, this habitat specialist of "cedar breaks," Ashe juniper and oaks, breeds only on or near the Edwards Plateau in Texas and winters in Mexico and Central America. From the mature Ashe juniper the female strips bark and binds it with spider webs to camouflage the outside of its nest. The male sings sunrise to sunset from high conspicuous perches on its nesting territory. Females have white throats and underparts. Juveniles have olive upperparts streaked with black and streaked sides to their throats.

black crown

golden cheeks with black outline

black eye line

black upperparts

2 white wing bars

black bib, throat, and chin

black streaking on sides

white underparts

MALE

• **SONG** 4–5 harsh buzzy notes, *bzzz-layzee-dayzee* or *tweeah-tweeah-tweesy*. Call is *tip*.

• **BEHAVIOR** Solitary or in pairs. Clings chickadee-like under branches as it forages. Gleans food from foliage, stems, and twigs. Eats mostly insects. Feeds at heights of 30 feet or less, hunting in middle to lower levels. Outside breeding season joins mixed foraging flocks. Returns to breeding grounds in mid-March and males begin territorial songs.

• **BREEDING** Monogamous and solitary.

• **NESTING** Incubation 12 days by female. Young altricial; brooded by female; stay in nest 9 days, fed by both sexes. 1 brood per year.

• **POPULATION** Rare; limited to hill country of central Texas.

2 white wing bars

dark olive-green upperparts and crown with black streaking

blackish eye line

light golden cheeks without outline

black streaks on sides

streaky blackish bib

FEMALE

Similar Birds

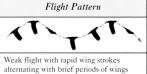

BLACK-THROATED GREEN WARBLER ♀ Juvenile female • olive cap; unstreaked olive-green upperparts; olive auricular patch; greenish olive rump.

• **CONSERVATION** Federally endangered. One of the rarest songbirds in North America. Vulnerable to Blue Jay predation, cowbird parasitism, and habitat destruction. Neotropical migrant.

Flight Pattern

Weak flight with rapid wing strokes alternating with brief periods of wings pulled to sides.

Nest Identification

Shape   Location

Bark pieces, grasses, spider's silk, and rootlets, with lining of feathers and hair • in fork of tree, usually 15–20 feet above ground • built by female • 3–5 white to creamy white eggs, with brown and gray dots and flecks; generally ovate to short ovate, 0.75 x 0.5 inches.

Plumage Sexes differ	Habitat	Migration Migratory	Weight 0.4 ounce

DATE _____ TIME_____ LOCATION _____

Family PARULIDAE	Species *Dendroica virens*	Length 4.75–5 inches	Wingspan 7.5–8 inches

BLACK-THROATED GREEN WARBLER

Like many in its family, the individual Black-throated Green Warbler sings two different songs, but in two different contexts: one in the vicinity of the female or nest and the other near the territorial boundaries or when stimulated by another male. It is the only warbler in eastern North America with bold yellow cheeks. The female is similar to the male but shows fewer black streaks on the sides of her body, less black on her throat, and has a yellowish chin and upper throat. The juvenile is similar to the female but has a white throat and lacks the black on its breast.

olive-green auricular patch

yellow- and olive-green upperparts with black streaking on back

MALE

bright yellow forehead and sides of face

black chin, throat, and upper breast

white underparts

yellow wash on flanks

2 white wing bars

black streaking on flanks and sides

FEMALE

yellowish chin

black throat veiled with whitish feather tips

- **SONG** A throaty *trees-trees-whispering-trees* (the territorial/male interaction song) and a hoarse *zay-zay-zay-zoo-zeee* (the pair bonding/nest vicinity song). Call is a flat soft *tsip*.
- **BEHAVIOR** Solitary or in pairs. Forages at mid-level in vegetation and in the interior of branches, usually not at the tips. Gleans from twigs and foliage; hover-gleans and may hawk flying prey. Eats adult insects, caterpillars, larvae, and some berries, particularly in migration.
- **BREEDING** Monogamous. Solitary.
- **NESTING** Incubation 12 days by female. Young altricial; brooded by female; remain in nest 8–10 days, fed by both sexes, but female does more. 1–2 broods per year.
- **POPULATION** Fairly common in a variety of habitats of conifer, mixed deciduous-conifer, and deciduous woodlands. Some winter regularly in southern Florida; casual to accidental in the West. Numbers decreasing in the Great Lakes areas and in parts of New England.
- **CONSERVATION** Neotropical migrant. Vulnerable to habitat loss. Rare host to cowbird parasitism.

Similar Birds

GOLDEN-CHEEKED WARBLER
Gray to black upperparts with black streaking; black or black-streaked crown; yellow face; black eye line connected to the dark color of nape; black ear patch; white crissum • restricted range in Texas.

Flight Pattern

Somewhat weak flight with rapid wing strokes, alternating with brief periods of wings pulled to sides. Sallies from perch, takes insect in air, and returns to perch.

Nest Identification	
Shape Location	Dead grasses, plant fibers, and stems, with lining of animal hair, flower stems, and feathers • usually in crotch of small or large evergreen or in hardwood tree on horizontal branch, 3–80 feet above ground • built by both sexes • 3–5 gray-white or creamy white eggs, with brown and purple dots and blotches, often wreathed; oval to short oval, 0.65 x 0.5 inches.

Plumage Sexes differ	Habitat	Migration Migratory	Weight 0.3 ounce

DATE _____ TIME_____ LOCATION _____

Family PARULIDAE	Species *Dendroica townsendi*	Length 4.75–5 inches	Wingspan 7.5–8 inches

TOWNSEND'S WARBLER

The western counterpart of the Black-throated Green Warbler nests in high pines and spruces of the Pacific Northwest. The bright yellow underparts and yellow face with black cheek patch are difficult to see because the bird forages and sings in the tops of the mature conifers. Townsend's Warbler often hybridizes with the Hermit Warbler where ranges overlap.

- **SONG** Variable. Raspy high *weezy, weezy, weezy, tweea*, rising in pitch but dropping at the end. Call is high sharp *tsik*.
- **BEHAVIOR** Solitary or in pairs. Gregarious after breeding season; joins mixed-species foraging flocks. Aggressive toward other species. Sometimes hover-gleans from branches and foliage. Eats insects, caterpillars, and spiders.
- **BREEDING** Monogamous. Solitary.
- **NESTING** Breeding biology poorly known. Incubation estimated at 12 days by female. Altricial young brooded by female; stay in nest estimated 8–12 days. Fed by both sexes; female may do more. 1 brood per year.
- **POPULATION** Fairly common in coniferous and mixed coniferous-deciduous forests. Casual to accidental in winter and in migration in the East. May be increasing slightly and expanding range southward in Washington and Oregon.
- **FEEDERS** Mixture of peanut butter, marshmallows, and cheese.
- **CONSERVATION** Neotropical migrant. Degree of cowbird parasitism unknown. Subject to forest fragmentation by logging.

blackish ear patch with wide yellow trim
olive-green upperparts with black streaks
dark blackish crown
2 white wing bars
black chin, throat, and upper breast
white in outer 2–3 tail feathers
yellow breast
white belly
yellowish sides with black streaking

MALE

olive crown with black streaking
narrow black streaking on back
2 thin white wing bars
yellow chin and throat
olive cheeks
necklace of black streaks on lower throat
thin black streaks on sides and flanks

FEMALE

Similar Birds

BLACK-THROATED GREEN WARBLER ♂
Yellow cheeks and face without dark ear patches; whitish chest; olive back with black streaking; yellowish wash on undertail coverts • eastern breeding range has almost no overlap. ♀

HERMIT WARBLER ♂
Lacks black cheeks and crown; yellow restricted to breast and sides; fine black streaking on sides and flanks. ♀

Flight Pattern

Relatively weak flight on rapidly beating wings, alternating with brief periods of wings pulled to sides.

Nest Identification

Shape ◄ Location ⬧

Bark pieces, plant fibers, lichens, grasses, and cocoon materials, with lining of feathers and animal hair • across limb of conifer, high above ground • built by both sexes • 3–5 white eggs, with fine dots of brown; short ovate, 0.7 x 0.5 inches.

Plumage Sexes differ	Habitat 🌲 🐾	Migration Migratory	Weight 0.3 ounce

DATE _____ TIME _____ LOCATION _____

Family PARULIDAE	Species *Dendroica occidentalis*	Length 5 inches	Wingspan 7.75 inches

HERMIT WARBLER

This bird is difficult to spot because it spends its time in the tops of tall fir and pine trees. It exhibits a marked partiality to conifers when foraging and nesting. Sometimes it can be drawn into the open when it hears a call or imitation of the Saw-whet Owl. This warbler generally has gray upperparts and white underparts with a brilliant yellow face. Males have a black throat. Females are similar to males but have a yellow chin and little or no black on the throat. Juveniles are similar to females; juvenile females have more olive to the upperparts.

slate-gray upperparts with black streaking

black nape with dark markings extending onto crown

yellow head

MALE

white outer tail feathers

faint streaking on sides

white underparts

black chin and throat

2 white wing bars

gray upperparts tinged olive

yellow face and chin

gray tail with white corners

varying degrees of black on throat

FEMALE

2 white wing bars

white underparts

- **SONG** Highly variable. A vibrant high *wheezy seadle, seadle, seadle, zeet-zeet*. Call is a flat *tsik* or *chip*.
- **BEHAVIOR** Solitary or in pairs. Territorial birds sing high up in conifers. Forages for food in high and mid-level branches of trees. Acrobatic, clinging upside down to pick insects off undersides of twigs. Eats adult insects, caterpillars, and spiders, which it gleans from branches and foliage; hover-gleans and sometimes hawks insects in midair. Sometimes hybridizes with Townsend's Warbler.
- **BREEDING** Monogamous. Solitary nester.
- **NESTING** Estimated incubation 12 days by both sexes. Young altricial; brooded by female; stay in nest estimated 8–10 days, fed by both sexes. 1–2 broods per year.
- **POPULATION** Fairly common. Stable in coniferous forests, especially in mountains. Casual in the East in migration.
- **CONSERVATION** Neotropical migrant. Infrequent cowbird host. May be displaced by Townsend's Warbler when both are sympatric. Vulnerable to habitat loss due to logging.

Similar Birds

♂ TOWNSEND'S WARBLER Black to dusky ear patches outlined by yellow face; black streaking on breast, sides, and flanks; more blackish crown; olive back with black streaking; olive rump; yellow breast.

♀

Flight Pattern

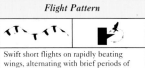

Swift short flights on rapidly beating wings, alternating with brief periods of wings pulled to sides. Hawks flying insects, returning to perch.

Nest Identification	Sticks, plant material, stems, and lichen, with lining of hair, feathers, fine plant stems, and bark pieces • on limb, usually 15–120 feet above ground • built by female • 3–5 white eggs, with red, brown, and lilac blotches, wreathed at larger end; ovate to short ovate, 0.66 x 0.51 inches.
Shape 🥚 Location 🌿	

Plumage Sexes differ	Habitat 🌳 🌿	Migration Migratory	Weight 0.3 ounce

DATE _____ TIME _____ LOCATION _____

| Family PARULIDAE | Species *Dendroica fusca* | Length 5 inches | Wingspan 8 inches |

BLACKBURNIAN WARBLER

Head and throat glowing like embers, the males are unmistakable. Juveniles and fall males are similar. It frequents coniferous or mixed deciduous-conifer forests in most of its breeding range; in the Appalachians, it is also found in lower drier forests of pine-oak-hickory.

brilliant orange head, throat, and upper breast

black nape and sides of crown

black triangular ear patch

MALE

black back with white streaking

white breast with pale ocher wash

black wings with large white patches

black streaking on sides

buff-white belly, flanks, and undertail coverts

- **SONG** Thin high-pitched ascending trill in 2–3 parts, ending with upslurred note that some people cannot hear: *seep seep seep seep titi zeeeeee*. Call is rich *tsip*.
- **BEHAVIOR** Solitary or in pairs. May join mixed foraging flocks after breeding. Gleans prey from branches, twigs, and foliage in treetops. Sometimes catches insects in flight. Eats insects, caterpillars, and some berries.

white patches in outer tail feathers

dark gray-olive upperparts

JUVENILE

pale orange-ocher supercilium and sides of head behind ear patch

FEMALE

pale orange to ocher throat and upper breast

2 broad white wing bars

white underparts with black streaks on sides and flanks

Similar Birds

TOWNSEND'S WARBLER
Juvenile female
- yellow throat and chest; olive crown and upperparts; entirely dark bill; more distinct dark streaking on sides.

CERULEAN WARBLER
Female and juvenile male • supercilium broadens behind eye; less distinct rounded ear patch; white or buff underparts; pale lines on back; dark streaks across back; shorter tail • eastern range.

- **BREEDING** Monogamous. Solitary nester.
- **NESTING** Incubation 11–12 days by female. Altricial young brooded by female; stay in nest estimated 9–12 days, fed by both sexes. 1 brood per year.
- **POPULATION** Fairly common in coniferous and mixed deciduous-conifer forests; stable. Strays to California in fall migration. Can be numerous in areas where there are spruce budworm outbreaks.
- **CONSERVATION** Neotropical migrant. Infrequent cowbird host. Vulnerable to loss of habitat due to land clearing. Hemlock infestations by insect pests could negatively impact.

Flight Pattern

Fairly swift direct flight on rapidly beating wings. Sallies forth from perch, taking insects in midair and returning to perch.

Nest Identification	
Shape ● Location 🪹	Small sticks, lichen, and plant down • lined with hair, bark pieces, and small roots • on horizontal branch, 20–50 feet above ground (but as high as 80 feet) • built by female • 4–5 white or greenish white eggs, with brown dots and splotches; oval to short oval, 0.68 x 0.49 inches.

| Plumage Sexes differ | Habitat 🌲 🌿 | Migration Migratory | Weight 0.4 ounce |

DATE _____ TIME_____ LOCATION _____

Family PARULIDAE	Species *Dendroica dominica*	Length 5.25 inches	Wingspan 8.5 inches

YELLOW-THROATED WARBLER

Some of these birds frequent the old oak trees of the Southeast and Mississippi Valley, where Spanish moss is abundant. Their habitat varies regionally from tall swampy bottomland hardwoods, to oak-pine woods on ridges, to lowland pine forests, to sycamores in riparian corridors. In all habitats, this long-billed warbler sings loudly from the tops of trees, and can be identified by the black face set off by a bold white supercilium and bright yellow chin and throat. The female is similar to the male but duller and has fewer black markings. Most migrate but southern populations are sedentary.

black-and-white head with white patch on sides of neck

white or yellow supraloral

white arc under eye, white stripe over eye

long black bill

blue-gray upperparts

bright yellow chin, throat, and breast

2 white wing bars

white underparts

black stripes on flanks, sides, and sides of breast

large white tail spots

- **SONG** Loud descending series of 3–4 measured whistles, followed by 2–3 weaker notes and more rapid notes, ending with sharper ascending note, *tweede-tweede-tweede-tweede-dee-da-m-deet.* Call note is high soft *tsip.*
- **BEHAVIOR** Solitary or in pairs. Somewhat sluggish and deliberate. Joins mixed-species feeding flocks after breeding season. Creeps along inner branches, twigs, and in foliage, foraging generally in the upper parts of trees; however, sometimes lower and even on the ground. Uses long bill and behavior similar to that of Brown Creeper to extract insects from bark crevices and pick them from the surface. Also catches insects in flight. Eats insects, caterpillars, and spiders.
- **BREEDING** Monogamous. Solitary nester.
- **NESTING** Breeding biology poorly known. Incubation by female estimated at 12–13 days. Altricial young brooded by female; stay in nest estimated 10 days, fed by female (possibly some by male). 1–2 broods per year.
- **POPULATION** Fairly common in habitat. Numbers stable overall; some expansion in the Northeast and noted decline in the Florida Panhandle and southern Alabama. Casual in the West during fall migration; rare to casual in southeastern Canada during spring migration.

Similar Birds

BLACKBURNIAN WARBLER
Juvenile fall male
- shorter bill; yellow-orange throat and supercilium; yellow patch on side of head; blackish back with white stripes; 2 white wing bars; dusky streaks on sides and flanks.

- **FEEDERS** Will eat bread crumbs and suet.
- **CONSERVATION** Neotropical migrant. Infrequent cowbird host. Vulnerable to habitat loss due to logging, land clearing, and development.

Flight Pattern

Fairly swift flight of short duration on rapidly beating wings. Sallies forth from perch, taking insects in air, and returns to perch.

Nest Identification	Plant down, stems, grasses, and cocoon material, with lining of feathers and fine plant material • tucked into Spanish moss or on or near end of branch, 10–100 feet above ground • built mostly by female • 4–5 grayish white or greenish white eggs, with lavender, reddish, and grayish flecks and splotches; subelliptical to short subelliptical, 0.68 x 0.51 inches.
Shape ☕ Location 🪹 🪺	

Plumage Sexes similar	Habitat 🌳 🌲	Migration Migratory	Weight 0.3 ounce

DATE _____ TIME_____ LOCATION _____

Family PARULIDAE	Species *Dendroica graciae*	Length 4.75 inches	Wingspan 7.75 inches

GRACE'S WARBLER

This energetic bird makes its summer home in the mountain pine and pine-oak forests of southwestern North America. Because it feeds in the tops of tall pine trees, it often is difficult to spot. Females are similar to males but duller in color and with more brown on the upperparts. In appearance and habitat this species is the western counterpart of the

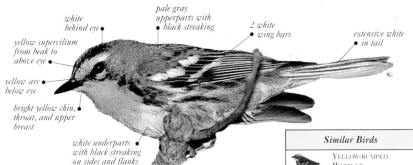

white behind eye

pale gray upperparts with black streaking

yellow supercilium from beak to above eye

2 white wing bars

extensive white in tail

yellow arc below eye

bright yellow chin, throat, and upper breast

white underparts with black streaking on sides and flanks

Yellow-throated Warbler; ranges do not overlap. Juveniles and adults show a brownish wash on the upperparts in fall plumage.

• **SONG** A vibrant warbling of slightly rising and accelerating notes, generally in 2 parts, *chu-chu-chu-chu-chichichichichichi*. Each male may give several variations. Call note is a slurred soft *chip*.

• **BEHAVIOR** Solitary or in pairs. Forages, sings, and nests almost exclusively in pines. Forages for food in tops of trees and catches insects in flight. Hops along limbs, gleaning food from bark and probing into clusters of needles and pine cones. Eats mainly insects and spiders.

• **BREEDING** Monogamous. Solitary.

• **NESTING** Breeding biology poorly known. Estimated incubation 11–12 days by female. Young altricial; brooded by female; young stay in nest estimated 8–10 days, fed by both sexes. 2 broods per year.

• **POPULATION** Fairly common to common in montane pine and mixed pine-deciduous forests. Casual to southern California.

• **CONSERVATION** Neotropical migrant. Infrequent host to cowbird parasitism. As a habitat specialist, vulnerable to loss of habitat due to logging and development.

Similar Birds

YELLOW-RUMPED WARBLER
Audubon's form • gray face and upperparts; broken white eye ring; yellow crown, chin, throat, side patch, and rump; black-streaked back; black breast, sides, and mottling on flanks; white belly and crissum; more white in greater wing coverts.

YELLOW-THROATED WARBLER
Southeast range does not overlap • triangular black face patch; white supercilium connects with white patch on back of face; white arc below eye; long bill; gray back lacks streaks.

Flight Pattern	

Fairly rapid flight with rapid wing strokes, alternating with brief period of wings pulled to sides. Sallies from perch to take flying insect, returns.

Nest Identification	
Shape 🥚 Location 🪺	Leaves, stems, down, bits of fabric, and cocoon material, with lining of mammal hair and feathers • on high branch, 20–60 feet above ground • built by female • 3–4 white or creamy white eggs, with blotches and fine dots of browns; oval to short oval, 0.6 x 0.45 inches.

Plumage Sexes similar	Habitat	Migration Migratory	Weight 0.3 ounce

DATE _____ TIME _____ LOCATION _____

Family PARULIDAE	Species *Dendroica pinus*	Length 5.25 inches	Wingspan 8.5 inches

PINE WARBLER

blackish eye line

yellow line over eyes

large bill

greenish olive upperparts with no streaking

yellow chin and throat

yellow breast has dark streaks on sides

2 white wing bars

long tail projects beyond undertail coverts

white belly and undertail coverts

white patches at ends of 2 outer tail feathers

JUVENILE FEMALE

True to its name, the long-tailed somewhat heavy-billed Pine Warbler inhabits open pine tree groves, where it conceals its nest among needles near the branch tips. It is distinguished from other warblers by its tendency to winter throughout much of its breeding range. Males and females are similar, both showing a white belly and undertail coverts, although females are duller in color with less yellow on their breasts. Juveniles have brownish to brownish olive upperparts with white wing bars, and underparts varying from white to yellowish with a brownish wash on the flanks.

- **SONG** Twittering musical trill similar to Chipping Sparrow but varying in speed, loudness, and pitch. Call is slurred *tsup*.
- **BEHAVIOR** Solitary or in pairs. Very vocal. Gregarious in winter; often joins mixed feeding flocks. Gleans food by creeping slowly and deliberately along branches, usually high in trees, but sometimes lower, even on ground. Often flies from tree to tree, diving for passing insects. Eats insects, caterpillars, and spiders. Also eats seeds, wild grapes, and some berries. Aggressive toward other species sharing same pine habitat.
- **BREEDING** Monogamous. Solitary.
- **NESTING** Incubation 10 days by both sexes. Young altricial; brooded by female; leave nest within 10 days, fed by both sexes. 2–3 broods per year in the South, 1 brood per year in the North.
- **POPULATION** Fairly common to common. Stable or increasing slightly, but some decline in coastal New England and Great Lakes region due to clearing of pines. Subject to loss in severe winters. Increases occur as pines mature. Casual in West.
- **FEEDERS** Peanut butter and cornmeal mixture.
- **CONSERVATION** Neotropical migrant. Infrequent host to cowbird parasitism. Vulnerable to fragmentation and clearing of pine forests.

Similar Birds

YELLOW-THROATED VIREO Heavier hooked bill; yellow spectacles; white belly and flanks; no streaking on sides or breast; gray rump and crissum; no white in tail corners; sluggish.

BAY-BREASTED WARBLER BLACKPOLL WARBLER Basic plumage • black streaking on back; much less white in tail corners; shorter tails with less extension from undertail coverts; paler cheeks contrast less with throat color.

Flight Pattern	
Weak flight, rapid wing beats alternated with brief period of wings pulled to sides. Sallies out to take flying insects, returns.	

Nest Identification	
Shape Location	Lined with feathers, weeds, grass, bark, pine needles, twigs, and spider webs • built on or near end of limb, 10–135 feet above ground • built by female • 3–5 off-white eggs, with brown specks near larger end; oval to short oval, 0.7 x 0.5 inches.

Plumage Sexes similar	Habitat 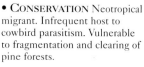	Migration Northern birds migrate	Weight 0.4 ounce

DATE _____ TIME_____ LOCATION _____

| Family PARULIDAE | Species *Dendroica discolor* | Length 4.75 inches | Wingspan 7.5 inches |

PRAIRIE WARBLER

Rather than the prairies as its name might imply, this bird can be found in brushy old fields, open pine stands, and sometimes in coastal mangroves in eastern and southern North America. Like many warblers, the male sings from an exposed perch at the tops of tall trees. Females are similar to males but duller in color. Juvenile females are duller still, with grayish olive upperparts, pale supercilium, and broken eye rings.

yellow sides of face with black streak through eyes, outlining ear patch

bright yellow eyebrow

olive-green upperparts with chestnut markings on back

2 light yellow wing bars

black streaking on sides

white patches on outer tail feathers

bright yellow underparts

- **SONG** An ascending trilling *zzee-zzee-zzee-zzee-zzee-zzee-zzee*, starting at one pitch and rising sharply over the last half of song. Call note is a rich smacking *tchick*.
- **BEHAVIOR** Solitary or in pairs. Joins mixed feeding flocks after breeding season. Tame. Active and restless. Constantly pumps or wags tail while feeding. Forages in low branches of trees and bushes and sometimes on ground. Catches some insects in flight but primarily gleans from foliage; sometimes hover-gleans. Eats mostly insects and spiders.
- **BREEDING** Monogamous; some males polygynous in midnesting season. Solitary nester.
- **NESTING** Incubation 11–14 days by female. Young altricial; brooded by female; stay in nest 8–11 days, fed by both sexes. Both sexes tend for additional 40–50 days. 2 broods per year.
- **POPULATION** Common but is declining.
- **CONSERVATION** Neotropical migrant. Frequently host to cowbird parasitism. Vulnerable to habitat loss that occurs with maturation of forests.

Similar Birds

PINE WARBLER
Yellow-green face; indistinct yellowish eye ring and supercilium; olive-green back without streaking; yellowish underparts with indistinct dusky streaking; extensive white tail spots; bobs tail but not as strongly.

Flight Pattern

Fairly fast flight with rapidly beating wings, alternating with brief periods of wings pulled to sides. May sally forth and take insects in flight.

Nest Identification

Shape Location

Grasses, stems, bark pieces, plant down, and leaves, bound with spider's silk and lined with feathers and mammal hair • hidden in tree or bush, usually 10–15 feet above ground (but ranges from 1–45 feet) • built by female • 4–5 white, creamy white, or greenish white eggs, with fine and large dots of brown, concentrated on larger end; oval to short oval, 0.6 x 0.48 inches.

| Plumage Sexes differ | Habitat | Migration Migratory | Weight 0.3 ounce |

DATE _____ TIME_____ LOCATION _____

Family PARULIDAE	Species *Dendroica palmarum*	Length 5.25 inches	Wingspan 8.5 inches

PALM WARBLER

This inhabitant of northern bogs pumps its tail up and down more than any other warbler. Two subspecies occur: the eastern form with strongly washed yellow underparts and the western form with whitish underparts with stronger streaking. Both nest on knolls of moss at the foot of small spruce or pine trees. A medium-distance migrant, the Palm Warbler winters in the South and frequents open habitats such as cultivated fields, marshes, pastures, parks, and gardens. Some winter in open pine woods or along their edges. The species is associated with palms only on some of its wintering areas and shows no inclination to seek them out. Fall adults and juveniles are drab, washed out, and lack the chestnut cap.

grayish to olive-brown upperparts

chestnut cap

white to yellowish wing bars

white spots on tail corners

yellow to whitish supercilium

chestnut to brownish streaks on sides of breast

greenish yellow undertail coverts and rump

streaked whitish underparts

WESTERN RACE

WINTER PLUMAGE

- **SONG** Monotone buzzlike fast trill, often stronger in middle, *zwee-zwee-zwee-zwee-zwee-zwee*. Call is forceful slurred *tsik*.
- **BEHAVIOR** Solitary or in pairs. Gregarious after breeding season, forming flocks and often mixing in foraging flocks with other species. Terrestrial; searches for food on ground or along beaches during migration, particularly among twigs and cones from conifers. Also foliage-gleans and hover-gleans in shrubs and trees; sometimes hawks prey in flight. Eats insects and caterpillars, also bayberries and raspberries.
- **BREEDING** Monogamous. Solitary.
- **NESTING** Incubation 12 days by both sexes. Young altricial; brooded by female; stay in nest 12 days, fed by both sexes. 2 broods per year.
- **POPULATION** Fairly common to common. Stable with some decline noted in wintering numbers in Florida.
- **CONSERVATION** Neotropical migrant. Rare cowbird host; buries eggs of parasite in floor of nest. Vulnerable to loss of habitat due to forest fragmentation.

Similar Birds

CAPE MAY WARBLER ♀
Pale lemon supercilium; white undertail coverts; does not wag short tail.

YELLOW-RUMPED WARBLER
Myrtle form, basic plumage • brown to gray upperparts with black streaking on back; white supercilium; bright yellow rump; streaked underparts; does not pump tail.

Flight Pattern

Weak flight; rapid wing beats alternate with brief periods of wings pulled to sides. Sallies from perch to take insects in air.

Nest Identification	
Shape ⬥ Location ▬ 🦕	Grass and shredded bark, lined with feathers • built on or near ground or up to 4 feet above ground in coniferous tree • built by female • 4–5 white to creamy eggs, with brown markings; ovate, short ovate, or elongated ovate, 0.7 x 0.5 inches.

Plumage Sexes similar	Habitat ▲▲ ▲	Migration Migratory	Weight 0.4 ounce

DATE _____ TIME_____ LOCATION _____

Family PARULIDAE	Species *Dendroica castanea*	Length 5.5 inches	Wingspan 8.5 inches

BAY-BREASTED WARBLER

The male's warm chestnut and creamy markings help identify this native of northern coniferous forests. It is one of the largest warblers. Females are duller and have a gray rump. Juveniles and winter adults have olive upperparts with streaking

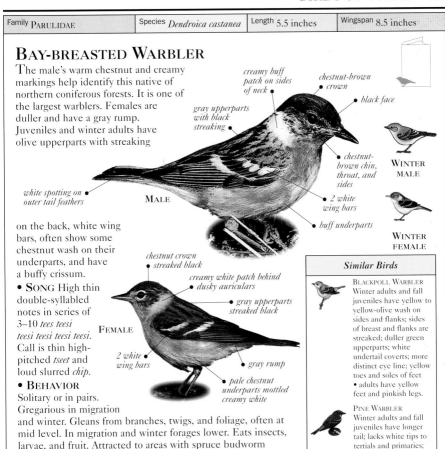

creamy buff patch on sides of neck

chestnut-brown crown

black face

gray upperparts with black streaking

chestnut-brown chin, throat, and sides

WINTER MALE

white spotting on outer tail feathers

MALE

2 white wing bars

buff underparts

WINTER FEMALE

on the back, white wing bars, often show some chestnut wash on their underparts, and have a buffy crissum.

chestnut crown streaked black

creamy white patch behind dusky auriculars

gray upperparts streaked black

FEMALE

2 white wing bars

gray rump

pale chestnut underparts mottled creamy white

- **SONG** High thin double-syllabled notes in series of 3–10 *tees teesi teesi teesi teesi teesi.* Call is thin high-pitched *tseet* and loud slurred *chip.*
- **BEHAVIOR** Solitary or in pairs. Gregarious in migration and winter. Gleans from branches, twigs, and foliage, often at mid level. In migration and winter forages lower. Eats insects, larvae, and fruit. Attracted to areas with spruce budworm outbreaks. Wags tail slightly as it forages.
- **BREEDING** Monogamous. Solitary nester.
- **NESTING** Incubation 12–13 days by female. Young altricial; brooded by female; leave nest at 10–12 days, fed by both sexes. 1 brood per year.

Similar Birds

BLACKPOLL WARBLER Winter adults and fall juveniles have yellow to yellow-olive wash on sides and flanks; sides of breast and flanks are streaked; duller green upperparts; white undertail coverts; more distinct eye line; yellow toes and soles of feet • adults have yellow feet and pinkish legs.

PINE WARBLER Winter adults and fall juveniles have longer tail; lacks white tips to tertials and primaries; unstreaked olive to olive-brown back; olive cheek patch contrasts with paler throat; more elongated tail spots.

- **POPULATION** Abundant to common in boreal coniferous forests and adjoining deciduous second growth.
- **CONSERVATION** Neotropical migrant. Rare cowbird host. Vulnerable to habitat loss due to logging.

Flight Pattern

Relatively weak flight with rapid wing strokes alternating briefly with wings pulled to sides.

Nest Identification

Shape ▼ Location 🌿 🌳 🌲

Sticks, grasses, roots, mosses, and stems, lined with pieces of bark and rabbit hair • on branch of tree or bush, 4–40 feet above ground • built by female • 4–6 white, greenish white, or bluish white eggs, with lavender or brown splotches at larger end; varying from ovate to elongate ovate, 0.7 x 0.5 inches.

Plumage Sexes differ	Habitat 🌾 🪨	Migration Migratory	Weight 0.5 ounce

DATE _____ TIME_____ LOCATION _____

| Family PARULIDAE | Species *Dendroica striata* | Length 5.25 inches | Wingspan 8.5 inches |

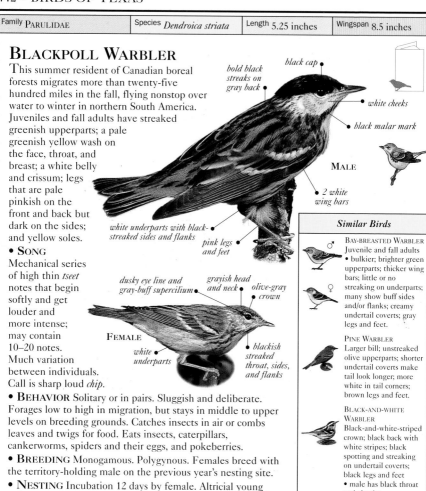

BLACKPOLL WARBLER

This summer resident of Canadian boreal forests migrates more than twenty-five hundred miles in the fall, flying nonstop over water to winter in northern South America. Juveniles and fall adults have streaked greenish upperparts; a pale greenish yellow wash on the face, throat, and breast; a white belly and crissum; legs that are pale pinkish on the front and back but dark on the sides; and yellow soles.

bold black streaks on gray back

black cap

white cheeks

black malar mark

MALE

2 white wing bars

white underparts with black-streaked sides and flanks

pink legs and feet

dusky eye line and gray-buff supercilium

grayish head and neck

olive-gray crown

FEMALE

white underparts

blackish streaked throat, sides, and flanks

- **SONG** Mechanical series of high thin *tseet* notes that begin softly and get louder and more intense; may contain 10–20 notes. Much variation between individuals. Call is sharp loud *chip*.

Similar Birds

BAY-BREASTED WARBLER ♂ ♀ Juvenile and fall adults • bulkier; brighter green upperparts; thicker wing bars; little or no streaking on underparts; many show buff sides and/or flanks; creamy undertail coverts; gray legs and feet.

PINE WARBLER Larger bill; unstreaked olive upperparts; shorter undertail coverts make tail look longer; more white in tail corners; brown legs and feet.

BLACK-AND-WHITE WARBLER Black-and-white-striped crown; black back with white stripes; black spotting and streaking on undertail coverts; black legs and feet • male has black throat and cheeks.

- **BEHAVIOR** Solitary or in pairs. Sluggish and deliberate. Forages low to high in migration, but stays in middle to upper levels on breeding grounds. Catches insects in air or combs leaves and twigs for food. Eats insects, caterpillars, cankerworms, spiders and their eggs, and pokeberries.
- **BREEDING** Monogamous. Polygynous. Females breed with the territory-holding male on the previous year's nesting site.
- **NESTING** Incubation 12 days by female. Altricial young brooded by female; stay in nest 11–12 days, fed by both sexes. 1–2 broods per year.

- **POPULATION** Abundant in northern boreal coniferous forests. May be declining in southern part of breeding range.
- **CONSERVATION** Neotropical migrant. Vulnerable to habitat loss from logging and forest fragmentation.

Flight Pattern

Fairly swift direct flight on rapidly beating wings.

Nest Identification

Shape ⬦   Location 🐦

Lined with spruce sprigs, twigs, bark, dried grass, feathers, weeds, moss, and lichen • on branch near trunk, 2–33 feet above ground • built by female • 3–5 white to off-white eggs, with brown or lavender markings, occasionally wreathed; oval to long oval, 0.72 x 0.53 inches.

| Plumage Sexes differ | Habitat 🌳 🏵 | Migration Migratory | Weight 0.5 ounce |

DATE _____ TIME_____ LOCATION _____

Family PARULIDAE	Species *Dendroica cerulea*	Length 4.5 inches	Wingspan 7.25 inches

CERULEAN WARBLER

Although its buzzy song can be heard from dawn until dusk, this bird, one of the smallest warblers, is difficult to spot, as it stays hidden in dense foliage in the crowns of tall deciduous trees. This habit of remaining high in mature trees has made studies of its natural history difficult, and its breeding biology and feeding habits are poorly known. Juveniles are similar to females.

- **SONG** A series of accelerating buzzy notes on the same or slightly ascending pitch, ending in a drawn-out buzz, *zray, zray, zray, zray, zeeeeeee,* reminiscent of the slower second song of the Northern Parula. Call is a slurred *chip.*

- **BEHAVIOR** Solitary or in pairs. Vigorous and persistent singer on breeding grounds. Eats mainly insects, larvae, and spiders. Very active and acrobatic forager but sometimes moves sluggishly, gleaning food off leaves and branches while staying hidden in trees. Also catches insects in flight.

- **BREEDING** Monogamous. Solitary nester.

- **NESTING** Incubation about 12–13 days by female. Altricial young brooded by female; stay in nest estimated 8–10 days, fed by both sexes. 1–2 broods per year.

- **POPULATION** Fairly common to uncommon in mature deciduous forest. Declining dramatically, particularly in the heart of range, but range is expanding north and northeast, on the Atlantic coastal plain, and the Piedmont.

- **CONSERVATION** Neotropical migrant. Moderate host to cowbird parasitism. Vulnerable to habitat loss and forest fragmentation.

white tail spots

bluish to blue-gray upperparts with black streaking on back

2 white wing bars

black streaking on flanks and sides

bluish black chest band

white underparts

MALE

blue-gray to greenish mantle

bluish green crown

whitish supercilium widens behind eye

white tail spots

FEMALE

pale yellowish buff breast and throat

Similar Birds

The small and short-tailed male is the only warbler with a blue back, black necklace, and white throat.

♀ **BLACKBURNIAN WARBLER** Female and juvenile • pale orange supercilium broadens behind eye; white or buff underparts; longer tail; triangular cheek patch; pale lines and dark streaking on back.

Flight Pattern

Relatively weak flight with quick wing strokes alternating with brief periods of wings pull to sides; repeated.

Nest Identification

Shape ⌒ Location 🪹

Stems, grasses, mosses, bark pieces, and spider's silk, with lining of mammal hair and mosses • far out on branch of tree, usually 30–60 feet above ground • built by female • 3–5 grayish or creamy white eggs, with fine dots or splotches of brown, usually loosely wreathed; oval to short oval, 0.7 x 0.5 inches.

Plumage Sexes differ	Habitat 🌲 🌿 🌳	Migration Migratory	Weight 0.3 ounce

DATE _____ TIME_____ LOCATION _____

| Family PARULIDAE | Species *Mniotilta varia* | Length 5 inches | Wingspan 8.5–9 inches |

BLACK-AND-WHITE WARBLER

This mostly black-and-white striped bird feeds nuthatch-style, moving up and down the trunks of trees and crawling over and under branches, a foraging behavior unlike any other warbler. It is one of the earliest warblers to return to the breeding grounds in early spring, because its bark-gleaning foraging habit does not require it to linger on wintering grounds until the leaves begin to develop. Females are similar to males but have cream-colored flanks and creamy whitish rather than black cheeks. Juveniles are similar to females.

bold black-and-white stripes on head and most of body

distinctive white stripe over and under each eye

slightly curved slim bill

black cheeks and throat

2 white wing bars

white belly

JUVENILE

• **SONG** Repetitive thin high-pitched series of 6–10 *wee-sea, wee-sea* notes like the sound of a turning squeaky wheel. Sometimes a trill is added as an ending to the cadence. Has call of an abrasive *chip* or *tink*, and a *seap*.

• **BEHAVIOR** Solitary or in pairs. Probes into bark crevices with long bill; does not prop body on tree with tail as do woodpeckers and creepers. Eats adult insects, caterpillars, and spiders. Occasionally hawks and hover-gleans. If flushed from ground nest, female performs distraction display, dragging wings with tail spread.

• **BREEDING** Monogamous. Solitary.

• **NESTING** Incubation 10–12 days by female. Young altricial; brooded by female; remain in nest 8–12 days but still not able to fly well; fed by both sexes. 1–2 broods per year.

• **POPULATION** Widespread in mature and second-growth deciduous or mixed deciduous-conifer woodlands with large trees. Declining in the Midwest and Great Lakes region because of habitat loss and cowbird parasitism. Vagrant in the West during migration as far north as Alaska.

• **CONSERVATION** Neotropical migrant. Common host to cowbird eggs. Vulnerable to forest fragmentation and habitat loss due to logging operations in mature forests.

Similar Birds

BLACK-THROATED GRAY WARBLER ♂ Small yellow spot between eye and bill; blackish crown; gray back with black streaking; white undertail coverts; lacks central crown stripe.

BLACKPOLL WARBLER ♂ Black crown; white cheeks; gray back with black streaking; white throat; white undertail coverts.

Flight Pattern

Relatively weak flight with rapid wing strokes alternating with brief periods of wings pulled to sides; repeated.

Nest Identification

Shape 🥄   Location ▬ 🌿 🌿

Grasses, bark pieces, dead leaves, rootlets, and pine needles, lined with moss and mammal hair • on ground, near base of tree or bush, or in small hollow of rock, stump, or log • built by female • 4–6 creamy white or white eggs, flecked with brown; short subelliptical to subelliptical, 0.67 x 0.52 inches.

| Plumage Sexes similar | Habitat 🌳🌳 | Migration Migratory | Weight 0.4 ounce |

DATE _____ TIME_____ LOCATION _____

Family PARULIDAE	Species *Setophaga ruticilla*	Length 5 inches	Wingspan 8 inches

AMERICAN REDSTART

Birders enjoy watching this vivacious bird as it flits to catch insects or sits on a perch, partially spreading and drooping its wings and spreading its tail. Other warblers pump or flick their tails, but this bird fans its tail and holds it there for a second. The male's tail can be either orange and black or dusky olive-gray. This woodland inhabitant is one of the most common warblers nesting in North America. Juvenile males look like females but with an orange wash on the sides.

glossy black overall

orange patches on wings, sides, and tail

white belly and undertail coverts

MALE

FEMALE

thin white supercilium and eye ring

grayish olive upperparts

whitish underparts from chin to tip of undertail coverts

yellow patches on sides, wings, and tail

- **SONG** Variable. Sings often and through the heat of midday. Basic song is 4–8 high-pitched, somewhat coarse notes, with explosive accented lower-ending *zeet-zeet-zeet-zeet-zeeeah*. Other songs have unaccented ending. Some are reminiscent of the Yellow, Chestnut-sided, and Black-and-white Warblers. Territorial males have repertoire of several songs. Call is slurred thin *chip*.
- **BEHAVIOR** Solitary or in pairs. Tame. Conspicuous. Sings often. Responds to squeaking or pishing by birders. Sallies into air to catch insects, perching between hawking events like a small flycatcher. Gleans food from branches and foliage; hover-gleans. Eats insects, caterpillars, spiders, berries, fruit, and seeds.
- **BREEDING** Monogamous. Solitary nester.
- **NESTING** Incubation 11–12 days by female. Altricial young brooded by female; stay in nest 9 days, fed by both sexes. 1–2 broods per year.
- **POPULATION** Common to fairly common in wet deciduous and mixed conifer-deciduous woodlands with understory, woodland edges, riparian woodlands, and second growth. Widespread but declining in the Midwest, Great Lakes, the Northeast, and the Maritime Provinces. Rare to uncommon migrant in the West to California.
- **CONSERVATION** Neotropical migrant. Common cowbird host. Vulnerable to habitat loss caused by deforestation or maturation of second-growth forests.

FIRST SPRING MALE

Similar Birds
None in range.

Flight Pattern
Somewhat weak flight on rapidly beating wings, alternating with brief periods of wings pulled to sides. Flies into air from perch to take flying insects, and returns.

Nest Identification	
Shape (cup) Location (tree/bush)	Grasses, pieces of bark, rootlets, and plant down, decorated with lichens, birch bark, and spider's silk, and lined with feathers • in fork of tree or bush, usually 10–20 feet above ground (but ranges from 4–70 feet) • built by female • 2–5 off-white, greenish white, or white eggs, flecked and dotted with browns or grays; ovate, occasionally short ovate, 0.63 x 0.48 inches.

Plumage Sexes differ	Habitat	Migration Migratory	Weight 0.3 ounce

DATE _____ TIME_____ LOCATION _____

Family PARULIDAE	Species *Protonotaria citrea*	Length 5.25 inches	Wingspan 8.5 inches

PROTHONOTARY WARBLER

The male builds several nests, then sings continuously until the female arrives to choose a nest and complete it. This is the only eastern warbler that nests in tree hollows, a trait it shares with just one other North American warbler, the western Lucy's Warbler. It was once called the "Golden Swamp Warbler," describing the bird and its dark backwater haunts.

• **SONG** A bold ringing repetitive *zweet*, slightly up-slurred as *sweet, sweet, sweet, sweet*. Call is loud *chip-chip*.

• **BEHAVIOR** Solitary or in pairs. Gregarious in winter, roosting communally. Tame, noisy, and conspicuous. Deliberate in its feeding, gleaning food and probing crevices with its bill. Picks food off floating logs and branches and out of water. Also forages in trees while grasping trunk like a nuthatch. Eats insects, spiders, larvae, and seeds. Takes small crustaceans and snails. Inquisitive; will come to squeaking and pishing by birders.

• **BREEDING** Monogamous. Solitary nester.

• **NESTING** Incubation 12–14 days by female. Altricial young brooded by female, fed by both sexes; first flight at 11 days. 2 broods per year in the South.

• **POPULATION** Fairly common in swampy lowland forest, river-bottom woodlands subject to flooding, and riparian corridors along streams. Accidental to rare in the West.

• **BIRDHOUSES** Nest boxes.

• **CONSERVATION** Neotropical migrant. Common cowbird host. Destruction of mangrove swamps and wetland drainage reduce populations. Competition from other cavity nesters that destroy eggs or usurp cavities.

golden yellow head, neck, and underparts

large dark eyes

olive-green back

long black bill

blue-gray wings

chunky body

short blue-gray tail with large white patches

white undertail coverts

MALE

greenish yellow crown and nape

greenish back

gray wings, rump, uppertail coverts, and tail

bright yellow throat, face, and breast

FEMALE

white belly and undertail coverts

white spots on inner web of tail feathers

Similar Birds

YELLOW WARBLER
Bright yellow underparts; orange-yellow forehead and front of crown; reddish streaking on underparts; yellow-olive wings; yellow spots in tail • appears completely yellow from a distance.

BLUE-WINGED WARBLER
Blue-gray wings with 2 white wing bars; black eye line; shorter bill; yellow head and underparts; olive back; no white spots in tail.

Flight Pattern
Rapid direct flight, often low over water, on quickly beating wings.

Nest Identification	
Shape ◣²	Grasses, moss, leaves, and sticks, lined with feathers and rootlets • in natural hollow or woodpecker cavity in snag, tree, post, or nest box, near water and usually 5–10 feet above ground (but range from 2–32 feet) • male builds dummy nests; female selects and completes one • 4–6 pinkish or cream eggs, with brown and gray dots; short elliptical to elliptical, 0.8 x 0.57 inches.
Location	

Plumage Sexes differ	Habitat	Migration Migratory	Weight 0.5 ounce

DATE _____ TIME_____ LOCATION _____

Family PARULIDAE	Species *Helmitheros vermivorus*	Length 5.25 inches	Wingspan 8.5 inches

WORM-EATING WARBLER

Similar to a sparrow in color, size, and habits, the Worm-eating Warbler's steady diet of moth caterpillars and worms has earned this bird its name. An inhabitant of deciduous forests, it seldom is observed combing the forest floor for food; rather, it usually forages in the understory vegetation, where it often probes for food in clusters of dead leaves. While primarily a solitary bird, the Worm-eating Warbler sometimes is known to associate loosely with foraging flocks of mixed bird species.

buff-colored head with 2 pairs of bold dark stripes

brownish olive upperparts

long spikelike bill

buff-colored underparts

- **SONG** A buzzy insectlike fricative trill, often beginning softly and fading away at the end with a series of *chip* notes. Song is similar to the Chipping Sparrow's but more rapid and given in a thick shaded wooded habitat. Call is a *zit-zit*.

- **BEHAVIOR** Solitary or in pairs. More often heard than seen in the breeding season. Most often observed foraging alone for insects, spiders, and some worms. Gleans food by moving along branches like a Black-and-white Warbler, but specializes in probing clusters of dead leaves for food. Usually forages in low to middle levels, but sometimes in treetops; rarely in leaf litter on ground. Frequents deciduous woodlots on slopes, along ravines, or mountain sides. When flushed from nest, female drags wings and spreads tail, running on ground in distraction display. Mixed flocks postbreeding season.

- **BREEDING** Monogamous. Solitary.

- **NESTING** Incubation 13 days by female. Young altricial; brooded by female; stay in nest 10 days, fed by both sexes. 1–2 broods per year.

- **POPULATION** Fairly common to common in ravines, hillsides, and mountainsides in thick deciduous woodlands. Stable in most of its range but regional declines noted. Casual to rare vagrant in migration in the West to California.

- **CONSERVATION** Neotropical migrant. Frequent host to cowbird parasitism. Vulnerable to habitat loss due to forest fragmentation.

Similar Birds

SWAINSON'S WARBLER Larger; longer bill; browner upperparts; grayish buff underparts; brown cap without stripes; pale supercilium; thin dark eye line.

Flight Pattern

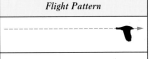

Fairly fast direct flight on rapidly beating wings.

Nest Identification	
Shape ◖ Location ▬	Lined with dead leaves, animal hair, fungus, moss, and tree stems • often built on sloping ground near base of deciduous shrubs or saplings or on ridges of leaves on forest floor • built by female • 4–6 white eggs, with brown spots or blotches, often wreathed; short ovate, 0.7 x 0.55 inches.

Plumage Sexes similar	Habitat 🐾	Migration Migratory	Weight 0.7 ounce

DATE _____ TIME_____ LOCATION _____

Family PARULIDAE	Species *Limnothlypis swainsonii*	Length 5.25 inches	Wingspan 8.5 inches

SWAINSON'S WARBLER

This recluse hides in dense thickets, except when the male perches to sing, which he does with his head thrown back and his bill lifted in the air. It is found in two habitats: in the low coastal and river-bottom country of the Southeast it inhabits canebrakes and thickets in swamps and among hardwoods; in

brown and olive upperparts

brownish eye line

tawny brown cap

white eye stripe

long pointed bill

grayish white underparts

the Southern Appalachians it is found in laurel and rhododendron thickets in moist montane forests.

• **SONG** Bold clear *whee-whee-whee, whip-poor-will*, with the opening notes down-slurred and the last 3 clear and more rapid. Begins like that of the Louisiana Waterthrush but lacks sputtering downward trill at the end. Call is loud clear *chip*.

• **BEHAVIOR** Solitary or in pairs. Tame. Sings from concealed perch or from ground; voice has a ventriloquial quality. May sing continuously for 10–15 minutes, then be silent for an hour or more. Forages frequently on ground, walking slowly and turning over leaves with its bill or probing into leaves or ground for food. Eats insects, caterpillars, and spiders. A skulking bird in dense undergrowth, it is difficult to see. Sometimes detected by the noise it makes tossing leaves.

• **BREEDING** Monogamous. Solitary nester. Sometimes in loose colonies in prime lowland habitat.

• **NESTING** Incubation 13–15 days by female. Young altricial; brooded by female; stay in nest 10–12 days, fed by both sexes. 1–2 broods per year.

• **POPULATION** Uncommon in thickets in swamps, canebrakes, and moist woodlands.

• **CONSERVATION** Neotropical migrant. Increasing host to cowbird parasitism. Vulnerable to habitat loss as wetlands are drained and river-bottom forests are cleared for agricultural use.

Similar Birds

WORM-EATING WARBLER Shorter bill; buff-colored head with 2 pairs of blackish stripes; brownish olive upperparts; buff-colored underparts.

Flight Pattern

Fairly swift short direct flights on rapidly beating wings.

Nest Identification

Shape ◗   Location ⬤

Mass of leaves, pine needles, mammal hair, grasses, Spanish moss, and rootlets • in fork of bush or vines, 2–10 feet above ground • built by female • 2–5 white eggs, occasionally with brown speckles; elliptical, 0.76 x 0.59 inches • only North American warbler besides Bachman's to lay unmarked white eggs.

Plumage Sexes similar	Habitat 🌲 🏕 🌾 ⛰ 🍂 〜	Migration Migratory	Weight 0.7 ounce

DATE _____ TIME_____ LOCATION _____

Family PARULIDAE	Species *Seiurus aurocapillus*	Length 6 inches	Wingspan 9 inches

OVENBIRD

In the leaf litter under tall deciduous trees, the female bird builds a small oven-shaped nest with a side entrance. Unlike many warblers, it does not often forage in live vegetation; instead it walks on the ground, foraging among the leaf litter and twigs, its wings partially drooped and its tail cocked upward and sometimes quickly raised and slowly lowered. It is sometimes called the Wood Wagtail because it moves its tail up and down. Most singing is done from an elevated perch, and the song of one territorial male initiates a response song from each neighbor, which in turn stimulates another to do so, until a wave of Ovenbird songs sweeps across the woodlot.

brownish orange stripe, edged in black, over head from bill to nape

white eye ring

olive-brown upperparts

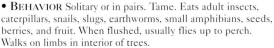

- **SONG** More often heard than seen. Sings a loud and repetitive *TEAcher-TEAcher-TEAcher*, rising and becoming more emphatic. There is regional variation, with some birds singing *teach-teach-teach-teACH!* From a distance the song sounds like two stones being tapped together harder and harder. Call note is a loud sharp *tsick*.

pale pink legs and feet

white underparts with dark brown splotching

- **BEHAVIOR** Solitary or in pairs. Tame. Eats adult insects, caterpillars, snails, slugs, earthworms, small amphibians, seeds, berries, and fruit. When flushed, usually flies up to perch. Walks on limbs in interior of trees.
- **BREEDING** Monogamous. Solitary nester.
- **NESTING** Incubation 11–14 days by female. Young altricial; brooded by female; remain in nest 8–11 days, fed by both sexes. 1–2 broods per year (occasionally 3 in regions with spruce budworm outbreaks).
- **POPULATION** Common to fairly common in mature deciduous forests; rarely in pine forests. Rare in the west of the Rockies in migration; rare to casual on southern Atlantic Coast and Gulf Coast in winter.
- **CONSERVATION** Neotropical migrant. Host to cowbird parasitism. Significant declines documented in the northeast beginning in the 1970s but now increasing in much of its range.

Similar Birds

LOUISIANA WATERTHRUSH
NORTHERN WATERTHRUSH
White to yellowish supercilium; lack eye ring and black border to crown; brownish upperparts; usually near water; habitual tail bobbing.

Flight Pattern
Relatively swift, short direct flight on rapidly beating wings.

Nest Identification	
Shape ⬤ Location ▬	Leaves, grasses, stems, rootlets, mosses, and hair • in slight hollow on ground of forest, concealed by leaves on top of nest, creating a dome • built by female • 3–6 white eggs, with gray or brown flecks; subelliptical to short subelliptical, 0.79 x 0.6 inches.

Plumage Sexes similar	Habitat 🌳 🌾	Migration Migratory	Weight 0.7 ounce

DATE _____ TIME_____ LOCATION _____

Family PARULIDAE	Species *Seiurus noveboracensis*	Length 5.75 inches	Wingspan 8.75 inches

NORTHERN WATERTHRUSH

Northern lakeshores, slow-running streams, and bogs are the most common habitats of the Northern Waterthrush. Walking, rather than hopping, along the ground, the Northern Waterthrush often is observed repeatedly bobbing the rear part of its body and its tail while searching for food. An early migrant, the Northern Waterthrush generally begins traveling southward by mid-July.

pale yellow to whitish supercilium

olive-brown to gray-brown upperparts

heavily streaked throat, upper breast, and sides

pale yellow to whitish underparts

• **SONG** Begins with loud insistent notes, tapering to rapidly whistled lower tones, *twit twit twit twit sweet sweet sweet chew chew chew*, with the individual notes grouped in series of 3's and 4's. Call is a very loud ringing metallic *chink*.

• **BEHAVIOR** Solitary or in pairs. Terrestrial but often sings from elevated perches and walks, bobbing, on branches. Forages on ground by picking up leaves with its bill and tossing them aside or turning them over. Eats aquatic and terrestrial adult insects, caterpillars, and case worms; also sometimes slugs, mollusks, crustaceans, and small fish. Frequents areas with dense shrub and slowly moving or still water.

• **BREEDING** Monogamous. Solitary.

• **NESTING** Breeding biology poorly known. Estimated incubation 13 days by female. Young altricial; brooded by female; stay in nest estimated 10 days, fed by both sexes. 1 brood per year.

• **POPULATION** Generally common in wooded swamps, forests with standing water, bogs, and thickets with slowly running or standing water. Rare to uncommon in migration in the Southwest to California. Rare to casual in winter in the US, except for southern Florida where it is uncommon.

• **CONSERVATION** Neotropical migrant. Uncommon host to cowbird parasitism. Some declines in southern portions of breeding range in New England portions. Vulnerable to habitat loss due to deforestation and drainage.

Similar Birds

LOUISIANA WATERTHRUSH Longer stouter bill; white supercilium broadens behind eye; fewer and less-contrasting streaks on underparts; unmarked white throat; contrasting pinkish buff wash on flanks; bright pink legs and feet; more deliberate and exaggerated tail bobbing with a circular body motion; song differs.

Flight Pattern
Fairly swift direct flight for short distances on rapidly beating wings.

Nest Identification	
Shape	Location	Lined with grass, animal hair, moss, twigs, pine needles, bark strips, and roots • often built in moss-covered stumps near water • 0–2 feet above ground • built by female • 3–6 cream or buff-white eggs, with brown or gray spots or speckles; ovate to short ovate, 0.8 x 0.57 inches.

Plumage Sexes similar	Habitat	Migration Migratory	Weight 0.8 ounce

DATE _____ TIME_____ LOCATION _____

Family PARULIDAE	Species *Seiurus motacilla*	Length 6 inches	Wingspan 9 inches

LOUISIANA WATERTHRUSH

The less common of the two waterthrush species frequents fast-running streams and floodplain river swamps, where it hides its nests on streamside banks, under tree roots, or in rock crevices. This bird has a nesting range from Minnesota to New England and as far south as Texas and Georgia. In spring it is one of the earliest warblers to arrive on the nesting grounds and one of the first to depart in late summer and early fall.

darker crown

long stout bill

broad gray-buff stripe broadens behind eye and becomes white

olive-gray to olive-brown upperparts

unstreaked white throat and chin

olive-striped breast, sides, and flanks

white or buff-white underparts

pinkish buff flanks contrast with white underparts

bright pink legs and feet

- **SONG** Loud and clear, beginning with 3–4 high-pitched downslurred notes, followed by a brief rapid medley of jumbled notes that cascade up and down prior to fading away, *SWEER SWEER SWEER chee chi-wit-it chit swee-yuu*. The combination of slurred opening notes and ending twittering is diagnostic. Call is a loud bright *chik*.
- **BEHAVIOR** Solitary or in pairs. Sings on ground or from elevated perch in trees. Bobs rear and tail while walking. Terrestrial, primarily foraging on ground, along stream banks, on rocks and logs in water, and in the stream shallows. Bobs up and down while foraging, much like a sandpiper, with a slow circular exaggerated motion. Dines on adult aquatic and terrestrial insects, caterpillars, mollusks, snails, and small fish. Territories are linear along stream.
- **BREEDING** Monogamous. Solitary.
- **NESTING** Incubation 12–14 days by female. Young altricial; brooded by female; remain in nest 9–10 days, fed by both sexes. 1 brood per year.
- **POPULATION** Uncommon to fairly common. Restricted habitat specialist along fast-flowing streams within woodlands, often in mountains or hilly terrain, or in floodplain forests and swamps in lower country. Casual in the West during migration.
- **CONSERVATION** Neotropical migrant. Frequent host to cowbird parasitism. Deforestation and stream siltation negatively impact both breeding and wintering areas.

Similar Birds

NORTHERN WATERTHRUSH Narrow buff to white eye stripes of uniform color and width; smaller bill; streaked and spotted throat; pale yellow to white underparts with darker, more uniform streaking; olive-brown to gray-brown upperparts; dull pink legs and feet; different voice.

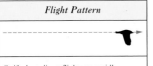

Flight Pattern

Swift short direct flights on rapidly beating wings.

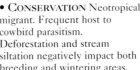

Nest Identification	
Shape Location	Lined with roots, fern stems, grass, animal fur, dead leaves, moss, and twigs • 0–2 feet above ground, on bank, rock crevice, or roots of tree, no further than 3–6 feet from water • built by both sexes, but female does more • 4–6 white or cream-colored eggs, with brown and gray specks or blotches; oval to short oval, 0.78 x 0.6 inches.

Plumage Sexes similar	Habitat	Migration Migratory	Weight 0.7 ounce

DATE _____ TIME_____ LOCATION _____

Family PARULIDAE	Species *Oporornis formosus*	Length 5.25 inches	Wingspan 8.25 inches

KENTUCKY WARBLER

This retiring, short-tailed chunky bird is named for the
state where it was first encountered, but it is common
throughout most of the damp shaded woodlands in
southeastern North America. The female is especially
wary and will sometimes abandon her nest if she is
threatened. She appears similar to the male, but her
black areas are duller. Juvenile females have dark
olive plumage in place of black.

short tail

bright olive upperparts

long pink legs and feet

black crown

bold yellow spectacles

black on face and sides of neck

yellow underparts

• **SONG** Loud and rich. A rolling melody of
5–8 notes with 2 syllables, *churry-churry-churry-
churry-churry*, but sometimes 3 syllables, with
an upward inflection at the end of each
phrase. Reminiscent of the Carolina
Wren, but drier sounding, and
although the wren may give 2-
syllabled notes, more often
has 3-syllabled notes in its
song series. Has call of
low abrasive *chuck chuck*.

• **BEHAVIOR** Solitary or
in pairs. Rather secretive;
more often heard than
seen. Terrestrial, but also
forages and sings in low to
middle levels of vegetation.
Hops or runs on ground while
flicking its tail, which is usually
partially cocked upward. Forages for food
by picking over foliage and branches and overturning leaves.
Jumps up to pick insects off bottom side of leaves. Eats adult
insects, spiders, and caterpillars.

• **BREEDING** Monogamous. Solitary nester.

• **NESTING** Incubation 12–13 days by female. Altricial young
brooded by female; stay in nest 8–10 days, fed by both sexes,
but female does more. 1 brood per year.

• **POPULATION** Common in moist woodlands with dense
understory; large tracts are optimum. In migration, casual to rare in
the Southwest to California.

• **CONSERVATION** Neotropical
migrant. Frequent cowbird host.
Vulnerable to deforestation;
sensitive to forest fragmentation
and overbrowsing by deer.

Similar Birds

COMMON
YELLOWTHROAT
First fall male • some
black on sides of face;
olive-gray to olive-
brown upperparts; paler
yellow underparts;
whitish belly; brownish
flanks; longer tail.

Flight Pattern

Swift short direct flights with rapidly
beating wings.

Nest Identification

Shape ◥   Location ▬

Grasses, stems, vines, and leaves • lined with mammal hair and rootlets • on
ground, near base of tree or bush, or clump of vegetation, sometimes in fork of
low shrub • build by both sexes • 3–6 white or creamy white eggs, with brown
flecks and splotches; short oval to long oval, 0.75 x 0.58 inches.

Plumage Sexes similar	Habitat 🐦 🌳	Migration Migratory	Weight 0.5 ounce

DATE _____ TIME_____ LOCATION _____

Family PARULIDAE	Species *Oporornis philadelphia*	Length 5.25 inches	Wingspan 8.25 inches

MOURNING WARBLER

The eastern counterpart to MacGillivray's Warbler was named for the way its black breast and gray hood resemble a person in mourning. Usually skulking in the undergrowth of damp woodlands, the male will fly up from the bushes to sing and is more often heard than seen. The female is similar to the male but has a paler dusky hood, light grayish throat, and a more distinct eye ring. Juveniles have pale yellowish throats and broken thin white eye rings. Traveling over eastern Mexico, this bird circumnavigates the western Gulf of Mexico, making it one of the latest spring migrants of all North American warblers.

- **SONG** Typically a 2-part song, with the second part lower in pitch, *cherrie, cherrie, chorrie, chorrie*. Individual and regional variations exist. Call is a sharp raspy *chit*, sometimes given in a series.
- **BEHAVIOR** Solitary or in pairs. Secretive. Sings often in migration and on breeding grounds. Will respond to pishing by birders. Terrestrial, forages low in vegetation hidden in undergrowth. Hops and flicks wings and tail. Gleans insects and spiders.
- **BREEDING** Monogamous. Solitary nester.
- **NESTING** Incubation 12 days by female. Altricial young brooded by female; remain in nest 7–9 days, fed by both sexes. 1 brood per year.
- **POPULATION** Fairly common in dense shrubbery in open deciduous woodlands, dense second growth, bog, and marsh edges.
- **CONSERVATION** Neotropical migrant. Infrequent host to cowbirds.

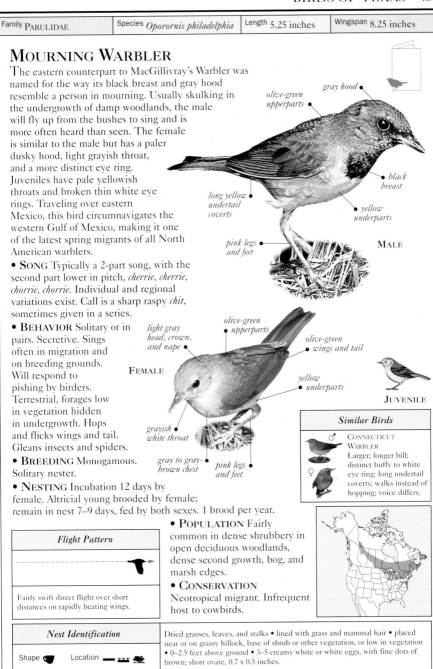

gray hood

olive-green upperparts

black breast

long yellow undertail coverts

yellow underparts

pink legs and feet

MALE

olive-green upperparts

light gray head, crown, and nape

olive-green wings and tail

yellow underparts

FEMALE

JUVENILE

grayish white throat

gray to gray-brown chest

pink legs and feet

Similar Birds

♂ CONNECTICUT WARBLER Larger; longer bill; distinct buffy to white eye ring; long undertail coverts; walks instead of hopping; voice differs. ♀

Flight Pattern
Fairly swift direct flight over short distances on rapidly beating wings.

Nest Identification	
Shape ◗ Location ▬ ✦✦✦ ❀	Dried grasses, leaves, and stalks • lined with grass and mammal hair • placed near or on grassy hillock, base of shrub or other vegetation, or low in vegetation • 0–2.5 feet above ground • 3–5 creamy white or white eggs, with fine dots of brown; short ovate, 0.7 x 0.5 inches.

Plumage Sexes differ	Habitat 🌿🌿 〰️ ⛰️	Migration Migratory	Weight 0.5 ounce

DATE _____ TIME_____ LOCATION _____

Family PARULIDAE	Species *Oporornis tolmiei*	Length 5.25 inches	Wingspan 8.25 inches

MacGillivray's Warbler

The western counterpart to the Mourning Warbler remains hidden in thick vegetation on or close to the forest floor until breeding season, when the male becomes more conspicuous and perches to sing in a higher, more exposed position above the thickets, bill pointed toward the sky. Both sexes have legs that are basically pink, but the male's legs do vary from grayish pink to brownish pink. Juveniles are similar to females.

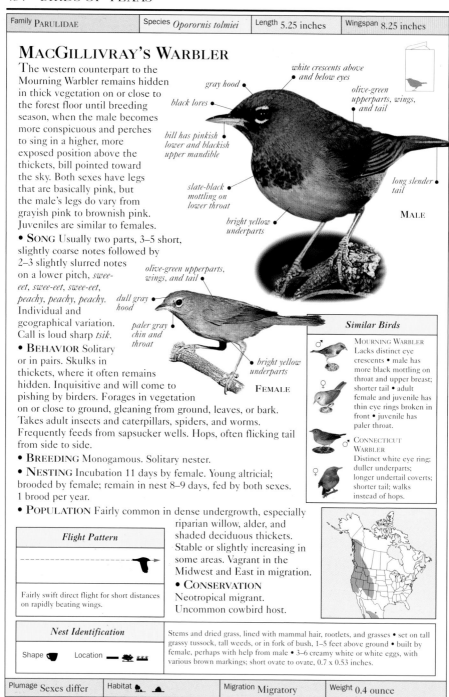

white crescents above and below eyes

gray hood

olive-green upperparts, wings, and tail

black lores

bill has pinkish lower and blackish upper mandible

slate-black mottling on lower throat

bright yellow underparts

long slender tail

MALE

olive-green upperparts, wings, and tail

dull gray hood

paler gray chin and throat

bright yellow underparts

FEMALE

• **SONG** Usually two parts, 3–5 short, slightly coarse notes followed by 2–3 slightly slurred notes on a lower pitch, *swee-eet, swee-eet, swee-eet, peachy, peachy, peachy.* Individual and geographical variation. Call is loud sharp *tsik.*

• **BEHAVIOR** Solitary or in pairs. Skulks in thickets, where it often remains hidden. Inquisitive and will come to pishing by birders. Forages in vegetation on or close to ground, gleaning from ground, leaves, or bark. Takes adult insects and caterpillars, spiders, and worms. Frequently feeds from sapsucker wells. Hops, often flicking tail from side to side.

• **BREEDING** Monogamous. Solitary nester.

• **NESTING** Incubation 11 days by female. Young altricial; brooded by female; remain in nest 8–9 days, fed by both sexes. 1 brood per year.

• **POPULATION** Fairly common in dense undergrowth, especially riparian willow, alder, and shaded deciduous thickets. Stable or slightly increasing in some areas. Vagrant in the Midwest and East in migration.

• **CONSERVATION** Neotropical migrant. Uncommon cowbird host.

Similar Birds

MOURNING WARBLER
Lacks distinct eye crescents • male has more black mottling on throat and upper breast; shorter tail • adult female and juvenile has thin eye rings broken in front • juvenile has paler throat.

CONNECTICUT WARBLER
Distinct white eye ring; duller underparts; longer undertail coverts; shorter tail; walks instead of hops.

Flight Pattern

Fairly swift direct flight for short distances on rapidly beating wings.

Nest Identification

Shape ◥   Location ▬ 🌿 ✸✸✸

Stems and dried grass, lined with mammal hair, rootlets, and grasses • set on tall grassy tussock, tall weeds, or in fork of bush, 1–5 feet above ground • built by female, perhaps with help from male • 3–6 creamy white or white eggs, with various brown markings; short ovate to ovate, 0.7 x 0.53 inches.

Plumage Sexes differ	Habitat 🌳 ⛰	Migration Migratory	Weight 0.4 ounce

DATE _____ TIME _____ LOCATION _____

Family PARULIDAE	Species *Geothlypis trichas*	Length 5 inches	Wingspan 8 inches

COMMON YELLOWTHROAT

One of the most numerous and widespread warblers usually stays close to the ground, concealed in vegetation. The amount of yellow on the underparts, the shade of olive on the upperparts, and the color of the pale border between the mask and crown all vary with geography.

black mask, bordered by thin blue-gray or white band

olive-gray to olive-green upperparts

JUVENILE

- **SONG** Bold rhythmic *wichity wichity wich;* varies with range. Sharp raspy call of *chuck* or *djip;* sometimes flat *pit* note.

MALE

bright yellow chin, throat, breast, and undertail coverts

- **BEHAVIOR** Solitary or in pairs. Wrenlike; skulks in vegetation, climbs vertically on stems, cocks and flicks tail, and

brownish-washed flanks

white belly

dusky to gray-brown forehead, lores, and ear patch

dull olive upperparts

pale gray to buff eye ring

pale yellow upper breast, throat, and chin

dull whitish lower breast and belly

dull yellow undertail coverts

FEMALE

droops and flicks wings. Hops on ground, gleaning from foliage, twigs, and grass. Eats insects, caterpillars, and spiders. Sometimes hover-gleans and hawks flying insects.

- **BREEDING** Monogamous. Solitary. Often polygamous.
- **NESTING** Incubation 12 days by female. Young altricial; brooded by female; stay in nest 8–10 days, fed by both sexes. 2 broods with single female per year; more if polygamous.
- **POPULATION** Common to abundant in marshes, brushy fields, hedgerows, woodland edges, and second growth brush. Some decline in the South, Texas, and San Francisco Bay.
- **CONSERVATION** Neotropical migrant. Frequent cowbird host. Vulnerable to habitat loss caused by wetland drainage and stream channelization.

Similar Birds

NOTE Black mask separates adult males from other North American warblers.

CONNECTICUT WARBLER
♀ Female and juvenile are larger; chunkier; bolder white eye ring; longer wings; browner upperparts; yellow underparts; long undertail coverts; short tail; walk on ground or limbs.

MACGILLIVRAY'S WARBLER
♀ Female and juvenile are hooded; yellow underparts; broken white eye ring; longer wings.

MOURNING WARBLER
♀ Female and juvenile have brownish hood; yellow underparts; short tail • female has yellow throat; eye ring either complete or broken.

Flight Pattern

Slow weak jerky flight with rapid wing beats, alternating with brief periods of wings pulled to sides. Sallies from perch to take insects in midair, returning to perch.

Nest Identification

Shape Location

Dried grasses, dried leaves, stems, bark chips, and sedges • lined with fine grasses, hair, and bark fibers • atop small pile of weeds or grass or atop cattails, sometimes in small shrub, less than 3 feet above ground • built by female • 3–6 creamy white or white eggs, flecked with black, grays, and browns, mostly at larger end; oval to short oval, 0.7 x 0.5 inches.

Plumage Sexes differ	Habitat	Migration Migratory	Weight 0.4 ounce

DATE _____ TIME _____ LOCATION _____

Family PARULIDAE	Species *Geothlypis poliocephala*	Length 5.5 inches	Wingspan 8.5 inches

GRAY-CROWNED YELLOWTHROAT

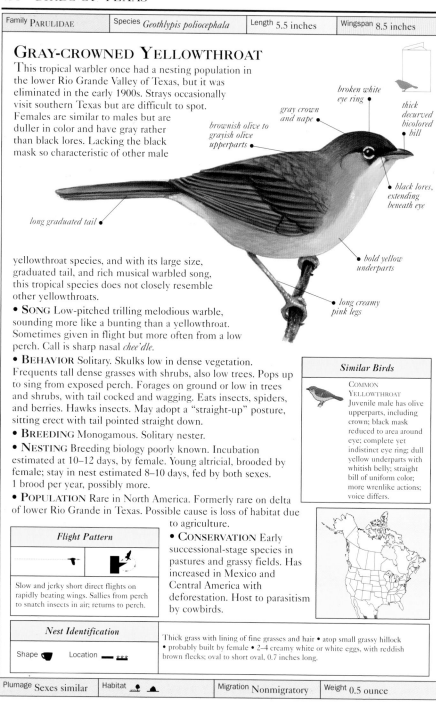

This tropical warbler once had a nesting population in the lower Rio Grande Valley of Texas, but it was eliminated in the early 1900s. Strays occasionally visit southern Texas but are difficult to spot. Females are similar to males but are duller in color and have gray rather than black lores. Lacking the black mask so characteristic of other male

broken white eye ring

gray crown and nape

brownish olive to grayish olive upperparts

thick decurved bicolored bill

black lores, extending beneath eye

long graduated tail

bold yellow underparts

long creamy pink legs

yellowthroat species, and with its large size, graduated tail, and rich musical warbled song, this tropical species does not closely resemble other yellowthroats.

- **SONG** Low-pitched trilling melodious warble, sounding more like a bunting than a yellowthroat. Sometimes given in flight but more often from a low perch. Call is sharp nasal *chee'dle*.
- **BEHAVIOR** Solitary. Skulks low in dense vegetation. Frequents tall grasses with shrubs, also low trees. Pops up to sing from exposed perch. Forages on ground or low in trees and shrubs, with tail cocked and wagging. Eats insects, spiders, and berries. Hawks insects. May adopt a "straight-up" posture, sitting erect with tail pointed straight down.
- **BREEDING** Monogamous. Solitary nester.
- **NESTING** Breeding biology poorly known. Incubation estimated at 10–12 days, by female. Young altricial, brooded by female; stay in nest estimated 8–10 days, fed by both sexes. 1 brood per year, possibly more.
- **POPULATION** Rare in North America. Formerly rare on delta of lower Rio Grande in Texas. Possible cause is loss of habitat due to agriculture.
- **CONSERVATION** Early successional-stage species in pastures and grassy fields. Has increased in Mexico and Central America with deforestation. Host to parasitism by cowbirds.

Similar Birds

COMMON YELLOWTHROAT
Juvenile male has olive upperparts, including crown; black mask reduced to area around eye; complete yet indistinct eye ring; dull yellow underparts with whitish belly; straight bill of uniform color; more wrenlike actions; voice differs.

Flight Pattern

Slow and jerky short direct flights on rapidly beating wings. Sallies from perch to snatch insects in air; returns to perch.

Nest Identification

Shape ⬩   Location ▬ ⚬⚬⚬

Thick grass with lining of fine grasses and hair • atop small grassy hillock • probably built by female • 2–4 creamy white or white eggs, with reddish brown flecks; oval to short oval, 0.7 inches long.

Plumage Sexes similar	Habitat 🌱 ⛰	Migration Nonmigratory	Weight 0.5 ounce

DATE _____ TIME_____ LOCATION _____

Family PARULIDAE	Species *Wilsonia citrina*	Length 5.25 inches	Wingspan 8 inches

HOODED WARBLER

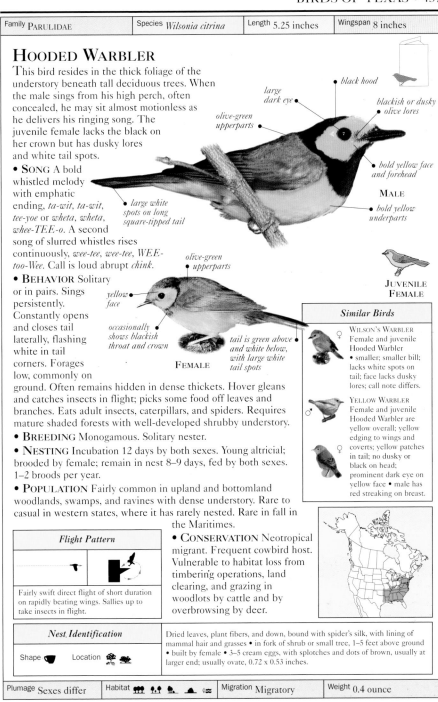

This bird resides in the thick foliage of the understory beneath tall deciduous trees. When the male sings from his high perch, often concealed, he may sit almost motionless as he delivers his ringing song. The juvenile female lacks the black on her crown but has dusky lores and white tail spots.

large dark eye

olive-green upperparts

black hood

blackish or dusky olive lores

bold yellow face and forehead

MALE

bold yellow underparts

- **SONG** A bold whistled melody with emphatic ending, *ta-wit, ta-wit, tee-yoe* or *wheta, wheta, whee-TEE-o*. A second song of slurred whistles rises continuously, *wee-tee, wee-tee, WEE-too-Wee*. Call is loud abrupt *chink*.

large white spots on long square-tipped tail

olive-green upperparts

yellow face

occasionally shows blackish throat and crown

FEMALE

tail is green above and white below, with large white tail spots

JUVENILE FEMALE

- **BEHAVIOR** Solitary or in pairs. Sings persistently. Constantly opens and closes tail laterally, flashing white in tail corners. Forages low, commonly on ground. Often remains hidden in dense thickets. Hover gleans and catches insects in flight; picks some food off leaves and branches. Eats adult insects, caterpillars, and spiders. Requires mature shaded forests with well-developed shrubby understory.
- **BREEDING** Monogamous. Solitary nester.
- **NESTING** Incubation 12 days by both sexes. Young altricial; brooded by female; remain in nest 8–9 days, fed by both sexes. 1–2 broods per year.
- **POPULATION** Fairly common in upland and bottomland woodlands, swamps, and ravines with dense understory. Rare to casual in western states, where it has rarely nested. Rare in fall in the Maritimes.
- **CONSERVATION** Neotropical migrant. Frequent cowbird host. Vulnerable to habitat loss from timbering operations, land clearing, and grazing in woodlots by cattle and by overbrowsing by deer.

Similar Birds

WILSON'S WARBLER
Female and juvenile Hooded Warbler
• smaller; smaller bill; lacks white spots on tail; face lacks dusky lores; call note differs.

YELLOW WARBLER
Female and juvenile Hooded Warbler are yellow overall; yellow edging to wings and coverts; yellow patches in tail; no dusky or black on head; prominent dark eye on yellow face • male has red streaking on breast.

Flight Pattern	
Fairly swift direct flight of short duration on rapidly beating wings. Sallies up to take insects in flight.	

Nest Identification	
Shape ◢ Location 🌿 🌳	Dried leaves, plant fibers, and down, bound with spider's silk, with lining of mammal hair and grasses • in fork of shrub or small tree, 1–5 feet above ground • built by female • 3–5 cream eggs, with splotches and dots of brown, usually at larger end; usually ovate, 0.72 x 0.53 inches.

Plumage Sexes differ	Habitat 🌳 🌿 🌲 ⛰ 〰	Migration Migratory	Weight 0.4 ounce

DATE _____ TIME _____ LOCATION _____

Family PARULIDAE	Species Wilsonia pusilla	Length 4.75 inches	Wingspan 7.5 inches

WILSON'S WARBLER

Making its home in the thick damp woodlands and bogs of western North America, this active warbler has a wide nesting range, from Alaska to New Mexico, in the boreal forest from the Pacific to the Atlantic coast in Canada, and south into the New England states. The female is similar to the male but lacks the black cap or has only a light gray-black wash on her crown. Juvenile females lack the black crown altogether.

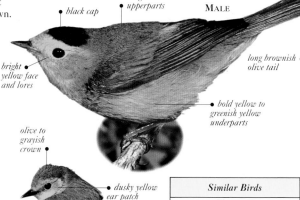

black cap

olive-green upperparts

MALE

long brownish olive tail

bright yellow face and lores

bold yellow to greenish yellow underparts

• **SONG** Quick series of slurred *chee-chee-chee* notes, dropping in pitch at the end. Subject to much individual and regional variation. Call is abrasive nasal *chimp*.

• **BEHAVIOR** Solitary or in pairs. Tame and inquisitive; responds to pishing by birders. Energetic. Moves tail up and down or in a circular fashion, similar to a gnatcatcher, as it picks food off foliage by gleaning and hover-gleaning. Also catches insects in flight. Eats spiders, insects, and berries.

olive to grayish crown

dusky yellow ear patch

FEMALE

• **BREEDING** Monogamous. Solitary in coastal areas. Forms loose colonies and is polygynous at high elevations.

• **NESTING** Incubation 10–13 days by female. Young altricial; brooded by female; stay in nest 8–11 days, fed by both sexes. 1 brood per year.

• **POPULATION** Common to fairly common in dense moist woodlands, willow and alder bogs, riparian corridors, and dense brushy ground cover in moist situations. Much more numerous in the West than in the East.

• **CONSERVATION** Neotropical migrant. Uncommon cowbird host, except in the coastal lowlands of California. Vulnerable to habitat loss from destruction of lowland riparian thickets.

Similar Birds

HOODED WARBLER White spots on tail, which it constantly flicks open and closed; longer bill; dark dusky lores; black hood in males, with suggestion of hood in many females.

YELLOW WARBLER ♀ Female and juvenile • yellow edging to wings and wing coverts; yellow spots in tail; short tail with undertail coverts reaching closer to tip; more subdued tail wag.

Flight Pattern
Swift flight of short duration on rapidly beating wings. Sallies forth from perch to take insects in midair before returning.

Nest Identification	
Shape ⬤ Location ▬ ⬤⬤⬤ 🌳	Dried leaves, stalks, moss, and grass, with lining of fine grasses • atop grassy tussock, pile of moss, or sedges, or set at base of tree or bush, or in low shrub • 0–3 feet above ground • built by female • 4–7 creamy white or white eggs, with flecks of brown, sometimes wreathed; oval to short oval, 0.6 inch long.

Plumage Sexes differ	Habitat 🌳🌳 🌲 〰️ 🔺	Migration Migratory	Weight 0.3 ounce

DATE _____ TIME_____ LOCATION _____

Family PARULIDAE	Species *Wilsonia canadensis*	Length 5–6 inches	Wingspan 7.5–8.75 inches

CANADA WARBLER

This bird sings frequently from the dense forest undergrowth it favors, or from an exposed perch just above it, with a jumbled warbling song that defies a fitting mnemonic. It actively forages for insects by flushing them from the foliage and chasing them. Males have been observed in "anticipatory feeding," offering insects to the unhatched eggs in the well-concealed nest on the ground. Canada Warblers are more often seen than heard on the breeding grounds, but a bird often will reveal itself, coming close to squeaking and pishing sounds made by birders. This early fall migrant heads southward before many other warblers begin their migrations. During migration they are often seen in pairs, and may be traveling with their mate of the season.

yellow supraloreal stripe

whitish eye ring forms spectacles

black necklace on breast

lacks wing bars

MALE

- **SONG** *Chip* followed by explosive staccato series of short notes ending with 3-note phrase, the last note rising in pitch. Song carries well and is given often on breeding grounds.
- **BEHAVIOR** Skulks in the undergrowth; often concealed when perched. Frequently found in low, dense, luxuriant undergrowth under mixed hardwoods. Gleans insects from foliage, stems, and ground; sometimes flycatches.
- **BREEDING** Solitary nester.
- **NESTING** Incubation 12 days by female. Altricial young fledge at 10–12 days. Probably 1 brood per year.
- **POPULATION** Common to fairly common in breeding range and in migration in the East; casual to accidental elsewhere. Declining.

gray upperparts, wings, and tail

pinkish legs and feet

black lores

spectacles

yellow underparts with faint gray streaking on breast

white undertail coverts

pinkish legs and feet

FEMALE

Similar Birds

MAGNOLIA WARBLER
♂ Black streaking extends onto sides; yellow rump; white wing patch or bars; white patches in ♀ tail; white supercilium; black lores and cheeks.

- **CONSERVATION** Neotropical migrant. Host to Brown-headed Cowbirds. Vulnerable to disturbance of mature forest on wintering ground. Habitat loss and forest fragmentation negatively affecting populations.

Flight Pattern
Direct flight with rapid somewhat fluttering wing beats.

Nest Identification	
Shape ⌣ Location ▬ 🐦	Generally on the ground • bulky cup of dead leaves, grasses, dried plants, and ferns • lined with finer grasses and rootlets • on a bank, upturned tree roots, or mossy hummocks • built by female • 3–5 brown, buff, or creamy white eggs with speckled dots and small blotches of various shades of brown, gray, and purple; oval to short oval, 0.68 x 0.5 inches.

Plumage Sexes differ	Habitat 🌿 🏕 ⛰	Migration Migratory	Weight 0.4 ounce

DATE _____ TIME_____ LOCATION _____

Family PARULIDAE	Species *Myioborus pictus*	Length 5.5 inches	Wingspan 8.5 inches

PAINTED REDSTART

Easily identified by its conspicuous scarlet breast and white wing patches, this native of Mexico and Central America also nests in the wooded pine-oak foothills and mountain canyons of the Southwest. It often spreads its tail and droops its wings while hopping over stumps and branches. In the dark shadowed habitats the redstart frequents, the resulting white flashes may attract the attention of the bird's mate, foraging nearby. The white flashes may also startle insects into revealing themselves as prey. In flight this bird shows a white crissum with black scalloping. Juveniles are duskier and lack the red underparts until early fall.

black head and upperparts

white arc beneath eye

white wing patches

black bill

black throat and upper breast

bold scarlet lower breast and upper belly

black sides and flanks

black feet and legs

3 white outer tail feathers

• **SONG** A full melodic low-pitched warble, *weacher, weacher, weacher chee*, the last note emphatic and single-syllabled, but all preceding notes 2-syllabled. Songs are given rather slowly, with much variation by a single male and between singers. Females may duet with male. Has call note of squeaky down-slurred *peep*.

• **BEHAVIOR** Solitary or in pairs. Tame and inquisitive. Hops on ground, logs, rocks, and branches, often turning sideways with each hop and flashing tail open or spreading it open with wings partially spread. Eats only insects. Forages actively on ground, in lower to middle levels of vegetation, and sometimes high in trees. Gleans, hover-gleans, and catches insects in flight. May join mixed-species foraging flocks outside breeding season.

• **BREEDING** Monogamous. Solitary nester.

• **NESTING** Incubation 13–14 days by female. Young altricial; brooded by female; stay in nest 9–13 days, fed by both sexes. 1–2 broods per year.

• **POPULATION** Fairly common to common in montane canyons of shaded pine-oak habitat. Rare in southern California. Accidental to rare elsewhere outside breeding range.

• **CONSERVATION** Neotropical migrant. Rare host to cowbird parasitism. Vulnerable to habitat loss because of logging and also from overgrazing in woodlots.

Similar Birds

Unmistakable; no other North American warbler resembles it.

SLATE-THROATED REDSTART
Accidental vagrant
• slate-gray wings, lacking white patches; slate-gray upperparts and face; dark chestnut crown patch; lacks white arc beneath eye; less white in tail; black-scalloped white crissum.

Flight Pattern

Weak fluttering flight of short duration on rapidly beating wings. Sallies from perch to snatch insects in air, returns to perch.

Nest Identification

Shape   Location

Stalks and bark pieces • cup often roofed • lined with grasses and hair • built on ground, sheltered by large rock, grassy tussock, tree roots, shrub, or side of bank • built by female • 3–4 creamy white eggs, with specks of brown, mostly at larger end, not wreathed; oval to short oval, 0.7 x 0.55 inches.

Plumage Sexes similar	Habitat	Migration Migratory	Weight 0.3 ounce

DATE _____ TIME_____ LOCATION _____

Family PARULIDAE	Species *Icteria virens*	Length 7.25 inches	Wingspan 9–10 inches

YELLOW-BREASTED CHAT

The largest North American warbler is named for its song, which resembles bizarre loud chattering. The large size, stocky body, thick bill, and long tail are unusual for a warbler, yet DNA studies confirm its taxonomic placement within this family. Unlike other warblers, it often sings at night in addition to its daytime vocalizations, a trait shared with some of the mimic thrushes. The female is similar to the male but has gray lores.

• **SONG** A clashing mixture of prattles, whistles, catlike sounds, clucking, screeching, and *caw* notes, both musical and harsh. Pacing is slow, hesitant, and unwarbler-like, more like a mockingbird or thrasher. Has the lowest voice of any American wood warbler. Some songs given in hovering mothlike display flights. Call notes are harsh *cheow* or nasal *hair.*

olive-green to olive-gray upperparts

blackish auriculars

white spectacles

thick curved bill

long graduated tail

white belly and crissum

black lores

white malar mark

bright yellow throat and breast

• **BEHAVIOR** Solitary or in pairs. Acts more like a mockingbird than a warbler. Shy, skulking, and secretive. Often remains hidden in thick foliage. Best seen when male sings from an exposed perch or is displaying. Display flight lasts several seconds, head held high, tail pumping, legs dangling, and singing all the while. Forages low in dense brushy shrubbery and sometimes on the ground, gleaning insects, larvae, berries, and fruits. The only warbler known to hold food in its feet.

• **BREEDING** Monogamous. Solitary nester or small colonies.

• **NESTING** Incubation 11–12 days by female. Altricial young brooded by female; stay in nest 8–11 days, fed by both sexes. 2 broods per year.

• **POPULATION** Common in dense thickets, brush, or scrub, especially along swamp margins and streams. Significant decline over much of its eastern range.

Similar Birds
No similar species in North America.

• **CONSERVATION** Neotropical migrant. Common host to Brown-headed Cowbird. Vulnerable to habitat loss due to land development and clearing, urbanization, and natural succession from old fields to maturation of forests.

Flight Pattern
Weak direct flights of short duration. In singing display, flies with legs dangling and wings flapping limply.

Nest Identification	
Shape ⬠ Location ⬠	Dried stems, leaves, grasses, and bark pieces, lined with soft grasses, stems, and leaves • in bush, vines, or thorny shrub, 2–8 feet above ground • built by female • 3–6 white or creamy white eggs, with flecks of rust or violet, concentrated at larger end; oval, 0.86 x 0.67 inches.

Plumage Sexes similar	Habitat	Migration Migratory	Weight 0.9 ounce

DATE _____ TIME_____ LOCATION _____

| Family THRAUPIDAE | Species *Piranga flava* | Length 8 inches | Wingspan 12.75 inches |

HEPATIC TANAGER

Named for the liver-red plumage of the male, this tropical bird has a small summer range in the southwestern mountain forests of North America. Not shy around humans, the male perches in tall trees to sing a sing-song series of musical phrases, similar to those of the Black-headed Grosbeak, but faster. The adult male retains his red plumage throughout the year. The combination of dark bill and dusky gray auriculars in both sexes are good field marks to separate them from other tanager species. Juveniles are similar to females but have paler underparts with buffy wing bars and are heavily streaked with brown.

grayish cheek patch

orange-red to dark red overall

blackish bill

grayish wash on back and flanks

MALE

grayish cheek patch

olive-green upperparts

yellow underparts

grayish wash on flanks

FEMALE

- **SONG** Clear bold musical phrases in back-and-forth sing-song pattern. Call note is a loud *chip* or *chuck*, similar to the Hermit Thrush.
- **BEHAVIOR** Solitary or in pairs. Often joins mixed-species foraging flocks after the nesting season. Forages for food in upper foliage of tall trees where it gleans from branches, stems, and leaves. Sometimes catches insects in flight. Eats insects and fruit. Sings often and is often detected by calls or song. Restless and active. Often flies considerable distances, moving rapidly from one tree to the next or traveling all the way across mountain canyons.
- **BREEDING** Monogamous. In courtship display male moves head back and forth and lifts bill to sky, showing off his bright throat.
- **NESTING** Breeding biology poorly known. Estimated incubation 13–14 days by female. Young altricial; brooded by female; stay in nest estimated 13–15 days, fed by both sexes. 1 brood per year.
- **POPULATION** Uncommon to fairly common in pine and pine-oak in mountain canyons. Accidental on Gulf Coast.
- **CONSERVATION** Neotropical migrant. Rare host to cowbird parasitism.

Similar Birds

♂ SUMMER TANAGER Large yellow-brown bill; lacks grayish cheek patch • male displays ♀ brighter reds.

Flight Pattern
Relatively swift direct flight on rapidly beating wings.

Nest Identification	
Shape ⌣ Location 🌳 🌿	Forbs, grasses, stems, and flower petals with lining of soft grass • in fork, toward end of limb, 15–50 feet above ground • built mostly by female, but male may bring materials • 3–5 bluish greenish eggs with brownish markings, often wreathed; oval to short oval, 1.0 x 0.75 inches.

| Plumage Sexes differ | Habitat ▲ 🌿 🌱 | Migration Migratory | Weight 1.3 ounces |

DATE _____ TIME_____ LOCATION _____

Family THRAUPIDAE	Species *Piranga rubra*	Length 7.75 inches	Wingspan 11–12 inches

SUMMER TANAGER

Males are easily identified by their brilliant red plumage. This bird is the most common North American tanager in its range, which is the most extensive tanager range across the eastern and southern United States. Males retain the bright red plumage all year long. Females have olive-green upperparts and orange-yellow underparts. First spring males are a mixture of reds and yellow-greens, usually with red on the head, back, and uppertail coverts.

- **SONG** Melodic leisurely warbling of 5–7 phrases; sing-song, back-and-forth, and robinlike. Call is a repeated *pick-a-tuck*.
- **BEHAVIOR** Solitary or in pairs. Forages at middle to high levels in trees; picks food off leaves. Eats mostly bees and wasps, which it takes expertly in midair, and often raids wasp nests and beehives. Also eats other insects, grubs, caterpillars, and fruit. Often found near water, including bottomland hardwood and riparian forest, but also pine-oak forest in the East; primarily riparian in the West.
- **BREEDING** Monogamous. Solitary.
- **NESTING** Incubation 11–12 days by female. Altricial young brooded by female; leave nest at 13–14 days, fed by both sexes. 1–2 broods per year.
- **POPULATION** Common in deciduous and mixed conifer-deciduous forests, especially oaks. Some declines in the East.
- **FEEDERS** Mixture of peanut butter and cornmeal.
- **CONSERVATION** Neotropical migrant. Uncommon cowbird host. Vulnerable to habitat loss and forest fragmentation.

bright rosy red overall

large yellowish bill

MALE

yellowish bill

olive-green upperparts

orange-yellow underparts

FEMALE

FIRST SPRING MALE

Similar Birds

NORTHERN CARDINAL ♂
Red crest; black face and chin; large cone-shaped reddish bill.

HEPATIC TANAGER ♂ ♀
Duller darker red color; blackish bill; grayish cheek patch; gray wash on flanks, back, and wing coverts.

Flight Pattern
Swift direct flight with quick wing strokes. Sallies forth to take insects on the wing.

Nest Identification	
Shape ⌒ Location 🌿 🌳	Bark pieces, forbs, grass, and leaves, with lining of soft grasses • far out on limb, 10–35 feet above ground • built by female • 3–5 light blue or green eggs, marked with browns, occasionally wreathed or capped; oval to short oval, sometimes long oval, 0.9 x 0.75 inches.

Plumage Sexes differ	Habitat 🌾 🌳	Migration Migratory	Weight 1.0 ounce

DATE _____ TIME_____ LOCATION _____

| Family THRAUPIDAE | Species *Piranga olivacea* | Length 7 inches | Wingspan 11–12 inches |

SCARLET TANAGER

No other bird in North America has the breeding male's unique plumage of a rich scarlet body with black wings and tail. When the male arrives on the breeding grounds, he perches at the tops of tall trees and sings to defend his territory and attract a mate. In the molt following the breeding season, the male retains his black wings and tail, but his plumage becomes a mixture of green, yellow, and red patches, later becoming dull green and yellow, appearing similar to the female bird. Juveniles and first fall males are similar in appearance to the adult female.

bright scarlet overall

black wings and tail

tan to creamy pink bill with blackish culmen

MALE

• **SONG** A breathy, coarse series of 4–5 notes, somewhat rapidly delivered, *querit-queer-query-querit-queer*. Pattern is sing-song and back-and-forth, somewhat like a robin with a sore throat. Has call of *chip-burrr*.

• **BEHAVIOR** Solitary or in pairs. May forage for food on ground but more often high in tops of trees. Eats insects, including wasps, bees, and caterpillars. Also takes berries and fruit. Gleans food from branches and foliage and frequently hawks insects. Frequents drier forests, often pine and pine-oak.

pale broken eye ring

dull green upperparts

blackish wings and tail

FALL MALE

lemon-yellow underparts

FEMALE

• **BREEDING** Monogamous; solitary or in pairs. Male displays by perching below female, opening his wings and showing off his scarlet back.

• **NESTING** Incubation 13–14 days by female. Young altricial; brooded by female; stay in nest 9–11 days, fed by both sexes. 1 brood per year.

• **POPULATION** Fairly common in deciduous and mixed conifer-hardwood forests. Some recent declines. Casual in West.

• **FEEDERS** Will come to feeders for mixture of bread crumbs, cornmeal, and peanut butter.

Similar Birds

♂ **WESTERN TANAGER** Male has additional yellow upper wing bar • females and winter males are similar to their counterparts but have white wing bars. ♀

• **CONSERVATION** Neotropical migrant. Vulnerable to loss of habitat and forest fragmentation, as it requires large areas of forest for breeding. Fairly common host to cowbird parasitism.

Flight Pattern	

Swift rapid flight with quick wing strokes. Sallies forth to take insects in flight.

Nest Identification	
Shape 🥄 Location 🐦 🔖	Forbs, grasses, sticks, rootlets, and twigs, with lining of soft grasses and conifer needles • far out on limb, 5–70 feet above ground • built by female • 2–5 bluish greenish eggs, marked with brown, often wreathed; oval to short oval, 0.9 x 0.7 inches.

| Plumage Sexes differ | Habitat 🐦 🌲 | Migration Migratory | Weight 1.0 ounce |

Family THRAUPIDAE	Species *Piranga ludoviciana*	Length 7.25 inches	Wingspan 11–12 inches

WESTERN TANAGER

One of only two North American tanagers with distinct wing bars, this bird frequents the coniferous forests of the western mountain region, where it is one of the most colorful species present. It has on rare occasions hybridized with its close cousin, the Scarlet Tanager. In the molt after the breeding season, the male's red head fades to a yellowish color with fine streaking on the crown. The female's olive-gray back contrasts sharply with the yellow-green rump, uppertail coverts, and nape. Juveniles resemble females but with head and body streaked dark brown.

red head, throat, and upper breast

yellow uppertail coverts, rump, and lower back

creamy pinkish orange bill with dark culmen

upper yellow and lower white wing bars

black tail

yellow underparts

MALE

WINTER MALE

- **SONG** A hoarse vireo-like series of 3–4 phrases, *che-ree, che-ree, che-weeu, cheweeu*. Call is *pit-ick, pri-tick-tick*.
- **BEHAVIOR** Solitary or in pairs. Forages in trees and on ground, gleaning food from bark, limbs, foliage, and soil. Eats fruit and insects, including wasps and bees. Hawks insects in flight. Bathes in birdbaths. Frequent singer often first detected by vocalizations. In postbreeding season, often joins mixed-species foraging flocks.
- **BREEDING** Monogamous. Solitary.
- **NESTING** Incubation 13 days by female. Altricial young brooded by female; stay in nest 13–15 days, fed by both sexes. 1 brood per year.
- **POPULATION** Fairly common in coniferous and pine-oak forests, particularly in mountain canyons. Casual in East in winter.

yellow-olive head

olive-gray back, shoulders, and wing coverts

FEMALE

pale broken eye ring

thin yellow and white wing bars

yellowish underparts

Similar Birds

FLAME-COLORED TANAGER ♀ Dark bill; dusky auriculars; bolder whitish wing bars; white tail corners; darkly streaked back.

♂ SCARLET TANAGER Females and winter ♀ males are similar to their counterparts but have olive backs and lack the wing bars.

- **FEEDERS** Fresh oranges, dried fruit, bread crumbs.
- **CONSERVATION** Neotropical migrant. Uncommon cowbird host. Vulnerable to loss of habitat and forest fragmentation.

Flight Pattern
Swift direct flight on rapidly beating wings. Sallies forth from perch to take insects in flight.

Nest Identification	
Shape ⌣ Location 🌿🌳	Rootlets, sticks, and moss, with lining of plant down and mammal hair • far out on branch, 6–65 feet above ground • built mostly by female • 3–5 bluish eggs, marked with browns, often wreathed; oval to short subelliptical, 0.9 x 0.66 inches.

Plumage Sexes differ	Habitat 🌿🌲	Migration Migratory	Weight 1.0 ounce

DATE _____ TIME_____ LOCATION _____

Family EMBERIZIDAE	Species *Sporophila torqueola*	Length 4.5 inches	Wingspan 8 inches

WHITE-COLLARED SEEDEATER

A native of Mexico and Central America, this bird has a small nesting range in southern Texas, one that decreased early in the 20th century. In local grassy habitats, weedy fields and overgrown lots, canebrakes, and similar habitats near the river in the lower Rio Grande Valley, small groups of this little seedeater, with its stubby swollen bill, can still be found. It can sometimes be seen with large flocks of other seed-eating birds. In flight it shows a white base to the primaries. Females are duller in color with buffy underparts, brown upperparts, and paler wing bars and lack the collar and cap. Juvenile males have the pattern of the males with the coloration of the females.

black cap

white crescent under eye

partial buff collar

black upperparts and wings

thick short curved bill

2 white wing bars

black rounded tail

MALE

buff-white underparts

• **SONG** A 2-part song with first notes high-pitched, followed by series of lower notes, *sweet sweet sweet sweet wit-wit-wit-wit*, often ending in a buzzy trill. Call is a high-pitched *wink*.

• **BEHAVIOR** In pairs or small groups. More gregarious after the breeding season, forming flocks and often foraging with other species. Eats seeds and insects. Males often sing from exposed perches on weed stalks, cane, fences, and utility wires. Some populations found in overgrown weedy and grassy lots in small towns. Frequents marshes with dense stands of grass.

• **BREEDING** Monogamous. Solitary.

• **NESTING** Incubation 13 days by female. Young altricial; brooded by female; leave nest at 9–11 days, fed by both sexes. 1–2 broods per year.

short thick curved bill

FEMALE

tawny brown upperparts

brownish black wings with cinnamon edging and 2 thin wing bars

cinnamon tail

buffy underparts

FIRST WINTER MALE

• **POPULATION** Rare and local in the lower Rio Grande Valley of Texas.

• **CONSERVATION** Declines with loss of habitat due to land clearing, agriculture, and development. Uncommon host to cowbird parasitism.

Flight Pattern

Weak bouncy fluttering flight, with series of rapid wing strokes alternating with wings pulled to sides.

Nest Identification	
Shape Location	Sticks, rootlets, plant stems, and grass, with lining of plant down and mammal hair • in fork of bush or small tree or in weeds, 3–5 feet above ground • built by female • 2–4 pale blue to pale gray eggs, with brown markings, concentrated at larger end; subelliptical toward elliptical oval, 0.64 x 0.5 inches.

Plumage Sexes differ	Habitat	Migration Nonmigratory	Weight 0.3 ounce

DATE _____ TIME_____ LOCATION _____

Family EMBERIZIDAE	Species *Arremonops rufivirgatus*	Length 6.25 inches	Wingspan 9 inches

OLIVE SPARROW

A native of Mexico, this bird has a small nesting range along the lower Rio Grande Valley in southern Texas. It is difficult to spot, as it often remains hidden in low thickets and dense undergrowth. It may be first detected by its noisy towheelike scratching in the leaf litter or by its accelerating song, likened to a bouncing ball. The male sings only from a low concealed perch. Juveniles have streaked dark brown upperparts and pale buff underparts streaked with dark brown, except on the whitish belly and throat.

wide brown stripe on each side of crown

dark line through eye

drab olive upperparts

white chin and throat

white belly

buff breast, sides, flanks, and undertail coverts

• **SONG** A repetitive accelerating series of *chip* notes, preceded by one or two introductory notes, *chip, chip, chip-chip-chip-chip-chip-chip*. Call is an insectlike *speeee* or a sharp *tsik*.

• **BEHAVIOR** Solitary or in pairs. Skulks on ground and in underbrush. Forages low in trees, bushes, and on the ground, gleaning, scratching, and picking food off ground. Eats seeds and insects.

• **BREEDING** Monogamous. Solitary.

• **NESTING** Breeding biology poorly known; species virtually unstudied in the field. Estimated incubation 10–12 days by female. Young altricial; brooded by female; stay in nest estimated 9–11 days, fed by both sexes. 2 broods per year.

• **POPULATION** Common in thickets, especially riparian thickets, and thorn scrub, although numbers are decreasing due to loss of habitat.

• **CONSERVATION** Infrequent cowbird host. Vulnerable to habitat loss because of clearing of riparian forests, brushlands, and scrublands for agriculture, grazing, and development.

Similar Birds

GREEN-TAILED TOWHEE
Larger; reddish cap; blackish line borders white mustache and separates it from white throat; gray head and underparts; lacks eye stripe.

Flight Pattern

Short flights with series of rapid wing beats alternating with wings pulled to sides for brief periods; repeated.

Nest Identification

Shape   Location

Dried grasses, sticks, stems, leaves, and bark pieces, with lining of mammal hair and finer material • entrance on side • in bush or cactus, 2–5 feet above ground or on ground • built by female • 2–5 white eggs, unmarked; ovate, 0.7 inch long.

Plumage Sexes similar	Habitat	Migration Nonmigratory	Weight 0.8 ounce

DATE _____ TIME_____ LOCATION _____

| Family EMBERIZIDAE | Species *Pipilo chlorurus* | Length 7.25 inches | Wingspan 10 inches |

GREEN-TAILED TOWHEE

The smallest of the towhees, this bird lives in the low brush of high mountain plateaus in southwestern North America. If an intruder approaches its nest, it leaves the nest and scampers through the undergrowth like a small mammal, hoping to distract the predator. Its habit of staying on or near the ground sometimes makes it a difficult species to observe, but males do choose prominent perches to deliver their territorial songs. Juveniles are streaked overall and have buffy white underparts and brownish upperparts with two faint wing bars.

- **SONG** A varied series of chip notes, *chu-weet-chur, cheee-chur,* accelerating to a trill. Calls a nasal *meew* and *chink.* Somewhat similar to Fox Sparrow.

reddish cap

white lores

gray face

olive-green upperparts

white throat bordered by a dark and a white stripe

gray breast

buffy flanks

wings and tail edged with yellow-olive

whitish belly

- **BEHAVIOR** Solitary or in pairs. May form loose flocks with other species in winter. Forages for food on ground by scratching under foliage with both feet simultaneously, which is called double-scratch feeding. Eats seeds, fruit, and insects and their larvae. Secretive and easily overlooked. May be detected by the loud noises it makes rustling leaves on the ground as it scratches for food.

- **BREEDING** Monogamous. Solitary.
- **NESTING** Breeding biology poorly known. Estimated incubation 11–13 days by female. Young altricial; brooded by female; stay in nest estimated 10–12 days, fed by both sexes. 2 broods per year.
- **POPULATION** Fairly common in mountain thickets, chaparral, scrublands, and riparian scrub. Casual across the East.
- **FEEDERS** Visits feeding stations that have seed, grains, and bread crumbs.
- **CONSERVATION** Neotropical migrant. Uncommon cowbird host. Vulnerable to habitat loss because of land clearing, grazing, and development.

Similar Birds

OLIVE SPARROW Smaller; brown-striped crown; buff breast; dark thin eye line • inhabits lower Rio Grande Valley.

Flight Pattern
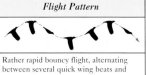
Rather rapid bouncy flight, alternating between several quick wing beats and wings pull to sides; repeated.

Nest Identification	
Shape ◖ Location ▬ 🐦	Sticks, bark chips, and grass, with lining of hair and fine plant materials • on ground, near base of bush or low in shrub or cactus, less than 28 inches above ground • built by female • 2–5 white eggs, flecked and dotted with brown; short oval, 0.9 x 0.65 inches.

| Plumage Sexes similar | Habitat ▲ ⤴ | Migration Migratory | Weight 1.0 ounce |

DATE _____ TIME_____ LOCATION _____

Family EMBERIZIDAE	Species *Pipilo maculatus*	Length 7–7.5 inches	Wingspan 10–11 inches

SPOTTED TOWHEE

This bird is the western counterpart of the Eastern Towhee, and until recently they were considered one species, the Rufous-sided Towhee. The white spotting on the upperparts, wings, and tail shows geographical variation. The white on the undersides of the tail corners flash in flight. Juveniles are brown with two white wing bars and darker brown streaking on the upperparts and underparts.

MALE
blackish head and chest
blackish olive upperparts
red eyes
black wings with 2 white wing bars and white spots
blackish bill
black tail with white tips on underside of outer tail feathers
cinnamon-rufous sides, flanks, and undertail coverts
white belly and median underparts
creamy pink legs and feet

dark brown head, neck, breast, and upperparts
white spotting on back
dark brown tail with white tips on underside of outer tail feathers
FEMALE
dark brown wings with 2 white wing bars and white spots
JUVENILE

• **SONG** Interior populations give 2 introductory *chip* notes, followed by a trill, similar to Bewick's Wren. Pacific Coast birds deliver a fast or slow trilling. Call is slurred nasal mewing *guee*.

• **BEHAVIOR** Solitary or in pairs. Small family groups stay together after nesting season. Males sing from elevated perches. Forages by double-scratching in leaf litter on ground beneath dense thickets, pulling both legs sharply backward at the same time. Eats insects, caterpillars, spiders, seeds, and fruit; sometimes small lizards or snakes. If approached too closely, female scurries from nest in the manner of a small rodent to distract intruder.

• **BREEDING** Monogamous. Solitary.

• **NESTING** Incubation 12–14 days by female. Young altricial; brooded by female; stay in nest 9–11 days, fed by both sexes, but mostly by male. 2 broods per year.

• **POPULATION** Common to fairly common in chaparral, brushy thickets, and forest edge.

• **FEEDERS** Mixture of oats, suet, and flax seeds.

• **CONSERVATION** Vulnerable to loss of habitat due to land clearing, grazing, and development. Fairly common host to cowbird parasitism.

Similar Birds

♂ **EASTERN TOWHEE** Lacks white spotting on back and scapulars • male has blacker upperparts • female has ♀ paler brown head, breast, and upperparts.

Flight Pattern

Short bounding flights with several rapid wing strokes followed by wings pulled to sides.

Nest Identification

Shape ◖   Location ▬ 🌿 🌳

Twigs, leaves, rootlets, grass, and bark • lined with grasses • on ground, sheltered by bush or grassy tussock, occasionally in low shrub or tree • built by female • 2–6 gray-brown or creamy white eggs, flecked and dotted with purple, red-brown, and gray; ovate, 0.95 x 0.7 inches.

Plumage Sexes differ	Habitat 🌲 🔺 ✈	Migration Some migrate	Weight Undetermined

DATE _____ TIME_____ LOCATION _____

Family EMBERIZIDAE	Species *Pipilo erythrophthalmus*	Length 7–7.5 inches	Wingspan 10–11 inches

EASTERN TOWHEE

Sometimes called a Ground Robin in the South, this is the eastern counterpart of the Spotted Towhee. Until recently these birds were classified as one species, the Rufous-sided Towhee. The two species hybridize where their ranges overlap along rivers in the Great Plains. The smaller Florida race has whitish eyes instead of red like most other races. In flight the white undertail corners flash conspicuously. Juveniles are brown overall with pale chins and dark streaking on underparts and upperparts.

black upperparts and hood

red eyes

MALE

white outer tail feathers

tawny buff undertail coverts

rufous sides

white underparts

distinct white patch at base of primaries and distinct white tertial edges

• **SONG** A clear whistled *drink-your-teeeaaa*, with the "tea" trilled. Much individual variation, with some birds leaving off the introductory note and some omitting the ending trill. Has calls of *toe-WHEEE* and *che-wink* or *wank*.

• **BEHAVIOR** Solitary or in pairs. Secretive; stays low in underbrush and on ground. Frequents brushy thickets, woodland edges, and riparian areas. Males are conspicuous when singing, often choosing an exposed perch. Usually detected by the rustle of dry leaves on ground; forages by double-scratching, pulling both legs sharply backward at once. Eats insects, caterpillars, small salamanders, fruits, and seeds.

brown upperparts and hood

white outer tail feathers

tawny buff undertail coverts

rufous sides

white patch at base of primaries and white tertial edges

white underparts

FEMALE

JUVENILE

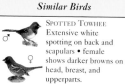

• **BREEDING** Monogamous. Solitary. Courting male chases female and fans tail to show off white spots on outer feathers.

• **NESTING** Incubation 12–13 days by female. Young altricial; brooded by female; stay in nest 10–12 days, fed by both sexes, more by male. 2–3 broods per year.

• **POPULATION** Common to fairly common. Major decline in Northeast in last half of 20th century.

Similar Birds

SPOTTED TOWHEE
Extensive white spotting on back and scapulars • female shows darker browns on head, breast, and upperparts.

• **FEEDERS** Mixture of oats, suet, and seeds.

• **CONSERVATION** Declines in Northeast poorly understood; vulnerable to loss of habitat, clearing of land, development, and pesticides in food chain. Frequent cowbird host.

Flight Pattern

Short bouncy flights with tail spread; series of rapid wing beats alternating with wings pulled to sides; repeated.

Nest Identification

Shape Location

Sticks, rootlets, grass, bark, and leaves, with lining of soft grasses • on ground, sheltered by grassy tussock or bush, occasionally in low bush or tree, 1–5 feet above ground (but up to 20 feet) • built by female • 2–6 creamy white or grayish eggs; oval, 0.9 x 0.66 inches.

Plumage Sexes differ	Habitat	Migration Northern birds migrate	Weight 1.5 ounces

DATE _____ TIME_____ LOCATION _____

Family EMBERIZIDAE	Species *Pipilo fuscus*	Length 8 inches	Wingspan 11–11.5 inches

CANYON TOWHEE

This sparrowlike bird was formerly lumped with the very similar California Towhee and together they were called the Brown Towhee. Now considered a separate species, the Canyon Towhee is paler with a more rufous cap and a dark central chest spot. Not as strongly territorial as the California Towhee, it shows little aggressive interactions when defending its nesting area. Juveniles are similar to adults but have streaked underparts, two cinnamon wing bars, and, darker streaked upperparts.

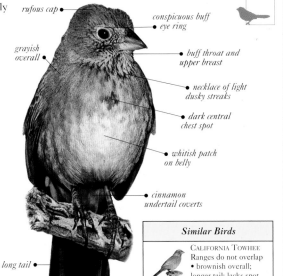

rufous cap

grayish overall

conspicuous buff eye ring

buff throat and upper breast

necklace of light dusky streaks

dark central chest spot

whitish patch on belly

cinnamon undertail coverts

long tail

• **SONG** 1–2 introductory chips, followed by series of accelerating chips, *chwee, chwee, chilly, chilly, chilly.* Call is nasal slurred *chedep* or *chee-yep;* also a light *ssip.*

• **BEHAVIOR** Solitary or in pairs. Often in small groups after breeding season. Stays low in brush or on ground. Hops rather than walks. Forages by double-scratching on ground in soil or leaf litter. Eats grain, insects, and seeds. Females sit tightly on nest, and, when flushed by intruder, scurry away with wings drooped like a small rodent to lure interloper from nest site.

• **BREEDING** Monogamous. Solitary nester. Pair mates for life.

• **NESTING** Incubation 11 days by female. Young altricial; brooded by female; stay in nest 8–9 days, fed by both sexes. 2–3 broods per year.

• **POPULATION** Common on the lower slopes of mountain canyons covered with brush, juniper, or piñon.

• **FEEDERS** Will come to feeders for seeds.

• **CONSERVATION** Uncommon host to parasitism by cowbirds.

Similar Birds

CALIFORNIA TOWHEE
Ranges do not overlap • brownish overall; longer tail; lacks spot between breast and belly; brownish crown contrasts little with head and nape; cinnamon lores contrast with face; dusky brown underparts.

ABERT'S TOWHEE
Cinnamon-brown upperparts; paler cinnamon undertail coverts and mottled cinnamon-brown; lacks spot between breast and belly; cinnamon-brown crown.

Flight Pattern

Short flights with rapidly beating wings alternating with wings pulled briefly in to sides.

Nest Identification	Stems, grass, and sticks, with lining of leaves, bark pieces, and mammal hair • in thickest part of tree, usually 3–12 feet above ground • built mostly by female • 2–6 light green or blue eggs, with various splotches, dots, and flecks of black and brown; ovate, 0.92 x 0.68 inches.
Shape ◗ Location 🌱 🌿 🌳	

Plumage Sexes similar	Habitat ▲ ▲	Migration Nonmigratory	Weight 1.6 ounces

DATE _____ TIME_____ LOCATION _____

Family EMBERIZIDAE	Species *Aimophila cassinii*	Length 6 inches	Wingspan 9 inches

CASSIN'S SPARROW

When another male invades its territory, this drab-looking sparrow will rise from its cactus perch and perform its exquisite fluttering territorial song flight some fifteen to thirty feet above the ground. In flight the white tips on its outer tail feathers are conspicuous. Adults are similar to juveniles but have whiter underparts with less streaking on the breast, sides, and flanks.

grayish head with brownish streaking on crown

grayish upperparts with black and brownish streaks

2-toned bill with straight dark gray culmen

long rounded dark grayish brown tail

whitish gray chin and throat, bordered by thin dark malar mark

buffy white underparts

JUVENILE

brown streaking on flanks

BREEDING ADULT

- **SONG** Slightly quivering sweet trill, preceded and followed by 2 notes. Call note is *pit.* Fluttering skylarking display flights. Sometimes sings at night.
- **BEHAVIOR** Solitary or in pairs. Small groups after nesting season. May join mixed foraging flocks in winter. Except when singing, skulks and forages under cover of tall grasses and bushes. Forages by scratching on ground, gleaning food from grassy vegetation and substrate. Eats seeds, insects, caterpillars, and flower buds. Like some other species living in arid regions, it apparently gains all the water it requires from its diet.
- **BREEDING** Monogamous. Solitary.
- **NESTING** Breeding biology poorly known. Estimated incubation 12–14 days by female. Young altricial; brooded by female; remain in nest estimated 9–11 days, fed by both sexes. 1–2 broods per year.
- **POPULATION** Fairly common in arid grasslands with scattered thorn shrubs and cacti. Casual in the far West and the East in migration.
- **FEEDERS** Ground corn, sorghum, and other grains.

Similar Birds

BOTTERI'S SPARROW Rusty brown-streaked gray upperparts; black streaking on uppertail coverts; buffy wash on breast, sides, and flanks, lacking streaks; lacks white tail tips.

BREWER'S SPARROW Smaller; more slender body; cleft tail; smaller pinkish bill • western range.

- **CONSERVATION** Neotropical migrant. Uncommon host to cowbird parasitism. Vulnerable to habitat loss due to overgrazing, land clearing for agricultural use, and for development.

Flight Pattern

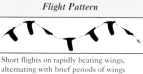

Short flights on rapidly beating wings, alternating with brief periods of wings pulled to sides.

Nest Identification

Shape ◗   Location ▬ ••• 🌳

Forbs, grass, and occasionally flowers, with lining of soft grass, rootlets, and hair • on grassy tussock sheltered by bush or low in cactus or bush • up to 1 foot above ground • built by female • 3–5 plain white eggs; oval, 0.8 x 0.6 inches.

Plumage Sexes similar	Habitat 🌿 ✈	Migration Migratory	Weight 0.7 ounce

DATE _____ TIME_____ LOCATION _____

| Family EMBERIZIDAE | Species *Aimophila botterii* | Length 6 inches | Wingspan 9 inches |

BOTTERI'S SPARROW

This large sparrow is a native of Mexico, its permanent range extending into southernmost Texas and its breeding range in summer into southeastern Arizona. Spending most of its time on the ground, it often will run rather than fly to escape danger. It can be distinguished from Cassin's Sparrow by its long brown tail and whitish breast, and when flushed, by the lack of white in the tips of its outer tail feathers. Juveniles are buffier overall and have buffy underparts with streaking on the breast, sides, and flanks.

large bill with decurved culmen

whitish or grayish buff underparts

grayish upperparts with rufous and black streaking

rusty wash on wings and tail

JUVENILE

long rounded dusky brown tail

brownish buff on flanks and crissum

• **SONG** A high abrasive series of hesitant chips, followed by a bouncing-ball trill. Call is a thin *chick*.

• **BEHAVIOR** Solitary or in pairs. Small groups after nesting season. Shy, elusive, and retiring. Hard to see. When flushed, flies short distance before dropping back into cover. Forages on ground for food. Eats insects and seeds. Males sing from low exposed perches and sometimes on the wing between perches.

• **BREEDING** Monogamous. Solitary.

• **NESTING** Breeding biology poorly known. Estimated incubation 12–14 days by female. Young altricial; brooded by female; stay in nest estimated 9–11 days, fed by both sexes. 1–2 broods per year.

• **POPULATION** Uncommon in grasslands with scattered shrubs and bushes. Declining due to loss of habitat, especially in southern Texas.

• **CONSERVATION** Neotropical migrants in western population. Extent of cowbird parasitism unknown. Population declines due to overgrazing from as early as 1880s, land clearing, and development.

Similar Birds

CASSIN'S SPARROW
Dusky tail; white tips on outer tail feathers; dusky streaking on flanks; bill with straight culmen; dark spots and subterminal dark barring on upperparts; grayer underparts.

GRASSHOPPER SPARROW
Chunkier; buffy loral region; short tail; buffier underparts; buffy streaking on upperparts.

Flight Pattern

Short flights on rapidly beating wings alternating with brief periods of wings pulled to sides.

Nest Identification

Shape ◖ Location ▬ ⁂

Grasses and rootlets, with lining of finer materials • on ground or grassy tussock, usually sheltered by tall grass or shrub • built by female • 2–5 plain bluish white eggs; oval to short oval, 0.8 x 0.57 inches.

| Plumage Sexes similar | Habitat ⬥ ⤝ | Migration Texas birds do not migrate | Weight 0.7 ounce |

DATE _____ TIME_____ LOCATION _____

Family EMBERIZIDAE	Species *Aimophila ruficeps*	Length 6 inches	Wingspan 9 inches

RUFOUS-CROWNED SPARROW

The black "whisker" lines on each side of its face, white eye ring, and lack of a white supercilium distinguish this bird from the similar Chipping Sparrow. The wary Rufous-crowned Sparrow will run and hide from danger, rather than fly. Despite this tendency, the sparrow is often conspicuous and easily observed when not approached too closely. It will, however, come out into the open in response to a squeaking noise. Juveniles have buffier upperparts and underparts, with streaking on the breast, and often show two narrow white wing bars.

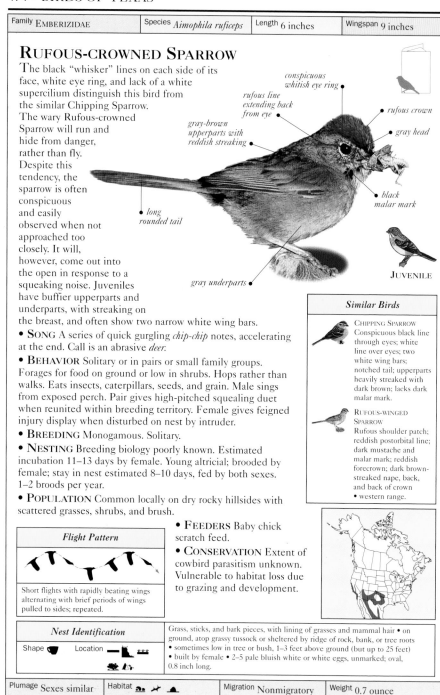

conspicuous whitish eye ring

rufous line extending back from eye

gray-brown upperparts with reddish streaking

rufous crown

gray head

black malar mark

long rounded tail

gray underparts

JUVENILE

- **SONG** A series of quick gurgling *chip-chip* notes, accelerating at the end. Call is an abrasive *deer*.
- **BEHAVIOR** Solitary or in pairs or small family groups. Forages for food on ground or low in shrubs. Hops rather than walks. Eats insects, caterpillars, seeds, and grain. Male sings from exposed perch. Pair gives high-pitched squealing duet when reunited within breeding territory. Female gives feigned injury display when disturbed on nest by intruder.
- **BREEDING** Monogamous. Solitary.
- **NESTING** Breeding biology poorly known. Estimated incubation 11–13 days by female. Young altricial; brooded by female; stay in nest estimated 8–10 days, fed by both sexes. 1–2 broods per year.
- **POPULATION** Common locally on dry rocky hillsides with scattered grasses, shrubs, and brush.
- **FEEDERS** Baby chick scratch feed.
- **CONSERVATION** Extent of cowbird parasitism unknown. Vulnerable to habitat loss due to grazing and development.

Similar Birds

CHIPPING SPARROW Conspicuous black line through eyes; white line over eyes; two white wing bars; notched tail; upperparts heavily streaked with dark brown; lacks dark malar mark.

RUFOUS-WINGED SPARROW Rufous shoulder patch; reddish postorbital line; dark mustache and malar mark; reddish forecrown; dark brown-streaked nape, back, and back of crown • western range.

Flight Pattern

Short flights with rapidly beating wings alternating with brief periods of wings pulled to sides; repeated.

Nest Identification		
Shape	Location	Grass, sticks, and bark pieces, with lining of grasses and mammal hair • on ground, atop grassy tussock or sheltered by ridge of rock, bank, or tree roots • sometimes low in tree or bush, 1–3 feet above ground (but up to 25 feet) • built by female • 2–5 pale bluish white or white eggs, unmarked; oval, 0.8 inch long.

Plumage Sexes similar	Habitat	Migration Nonmigratory	Weight 0.7 ounce

DATE _____ TIME_____ LOCATION _____

Family EMBERIZIDAE	Species *Spizella arborea*	Length 6.25 inches	Wingspan 9.75 inches

AMERICAN TREE SPARROW

After nesting near the frigid tundra regions, flocks of these sparrows migrate south and can be found primarily in the United States during the winter. Sometimes traveling in flocks of thirty-five to forty birds, but often smaller, they scout out food supplies and willingly come to outdoor feeders. Males often winter farther north than females and juveniles. Males sing during courtship and also to claim territory.

rufous crown

gray head and nape

rufous stripe behind eye

dark upper and yellow lower mandibles

gray chin, throat, breast, and underparts

black and rufous streaking on scapulars and back

dark central spot on breast

white trim on outer webs of outer tail feathers

rufous patches on sides of breast, sides, and flanks

notched tail

Juveniles have paler upperparts and streaking on the head, breast, and sides. These birds spend their summers in open landscapes and their winters near the forest edge.

- **SONG** Several long clear introductory notes followed by a variable trilled melody. Has a call of *tweedle-eet, tweedle-eet.*
- **BEHAVIOR** In pairs on breeding grounds. In flocks in winter. Relatively tame and conspicuous. Forages for food by scratching on ground, foliage, or snow. Eats mostly seeds. Also eats insects and caterpillars in summer, as well as some berries and catkins of willow.
- **BREEDING** Monogamous. Solitary.
- **NESTING** Incubation 12–13 days by female. Young altricial; brooded by female; stay in nest 8–10 days, fed by both sexes. 1 brood per year.

JUVENILE

WINTER PLUMAGE

Similar Birds

FIELD SPARROW
Smaller; pink upper and lower mandibles; clear buff breast lacks black central spot.

- **POPULATION** Fairly common in weedy fields, open areas of brush and scattered trees, groves of small conifers, mixed conifer-deciduous groves, and marshes.
- **FEEDERS** Feeds on wild birdseed mixture.

Flight Pattern

Short flight on rapidly beating wings alternating with brief periods of wings pulled to sides; repeated.

Nest Identification

Shape 〔 Location ▬ ⚬⚬⚬ 🌲 🐦

Stems, bark pieces, moss, and grass, with lining of feathers, fur, and hair • atop clump of grass or moss, rarely low in shrub or tree • 1–5 feet above ground • built by female • 3–7 light blue or greenish white eggs, with brown spots and flecks; oval, 0.75 x 0.56 inches.

Plumage Sexes similar	Habitat ▬ ▲ 🐦	Migration Migratory	Weight 0.7 ounce

DATE _____ TIME_____ LOCATION _____

Family EMBERIZIDAE	Species *Spizella passerina*	Length 5.5 inches	Wingspan 8–9 inches

CHIPPING SPARROW

Its bold chestnut cap, bordered by a long white superciliary stripe during breeding season, helps identify this tiny sparrow. Named for its song and call, it sings from its high perch during the day, and sometimes even at night, or calls as it forages for food in trees, gardens, and backyards. One of the tamest sparrows, it will take food from human hands. Juveniles lack the white eyebrow and

chestnut cap

gray nape and cheeks

white supercilium

black bill

light brown upperparts with black or brown streaking

black line extends from bill through eye to ear

long slightly notched tail

2 white wing bars

gray underparts

JUVENILE

WINTER PLUMAGE

chestnut cap but have a streaked crown and nape, streaked underparts, and buffy wing bars. Winter birds have brown-streaked crowns, brown faces, and dark lores.

- **SONG** A repetitive series of trilled chip notes, *chip-chip-chip-chip-chip-chip-chip*, all the same pitch. Has a call of *seek*.
- **BEHAVIOR** Solitary or in pairs. In small family groups after breeding season. May join mixed-species foraging flocks in winter. Forages on ground and picks off foliage. Eats seeds, insects, their caterpillars, and spiders.
- **BREEDING** Monogamous. Solitary. A few males polygynous.
- **NESTING** Incubation 11–14 days by female. Young altricial; brooded by female; stay in nest 8–12 days, fed by both sexes. 2 broods per year.
- **POPULATION** Common and widespread in open mixed coniferous-deciduous forests, forest edges, gardens, lawns, and short-grass fields.
- **FEEDERS** Comes to feeders for breadcrumbs and seeds.
- **CONSERVATION** Neotropical migrant. Common host to cowbird parasitism.

Similar Birds

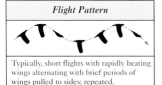

CLAY-COLORED SPARROW
Black-streaked brown crown with gray center stripe; buffy brown cheek patch bordered by dark postocular stripe and dark mustache mark; pale grayish eyebrow; whitish chin and submustachial stripe separated by buffy malar mark; whitish underparts with buffy wash on breast.

Flight Pattern

Typically, short flights with rapidly beating wings alternating with brief periods of wings pulled to sides; repeated.

Nest Identification	
Shape Location	Grass, forbs, weed stalks, and rootlets, with lining of mammal hair and grass • on branch or vine tangle, rarely on ground • most often 3–11 feet above ground (but up to 60 feet) • built by female • 2–5 bluish green eggs, marked with dark browns, blues, and blacks, often wreathed; subelliptical to short subelliptical, 0.7 x 0.5 inches.

Plumage Sexes similar	Habitat	Migration Migratory	Weight 0.4 ounce

Family EMBERIZIDAE	Species *Spizella pallida*	Length 5.5 inches	Wingspan 8 inches

CLAY-COLORED SPARROW

The male bird perches to claim its territory while singing its buzzy insectlike song across the grasslands. Wintering primarily in the highlands of central Mexico, this tiny bird flies north to summer in the prairies of Canada and the northern United States. In flight this frequent visitor to backyard feeders shows a dark buff rump. Juveniles have a gray nape, buffy brown cheek patch, and streaked underparts.

white supercilium

brown crown with black streaks

whitish stripe in middle of crown

white malar stripe

dark stripe from behind eye

JUVENILE

dark mustache stripe

light brown back with dark streaks

brown ear patches

pale gray-white underparts with buffy wash on breast

2 white wing bars

- **SONG** Insectlike repetitive *bzzz-bzzzz-zeee-zeee*. Has a call of *chip* or *sip*.
- **BEHAVIOR** In pairs during breeding season. Small family groups prior to fall migration. Males vigorously defend small territory. Sings often and well into the heat of July. Forages on ground or low in trees. Eats seeds and insects. May join mixed-species feeding flocks with other sparrows in winter.
- **BREEDING** Monogamous. Solitary.
- **NESTING** Incubation 10–12 days by both sexes, but female does more. Young altricial; brooded by female; stay in nest 8–9 days, fed by both sexes. 1–2 broods per year.
- **POPULATION** Fairly common in brushy weedy fields, riparian thickets, and forest edges. Slight decline over recent decades due to loss of habitat after human populations increased in the North and East. Rare to casual visitor in migration and winter on both coasts, the Southwest, and southern Florida.
- **FEEDERS** Will come to feeding stations for breadcrumbs, cracked corn, sunflower seeds, and millet.
- **CONSERVATION** Neotropical migrant. Common host to cowbird parasitism. Vulnerable to habitat loss due to development and land clearing for agriculture.

Similar Birds

CHIPPING SPARROW
Winter adults have gray rump; brown crown with black streaking and whitish central crown stripe; gray underparts • first winter birds have buffy underparts.

BREWER'S SPARROW
Lacks whitish crown stripe; blacker streaking on upperparts; paler brown ear patch lacks black outline; whitish eye ring.

Flight Pattern

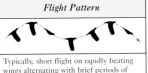

Typically, short flight on rapidly beating wings alternating with brief periods of wings pulled to sides.

Nest Identification	Sticks, grass, forbs, and rootlets, with lining of mammal hair and rootlets • atop grassy tussock, on ground sheltered by bush, or low in branch of shrub or tree • less than 5 feet above ground • built by female • 3–5 bluish green eggs, marked with dark browns and blacks, often wreathed; ovate, 0.67 x 0.5 inches.
Shape 🥚 Location ▬ 🪹 🐦	

Plumage Sexes similar	Habitat 🌿 ▬ 🌾 🌲	Migration Migratory	Weight 0.4 ounce

DATE _____ TIME _____ LOCATION _____

Family EMBERIZIDAE	Species *Spizella breweri*	Length 5.5 inches	Wingspan 8 inches

BREWER'S SPARROW

At sunrise and just before sunset, countless territorial males sing continuous choruses, their buzzing trill spreading across the Great Basin of the western United States. The Timberline Sparrow, an isolated subspecies that nests above the timberline in the subalpine

pale brown ear patch with dark borders

brown crown with fine black streaking

brown upperparts with black streaking

grayish white eyebrow

pale lores

whitish eye ring

dark malar stripe

grayish white throat and underparts

dark brown wings with buff wing bars

zone of the Canadian Rockies north into southeastern Alaska, may be a separate species. Shy and wary on the nesting grounds, this sparrow is tame during other times of the year and often visits gardens and outdoor feeders. Juveniles are similar to adults but are buffier overall with streaked underparts; both juveniles and adults show a buffy brown rump.

JUVENILE

• **SONG** An insectlike long-continuing buzzing trill, with each sequence of the song given on different pitches, one sequence following another in long sessions without pauses. Call is *tsip*.

• **BEHAVIOR** Solitary or in pairs. In small family groups after breeding season. In winter, may join mixed-species foraging flocks with other sparrows and buntings. Forages on or near ground for food. Eats mostly insects in spring and summer. In fall and winter, eats mostly seeds. Found almost anywhere that sagebrush occurs. When disturbed by intruder, incubating or brooding female often runs rather than flies from nest.

• **BREEDING** Monogamous. Solitary.

• **NESTING** Incubation 11–13 days, mostly by female, but some by male. Young altricial; brooded by female; stay in nest 8–9 days, fed by both sexes. 1–2 broods per year.

• **POPULATION** Common in arid brushland, sagebrush flats, mountain meadows, and also in thickets. Accidental in the East.

• **FEEDERS** Will come for baby chick scratch feed.

• **CONSERVATION** Neotropical migrant. Infrequent host to cowbird parasitism.

Similar Birds

CHIPPING SPARROW
Winter • dark streaking on rufous crown; gray rump; bold white wing bars; less contrasting eyebrow stripe; lacks white eye ring and dark malar mark.

CLAY-COLORED SPARROW
Whitish or buffy white central stripe; buffier streaking on upperparts; buffier washes on underparts; gray nape; buffier cheek patch; lacks white eye ring.

Flight Pattern

Short flights with rapid wing beats alternating with brief periods of wings pulled to sides; repeated.

Nest Identification

Shape 〈icon〉 Location 〈icons〉

Forbs and dried grasses, with lining of rootlets and mammal hair • in bush or cactus • usually less than 4 feet above ground • built by female • 3–5 bluish green eggs, with dark brown dots and specks; subelliptical to ovate, 0.7 x 0.5 inches.

Plumage Sexes similar	Habitat 〈icons〉	Migration Migratory	Weight 0.5 ounce

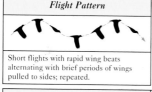

DATE _____ TIME _____ LOCATION _____

Family EMBERIZIDAE	Species *Spizella pusilla*	Length 5.75 inches	Wingspan 8.5 inches

FIELD SPARROW

This sparrow stays near the ground in fields and open woodlands. When defending its nest, the male flies from tree to tree singing a melody that accelerates like the bouncing of a dropped rubber ball. The clearing of the primeval eastern forest provided thousands of acres of habitat ideally suited for this

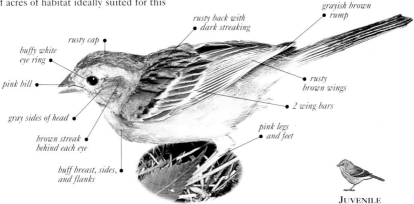

grayish brown rump

rusty back with dark streaking

rusty cap

buffy white eye ring

pink bill

rusty brown wings

2 wing bars

gray sides of head

pink legs and feet

brown streak behind each eye

buff breast, sides, and flanks

JUVENILE

small sparrow. Now, as the old farms become suburbs or succumb to the woodlots brought on by ecological succession, this bird is declining in this range.

- **SONG** A pleasant *seea-seea-seea-wee-wee-wee*, which begins with separate clear whistled notes and accelerates, either ascending, descending, or staying on the same pitch. Call is abrasive *chip*.
- **BEHAVIOR** Solitary or in pairs in breeding season. In small family flocks after nesting. In winter, forms flocks that may join mixed-species foraging flocks. Forages on ground or low in shrubbery for insects, caterpillars, seeds, and spiders. Tame and curious; responds to squeaking and pishing by birders.
- **BREEDING** Monogamous. Solitary.
- **NESTING** Incubation 10–17 days by female. Young altricial; brooded by female; stay in nest 7–8 days, fed by both sexes. Male tends and feeds fledglings while female incubates second clutch. 2–3 broods per year.
- **POPULATION** Fairly common in old fields, open brushy woodlands, thorn scrub, and forest edge. Casual in West. Uncommon in the Maritimes.
- **FEEDERS** Small grain.
- **CONSERVATION** Common host to cowbird parasitism.

Similar Birds

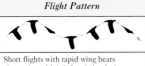

CLAY-COLORED SPARROW
Brown crown with central stripe; buffy cheek patch; buffy brown malar mark; gray nape; buffy edges and streaks on upperparts; whitish underparts with buffy wash on chest and flanks; 2 buffy wing bars.

Flight Pattern
Short flights with rapid wing beats alternating with brief periods of wings pulled to sides; repeated.

Nest Identification	
Shape 🐦 Location ▬ ✶✶✶ 🌿	Fine grasses, leaves, and dried grass, with lining of mammal hair and rootlets • atop grassy tussock or clump of vegetation, sometimes in vine or bush • less than 3 feet above ground • built by female • 2–6 creamy pale greenish bluish white eggs, marked with browns, occasionally wreathed; short subelliptical, 0.7 x 0.53 inches.

Plumage Sexes similar	Habitat 🌿 ▬ ▲	Migration Northern birds migrate	Weight 0.4 ounce

DATE _____ TIME_____ LOCATION _____

Family EMBERIZIDAE	Species *Spizella atrogularis*	Length 5.75 inches	Wingspan 9 inches

BLACK-CHINNED SPARROW

The black chin of the breeding male combined with the rusty back and gray body set this bird apart from similar sparrows. Females are similar to males but have a plain gray head and underparts, sometimes with a trace of black on the chin. Juveniles are similar to females and winter birds, but have light streaking on their underparts and a brownish wash on their heads. Although primarily nonmigratory, birds in the northern parts of the range do migrate.

- **SONG** A series of 2 or more clear chips run into a bouncing-ball trill of *sweet-sweet-swee-I-iiiiiiiiir*; similar to the song of a Field Sparrow. Has a call of high thin *seep*.

- **BEHAVIOR** Solitary or in pairs. After breeding season and in winter, sometimes in small family groups. Shy and retiring. Male chooses prominent singing perch. Forages for food in brush and on ground. Eats insects and seeds. Little is known of its biology.

- **BREEDING** Monogamous. Loose colonial.

- **NESTING** Incubation 13 days, mostly by female. Young altricial; brooded by female; stay in nest estimated 8–12 days, fed by both sexes. 1–2 broods per year.

- **POPULATION** Uncommon and local in chaparral, sagebrush, and arid scrub on grassy slopes in foothills and mountains.

- **CONSERVATION** Neotropical migrant. Uncommon host to cowbird parasitism. Vulnerable to habitat loss because of development, land clearing, overgrazing, and fire retardation leading to maturing of chaparral habitat. Species requires open, early stage of post-fire chaparral habitat development.

bright pink bill

black chin and lores

gray overall

whitish gray belly

rusty back and scapulars with black streaking

brown wings with paler-edged coverts

MALE

long dark tail

rusty back and scapulars with dark streaking

brown wings with paler edging on coverts

bright pink bill

gray overall

whitish gray belly

long dark gray tail

FEMALE

JUVENILE

Similar Birds

DARK-EYED JUNCO "Gray-headed Junco" race • gray overall; pink bill; black lores extending mask to back of eye; chestnut back; white outer tail feathers.

Flight Pattern

Flights of short duration on rapidly beating wings alternating with brief periods of wings pulled to sides.

Nest Identification

Shape [icon]   Location [icon]

Stems and grasses, with lining of rootlets, hair, and feathers • set low in bush, 1.5–3 feet above ground • built by female • 2–5 light blue eggs, unmarked; subelliptical, ovate, or rounded ovate, 0.7 x 0.53 inches.

Plumage Sexes differ	Habitat ▲ ▲	Migration Northern birds migrate	Weight 0.4 ounce

DATE _____ TIME_____ LOCATION _____

Family EMBERIZIDAE	Species *Pooecetes gramineus*	Length 5.5–6.75 inches	Wingspan 10–11.25 inches

VESPER SPARROW

This bird is named for the time of day it usually sings its best and most continuous choruses, which is at twilight when many other songbirds have become silent. Its song is not limited to the vespers hour, however, for during nesting season, it sings throughout the day from the highest perch available in its territory. This sparrow, with chestnut lesser coverts on its shoulder and white outer tail feathers, has a vast geographical distribution, its home habitats ranging from dry grasslands and farmlands to sagebrush flats. Juveniles resemble adults but have more extensive streaking on the underparts.

brown ear patch bordered behind and below with white

white eye ring

upperparts streaked gray-brown

grayish brown streaking on breast, throat, and sides

chestnut patch at bend of wing, with row of black spots beneath

white underparts

white outer tail feathers

long notched tail

- **SONG** Two drawled clear notes followed by two higher notes, then a short descending trill. Call is a high thin *tssit*.
- **BEHAVIOR** Solitary or in pairs. May form small family groups after breeding season. May join loose flocks in winter. Walks on ground. Runs from danger instead of flying. Forages on ground, in grasses, and in low shrubbery for insects and seeds. Very fond of dust baths. Neither bathes in nor drinks water, meeting all internal water needs through diet.
- **BREEDING** Monogamous. Solitary or loose colonies.
- **NESTING** Incubation 11–13 days by both sexes, but female does more. Young altricial; brooded by female; stay in nest 7–14 days, fed by both sexes. Fledglings tended and fed by male while female starts another nest. 1–3 broods per year.
- **POPULATION** Uncommon to fairly common. Numbers declining in the East as habitat is lost to development and because logged areas become older and less suitable for nesting.
- **CONSERVATION** Neotropical migrant. Common host to cowbird parasitism. Nesting sites are being lost due to agricultural mowing and other operations.

Similar Birds

SAVANNAH SPARROW
Shorter tail; yellow supercilium; pale central crown stripe; central "stickpin" spot on chest; lacks chestnut lesser coverts; lacks white eye ring and outer tail feathers.

Flight Pattern

Short flights on rapidly beating wings alternating with brief periods of wings pulled to sides; repeated.

Nest Identification	
Shape ◄ Location ▬ ✶✶✶	Dry grasses, weed stalks, and rootlets, lined with finer grasses and animal hair • in scraped-out depression on ground • hidden under vegetation, in field, near tall grass clump, on sand or dirt • built by female • 2–6 creamy white or pale greenish white eggs with brown markings; oval, 0.8 x 0.6 inches.

Plumage Sexes similar	Habitat	Migration Migratory	Weight 1.0 ounce

DATE _____ TIME _____ LOCATION _____

Family EMBERIZIDAE	Species *Chondestes grammacus*	Length 5.75–6.75 inches	Wingspan 10.5–11 inches

LARK SPARROW

This sparrow, with its harlequin head pattern, has a lovely voice and sings from the ground, a perch, or while flying, sometimes even at night. Frequenting the open prairies and other open habitats, mostly west of the Mississippi River, it can be identified by the dark spot in the center of its breast and the long rounded tail with extensive white edging. Juveniles are similar to adults but more washed-out with an ill-defined head pattern, buffier coloration, dark brown streaking on the white throat, and white underparts with a buffy wash on the sides of the breast.

black, white, and chestnut-brown stripes on head

chestnut ear patches

white mustache

brown and black streaking on back

black malar mark

whitish underparts with buff wash on flanks

• **SONG** Long, pleasant bubbling melody, beginning with 2 loud clear notes followed by series of chips, buzzes, and trills. Call is repetitive sharp metallic *tik*, often given in flight.

• **BEHAVIOR** Solitary or in pairs. Gregarious. Feeds in flocks, even during breeding season. Forages for food on ground and low in trees and shrubs. Eats seeds, insects, and caterpillars. Females on nest perform distraction display when disturbed, scurrying away with wings fluttering and tail spread. Prior to copulating, male often passes to female a twig or grass stem, which she holds.

• **BREEDING** Monogamous. Occasionally polygamous. Often in loose colonies. Male displays while swaggering on the ground in front of female, his tail spread, showing off its white feathers.

long rounded black tail with white edging

JUVENILE

• **NESTING** Incubation 11–12 days by female. Young altricial; brooded by female; remain in nest 9–10 days, fed by both sexes. 1 brood per year.

• **POPULATION** Common in cultivated areas, fields, pastures, grassland, prairie, and savanna. Range has declined east of the Mississippi River due to loss of habitat. Casual to East Coast.

Similar Birds

Head pattern is distinctive; not likely to be confused with other sparrows.

• **FEEDERS** Small grains.

• **CONSERVATION** Neotropical migrant. Uncommon cowbird host. Vulnerable to habitat loss due to land clearing, development, overgrazing, and nest losses resulting from agricultural operations.

Flight Pattern

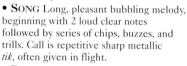

Short fluttering flight on rapidly beating wings alternating with brief periods of wings pulled to sides.

Nest Identification

Shape ☕   Location ▬ ▬▬ 🐦🌳

Sticks, grass, and forbs • lined with rootlets and grasses • atop grassy tussock shaded by bush, or low in tree, sometimes in shrub or bush or in abandoned nest • 3–30 feet above ground • built by female • 3–6 creamy to grayish white eggs, marked with dark browns and blacks, often wreathed; oval, 0.8 x 0.62 inches.

Plumage Sexes similar	Habitat 🌿 ▬	Migration Migratory	Weight 1.0 ounce

DATE _____ TIME_____ LOCATION _____

Family EMBERIZIDAE	Species *Amphispiza bilineata*	Length 5.5 inches	Wingspan 8.5 inches

BLACK-THROATED SPARROW

Its bold black throat and the white stripes above its eye extending from its bill are good clues for identifying this sparrow. As long as it is able to get water from its diet, it thrives in the desert country, surviving long periods of time without drinking water. Accessible water is necessary, however, in the heat of the summer through autumn, until the rains begin and green vegetation develops. It has not adapted well to the transition of habitats as some of its range has been developed into suburbs. Juveniles lack the black chin, throat, and breast of adults and are streaked with brown on the breast and sides.

brownish gray head

white eyebrow

white mustache

brownish gray upperparts

black lores, chin, throat, and chest

whitish underparts

gray-buff wash on sides, flanks, and crissum

rounded black tail with white trim on outer tail feathers and white tips

JUVENILE

- **SONG** A high bell-like song with 2 introductory notes followed by a trill *queat-queat, toodle-oodle-oodle*; variable. Call is an abrasive *chip* or high sweet tinkling twitters.
- **BEHAVIOR** Solitary or in pairs. Sometimes forms small family groups after nesting season. Joins mixed-species foraging flocks in winter. Fairly tame and curious. Responds to pishing by birders. Forages for food on ground and in low vegetation. Eats seeds, spiders, and insects. Walks or runs, often with tail cocked upward. Timing of breeding varies annually, apparently based on seasonal rainfall amounts and food availability.
- **BREEDING** Monogamous. Solitary.
- **NESTING** Breeding biology poorly known. Estimated incubation 12–15 days by female. Young altricial; brooded by female; stay in nest estimated 10–11 days, fed by both sexes. 2 broods per year.
- **POPULATION** Fairly common in desert and semidesert scrub, especially on rocky uplands. Declining in some areas due to development of habitat. Accidental in the East.
- **CONSERVATION** Neotropical migrant. Uncommon host to cowbird parasitism. Vulnerable to habitat loss caused by combination of land clearing and development.

Similar Birds

SAGE SPARROW Juvenile similar to juvenile Black-throated Sparrow • white eyebrow stripe and white eye ring; sandy gray-brown crown, nape, and back; fine dusky streaks on chest; traces of central dark spot on chest; tail lacks white edging and tips; brown streaking on sides and flanks.

Flight Pattern

Typically, short-duration flights on rapidly beating wings alternating with brief periods of wings pulled to sides; repeated.

Nest Identification	
Shape ◥ Location 🌳 🌵	Forbs and grass, with lining of mammal hair and plant fibers • in middle of bush or cactus, less than 10 feet above ground • built by female • 2–4 plain white or pale blue eggs; oval, 0.7 x 0.52 inches.

Plumage Sexes similar	Habitat 〰 〰 🌵 ✈	Migration Northern birds migrate	Weight 0.5 ounce

DATE _____ TIME_____ LOCATION _____

Family EMBERIZIDAE	Species *Amphispiza belli*	Length 6.25 inches	Wingspan 8.25 inches

SAGE SPARROW

This shy sparrow of coastal California and the Great Basin area west of the Rocky Mountains most often skulks and hides under dense scrub. It often flicks its tail as it walks on the ground; when it runs, it usually holds its tail perpendicular to its back, wrenlike. Males perch to sing conspicuously on the top of a bush. The coastal subspecies Bell's Sparrow has much darker gray upperparts with more distinct facial markings than the paler interior race, with its sandier upperparts with faint streaking. Although the species is primarily migratory, the coastal race is not. Juveniles are duller overall and have more heavily streaked upperparts and underparts.

light to dark gray upperparts, with or without dusky streaking

white eye ring and supraloral streak

gray head

white chin and throat

brown to black malar mark borders white submustachial stripe

black central spot on breast

white underparts

dusky streaking on sides and flanks

JUVENILE

• **SONG** A jumbled series of phrases with a seesaw rhythm, *twee-si-tity-slip, twee-si-tity-slip*, high, thin, and tinkling. Has a high faint call note of *tik* or *tik-tik*.

• **BEHAVIOR** Solitary or in pairs. Small flocks after breeding season. Inconspicuous and wary. Difficult to observe. Often found near water. Stays low in shrubbery or on ground, except to sing. Forages mainly on ground. Eats insects, caterpillars, and seeds. Male twitches tail while singing and when scolding intruders. Runs or flies away low over or within vegetation.

• **BREEDING** Monogamous. Solitary.

• **NESTING** Incubation 12–16 days by female. Young altricial; brooded by female; stay in nest 9–11 days, fed by both sexes. 2 broods per year.

• **POPULATION** Common and widespread in the Great Basin in sagebrush and alkaline flats. Coastal subspecies fairly common to common in montane chaparral. Accidental in East.

• **FEEDERS** Will come to feeders for baby chick scratch feed.

• **CONSERVATION** Uncommon host to cowbird parasitism. Vulnerable to habitat loss due to land clearing and development, overgrazing by cattle. The endemic San Clemente Island (California) subspecies is endangered.

Similar Birds

LARK SPARROW
Brown ear patches; harlequin head pattern; white tail corners; black spot in center of white chest; does not bob tail.

BLACK-THROATED SPARROW
Juvenile similar to juvenile Sage Sparrow • gray head, nape, and ear patch; white supercilium; white throat and broad mustache; brown-streaked breast and sides; white edges and outer tips to tail.

Flight Pattern

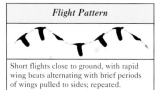

Short flights close to ground, with rapid wing beats alternating with brief periods of wings pulled to sides; repeated.

Nest Identification	
Shape 🔻 Location 🪺 ▬	Twigs, grass, and bark chips, with lining of grasses, forbs, feathers, fur, and seeds • set deep in shrub, less than 4 feet above ground • sometimes in scrape on ground, sheltered by bush • built by female • 2–5 bluish white eggs, marked with dark browns and black, occasionally wreathed; ovate, 0.8 x 0.65 inches.

Plumage Sexes similar	Habitat ⤲ ▲	Migration Most migrate	Weight 0.7 ounce

DATE _____ TIME_____ LOCATION _____

Family EMBERIZIDAE	Species *Calamospiza melanocorys*	Length 7 inches	Wingspan 11 inches

LARK BUNTING

In the spring hundreds of these birds fly in choreographed circles and shapes like a rolling wheel of birds. As they move across the prairie, birds from the rear fly to the front over birds settling into vegetation. They remain in flocks as they return to their nesting grounds on the sagebrush plains. Males and females have similar winter plumage, but males show black primaries. Juveniles are similar to winter adults. This is the state bird of Colorado.

- **SONG** Flutelike warbling melody of full whistles and trills. Often sings in groups. Call is *hoo-ee*.
- **BEHAVIOR** In pairs or flocks. Gregarious; in flocks most of year. Forages on ground and in low vegetation. Eats insects, caterpillars, and seeds. Territorial males ascend 20–30 feet with white wing patches flashing, pour out song, and descend with jerky butterfly movements to ground. Neighboring males often join in display flights.
- **BREEDING** Monogamous. Some are polygynous. Loose colonies. Displaying male fluffs out feathers and crest and sings.
- **NESTING** Incubation 11–12 days by female; some males help. Altricial young brooded by female; stay in nest 8–9 days, fed by both sexes. 2 broods per year.
- **POPULATION** Common in grasslands, dry plains, prairies, sagebrush flats, and meadows. Rare to casual on Pacific Coast in fall and winter. Casual in the East in fall and winter.
- **FEEDERS** Occasionally attends feeders that supply small grains and seeds.
- **CONSERVATION** Neotropical migrant. Uncommon host to cowbird parasitism. Historical population declines in northern and eastern parts of breeding range caused by loss of the bird's prairie habitat.

black or slate-gray overall
bluish gray bill
large white wing patches

MALE

short tail with white tips on all but central tail feathers

bluish gray bill
FEMALE
streaked gray-brown upperparts
white wing patch with hint of buff
short tail

WINTER PLUMAGE

unstreaked belly
white underparts with dusky streaking

Similar Birds

BOBOLINK ♂
White on back, rump, uppertail coverts, and wings; buffy ocher hindneck.

Flight Pattern
Strong flight with shallow wing beats alternating with brief periods of wings pulled to sides.

Nest Identification	
Shape ◗ Location ▬ ⁎⁎⁎	Grass, forbs, and fine roots • lined with hair and plant down • in grassy depression • built by female • 3–7 pale blue or greenish blue eggs, occasionally spotted with reddish browns; oval, 0.9 inch long.

Plumage Sexes differ	Habitat ▬ ✦ ▄	Migration Migratory	Weight 1.1 ounces

DATE _____ TIME_____ LOCATION _____

Family EMBERIZIDAE	Species *Ammodramus savannarum*	Length 4.75–5.5 inches	Wingspan 8–8.5 inches

GRASSHOPPER SPARROW

These birds are named for their insectlike song. The male claims his territory by singing from a low exposed perch during the day. Hidden in tall grasses, this bird runs rather than flies from danger. Because it nests on the ground in cultivated grasslands, lives are lost when the crop is mowed; after mowing, predators take eggs, young, and adults.

dark crown with pale stripe through center

yellow lore

white eye ring

gray-brown streaking on upperparts

buff breast, sides, flanks, and undertail coverts

yellow at bend of wings

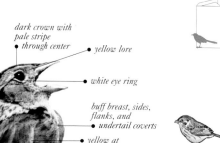

JUVENILE

white belly

- **SONG** High thin insectlike buzzing with 2 notes then a trill, *pit-tuck, zeeeeeeeeeeee.* At dusk may sing with more squeaky buzzy notes and trills. Call is soft insectlike *tisk*.

- **BEHAVIOR** Solitary or in pairs. May form small family groups after breeding season. Forages on ground and from low vegetation. Eats insects, worms, snails, seeds, and grains. Males sing from any exposed perch. When disturbed on nest, female flutters away in distraction display.

- **BREEDING** Monogamous Loose colonies.

- **NESTING** Incubation 11–12 days by female. Young altricial; brooded by female; stay in nest 9 days, fed by both sexes. 2–3 broods per year.

- **POPULATION** Common in cultivated fields, grasslands, prairies, savanna, and palmetto scrub. Declining in eastern part of its range.

- **CONSERVATION** Neotropical migrant. Uncommon host to cowbird parasitism. Declining due to changes in grasses grown and losses to agricultural operations. Threatened or endangered in Florida and parts of the Appalachian Mountains.

Similar Birds

BAIRD'S SPARROW
Buffy orange crown and supercilium; dark spot in each rear corner of ear patch; blackish malar mark; necklace of dark brown streaks on breast; chestnut scapulars with pale edging forming scaly appearance on upperparts.

HENSLOW'S SPARROW
Greenish buff head and nape; blackish crown stripes; black-bordered ear patch; rusty brown upperparts edged whitish and streaked black; dark brown streaking on breast, sides, and flanks • juvenile is paler and more washed with buffy head, nape, upperparts, and underparts; faint dusky streaking on sides • eastern range.

short notched tail

Flight Pattern
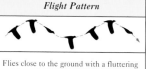
Flies close to the ground with a fluttering rapid undulating flight, similar to a wren.

Nest Identification	Dried grass with lining of rootlets, hair, and grass, partially domed on one side • in slight hollow on ground, sheltered by tall grasses • built by female • 3–6 creamy white eggs with flecks and dots of reddish brown, occasionally wreathed; ovate, 0.8 x 0.56 inches.
Shape ◗ Location ▬	

Plumage Sexes similar	Habitat ▃▃ ♠	Migration Migratory	Weight 0.8 ounce

DATE _____ TIME_____ LOCATION _____

Family EMBERIZIDAE	Species *Ammodramus bairdii*	Length 5.5 inches	Wingspan 8.5 inches

BAIRD'S SPARROW

On nesting grounds males establish territories by perching on a tussock or shrub and singing. In the 1870s this bird was one of the most abundant in the prairies of its region, but remnant populations now cling to the habitat remains. When frightened it scurries mouselike through the grass and hides. The best field marks on this elusive sparrow are the broad buff-ocher central crown stripe and the necklace of brownish black streaks across the chest.

short spiky tail with pale edges

dark spot at each rear corner of auriculars

flat ocherous crown with black stripes and wide ocher center stripe

large bill

black mustache

buffy brown, rufous, and black upperparts

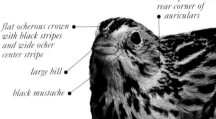

buffy wash on streaked sides and flanks

band of fine black streaks on breast

Similar Birds

GRASSHOPPER SPARROW
Plain buff face and chest; pale narrow central crown stripe; dark postocular stripe; auriculars outlined above and on rear with dark border • juvenile has buffy wash on streaked breast and sides.

SAVANNAH SPARROW
More extensive streaking on underparts; large central "stickpin" on chest (typically); conspicuous white to yellow narrow crown stripe; yellowish to white supercilium.

Underparts are white. Juveniles are more washed out and paler with less streaking on the underparts.

- **SONG** Silvery tinkling bell-like 2–3 notes, then lone warbled note, then trilling *zip-zip-zip-zr-r-rrrrrrrr*. Call is abrasive *chip*.
- **BEHAVIOR** Solitary or in pairs. Difficult to observe unless singing. Flushed birds fly up and drop, running to hide. Forages on ground. Eats seeds, insects, and spiders.
- **BREEDING** Monogamous. Loose colonies.
- **NESTING** Incubation 11–12 days by female. Young altricial; brooded by female; stay in nest 8–10 days, fed by both sexes. 1 brood per year.
- **POPULATION** Uncommon and local on short-grass prairie and grasslands. Declining. Accidental on both coasts.
- **CONSERVATION** Neotropical migrant. Vulnerable to loss of prairie habitat.

Flight Pattern

Short flights low over grasses with rapid wing beats alternating with brief periods of wings pulled to sides.

Nest Identification	
Shape 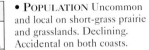 Location 	Dried grass and forbs, with lining of mammal hair and soft grass • in slight depression, set in tall grasses or near bush • built by female • 3–6 white to grayish white eggs, with lilac and reddish brown markings; oval, 0.8 inch long.

Plumage Sexes similar	Habitat 	Migration Migratory	Weight 0.8 ounce

DATE _____ TIME_____ LOCATION _____

| Family EMBERIZIDAE | Species *Ammodramus henslowii* | Length 4.75–5.25 inches | Wingspan 7–7.5 inches |

HENSLOW'S SPARROW

Upon arrival at the nesting grounds, the male begins singing day or night, rain or shine, perched or concealed. He cocks his tail down, elevates his head, and expels with a bodily shudder one of the shortest songs of any songbird. Occasionally, these sparrows battle one another in defense of territory. Their plumage serves as camouflage in the marshes and meadows. Juveniles resemble adults but are buffier and paler and have only faint streaking on their underparts.

• **SONG** Sings *flee-LICK*, like an explosive bird hiccup, with emphasis on the second note. Call is a thin high *tsip*.

flat greenish ocherous head with black stripes

green wash on neck and nape

large grayish bill

reddish back and wings with black streaking and white to buff edging

buff-green mustache, bordered black on both sides

conspicuous streaking on breast and sides

whitish underparts with buff wash on chest, sides, and flanks

short notched tail

JUVENILE

• **BEHAVIOR** Solitary or in pairs. Unobtrusive, secretive, and easily overlooked, except for the persistent song of the male, from low concealed or higher exposed perches. Singing males allow reasonably close approach. Forages and skulks on ground among vegetation. Eats insects, caterpillars, and seeds.
• **BREEDING** Monogamous. Loose colonies.
• **NESTING** Incubation 11 days by female. Young altricial; brooded by female; stay in nest 9–10 days, fed by both sexes. 2 broods per year.
• **POPULATION** Uncommon in weedy meadows, grassy fields (especially wet), and reclaimed strip mine benches in pine-grass savannas in the West. Declining, particularly in the Northeast.

Similar Birds

GRASSHOPPER SPARROW Brown to buffy head; pale central crown stripe; dark postocular stripe; buffy wash on white underparts, particularly on chest, sides, flanks, and crissum; lacks streaking on underparts.

• **CONSERVATION** Some concern has been recorded. Uncommon host to cowbird parasitism. Vulnerable to habitat loss due to grazing, agricultural mowing operations, land clearing, and development.

Flight Pattern

Weak fluttering flight with jerking of tail, low over vegetation. Alternates rapid series of wing beats with brief periods of wings pulled to sides.

Nest Identification

Shape ● Location ▬ ⁂

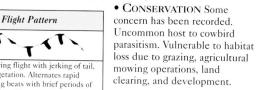

Grass and forbs, with lining of fine grass and hair • on ground in slight hollow or sheltered by grassy clump or weeds • built by female • 3–5 creamy or pale greenish white eggs, marked with reddish browns, often wreathed; oval, 0.7 x 0.55 inches.

| Plumage Sexes similar | Habitat | Migration Migratory | Weight 0.5 ounce |

DATE _____ TIME_____ LOCATION _____

Family EMBERIZIDAE	Species *Ammodramus leconteii*	Length 4.5–5.25 inches	Wingspan 6.5–7.25 inches

LE CONTE'S SPARROW

One of the smallest sparrows, this bird is most often found in prairie wetlands. A secretive bird, Le Conte's Sparrow often scurries mouselike in thick cover when flushed, rarely flying, and only a few feet at a time when it does. The species has declined in some parts of its range with the disappearance of damp fields and other similar habitats. This sparrow is a casual migrant in the Northeast and West, traveling only short distances off the main migration pathways. Juveniles are buffier overall and are heavily streaked on their underparts.

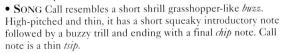

white central crown stripe

bright broad buff-orange eyebrows

thin bill

grayish ear patches

dark brown-streaked orange-buff sides and breast

chestnut streaks on nape

straw-colored streaks on back

bristly tail

• **SONG** Call resembles a short shrill grasshopper-like *buzz*. High-pitched and thin, it has a short squeaky introductory note followed by a buzzy trill and ending with a final *chip* note. Call note is a thin *tsip*.

• **BEHAVIOR** Solitary or in pairs. Secretive. Skulking. Walks and runs on ground to forage within matted vegetation, often in wet grasslands and bogs. In winter months, combs ground for seeds from grass and weeds. During summer, eats wide variety of insects, seeds, and spiders. Territorial male sings from exposed perch, with head pulled back and bill pointed skyward.

• **BREEDING** Monogamous. Solitary.

• **NESTING** Incubation 12–13 days by female. Young altricial; brooded by female; stay in nest estimated 8–10 days, fed by both sexes. 1–2 broods per year.

• **POPULATION** Fairly common and somewhat local in wet meadows, bog, and marsh edges. Declining in parts of range.

• **CONSERVATION** Uncommon host to cowbird parasitism. Vulnerable to loss of habitat due to draining of wetlands and development of habitat for agriculture.

Similar Birds

NELSON'S SHARP-TAILED SPARROW
Broad blue-gray crown stripe; unstreaked blue-gray nape; less color contrast on upperparts; olive-brown body with whitish streaks; frequents marsh habitat.

GRASSHOPPER SPARROW
Whitish to buff eyebrows; brown, black, and buff nape; brown auricular patch with dark borders; whitish underparts with buffy wash on chest and sides; lacks streaks on breast and sides.

Flight Pattern

Alternates of rapid wing beats with brief periods of wings pulled to sides; flies short distances before dropping back into grass.

Nest Identification	
Shape 🥄 Location ▬ •••	Grass, rushes, and stems, lined with fine materials • usually on or near ground • built by female • 3–5 grayish white eggs with brown spots; ovate, 0.7 x 0.53 inches.

Plumage Sexes similar	Habitat 🌱 〰	Migration Migratory	Weight 0.5 ounce

DATE _____ TIME _____ LOCATION _____

Family EMBERIZIDAE	Species *Ammodramus nelsoni*	Length 4.75 inches	Wingspan 7.25 inches

NELSON'S SHARP-TAILED SPARROW

Its streaked plumage serves as camouflage in the dense freshwater marsh grasses it inhabits in Canada, the northern prairie marshes of the US, and parts of Maine. When frightened, it scampers mouselike, with its head held low, and does not fly. It recently was determined to be a separate species from the Saltmarsh Sharp-tailed Sparrow; both were formerly lumped together under the name Sharp-tailed Sparrow. Adults show whitish or gray streaking on scapulars. Juveniles have buffier underparts and buffy heads without the gray auriculars and nape and lack streaking on the breast and flanks.

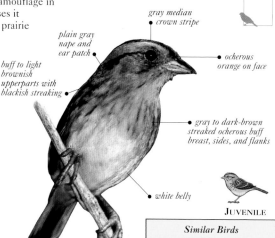

gray median crown stripe

plain gray nape and ear patch

buff to light brownish upperparts with blackish streaking

ocherous orange on face

gray to dark-brown streaked ocherous buff breast, sides, and flanks

white belly

JUVENILE

• **SONG** An explosive wheezy descending *p-tssssshh-uk*, like the sound of cold water tossed on hot metal.

• **BEHAVIOR** In pairs or small groups. Secretive. Difficult to observe unless male is singing, which it does from conspicuous perches. Curious, and will come up in vegetation and draw closer to pishing and squeaking by birders. Walks around on ground and picks up food or gleans from vegetation. Eats insects, their caterpillars, various seeds, and small snails. Males loosely territorial or nonterritorial. Flushed birds usually fly short distance before dropping back down into dense cover.

• **BREEDING** Polygamous. Loose colonies.

• **NESTING** Incubation 11 days by female. Young altricial; brooded by female; stay in nest 10 days, fed mostly by female. 1 brood per year.

• **POPULATION** Fairly common in wet meadows, freshwater marshes, and tule beds. Numbers decline with habitat drainage.

• **CONSERVATION** Rare host to cowbird parasitism. Vulnerable to loss of habitat due to marsh draining and agricultural practices, including cattle grazing.

Similar Birds

LE CONTE'S SPARROW
Bold dark brown stripes on sides; white median crown stripe; gray nape with chestnut streaking; straw-colored streaking on back and scapulars; lives in prairies
• juveniles have heavily streaked underparts.

SALTMARSH SHARP-TAILED SPARROW
Larger orange-buff facial triangle contrasts sharply with body; larger bill; black-streaked supercilium behind eye
• juveniles have heavily streaked underparts
• eastern range.

Flight Pattern

Short flights low over vegetation, with rapid wing beats alternating with brief periods of wings pulled to sides; repeated.

Nest Identification	
Shape ◥ Location ▬ ∭ ⁂	Dried grasses and stems • atop grassy tussock or on pile of reeds • built by female • 3–7 light green eggs, with heavy brown spotting; oval, 0.76 x 0.57 inches.

Plumage Sexes similar	Habitat ⤳	Migration Migratory	Weight Undetermined

DATE _____ TIME_____ LOCATION _____

Family EMBERIZIDAE	Species *Ammodramus maritimus*	Length 5.25–6.5 inches	Wingspan 8–8.5 inches

SEASIDE SPARROW

This shy bird makes its home in the salt marshes of the eastern coasts. Like many sparrows, the male perches atop reeds, grasses, or fences to sing his territorial song. Walking or running on the ground, its large feet prevent it from sinking in the soft marsh mud. There is much variation in size and color across the range, but the most widespread race, *A. m. maritimus*, is pictured here. Another race, *A. m. nigrescens*, is darkest, with the heaviest streaking on the underparts, and was formerly recognized as the species Dusky Seaside Sparrow. Found only near Titusville, Florida, it became extinct in 1987. Another species, *A. m. mirabilis*, called Cape Sable Sparrow, also found only in the Florida Everglades, is listed as federally endangered. All races show rufous greater primary coverts. Juveniles are duller with finer streaking on the underparts.

yellow supraloral streak

long bill with thick base and spiky tip

grayish olive upperparts with streaking

white throat

dark malar stripe separating throat and white mustache

white or buff breast with dusky gray streaking

short pointed tail

- **SONG** Harsh buzzy *oka-cheee-weee*, reminiscent of Red-winged Blackbird. Call note is *chip*.
- **BEHAVIOR** In pairs or small groups. Forages on ground, gleaning food as it walks upright, like a small rail; also wades, rail-like, in shallow water. Eats small snails, terrestrial and aquatic insects, crabs and other small crustaceans, and some seeds. Males fly 20–30 feet high in fluttering skylarking display flights and slowly descend back down to a perch — singing all the while.
- **BREEDING** Monogamous. Loose colonies.
- **NESTING** Incubation 12–13 days by female. Young altricial; brooded by female; stay in nest 8–10 days, fed by both sexes. 1–2 broods per year.
- **POPULATION** Fairly common in coastal salt marshes but declining from destruction of this habitat.
- **CONSERVATION** Rare host to cowbird parasitism. Destruction of coastal marshes, application of DDT in the 1970s, and flooding of marshes for mosquito control led to the extinction of one race and contributed to the near extinction of another in Florida, as well as the significant decline of other populations.

JUVENILE

Similar Birds

SALTMARSH SHARP-TAILED SPARROW Smaller; paler; buffier in overall color; ocherous orange triangle frames gray ear patch; whiter underparts with sharper dark streaking on breast, sides, and flanks; black crown patch; gray nape.

Flight Pattern

Short flights low over vegetation on rapidly beating wings alternating with brief periods of wings pulled to sides.

Nest Identification	
Shape ● Location ▦ ⩊	Dried grass and sedges • lined with soft finer grasses • attached to marsh reeds or set on clump of grass, from 9–11 inches to 5 feet above mud (but up to 14 feet) • built by female • 3–6 white to pale greenish eggs, marked with reddish browns; short ovate to elongated ovate, 0.8 x 0.6 inches.

Plumage Sexes similar	Habitat ___	Migration Northern birds migrate	Weight 0.8 ounce

DATE _____ TIME_____ LOCATION _____

Family EMBERIZIDAE	Species *Passerella iliaca*	Length 6.75–7.5 inches	Wingspan 10.5–11.75 inches

FOX SPARROW

Named for its rufous coloring, particularly on the rump and tail, the Fox Sparrow is one of the largest of all sparrows. There is much variation in size and coloration over the wide breeding range. The most richly plumaged birds breed in the boreal forests from Alaska to Newfoundland and are the forms seen in winter in the southeastern US, such as the *P. i. zaboria* pictured here. In the western mountain races, birds have gray heads and backs, while northwestern Pacific coastal races are sooty brown with dark brown rumps and tails. While mostly solitary, this sparrow sometimes is observed associating with other sparrows. Migrates in late March and early November, generally traveling at night.

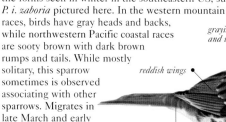

stout conical bill
with darker upper
• mandible

grayish nape
and upper back •

reddish wings •

reddish tail •
and rump

large rufous to
brown spot on
• central breast

• underparts heavily
marked with
triangular spots

• **SONG** Each male has a large repertoire of songs, singing one after the other until his entire suite is exhausted before beginning again. Rich flutelike sweet melody in northern reddish races; other races include grating trills. Variable, each phrase rises in pitch then falls on closing notes. Call is loud *smack* or drawn-out *stsssp*.

• **BEHAVIOR** Solitary or in pairs in breeding season. Small flocks in migration and on wintering grounds. Forages by double-scratching, towheelike, on ground and digging small holes by kicking backward with claws. Eats weed seeds, wild fruits and berries, insects, spiders, millipedes, and small snails.

• **BREEDING** Monogamous. Solitary.

• **NESTING** Incubation 12–14 days by female. Young altricial; brooded by female; stay in nest 9–11 days, fed by both sexes. 2 broods per year.

• **POPULATION** Uncommon to common in deciduous or conifer forest, undergrowth, chaparral, montane thicket, and riparian woodland. Declining in East.

• **FEEDERS** Birdseed and breadcrumbs attract it to ground underneath feeders.

• **CONSERVATION** Rare cowbird host. Vulnerable to habitat loss due to logging operations and development.

Similar Birds

HERMIT THRUSH
Reddish tail; lacks streaking on brownish back; brown to gray-brown upperparts; whitish gray underparts; thin bicolored bill with dark tip and creamy pinkish yellow base; spotted breast, sides, and flanks.

Flight Pattern

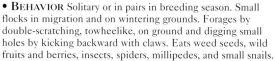

Short flights on rapidly beating wings alternating with brief periods of wings pulled to sides.

Nest Identification		
Shape ◥ Location ━ ◆ ◭ ◈	Lichen, roots, bark, leaves, twigs, grass, feathers, and animal fur • lined with grass and moss • on ground or in shrub, rarely on branch of tree • 0–3 feet above ground (rarely up to 20 feet) • built by female • 2–5 pale green to greenish white eggs, with reddish brown markings; oval, 0.9 inch long.	

Plumage Sexes similar	Habitat 🌳 🍃 ▲ ▲ 🌿	Migration Migratory	Weight 1.1 ounces

DATE _____ TIME_____ LOCATION _____

| Family EMBERIZIDAE | Species *Melospiza melodia* | Length 5.75–7.5 inches | Wingspan 8.25–12.5 inches |

SONG SPARROW

Even with its drab plumage, this bold songbird is easy to spot when it perches in the open, trilling its pleasant melody. In flight it pumps its tail up and down. Inhabiting a wide range, this bird is found throughout most of North America and is perhaps the continent's most variable species, with approximately thirty-one subspecies recognized. The Aleutian race, *M. m. maxima*, is so large and dark it looks like a different species. Because of the work of Ohio bird biologist Margaret Morse Nice, the biology of this bird may be the best-known of any songbird on the continent. Juveniles are similar to adults but appear buffier overall with finer streaking.

dark malar stripe borders white throat

brownish, grayish, or brownish gray upperparts, usually streaked

broad grayish eyebrow

streaking on sides and breast meet in center and form "stickpin"

whitish underparts

pinkish legs and feet

long rounded tail

ALEUTIAN RACE

- **SONG** Whistles 2–3 clear introductory notes, followed by a trill. Much variation in each individual's song and between individuals. Call is *chimp* or *what* and a high thin *ssst*.
- **BEHAVIOR** Solitary or in pairs. May be in small loose flocks in winter, often with other species of sparrows. Forages in trees, bushes, and on ground by picking food off foliage, grass, and soil; also scratches on ground. Eats insects, larvae, grains, seeds, berries, and some fruits. Coastal species take small mollusks and crustaceans. Males sing from exposed perches to claim territory.
- **BREEDING** Monogamous. Polygynous in some cases. Male vigorously defends territory and battles with other males. Often chases invading birds from territory.
- **NESTING** Incubation 12–14 days by female. Young altricial; brooded by female; stay in nest 9–16 days, fed by both sexes. 2–3 broods per year (occasionally 4 in southern parts of range).
- **POPULATION** Widespread and abundant to common in brushy areas, thickets, riparian scrub, weedy fields, urban/suburban lawns, and forest edge.
- **FEEDERS** Birdseed.
- **CONSERVATION** Species is one of the most frequent victims of parasitism by the Brown-headed Cowbird.

Similar Birds

SAVANNAH SPARROW Yellowish above eye; shorter notched tail; pinker legs; finer streaking on upperparts; central "stickpin" on chest.

LINCOLN'S SPARROW Smaller; buff wash on chest; more distinct markings; finer streaking on throat, breast, sides, and flanks; lacks central "stickpin" on chest.

Flight Pattern

Short flights close to ground, tail pumping up and down. Alternates rapid wing beats with brief periods of wings pulled to sides.

Nest Identification

Shape 🦃   Location ━ 🌿🔺 🌾

Grass, forbs, leaves, and bark strips, with lining of fine materials • usually on ground, sheltered by grassy tussock or reeds • sometimes in bush or tree, 2–4 feet above ground (but up to 12 feet) • built by female • 2–6 greenish white eggs, marked with reddish browns; oval to short oval, 0.8 x 0.61 inches.

| Plumage Sexes similar | Habitat | Migration Northern birds migrate | Weight 0.7 ounce |

DATE _____ TIME_____ LOCATION _____

Family EMBERIZIDAE	Species *Melospiza lincolnii*	Length 5.25–6 inches	Wingspan 7.25–8.75 inches

LINCOLN'S SPARROW

This inhabitant of northern bogs and mountain meadowlands is skittish, often raising its slight crest when disturbed. It is sometimes overlooked because of its furtive habits and similarity to the Song Sparrow, with which it may compete when nesting territories overlap. This sparrow can be distinguished by its sweet gurgling melody that sounds similar to that of a House Wren or Purple Finch, and by the buffy band crossing the chest and separating the white chin and throat from the white lower breast and belly. Juveniles are paler and buffier overall with more streaking on their underparts.

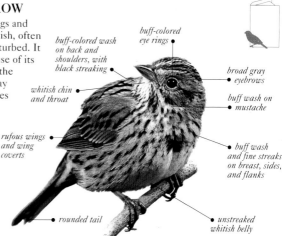

buff-colored wash on back and shoulders, with black streaking

whitish chin and throat

rufous wings and wing coverts

buff-colored eye rings

broad gray eyebrows

buff wash on mustache

buff wash and fine streaks on breast, sides, and flanks

rounded tail

unstreaked whitish belly

• **SONG** Features rapid bubbling trilled notes, with last notes harsher, louder, and lower in pitch, *chur-chur-chur-wee-wee-wee-wee-wah*. Alarm call is a flat-toned repetitious *tschup*. Calls also include a sharp buzzlike *zeee*.

• **BEHAVIOR** Solitary or in pairs. Sometimes joins mixed-species foraging flocks on wintering grounds. Secretive. Skulks low in thickets or on ground. Kicks backward with both feet like a towhee as it scratches among leaves on the ground; feeds on insects and small grains, as well as seeds from weeds and grasses. In migration, often found in brushy tangles near water. Often sings from a concealed perch during spring migration.

• **BREEDING** Monogamous. Solitary.

• **NESTING** Incubation 12–14 days by female. Young altricial; brooded by female; stay in nest 9–12 days, fed by both sexes. 1–2 broods per year.

• **POPULATION** Uncommon to fairly common in bogs, wet meadows, riparian thickets, and mountain meadows. Uncommon to fairly common in thickets and weedy fields in winter.

• **FEEDERS** Attracted by seed, particularly in migration.

• **CONSERVATION** Neotropical migrant. Rare host to cowbird parasitism. Vulnerable to loss of habitat because of logging operations and development.

Similar Birds

SONG SPARROW
Longer tail; thicker bill; thicker malar stripe; heavier streaking on underparts; central "stickpin" on chest; white underparts lack buffy wash on chest; brown upperparts with rufous and black streaking.

SWAMP SPARROW
Duller breast with thinner blurry streaks; gray head; rufous-brown crown with gray central stripe; unstreaked white throat; rufous wings and primary coverts.

Flight Pattern

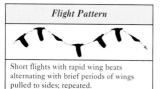

Short flights with rapid wing beats alternating with brief periods of wings pulled to sides; repeated.

Nest Identification

Shape Location

Grass or sedge lined, sometimes with hair • often built in grass, hollow depressions, or moss • built by female • 3–6 pale green to greenish white eggs, with reddish brown markings; oval to short oval, 0.8 x 0.6 inches.

Plumage Sexes similar	Habitat	Migration Migratory	Weight 0.8 ounce

DATE _____ TIME_____ LOCATION _____

Family EMBERIZIDAE	Species *Melospiza georgiana*	Length 4.75–5.75 inches	Wingspan 7.5–8 inches

SWAMP SPARROW

This small stocky sparrow will nest anywhere within its range where there is sufficient emergent dense vegetation in marshes, bogs, wet meadows, or sluggish streams. As nestlings learn to fly, they must stay above the water, so as not to be eaten by turtles, frogs, or fish. Adult females are similar to males but have brown-striped crowns. Juveniles are buffy with reddish wings and tails and heavily streaked underparts. Immatures resemble winter adults with tan buff sides, gray central crown stripe, and buffy wash overall.

reddish crown

deep rufous upperparts with black streaking

deep rufous wings

gray face

whitish throat

gray breast

whitish belly

JUVENILE WINTER PLUMAGE

• **SONG** A bold slow melodious musical trill of either sharp single-note or slurred double-note phrases, *peat-peat-peat-peat-peat-peat-peat*. Has a call of *zeee* or *chip*.

• **BEHAVIOR** Solitary or in pairs in breeding season. May form loose flocks in winter. Secretive and skulking in dense vegetation or on ground. Curious, it will come to pishing or squeaking by birders. Forages by wading in water and picking up food with bill or by gleaning prey from vegetation or ground. Eats insects and seeds. Male sings to claim territory.

• **BREEDING** Monogamous. Loose colonies. Male often feeds incubating or brooding female while on nest.

• **NESTING** Incubation 12–15 days by female. Young altricial; brooded by female; stay in nest 11–13 days, fed by both sexes. 2 broods per year.

• **POPULATION** Common in marshes, bogs, and riparian stands of reeds, cattails, and sedges. Rare in the West. Some population declines due to loss of marsh habitat.

• **CONSERVATION** Neotropical migrant. Common host to cowbird parasitism. Vulnerable to habitat loss due to draining of wetlands, livestock overgrazing, and development.

Similar Birds

WHITE-THROATED SPARROW Stockier; larger; yellow supraloral spot; whitish or buff supercilium; two whitish wing bars; gray underparts; white-and-black- or brown-and-tan-striped crown.

LINCOLN'S SPARROW Buffy back and shoulders with black streaking; buffy breast band, sides, and flanks; black streaking on throat, breast, sides, and flanks; broad gray supercilium; brown crown with black streaks; buffy eye ring.

Flight Pattern

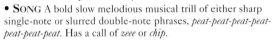

Short flights low over vegetation on rapidly beating wings alternating with brief periods of wings pulled to sides.

Nest Identification

Shape 🐦 Location 〽️🌿

Dry thick grasses with lining of finer grasses • set in reeds, usually 0–5 feet above water • in some areas, in bush near water, 1–6 feet above ground • built by female • 3–6 greenish white eggs, marked with reddish browns; short subelliptical, 0.8 x 0.57 inches.

Plumage Sexes differ	Habitat 〰️ 〜	Migration Migratory	Weight 0.8 ounce

DATE _____ TIME_____ LOCATION _____

Family EMBERIZIDAE	Species *Zonotrichia albicollis*	Length 6.25–7.5 inches	Wingspan 8.75–10 inches

WHITE-THROATED SPARROW

The song of the White-throated Sparrow is heard in the Canadian wilderness and in the northeastern US where it breeds in woodland undergrowth, clearings, and gardens. Distinguishing marks include a broad yellow eyebrow, or supraloral stripe in the front of the eye, which tapers to either white or tan, and a sharply outlined white throat. Although it is common and widespread, sightings of this bird are rare in the West.

black or brown borders crown stripes and eye line

rusty brown upperparts

yellow supraloral stripe

dark bill

white throat

2 white wing bars

grayish underparts with diffuse streaking

• **SONG** A thin whistle, starting with 2 single notes followed by 3 triple notes: *poor-sam-peabody, peabody, peabody* or *pure-sweet-Canada, Canada, Canada*. Calls include a grating *pink* and a drawled lisping *tseep*. Territorial birds often sing at night. Some black-and-white-striped females sing.

JUVENILE

TAN-STRIPED

• **BEHAVIOR** Solitary or in pairs. In winter joins flocks of other White-throats and mixed species. Hops on ground or forages in shrubs and trees. Scratches among leaves for food. Eats mostly weed seeds, fruit from trees, tree buds, and insects. May hawk insects in midair. Attracted by pishing and squeaking by birders. Two adult color morphs are based on head striping: black-and-white-striped and brown-and-tan-striped. Field studies show that white-striped males tend to mate with tan-striped females, and tan-striped males tend to mate with white-striped females.

• **BREEDING** Monogamous. Solitary.

• **NESTING** Incubation 11–14 days by female. Young altricial; brooded by female; stay in nest 7–12 days, fed by both sexes. 1–2 broods per year.

• **POPULATION** Common and widespread in conifer and mixed-conifer forest, forest edge and clearings, and thickets. Rare in the West.

• **FEEDERS** Seeds and grains.

• **CONSERVATION** Uncommon host to cowbird parasitism. Vulnerable to habitat loss due to logging operations.

Similar Birds

WHITE-CROWNED SPARROW Black-and-white-striped crown; pink bill; lacks whitish throat contrasting with gray breast; lacks yellow supraloral spot; tertials lack bright rufous coloring.

HARRIS'S SPARROW Winter adult and juvenile • slightly larger; pink bill; crown varies from tan with black stippling, to black with white spotting, to black; face buffy tan; chin varies from white to blackish; throat white, black-and-white, or black; blackish band crossing upper breast.

Flight Pattern

Relatively short flights with rapid wing beats alternating with brief periods of wings pulled to sides; repeated.

Nest Identification	
Shape 🥣 Location 🪺 ▬	Lined with coarse grass, wood chips, twigs, pine needles, roots, and other fine materials • often found at edge of clearing • 0–3 feet above ground • built by female • 3–6 greenish, bluish, or cream-white eggs with reddish brown markings; subelliptical or long elliptical, 0.8 x 0.6 inches.

Plumage Sexes similar	Habitat 🌳 🌿 🔺 🌱	Migration Migratory	Weight 0.9 ounce

DATE _____ TIME_____ LOCATION _____

Family EMBERIZIDAE	Species *Zonotrichia querula*	Length 6.75–7.75 inches	Wingspan 10.25–11.75 inches

HARRIS'S SPARROW

This large sparrow is named after Edward Harris, one of John James Audubon's expedition partners. Where it nested was one of the great ornithological mysteries of the early 20th century. The nest was seen and documented in 1931, making this the last songbird to have its nesting information recorded. In winter, breeding plumage is replaced by a buffy face, all or mostly black crown, black chin, and throat that varies from all black to having a white band through it. The amount of black on the winter bird is under hormonal control and signals social dominance; the more black the higher its rank in the pecking order of the flock. Juveniles are similar to winter adults but show less black on the crown and upper breast and have a white throat bordered by a black malar mark.

black crown, face, and bib
black auricular spot
brown back and sides, streaked blackish brown
2 buffy to white wing bars
pink-orange bill
pale gray cheeks and nape
white underparts

- **SONG** Repeated clear tremulous whistles in 1 pitch, followed at an interval by several clear notes in another pitch. Calls sound like a loud metallic *spink* and a drawn-out *tseep*.
- **BEHAVIOR** Solitary or in pairs. Shows faithfulness to wintering territories. Forages on ground by kicking and scratching among leaf litter and dry weed stalks. Bulk of diet is wild fruits, grains, and seeds from grass and weeds; also eats insects, spiders, and snails. Breeds among stunted trees and shrubs in taiga-tundra ecotone.
- **BREEDING** Monogamous. Solitary.
- **NESTING** Incubation 12–15 days by female. Altricial young brooded by female; stay in nest estimated 7–12 days, fed by both sexes. 1 brood per year.
- **POPULATION** Common to fairly common on restricted breeding and wintering grounds. Rare to casual in winter elsewhere.
- **FEEDERS** Grains, mixed birdseed, suet, breadcrumbs.

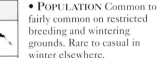

JUVENILE

WINTER PLUMAGE

Similar Birds

WHITE-CROWNED SPARROW
Black-and-white-striped crown; pink bill; mostly gray underparts; brown upperparts with blackish brown streaks on back and shoulders; 2 white wing bars; brown rump • juvenile similar to adult but with gray-and-brown-striped head.

WHITE-THROATED SPARROW
Distinctly outlined white throat; dark bill; black-and-white- or brown-and-tan-striped crown; broad eyebrow yellow in front of eye, remainder is white or tan; 2 white wing bars.

Flight Pattern

Series of rapid wing beats alternating with brief periods of wings pulled to sides; repeated.

Nest Identification	
Shape 🥄 Location ▬	Lined with grass and coarse roots • in depression on ground under stunted woody vegetation or moss hummock • built by female • 3–5 white to greenish white eggs with brown markings; ovate to elliptical ovate, 0.9 x 0.7 inches.

Plumage Sexes similar	Habitat 🐾 ▲ ▬	Migration Migratory	Weight 1.4 ounces

DATE _____ TIME _____ LOCATION _____

Family EMBERIZIDAE	Species *Zonotrichia leucophrys*	Length 6.5–7.5 inches	Wingspan 9.25–10.25 inches

WHITE-CROWNED SPARROW

This bold bird is easy to identify, with conspicuous black stripes on its white crown, a pink to dull yellow bill, and a pale gray throat. Like many sparrows, the male sings to claim its territory and duels to defend its ground. His songs may even continue into the night. As is usual with a wide geographical range, there is morphological and behavioral variation. The most striking subspecies differences include bill color and white versus black supralorals. Juveniles have heavily streaked underparts and a brown-and-buff-streaked head. Immatures have a brown-and-tan-striped head and unstreaked underparts.

white supercilium

black postocular stripe

brownish upperparts with blackish brown streaking

2 white wing bars

brownish wash on sides and flanks

white crown with bold black stripes

pink to dull yellow bill

whitish gray throat

grayish underparts become white on belly

JUVENILE

FIRST WINTER

- **SONG** A melancholy whistled *poor-wet-wetter-chee-zee*. Has call note of *pink* or sharp *tseek*.
- **BEHAVIOR** Solitary or in pairs. In small family groups after breeding season. Forms flocks in winter. Males sing from exposed perches; sometimes in spring on wintering grounds. Gleans food from vegetation; hops on ground and forages by scratching. Eats seeds, insects, caterpillars, and parts of plants.
- **BREEDING** Monogamous. Individuals in some nonmigratory populations may pair for life. Some polygynous.
- **NESTING** Incubation 11–14 days by female. Young altricial; brooded by female; stay in nest 7–12 days, fed by both sexes. Male continues to feed young while female starts another nest. 2–4 broods per year (largest number of broods in southern populations; 1 brood in far north).
- **POPULATION** Common to fairly common in woodlands, thickets, wet meadows, and chaparral.
- **FEEDERS** Baby chick scratch and seeds.
- **CONSERVATION** Neotropical migrant. Uncommon host to cowbird parasitism. Vulnerable in the West to habitat loss because of land development and logging.

Similar Birds

WHITE-THROATED SPARROW
More rufous-brown upperparts; mostly dark bill; well-defined white throat patch; yellow spot between eye and bill; gray underparts; two white wing bars; black-and-white- or brown-and-tan-striped cap.

HARRIS'S SPARROW
Winter adult and juvenile • slightly larger; pink bill; crown varies from tan with black stippling, to black with white spotting, to black; face buffy tan; chin varies from white to blackish; throat white, black-and-white, or black; blackish band crossing upper breast.

Flight Pattern
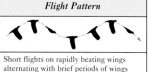
Short flights on rapidly beating wings alternating with brief periods of wings pulled to sides; repeated.

Nest Identification	
Shape Location ▬ ✸✸✸ ▲▾	Grass, sticks, rootlets, and forbs • lined with soft grasses, feathers, and hair • on clump of grass or moss, sheltered by bush, or in small tree • 0–5 feet above ground (but up to 30 feet) • built by female • 2–6 light blue or green eggs marked with reddish browns; ovate to short ovate or long ovate, 0.8 x 0.6 inches.

Plumage Sexes similar	Habitat ♦ 🐾 ▲ △	Migration Northern birds migrate	Weight 1.0 ounce

DATE _____ TIME_____ LOCATION _____

Family EMBERIZIDAE	Species *Junco hyemalis*	Length 5.75–6.5 inches	Wingspan 9.25–10 inches

DARK-EYED JUNCO

In 1973 the American Ornithologists' Union grouped under one heading what was once considered five different junco species. Thus, the Dark-eyed Junco is composed of geographic races that differ in color and range but are closely related and have similar habits. All races of the species complex have white outer tail feathers; a black, gray, or brown hood; and white lower breast, belly, and undertail coverts. All have similar songs; all but one have a pink bill. Females tend to be paler and sometimes browner on the back. Juveniles have streaked upperparts and underparts.

gray upperparts

dark gray hood

white outer tail feathers

SLATE-COLORED MALE

SLATE-COLORED JUVENILE

brownish gray hood

brownish gray upperparts

SLATE-COLORED FEMALE

OREGON MALE

PINK-SIDED MALE

WHITE-WINGED MALE

GRAY-HEADED MALE

- **SONG** Melodic trill, varied in pitch and tempo and from dry *chip* notes to tinkling bell-like sounds, similar to Chipping Sparrow. Call is abrasive *dit* produced with sucking smack. Twitters in flight.
- **BEHAVIOR** Solitary or in pairs. In small family groups after breeding season. In spring and fall may join mixed-species foraging flocks; forms flocks in winter. Forages by gleaning from vegetation and scratching on ground. Hops. Eats seeds, grains, berries, insects, caterpillars, and some fruits; occasionally hawks flying insects. The larger males often winter farther north or at higher elevations than juveniles and females.
- **BREEDING** Monogamous. Solitary.
- **NESTING** Incubation 11–13 days by female. Altricial young brooded by female; leave nest at 9–13 days, fed by both sexes. 1–3 broods per year.
- **POPULATION** Common to fairly common in coniferous and mixed conifer-deciduous forests and bogs; winter habitats vary.
- **FEEDERS** Breadcrumbs, nuts, and seeds.
- **CONSERVATION** Uncommon cowbird host. Vulnerable to habitat loss due to logging operations.

Similar Birds

YELLOW-EYED JUNCO Yellow eyes; black lores; rufous-trimmed greater coverts and tertials; gray head and nape; gray throat and underparts paler than head; white belly
- limited southwest range.

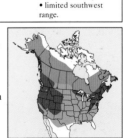

Flight Pattern

Short flights with white outer tail feathers flashing conspicuously. Alternates several rapid wing beats with brief periods of wings pulled to sides.

Nest Identification	Grass, weeds, and leaves, with lining of fine grass, hair, and feathers • on ground, sometimes in cavity, sheltered by bush, tree roots, log, occasionally in shrub or tree, 0–20 feet above ground • male gathers materials and female builds
Shape ● Location ▬ ▲ ▲	• 3–6 whitish to bluish white eggs, with markings of brown and gray, sometimes concentrated at larger end; oval to short or long oval, 0.8 x 0.56 inches.

Plumage Sexes differ	Habitat 🌱🌳 ▲	Migration Northern birds migrate	Weight 0.7 ounce

DATE _____ TIME_____ LOCATION _____

Family EMBERIZIDAE	Species *Calcarius mccownii*	Length 6 inches	Wingspan 10 inches

McCown's Longspur

During years of heavy rainfall, this inhabitant of arid short-grass plains will desert its nesting grounds. A monogamous species, males and females are often together, walking side by side. Winter males are similar to breeding females but show deeper chestnut in the median coverts and more black in the breast band. Winter females are buffy with broad buffy eyebrows. Juveniles are paler with a scaly-backed look and streaked heads and underparts. All plumages show a white tail with a black inverted T-shaped pattern.

• **SONG** High-spirited warbling and twittering on breeding grounds. Call sounds like dry rattle or double-noted *churrip-churrip.*

• **BEHAVIOR** In pairs on breeding grounds. Forms large flocks in winter. Forages on ground and makes daily visits to water, including irrigation reservoirs, with other species. Eats weed seeds, variety of insects, and caterpillars. This species frequents drier prairies and stubble fields than other longspurs.

• **BREEDING** Monogamous. Solitary.

• **NESTING** Incubation 12 days by female. Altricial young brooded by both sexes; stay in nest 10–12 days, fed by both sexes; remain with parents 3 more weeks. 2 broods per year.

• **POPULATION** Fairly common locally. Stable with increase possible on dry short-grass prairies. Ranges have shrunk since 1800s. Casual to California coast and southern Oregon. Accidental to East Coast. Rare in interior California and Nevada.

• **CONSERVATION** Uncommon cowbird host. Vulnerable to habitat loss.

MALE

black crown

buff- and brown-streaked upperparts

stout thick bill

white face and throat

chestnut wing bar

black malar stripe

black crescent on breast

gray sides and nape

white underparts

WINTER MALE

white face with tan auriculars

tawny upper wing bar

white tail marked with dark inverted T shape

WINTER FEMALE

buff-tipped feathers produce scalloped effect on brown breast

FEMALE

Similar Birds

♂ CHESTNUT-COLLARED LONGSPUR White tail with black triangle • breeding male has black belly and chestnut collar • winter birds buffy overall; ♂ male with black mottling on breast and ♀ white spot on shoulder.

Flight Pattern

Series of rapid wing beats alternating with brief periods of wings pulled to sides; repeated.

Nest Identification

Shape ▬ Location ▬ ▬

Grass lined with occasional weeds, roots, and lichen • in scrape on ground • scratched out by both and built by female • 2–4 white to pale olive eggs, with brown and lavender markings; oval, elliptical, or pyriform; 0.8 x 0.6 inches.

Plumage Sexes differ	Habitat ▬	Migration Migratory	Weight 0.8 ounce

DATE _____ TIME_____ LOCATION _____

Family EMBERIZIDAE	Species *Calcarius lapponicus*	Length 6–7 inches	Wingspan 10.5–11.75 inches

LAPLAND LONGSPUR

In winter this bird is commonly in the company of Horned Larks, Snow Buntings, and other longspurs on barren snow-swept fields throughout the north and central US, sometimes in large flocks. Resembling a House Sparrow, it is seen often. In all plumages the outer two tail feathers are partly white and partly black. Females are duller in color with rufous greater wing coverts and edging on the tertials, and a bold dark triangle outlines buff ear patches. Juveniles are similar to females but with heavy streaking on the head, back, and underparts.

- **SONG** Liquid warbling Bobolink-like song given in flight. Call is melodious *tee-lee-oo* or *tee-dle* or dry rattling *drit-ri-it*.
- **BEHAVIOR** In pairs or small family groups in summer. Forages on ground for insects and spiders; also eats seeds from grass and sedges; mostly weed seeds in winter. Migrates in flocks in late fall and early spring. Flocks number in the thousands on US wintering grounds. Courting tundra male may sing while chasing female on ground; gives skylarking flight song, rising from ground in front of female, singing above her, and gliding back down with tail and wings spread.
- **BREEDING** Monogamous. Solitary.
- **NESTING** Incubation 10–14 days by female. Young altricial; brooded by female; stay in nest 8–10 days, fed by both sexes. Fledglings are divided equally between the sexes; each tends its half of the brood. 1 brood per year.
- **POPULATION** Common to abundant on arctic tundra in summer; prairies, grassy fields, stubble fields, and dune areas along shorelines. Widespread.

black crown, lores, cheeks, throat, and breast

reddish brown nape

broad white stripe extends from eye to sides of breast

white underparts with black streaking on sides and flanks

MALE

blackish brown crown

tan auriculars bordered blackish

chestnut nape with blackish streaking

broad white supercilium

FEMALE

WINTER MALE   **WINTER FEMALE**

Similar Birds

SMITH'S LONGSPUR Winter • rich buff nape and underparts; thin dusky streaking on underparts; white shoulder patch, often hidden; 2 white outer tail feathers tipped black on distal third of outer web; small thin bill; buffy supercilium.

Flight Pattern

Rapid wing beats alternating with brief periods of wings pulled to sides.

Nest Identification	Fine grass and feathers • lined with grass and moss • in scrape or shallow depression • built by female • 4–7 greenish white to pale gray-green eggs, with brown and black markings; elliptical to oval, 0.8 x 0.6 inches.
Shape ☙ Location ▬	

Plumage Sexes differ	Habitat ⌇ ▲ ☙	Migration Migratory	Weight 1.0 ounce

DATE _____ TIME_____ LOCATION _____

| Family EMBERIZIDAE | Species *Calcarius pictus* | Length 5.75–6.5 inches | Wingspan 10–11 inches |

SMITH'S LONGSPUR

This bird is most often observed during winter months, foraging in pastures and other open areas, including airports, in the Midwest and farther south. Winter flocks often do not closely associate with other foraging longspurs, pipits, or Horned Larks. Smith's Longspur is not wary and allows close approach, but if pushed to flight the birds fly up in a zigzag, giving clicking call notes. The white outer tail feathers bordering the black tail are conspicuous in flight.

• **SONG** Generally heard in spring migration and around breeding grounds. Series of rapid sweet melodious warbles ending in *wee-chew!*, like the ending of a Chestnut-sided Warbler's song. Call sounds like a dry tickling rattle.

• **BEHAVIOR** In pairs on breeding grounds in arctic tundra. In small flocks, pairs, or as individuals on wintering grounds. Somewhat secretive but tame and easily approached. On tundra, eats seeds, insects, and spiders. Feeds mostly on seeds in winter. Seldom seen by biologists or birders due to high arctic breeding range and inconspicuous flock size, so its biology is poorly known.

• **BREEDING** Monogamous. Solitary.

• **NESTING** Incubation 11–13 days by female. Young altricial; brooded by female; leave nest at 7–9 days, with flight 14 days later, fed by both sexes. 1 brood per year.

• **POPULATION** Generally uncommon, especially in migration and winter. Casual vagrant to the Atlantic Coast. Casual to California.

black-and-white head with white ear patch entirely bordered by black

buff-colored nape and underparts

thin bill

MALE

white shoulder patch

yellowish legs and feet

black tail bordered by 2 mostly white outermost tail feathers

brown-streaked tawny crown

broad buffy supercilium

dusky auriculars bordered dark brown

thin brown malar mark

buffy underparts with thin dark brown streaking

FEMALE

WINTER MALE

WINTER FEMALE

Similar Birds

LAPLAND LONGSPUR ♂ Winter plumage • white underparts; black legs and feet; thick pinkish bill with black tip; rufous greater coverts; outer 2 tail feathers black-and-white ♀ • winter male has scalloped blackish bib; streaked black crown.

Flight Pattern

Swift erratic zigzag flight when flushed, then undulating flight with series of rapid wing beats alternating with brief periods of wings pulled to sides.

Nest Identification	
Shape 🪹 Location ▬	Lichen, animal hair, and feathers • lined with grass and sedge • on ground in shallow depression • built by female • 4–6 pale tan to pale green eggs, with lavender and dark brown markings, or grayish eggs, marked with dark brown and lavender; subelliptical to short subelliptical, 0.8 x 0.6 inches.

| Plumage Sexes differ | Habitat ◢◣ | Migration Migratory | Weight 1.0 ounce |

DATE _____ TIME_____ LOCATION _____

Family EMBERIZIDAE	Species *Calcarius ornatus*	Length 5.75–6.5 inches	Wingspan 10–10.75 inches

CHESTNUT-COLLARED LONGSPUR

All the longspurs are named for the long claw on their hind toe. The male is conspicuous as it rises from the ground, circles and sings above its territory, then glides down on rapidly beating wings, hanging as if to land with wings extended above its back. Males may repeat this several times before landing. In flight the white tail with its black terminal triangle is distinctive.

- **SONG** Soft sweet tumbling warble, similar to song of Western Meadowlark, given only on breeding grounds. Call is nasal *kit-tal, kit-tal*.
- **BEHAVIOR** In pairs or small family groups in summer. Flocks can number more than 100 birds in winter, often including pipits and Horned Larks. Eats weed seeds and insects. Males may attack other birds and ground squirrels that approach the nest. Female has unique distraction display when intruders close to nest, fluttering 2–3 feet into air in aerial "jumps."
- **BREEDING** Monogamous. Solitary.
- **NESTING** Incubation 10–13 days by female. Young altricial; brooded by female; stay in nest 10 days, first flight at 9–14 days, fed by both sexes. 2 broods per year.
- **POPULATION** Fairly common in moist upland prairies; winters in grassy and stubble fields. In migration, casual east and west of range.
- **CONSERVATION** Uncommon host to cowbird parasitism. Vulnerable to habitat loss due to agriculture and development.

black-and-white head

chestnut collar

buffy yellow face

upperparts streaked with black, buff, and brown

bold black breast and upper belly

single white wing bar

MALE

very short primary projection

whitish lower belly and undertail coverts

WINTER MALE

WINTER FEMALE

white tail with blackish triangle

chestnut wash on nape

buff upperparts with brownish streaking

whitish buff underparts with faint streaking

FEMALE

Similar Birds

♂ MCCOWN'S LONGSPUR
Gray hindneck; white face with black malar mark; black crescent on chest; white underparts;
♀ chestnut wing bar; white tail with inverted black T; larger heavy pink bill; longer primary
♂ projection • females and winter-plumaged birds have tail pattern of breeding male; white underparts without
♀ streaking; buffy wash on sides and flanks • winter male has mottled blackish chest.

Flight Pattern	

Swift flight on rapidly beating wings alternating with brief periods of wings pulled to sides.

Nest Identification	
Shape	Location	Grass • lined with finer grass and sometimes with feathers and hair • in hollow on ground, usually hidden in grasses • built by female • 4–5 whitish eggs, marked with brown, black, and purple, occasionally wreathed; oval, 0.8 x 0.6 inches.

Plumage Sexes differ	Habitat	Migration Migratory	Weight 0.7 ounce

DATE _____ TIME_____ LOCATION _____

Family CARDINALIDAE	Species *Cardinalis cardinalis*	Length 7.5–9.25 inches	Wingspan 10–12 inches

NORTHERN CARDINAL

The official bird of seven US states sings a variety of cheerful melodies year-round. The male fights other birds to defend his territory and sometimes tries to attack his own reflection in windows, automobile mirrors, chrome, and hubcaps. Having adapted to suburban areas, these birds visit backyard feeders regularly and sometimes take food from the hand. Juveniles resemble the adult female but have a blackish instead of reddish bill.

• **SONG** Variable. Variety of gurgling and clear whistled melodies. More than 25 different songs. Best-known phrases include *whoit cheer, whoit cheer, cheer-cheer-cheer; cheer, whoit-whoit-whoit-whoit; wheat-wheat-wheat-wheat;* and *bir-dy, bir-dy, bir-dy, bir-dy.* Female in courtship duets with male after territory is established and prior to nesting. Call is abrasive metallic *chip* or *pik.*

• **BEHAVIOR** Solitary or in pairs during breeding season. Gregarious at other times, forming flocks in winter or joining mixed-species foraging flocks. Forages in trees, bushes, and on ground. Eats insects, seeds, grains, fruits, and snails. Drinks sap from holes drilled by sapsuckers. Hops rather than walks on ground.

• **BREEDING** Monogamous. Solitary. Male feeds female during courtship and while incubating.

• **NESTING** Incubation 12–13 days, mostly by female. Young altricial; brooded by female; stay in nest 9–11 days, fed by both sexes. Male may continue to tend fledglings while female begins incubating new set of eggs. 2–4 broods per year.

• **POPULATION** Abundant and widespread in woodland edges, undergrowth, thickets, and residential areas. Range has expanded north in the last century, partly due to increase of feeding stations. Casual in West.

• **FEEDERS** Cracked corn, sunflower seeds, birdseed. Will bathe in birdbaths.

• **CONSERVATION** Common cowbird host, especially in the central portion of its range.

black mask through eyes

accentuated crest

cone-shaped reddish bill

red overall

black patch at base of bill extends onto throat

MALE

red tip

buffy golden brown head and underparts

dusky lores and patch at base of bill

buffy olive upperparts

FEMALE

buff-brown underparts

red wash on wings and tail

JUVENILE

Similar Birds

PYRRHULOXIA ♀
Resembles female and juvenile Northern Cardinal; stubby sharply curved yellowish bill; red eye ring; red tip to long gray crest; grayish upperparts; red edging to primaries; reddish wash on throat and underparts.

Flight Pattern

Short flight just above vegetation or below canopy; rapidly beating wings alternate with brief periods of wings pulled to sides.

Nest Identification	
Shape  Location	Twigs, weeds, grass, bark strips, and leaves • lined with hair and grass • in fork of low tree or bush or set in tangled twigs or vines • usually less than 5 feet above ground (but up to 15 feet) • built by female • 3–4 pale greenish, bluish, or grayish eggs with dots and flecks of gray, purple, and brown; oval, 1.0 x 0.7 inches.

Plumage Sexes differ	Habitat	Migration Nonmigratory	Weight 1.6 ounces

DATE _____ TIME_____ LOCATION _____

Family CARDINALIDAE	Species *Cardinalis sinuatus*	Length 8.75 inches	Wingspan 11.25 inches

PYRRHULOXIA

This long-crested bird of southwestern North America and Mexico looks like a gray cardinal with a parrotlike bill. Both the male and female aggressively defend their two- to three-acre territory until it is established, whereupon it becomes the duty of the male to maintain it. The female is similar to the male but has a buffy gray breast, a red tip to her gray crest, red washes on her throat and the midline of her breast and belly, and red edging to her primaries. In winter the yellow bill of both sexes turns grayish yellow. In flight the underwing coverts flash red.

• **SONG** Varied series of rich loud whistles, *chewee, chewee, chewee; wheet-wheet-wheet*, very similar to Northern Cardinal. Call is sharp metallic *plik* or *chink*.

• **BEHAVIOR** Solitary or in pairs during breeding season. Gregarious at other times, forming flocks in winter. Often joins mixed-species foraging flocks in winter. Forages for food in trees, bushes, and on ground but spends much time on ground, where it hops instead of walks. Eats flower spikes, various fruits, berries, seeds, insects, and larvae. Male sings from exposed perch.

• **BREEDING** Monogamous. Solitary.

• **NESTING** Incubation 14 days by female. Young altricial; brooded by female; leave nest at 10–11 days, fed by both sexes. 1 brood per year.

• **POPULATION** Fairly common in thorn scrub, arid brushlands, mesquite thickets, and ranchlands.

• **FEEDERS** Will come to feeders and birdbaths.

• **CONSERVATION** Uncommon cowbird host.

conspicuous red-tipped gray crest

red face

thick stubby sharply curved yellow bill

gray head, back, and upperparts

dark gray wings with red edging on primaries

red mottling from throat to center of belly

red tail feathers

pale gray underparts

MALE

red-tipped gray crest

thick stubby sharply decurved yellow bill

red eye ring

buff-gray breast and underparts

FEMALE

Similar Birds

NORTHERN CARDINAL ♀ Female and juvenile have buffy olive upperparts; red wings, wing coverts, and tail; buffy olive crest with reddish tip; dusky lores and patch at base of bill; buffy brown underparts • female has cone-shaped reddish bill • juvenile has cone-shaped blackish bill.

Flight Pattern

Short flights low over vegetation, with rapid wing beats alternating with brief periods of wings pulled to sides.

Nest Identification

Shape ◖   Location 🌿

Thorny twigs, weeds, grass, and bark pieces, lined with rootlets and fine materials • in shrub or thicket • 5–15 feet above ground • built by female • 3–4 grayish white or greenish white eggs with brown dots and flecks; oval, 1.0 x 0.7 inches.

Plumage Sexes differ	Habitat 🦋 ⚘ ⚘ 🌱 🌳 🌵	Migration Nonmigratory	Weight 1.3 ounces

DATE _____ TIME_____ LOCATION _____

Family CARDINALIDAE	Species *Pheucticus ludovicianus*	Length 7–8.5 inches	Wingspan 12–13 inches

ROSE-BREASTED GROSBEAK

This bird's clear notes are delivered in robinlike phrases, but the song is sweet. Males sing constantly, even while sparring to win a female. In flight the male shows rosy red wing linings, a white rump, and black-tipped white uppertail coverts; females flash yellow wing linings. First fall males have less streaking on underparts than females, buffy wash across the breast, and rose-red wing linings. First spring males are similar to adult males but with brown edges to the black plumage.

- **SONG** Rich warbled melodious phrases interspersed with call notes. Squeaky abrasive call, *eek*.
- **BEHAVIOR** Solitary or in pairs in breeding season. Flocks in migration and winter. Forages in trees, shrubs, and on ground. Eats seeds, insects, caterpillars, tree flowers, fruits, and berries. Hover gleans high in trees at branch tips; females more often than males.
- **BREEDING** Monogamous. Solitary. Male and female rub bills to display affection during courtship.
- **NESTING** Incubation 13–14 days by both sexes. Altricial young brooded by both sexes, more by female; stay in nest 9–12 days, fed by both sexes. Male may tend while female begins second nesting. 1–2 broods per year.
- **POPULATION** Common to fairly common in deciduous forest, woodland, and second growth. Rare migrant in West. Rare to accidental in winter on southern California coast.
- **FEEDERS** Use increases during migration.
- **CONSERVATION** Neotropical migrant. Common cowbird host. Vulnerable to habitat loss due to logging.

black head and back

white or buff-colored bill

white shoulder patch

white wing patch

black throat

white underparts with rosy red triangular patch on breast

JUVENILE MALE

black tail with white inner webs to outer tail feathers

MALE

white eyebrow

brownish upperparts with dark streaking

2 broad white wing bars

FIRST SPRING MALE

white mustache and throat

FEMALE

whitish to buff underparts with brownish streaking

Similar Birds

BLACK-HEADED GROSBEAK ♀ Buff to white supercilium; pale cinnamon chest with fine streaking on sides and flanks; upperparts have buffy mottling and streaking; lemon-yellow underwing coverts.

Flight Pattern

Swift flight on rapidly beating wings with brief periods of wings pulled to sides.

Nest Identification

Shape 🍵   Location 🌿 🌳

Twigs, weeds, and leaves • lined with fine twigs, rootlets, and mammal hair • in vines, low tree, or shrub, 5–15 feet above ground (but up to 50 feet) • built mostly by female, but male helps • 3–5 light greenish or bluish eggs marked with reddish brown; oval, 1.0 x 0.7 inches.

Plumage Sexes differ	Habitat 🪶 🌿	Migration Migratory	Weight 1.6 ounces

DATE _____ TIME_____ LOCATION _____

Family CARDINALIDAE	Species *Pheucticus melanocephalus*	Length 7–8.5 inches	Wingspan 12–13 inches

BLACK-HEADED GROSBEAK

Easily observed in western woodlands, this tame bird attends feeders and sometimes takes food from the hand. Both sexes aggressively defend their territory from other grosbeaks. Lemon wing linings are conspicuous in flight. First fall males have rich cinnamon-buff underparts, blackish brown cheek patches, white eyebrow and mustache, and white tips to tertials.

• **SONG** Rich back-and-forth series of warbled phrases, robinlike. Similar to Rose-breasted Grosbeak but lower pitched. Female sings less with more variations. Call is high squeaky *plik*.

• **BEHAVIOR** Solitary or in pairs in breeding season. Gregarious in migration and winter; may form flocks. Forages in trees, bushes, and on ground. Eats seeds, insects, caterpillars, berries, and fruits. Some hybridize with Rose-breasted Grosbeak where ranges overlap in Great Plains. Both sexes may sing "whisper" songs while incubating and brooding.

• **BREEDING** Monogamous. Solitary.

• **NESTING** Incubation 12–14 days by both sexes. Altricial young brooded by both sexes, more by female; stay in nest 11–12 days, fed by both sexes. 1 brood per year.

• **POPULATION** Common to fairly common in open woodlands, especially pine-oak and oak, forest edge, and riparian woodlands. This bird is casual in migration and winter to the Midwest and the East.

• **FEEDERS** Various seeds.

• **CONSERVATION** Neotropical migrant. Uncommon cowbird host. Vulnerable to habitat loss due to logging and fires.

black head

cinnamon-orange hind collar and postocular stripe

large dark conical bill

black upperparts with brown edging to feathers

MALE

2 white wing bars

white patch at base of primaries

cinnamon underparts

cinnamon rump

brown head and upperparts with dark streaking

white median crown stripe

white supercilium and mustache

2 white wing bars

black tail with white inner webs to outer tail feathers

pale cinnamon throat and underparts

lemon wash on belly

fine brown streaks on sides and flanks

FEMALE

white undertail coverts

JUVENILE MALE

Similar Birds

ROSE-BREASTED GROSBEAK ♀ Heavier streaked white to buffy underparts; darker upperparts; brown edging to feathers on back; gray to pale creamy pink bill; paler upper mandible.

Flight Pattern

Short flights with rapid wing beats alternating with brief periods of wings pulled to sides.

Nest Identification

Shape   Location

Sticks, weeds, rootlets, and pine needles, lined with finer materials • in dense part of tree or shrub, usually near water, about 4–25 feet above ground • built by female • 3–4 light greenish or bluish eggs dotted with reddish brown; oval, 1.0 x 0.7 inches.

Plumage Sexes differ	Habitat	Migration Migratory	Weight 1.5 ounces

DATE _____ TIME_____ LOCATION _____

Family CARDINALIDAE	Species *Guiraca caerulea*	Length 6.25–7.5 inches	Wingspan 10.5–11.5 inches

BLUE GROSBEAK

Often seen flocking in southern fields in spring, this grosbeak, with its deep blue plumage, may appear black from a distance or on a cloudy day. Not shy, it hops on the ground, wagging or spreading its tail, and sings from a conspicuous perch. In nesting season the male attacks other pairs to defend its territory. Females may be mistaken for female Brown-headed Cowbirds, but the large triangular bill and brown wing bars are distinctive, as is their behavior of raising a slight crest and flicking and spreading their tails. Females have a gray-brown rump that can show a bluish cast.

MALE

black lores and face around base of bill

deep rich blue overall

blackish wings and tail

thick conical bill with blackish upper mandible and silver-gray lower mandible

2 chestnut wing bars

FIRST SPRING MALE

• **SONG** Series of deep rich slightly scratchy warbles that rise and fall in pitch, resembling the Purple Finch. Call is explosive metallic *pink*.

• **BEHAVIOR** Solitary or in pairs during breeding season. More gregarious in other seasons; forms flocks. Hops on ground to forage; gleans from weeds, bushes, and low in trees. Eats mostly insects in summer; also fruits, seeds, grains, and land snails. May fly considerable distances across fields from one song perch to the next.

darker brown streaking on back

dull brown overall

2 cinnamon to chestnut wing bars

paler cinnamon buff on throat

cinnamon buff underparts

FEMALE

• **BREEDING** Monogamous. Solitary.

• **NESTING** Incubation 11–12 days by female. Young altricial; brooded by female; leave nest at 9–10 days, fed mostly by female. 2 broods per year.

Similar Birds

INDIGO BUNTING
Smaller; bright blue overall; smaller bill; lacks chestnut wing bars • female is smaller with smaller bill; brown overall with faint streaking on breast and narrow brown wing bars.

BLUE BUNTING
Smaller; blue-black overall; smaller bill with rounded culmen; lacks chestnut wing bars • female has brown plumage overall; lacks wing bars • casual in Texas.

• **POPULATION** Uncommon to fairly common in overgrown fields, riparian thickets, brushy rural roadsides, and woodland edges. Range is expanding in central and northeastern US.

• **FEEDERS** Seeds and grains.

• **CONSERVATION** Neotropical migrant. Fairly common cowbird host.

Flight Pattern

Swift flight with rapid wing beats alternating with brief periods of wings pulled to sides.

Nest Identification	
Shape Location	Twigs, weeds, rootlets, snakeskin, leaves, bark, bits of paper, and string, with lining of finer materials • low in tree, bush, or weed clump • 3–12 feet above ground • built by female • 3–5 light blue eggs occasionally marked with brown; oval, 0.9 x 0.7 inches.

Plumage Sexes differ	Habitat	Migration Migratory	Weight 1.0 ounce

DATE _____ TIME_____ LOCATION _____

Family CARDINALIDAE	Species *Passerina amoena*	Length 5.25–5.75 inches	Wingspan 8–9 inches

LAZULI BUNTING

This small turquoise bird is the western counterpart to the Indigo Bunting of eastern North America. Seen in open forests, riparian thickets, chaparral, and arid brushy canyons, the male sings to claim his territory and spreads and flutters his wings to show off his plumage and attract females. The winter plumage of the male shows the blue on its head and upperparts heavily washed with brown.

- **SONG** Various phrases, some paired and somewhat buzzy, *see-see-sweet, sweet-zee-see-zeer.* Call is "wet" *plik.*
- **BEHAVIOR** Solitary or in pairs during breeding season. Gregarious at other times, in flocks and mixed-species foraging flocks with other buntings and sparrows. Forages on ground and low in trees and bushes. Eats mainly seeds; also insects and caterpillars, especially in summer. At end of breeding season many join flocks and move to higher elevations. Hybrids occur where range overlaps with Indigo Bunting. Aggressively defends territory.
- **BREEDING** Mostly monogamous; some males polygamous.
- **NESTING** Incubation 12 days by female. Young altricial; brooded by female; stay in nest 10–12 days, fed by both sexes, but female does more. 2–3 broods per year.
- **POPULATION** Fairly common. Logging and agricultural change in 20th century promoted range and population expansion. Casual throughout the East.
- **FEEDERS** Comes for small seeds and grains.
- **CONSERVATION** Neotropical migrant. Uncommon host to parasitism by cowbirds. Disappearing due to development.

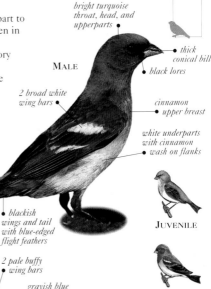

MALE

bright turquoise throat, head, and upperparts

thick conical bill

black lores

2 broad white wing bars

cinnamon upper breast

white underparts with cinnamon wash on flanks

blackish wings and tail with blue-edged flight feathers

JUVENILE

grayish brown head and upperparts

thick conical bill

2 pale buffy wing bars

grayish blue uppertail coverts and rump

FIRST SPRING MALE

buff wash on throat and breast

FEMALE

white underparts

blackish wings and tail with blue-edged flight feathers

Similar Birds

INDIGO BUNTING
Male bright blue overall • female lacks pale wing bars; warm brown to pale buffy brown underparts; dusky streaking on chest.

VARIED BUNTING
Stubbier bill; lacks buff wash on flanks; lacks pale wing bars.

Flight Pattern

Typically, short flights on rapidly beating wings alternating with brief periods of wings pulled to sides.

Nest Identification	
Shape 🥄 Location 🌿 🌱 🌳	Grass, weeds, and leaves, with lining of finer grass and mammal hair • in fork of bush or small tree • 2–4 feet above ground (but up to 10 feet) • built by female • 3–5 plain pale bluish white eggs; short oval to oval, 0.8 x 0.5 inches.

Plumage Sexes differ	Habitat 🏞️ ⛰️ 🌾 ✈️ 🏔️	Migration Migratory	Weight 0.8 ounce

DATE _____ TIME_____ LOCATION _____

Family CARDINALIDAE	Species *Passerina cyanea*	Length 5.25–5.75 inches	Wingspan 8–9 inches

INDIGO BUNTING

The male's distinctive plumage looks blue in sunlight and almost black in shade or backlighting. Populations are expanding with the creation of disturbed habitat after logging, highway and power line construction, and farmland abandonment. Its breeding range now includes much of the Southwest.

blue-purple sheen to head

deep-colored bright blue overall

dark blue to black lores

MALE

blue edging to blackish wings and tail

- **SONG** Series of varied measured strident phrases, usually paired, *sweet-sweet, sweeter-sweeter, here-here*, often with an added trilled ending. Call is a "wet" *spit* or *plik*.
- **BEHAVIOR** Solitary or in pairs during breeding season. Gregarious at other times; in flocks in winter, often with other buntings, sparrows, and finches. Forages in trees, shrubs, and on ground. Eats variety of insects and larvae, especially in summer; also dandelion seeds, weed seeds, grass seeds, small grains, and wild berries. Males defensive of territory; often engage in colorful chases with other males.

JUVENILE

WINTER MALE

- **BREEDING** Monogamous. Solitary. Some males polygynous when outnumbered by females.

brown head and upperparts

2 tawny buff wing bars

whitish throat and underparts

buffy brown-washed chest and flanks with dusky streaks

tertials edged with contrasting buff

FEMALE

darker brown wings and tail with blue-edged feathers

- **NESTING** Incubation 12–14 days by female. Young altricial; brooded by female; leave nest at 9–12 days, fed mostly by female; some males bring food. 2 broods per year.
- **POPULATION** Fairly common to common. Abundant in some deciduous forest edges, old fields, clearings, and agricultural areas.

Similar Birds

BLUE GROSBEAK
Larger; large triangular bill; tan wing bars.

VARIED BUNTING ♀
Olive-brown to tawny-brown overall; brown rump; bill with more decurved culmen; narrower tertial edges with less buffy contrast; lacks streaking on underparts; lacks brown wing bars.

Expanding.
- **FEEDERS** Comes for small seeds and grains.
- **CONSERVATION** Neotropical migrant. Common host to cowbird parasitism. Some habitat loss due to maturation of cut-over forests.

Flight Pattern

Short flight low over vegetation with rapid wing beats alternating with brief periods of wings pulled to sides.

Nest Identification	
Shape Location	Weeds, bark, and fine materials, lined with grass and leaves • in weed clump, dense shrub, or low tree • 1–15 feet above ground • built by female • 3–4 pale bluish white to white eggs, sometimes with brown or purple spotting; short oval to short subelliptical, 0.8 x 0.5 inches.

Plumage Sexes differ	Habitat	Migration Migratory	Weight 0.5 ounce

DATE _____ TIME_____ LOCATION _____

Family CARDINALIDAE	Species *Passerina versicolor*	Length 5–5.5 inches	Wingspan 8–8.5 inches

VARIED BUNTING

If this bird is seen in the open on a sunny day, the exquisite colors in the male's breeding plumage are striking: varied reds, violet-blues, deep purples, and blacks. When seen from a distance or in poor light, however, it appears black overall. In the molt to basic plumage following the breeding season, males show brownish rather than plum-colored plumage, and the red nape is faded and washed with browns, while the forecrown, face, and rump retain some blue. Juveniles resemble females but show narrow buff wing bars and a brighter brown body.

slightly curved grayish bill

deep violet-blue face, crown, and hind collar

plum-purple throat, breast, and back

deep purple on lower belly and undertail coverts

deep red nape

blue-edged black wings and tail

royal blue rump

MALE

- **SONG** Various high-pitched slightly scratchy thin warbles similar to the song of the Painted Bunting. Call is a "wet" *spik*.
- **BEHAVIOR** Solitary or in pairs during breeding season. Solitary or in small groups at other times. Shy and secretive. Remains hidden in thickets close to ground and often distances itself from human habitation. Forages in low dense vegetation or on ground. Takes some insects but major diet is seeds. Bonded pairs spend much time together. Male sings from exposed perch. Natural history is poorly studied.
- **BREEDING** Monogamous. Solitary.
- **NESTING** Breeding biology poorly known. Incubation 12–13 days by female. Young altricial; brooded by female; stay in nest estimated 12 days, fed by both sexes. 1–2 broods per year.
- **POPULATION** Common locally in mesquite chaparral, dry washes, and arid thorn scrub, often near water.
- **CONSERVATION** Neotropical migrant. Rare host to cowbird parasitism. Vulnerable to habitat loss from agriculture and development.

gray-brown upperparts

slightly curved grayish bill

faint bluish sheen on wings and tail

pale buff underparts

FEMALE

WINTER PLUMAGE

Similar Birds

LAZULI BUNTING ♀
Gray-brown head and upperparts; white underparts; buffy wash on throat and breast; gray-blue rump; 2 narrow buffy white wing bars.

INDIGO BUNTING ♀
Brown head and upperparts; blue-tinged rump; tertials edged with buff; 2 tawny buff wing bars; whitish throat and underparts; chest and flanks washed buffy brown with dusky streaks.

Flight Pattern
Short flights close to vegetation, with rapid wing beats alternating with brief periods of wings pulled to sides.

Nest Identification	Stalks, grass, cotton, snakeskin, and paper, with lining of rootlets, grass, and hair • in fork of low tree or bush, usually 2–10 feet above ground • built by both sexes • 3–4 white to light blue eggs, characteristically unmarked; short to oval subelliptical, 0.7 x 0.5 inches.
Shape Location	

Plumage Sexes differ	Habitat	Migration Migratory	Weight 0.4 ounce

DATE _____ TIME_____ LOCATION _____

Family CARDINALIDAE	Species *Passerina ciris*	Length 5–5.5 inches	Wingspan 8–8.5 inches

PAINTED BUNTING

Flaunting one of the most brilliant plumages of all North American songbirds, the male is easy to identify by the dark blue head, lime-green back, and red rump and underparts. The green and yellow-green coloring of the female and juvenile serves as camouflage in the dense riparian thickets, woodland edges, and scrubby brushy areas. Males can be highly aggressive and sometimes kill one another in territorial battles. Their striking colors and warbled song have made them a popular cage bird in Mexico, Central America, and the Caribbean. Before laws prevented it, they were sold as cage birds in the United States, sometimes under the name "nonpareil." The first spring male is similar to the female but is brighter overall and has a bluish wash on the head.

deep blue-violet head and hindneck

bright lime-green back

red eye ring

scarlet underparts

MALE

dark mouse-gray tail and wings with reddish edges

JUVENILE

bright green upperparts

gray-green tail and wings

FEMALE

yellow-green underparts

olive-washed flanks and chest

• **SONG** High-pitched musical measured warble *pew-eata, pew-eata, I eaty you too*. Call is 2-note *chip* or a "wet" *plik*.

• **BEHAVIOR** Solitary or in pairs during breeding season. Gregarious in other seasons, forming flocks and joining mixed-species foraging flocks. Shy, secretive, and often difficult to see. Male sings from exposed perch. Most often hops on ground. Forages on ground and low in trees and shrubs. Eats seeds, insects, and caterpillars.

• **BREEDING** Mostly monogamous, but some males polygynous.

• **NESTING** Incubation 11–12 days by female. Young altricial; brooded by female; stay in nest 12–14 days, fed by both sexes, but female does more. 2–3 broods per year.

• **POPULATION** Common in riparian thickets and shrubby habitats. Casual north of range.

• **FEEDERS** Birdseed and sunflower seeds; uses birdbaths.

• **CONSERVATION** Neotropical migrant. Common cowbird host. Declining on the East Coast, where the species is losing habitat to development.

Flight Pattern
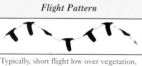
Typically, short flight low over vegetation, with rapid wing beats alternating with brief periods of wings pulled to sides.

Nest Identification	
Shape 🥣 Location 🌳 🌲	Stalks, leaves, and grasses, with lining of rootlets, snakeskin, and animal hair • in dense part of bush, in low tree, or in vines or moss • 3–6 feet above ground (but up to 25 feet) • built by female • 3–5 pale blue eggs marked with reddish brown, concentrated at larger end; oval to short oval, 0.8 x 0.6 inches.

Plumage Sexes differ	Habitat 🌾 ✈ 🌲 〰	Migration Migratory	Weight 0.8 ounce

DATE _____ TIME_____ LOCATION _____

Family CARDINALIDAE	Species *Spiza americana*	Length 6–7 inches	Wingspan 9–11 inches

DICKCISSEL

This bird is named for its song of *dick-dick-dick-cissel.*
Often flying in flocks over grassy prairies, the
Dickcissel, with its black bib and yellow breast,
looks like a small meadowlark. Females are
similar to males but lack the black bib and
have duller chestnut wing patches.

- **SONG** Staccato *dick-dick-dick-cissel.* Has an
insectlike call of *bzzrrrt.*

- **BEHAVIOR** Solitary or in pairs during
breeding season. Gregarious at other
times, forming wintering flocks
numbering thousands of birds. Joins
communal roosts after breeding season.
Male sings from exposed perches and
in flight. Forages on ground. Eats
grains, seeds, and insects.

- **BREEDING** Polygamous, although
some birds are monogamous.

- **NESTING** Incubation 12–13 days
by female. Altricial young brooded
by female; stay in nest
7–10 days, fed by female.
1–2 broods per year.

- **POPULATION**
Common to abundant
in grasslands,
meadows, savannas,
and fields. Local
and irregular east
of Appalachians.
Rare in migration
on Atlantic and
Pacific Coasts.
Casual in winter
in the East.

- **FEEDERS** Birds in northern
part of range come to feeders.

yellowish eyebrow
becomes whitish
behind eye

thick stout bill
with blackish
upper mandible

white chin

thin blackish
malar stripe

black bib

bold yellow breast

chestnut wing coverts

brown auricular
patch and crown

brown
upperparts

black
streaking
on back

dusky white
underparts

JUVENILE

WINTER
MALE

MALE

WINTER
FEMALE

yellowish eyebrow
becomes whitish
behind eye

grayish-brown
auricular patch

grayish-brown upperparts

blackish
streaking on back

thin dark
brown
malar stripe

chestnut
wing
coverts

white throat,
chin, and
mustache

FEMALE

dusky white
underparts

yellow breast

Similar Birds

HOUSE SPARROW ♀
Similar to female
Dickcissel • stubbier
yellowish bill; buffy
supercilium; brown
postocular stripe; single
white wing bar; lacks
pale throat with dark
malar stripe; lacks
streaking on flanks.

- **CONSERVATION** Neotropical
migrant. Frequent host to
cowbird parasitism. Nests and
young lost annually to the
mowing of fields for hay.
Thousands are killed annually
on wintering grounds for the
protection of rice plantations.

Flight Pattern

Series of rapid wing beats alternating with
brief periods of wings pulled to sides.
Often flies in large flocks in compact
undulating formation.

Nest Identification

Shape ◣   Location 🌳 🌿 ▭▭

Grasses, stems, and leaves, with lining of soft rootlets, grasses, and hair • low
in tree or bush, sometimes atop grassy tussock or on ground in field • 0–6 feet
above ground • built by female • 3–5 plain pale blue eggs; oval to long oval,
0.8 x 0.6 inches.

Plumage Sexes differ	Habitat ___ ▲	Migration Migratory	Weight 1.0 ounce

DATE _____ TIME_____ LOCATION _____

Family ICTERIDAE	Species *Dolichonyx oryzivorus*	Length 6.25–8 inches	Wingspan 10.25–12.5 inches

BOBOLINK

In northern meadows and farmland, this bird is known for its cheerful bubbling *bob-o-link* song and handsome plumage. It is said the male wears his breeding plumage upside down, as he has black underparts with a buff nape and hindneck and white scapulars and rump. In all plumages, birds are adorned with sharply pointed tail feathers, unusual for songbirds. All fall-plumaged birds and juveniles are similar to the female but have brighter yellow-buff underparts with less streaking.

buff-colored hindneck

black face and crown

black back

narrow buff stripe in center of back

white scapulars

white rump

MALE

- **SONG** Lively bubbling cascade of notes, starting with low reedy notes and rollicking upward, *bob-o-link, bob-o-link, pink, pink, pank, pink*. Call is clear *pink*.

black underparts and wings

buff-edged tertials and wing coverts

black tail

- **BEHAVIOR** Gregarious; in flocks numbering up to thousands. Males sing from perch or in flight display, circling low over fields. In summer eats insects and caterpillars, grass and weed seeds, and grains; eats seeds and grains in migration and winter.

- **BREEDING** Strongly polygynous.

- **NESTING** Incubation 13 days by female. Altricial young brooded by female; stay in nest 10–14 days, fed by both sexes. 1 brood per year.

blackish brown crown with buff central crown stripe

pinkish bill

black streaking on back, rump, sides, and flanks

golden buff overall

WINTER MALE

- **POPULATION** Fairly common to common in tall grass, wet meadows, prairie, hay fields, and grain fields. Decline in the East during 20th century. Rare in the fall on West Coast.

- **CONSERVATION** Neotropical migrant. Rare cowbird host. Vulnerable to destruction of nests and young by mowing of hayfields. Has declined in the Southeast from former 19th-century market hunting for food and from continued destruction to protect rice plantations. Similar killing currently exists on expanding rice plantations on wintering grounds in South America.

FEMALE

Similar Birds

LARK BUNTING ♂
Entirely black except for large white shoulder patches, white edging to tertials and inner secondaries, and white tips to outer tail feathers.

Flight Pattern

Strong undeviating and slightly undulating flight on rapidly beating wings. Male has display flight with shallow wing strokes on rapidly fluttering wings.

Nest Identification

Shape ⌣ Location ▬ ✳✳✳

Coarse grasses and weed stalks, lined with finer grasses • in slight depression on ground in tall grass, weeds, or clover, sometimes in rut made by tractors and combines • female digs scrape and then builds nest • 4–7 eggs, irregularly blotched with browns, purple, and lavender; oval to short oval. 0.82 x 0.62 inches.

Plumage Sexes differ	Habitat	Migration Migratory	Weight 1.7 ounces

DATE _____ TIME_____ LOCATION _____

Family ICTERIDAE	Species *Agelaius phoeniceus*	Length 7.5–9.5 inches	Wingspan 12–14.5 inches

RED-WINGED BLACKBIRD

Believed one of the most numerous land birds in North America, the Red-winged Blackbird is known for aggressively defending its territory from intruders. Many geographical races exist across its extensive range. Females, identifiable by dark brown upperparts and heavily streaked underparts, sometimes show a red tinge on wing coverts, chin, and throat. Males resemble females at a year old but have less streaking and some red on their epaulettes; they develop glossy black plumage after their second year.

red shoulder patches (epaulettes) with broad buff-yellow distal tips

black overall, including wings and tail

MALE

- **SONG** Gurgling reedy *konk-la-ree* or *gurr-ga-leee*. Calls: low *clack*, sharp nasal *deekk*, and metallic *tiink*.
- **BEHAVIOR** Gregarious. Small breeding colonies in summer. Winter flocks often segregated by sex and age. Runs or hops while foraging on ground. Eats mostly seeds, grains, berries, and wild fruit; in summer also eats insects, caterpillars, grubs, spiders, mollusks, and snails. Male's social dominance is proportional to amount of red displayed.
- **BREEDING** Colonial. Some males polygynous.
- **NESTING** Incubation 11–12 days by female. Altricial young brooded by female; stay in nest 10–14 days, fed mostly by female. 2–3 broods per year.
- **POPULATION** Abundant to common in fields, riparian thickets and scrub, freshwater and brackish marshes.

brown crown

dusky tan face

broad dusky tan supercilium

brown upperparts with dark streaks

FIRST YEAR MALE

thin brown malar mark

dark brown postocular stripe

2 thin tan wing bars

dusky white underparts heavily streaked with brown

FEMALE

Similar Birds

♂ TRICOLORED BLACKBIRD
Longer, more slender body • male's red epaulettes have whitish borders • females have darker bodies; heavier streaks on underparts; blackish bellies; lack chestnut and buff edges to upperparts; lack pink coloring on throat • West Coast only.

♀

- **FEEDERS** Will attend for breadcrumbs and birdseed.
- **CONSERVATION** Vulnerable to pesticides in food chain and to habitat loss due to the drainage of wetlands. Nests and young are destroyed by mowing operations.

Flight Pattern

Strong flight on rapidly beating wings; displaying males fly with slow stiff shallow wing beats with epaulettes raised.

Nest Identification

Shape

Location

Dried cattail leaves and sedges, lined with fine grasses and rushes • fastened to stalks or twigs with plant fibers • in cattails, bushes, trees, dense grass, or on ground, preferably near or over water • built by female • 3–5 (usually 4) pale blue-green eggs spotted or with zigzag lines of black, browns, and purple; oval, 0.97 x 0.75 inches.

Plumage Sexes differ	Habitat	Migration Migratory	Weight 2.3 ounces

DATE _____ TIME_____ LOCATION _____

Family ICTERIDAE	Species *Sturnella magna*	Length 9–11 inches	Wingspan 13.5–17 inches

EASTERN MEADOWLARK

A common inhabitant of fields and meadows, the Eastern Meadowlark often is observed flicking its tail open and shut while walking through grass and weeds and along roadsides. Clearing of forests in eastern North America has led to the expansion of its breeding range. Fall-plumaged birds show narrow buffy mottling in the black breast band and a buffy wash on the face, supercilium, flanks, and undertail coverts. Juveniles have black spotting on the chest, sides, and flanks.

black-and-white-striped crown

white face with black postocular stripe

brown upperparts streaked with buff and black

chunky body

yellow breast and belly with broad black V on chest

white outer tail feathers

white sides and flanks with black spots and streaks

• **SONG** A plaintive *tee-you, tee-airrr,* or *spring-o'the-year.* Call given on ground or in flight is high buzzy *zzzzrrt,* and a nasal *sweeink* also is given in flight.

white undertail coverts with dusky streaking

• **BEHAVIOR** Solitary or in pairs during summer. Gregarious during other seasons, forming small flocks in winter. Eats mostly insects, especially in summer. Also eats grains, weed and grass seeds, and tender sprouts of spring plants.

• **BREEDING** Monogamous. Solitary. Some males polygynous.

• **NESTING** Incubation 13–14 days by both sexes. Young altricial; brooded by female; stay in nest 11–12 days, fed by both sexes, but female does more. Male may take over brood while female starts second nest. 2 broods per year.

• **POPULATION** Common in meadows, fields, grasslands, and savanna. Decline reported in the East during last quarter of the 20th century.

• **CONSERVATION** Common host to cowbird parasitism. Nests and young destroyed by mowing operations. Vulnerable to habitat loss due to natural succession of abandoned fields, as well as from overgrazing, development, and grassland habitat fragmentation.

Similar Birds

WESTERN MEADOWLARK Paler upperparts lack dark centers in most feathers; yellow of throat, especially that of breeding males, extends into submustachial region; sides of crown and postocular stripe usually brownish; most have less white in outer tail feathers.

Flight Pattern

Several rapid shallow stiff wing beats followed by short glides close to landscape.

Nest Identification

Shape ⬤   Location ✱✱✱

Lined with grass, plant stems, and pine needles • domed or partially domed • often next to dense clump of grass or weeds on damp or wet ground • built by female • 3–7 white eggs, suffused with pink, with brown and lavender spots and speckles; oval to short or long oval, 1.1 x 0.8 inches.

Plumage Sexes similar	Habitat ◢ ▂▂	Migration Northern birds migrate	Weight 3.6 ounces

DATE _____ TIME_____ LOCATION _____

Family ICTERIDAE	Species *Sturnella neglecta*	Length 9–11 inches	Wingspan 13.5–17 inches

WESTERN MEADOWLARK

Its distinctive song often is the only way to distinguish this bird from the Eastern Meadowlark, which is strikingly similar in appearance. Both birds are known to be interspecifically territorial and nest in the same area, interbreeding in regions where their ranges overlap. Under such circumstances some males sing the songs of both species, creating a tricky identification challenge for the observer. Breeding adults show bright yellow plumage from throat to belly, with a black V on the chest. Fall-plumaged birds show a pale buffy wash on the face, sides, and flanks, and the yellow in submustachial regions is much reduced or veiled, as is the black breast band. Juveniles are paler and instead of the black V show a streaked necklace.

dark brown stripes on crown

yellow of throat extends well into submustachial area

dark brown postocular stripe

black V on chest

chunky body

black spots and streaks on sides and flanks

short wide tail with white outer feathers

• **SONG** Repeated bubbling flutelike notes, varying in length, *shee-oo-e-lee shee-ee le-ee*, accelerating toward the end. Call is a low *chuk*. Flight note is a nasal *whew*.
• **BEHAVIOR** Solitary or in pairs during breeding season. Gregarious at other times, forming small to large flocks in winter, which forage and roost together on the ground. Walks on ground. Sings from ground or exposed perches, including fence posts, shrubs, trees, and utility wires. Forages primarily in vegetation on ground. Eats mostly insects and larvae, spiders, and some snails; also seeds of grains, grasses, and weeds. Winter birds often forage in shorter grasses along roadsides.
• **BREEDING** Monogamous. Solitary. Some males polygynous.
• **NESTING** Incubation 13–15 days by female. Young altricial; brooded by female; stay in nest 11–12 days, fed by both sexes but more by female. 2 broods per year.
• **POPULATION** Fairly common to common in cultivated fields, pastures, grasslands, and savanna. Range expanding in the Northeast.
• **CONSERVATION** Neotropical migrant. Uncommon cowbird host. Nest and young destroyed by mowing operations.

Similar Birds

EASTERN MEADOWLARK Darker body; dark centers to feathers on upperparts; yellow of throat generally does not reach submustachial area, barely does so on males; more extensive white on outer tail feathers; black crown and postocular stripes; voice differs.

Flight Pattern

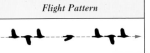

Flies low over landscape, with series of rapid shallow stiff wing beats followed by short glide.

Nest Identification

Shape 🪹   Location ▬ ▬ ▬

Dried grass and plant stems; domed or partially domed • lined with grasses and pine needles • against clump of grass or weeds • built by female • 3–7 white eggs, suffused with pink, with brown and lavender spots and speckles; oval or short to long oval, 1.1 x 0.8 inches.

Plumage Sexes similar	Habitat 🌿	Migration Northern birds migrate	Weight 4.0 ounces

DATE _____ TIME_____ LOCATION _____

Family ICTERIDAE	Species *Xanthocephalus xanthocephalus*	Length 8.75–11 inches	Wingspan 14–17 inches

YELLOW-HEADED BLACKBIRD

Brilliant yellow plumage and white wing patches contrasting with its all-black body make this robin-sized marsh bird easy to identify. Often nesting in colonies, it is highly aggressive in defending its grounds and will attack other birds and even human intruders, especially if young are in the nest. The song of the male is considered by many to be the poorest vocalization of any North American songbird. Males are larger than females, and the white wing patch is conspicuous in flight. Juveniles show dark brown upperparts with cinnamon-buff edging to the body feathers, pale buff underparts with a cinnamon wash on the flanks, an ocherous buff head and breast, a whitish throat, and dusky brown auriculars.

yellow head, throat, and breast

black body

black loreal mask

white wing patch

MALE

- **SONG** High-pitched raspy honking gurgle, ending with a descending buzz, *klee-klee-klee-ko-kow-w-w-w,w,w,w.* Call is hoarse *ka-aack.*

- **BEHAVIOR** Gregarious; forms breeding colonies and flocks outside breeding season. Flocks forage and roost together and range from small to enormous, containing millions in winter. Males often segregate from females and juveniles in separate winter flocks. Conspicuous. Forages in mud near water and in fields. Walks on ground. Eats insects, larvae, snails, grains, and seeds.

dusky brown crown and cheeks

yellowish eyebrow

dusky brown upperparts

yellowish lower cheek, throat, and breast

dusky brown belly with white streaking

dusky brown crissum

FEMALE

- **BREEDING** Polygynous. Colonial.

- **NESTING** Incubation 11–13 days by female. Young altricial; brooded by female; stay in nest 9–12 days, fed by both sexes, but mostly by female. 2 broods per year.

- **POPULATION** Common in freshwater marshes, reedy lakes and irrigation ditches, and open farmlands. Rare to casual in migration and in winter to the East Coast. Casual spring migrant to southeastern Alaska.

- **CONSERVATION** Neotropical migrant. Rare host to cowbird parasitism. Vulnerable to loss of habitat due to draining of wetlands and freshwater marshes.

Flight Pattern
Strong direct flight with rapid wing beats.

Nest Identification	
Shape ● Location ⅄⅄⅄	Grasses, reeds, cattails, and bulrushes, with partial canopy that shrinks into tight basket when dry • over water in marsh vegetation • 0.5–3 feet above surface • built by female • 3–5 light gray or green eggs with brownish or grayish markings; oval to long oval, 1.0 x 0.8 inches.

Plumage Sexes differ	Habitat	Migration Migratory	Weight 2.8 ounces

DATE _____ TIME_____ LOCATION _____

Family ICTERIDAE	Species *Euphagus carolinus*	Length 8.25–9.75 inches	Wingspan 13–15 inches

RUSTY BLACKBIRD

This bird is named for the rusty wash on its fall and winter plumage. Only birds in juvenile plumage have dark eyes; older birds in immature plumage have yellow eyes like adults. Juvenile plumage resembles that of winter adults. Fall males have a blackish loreal mask that contrasts with the rufous wash on the rest of the plumage. The fall female has a gray rump and cinnamon-gray supercilium and underparts. Flying in large flocks from their wintering grounds, these birds will swoop down to forage behind tractors and plows.

faint iridescent green on head

black overall

black wings and tail with bluish sheen

blackish bill

yellow eyes

MALE

blackish legs

WINTER MALE

WINTER FEMALE

- **SONG** A high-pitched creaky *koo-a-lee-m-eek, koo-a-lee—-eek.* Has call notes of *chuck* or *kick.*
- **BEHAVIOR** In pairs during breeding season. Gregarious. After nesting season forms small flocks that forage and roost communally. Forms large flocks in migration and winter and joins mixed flocks with other blackbird species and starlings. Forages on ground of wet woodlands and agricultural lands or wades in marshes and small pools of water. Eats insects, caterpillars, crustaceans, small fish, salamanders, and snails. Also eats grains, seeds, and fruits.
- **BREEDING** Monogamous. Pairs.
- **NESTING** Incubation 14 days by female; male feeds incubating female on nest. Young altricial; brooded by female; stay in nest 11–14 days, fed by both sexes. 1 brood per year.

darker gray wings and tail with greenish blue sheen

FEMALE

slate-gray overall

Similar Birds

BREWER'S BLACKBIRD Most males are black throughout year, with purplish gloss on head and neck and blue-green sheen on body, wings, and tail • female has dark eyes • some variant fall males have buff-brown edging on head and body but never on wing coverts or tertials.

- **POPULATION** Fairly common in wet coniferous woodlands, bogs, riparian habitats, and swamps. Rare in the West.
- **CONSERVATION** Rare host to cowbird parasitism.

Flight Pattern

Strong direct flight on rapidly beating wings.

Nest Identification	
Shape  Location	Grasses, moss, and twigs, with inner cup of mud lined with soft grasses and rootlets • over water in dense bush or conifer, usually 2–8 feet above ground (but up to 20 feet) • built by female • 4–5 light blue-green eggs, with brown and gray splotches; oval, 1.0 x 0.75 inches.

Plumage Sexes differ	Habitat	Migration Migratory	Weight 2.3 ounces

DATE _____ TIME_____ LOCATION _____

Family ICTERIDAE	Species *Euphagus cyanocephalus*	Length 8.75–10.25 inches	Wingspan 14–16 inches

BREWER'S BLACKBIRD

purplish sheen on head and neck

yellow eyes

MALE

greenish blue sheen on body and wings

black overall

FALL MALE

Huge flocks can be seen flying over farm fields during plowing season, and the species has expanded its range and abundance with the spread of agriculture. One of the most common blackbirds, the male's plumage remains glossy black year-round. In fall, some males acquire buffy edging on the head and body feathers but never on the wing coverts or tertials. Juveniles resemble females but lack the green sheen on wings and tail.

dark brown eyes

dark gray-brown overall

green sheen on wings and tail

FEMALE

- **SONG** Breathy, creaky *ke-see*. Call is gruff *check*.
- **BEHAVIOR** In pairs during breeding season. Gregarious. Forms large foraging and roosting flocks in migration and winter. Often joins mixed-species foraging flocks with other blackbirds in winter. Nests in small to large colonies. Head bobs forward while walking. Follows farm tractors and plows. Forages on ground. Eats insects; caterpillars; and some fruits, seeds, and grains.
- **BREEDING** Monogamous. Some males polygynous. Can be loosely colonial.
- **NESTING** Incubation 12–14 days by female, guarded by male. Altricial young brooded by female; stay in nest 13–14 days, fed by both sexes. 1–2 broods per year.
- **POPULATION** Common in open habitats, shrub/scrub, riparian woodlands, farms, and around human habitation. Extending range north and east.
- **CONSERVATION** Neotropical migrant. Common cowbird host.

Similar Birds

BROWN-HEADED COWBIRD ♀
Smaller; slimmer; pale face pattern; shorter, deeper-based bill; shorter tail.

RUSTY BLACKBIRD
Faint greenish sheen on head; longer bill • female slate-gray overall with yellow eyes • in winter, rusty edging to feathers on back, wing coverts, and tertials • winter male has black loral mask; shows cinnamon edging to head, throat, breast, supercilium, and mustache • winter female has buff eyebrow; gray rump; buffy gray underparts.

Flight Pattern

Strong swift direct flight on rapidly beating wings.

Nest Identification

Shape ◥

Location ▬ 🌿 🌾 🌱 🐾

Conifer needles, grasses, and sticks, with inside cup of mud or cow manure, lined with hair and rootlets • on ground in meadow or field or in marshes or trees, up to 150 feet above ground • built by female • 3–7 light green or grayish green eggs, with blotches of grayish brown; oval, 1.0 x 0.75 inches.

Plumage Sexes differ	Habitat ▬ 🐾 ≈ ▲	Migration Northern birds migrate	Weight 2.4 ounces

DATE _____ TIME_____ LOCATION _____

Family ICTERIDAE	Species *Quiscalus quiscula*	Length 11–13.5 inches	Wingspan 17–18.5 inches

COMMON GRACKLE

This gregarious bird has expanded its range by adapting to suburban areas. Outside the nesting season, noisy groups roost together at night, often with other species. Juveniles are sooty brown with dark brown eyes.

pale yellow eyes

faint iridescent purplish blue on head, neck, and breast

faint iridescent purple or deep bronze on back

long, sharply pointed black bill

- **SONG** Grating squeaky *coguba-leek*, like a creaking rusty hinge. Call is a bold *chuk*.
- **BEHAVIOR** Conspicuous. Nests, forages, and roosts in groups or flocks all year. Large postnesting season flocks can damage crops, and winter flocks may number in the hundreds of thousands. Walks on ground. Forages in trees, shrubs, grass, and croplands; may wade into water. Eats insects, worms, caterpillars, fruits, grains, seeds, small rodents, small fish, salamanders, and eggs and nestlings of other birds. Male displays by fluffing out shoulder feathers to make a ruffled collar, drooping his wings, and singing.

glossy black overall

MALE

long wedge-shaped tail

pale yellow eye

long, sharply pointed black bill

faint iridescent purple on head and neck

dull black overall

FEMALE

long wedge-shaped tail

- **BREEDING** Monogamous. Some males polygynous. Colonial.
- **NESTING** Incubation 13–14 days by female. Young altricial; brooded by female; stay in nest 16–20 days, fed by both sexes. 1–2 broods per year.
- **POPULATION** Abundant and widespread in open areas with scattered trees, open woodlands, agricultural areas, parks, and around human habitation. Casual in southern Alaska and in the Pacific states.
- **FEEDERS** Will come for small grains and seeds.
- **CONSERVATION** Rare host to cowbird parasitism. Birds feeding on crops and making a nuisance in large winter roosts sometimes are destroyed.

Similar Birds
♂ **GREAT-TAILED GRACKLE** **BOAT-TAILED GRACKLE** Lack glossy contrast between head and body; larger; longer tail • ♀ females have dark brownish upperparts and cinnamon or pale brown and buff underparts • Boat-tailed Grackle ranges along Atlantic and Gulf Coasts.

Flight Pattern
- - - - - - - - - - - - - →
Strong swift direct flight with rapid wing beats; holds tail folded in a V shape while flying.

Nest Identification	
Shape	Bulky mass of stems, sticks, grasses, and seaweed, with mud lining and softer lining of feathers, grasses, and bits of debris • high in tree, in shrub, set in marsh, in hollow of old tree, under eave of building, or among highway plantings, usually 2–12 feet above ground (but up to 100 feet) • built by female • 4–7 light brown or light green eggs, with brown and lilac markings; oval, 1.2 x 0.82 inches.
Location	

Plumage Sexes differ	Habitat	Migration Migratory	Weight 4.5 ounces

DATE _____ TIME_____ LOCATION _____

Family ICTERIDAE	Species *Quiscalus major*	Length 12–17 inches	Wingspan 18–23.5 inches

BOAT-TAILED GRACKLE

This large noisy grackle travels, eats, sleeps, and nests in groups. It frequents saltwater marshes and, except in Florida, is never found far inland. It walks the beaches, large keel-shaped tail held high above its back, wading into the water for food, examining the wrack line, or gleaning seeds and berries from dune vegetation. Brown eyes occur in western Gulf Coast races east to Mississippi; farther east adults have yellow eyes. Males are larger than females. Juveniles have dark eyes and are similar to respective adults; males lack the iridescent sheen; females have faint spotting and streaking on the breast.

iridescent blue-black overall

long keel-shaped tail

brown or yellow eyes

MALE

tawny cinnamon supercilium

darker brown crown

tawny brown face and throat

darker brown upperparts, wings, and tail

dusky brown auricular patch

tawny brown underparts

FEMALE

• **SONG** Abrasive loud repeated *jeeb, jeeb, jeeb*. Calls a noisy variety of harsh whistles, chucks, guttural rattles, raspy clicks, and wolf whistles.

• **BEHAVIOR** Gregarious. Steals food from other birds. Diet includes small fish, frogs, snails, aquatic and terrestrial insects, shrimp, small birds, eggs and nestlings of other birds, small reptiles, fruit, berries, grain, and seeds. Many in northernmost populations winter in Virginia.

• **BREEDING** Promiscuous. Loose colonies. Displaying male perches, spreads tail and wings, then bows toward female. Does not hybridize with Great-tailed Grackle in overlapping zone.

• **NESTING** Incubation 13–15 days by female. Altricial young brooded by female; stay in nest 12–15 days, fed by female. 2–3 broods per year.

• **POPULATION** Common in coastal salt marshes and adjacent open habitats, agricultural areas, and around human habitations; inland in Florida around lakes, canals, and freshwater marshes. Northeastern range expanding.

• **CONSERVATION** Vulnerable to loss of habitat caused by draining of marshes for agriculture and development.

Similar Birds

♂ ♀ **GREAT-TAILED GRACKLE** Larger; bright yellow eyes; longer bill; flatter crown • inland west of Mississippi River.

SMOOTH-BILLED ANI Dark eyes; thick curved bill; long graduated tail.

Flight Pattern

Strong direct flight on rapidly beating wings with long keeled tail extended behind.

Nest Identification

Shape ◢   Location ⊔⊔ ••• ☘ ❁

In marsh vegetation; bulky and built of dried stalks, grasses, and cattails, usually over or near water in marsh or on ground set in grass • in trees, built of Spanish moss, feathers, mud, cow dung, and bits of debris, 3–50 feet above ground • built by female • 3–5 pale blue to blue-gray eggs with splotches of black, brown, lilac, and gray; oval, 1.3 x 0.88 inches.

Plumage Sexes differ	Habitat ⊔⊔ ⩩≋ ≈≈ ⬤	Migration Northern birds migrate	Weight 7.5 ounces

DATE _____ TIME_____ LOCATION _____

Family ICTERIDAE	Species *Quiscalus mexicanus*	Length 10.5–18.5 inches	Wingspan 13.5–25 inches

GREAT-TAILED GRACKLE

The Great-tailed and Boat-tailed Grackles were once considered to be one species. Although these birds nest closely in coastal eastern Texas and western Louisiana, they do not interbreed. This bird often walks on the ground with its large keel-shaped tail cocked over its back. Walking in the open, males turn like weathervanes when a strong gust of wind strikes their tails. Males are larger than females. Juveniles are similar to females with a grayish brown belly but with streaked underparts and dark eyes.

iridescent purple on head and back

black overall

golden yellow eyes

iridescent purple on underparts

MALE

- **SONG** Loud chatters, squeaks, gurgles, shrieks, and piercing ascending whistles; high-pitched squeal of *may-reee, may-reee*. Flight call is *chak*.
- **BEHAVIOR** Gregarious, noisy; in groups and small flocks forage and roost together. Forages walking on ground and wading in water. Eats insects, snails, small fish, frogs, shrimp, small birds, eggs and nestlings, fruits, berries, seeds, and grains. Steals food from other birds; females pilfer nesting materials from each other.
- **BREEDING** Polygamous to promiscuous. Colonial. Male claims territory within colony and displays and sings in front of a group of females. Female chooses male.
- **NESTING** Incubation 13–14 days by female. Young altricial; brooded by female; stay in nest 20–23 days, fed by female. 1–2 broods per year.

very long keel-shaped tail

dark brown head and upperparts

thin dark brown malar mark

cinnamon-buff breast and throat

buff-cinnamon supercilium and border to auriculars

yellowish white eyes

faint iridescent purple on plumage

FEMALE

Similar Birds

♂ ♀ BOAT-TAILED
GRACKLE
Smaller; rounder head; smaller bill; smaller tail • brown-eyed birds occur where ranges overlap • only in the East.

♂ ♀ COMMON GRACKLE
Smaller; shorter tail; smaller bill • female is dull black.

- **POPULATION** Common in open areas with scattered trees, cultivated areas, marshes, riparian thickets, parks, and around human habitation. Agricultural irrigation in arid regions helping expand range.
- **CONSERVATION** Removes cowbird eggs from nest.

Flight Pattern

Strong direct flight with rapid wing beats and long keeled tail trailing behind.

Nest Identification

Shape ◖   Location 🪺 〰️ 🌿

In marsh vegetation, bulky and built of cattails, grasses, and dried rushes, less than 2 feet above water • in trees, built of Spanish moss, mud, cow dung, feathers, and bits of debris, 5–15 feet above ground • built by female • 3–4 light gray to light blue eggs, with reddish purple markings; oval, 1.3 x 0.9 inches.

Plumage Sexes differ	Habitat 🌿 〰️	Migration Northern birds migrate	Weight 6.7 ounces

DATE _____ TIME_____ LOCATION _____

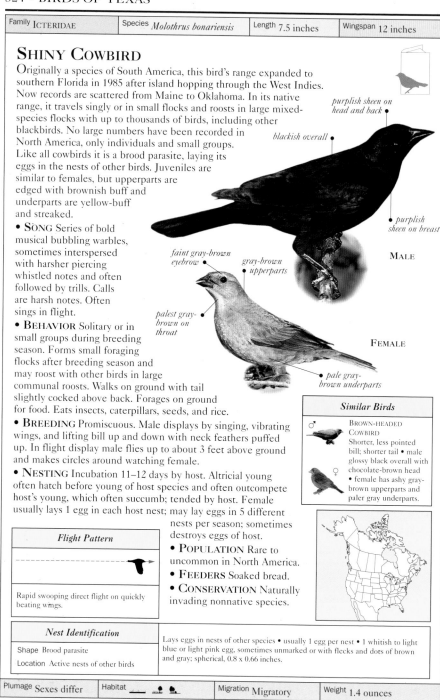

Family ICTERIDAE	Species *Molothrus bonariensis*	Length 7.5 inches	Wingspan 12 inches

SHINY COWBIRD

Originally a species of South America, this bird's range expanded to southern Florida in 1985 after island hopping through the West Indies. Now records are scattered from Maine to Oklahoma. In its native range, it travels singly or in small flocks and roosts in large mixed-species flocks with up to thousands of birds, including other blackbirds. No large numbers have been recorded in North America, only individuals and small groups. Like all cowbirds it is a brood parasite, laying its eggs in the nests of other birds. Juveniles are similar to females, but upperparts are edged with brownish buff and underparts are yellow-buff and streaked.

purplish sheen on head and back

blackish overall

purplish sheen on breast

MALE

faint gray-brown eyebrow

gray-brown upperparts

palest gray-brown on throat

FEMALE

pale gray-brown underparts

- **SONG** Series of bold musical bubbling warbles, sometimes interspersed with harsher piercing whistled notes and often followed by trills. Calls are harsh notes. Often sings in flight.
- **BEHAVIOR** Solitary or in small groups during breeding season. Forms small foraging flocks after breeding season and may roost with other birds in large communal roosts. Walks on ground with tail slightly cocked above back. Forages on ground for food. Eats insects, caterpillars, seeds, and rice.
- **BREEDING** Promiscuous. Male displays by singing, vibrating wings, and lifting bill up and down with neck feathers puffed up. In flight display male flies up to about 3 feet above ground and makes circles around watching female.
- **NESTING** Incubation 11–12 days by host. Altricial young often hatch before young of host species and often outcompete host's young, which often succumb; tended by host. Female usually lays 1 egg in each host nest; may lay eggs in 5 different nests per season; sometimes destroys eggs of host.
- **POPULATION** Rare to uncommon in North America.
- **FEEDERS** Soaked bread.
- **CONSERVATION** Naturally invading nonnative species.

Similar Birds

BROWN-HEADED COWBIRD Shorter, less pointed bill; shorter tail • male glossy black overall with chocolate-brown head • female has ashy gray-brown upperparts and paler gray underparts.

Flight Pattern

Rapid swooping direct flight on quickly beating wings.

Nest Identification

Shape Brood parasite

Location Active nests of other birds

Lays eggs in nests of other species • usually 1 egg per nest • 1 whitish to light blue or light pink egg, sometimes unmarked or with flecks and dots of brown and gray; spherical, 0.8 x 0.66 inches.

Plumage Sexes differ	Habitat	Migration Migratory	Weight 1.4 ounces

DATE _____ TIME_____ LOCATION _____

Family ICTERIDAE	Species *Molothrus aeneus*	Length 6.5–8.75 inches	Wingspan 10–13 inches

BRONZED COWBIRD

Both male and female have small neck ruffs, which fluff during breeding season and give the bird a hunchbacked look. Formerly called the Red-eyed Cowbird, this characteristic is visible only at close range. Flocks often follow cattle to eat insects that are kicked up. In the eastern race, the dark-eyed juveniles are blackish brown and similar to the female but lack the bluish sheen on upperparts. In the western race, the dark-eyed juvenile is paler brown than the female, which has gray-brown upperparts, paler gray-brown underparts, and an even paler gray-brown throat. Birds inhabiting the southernmost tip of Texas do not migrate.

bronze-greenish sheen on head and upper body

red eyes

erectile ruff on back of neck

large long bill

bluish sheen on wings and tail

purplish sheen on scapulars

black overall

MALE

red eyes

large long bill

dull blackish brown or gray-brown overall

FEMALE

- **SONG** Low guttural wheezy insectlike *glug-glug-glee*. Call is abrasive *chuk*.
- **BEHAVIOR** Solitary or in pairs or small groups during breeding season. During other seasons, forages in flocks and uses communal roosts. Males perch and sing from exposed sites to attract females. Turns over rocks with bill to find insects. Eats insects, seeds, and grains. Often found near human habitation.
- **BREEDING** Polygamous. Promiscuous.
- **NESTING** Incubation 10–12 days by host. Altricial young often hatch earlier than young of host species; tended by host. Female usually lays 1 egg in each nest; lays 8–10 eggs per year; may destroy host's eggs and any eggs laid in the nest by previous female cowbirds.
- **POPULATION** Common and local in open country with brushy scrub, agricultural areas, wooded canyons, and around human habitation.
- **FEEDERS** Small seeds and various grains.

Similar Birds

♂ ♀ **BROWN-HEADED COWBIRD** Smaller; dark eyes; smaller slimmer bill; distinct rounded forehead • male glossy black overall with brown head • female usually more ashy brown overall with trace of pale face pattern.

♂ ♀ **SHINY COWBIRD** Smaller; dark eyes; smaller bill • male glossy black with purple sheen on head, back, and breast • female has gray-brown upperparts; paler underparts; paler throat; faint pale gray eyebrow.

Flight Pattern

Swift somewhat swooping direct flight on rapidly beating wings.

Nest Identification	
Shape Brood parasite	Lays eggs in nests of other species • generally 1 egg in each nest • female lays 8–10 eggs per year • eggs usually glossy light blue-green, unmarked; spherical to oval, 0.8 x 0.68 inches.
Location Active nests of other birds	

Plumage Sexes differ	Habitat	Migration Most migrate	Weight 2.4 ounces

DATE _____ TIME_____ LOCATION _____

| Family ICTERIDAE | Species *Molothrus ater* | Length 7–8.25 inches | Wingspan 11.75–13.75 inches |

BROWN-HEADED COWBIRD

This common cowbird travels and roosts in large flocks with other blackbirds after breeding season; winter mixed-species flocks can number in the millions. Originally of the Great Plains, where it associated with bison, this species has expanded its range east and west, with the fragmentation of the eastern forest and the increase in range cattle and ranching. Like all cowbirds it is a brood parasite and lays its eggs in the nests of other birds. Juveniles resemble females but are paler overall; upperparts have pale edging, giving a scaly effect; underparts are streaky and throats gray-white.

black overall with faint green sheen

brown head

short conical bill

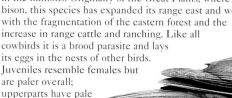

MALE

grayish brown upperparts

faint dusky malar mark

FEMALE

JUVENILE

• **SONG** Gurgling liquid *glug-glug-glee*, with tail spread, wings drooped, and a forward bow. Female's call is harsh rattle. Male in flight has high slurred *ts-eeeu!*

pale grayish brown underparts with faint streaking

• **BEHAVIOR** Solitary, in pairs, or small groups during breeding season; otherwise gregarious, foraging and roosting in flocks. Calls and displays from the ground or high exposed perches. Walks on ground to forage. Holds tail cocked over back. Eats insects, caterpillars, spiders, and various grains, seeds, and fruits.

• **BREEDING** Promiscuous.

• **NESTING** Incubation 10–13 days by host. Altricial young usually hatch before host's young and often outcompete them; tended by host. Female usually lays 1 egg in each nest; 10–36 eggs per year.

• **POPULATION** Common in woodlands, forest edge, agricultural areas, and around human habitation.

• **FEEDERS** Attends for small seeds and grains.

• **CONSERVATION** Neotropical migrant. Numbers reduced in Michigan by trapping to protect endangered Kirtland's Warbler in jack pine barrens nesting grounds.

Similar Birds

♂ BRONZED COWBIRD Slightly larger; much longer, larger bill; red eyes; ruff on nape • male has bronze-green sheen on head and upper body • female is dull blackish brown overall.

♀

♂ SHINY COWBIRD Male glossy black overall with purplish sheen on head, back, and breast • female has gray-brown upperparts; faint gray eyebrow; pale gray-brown underparts; paler gray throat.

♀

Flight Pattern

Swift somewhat swooping direct flight on rapidly beating wings.

Nest Identification	Lays eggs in nests of other species • usually 1 egg per nest • up to 36 eggs laid per female per nesting season • light blue eggs, often with brown flecks; oval, 0.84 x 0.64 inches.
Shape Brood parasite Location Active nests of other birds	

| Plumage Sexes differ | Habitat | Migration Northern birds migrate | Weight 1.7 ounces |

DATE _____ TIME_____ LOCATION _____

Family ICTERIDAE	Species *Icterus spurius*	Length 6–7.75 inches	Wingspan 9.25–10.25 inches

ORCHARD ORIOLE

This small oriole with its burnt-orange underparts is found in most of eastern North America in summer. It spends most of its time in trees in suburban and rural open stands and is often unwary when approached. Juveniles resemble females, and first spring males are similar to females but have a black chin and throat. Leaves breeding grounds in early fall.

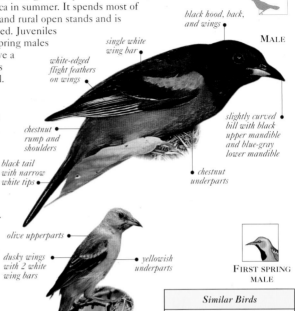

black hood, back, and wings

single white wing bar

white-edged flight feathers on wings

MALE

slightly curved bill with black upper mandible and blue-gray lower mandible

chestnut rump and shoulders

black tail with narrow white tips

chestnut underparts

• **SONG** Loud rich varied whistled notes, accelerating into a jumbled ending with a slurred *wheer!*, sounding like *look here, what cheer, wee yo, what cheer, whip yo, what wheer!* Calls sharp musical *chuk* and a dry chattering *chuh-huh-huh-huh.*

• **BEHAVIOR** Solitary or in pairs during breeding season. In small family groups after nesting. Vocal and often conspicuous. Relatively approachable. Forages at middle to high levels in trees and shrubs, often at tips of branches; hops from branch to branch. Eats insects; also berries, flower parts, nectar, and fruits.

olive upperparts

dusky wings with 2 white wing bars

yellowish underparts

FEMALE

FIRST SPRING MALE

• **BREEDING** Monogamous. Solitary and loose colonies.

• **NESTING** Incubation 12–14 days by female. Altricial young brooded by female, some by male; stay in nest 11–14 days, fed by both sexes. Mates often divide fledglings and care for them separately, but family group remains intact until fall migration. 1 brood per year.

Similar Birds

MALE: No other North American songbird is extensively black above and chestnut below.

HOODED ORIOLE ♀ Female and juvenile are larger; longer tail; longer bill; thinner lower wing bar; undertail coverts often washed yellow-orange • juvenile male has more extensive black bib.

• **POPULATION** Common to fairly common in open woodland, farmlands, scrub/mesquite, shade trees, and orchards. Species declining in parts of its western range.

• **FEEDERS** Fruit and nectar.

• **CONSERVATION** Neotropical migrant. Common host to cowbird parasitism.

Flight Pattern
Swift slightly swooping direct flight on rapidly beating wings.

Nest Identification	
Shape 🪹 Location 🌳 🌲	Intricately woven pouch of grasses with lining of plant down • hanging from fork of tree or bush, often hidden in cluster of leaves, 6–20 feet above ground (but up to 50 feet) • 3–7 light blue or gray eggs, splotched with gray, purple, or brown; oval, 0.8 x 0.57 inches.

Plumage Sexes differ	Habitat	Migration Migratory	Weight 0.7 ounce

DATE _____ TIME_____ LOCATION _____

Family ICTERIDAE	Species *Icterus cucullatus*	Length 7–8 inches	Wingspan 11.25–12 inches

HOODED ORIOLE

This bird flits from treetop to treetop and sometimes hangs upside down like a chickadee. It is associated with palm trees in its breeding range, most often nesting in them. The breeding male's orange-yellow head, black lores and bib, and white wing bars are distinctive. There is color variation in the males of different races, ranging from bright orange to bright yellow. Juveniles are similar to adult females. First spring males resemble females but have black lores and bib.

- **SONG** Throaty warbled whistles interspersed with chatter notes. Call is ascending whistled *wheat;* also series of chatters.

- **BEHAVIOR** Solitary or in pairs or small groups. Originally a riparian species; it now is often found around human habitation. Forages in trees and bushes. Eats insects and caterpillars. Uses bill to ingest nectar, piercing the flower's base and bypassing its stamens and style, thus not acting as a pollinator.

- **BREEDING** Monogamous. Solitary. Displaying male chases female and bows to her from branches.

- **NESTING** Incubation 12–14 days by female. Young altricial; brooded by female; stay in nest 14 days, fed by both sexes. 2–3 broods per year.

- **POPULATION** Common in riparian woodland, palm groves, arid scrub/mesquite, and around human habitation. West Coast range expanding northward with planting of palms and ornamental landscaping plants.

- **FEEDERS** Bread and fruit; also drinks sugar water mixture.

- **CONSERVATION** Neotropical migrant. Common cowbird host.

black lores and bib
orange-yellow head
black back
orange-yellow rump and uppertail coverts
long black slightly curved bill with blue-gray base of lower mandible
black wings with 2 white wing bars and white-edged flight feathers

MALE

graduated black tail with narrowly white-tipped outer tail feathers
orange-yellow underparts

pale yellow-green head
dark gray wings with 2 white wing bars and white-edged flight feathers
long slightly curved blue-gray bill

FEMALE

olive-greenish gray upperparts
yellow-green underparts

WINTER MALE

dark olive tail

Similar Birds

ORCHARD ORIOLE ♀
Female and juvenile male • smaller; shorter bill; wider lower white wing bar • juvenile male has smaller bib.

Flight Pattern

Strong rapid direct flight on rapidly beating wings.

Nest Identification

Shape   Location

Leaves and moss, with lining of moss, grasses, wool, hair, and feathers • hanging from branch, surrounded by Spanish moss or mistletoe, in palm, palmetto, or yucca, 12–45 feet above ground • built by female • 3–5 white, light yellow, or pale blue eggs, with dots of gray, brown, and purple; oval to long oval, 0.9 x 0.7 inches.

Plumage Sexes differ	Habitat	Migration Migratory	Weight 0.8 ounce

DATE _____ TIME_____ LOCATION _____

Family ICTERIDAE	Species *Icterus gularis*	Length 9–10 inches	Wingspan 13.5–15 inches

yellow-orange head

black back

black wings with white wing bar, white base to primaries, and white edging on tertials and secondaries

ALTAMIRA ORIOLE

The largest of the North American orioles, this bird intricately weaves a two-foot-long pendant-shaped nest. A native of Mexico, it has a small range in the southern tip of Texas, where it is a year-round resident. It resembles a larger version of the Hooded Oriole but with a larger bill and an orange shoulder patch in adults. A white wing patch shows in flight. The female is duller overall than the male. The immature is similar to the adult female but has an olive-brown back and tail and a white shoulder bar. The juvenile is similar to the immature but lacks the black lores and bib. This bird was formerly called Lichtenstein's Oriole.

black lores and bib

orange shoulder patches

yellow-orange underparts

yellow-orange rump

gray-green legs and feet

black tail with white tips to outermost tail feathers

- **SONG** Rapid series of 2–4 clear flutelike whistles, *chee-choo', chee-choo',* repeated. Male and female sing often. Call is nasal *yehnk!*
- **BEHAVIOR** In pairs for much of year. In family groups after breeding. Often with other orioles. Forages high in trees and in shrubs. Eats insects, caterpillars, and fruits and berries. The 14- to 26-inch-long, 6-inch diameter pendant nest may take the female 18 days to build and is the longest fibrous nest built by any bird north of Mexico. The entrance is at the top, and nest hangs in the open near the tip of a drooping branch from middle levels to high in a tree. Sometimes attached to a utility wire.
- **BREEDING** Monogamous. Solitary.
- **NESTING** Breeding biology poorly known. Estimated incubation 12–14 days by female. Young altricial; brooded by female; stay in nest estimated 12–14 days, fed by both sexes. Male takes over feeding of first brood while female begins construction of second nest. 2 broods per year.
- **POPULATION** Uncommon to fairly common and local in riparian woodlands, open woodlands, arid scrub, and mesquite in the lower Rio Grande Valley of southeastern Texas.
- **CONSERVATION** Frequent cowbird host. Vulnerable to habitat loss due to clearing for agriculture and development.

JUVENILE

Similar Birds

HOODED ORIOLE ♂
Smaller; more narrow bill; more extensive black bib • winter adults have olive-brown backs with fine black barring • all plumages and ages have white shoulder patches.

Flight Pattern	

Swift strong flight on rapidly beating wings.	

Nest Identification	
Shape ![shape] Location ![location]	Grasses and plant fibers, suspended from branch of tree or utility wire • built by female • 3–4 white eggs, heavily marked with browns; oval to long oval, 1.16 x 0.75 inches.

Plumage Sexes similar	Habitat 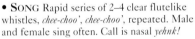	Migration Nonmigratory	Weight 2.1 ounces

Family ICTERIDAE	Species *Icterus graduacauda*	Length 8.5–9.5 inches	Wingspan 13.5–14.5 inches

AUDUBON'S ORIOLE

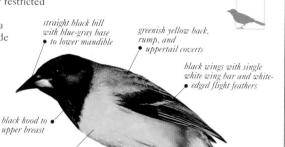

straight black bill with blue-gray base to lower mandible

greenish yellow back, rump, and uppertail coverts

black wings with single white wing bar and white-edged flight feathers

black hood to upper breast

bright lemon-yellow underparts

black tail with white tips to outer tail feathers

A tropical species almost entirely restricted to Mexico, this bird has a limited US range, along with the Altamira Oriole, along the lower Rio Grande Valley in southern Texas. It most often stays hidden in dense trees and thickets. The male and female are usually together and may stay that way throughout the year. Formerly called the Black-headed Oriole, this species is little known biologically. Females are similar to males but appear slightly duller. The immature resembles the adult female but shows an olive tail and gray-brown wings. The juvenile is similar to the immature but lacks the black hood and has an olive-green crown.

JUVENILE

- **SONG** Soft series of 3-note warbles, *peut-pou-it*, each note on a different pitch, with second note higher. Given infrequently. Call is a nasal *yehnk, yehnk!*, often repeated.
- **BEHAVIOR** In pairs most of the year. In small family groups following breeding. Somewhat shy and secretive. Spends much time foraging on ground. Eats insects and some fruits. Joins mixed foraging flocks with other orioles, jays, and tanagers.
- **BREEDING** Monogamous. Solitary.
- **NESTING** Breeding biology poorly known. Estimated incubation 12–14 days by female. Young altricial; brooded by female; stay in nest estimated 12–14 days, fed by both sexes. 1–2 broods per year.
- **POPULATION** Uncommon and local in the lower Rio Grande Valley of southern Texas. Frequents riparian thickets, scrub, forest undergrowth, and semiarid pine-oak woodlands. Population decline since the 1920s is a combination of habitat loss and related increased cowbird parasitism.
- **FEEDERS** Will come to nectar feeders and fruit such as sliced oranges.
- **CONSERVATION** Frequent host to cowbird parasitism. Vulnerable to habitat loss due to land clearing and alteration for agriculture and development.

Similar Birds

No other adult yellow oriole with black hood in its limited US range.

HOODED ORIOLE
Juveniles similar
• curved culmen;
2 white wing bars;
undertail coverts washed with yellow-orange.

Flight Pattern

Swift direct flight with rapid wing beats, low under the canopy.

Nest Identification

Shape Location

Woven of fresh green grass • hangs attached by top and side from small vertical terminal branch, 6–14 feet above ground • built by female • 3–5 light blue or grayish white eggs, speckled with browns or purples and scrawled with black lines; oval to long oval, 0.97 x 0.71 inches.

Plumage Sexes similar	Habitat	Migration Nonmigratory	Weight 0.8 ounce

DATE _____ TIME_____ LOCATION _____

Family ICTERIDAE	Species *Icterus galbula*	Length 7–8.25 inches	Wingspan 11.25–12.5 inches

BALTIMORE ORIOLE

The eastern counterpart to Bullock's Oriole was once thought conspecific with it and called the Northern Oriole. It is the state bird of Maryland. The male is the only bright orange-and-black oriole north of Florida. Some winter along the southeast Atlantic Coast and may find food in backyard feeders and gardens. Juveniles are similar to females but show a yellow-orange wash on the head and breast and grayish to whitish underparts. Juvenile males have more orange.

- **SONG** Disjointed measured 2-note whistled melodic phrases, some with long pauses, *hue-lee, hue-lee, hue-lee.* Call is rich *hue-lee.* Also a series of rattling chatter, *caw-caw-caw-caw-caw.*
- **BEHAVIOR** Solitary or in pairs in breeding season. In family groups after nesting, although some males remain solitary. May join mixed foraging flocks in winter and migration. Forages in bushes and trees, often high in canopy. Eats insects, caterpillars, berries, and fruits. Sips nectar.
- **BREEDING** Monogamous. Solitary. Displaying male spreads tail and wings, bows to female.
- **NESTING** Incubation 12–14 days by female. Altricial young brooded by female; stay in nest 12–14 days, fed by both sexes. 1 brood per year.
- **POPULATION** Common in deciduous woodlots, riparian woodlands, woodland edges and clearings, and around human habitation. Uncommon in winter in the Southeast. Rare in the West in migration.
- **FEEDERS** Oranges, peanut butter and suet, or nectar.
- **CONSERVATION** Neotropical migrant. Infrequent cowbird host (may eject eggs).

black hood and back

straight blue-gray bill with blackish culmen

black upper breast

orange-yellow shoulder patch

orange-yellow underparts and rump

narrow white lower wing bar

black wings with white edging to feathers

MALE

black tail with orange-yellow patches on distal half of outer tail feathers

FALL IMMATURE MALE

FALL IMMATURE FEMALE

variable amount of random black markings on head and throat

olive upperparts

yellow-olive rump

2 white wing bars

orange underparts

FEMALE

belly may have grayish wash

Similar Birds

♂ **BULLOCK'S ORIOLE**
Male has bright orange head, underparts, rump, and outer tail feathers; black crown, nape, eye line, throat, wings, and tail; large white wing patch • female and juvenile female have dark grayish eye line; yellowish head, throat, and breast; grayish white underparts; 2 thin white wing bars; olive-gray crown, nape, and upperparts • first spring male resembles adult female but shows black lores and bib.

Flight Pattern

Swift strong direct flight on rapidly beating wings; orange-yellow in dark tail flashes during flight.

Nest Identification

Shape   Location

Intricately woven from plant fibers, horse hair, yarn, cloth, and string • lined with grass, wool, and hair • hanging from end of drooping branch in deciduous tree, rarely in conifer, 25–30 feet above ground (but up to 60 feet) • built by female • 4 grayish white or light blue eggs, blotched and scrawled at large end with blacks and browns; oval to long oval, 0.9 x 0.61 inches.

Plumage Sexes differ	Habitat	Migration Migratory	Weight 1.2 ounces

DATE _____ TIME _____ LOCATION _____

| Family ICTERIDAE | Species *Icterus bullockii* | Length 7–8.25 inches | Wingspan 11.25–12.5 inches |

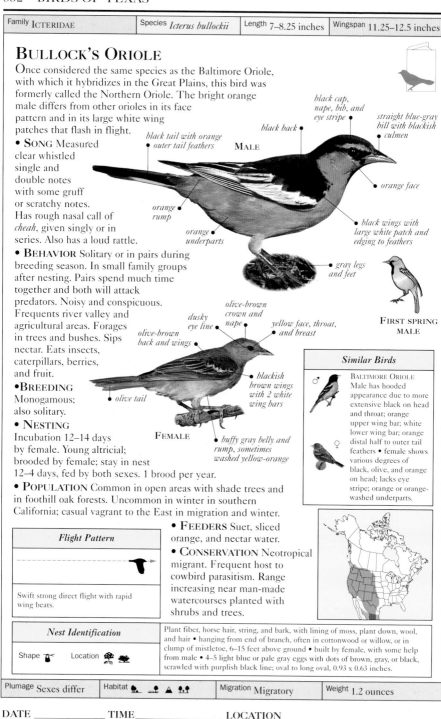

BULLOCK'S ORIOLE

Once considered the same species as the Baltimore Oriole, with which it hybridizes in the Great Plains, this bird was formerly called the Northern Oriole. The bright orange male differs from other orioles in its face pattern and in its large white wing patches that flash in flight.

- **SONG** Measured clear whistled single and double notes with some gruff or scratchy notes. Has rough nasal call of *cheah*, given singly or in series. Also has a loud rattle.

- **BEHAVIOR** Solitary or in pairs during breeding season. In small family groups after nesting. Pairs spend much time together and both will attack predators. Noisy and conspicuous. Frequents river valley and agricultural areas. Forages in trees and bushes. Sips nectar. Eats insects, caterpillars, berries, and fruit.

- **BREEDING** Monogamous; also solitary.

- **NESTING** Incubation 12–14 days by female. Young altricial; brooded by female; stay in nest 12–4 days, fed by both sexes. 1 brood per year.

- **POPULATION** Common in open areas with shade trees and in foothill oak forests. Uncommon in winter in southern California; casual vagrant to the East in migration and winter.

- **FEEDERS** Suet, sliced orange, and nectar water.

- **CONSERVATION** Neotropical migrant. Frequent host to cowbird parasitism. Range increasing near man-made watercourses planted with shrubs and trees.

Labels (Male):
black cap, nape, bib, and eye stripe
straight blue-gray bill with blackish culmen
black back
black tail with orange outer tail feathers
MALE
orange face
orange rump
orange underparts
black wings with large white patch and edging to feathers
gray legs and feet

FIRST SPRING MALE

Labels (Female):
olive-brown crown and nape
dusky eye line
olive-brown back and wings
yellow face, throat, and breast
blackish brown wings with 2 white wing bars
olive tail
FEMALE
buffy gray belly and rump, sometimes washed yellow-orange

Similar Birds

BALTIMORE ORIOLE Male has hooded appearance due to more extensive black on head and throat; orange upper wing bar; white lower wing bar; orange distal half to outer tail feathers • female shows various degrees of black, olive, and orange on head; lacks eye stripe; orange or orange-washed underparts.

Flight Pattern

Swift strong direct flight with rapid wing beats.

Nest Identification

Shape — Location —

Plant fiber, horse hair, string, and bark, with lining of moss, plant down, wool, and hair • hanging from end of branch, often in cottonwood or willow, or in clump of mistletoe, 6–15 feet above ground • built by female, with some help from male • 4–5 light blue or pale gray eggs with dots of brown, gray, or black, scrawled with purplish black line; oval to long oval, 0.93 x 0.63 inches.

| Plumage Sexes differ | Habitat | Migration Migratory | Weight 1.2 ounces |

DATE _____ TIME_____ LOCATION _____

Family ICTERIDAE	Species *Icterus parisorum*	Length 7.5–9 inches	Wingspan 10–13.5 inches

SCOTT'S ORIOLE

This subtropical bird, ranging from central Mexico into southwestern North America, sings constantly during the day in semidesert areas. It intricately weaves a nest, like many orioles, and often sews it onto yucca leaves or in a Joshua tree. The male is distinctive with a bright lemon-yellow rump and underparts and a black hood. Juveniles are similar to adult females but lack the black on head and chest. Immature males resemble adult females but have more black on the head and chest. The biology of this species is poorly known.

black hood and back

lemon-yellow shoulder patch

black wings with 2 white wing bars

white edging to flight feathers

straight black bill with blue-gray base to lower mandible

black upper breast

lemon-yellow underparts

black tail with yellow basal half to outer tail feathers

MALE

- **SONG** Various rich whistled phrases, suggesting Western Meadowlark. Call is grating *shack*.
- **BEHAVIOR** Solitary or in pairs during breeding season. In small groups after nesting. Sings often from conspicuous perch and forages in open among shrubs, trees, yucca, and agave. Eats insects and fruits. Uses bill to probe for nectar in flowers of cacti, agave, yucca, and other desert plants.
- **BREEDING** Monogamous. Solitary.
- **NESTING** Incubation 12–14 days by female. Altricial young brooded by female; stay in nest 14 days, fed by both sexes. 2 broods per year.

head, throat, and chest often mottled blackish, giving hooded effect

dark streaking on back

dusky cheeks

dark brown wings with 2 white wing bars

greenish yellow underparts

FIRST SPRING MALE

yellowish rump and uppertail coverts

olive tail with yellowish basal halves to outer tail feathers

FEMALE

Similar Birds

HOODED ORIOLE ♀
Immature, juvenile, and female • 2 narrow white wing bars; unstreaked back; lacks suggestion of hood; olive tail lacks yellow base to outer tail feathers • black bib and lores of immature male much more reduced than on immature male Scott's Oriole.

- **POPULATION** Fairly common in arid and semiarid habitats, palm oases, and oak-juniper and riparian woodlands. Uncommon in winter in southern California; casual in East to Louisiana and the western Great Lakes states.
- **CONSERVATION** Neotropical migrant. Rare host to cowbird parasitism. Breeding habitat lost to development.

Flight Pattern

Swift strong direct flight on rapidly beating wings, often close to the ground.

Nest Identification

Shape ● Location ❧ ❧ ♠

Yucca leaf fibers and grasses • lined with hair, grasses, and fine plant fibers • attached to dried yucca leaves or in Joshua tree, oak-junipers, or riparian tree • usually 4–20 feet above ground • built by female • 2–4 light blue eggs, splotched and dotted with grays, blacks, and reddish browns; oval to long oval, 0.94 x 0.67 inches.

Plumage Sexes differ	Habitat ↓↓ ↓ ⚘ ▲ ♠	Migration Migratory	Weight 1.3 ounces

DATE _____ TIME_____ LOCATION _____

Family FRINGILLIDAE	Species *Carpodacus purpureus*	Length 5.5–6.25 inches	Wingspan 9.25–10.5 inches

PURPLE FINCH

The male is easy to identify by its raspberry-colored plumage, brightest on the head, rump, and chest. Foraging in winter flocks, these birds depend on feeders when food supplies are scarce. Juveniles are similar to adult females; both have two white wing bars.

• **SONG** Rapid high-pitched rising and falling warble. Late winter/early spring males may sing in chorus. Call is *chur-lee*. Flight notes are sharp *tuck* or *pit*.

• **BEHAVIOR** Solitary or in pairs in nesting season. Male sings from exposed perch. Gregarious, tame. In flocks after breeding; joins mixed-species foraging flocks in winter with siskins and goldfinches. Forages in trees and hopping on ground. Eats seeds; some fruits, insects, and caterpillars in summer.

MALE

bright rosy red head

rosy supercilium

rosy red plumage with brown streaking on back and crown

pinkish edging to wings and 2 pinkish white wing bars

brown loreal mask extending onto auriculars

bright rosy red rump

white belly and undertail coverts

brown loreal mask extending onto auriculars

whitish eye line

brown malar mark

brown-gray upperparts with whitish streaks

grayish white underparts with brown streaking

deeply notched tail

FEMALE

• **BREEDING** Monogamous. Male displays by dancing around female and vigorously flapping his wings until he ascends to a foot above the ground.

• **NESTING** Incubation about 13 days by female. Altricial young brooded by female; stay in nest 14 days, fed by both sexes. 1–2 broods per year.

• **POPULATION** Fairly common in open coniferous and mixed coniferous-deciduous forests, in forest edge, and in suburbs; in Pacific states, in oak canyons and lower mountain slopes. Declining in the East.

• **FEEDERS** Millet and sunflower seeds.

Similar Birds

CASSIN'S FINCH ♂
Longer bill with straighter culmen; nape often slightly crested; gray-brown back; wings edged with pale pink; long primary projection; streaked undertail coverts; distinct streaks on sides and flanks • western range.

HOUSE FINCH ♂
Slender not chunky; less pointed bill with decurved culmen; indistinct facial pattern; brighter red on crown, rump, throat, and breast; dusky streaked underparts; squared tail.

• **CONSERVATION** Uncommon cowbird host. Vulnerable to habitat loss due to logging. Decrease in New England due to competition with House Sparrow; recent declines in East suggest same with House Finch.

Flight Pattern
Swift bounding flight with rapid wing beats alternating with brief periods of wings pulled to body.

Nest Identification	
Shape ⌒ Location 🌿 🌲	Twigs, weeds, rootlets, strips of bark, and string, with lining of moss, soft grasses, moss, and hair • on branch or in fork of tree, 6–40 feet above ground • built by female • 3–5 pale green-blue eggs, marked with black and brown; oval to short oval, 0.8 x 0.57 inches.

Plumage Sexes differ	Habitat 🌾 🪨 ⛰ 🏞	Migration Northern birds migrate	Weight 1.2 ounces

DATE _____ TIME_____ LOCATION _____

Family FRINGILLIDAE	Species *Carpodacus cassinii*	Length 6 inches	Wingspan 9.75 inches

CASSIN'S FINCH

Inhabiting the coniferous mountain forests of the West, these birds move in autumn with their young to lower elevations for the winter. Females have pale coloring and streaked undertail coverts that help distinguish them from other similar finches. In summer, this bird occurs at higher elevations than the Purple and House Finches. Juveniles closely resemble adult females

• **SONG** Long rich warbling, variable in pattern and length. Calls are clear *cheep, cheep, cheep* and *kee-up*, and a 3-syllabled flight note of *tee-dee-yip*.

• **BEHAVIOR** Solitary or in pairs during nesting season; forms family groups after breeding. Gregarious and tame. Forages on ground and high in trees; eats conifer seeds and buds, some insects in summer. Frequents salt licks and gathers at salted roadsides in winter. Nests in different sites each year.

• **BREEDING** Monogamous. Semicolonial.

• **NESTING** Incubation 12–14 days by female. Young altricial; brooded by female; stay in nest 14 days, fed by both sexes. 2 broods per year.

• **POPULATION** Fairly common in high montane open coniferous forests. In winter in deciduous woodlands, brushy scrublands, and second growth. Casual in winter to the West Coast and east to Minnesota, Oklahoma, and central Texas.

• **FEEDERS** Seeds.

• **CONSERVATION** Neotropical migrant. Rare cowbird host. Vulnerable to loss of habitat due to logging.

conspicuous red crown patch
rosy red head, throat, and breast
brown-streaked nape and back
large straight bill
indistinct brownish auriculars and submustachial mark
dark brown wings with 2 pinkish white wing bars, pinkish white coverts, and pinkish-edged flight feathers
rosy red rump
MALE
brown-streaked flanks and undertail coverts

whitish supercilium
gray upperparts with dusky streaking
deeply notched tail
white underparts with narrower dusky streaking
white undertail coverts with brown streaking
FEMALE

Similar Birds

PURPLE FINCH
More distinct whitish eyebrow and submustachial stripe; bill is shorter and more curved; lacks streaking on undertail coverts; crown does not contrast with nape and face
• sides of male are not distinctly streaked.

HOUSE FINCH
Smaller; more slender posture; less pointed bill; squared tail; red on crown does not contrast with nape and face
• male shows redder throat and breast
• female shows more brown underparts.

Flight Pattern

Swift bounding flight with rapid wing beats alternating with brief periods of wings pulled to sides.

Nest Identification	
Shape 🥃 Location 🪹	Twigs, weeds, rootlets, and strips of bark, with lining of fibers, soft grass, and hair • sometimes decorated with lichen • on branch of tree, 10–80 feet above ground • built by female • 4–6 blue-green eggs, dotted with brown and black, concentrated on larger end; subelliptical to long subelliptical, 0.8 x 0.57 inches.

Plumage Sexes differ	Habitat ▲ 🏕 🏔	Migration Northern birds migrate	Weight 0.9 ounce

DATE _____ TIME_____ LOCATION _____

Family FRINGILLIDAE	Species *Carpodacus mexicanus*	Length 6 inches	Wingspan 9.75 inches

HOUSE FINCH

- brown cap
- brown upperparts with paler brown streaking
- 2 narrow white wing bars
- squared tail

bright red to orange bib and front of head

MALE

brown-streaked underparts

Originally confined to the West, this finch was called a Linnet and introduced as a cage bird on Long Island, New York, in the 1940s. It became abundant in the East, surpassing the House Sparrow. Today, it is among the most widely distributed songbird species in North America. It often feeds with the Purple Finch, especially in winter. Some male variants are orange or yellow instead of red. Juveniles resemble adult females.

- **SONG** Varied rich high-pitched scratchy warble composed chiefly of 3-note phrases; many end with rising inflections. Both sexes sing, but male's song is longer, more complex, and more frequent. Call is nasal *chee* or *chee-wheet;* in flight a sharp nasal *nyee-ah.*
- **BEHAVIOR** Solitary or in pairs during nesting

grayish brown-streaked upperparts

2 narrow whitish buff wing bars

ORANGE VARIANT MALE

brown-streaked whitish buff underparts

FEMALE

season. Gregarious. Forms small family groups when young become independent. Larger foraging flocks in winter may join with other finches. Actively forages on ground, in fields, and in suburban areas. Eats mostly seeds but in summer takes insects and fruits. Drinks maple sap. Males are conspicuous and sing often. Studies indicate that the redder the male's plumage, the more desirable he is to females.

- **BREEDING** Monogamous. Solitary.
- **NESTING** Incubation 12–14 days by female. Altricial young brooded by female; stay in nest 11–19 days, fed by both sexes. 1–3 broods per year.
- **POPULATION** Abundant over much of North America in a wide variety of habitats, from arid scrub, wooded canyons, cultivated fields, and open woodlands to suburban yards and urban areas.
- **FEEDERS** Thistle, millet, sunflower, and other seeds.
- **CONSERVATION** Rare cowbird host in the West; fairly common host in the East.

Similar Birds

PURPLE FINCH ♂ Chunkier; notched tail; distinct rosy eyebrow and submustachial stripe; white crissum lacks streaking; crown does not contrast with face and nape • male shows raspberry-red on head, breast, and rump.

CASSIN'S FINCH ♂ Larger; notched tail; long straight bill; nape often slightly crested; bright red crown; pale pink-edged wings; streaked undertail coverts; distinct streaking on sides and flanks • western range.

Flight Pattern

Swift somewhat bounding flight with rapid wing beats alternating with brief periods of wings pulled to sides.

Nest Identification	
Shape 🐦	Twigs, grass, leaves, rootlets, bits of debris, and feathers • in tree hollow, cactus, on ground, under eaves of building, in bird boxes, abandoned nests, shrub, tree, etc. • built by female • 2–6 light blue eggs, spotted with lilac and black, often concentrated at larger end; oval to long oval, 0.8 x 0.57 inches.
Location	

Plumage Sexes differ	Habitat	Migration Some migrate	Weight 0.7 ounce

Family FRINGILLIDAE	Species *Loxia curvirostra*	Length 5.5–6.5 inches	Wingspan 10–10.75 inches

RED CROSSBILL

Crossbills take their name from the overlapping tips of the upper and lower mandibles. A resident of evergreen forests, they insert the crossed mandibles into conifer cones, forcing the scales apart while the tongue scoops the seed into the mouth. Nestlings have straight mandibles that cross gradually about three weeks out of the nest. Having abundant food year-round, this species begins nesting as early as January. Juveniles have weakly crossed mandibles, gray-olive upperparts heavily streaked dark brown, dark brown-streaked whitish underparts with yellowish wash, and buff-yellow rump. Subspecies of this bird vary in size, bill size, and vocalizations and may represent up to nine separate species.

MALE

dusky wings with reddish edging

mandibles crossed at tips

short notched dusky black tail

brick-red overall

whitish gray center to belly

dark undertail coverts with whitish edging

dusky black wings

dusky buff-yellow overall

FEMALE

JUVENILE

- **SONG** Series of 2-note phrases followed by trilled warble, *jitt, jitt, jitt, jitt, jiiaa-jiiaa-jiiaaaaa*. Calls vary among subspecies.
- **BEHAVIOR** In pairs during breeding season. Gregarious in small to large flocks most of year. Forages primarily in conifers, some on ground. Eats mostly seeds; also insects and caterpillars. Clings under branches and cones chickadee-like or crawls across limbs and cones like a small parrot, using bill and feet. Eats bits of mortar and is attracted to salt licks and to winter salt on the sides of roadways. Individuals and flocks fly high and are generally detected by their flight calls.
- **BREEDING** Monogamous. Solitary. Displaying male flies above female, vibrating wings and delivering flight song as he soars in circles overhead.
- **NESTING** Incubation 12–18 days by female. Altricial young brooded by female; stay in nest 15–20 days, fed by both sexes. 1–2 broods per year.
- **POPULATION** Fairly common in conifers and mixed forests. Wanderers, often depend on cone crop. Irruptive flights to Gulf states some winters.
- **FEEDERS** Sunflower seeds.
- **CONSERVATION** Vulnerable to habitat loss caused by logging operations.

Similar Birds

WHITE-WINGED CROSSBILL
White wing bars in all seasons • male pinkish red overall • female has dusky mottled olive-yellow upperparts; yellow rump; grayish underparts with yellowish wash.

Flight Pattern

Swift bounding flights, sometimes high above ground, on rapidly beating wings with brief periods of wings pulled to sides.

Nest Identification	
Shape Location	Twigs, pieces of bark, grass, and rootlets, with lining of finer grasses, feathers, fur, hair, and moss • on tree branch far out from trunk, 6–40 feet above ground • built by female • 3–4 light green or blue eggs spotted with browns and lilacs; oval to long oval, 0.8 x 0.58 inches.

Plumage Sexes differ	Habitat	Migration Nonmigratory	Weight 1.4 ounces

DATE _____ TIME_____ LOCATION _____

Family FRINGILLIDAE	Species *Carduelis pinus*	Length 4.5–5.25 inches	Wingspan 8.5–9 inches

PINE SISKIN

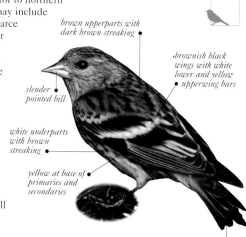

In fall and winter this is a common visitor to northern forests, where it forages in flocks that may include several thousand birds. When food is scarce these daytime migrants may travel as far south as Florida and central Mexico, flying in tightly formed flocks. In flight the yellow wing stripe at the base of the flight feathers and the yellow base to the outer tail feathers are conspicuous. Females are similar to males but with more washed-out yellow plumage. Juveniles resemble females but show a yellowish wash overall.

brown upperparts with dark brown streaking

brownish black wings with white lower and yellow upperwing bars

slender pointed bill

white underparts with brown streaking

yellow at base of primaries and secondaries

notched blackish tail with yellow base to outer tail feathers

• **SONG** Husky canary-like twittering warble, rising and falling in pitch and interspersed with a rapid ascending *ZZZzzzzzzzzzzrree!*, sounding like the equivalent of a bird with a chainsaw. Call is rising *tee-ee*. Flight note is hoarse descending *chee*.

• **BEHAVIOR** Tame, may allow close approach. Gregarious. In small groups or flocks year-round. Weakly territorial or not at all, with pairs nesting close to one another, often in the same tree. Forages on ground and in trees for seeds from alders, birches, spruce, and other trees. Also eats thistle seeds and weeds, some insects in summer. Nomadic in fall and winter. Attracted to salt licks and salt-treated winter highways. Feeds on sap at drill wells created by sapsuckers. Mountain populations descend to lower elevations prior to winter onset.

• **BREEDING** Monogamous. Semicolonial.

• **NESTING** Incubation 13 days by female. Young altricial; brooded by female; stay in nest 14–15 days, fed by both sexes. 2 broods per year.

• **POPULATION** Widespread and abundant in coniferous and mixed conifer-deciduous forests, in woodlands, parks, weedy fields, and near human habitation. Erratic irruptions in some winters bring large numbers far south of normal wintering range.

• **FEEDERS** Mixed seed, thistle, and black oil sunflower seed. Also will bathe and drink in birdbaths.

• **CONSERVATION** Fatalities high in winter; birds attracted to salt on roads become reluctant to fly.

Similar Birds

HOUSE FINCH ♀
Stubbier thicker bill; longer tail with squarish tip; 2 narrow white wing bars; lacks yellow at base of tail, primaries, and secondaries.

COMMON REDPOLL ♀
Red cap; black chin; 2 narrow white wing bars; lacks yellow plumage on wings and tail.

Flight Pattern

Flight is high and swift in compact flocks with long undulating sweeps.

Nest Identification

Shape 　Location

Bark, moss, feathers, and animal fur • lined with grass and twigs • usually hidden in conifer, placed far out from trunk • 10–50 feet above ground • built by female • 3–5 pale greenish blue eggs, with brown and black spots concentrated on larger end; short oval to short subelliptical, 0.7 x 0.5 inches.

Plumage Sexes similar	Habitat	Migration Migratory	Weight 0.5 ounce

DATE _____ TIME_____ LOCATION _____

Family FRINGILLIDAE	Species *Carduelis psaltria*	Length 4.5 inches	Wingspan 8 inches

LESSER GOLDFINCH

Smaller than the American Goldfinch, this bird is welcome in the Southwest because of its pleasant song and the amount of weed seeds it consumes. It can be distinguished from other goldfinches by the white patch at the base of the primaries, which shows as a white wing stripe in flight. All adult males have a black crown, but the color of the back varies with range: black-backed birds in the East and green-backed birds in the West. Juvenile males are similar to females but have a black forehead and black streaking on the crown.

black cap
dark greenish olive upperparts
long conical blackish bill
white wing bar
conspicuous white wing patch at base of primaries
bright yellow-green underparts
GREEN-BACKED MALE
black wings with white edges to tertials
yellow undertail coverts
JUVENILE MALE
FEMALE
BLACK-BACKED MALE
greenish olive upperparts

- **SONG** Complex warbling twittering exuberant series of *swee* notes. Call is mewing *tee-yee* and drawn-out nasal *zweeir.*
- **BEHAVIOR** In pairs or small flocks. Gregarious. Forages in flocks in brush, shrubs, and weedy fields. Frequents birdbaths and faucets. Eats weed seeds, other seeds, and insects.
- **BREEDING** Monogamous. Pairs stay together in winter; may mate for life. Male displays with singing flight song; feeds female during courtship.
- **NESTING** Late nester.

blackish wings with 2 white wing bars
dull yellowish green underparts
white tips to tertials and white base to primaries
notched blackish tail

Similar Birds

♂ AMERICAN GOLDFINCH Larger; stubby pinkish bill; whitish undertail coverts; blackish wings with 2 whitish to buff wing bars and white edging to tertials and secondaries; lacks white patch across base of primaries • in winter has brownish upperparts; grayish white underparts with buff wash on flanks.

Incubation 12 days by female, fed by male. Altricial young brooded by female; stay in nest 11–15 days. Both sexes feed regurgitated milky seed pulp. 1–2 broods per year.

- **POPULATION** Common in open habitats with scattered trees, brush fields, and woodland borders, especially near water and near human habitation. Casual in the Great Plains. Accidental vagrant in the East.
- **FEEDERS** Thistle, mixed seeds, and sunflower seeds.
- **CONSERVATION** Rare cowbird host.

Flight Pattern

High bouncy swift flight with rapid wing beats alternating with brief periods of wings pulled to sides.

Nest Identification	
Shape Location	Plant fibers, grasses, and bark pieces, with lining of feathers, cotton, and plant down • usually cradled across limb of tree or bush or occasionally set in tall weeds • 2–30 feet above ground • built by female • 3–6 light blue eggs, usually unmarked; ovate to rounded ovate, 0.61 x 0.45 inches.

Plumage Sexes differ	Habitat 	Migration Northern birds migrate	Weight 0.3 ounce

DATE _____ TIME_____ LOCATION _____

Family FRINGILLIDAE	Species *Carduelis tristis*	Length 5 inches	Wingspan 8.75–9 inches

AMERICAN GOLDFINCH

Often called the "wild canary" in the Southeast, the male in breeding plumage is a bright canary yellow. The female is more dull overall, while the young have whitish cinnamon wing bars and rump. Adult males in winter look more like the females and juveniles.

• **SONG** A jumbled series of musical warbles and trills often with a drawn-out *baybee* note. Flight song sounds like *per-chick-oree* or *po-tato-chips*.

• **BEHAVIOR** Occurs in flocks in nonbreeding season. In spring, feeds on the small seeds from dandelions. In the late summer breeding season, males engage in aerial displays of exaggerated roller coaster–like flights across the sky, singing *po-tato-chip* with each downward glide.

• **BREEDING** Monogamous. Among the very latest songbirds to nest each year. Territorial defense and mate selection begins in late summer and continues into early fall.

• **NESTING** Incubation 10–12 days by female. Young stay in nest

bright yellow

black cap

black wings with white double wing bars

MALE

black tail

extensive white edging on wing

JUVENILE

FEMALE
WINTER PLUMAGE

MALE
WINTER PLUMAGE

olive upperparts

pale yellow underparts

FEMALE

Similar Birds

YELLOW WARBLER ♂
Lacks wing bars and black wing and tail • breeds throughout much of the North, Southwest.

LESSER GOLDFINCH ♂
Yellow undertail coverts • ranges in the Northwest, Rockies, and much of the Southwest.

Flight Pattern

Undulating, roller coaster–like flight with several rapid wing beats and a pause.

11–17 days, fed by both sexes. 1–2 broods per year.

• **POPULATION** Common. Declining in eastern North America; stable in the West.

• **FEEDERS** Black (oil) sunflower seeds, thistle.

Nest Identification

Shape ● Location 🌳🌲⛺

Pliable vegetation lined with plant down • caterpillar webbing and spider silk often used to bind outer rim • usually along the edge of an open area • built by female • extremely well woven • 4–6 pale blue or bluish white eggs; subelliptical to oval, 0.6 inch long.

Plumage Sexes differ	Habitat	Migration Migratory	Weight 0.5 ounce

DATE _____ TIME_____ LOCATION _____

Family FRINGILLIDAE	Species *Coccothraustes vespertinus*	Length 7.75–8.5 inches	Wingspan 13–13.75 inches

EVENING GROSBEAK

Since the late nineteenth century the breeding range of this chunky bird has expanded eastward, supported by seed from new trees and by increased feeding stations. Fall migratory patterns are erratic; birds only leave breeding ranges when food supplies fail or populations become sizeable. Flocks may arrive in a region one winter and not return the next. In flight the short notched tail and large wing patches are distinctive.

- black crown on brownish head and nape
- yellow eyebrow and forehead
- dark brown and yellow overall
- large white or greenish yellow conical bill
- prominent white patch on black wings
- stocky body
- short notched black tail

MALE

- **SONG** Series of clipped warbled phrases, ending in shrill whistled note. Calls are loud piercing *clee-ip*, *peeer* and *chirp*. Flocks sound like chorus of amplified House Sparrows.
- **BEHAVIOR** Gregarious. Tame. Noisy. In groups and flocks during breeding season; pairs nest closely. Eats insects, including spruce budworm, while nesting; also eats buds, sap, and seeds from trees and shrubs; fruits and berries. In winter looks for salt and drinks water from melting snow.

- silver-gray crown, face, and back
- black malar mark
- white chin and throat
- gray-buff underparts and rump
- yellowish nape
- black wings with large white patches

FEMALE

- black uppertail coverts with white tips
- notched tail with white tip

JUVENILE

- **BREEDING** Monogamous. Semicolonial.
- **NESTING** Incubation 11–14 days by female; male feeds incubating female on nest. Young altricial; brooded by female; stay in nest 13–14 days, fed by both sexes. 1–2 broods per year.
- **POPULATION** Fairly common in breeding season in conifers and mixed woodlots; in mountains in West. Irregular in winter in woodlots, parks, second growth, suburban areas.
- **FEEDERS** Sunflower seeds; frequents birdbaths.
- **CONSERVATION** Rare cowbird host. Many killed on salt-treated highways in winter.

Similar Birds

AMERICAN GOLDFINCH♂
Smaller; black cap; pink conical bill; bright yellow upperparts and underparts; white undertail coverts; black wings; 2 white wing bars; white edging to tertials; notched black tail with white tips on inner webs.

Flight Pattern

Swift shallow bounding flight with rapid wing beats alternating with brief periods of wings pulled to sides.

Nest Identification	
Shape ⬬ Location 🌿 🌲	Frail structure of twigs, grass, moss, roots, and pine needles • lined with fine materials • built on horizontal branch of tree far out from trunk • usually 20–60 feet above ground (but up to 100 feet) • built by female • 3–5 pale blue to bluish green eggs, with brown, gray, and purple spotting; oval to short oval, 1.0 x 0.8 inches.

Plumage Sexes differ	Habitat 🌿 🪨 ⛰	Migration Some migrate	Weight 2.1 ounces

DATE _____ TIME_____ LOCATION _____

Family PASSERIDAE	Species *Passer domesticus*	Length 5.5–6.5 inches	Wingspan 9.5–10 inches

HOUSE SPARROW

This bird was introduced in New York City from Europe in the 1850s. By the early 20th century it was established over most of the continent. With the popularity of cars it began to decline; fewer horses meant less undigested grain to be gleaned from horse manure. Sometimes called the English Sparrow, it is the world's most widespread songbird. Juveniles resemble females but have browner upperparts, buffier underparts, and a pinkish bill.

• **SONG** Twittering series of chirps. Call is monotonous repeated *cheep-cheep-cheep.*

• **BEHAVIOR** Aggressive and noisy. In pairs during nesting season; family groups and flocks after breeding. Feeds and roosts in huge flocks. Hops. Forages on ground, in trees and shrubs, in urban and rural areas. Eats insects, caterpillars, seeds, grains, and fruits. Inspects car grilles for insects. Usurps nesting cavities from other species.

• **BREEDING** Monogamous. Some promiscuous. Males form circle around female and aggressively battle with each other.

• **NESTING** Incubation 10–14 days by both sexes, mostly by female. Altricial young brooded by female; stay in nest 14–17 days; both sexes feed by regurgitation. 2–3 broods per year.

• **POPULATION** Abundant and widespread in urban and cultivated areas and around human habitation; gradually declining.

• **FEEDERS AND BIRDHOUSES** Will come to feeders for small seeds and grains; nests in bird boxes.

• **CONSERVATION** Rare cowbird host. Out-competes other secondary-cavity nesters but loses to European Starlings.

gray crown and cheeks

chestnut nape joins postocular stripe

black bill

buff-brown back and wings with black streaking

black bib and lores

white submustache joins white half-collar

MALE

white wing bar

gray rump and tail

pale gray underparts

dusky postocular stripe below buff eyebrow

blackish-streaked buff-brown upperparts

dusky bill with yellowish base to lower mandible

white wing bar

brownish gray underparts

FEMALE

WINTER MALE

Similar Birds

EURASIAN TREE SPARROW
Reddish brown crown; white cheek with black patch; black loral mask and chin; black-streaked brownish upperparts; white wing bar has black upper border; dusky brown underparts • locally common only in and around St. Louis, Missouri, and Illinois.

Flight Pattern

Swift somewhat bounding flight with rapid wing beats alternating with brief periods of wings pulled to sides.

Nest Identification
Shape
Location

Grass, straw, weeds, cotton, bits of debris, twigs, and feathers • in tree hollow, under eaves of building or other sheltered areas, or in bird boxes; abandoned nests of other birds • on the backs of highway signs and billboards in the West • built by both sexes • 3–7 light green or blue eggs, dotted with grays and browns, concentrated toward larger end; oval to long oval, 0.9 x 0.7 inches.

Plumage Sexes differ	Habitat	Migration Nonmigratory	Weight 1.0 ounce

DATE _____ TIME_____ LOCATION _____

ACCIDENTAL, VAGRANT, & CASUAL SPECIES

The following section (pp. 544–554) contains 109 species for which the American Ornithologists' Union lists accepted records in Texas on an accidental, vagrant, or casual basis. Only those species listed on the current AOU Check-list of North American Birds (7th edition, 1998 and its 42nd Supplement, 2000) and the American Birding Association 1998–99 ABA Check-list Report, Birding 31: 518–524, are included. They appear in taxonomic order.

The species on the following pages fall into one of the following three designations depending on their abundance in this region:

Accidentals: Species that are represented by a single record or several records but have a normal range that is distant from this region. Therefore, these species are not expected to occur in this region.

Vagrants: Species with a natural range that is close to this region, that can be expected to be observed in the region on rare occasions.

Casuals: Species that have either a natural range that borders the region, or an extremely limited range within this region, and that may be expected to be recorded infrequently on an annual basis or over a period of several years.

PACIFIC LOON
Gavia pacifica
Length 26 inches

YELLOW-BILLED LOON
Gavia adamsii
Length 30–36 inches

YELLOW-NOSED ALBATROSS
Thalassarche chlororhynchos
Length 28–32 inches

BLACK-CAPPED PETREL
Pterodroma hasitata
Length 16 inches

STEJNEGER'S PETREL
Pterodroma longirostris
Length 12 inches

GREATER SHEARWATER
Puffinus gravis
Length 18–20 inches

MANX SHEARWATER
Puffinus puffinus
Length 12–15 inches

LEACH'S STORM-PETREL
Oceanodroma leucorhoa
Length 8–9 inches

BAND-RUMPED STORM-PETREL
Oceanodroma castro
Length 7.5–8.5 inches

RED-BILLED TROPICBIRD
Phaethon aethereus
Length 30–44 inches

BLUE-FOOTED BOOBY
Sula nebouxii
Length 32 inches

RED-FOOTED BOOBY
Sula sula
Length 26–28 inches

LITTLE EGRET
Egretta garzetta
Length 24 inches

JABIRU
Jabiru mycteria
Length 48–57 inches

GREATER FLAMINGO
Phoenicopterus ruber
Length 36–50 inches

TRUMPETER SWAN
Cygnus buccinator
Length 58–72 inches

WHITE-CHEEKED PINTAIL
Anas bahamensis
Length 18–20 inches

GARGANEY
Anas querquedula
Length 15 inches

KING EIDER
Somateria spectabilis
Length 18–25 inches

HARLEQUIN DUCK
Histrionicus histrionicus
Length 15–21 inches

BARROW'S GOLDENEYE
Bucephala islandica
Length 16–20 inches

SNAIL KITE
Rostrhamus sociabilis
Length 16–18 inches

CRANE HAWK
Geranospiza caerulescens
Length 18–21 inches

ROADSIDE HAWK
Buteo magnirostris
Length 13–16 inches

SHORT-TAILED HAWK
Buteo brachyurus
Length 15–17 inches

COLLARED FOREST-FALCON
Micrastur semitorquatus
Length 22–24 inches

PAINT-BILLED CRAKE
Neocrex erythrops
Length 7–8 inches

SPOTTED RAIL
Pardirallus maculatus
Length 10–11 inches

DOUBLE-STRIPED THICK-KNEE
Burhinus bistriatus
Length 18–20 inches

COLLARED PLOVER
Charadrius collaris
Length 5–6 inches

COMMON RINGED PLOVER
Charadrius hiaticula
Length 7.5 inches

EURASIAN DOTTEREL
Charadrius morinellus
Length 8.5 inches

WANDERING TATTLER
Heteroscelus incanus
Length 11 inches

SURFBIRD
Aphriza virgata
Length 10 inches

RED-NECKED STINT
Calidris ruficollis
Length 6.25 inches

SHARP-TAILED SANDPIPER
Calidris acuminata
Length 8.5 inches

PURPLE SANDPIPER
Calidris maritima
Length 9 inches

RUFF
Philomachus pugnax
Length 9–12.5 inches

LONG-TAILED JAEGER
Stercorarius longicaudus
Length 20–23 inches

LITTLE GULL
Larus minutus
Length 10–12 inches

BLACK-HEADED GULL
Larus ridibundus
Length 14–16 inches

HEERMANN'S GULL
Larus heermanni
Length 18–21 inches

BLACK-TAILED GULL
Larus crassirostris
Length 18–19 inches

MEW GULL
Larus canus
Length 16–18 inches

CALIFORNIA GULL
Larus californicus
Length 21–22 inches

THAYER'S GULL
Larus thayeri
Length 23–25 inches

ICELAND GULL
Larus glaucoides
Length 23–25 inches

SLATY-BACKED GULL
Larus schistisagus
Length 25–27 inches

YELLOW-FOOTED GULL
Larus livens
Length 27 inches

WESTERN GULL
Larus occidentalis
Length 24–27 inches

ELEGANT TERN
Sterna elegans
Length 16–17 inches

ROSEATE TERN
Sterna dougallii
Length 14–17 inches

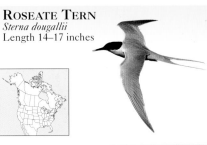

ARCTIC TERN
Sterna paradisaea
Length 14–17 inches

BRIDLED TERN
Sterna anaethetus
Length 14–15 inches

BLACK NODDY
Anous minutus
Length 12–13.5 inches

RUDDY GROUND-DOVE
Columbina talpacoti
Length 6–7 inches

RUDDY QUAIL-DOVE
Geotrygon montana
Length 8–10 inches

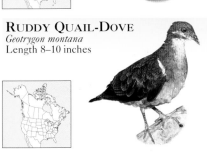

MANGROVE CUCKOO
Coccyzus minor
Length 12.5 inches

NORTHERN PYGMY-OWL
Glaucidium gnoma
Length 6–7 inches

MOTTLED OWL
Ciccaba virgata
Length 13–15 inches

STYGIAN OWL
Asio stygius
Length 15–17 inches

WHITE-THROATED SWIFT
Aeronautes saxatalis
Length 6–7 inches

GREEN-BREASTED MANGO
Anthracothorax prevostii
Length 4.75 inches

WHITE-EARED HUMMINGBIRD
Hylocharis leucotis
Length 3–4 inches

BERYLLINE HUMMINGBIRD
Amazilia beryllina
Length 3.75–4.25 inches

VIOLET-CROWNED HUMMINGBIRD
Amazilia violiceps
Length 4.25–4.5 inches

COSTA'S HUMMINGBIRD
Calypte costae
Length 3.5 inches

CALLIOPE HUMMINGBIRD
Stellula calliope
Length 2.75–3.25 inches

ELEGANT TROGON
Trogon elegans
Length 11–12.5 inches

RED-BREASTED SAPSUCKER
Sphyrapicus ruber
Length 8–9 inches

GREENISH ELAENIA
Myiopagis viridicata
Length 5–5.7 inches

TUFTED FLYCATCHER
Mitrephanes phaeocercus
Length 4.7–5.2 inches

BUFF-BREASTED FLYCATCHER
Empidonax fulvifrons
Length 4.5–5 inches

SULPHUR-BELLIED FLYCATCHER
Myiodynastes luteiventris
Length 8.5 inches

TROPICAL KINGBIRD
Tyrannus melancholicus
Length 8–9.25 inches

THICK-BILLED KINGBIRD
Tyrannus crassirostris
Length 9.5 inches

GRAY KINGBIRD
Tyrannus dominicensis
Length 9 inches

FORK-TAILED FLYCATCHER
Tyrannus savana
Length 14.5 inches

MASKED TITYRA
Tityra semifasciata
Length 8.5–9.5 inches

BLACK-WHISKERED VIREO
Vireo altiloquus
Length 6.25 inches

YUCATAN VIREO
Vireo magister
Length 5.7–6.2 inches

GRAY-BREASTED MARTIN
Progne chalybea
Length 7 inches

BLACK-CAPPED CHICKADEE
Poecile atricapilla
Length 5.5 inches

AMERICAN DIPPER
Cinclus mexicanus
Length 7.5 inches

NORTHERN WHEATEAR
Oenanthe oenanthe
Length 5.5–6 inches

ORANGE-BILLED NIGHTINGALE-THRUSH
Catharus aurantiirostris
Length 6.5 inches

WHITE-THROATED ROBIN
Turdus assimilis
Length 9.5 inches

RUFOUS-BACKED ROBIN
Turdus rufopalliatus
Length 9.5 inches

VARIED THRUSH
Ixoreus naevius
Length 9.5 inches

AZTEC THRUSH
Ridgwayia pinicola
Length 9.5 inches

GRAY SILKY-FLYCATCHER
Ptilogonys cinereus
Length 7.2–8.2 inches

OLIVE WARBLER
Peucedramus taeniatus
Length 5.25 inches

CONNECTICUT WARBLER
Oporornis agilis
Length 5.5 inches

RED-FACED WARBLER
Cardellina rubrifrons
Length 5 inches

SLATE-THROATED REDSTART
Myioborus miniatus
Length 6 inches

GOLDEN-CROWNED WARBLER
Basileuterus culicivorus
Length 5 inches

RUFOUS-CAPPED WARBLER
Basileuterus rufifrons
Length 5.25 inches

FLAME-COLORED TANAGER
Piranga bidentata
Length 7.25 inches

YELLOW-FACED GRASSQUIT
Tiaris olivacea
Length 4.25 inches

GOLDEN-CROWNED SPARROW
Zonotrichia atricapilla
Length 7 inches

YELLOW-EYED JUNCO
Junco phaeonotus
Length 6.25 inches

SNOW BUNTING
Plectrophenax nivalis
Length 6.25–7.25 inches

CRIMSON-COLLARED GROSBEAK
Rhodothraupis celaeno
Length 8.5 inches

BLUE BUNTING
Cyanocompsa parellina
Length 5.5 inches

BLACK-VENTED ORIOLE
Icterus wagleri
Length 8.5–9 inches

PINE GROSBEAK
Pinicola enucleator
Length 9–9.75 inches

WHITE-WINGED CROSSBILL
Loxia leucoptera
Length 6–6.75 inches

COMMON REDPOLL
Carduelis flammea
Length 5–5.5 inches

LAWRENCE'S GOLDFINCH
Carduelis lawrencei
Length 4.75 inches

GLOSSARY

• **AERIE**
A nest located on a cliff or high place, usually built by a raptor, a bird of prey.

• **AGAVE**
A desert plant with a spikelike flower, similar to a Yucca plant.

• **AIR SAC**
A series of thin-walled sacs, typically eight or nine (but ranging from six to fourteen, depending on the species) that in conjunction with the paired lungs comprise the bird's respiratory system.

• **ALAR BAR**
A contrasting line (bar) of plumage beginning in the alar region of the wing (where the wing bends at the wrist and on the leading edge) and running from that point at an angle toward the bird's body, stopping where the back of the wing joins the body. The effect is a patch or line of feathers that differ from the color of the wing feathers around it, thus producing a visible bar on the top of the wing. Sometimes the bar runs from the alula to the base of the wing on the front side (leading edge).

• **ALTERNATE PLUMAGE**
See Breeding Plumage.

• **ALTITUDINAL MOVEMENTS**
(Vertical migrations) A bird's regular seasonal vertical movement, often from the mountaintops in summer to lower regions or valleys during winter, with a return to higher elevations the following spring.

• **ALTRICIAL**
Term for young birds that hatch in a helpless state, usually naked with eyes closed, and are totally dependent on the parents.

• **ALULA**
A small group of feathers that protrude from the outermost joint of the wing. It has its own group of muscles and moves independently from the flight feathers. By adjusting the angle of the alula, the bird is able to regulate the air flow over the top of the wing, allowing it to alight or land at slower speeds without stalling.

• **ANHEDRAL**
The downward curve of a bird's wings when in flight.

• **ARBOREAL**
A tree-dwelling bird.

• **AURICULARS**
Feathers along the sides of the ears, often called ear coverts or ear patches.

• **AXILLARIES**
Rigid feathers along the underside of the wings where they connect to the body, corresponding to the underarm area in a human.

• **BASIC PLUMAGE**
See Winter Plumage.

• **BREEDING PLUMAGE**
(Alternate plumage) Seasonal alterations in appearance to attract birds of the opposite sex, such as changes in color or the addition of ornamental ruffs. This is accomplished by a feather molt from the basic, or winter, plumage.

• **CAMBIUM**
Plant tissue near the inner bark of a tree that produces lateral growth.

• **CATKIN**
A spike of flowers such as those found on a willow or birch tree.

- **CERE**
The fleshy area on top of the base of the upper bill that contains the nostrils. Present on the bills of some bird species, particularly among birds of prey.

- **CLUTCH**
The total number of eggs laid during a single nesting period; some birds lay several clutches in a nesting season.

- **COLONIAL**
The pattern of nesting close together with birds of the same species. Sometimes only a few nests packed close together constitute a colony, but some may hold hundreds or thousands of nesting pairs.

- **CONSPECIFIC**
Birds that are members of the same species.

- **CONGENERS**
Distinct bird species that are related to one another by being in the same genus.

- **COVERTS**
A covering of feathers overlaying the upper and lower part of the wings, covering the bases of the flight feathers (wing coverts); also on top of the tail feathers (uppertail coverts and undertail coverts).

- **CRECHE**
An aggregation of hatchlings of a nesting colony, living together while they are in a dependent state and fed and tended by the adult birds.

- **CREPUSCULAR**
Birds that feed and are active during twilight hours.

- **CRISSUM**
Feathers covering the base of the undertail, usually a different color from the rest of the underparts. Also called undertail coverts.

- **CROP**
Where food is stored in the esophagus for later digestion, or to be regurgitated and fed to hatchlings. Some birds, such as pigeons and doves, have a two-chambered crop that produces special milk to nourish their young.

- **CROWN**
Top of the head between the forehead and the back of the head or occiput.

- **CULMEN**
Top ridge of the upper mandible, darker on some birds than the side of the bill.

- **DABBLING**
Method of surface feeding by a relatively short-necked short-legged duck. It tips up the tail and body, then dips its bill and neck into water. These ducks are called dabblers. See Tipping-up.

- **DECURVED**
Sloped downward, usually referring to the bill.

- **DETRITUS**
Small particles of dead organic matter.

- **DIHEDRAL**
Wings held in a shallow V while bird is in flight.

- **DISTAL BAND**
A strip of color near the end of the tail, end of wing, or on the lower part of the leg.

- **DIURNAL**
Birds that feed and are active during the day.

- **ECLIPSE PLUMAGE**
Dull-colored plumage, similar to that of the female, into which many male ducks briefly molt in summer.

- **EXTIRPATED**
Exterminated or destroyed from a part of a species range.

- **EYE RING**
A circle around the eye, usually of a contrasting color.

- **EYE STRIPE OR EYEBROW**
See Supercilium.

- **FIELD MARKS**
Plumage or anatomical features of a bird that help to distinguish it from other similar species.

- **FLASHMARK**
Color or marking on plumage that is visible only when the bird is in flight.

- **FLEDGE**
The act of a young bird (nestling) leaving the nest. Also fledging.

- **FLEDGLING**
A young bird that has feathers and is old enough to have left the nest but is still dependent on adult birds for care and feeding.

- **GONYS**
A ridge on the lower mandible of a gull that causes the midline to appear angled. Sometimes shows a red patch during breeding season.

- **GORGET**
A small iridescent patch on the throat of a hummingbird.

- **GULAR SAC**
A large or small pouch in the upper throat that helps a bird regulate body temperature and sometimes holds undigested food. In a few species, such as the Magnificent Frigatebird, the pouch greatly expands for courtship display.

- **HAWKING**
The act of catching prey, usually insects, in flight. Generally done with the bill. Typical of flycatchers.

- **HERONRY**
(Rookery) The colonial nesting site for herons, egrets, and ibises.

- **HINDNECK**
The bird's nape or back of the neck.

- **HUMERAL**
The patch of feathers overlying the bone near the upperwing or shoulder area.

- **JIZZ**
The abstract combination of a bird's posture, plumage pattern, shape, size, and behavior that allows an experienced birder to recognize a species instantly without further examination.

- **LAMELLAE**
Miniature ridges inside the bill of a duck or water bird that resemble the teeth of a comb and serve as a strainer during feeding.

- **LARDER**
A place where a shrike impales and stores its prey on sharp branches or wire.

- **LEK**
A communal gathering place during breeding season where males of some species of birds display to attract the females. It contains numerous territories, each guarded by a different male.

- **LORES**
Space between the eyes and the base of the upper part of the bill on the side of the bird's face.

- **MALAR**
Refers to the cheek area along the side of the face. Field mark here is called malar mark or malar stripe.

- **MANDIBLE**
The lower half of the bill. Maxilla is the upper half; both halves collectively are called mandibles.

• **MANTLE**
The feathers covering the back and upperwing coverts; feathers of the back and folded wings.

• **MANUS**
The portion of a bird's wing that corresponds to the hand of a human. The fused bones of the palm and reduced digits bear the primary feathers and the alula.

• **MELANISTIC**
A bird that has a surplus of dark pigment in its plumage.

• **MIMIC THRUSH**
A member of the family Mimidae, which includes thrashers, catbirds, and mockingbirds.

• **MORPH**
When birds of the same species have two or more different colored plumages, that are independent of season, sex, age, or breeding. Color phases may or may not be related to range and climate.

• **NEOTROPICAL**
The New World tropical region that encompasses the northern portion of the Mexican rain forest and the Caribbean islands, and extends to the nontropical regions of South America.

• **NEW WORLD**
Earth's Western Hemisphere; includes North, South, and Central America.

• **NOCTURNAL**
Birds that feed and are active at night.

• **NON-PASSERINE**
Any of the birds that are not Passerines, which are the songbirds or perching birds. Includes loons, waterfowl, owls, shorebirds, hawks, woodpeckers, and doves.

• **NUCHAL PATCH**
A patch of contrasting color located on the back of the bird's neck or nape.

• **OCCIPITAL PATCH**
A patch of color located high on the back of the head. Higher on the head than the nuchal patch.

• **OCCIPUT**
The area on the back of a bird's head between the nape and the crown.

• **OCOTILLO**
A spiny desert shrub with red flower clusters at the tips of its branches.

• **OLD WORLD**
Earth's Eastern Hemisphere: Europe, Asia, and Africa.

• **ORBITAL RING**
See Eye Ring.

• **PALEARCTIC**
Faunal region surrounded by the Atlantic, Arctic, and Pacific Oceans; encompasses Asia north of the Himalayas, Europe, and Africa north of the Sahara desert.

• **PASSERINES**
Any of the birds belonging to the order Passeriformes, which comprise more than fifty percent of the world's birds. Highly evolved, these birds are able to sing and have three forward-pointing toes adapted for perching.

• **PEEP**
Birder's name for a group of small, similar-looking sandpipers; may have been derived from their high-pitched calls.

• **PELAGIC**
Birds that spend most of their time at sea and rarely are seen from shore.

• **PIEBALD**
Plumage that shows two contrasting colors.

• **PISHING**
Sound produced by birders to attract birds; made by clinching the teeth together and

forcing air out through the teeth and lips to create a noise that sounds like *pish-pish-pish*.

• POLYANDROUS
When female bird has two or more mates; female often larger, has brighter plumage, and defends her territory. Male of the species usually incubates and tends young.

• POLYGYNOUS
When a male bird takes two or more mates.

• POLYGAMOUS
When both male and female of a species may take two or more mates.

• POSTOCULAR STRIPE
A line that leads from behind the bird's eye to the auricular or ear patch.

• PRECOCIAL
Term for young birds that hatch with their eyes open, are down-covered, and are able to leave the nest within two days of hatching. These hatchlings may be either partially or not at all dependent on the parents for care and feeding.

• PRIMARIES
One of two sets of flight feathers, or remiges, located distally to the secondaries and joined to the manus of the wing.

• PROMISCUOUS
Birds, male or female, that come together solely for mating purposes and leave within a few hours to mate with other birds.

• PYRIFORM
Pear-shaped; often used to describe shape of egg.

• RAPTORS
A name applied to birds of prey – the hawks, falcons, eagles, kites, and owls.

• RECTRICES
The principal feathers that make up the tail. They range in number from eight to twenty-four, but the average in songbirds is twelve.

• REMIGES
Refers to flight feathers – primaries, secondaries, and tertials.

• RIPARIAN
Located on or near a river bank, stream bank, or other body of water.

• SCAPULARS
Feathers joined to the shoulder area of the bird and covering the top of the folded wing.

• SECONDARIES
One of two sets of flight feathers located between the body and the primaries and joined to the part of the wing that corresponds to the forearm of a human.

• SEMIALTRICIAL
Term for young birds that hatch with eyes either open or closed, are down-covered, and are incapable of leaving the nest; fed by parents.

• SEMICOLONIAL
Nesting pattern in which several birds of the same species nest close to one another, often within sight of each other's nests and do not behave aggressively toward one another.

• SEMIPRECOCIAL
Term for young birds that hatch with eyes open, are down-covered, and able to leave the nest soon after hatching, but remain in nest and are fed by parents.

• SKYLARKING
Elaborate territorial display flight given by a male songbird. It sings and often flutters in circles before swooping back to earth.

• SPATULATE
A long rounded spoonlike shape; sometimes used to describe bill or tail.

- **SPECULUM**
A small area of contrasting iridescent feathers located on the secondary feathers of the wings. Often seen in ducks.

- **SQUEAKING**
Sound produced by birders to attract birds; made by pursing the lips tightly together and sucking air in to make a high-pitched sound. This can be amplified by placing the lips on the back of the hand and sucking in a kissing fashion.

- **SUPERCILIUM**
Line above each eye; an eyebrow. Also called a superciliary stripe.

- **SUPERSPECIES**
Closely related species that are often separated from each other by geographic barriers. Without these barriers the two species probably would interbreed and become one.

- **SYMPATRIC**
Birds that inhabit the same range but remain distinct and separate species.

- **TAIGA**
Subarctic coniferous forests.

- **TARSUS**
The top of the foot behind the toes, often called the shank. Usually either bare or covered with scales, plates, or sometimes feathers.

- **TERTIALS**
The group of secondary feathers that are closest to the body; often a contrasting color.

- **TIPPING-UP**
Method of surface feeding by a duck, goose, or swan in which it raises its tail and dips its bill, head, and neck into the water. See Dabbling.

- **TOTIPALMATE**
All four toes joined together by webbing.

- **TYMPANI**
(Tympaniform membranes) Valves in the vocal organ of a bird that produce sound.

- **UNDERPARTS**
The plumage and coloring on the breast, belly, sides, flanks, and undertail coverts.

- **UPPERPARTS**
The plumage and coloring on the nape, back, shoulders, rump, and upper part of tail.

- **VANE**
Contoured flight feather that acts as a propeller. It consists of a central shaft surrounded by an inner and outer web.

- **VENT**
The opening of the cloaca, or anus; sometimes refers to a contrasting patch of feathers in this area.

- **WATTLE**
Fleshy piece of brightly colored skin that hangs from the lower bill; associated with turkeys and some chickens.

- **WILDTYPE**
A biological term based in genetics that describes the form that most individuals in a wild population take; description includes shape, color, patterns, and size.

- **WINGSTRIP**
A distinct line on the wing, usually of a contrasting color.

- **WINTER PLUMAGE**
(Basic plumage) Seasonal alteration in a bird's appearance produced by the fall molt.

INDEX

ACKNOWLEDGMENTS

The author would like to dedicate this book to his father, Fred J. Alsop, Jr., and thank his wife, Cathi Alsop, for her support during the writing of this book and for editing the final proofs of the range maps.

Southern Lights would like to thank: Ron Austing for photo coordination; Kristi Tipton for research on species profiles and range maps; Sandra Porter, Kristy Cuccini, Kelly Buford, and Anne Esquivel for species profile research; Jenny Cromie and Nina Costopoulos for editorial assistance; Holly Cross and R. Clay White for copyediting; Denise McIntyre and Rebecca Benton for proofreading; Marianne Thomas, Melissa Givens, George Griswold III, Jim Larussa, Will McCalley, Rick Tucker, and Christana Laycock for graphic assistance; Catherine O'Hare, Michelle Boylan, Taylor Rogers, Brad Reisinger, and Beth Brown for administrative support; and Charles (Chuck) Hunter of the US Fish and Wildlife Service, John C. Sterling, and Joseph DiCostanzo of the American Museum of Natural History for manuscript review and commentary.

m, 152f & m, 153f, 158, 159, 160, 163, 164, 167, 168f & m, 169, 170, 172, 174, 176, 180, 181, 182, 183, 184, 185, 188, 194, 200, 204, 210, 213, 214, 217, 222, 223, 226, 231, 237, 243, 244, 247, 250, 251, 252m, 253, 254, 255, 256, 257, 258, 259, 261, 263, 266, 267, 269, 271f & m, 276f & m, 277m, 278f, 280f & m, 283f & m, 286, 289f & m, 291, 294, 295, 297, 298f & m, 300, 303, 305, 307, 308, 319, 328, 329, 330, 331, 337, 339, 341, 344, 352, 357, 359, 361, 365, 366, 369, 370, 372f & m, 373, 377, 380, 382, 384, 385, 387f & m, 388m, 390f, 394, 396, 398, 400f & m, 401, 402, 404, 406, 408, 410, 412, 414, 415, 417, 418, 422, 424f & m, 425f & m, 426m, 427m, 428f & m, 429f & m, 432m, 435m, 436, 438, 439, 440, 441m, 444, 446f & m, 447, 449, 451, 452, 453f & m, 455f & m, 457f & m, 459f & m, 461, 463f & m, 464f & m, 468, 470f & m, 475, 476, 477, 479, 481, 482, 483, 486, 488, 492, 494, 495, 497, 498, 499f & m, 501f & m, 502m, 504f, 506f & m, 508f & m, 510m,

512f, 513m, 514f, 515f & m, 516, 520m, 522f & m, 526f & m, 527f & m, 528f, 531m, 534f & m, 536f & m, 540f & m, 541f & m, 542f, 544-rc-5, 545-le-1, 4, 5, 546-lc-1, 554-lc-4. **Rick & Nora Bowers** 83, 89, 110m, 143, 177, 232, 248, 249, 270, 284f & m, 304, 332f, 363, 364, 420, 421, 462m, 471, 487, 504m, 512m, 545-rc-3, 546-rc-2, 549-rc-5, 550-lc-3, rc-2, 551-lc-1, rc-1, 553-lc-3, 4. **Cornell Laboratory of Ornithology**/Allen Brooks 38t; L. Page Brown 132; George Sutton 37t. **Mike Danzenbaker** 54, 115m, 195, 203, 215, 233, 264, 265, 274f, 278m, 281f & m, 285, 302, 360, 367, 435f, 460, 474, 511f, 520f, 530, 544-lc-2, rc-3, 546-lc-2, 547-lc-1, 3, rc-1, 548-lc-1, 3, rc-4, 549-lc-5, 550-rc-5, 551-lc-3, 5, 552-lc-4, 5, rc-1, 2, 553-rc-1, 554-lc-5, rc-2. **DK Picture Library**/ 537f; Dennis Avon 153m, 236; Simon Battersby 12b; Peter Chadwick 29cr, 30b, 31tr, 31cl, 31cr; Mike Dunning 123; Frank Greenaway 139, 144; Cyril Laubscher 72, 80, 140, 175, 240, 542m; Karl & Steve Maslowski 314, 325, 376, 386f, 390m, 392f, 496, 514m, 552-lc-2; Jane Miller 162; Kim Taylor 95f & m; Jerry Young 252f.